CANON CROSSFIRE

Does
The Protestant Bible
Blow Up
The Case for Christianity?

ISBN Hardcover	979-8-9992090-0-9
ISBN Paperback	979-8-9992090-1-6
ISBN Large Print	979-8-9992090-2-3
ISBN Kindle	979-8-9992090-3-0
ISBN Audiobook	979-8-9992090-4-7

Except when quoting someone else quoting a Bible, my Bible citations are taken from: The Holy Bible, King James Version. Cambridge Edition: 1769; King James Bible Online, 2025. www.kingjamesbibleonline.org.

They also sell a 1611 KJV edition, source of the KJV cross-references: kingjamesbibleonline.org/King-James-Bible-Store/#!/KJV-1611-Bible-Hardcover/p/502257216.

CANON

CROSSFIRE

Does
The Protestant Bible
Blow Up
The Case for Christianity?

Matthew Mark McWhorter

ABOUT THE AUTHOR: I am a reformed corporate attorney, happily retired, living in Columbus, Ohio. I began this research as an atheist but ended as a Christian who accepts the Apocrypha.

All proceeds from this book will be donated.

Visit my website at CannonCrossFire.com.

If there are any errors, heresies, or blasphemies herein, they are mine alone, and all views expressed are mine alone. I have assumed that the only person who will ever read this is God. At judgment time, God may or may not care whether I have the correct answer to the topics I discuss herein. But there is no doubt whatsoever that He will care deeply about whether I was honest when discussing it.

Down in Georgia, there is a Matthew McWhorter with a Ph.D. in Roman Catholic Theology who (a) was also blessed with the name which is above every name except one (Philippians 2:9), but (b) teaches, writes and "conducts research on the integration of religio-philosophical psychology and the contemporary human sciences." Obviously, he is not the one to blame for my linguistic ineptitude, let alone my ideas.

This book is dedicated to all the early Church Fathers
who were tortured and killed for believing what they wrote
—the words which we now think of as "mere citations."

"The metric is 70% martyred."
(Page 484)

I am Alpha and Omega,
the beginning and the ending,
saith the Lord.

INTRODUCTION TO THE CASE

In my opinion, the case for Christianity would be lost by a Protestant[1] who believes that the Apocrypha[2] were never accepted as authentic Scripture by the early Church, the Apostles, or Jesus. After the Protestant has presented all the evidence for the authenticity, historicity, and truth of Christian claims for the actual Resurrection of Jesus Christ from the dead, as proclaimed in the Gospels, etc., a skeptic would be able to establish the Protestant's standard for acceptance and belief. Each piece of evidence in favor of the acceptance of the Apocrypha by the Apostles and their disciples would be presented, so as to be rejected as insufficient by such a Protestant. The judge would hear the Protestant's own voice tell her that the evidence for the Apocrypha is not enough, and explain all the reasons why it cannot be considered as sufficient proof of what the Apostles actually taught.

The case for Christianity would thus shift. It would no longer be a simple matter of Christians presenting evidence that meets or exceeds the traditional standards for proving historical or legal facts. Instead, it would require convincing the judge that the evidence proves that the Gospels and Epistles are authentic testimony and teaching from Apostles—even though the Protestant

---

[1] Generally speaking, by "Protestant" I just mean they who insist upon the Protestant canon (39 Old Testament Books). "Protestants" and "Jews" are just labels for extremely diverse groups (e.g., there are both Protestants and Jews who accept all the Apocrypha), and being clear about that in every single sentence is not feasible. I trust you can use your considerable intellect to decipher ancillary terminology from its context and figure out who I am talking about. (In addition, I over-capitalize religious terminology only to avoid giving offense.) While most of the discussion herein relates to those who deny that the early Church accepted the Apocrypha, the evidence should still be of interest to those who acknowledge that as a fact but reject the Apocrypha on theological grounds or limit their use in some way as secondary to other Scripture, etc.

The word "canon" means something like a measuring stick (a ruler, therefore a rule). In Biblical terms, it ends up being the official table of contents, applied as the "rule" that defines what is or is not included in the Bible as Scripture. A "canon list" is a list of the correct Books as claimed by early Father(s)—their lists often differed, so it is "so and so's canon list."

[2] I generally use the capitalized word "Apocrypha" to refer only to the Books of Susanna, Judith, Tobit, Baruch, Wisdom, Sirach, 1 Maccabees, and 2 Maccabees. These are some of the additional Books of the Catholic "Deuterocanon," which are part of the Catholic canon. All other books (putting aside other additions to Daniel and Esther, as well as the Epistle of Jeremiah (Baruch chapter 6), which I simply do not have space to cover in detail) would be considered "apocryphal" to both Catholics and Protestants—and outside of my scope. It is confusing to use the term this way, and impossible to use it consistently, but hopefully, the precise meanings will be obvious in context and will not distract from the point I am trying to make (which is mostly addressed to Protestants, hence my use of Protestant lingo).

"admits" that much the same evidence does not prove that the Apocrypha were authentic Apostolic teaching.

Rather than continue to try to explain how this could work, allow me to show you one way this becomes a problem, by turning to two tiny pieces of evidence: Susanna and Baruch.[3]

---

[3]   Just to get some things out of the way:

I cite Wikipedia and other free secondary sources on simple matters outside of my core research. I do so not because any of them are authoritative but to enable the reader to double check my work and (via Wikipedia's own notes) follow the matter back to primary sources. Citing obscure works looks like proof but, far too often, is an easy way to deceive someone.

Speaking of which, about 20% of modern authorial citations in this field are wrong, by my count from my own research. I believe I comfortably beat that metric herein, and I worked hard to assure myself that I was not taking any quotes out of context or misrepresenting what the author was actually saying. Undoubtedly, some mistakes are still included, but I sincerely doubt the mistakes can be numerous enough to matter to any fair analysis.

As for the style of my citations, while I am not proud of that part of my work, I hope that the effort I put into verifying the citations more than makes up for my lack of a consistent style. I generally do not cite pages for things like Bible commentaries, as the section references are more useful for those of us who cannot easily access a particular printing just to look something up.

All website links and citations were accurate when I created them in either 2024 or 2025. Websites were usually selected by Google and used because their content was representative on the point I am quoting them for, and not because their thoughts are unique. If they disappear or change their tune, then just Google the point they made, and you will find a thousand other sites saying the same sorts of things. I conducted no investigation into webpages, I merely cite to them for what I quote from them; beyond that their operators may all be devil-worshipping terrorists for all I know. For that matter, so too might be the authors of books I cite herein.

"Citation" and "reference" can mean different things to different authors, databases, and websites, and I generally track their meaning when I am talking about their work. Context should make it clear whether what is being discussed is an allusion or a full citation by name, etc. But notably, and very unfortunately, Biblia Patristica/biblindex.org uses "citation" to include everything, even vague allusions—which should never be confused with a real citation or quotation. Most of my use of the Biblindex data is to draw comparisons, where the important thing is that the data is consistent; so, even if the terminology is confusing, it generally does not matter.

Also, I did try to say things like "possible reference" or "John's Gospel may have referred to X" in order to make the point that these things are for you to decide, but it is often awkward to keep doing so. I trust that you, the reader, can keep such things straight and know that you need not agree with me on them.

Lastly, I did not consult a single scholar, Minister, Priest, or other knowledgeable source. I consider this a work of "outsider scholarship," and preferred to do my research without private engagement with any side in any of the debates I discuss herein.

THE PROLOGUE BEFORE THE OVERVIEW

HOW SUSANNA CAN DEFEAT THE CASE FOR CHRISTIANITY

Susanna is presented as a book in the 1611 King James Version of the Bible, but is Chapter 13 of Daniel in Catholic Bibles and the first chapter of Daniel in the Orthodox Bible.[4] Unfortunately, by not being a definitive "book," it can get lost in the discussion, which seems to lead to a massive amount of confusion and error when discussing the Apocrypha.

Consider Michael J. Kruger's *Canon Revisited: Establishing the Origins and Authority of the New Testament Books*—an attempt to prove that Christians have "good reasons" for believing in the authenticity of the New Testament canon.[5] He discusses the Apocrypha in a long footnote:[6]

> In the first few centuries of the church we have good evidence that <u>the dominant position (though not the only position) was an acceptance of the Jewish Old Testament canon</u>[7] <u>and not the Apocrypha</u>. This would include church fathers like Melito of Sardis, <u>Origen</u>, Eusebius, Athanasius, Cyril of Jerusalem, Epiphanius, Hilary of Poitiers, Gregory of Nazianzus, <u>Rufinus</u>, and <u>Jerome</u>. Thus, it appears that both the Jewish "church" and <u>the first centuries of the Christian church widely adopted the Old Testament books and not the Apocrypha</u> (of course there were minority opinions, but this does not contradict the model).

Emphasis added in order to emphasize just how incredibly wrong that statement really is. Professor Kruger's point is that the early Church accepted the 27 Books of the New Testament, and his goal is to show that we can trust the early Church to have identified the authentic Apostolic writings. But given Kruger's beliefs, for that to be true, the early Church had to also reject all the "wrong" books, i.e., all the Apocrypha. He cites ten witnesses (essentially

---

[4] Susanna is a complete story, is three times as long as the Book of Obadiah, and could easily be a full Book separated from "Daniel" (as, indeed, the KJV organizes it). From the other direction, Daniel is a collection of writings, i.e., an anthology. So, Susanna could also "fit" into Daniel.

[5] Kruger argues that we have good factual reasons for believing that the entire New Testament is authentic, beyond "mere self-authentication." As part of that, he offers proofs for all the Books, not just the Gospels. The book is a five-star must-read, in my opinion.

[6] As is so often the case, his entire thesis stands on a foundation that is briefly mentioned in a footnote: Ch. 6, note 11. If it matters, my copy of the book is from Crossway, 2012, first printing.

[7] Almost always, this and similar phrasing (whether from myself or other authors) means the canon as the Jews see it today—the same canon the Protestants keep. We will discuss later whether the Jews of antiquity really kept to that canon.

referring us to their canon lists) to disprove the claim that the early Church accepted the Apocrypha.

To see how wrong he is about that, we start with Rufinus, and we focus on Susanna. Here is Rufinus, in the year 400 AD, in his own words, as part of a disagreement with Jerome:

> There has been from the first in the churches of God and especially in that of Jerusalem, a plentiful supply of men who being born Jews have become Christians ... [and yet] has there been one who has dared to make havoc of the divine record handed down to the Churches by the Apostles and the deposit of the Holy Spirit? For what can we call it but havoc, when some parts of it are transformed, and this is called the correction of an error? For instance, the whole of the history of Susanna ... has by him [Jerome, says Rufinus (incorrectly)] been cut out, thrown aside and dismissed...[8]

Rufinus tells us that Susanna is Scripture to the early Church and always has been. But how do we know that Rufinus was correct? Partly, we can corroborate it with evidence from his enemy, Jerome. On whether Susanna is accepted as Scripture, they agree entirely.

First, we have Book 2 of Jerome's Apology Against Rufinus (402 AD):[9]

> ... In reference to Daniel ... We have four versions to choose from: those of Aquila, Symmachus, the Seventy [the Septuagint], and Theodotion. The churches choose to read Daniel in the version of Theodotion[10] [the modern Catholic/Orthodox version, with Susanna]. What sin have I committed in following the judgment of the churches? But when I repeat what the Jews say against the Story of Susanna ... which [is] not contained in the Hebrew Bible, the man who makes this a charge against me proves himself to be a fool and a slanderer; for I explained not what I thought but what they commonly say against us.[11]

---

[8] www.newadvent.org/fathers/27052.htm

[9] www.newadvent.org/fathers/27102.htm

[10] Theodotion's Greek Daniel superseded the Septuagint Greek version (also called the Seventy, or LXX: from the second century BC) that had been used by the Church until 150 AD. Both included Susanna—the Church just started with one version and switched to another. And, according to Kruger's witnesses, no one in the Church of 400 AD had yet to even advocate for using a version without Susanna. Rufinus misunderstood what Jerome wrote, as Jerome does not actually call for the rejection of Susanna: "... Leaving this for the reader to pronounce upon as he may think fit ..." tertullian.org/fathers/jerome_preface_daniel.htm. (The Hebrew Daniel (without Susanna) was not being used by Christians; only a handful could even read it. Among them was Jerome, who translated it into Latin so that others could start to use it.) All this is endlessly misunderstood, e.g., the Orthodox Study Bible (Intro, p. vi, 2008 ed.) claims to have the original Bible because they have the Septuagint—but they are wrong, they too have the Theodotion Daniel.

[11] That last sentence is a detail forgotten, or misunderstood, by roughly 100% of authors 100% of the time when discussing these things. But what Jerome said to Rufinus is applicable to anyone else who claims Jerome matched the Jewish/Protestant canon: "I repeat what the Jews say against

Jerome also wrote a Prologue to Daniel, where he tells us:

> I also wish to emphasize to the reader the fact that it was not according to the Septuagint version but according to the version of Theodotion himself that the churches publicly read Daniel. ... all the churches of Christ, whether belonging to the Greek-speaking territory or the Latin, the Syrian or the Egyptian, publicly read this edition...[12]

So, Jerome repeatedly confirms that the early Church is not following the Jewish/Protestant canon and accepts Susanna as Scripture.[13] Thus, everyone in the dispute is agreeing that to the early Church, Susanna is Scripture and always had been.

But also, there is much earlier corroborating evidence to further confirm it, from a discussion 150 years before Jerome and Rufinus wrote:

> Letter from Africanus to Origen: "... you referred to that prophecy of Daniel which is related of his youth [i.e., the story of Susanna]. ... I cannot understand how it escaped you that this part of the book is spurious. ... this section, along with the other two at the end of it, is not contained in the Daniel received among the Jews ..."[14]

> Letter from Origen to Africanus: "... You begin by saying, that ... I did this as if it had escaped me that this part of the book was spurious. ... In answer to this, I have to tell you what it behooves us to do in the cases not only of the History of Susanna, which is

---

the Story of Susanna ... the man who makes this a charge against me proves himself to be a fool and a slanderer; for I explained not what I thought but what they commonly say against us." So sayeth Jerome. It is clear from Rufinus and Jerome that anyone calling for the removal of Susanna in 400 AD would have found it a very unpopular position, which is presumably (a) part of why Jerome does not quite take that stance and (b) part of why Rufinus jumps to the mistaken conclusion that his enemy really was advocating to get rid of it. In any event, Jerome is, himself, evidence that there is still no actual controversy within the Church over Susanna, just the beginning of one that will play out later due to Jerome's influence.

[12] www.tertullian.org/fathers/jerome_daniel_02_text.htm

[13] As full, complete, 100%, canonical Scripture. Neither Jerome nor Rufinus (nor anyone else) says that the early Church sees Susanna as "Ecclesiastical" or just "to be read" or "not to confirm doctrine" or anything of the sort. As far as the evidence shows, Susanna was just a piece of Daniel, even if the Jews did not accept it. Until Jerome, it was treated like everything else in Daniel, without any distinction whatsoever.

[14] www.newadvent.org/fathers/0413.htm. Note that Africanus is not really evidence of his view for any other Christian but himself: his letter is a request for an answer to the issues he is raising and gives no sign that anyone else within the Church was debating any of this at that time. Regardless, he ends the letter with: "I have struck the blow; do you give the echo; answer, and instruct me." Origen's letter back to him appears to have been the end of it.

found in every Church of Christ in that Greek copy which the Greeks use, but is not in the Hebrew …"[15]

We will discuss Origen's explanation of why the Church did not use the Hebrew Scriptures in detail shortly, but for now the "why" does not matter. Origen tells us that every Church of Christ held Susanna as Scripture, while knowing that Susanna is not in the Hebrew version of Daniel—and telling us so 150 years before Jerome and Rufinus also tell us so.

The position of the early Church is crystal clear—in fact, it is crystal clear just from the Fathers cited by Kruger (let alone all the other evidence). Susanna was Scripture, full Christian Scripture, regardless of the Jewish canon, and regardless of it not being written in the Hebrew language or anything else. The early Church fully accepted this Apocrypha along with the Jewish/Hebrew Scriptures (as the Jews of its time (or our time) define them, and as Protestants accept them). The evidence for that includes each and every one of the other Fathers on Kruger's list:

> Athanasius repeatedly refers to Susanna as Scripture, e.g. "it is equally plain from what follows that … in the same Scriptures … And in Daniel, 'Susanna cried out with a loud voice and said, O everlasting God, that know the secrets, and know all things before they be.' Thus, it appears that …"[16]
>
> Epiphanius: "God knoweth all things before they be, as scripture says" (Susanna 42).[17]
>
> Eusebius: "At this time also Africanus… was well known. There is extant an epistle of his to Origen, expressing doubts of the story of Susannah in Daniel, as being spurious and fictitious. Origen answered this very fully."[18]
>
> Cyril of Jerusalem: "And if further a man peruse all the books of the Prophets, both of the Twelve, and of the others, he will find many testimonies concerning the Holy Ghost; … The chaste Susanna was condemned as a wanton; …We bring this forward as a testimony... And indeed it were easy to collect very many texts out of the Old Testament, and to discourse more largely concerning the Holy Ghost."[19]
>
> Hilary of Poitiers: "...refute their vain and pestilent teaching by the witness of the evangelists and apostles. ... They say that the Father has prescience of all things, as the blessed Susanna says, O eternal God, that know secrets, and know all things before they be; that He is incomprehensible, as it is written ..."[20]

---

[15] www.newadvent.org/fathers/0414.htm; there is earlier evidence for Suzanna as well, from Fathers not on Kruger's list.

[16] Four Discourses against the Arians 1, 12-13. www.newadvent.org/fathers/28161.htm.

[17] Panarion, Section 2, Heresy 30, Ebionites 9, 2. Not available online.

[18] Church History 6, 31, 1: www.newadvent.org/fathers/250106.htm.

[19] Catechetical Lecture 16: 29-32 www.newadvent.org/fathers/310116.htm

[20] On the Trinity Book 4: 7-8. www.newadvent.org/fathers/330204.htm.

> Gregory of Nazianzus refers to Susanna as part of Daniel and, therefore, as Scripture. "Passing by the elders in the book of Daniel; for it is better to pass them by, together with the Lord's righteous sentence and declaration concerning them, that wickedness came from Babylon from ancient judges." [Susanna 5 (Daniel 13:5)][21]

That is nine out of the ten people on Kruger's list who are on the record as considering Susanna (Apocrypha) as full Christian Scripture, and the absence of Melito of Sardis is because he never said anything about Susanna. We have very little from Melito, so that is not surprising. However, his canon list uses the Septuagint name for Daniel—and the Septuagint version of Daniel definitely included Susanna. Thus, based on the words of his list—which is (a) the only statement from Melito himself that we possess on the subject, and (b) why Kruger cited to Melito—the evidence shows that his Daniel would have included Susanna.

So yes, there was debate with the Jews. Yes, there are individuals within the Church (Africanus and Jerome) who seem to want to agree with the Jews. Yes, accepting Susanna does not mean that all the other Apocrypha were accepted. Yes, yes, yes…

But the factual inquiry is as simple and conclusive as it could possibly be. The evidence shows us that there is no dispute or argument over the early Church's position on Susanna. Every single ancient source that Kruger himself is citing is telling us that the early Church saw it as canonical Scripture. Unanimously. There is not even a "minority view." Jerome tells us that Susanna is accepted and publicly read by "all the churches of Christ, whether belonging to the Greek-speaking territory or the Latin, the Syrian or the Egyptian." He could not have been more specific or certain on that point.

Kruger's case for the authenticity of the New Testament was based on "an acceptance of the Jewish Old Testament canon and not the Apocrypha." But according to his own witnesses, for 400 years—at least sixteen generations, and the same time period from the Pilgrims to us today—"all the churches of Christ" (as Jerome says) and "every Church of Christ" (as Origen says) accepted Susanna as "the divine record handed down to the Churches by the Apostles and the deposit of the Holy Spirit" (as Rufinus says).

---

[21] Oration 2, 64. www.newadvent.org/fathers/310202.htm.

Susanna, alone, kills the horse. As far as Kruger's case for Christianity is concerned, the rest of this book is just me repeatedly beating that dead horse's corpse, of course.[22]

Three key points to consider. First, a brief interlude to discuss wordsmithing. What we often hear is that the name "Daniel" in a Protestant Bible matches the name "Daniel" on an ancient canon list. Some go further and mistakenly handwave Susanna away by claiming it is just part of a "textual variation" of Daniel. While true, such things are completely irrelevant to all discussion of Susanna.

We are discussing Susanna, not Daniel. The question is whether a list's mention of "Daniel" is referencing the Daniel that includes Susanna or not. When focusing on Susanna, every other word of Daniel is the irrelevant textual variation! We do not care in the slightest about the "rest of" Daniel. Yes or no, "Professor," did the list's mention of "Daniel" include Susanna?

The answer is always yes and can only ever be yes. The explanation that "they thought Susanna was part of Daniel" forms the actual proof: if it was a part of Daniel, it was accepted. The author of the list did not mean solely the Protestant Daniel, and (except for Melito and unknown authors) his own use of the term proves that. For the others, the evidence may be circumstantial, but it is still the evidence. The lists should, therefore, say "Daniel [and Susanna]" because the word "Daniel" meant (to the Father who wrote it) what to Protestants would be said as "Daniel and Susanna." The modern translator should be trying to convey the correct modern English meaning of the Father's Greek word "Daniel." Instead, they bury it in a footnote and confuse everyone.

In fact, Protestant scholars go to great lengths to stress this exact concept all the time when discussing the canon—it is just that they do not do so with Susanna. Instead, they do so with a different lady: Ruth. Read any discussion of the canon lists that are just numbers (such as Josephus, in which he mentions "22 books") or read any discussion of a list that specifically mentions the book "Judges" (without mentioning the Book of Ruth):

---

[22] If we seek the first list, or Bible, or Church or Father that does not accept Susanna, it would be from someone influenced by Jerome's ideas in a later era. Edmon Gallagher (e.g., at www.academia.edu/14345165/) calls the "obelus" (the marking Jerome used to note that Susanna was not in the Hebrew Daniel) a "death warrant" for Susanna—but a death warrant is not an execution until it is actually carried out. So, then, who first takes it out? What is the first Bible whose Daniel does not have it, or the first canon list that really excludes it, or the first person to openly say it is not Scripture, etc.? I have long sought the answer, but no one seems to say. I did not find anything through 450 AD in my own searches.

inevitably, as part of arguing that the references are actually to all 39 books of the Protestant canon as they are currently thought of and named, someone expresses the idea that Judges and Ruth were thought of as one book by the ancients, so therefore Ruth is part of that canon.[23]

Exactly! The ancients also thought of Daniel and Susanna as one Book. The same logic that identifies Ruth was part of a canon list that only indicates Judges makes Susanna part of the early Church's canon lists when they said Daniel.[24] The only difference is that the scholars *stress* the inclusion in one context and *dismiss* the inclusion in another.

But the result is inarguable: the canon lists of the early Church used the word Daniel to refer to a Book that included both Daniel and Susanna.

Second, I shall preach a gospel of being "fair and consistent"—but not out of a spirit of Christian goodness. It is simply a practical necessity because this is the case for Christianity. Notably, the case presupposes that the judge will always rule based on evidence, not speculation. I.e., the evidence shows that Jesus Christ rose from the dead—and the evidence wins despite endless speculation otherwise.

For example, the judge will rule that someone's use of the word "Matthew" refers to the physical Book we call "Matthew" because the ordinary meaning of a word stands, absent sufficient evidence to the contrary. So, too, will the Septuagint name for Daniel refer to the Septuagint Book (with Susanna). There is plenty of evidence proving the ordinary meaning of the term Melito used, and that definition would be the basis of the ruling in an

---

[23] E.g., "He limits the number of canonical books in these three divisions to twenty-two. This would be the same as the current twenty-four – Ruth was attached to Judges, and Lamentation attached to Jeremiah." blogs.blueletterbible.org/blb/2012/05/29/josephus-historical-evidence-of-the-old-testament-canon/.

[24] There is actually far earlier evidence of this practice for Susanna than for Ruth: Origen (a Christian) is the first to mention this alleged Jewish practice for Ruth, and he does so 200 years after Christ. Compare this to Irenaeus, who was writing well before Origen in Against Heresy IV, 26, 3: "hear those words, to be found in Daniel the prophet: ..." and then quoting Susanna 52-53. www.newadvent.org/fathers/0103426.htm). In addition, indirect evidence for Susanna would include the Church's use of the Septuagint version of Daniel (which included Susanna), etc.

Moreover, Origen is also better evidence for Susanna than he is for Ruth because it is Origen talking about his own church (in fact, there is still ongoing debate over whether the Jews actually did combine Judges and Ruth). If a judge accepts what Origen says about Ruth as proof, then a judge is certainly going to accept what Origen says about Susanna.

evidentiary hearing. While speculation and debate to the contrary exists, meaningful evidence does not.[25]

Third, I will discuss Susanna itself in more detail later, including all the evidence from the centuries before the canon lists. However, if it seems to you that it would be a good idea to look into the possibility that the evidence from the period before the lists does not match what the lists indicate about Susanna, then please realize that you have proven to yourself that relying only on canon lists is a mistake for ignorant fools—because the fact that Susanna is on all of them did not satisfy you either. So, inclusion/exclusion by canon lists should never be the end of the inquiry for any other Book or timeframe.

But actually, for purposes of Kruger's case, the "even earlier" Church is completely irrelevant. Because the point here is not actually about Susanna; it is what Susanna shows us about Kruger's claim. No one is trying to prove that Susanna was Scripture. In fact, Kruger is the only Christian involved in the case, and he alone cares about such metaphysical "nonsense." The opponent just wants to defeat the case and is using Susanna to do so.

The opponent's point is that, because of Susanna, not a single one of the ten witnesses actually evidences the claim that Kruger was trying to prove: the "acceptance of the Jewish Old Testament canon and not the Apocrypha." In effect, after ten witnesses have come and gone, Kruger has not yet presented a single shred of evidence to prove his claim.

So, then, what could earlier evidence prove? Simply that the early Church was entirely and completely wrong. After all, that is precisely what Jerome was saying: everyone had been unanimously accepting Susanna for centuries, but the Jews say that they should not have done so. Recall that Rufinus says that it "is called the correction of an error." And per Jerome, those who might be wrong were "all the churches of Christ, whether belonging to the Greek-speaking territory or the Latin, the Syrian or the Egyptian."

Kruger would only disprove his claim that the early Church correctly identified the authentic Books handed down by the Apostles. Even if he won the "case against the Apocrypha," he would lose the case for Christianity.[26]

---

[25] Thus, I devote less time to dealing with endless speculation than other books on the canon. I simply go with the position that I feel would win in the actual case for Christianity, based on the evidence.

[26] The same thing would happen, of course, if a judge ruled that Melito's reference is insufficiently proved. What, then, is proved, except that the Church and the later nine Fathers were mistaken? This is actually why a judge would never even rule on it: either way, Kruger loses. Case dismissed.

CANON LISTS AND SUSANNA

Below is a chart of every early canon list and whether Susanna is canon on each. For Christians, it is unanimous.

FATHER/LIST/BOOK	Year	SUSANNA CANONICAL?	EVIDENCE
MELITO OF SARDIS	170	CANON FOR JEWS?	SEPTUAGINT NAME
MURATORIAN CANON	170	N/A	NT LIST
CLEMENT OF ALEXANDRIA	203	CANON	GREEK DANIEL
ORIGEN (JEWISH LIST)	220	NOT FOR JEWS	SEE THE LETTER
ORIGEN (TO AFRICANUS)	248	CANON	SEE THE LETTER
ORIGEN (CITATIONS)	250	CANON	PREP GOSPEL 6, 11
EUSEBIUS (APPROVAL)	324	CANON	CH. HISTORY 6, 31, 1
~~THE NICENE COUNCIL~~	325	~~UNKNOWN~~	~~UNKNOWN~~
CODEX CLAROMONTANUS	349	CANON	VERSES DAN. 1600
CODEX VATICANUS	*350*	*CANON*	*DANIEL CHAPTER 1*
CODEX SINAITICUS	*350*	*UNKNOWN*	*ALL DANIEL MISSING*
CYRIL OF JERUSALEM	350	CANON	LECTURE 16: 29-32
ST CATHERINE'S SYRIAC	350	CANON	AS SYRIAC DANIEL
CHELTENHAM LIST	360	CANON	DANIEL 1350 LINES
~~COUNCIL OF LAODICEA~~	363	~~CANON~~	~~AS DANIEL~~
ATHANASIUS	367	CANON	4 D. ARIANS 1, 12-13
HILARY OF POITIERS	367	CANON	ON TRINITY 4: 7-8
GREGORY OF NAZIANZUS	380	CANON	ORATION 2, 64
AMPHILOCHIUS OF ICONIUM	380	CANON	ORATIO IN ILLUD
APOSTOLIC CANONS	380	CANON	BOOK 2, 51
~~THE COUNCIL OF ROME~~	382	~~CANON~~	~~AS DANIEL~~
EPIPHANIUS PANARION 8.6.1	385	CANON FOR JEWS	SEPTUAGINT
EPIPHANIUS PAN.76.22.5	385	CANON	2, 30, 9, 2
JEROME (HELMETED)	390	CANON	APOLOGY 2, 33
EPIPHANIUS DE MENS. 4-5	392	CANON FOR JEWS	SEPTUAGINT
THE COUNCIL OF HIPPO – 70 BISHOPS	**393**	**CANON**	**AS DANIEL**
AUGUSTINE	397	CANON	HOLY VIRGIN. 19
COUNCIL OF CARTHAGE - 44-48 BISHOPS	**397**	**CANON**	**AS DANIEL**
JEROME (SOLOMON)	398	CANON	APOLOGY 2, 33
RUFINUS	400	CANON	APOLOGY 2, 33
JEROME (TOBIT/JUDITH)	404	CANON	APOLOGY 2, 33
POPE INNOCENT I	405	CANON	AS DANIEL
COUNCIL OF CARTHAGE - 217 BISHOPS	**419**	**CANON**	**AS DANIEL**
CODEX ALEXANDRINUS	*450*	*CANON*	*DANIEL CH.1*
CODEX EPHRAEMI R.	*450*	*UNKNOWN*	*ALL DANIEL MISSING*

Explanations and discussion about the individual lists will come later in the book (but in case you are wondering, the stricken-out councils probably did not issue those canon lists: the much later evidence is dubious). Note that it is the canon list that is the evidence of Susanna's canonicity. The other writings just evidence what the label "Daniel" meant, so that we correctly interpret the meaning of the words of the canon lists. This case for Susanna is a "canon list case" as much as the case for any other Book, in that we look to the Greek (etc.) words of the list but need external proof of their meaning.

Clearly, the evidentiary "arrow" of the canon lists points to Susanna every bit as much as it does to any other Old or New Testament Books.[27] Lose sight of this at your peril. The case for Christianity is based on the claim that the New Testament is authentic Apostolic testimony. Kruger was trying to prove that, and he failed. The canon lists are the very best evidence for his view, and yet what they evidence is that not one single person in the early Church held to the canon that Kruger claims they held—not even Jerome.

However, Susanna is not a full-length Book, and sometimes scholars try to distinguish it on that basis. I do not believe that such a tactic works in a real case, but I need not argue the point. Instead, let us turn to Baruch.[28]

HOW BARUCH CAN DEFEAT THE CASE FOR CHRISTIANITY

The early Church accepted Baruch, according to nine of the ten Fathers that Kruger cites, let alone all the other Fathers. The first and only Father we know of who may have rejected Baruch is Jerome, 360 years after Christ.

Jerome again evidences this in what he tells us about Baruch. He is really a tenth witness to the Church's unanimous position; he just may not agree with it, so he ends the unanimity. Jerome is very clear that "the Hebrews" reject Baruch, but pointedly does not say that the Church rejects Baruch. Instead, he gives clear evidence that his Christian peers do not agree with the Jews:

> And the Book of Baruch, his scribe,[29] which is neither read nor found among the Hebrews, we have omitted, standing ready, because of these things, for all the curses

---

[27] And it points more to Susanna than for some: e.g., Susanna is on every single list, but both Old Testament Books (notably Esther) and New Testament Books are missing on various canon lists.

[28] The other "longer form" pieces of Daniel and Esther raise essentially the same issue as Susanna, just with different evidence in support of their acceptance by the early Church. However, I do not have space in this book to discuss their evidence in detail.

[29] Jeremiah may have been illiterate, and the Book of Jeremiah was actually written by Baruch as his scribe. This interconnected "dual authorship" is at the heart of the practice of calling Baruch "Jeremiah" (and similar practices shared by Lamentations and the Epistle (Baruch Chapter 6)). The Book of Baruch does not pretend to be by Jeremiah and begins by saying "And these are the words of the book, which Baruch … wrote in Babylon." On the other hand, Jeremiah is an

from the jealous, to whom it is necessary for me to respond through a separate short work. And I suffer because you think this.[30]

Nowhere does Jerome mention a single predecessor who agrees with the Jewish view. If read carefully, he does not even say that he agrees with it. For the purposes of this book, I assume he does, but he does not actually say so (and he accepts Baruch as Prophecy in other writings).

So (a) focus on Baruch, not Apocrypha, and (b) understand that (in the case of Fathers who make no express mention of the name Baruch) the Book of Baruch was considered part of the Book of Jeremiah by the early Church (similar to how Susanna was considered part of Daniel, or Ruth was considered part of Judges, or even how Lamentations was also considered part of Jeremiah).[31] Eight of Kruger's ten Fathers expressly quote verses from Baruch as Scripture, or Prophecy, or the word of God, etc. A few specifically say that the quotes came from the Book of Baruch, but others say that the quotes came from Jeremiah.

A citation from the Book of Baruch as coming from Jeremiah is confirmation that the Father did, in fact, see it as part of Jeremiah. The canon list is the proof that (like everyone else) he thought that Jeremiah was "canon." Thus, the citation is just proof that the Jeremiah on his canon list included Baruch, too.

Note that the canon list case for Baruch has something that even Susanna did not: Baruch is explicitly mentioned by name as a canonical Book on several lists.

---

anthology that collects shorter writings; so as with Susanna and Daniel, the question is whether Baruch is part of the collection. Sorting all that out is an issue for a later discussion; at the moment, all we care about is that the early Church considered the Book of Baruch to be part of the Book of Jeremiah. I.e., Baruch was canon to the early Church, every bit as much as the "rest of" Jeremiah.

[30] www.tertullian.org/fathers/jerome_preface_jeremiah.htm

[31] See below for additional citation evidence for the practice in the period between Christ and the year 200. As for the Jews before Christ, many experts believe that the same person translated (from Hebrew into Greek) Jeremiah, Baruch, and the Epistle, which would also be evidence that they were on the same scroll. There is even a piece of possible Biblical evidence: in Daniel 9:2, Daniel explicitly mentions Jeremiah and, then, in 9:5 and 9:8, may have quoted from Baruch (i.e., the Baruch part of Jeremiah) in his prayers. (Compare Daniel 9:8 "O Lord, to us belongeth confusion of face, to our kings, to our princes, and to our fathers, because we have sinned against thee" and Baruch 1:15-17: "15And ye shall say, To the Lord our God belongeth righteousness, but unto us the confusion of faces, ..., 16And to our kings, and to our princes, and ... to our fathers: 17For we have sinned before the Lord"). There are other possible quotes and allusions by Daniel as well. (But like everything else with the canon discussion, the Biblical evidence is debated.)

Athanasius separates Baruch from Jeremiah, and his canon list expressly declares Baruch to be Scripture (and not in his third category).[32]

Rufinus (a) does not list Baruch as Ecclesiastical, and (b) in the exact same book, (see Section 38) he quotes from Baruch. "Which also the Prophet foretold when he said, This is our God: ... Afterward He showed Himself upon the earth, and conversed with men." (Baruch 3:35-37).[33]

Origen quotes from Baruch as part of his homily on Jeremiah: "... about which it is written: Hear Israel. Why is it that you are in the land of enemies ... If you have walked in the way of God, you would have dwelt in peace forever." (Baruch 3:9-13).[34]

Hilary of Poitiers lists Jeremiah as canon and quotes from Baruch as Jeremiah, e.g., "...listen now to Jeremiah inculcating the same truth as they:— This is our God ... Afterward did He show Himself upon earth and dwelt among men. ... Jeremiah proclaims God seen on earth and dwelling among men..." (Baruch 3:35-37).[35]

Eusebius does not have his own Old Testament canon list, but he cites to Baruch as inspired prophecy, e.g.: "It is prophesied that the God of the Prophets...will some Day afterwards be seen on Earth, and mingle among Men. I need add nothing to these inspired words, which so clearly support my argument." (Baruch 3:29-37).[36]

Epiphanius' Christian list (in his Panarion) does not specifically mention Jeremiah or Baruch, but his reference to 27 Books is read by all to incorporate the 27 Books on his Jewish list in the same work, which does mention Baruch by name as part of Jeremiah. He then quotes from Baruch as Scripture throughout the same book: "But the scripture says...he alone is Son by nature, not grace—for "He hath found out every path of understanding" (Baruch 3:32) and "none shall be declared his equal."" (Baruch 3:35).[37]

---

[32] See www.bible-researcher.com/athanasius.html.

[33] Commentary on the Apostles' Creed, 5, www.newadvent.org/fathers/2711.htm

[34] Homily 7 on Jeremiah, 3.3, not available online. Origen's situation is more complicated than I allude to above. He is the first to separate Baruch from Jeremiah, and his list (which is a Jewish list, not a Christian one—see later discussion) does not specifically mention it by name. It does mention the Epistle of Jeremiah (Baruch Chapter 6, to Catholics), which makes the absence of Baruch odd. Many think it is a copyist's mistake: either both should be off the list or on it, in the usual practice. On the other hand, he may have meant to leave it off the Jewish list as not being canon to the Jews, which (as will be discussed) does not mean that he does not accept it as canon for Christians. It makes sense to me that he (as the first to separate Baruch) might do so because he knew that the Jews did not accept it, without realizing (at the time of his writing) that they also rejected the Epistle—but no one else ever mentions that idea, so perhaps I am wrong. In any event, there is nothing in Origen's writings to show that he did not consider Baruch part of the Christian canon. He cited to it 16 times, including the "it is written" noted above (which notably occurs in a homily on Jeremiah, without mentioning whether he takes it from Jeremiah or Baruch). See also the discussion in Chapter 3, footnote 68, p. 87 of Gallagher and Meade.

In addition, note that Athanasius states that Baruch was handed down to him in the Church at Alexandria more than a century after Origen (a predecessor of his in the Church at Alexandria)— evidence that Origen continued to teach Baruch as canon for Christians. See his statement at www.bible-researcher.com/athanasius.html.

[35] On the Trinity, 4, 42 (www.newadvent.org/fathers/330204.htm).

[36] Demonstratio Evangelica, 6.19 www.ccel.org/ccel/pearse/morefathers/files/eusebius_de_08_book6.htm.

[37] Panarion, Section 4, Heresy 49, Arians, 53, 7 (not available online).

Gregory of Nazianzus lists Jeremiah as canon and quotes from Baruch (without naming a Book), e.g.: "Since I have ...solved in the mass the objections and oppositions drawn from Holy Scripture, ... yet we have not yet gone through the passages in detail, because of the haste of our argument. ... In what passage? Why, in this: This is your God; ... after this did He show Himself upon earth, and conversed with men." (Baruch 3:35-3:37).[38]

Cyril of Jerusalem specifically lists Baruch as canon in his list.[39]

Melito lists Jeremiah but is not known to have ever mentioned Baruch or to have quoted from the Book (he also does not list Lamentations, so the only way for his list to include Lamentations is to apply the logic that the Book of Jeremiah included Lamentations, the exact same logic as for Baruch). There is citation evidence from others contemporaneous with Melito, as well as the general evidence about use of the Septuagint (the names on Melito's list are the Septuagint names of Books, not the Hebrew), which point to the inclusion of Baruch.

Jerome alone may reject Baruch. He actually never says so expressly, and he seems to accept it in some writings (e.g., calling Baruch a prophet in Letter 77, 4).[40] But for the purposes of this book, I grant that Jerome stands for the rejection of Baruch.

Now another brief interlude on wordsmithing. We are often told that the name Jeremiah on some ancient canon list includes Lamentations because Lamentations was often included as "part of Jeremiah." Exactly! Just as Lamentations was "always canon," so was Baruch. It is literally the exact same claim, although the evidence is sometimes different. Compare and contrast:

Why is Lamentations canon? "Lamentations was attached to the Book of Jeremiah... Therefore, its canonical status was not in doubt."[41]

Why do some claim Baruch is "not really" canon? "The Roman Catholic Deuterocanon also includes Baruch, but we have seen that in this early period this work was often considered a part of Jeremiah."[42]

Note carefully the stress put on this in one quote and the dismissiveness put on it in the other, even though the situation is identical.

Does it matter that the Fathers considered Baruch part of Jeremiah? In a discussion about whether the early Church accepted Apocrypha as Scripture, it most certainly does: they accepted Baruch because they accepted Jeremiah. Does it matter if the Fathers were "mistaken" to think that Baruch was part of Jeremiah? No, not in the slightest. We are discussing whether Apocrypha were canon to the early Church and the answer is that Baruch was canon. There endeth all discussion. If you believe that it was a mistake, and that there is a

---

[38] Oration 30, 13 (Fourth Theological Oration) Section 1 www.newadvent.org/fathers/310230.htm

[39] www.bible-researcher.com/cyril.html

[40] The letter is available at www.newadvent.org/fathers/3001077.htm

[41] www.blueletterbible.org/Comm/stewart_don/faq/right-books-in-old-testament/question17-new-testament-quote-old-testament.cfm.

[42] Gallagher and Meade, p. 5 (as will also be discussed below).

good reason to get rid of it or place it in a separate section of the Bible, that is up to you (and will be discussed a bit later)—but the point is that it was/is a later theological decision. The evidence (all from Kruger's witnesses, I remind you) does not identify anyone who felt that way until Jerome, and as far as I could find, no one else felt that way until after at least 450 AD (30 years after Jerome's death). The early Church accepted Baruch.[43]

Something else is also clear, when we look solely at Baruch and not at the Apocrypha as a group: with respect to Baruch (and, in fact, Susanna, as briefly mentioned above) there is no third category (the three categories being Scripture, not Scripture, and something in between = Apocrypha), no Ecclesiastical, no "only to be read and not to be used to confirm doctrine," nothing like that at all. Baruch is either full canonical Scripture or it is not, and it is that way for every single Father, including Athanasius, Rufinus, and Jerome (the three Fathers most often cited as support for a "third category" of Books), and also including Epiphanius, Cyril of Jerusalem, Gregory of Nazianzus, Amphilochius of Iconium,[44] and the Apostolic Canons[45] (additional Fathers occasionally cited as support for a third category).[46]

A claim that the Apocrypha were only ever "Ecclesiastical" and never considered full Scripture by the early Church is as easily disproven by the canon lists as Kruger's claim that the Apocrypha were never accepted at all.

My point in covering this at the beginning is to stress that it does not matter how many canon lists someone claims to have that (they say) show that

---

[43] As with Susanna, there is no real debate on this. In fact, it is often acknowledged in the footnotes of Protestant books on the canon (see e.g., Gallagher's blog, where he notes offhand that "Rufinus had assumed the presence of Baruch within Jeremiah" (sanctushieronymus.blogspot. com/search/label/Baruch). However, as I discuss below, it is often done in a dismissive way that leads to confusion, such as we see with Kruger, Gallagher and Meade, etc.

[44] His list only says Jeremiah, but he cites to Baruch in other works (Homily 1, On the Nativity, 1.2.50-52, not available online) as "other sayings of the prophet," i.e., Jeremiah.

[45] A list that is part of a book called the Apostolic Constitutions. The list merely says "the 16 books of the prophets," but that number would presumably include Jeremiah, with Baruch as part of Jeremiah. The book elsewhere cites to Jeremiah and Baruch repeatedly, e.g., Book 6, 4, 23 ("For says He [God]: ... And again: Blessed are we, O Israel, because those things that are pleasing to God are known to us." Baruch 4:4), even mentioning that the Jews of 380 AD still accept Baruch: "For even now, on the tenth day of the month Gorpiæus, when they assemble together, they read the Lamentations of Jeremiah, in which it is said ... and Baruch, in whom it is written, "This is our God; ... Afterwards He was seen upon earth, and conversed with men." And when they read them, they lament and bewail..." (Baruch 3:35-37). Book 5, 3, 20. Newadvent .org/fathers/07156.htm and newadvent.org/fathers/07155.htm.

[46] As with Susanna, the first support for such a categorization of Baruch would come either in the Middle Ages or, perhaps, even after the Reformation (Sorry, but I could not find any mention of when precisely that first occurs. I found no evidence for it before 450 AD).

the Protestant/Jewish canon was the early Church's canon. The lists actually show the exact opposite. Just focus on Susanna and Baruch, and you will see that the claim is provably false. In fact, the canon lists prove that the early Church's Scriptures differed from the "Jewish canon" and included Apocrypha—at the very least, Susanna and Baruch.

Note that I said "provably false." The claim can be disproved using the claimant's own evidence and their own standards of proof. And the case for Christianity can be lost just as easily over Baruch as with Susanna.

CANON LISTS AND BARUCH

Below is a chart of every canon list, and whether Baruch is canon on each. For Christians, it is unanimous, except for Jerome.

FATHER/LIST/BOOK	Year	BARUCH CANONICAL?	NAME
MELITO OF SARDIS	170	CANON FOR JEWS?	JEREMIAH
MURATORIAN CANON (NT LIST)	170	N/A	N/A
CLEMENT OF ALEXANDRIA	203	CANON	JEREMIAH
ORIGEN (JEWISH LIST)	220	NOT FOR JEWS?	BARUCH? .
ORIGEN (LETTER)	248	N/A	N/A
ORIGEN (CITATIONS)	250	CANON	BARUCH
EUSEBIUS (CITES W/ APPROVAL)	324	CANON	JEREMIAH
THE NICENE COUNCIL	325	UNKNOWN	UNKNOWN
CODEX CLAROMONTANUS	349	CANON	JEREMIAH
CODEX VATICANUS	*350*	*CANON*	*BARUCH*
CODEX SINAITICUS	*350*	*CANON*	*BARUCH*
CYRIL OF JERUSALEM	350	CANON	BARUCH
ST CATHERINE'S SYRIAC MS 10	350	CANON?	JEREMIAH
CHELTENHAM LIST	360	CANON?	JEREMIAH?
THE COUNCIL AT LAODICEA	363	CANON	BARUCH
ATHANASIUS	367	CANON	BARUCH
HILARY OF POITIERS	367	CANON	JEREMIAH
GREGORY OF NAZIANZUS	380	CANON	JEREMIAH
AMPHILOCHIUS OF ICONIUM	380	CANON	JEREMIAH
THE APOSTOLIC CANONS	380	CANON	BARUCH
THE COUNCIL OF ROME	382	CANON	JEREMIAH
EPIPHANIUS PANARION 8.6.1-4	385	CANON FOR JEWS	BARUCH
EPIPHANIUS PAN. 76.22.5	385	CANON	BARUCH
JEROME (HELMETED PREFACE)	390	NOT CANON	BARUCH
EPIPHANIUS DE MENS. 4-5	392	NOT FOR JEWS	BARUCH
THE COUNCIL OF HIPPO – 70 BISHOPS	393	CANON	JEREMIAH
AUGUSTINE	397	CANON	JEREMIAH
THE COUNCIL OF CARTHAGE - 44-48 BISHOPS	397	CANON	JEREMIAH
JEROME (SOLOMON)	398	NOT CANON	BARUCH
RUFINUS	400	CANON	JEREMIAH

FATHER/LIST/BOOK	Year	BARUCH CANONICAL?	NAME
JEROME (TOBIT/JUDITH)	404	NOT CANON	BARUCH
POPE INNOCENT I	405	CANON	PROPHETS (JER.)
THE COUNCIL OF CARTHAGE - 217 BISHOPS	**419**	**CANON**	**JEREMIAH**
CODEX ALEXANDRINUS	*450*	*CANON*	*JEREMIAH*
CODEX EPHRAEMI RESCRIPTUS	*450*	*UNKNOWN*	*UNKNOWN*

So, given what the evidence actually is, how did Kruger come to be citing witnesses who disprove his claim? My guess is that Susanna and Baruch were pieces of trivia rattling around in the back of his brain, and he simply never realized that the trivia ruined his case. It takes an actual opponent digging through the evidence to point out that the footnotes in the canon debate are the smoking gun that defeats the case for Christianity.

Kruger is not exceptional for making this mistake. Nearly all canon scholars trivialize and then promptly forget the smoking gun. Kruger is exceptional because he entered the arena to make the case for Christianity. His footnote is the foundation of his proof of Christian beliefs, so his error is not just the usual mistaken detail buried in one footnote among hundreds.[47]

Often, the verbal gymnastics involved in the canon debate are so pervasive that authors even go on to fool themselves. Take, for example, *The Biblical Canon Lists from Early Christianity* by Edmon L. Gallagher and John D. Meade—a book we know Kruger read, since he gives the book a nice little blurb on the back cover:

> 'Gallagher and Meade have provided a useful and much-needed tool in the study of the biblical canon. No doubt it will be a key resource for anyone wishing to explore the reception history of either the Old or New Testament.' Michael Kruger, Journal of Theological Studies.[48]

Consider an early mention of Baruch in Gallagher and Meade. It is, of course, in a footnote (footnote 18, Chapter 1, p. 5):

---

[47] In fact, Kruger's peers, students, and even enemies (let alone proofreaders and fact checkers) are also so accustomed to seeing the usual erroneous statements that (as far as I know) no one even noticed the problem it creates.

[48] I agree entirely with the blurb, and as you will see many times below, the book is my go-to reference for canon lists. It is another five-star must-read, despite all my arguing with their opinions. Just read the book carefully and sort wheat from chaff—as you should do with any book, including this one. If it matters to someone trying to find an exact citation, my copy is from Oxford University Press, first paperback edition, 2019.

The Roman Catholic deuterocanon also includes Baruch, but we have seen that in this early period this work was often considered a part of Jeremiah. In this way, it was also included by Augustine, but also by other Christians who did not include the other books of the deuterocanon (i.e., Tobit, Judith, etc.). The term deuterocanonical was coined by Sixtus of Siena in his Bibliotheca Sancta (Venice, 1566, p. 10). The term refers to books that were not recognized as authoritative until a later time, and for Sixtus the deuterocanonical books include more books and sections of books than are commonly included under that label today.

That footnote is so misleading (inadvertently, I am sure) that, apparently, Kruger could read it without realizing what it does to his beloved model. Even worse, it is so misleading that the authors contradict themselves in their own footnote. They begin by saying:

The Roman Catholic deuterocanon also includes Baruch, but we have seen that in this early period this work was often considered a part of Jeremiah. [49]

In other words (in better words!), since it was considered part of Jeremiah, it was inarguably[50] considered canon by everyone, except for Jerome and only except for Jerome. Yet the authors minimize this crucial fact, which is actually an important point not to be missed.

In this way, it was also included by Augustine, but also by other Christians who did not include the other books of the deuterocanon (i.e., Tobit, Judith, etc.).

In other words, Baruch was an Apocrypha/Deuterocanonical book that was included on every single canon list except for Jerome's. Note the editorial choice to mention Augustine by name rather than someone centuries earlier— that, too, is part of the dismissiveness. They are not wrong, but they are also

---

[49] Gallagher and Meade's use of the phrase "often considered a part of Jeremiah" is accurate, but note that those who did not consider it part of the Book of Jeremiah (such as Athanasius) still believed it was Scripture as the Book of Baruch. The only possibility I have found for someone agreeing with Jerome before 450 AD (a generation after Jerome's death) is noted in passing by Gallagher's blog (sanctushieronymus.blogspot.com/search/label/Baruch), referencing a colophon (a note left by a monk who copied Jerome's Biblical translations) that "dates to maybe the fifth century" and "comes in a manuscript containing Jerome's version of Jeremiah, without Baruch." However, even if the fifth century dating of the colophon is correct, it still might not be before 450 AD, which is the referential end date for this book. (Note that what we are looking for are Bibles or canon lists or other notes that can be shown to exclude the "Old Latin" Book of Baruch, which was sometimes included with Jerome's (newer Latin) translation of Jeremiah. See e.g., the Codex Cavensis (or Biblia de Danila), which has both, per Gallagher and Meade, p. 256.)

[50] As noted above, I speak of an actual case for Christianity. That a scholar can argue anything is inarguable, just as it is for lawyers. In actual cases, however, the point is reached where the judge tells both to shut up. The evidence for Baruch is inarguable by any judicial standard.

not stressing that it was always accepted by everyone. In fact, among the many that get confused by this endless dismissiveness are the gentlemen who wrote the footnote, because they go on to say:

> The term deuterocanonical was coined by Sixtus of Siena in his Bibliotheca Sancta (Venice, 1566, p. 10). The term refers to books that were not recognized as authoritative until a later time…[51]

At a minimum, the term Deuterocanonical expressly encompasses both (a) "books that were not recognized as authoritative until a later time" (if such is true) and (b) Baruch. Thus, the authors instantly forgot what they had just said about Baruch and what it and its history do to most such generalized claims about Apocrypha and Deuterocanonical books (even just definitions).[52]

So, that is what happens. We have Level One (understanding that Baruch was accepted as a matter of trivia) moving up to Level Two (a generalization about the Apocrypha that ignores Baruch as mere trivia) then becoming the basis for Level Three (a claim that the generalization is entirely true)—which is easily disproved by opponents who investigate Level One.

I could continue endlessly with all the examples I have found, but to keep this short I will pick a random one instead. Consider this, from William Webster at christiantruth.com/articles/canon/, which was carefully selected by performing a sophisticated statistical analysis of the leading global archive of all known discussions of the Apocrypha (i.e., this was the first thing at the top of my Google search): "Origen and Athanasius who were from Alexandria both reject the Apocryphal books as being canonical. There are a couple that Athanasius does receive such as Baruch but he mistakenly thought such a work was part of canonical Jeremiah." Webster structured his thoughts as "Bold statement that is not true. And here is my own trivialized proof that it is false." Such a technique is not dishonest or even necessarily deceptive—after all, every book with footnotes does this on practically every single page. "The

---

[51] Note, incidentally, that a claim that "the Apocrypha were recognized as authoritative at a later time" itself implies that the rest of the canon was, somehow, recognized earlier. But there was no Ecumenical Council that recognized the Protestant canon either. The only way to try to claim that Apocrypha came later is if the Protestant canon was canon earlier, which is to acknowledge that consensus is the standard for judging the early Church's canon, whether Old Testament, New Testament, or Apocrypha. Below, we will see Kruger make the point that only consensus determined the New Testament canon.

[52] A neutral definition of the Deuterocanon is just the Books Catholics accept and Protestants do not. Anyone varying from a neutral definition always seems to go on to fool themselves.

sky is blue. Footnote: Except when it is not, such as when there is cloud cover."

However, in some contexts this way of thinking can become very misleading. And here, the fact to remember is that the canon lists are clear evidence that the Fathers and the early Church accepted Apocrypha. No matter how many times you hear something like Webster's first sentence, Webster's second sentence makes it clear that Athanasius, the "Father of the Canon," is actually an example of how every single Father accepted at least some of the Apocrypha. What Webster's two sentences combine to say is not that Athanasius rejected all of the Apocrypha (though that is what he expressly stated in the first sentence), but that Athanasius' acceptance of Apocrypha like Baruch was "mistaken." Those are not the same thing!

And again we see how authors forget 'mere details' when they use this confusing thought structure: read both of Athanasius' and Origen's lists carefully and you will see that both expressly include the Epistle of Jeremiah.[53] That makes something of a mockery of Webster's claim that "both reject the Apocryphal books as being canonical" – because both Athanasius and Origen expressly accept that one.[54] Webster mistakenly forgot to note that his belief is that Origen was also "mistaken," not just Athanasius.

Now of course, this particular confusion is just one example of how the canon can undermine the case for Christianity, and we are discussing what might only be Kruger's first attempt. He or someone else could go back down to Level One (i.e., the actual evidence, rather than relying on an abstraction or a generalization) and try to build an argument that remembers Susanna and Baruch and is based on all the evidence, including all the earlier writings (beyond just the canon lists), etc. What would happen then?

They would always lose, just not as instantly as Kruger did with his first attempt. Such is my opinion, anyway! But decide for yourself. For the love of God—literally, for the love of God—do not let my personal views keep you from considering the evidence properly. Tweak whatever I miswrote and figure out the actual truth. That, after all, is the only part of this that matters.

---

[53] The Epistle of Jeremiah is included as chapter 6 of the Catholic Book of Baruch, but historically it is a separate writing that has its own unique history and evidentiary support (and is not a minor piece of it, despite being set off as only one chapter: it is 73 verses long, more than half as long as the "rest of" the Book of Baruch's 140 verses).
[54] See bible-researcher.com/origen.html and bible-researcher.com/athanasius.html. I will discuss other problems involved with citing to Origen later.

This book is not concerned with the theological decision of what modern Christians should accept as "the" canon, and it is not an argument with anyone. It is just a review of the evidence, with a focus on what the evidence would then be held to prove, given the claims made in the case for Christianity—where the evidence for the Apocrypha is never trivial and never to be dismissed or handwaved away. Whatever it is, it is.

Of course a Protestant has every right to claim that the evidence is not enough to prove that the Books were really accepted, and does not prove that the Books were authentic Apostolic teaching, etc.—but understand that the opponents in the case for Christianity do not care about whether Apocrypha should be "Scripture." They are introducing the Apocrypha into the discussion so that the Protestant will testify that the evidence is insignificant, unreliable, or insufficient. Because as soon as the Protestant is done testifying to that, the skeptics are going to compare it to the evidence in the case for Christianity, to show the judge that the Protestant "admits" that the case for Christianity is not proved. It is this comparison of (a) whatever the evidence for the Apocrypha is, to (b) the evidence being cited in the case for Christianity, that (c) determines whether there is really enough evidence to prove that Jesus Christ rose from the dead—e.g., whether we have the true authentic Apostolic eye-witness testimony that we claim to have.

The rest of this book goes through all the evidence in order to unconfuse people about what the evidence for the Apocrypha actually is, show how it interrelates, and how it would be used in an actual case for Christianity. In effect, I have reviewed the "evidence file" for the case for Christianity. This is my report on what one aspect of the case would entail and what you would need to be ready to deal with.

With that, let's get started and finally move on to the initial overview.

OVERVIEW FROM ORIGEN:
"SUSANNA IS FOUND IN EVERY CHURCH"

Rather than give you my own biased and misleading overview of the canon debate, I will skip that universal practice (can I get an "Amen!"?) and simply continue with the evidence: specifically, a longer quotation from the letter about Susanna that Origen wrote to Africanus in 248 AD (200 years after Christ and 150 years before Jerome and Rufinus). I do so because it is, itself, an overview. It specifically discusses whether Susanna is canon (without using the term) and whether it ought to be. And Origen is one of the absolutely crucial Fathers in the canon debate:

> Origen is the main source of information on the use of the texts that were later officially canonized as the New Testament. ... Origen is not the originator of the idea of biblical canon, but he certainly gives the philosophical and literary–interpretative underpinnings for the whole notion.[55]

The letter will also quickly show us which side Origen was on—and why. Note that we are not concerned about whether Origen's position or the Church's position was right; we only want to know what their position was and why they held it. Hence the frequent use of "..."—but for the substance of what Origen said about Susanna, you can always read the whole thing:[56]

> Origen to Africanus, ... Your letter, from which I learn what you think of the Susanna in the Book of Daniel, which is used in the Churches, although apparently somewhat short, presents in its few words many problems...
>
> 2. You begin by saying, that when, in my discussion with our friend Bassus, I used the Scripture which contains the prophecy of Daniel when yet a young man in the affair of Susanna, I did this as if it had escaped me that this part of the book was spurious. You say that you ... find fault with it as a more modern composition, and a forgery; ...
>
> In answer to this, I have to tell you what it behooves us to do in the cases not only of the History of Susanna, which is found in every Church of Christ in that Greek copy which the Greeks use, but is not in the Hebrew, ... but of thousands of other passages also which I found in many places when with my little strength I was collating the Hebrew copies with ours. ....
>
> 3. And in many other of the sacred books I found sometimes more in our copies than in the Hebrew, sometimes less. ...

---

[55] wikipedia.org/wiki/Origen.
[56] Available online at www.newadvent.org/fathers/0414.htm. I would also recommend a brief update discussing the modern scholarship on the substantive issues, posted by Gallagher on his blog at sanctushieronymus.blogspot.com/search/label/Susanna.

4. ... But why should I enumerate all the instances I collected with so much labour, to prove that the difference between our copies and those of the Jews did not escape me? ... And, forsooth [*i.e., the rest of this sentence is sarcasm*], when we notice such things, we are immediately to reject as spurious the copies in use in our Churches, and enjoin the brotherhood to put away the sacred books current among them, and to coax the Jews, and persuade them to give us copies which shall be untampered with, and free from forgery! Are we to suppose that that Providence which in the sacred Scriptures has ministered to the edification of all the Churches of Christ, had no thought for those bought with a price, for whom Christ died...?

5. In all these cases consider whether it would not be well to remember the words, "You shall not remove the ancient landmarks which your fathers have set." ... I make it my endeavour not to be ignorant of their various readings, lest in my controversies with the Jews I should quote to them what is not found in their copies... For if we are so prepared for them in our discussions, they will not, as is their manner, scornfully laugh at Gentile believers for their ignorance of the true reading as they have them. ....

7. Moreover, I remember hearing from a learned Hebrew, said among themselves to be the son of a wise man, and to have been specially trained to succeed his father, with whom I had intercourse on many subjects, the names of these elders, just as if he did not reject the History of Susanna ...

8. And I knew another Hebrew, who told about these elders such traditions as the following: that they pretended to the Jews in captivity, who were hoping by the coming of Christ to be freed from the yoke of their enemies, that they could explain clearly the things concerning Christ...and that they so deceived the wives of their countrymen. ...

9. But probably to this you will say, Why then is the History not in their Daniel, if, as you say, their wise men hand down by tradition such stories? The answer is, that they hid from the knowledge of the people as many of the passages which contained any scandal against the elders, rulers, and judges, as they could, some of which have been preserved in uncanonical writings (Apocrypha). ... Now we know very well that tradition says that Esaias the prophet was sawn asunder; and this is found in some apocryphal work, which probably the Jews have purposely tampered with, introducing some phrases manifestly incorrect, that discredit might be thrown on the whole.

... Wherefore I think no other supposition is possible, than that they who had the reputation of wisdom, and the rulers and elders, took away from the people every passage which might bring them into discredit among the people. We need not wonder, then, if this history of the evil device of the licentious elders against Susanna is true, but was concealed and removed from the Scriptures by men themselves not very far removed from the counsel of these elders.

...What I have said is, I think, sufficient to prove that it would be nothing wonderful if this history were true, and the licentious and cruel attack was actually made on Susanna by those who were at that time elders, and written down by the wisdom of the Spirit, but removed by these rulers of Sodom, as the Spirit would call them. ...

13. ... Tobias (as also Judith), we ought to notice, the Jews do not use. They are not even found in the Hebrew Apocrypha, as I learned from the Jews themselves.

However, since the Churches use Tobias,[57] you must know that even in the captivity some of the captives were rich and well to do. Tobias himself says...

This, then, is my defense. I might, especially after all these accusations, speak in praise of this history of Susanna, dwelling on it word by word, and expounding the exquisite nature of the thoughts. Such an encomium, perhaps, some of the learned and able students of divine things may at some other time compose. This, however, is my answer to your strokes, as you call them. Would that I could instruct you! But I do not now arrogate that to myself. ...

A couple of specific items to note for discussion later in this book:

(A) In section 13, Origen notes that the Christian Churches accept Tobit (Tobias) and Judith with full knowledge that the Jews of his time claimed that these books were not even Apocrypha to them, let alone Scripture.

(B) Origen uses Tobit as full Scripture in order to prove that Susanna is also Scripture. He uses Tobit (alleged Apocrypha) to prove that part of Daniel (Canon) is authentic Scripture. Africanus, on the other hand, cites to Tobit to question whether Susanna is authentic Scripture.[58] I.e., both sides of the discussion agree entirely that Tobit is full Scripture, not Apocrypha, and they use it confirm the most important doctrine, dogma, etc. of them all: what is Scripture.

At no point does Origen express any concept whereby a book accepted by the Churches as Scripture would be seen as wrong, inferior (Ecclesiastical or "only to be read" or "not to be used to confirm doctrine") or in any way second class because those who "scornfully laugh at Gentile believers for their ignorance of the true reading as they have them" say it is not Scripture. To the contrary, he uses just such a book (Tobit) as a "canon within the canon" to determine what else is included as Scripture.[59]

---

[57] Origen also refers to Tobit as Scripture repeatedly in other works; see e.g., First Principles 3, 2, 4 ("... such a statement will perhaps appear incredible, unless it be confirmed by the testimony of holy Scripture. ...That certain thoughts are suggested to men's hearts either by good or evil angels, is shown both by the angel that accompanied Tobias..." www.newadvent.org/fathers/04123.htm) and On Prayer 6 ("the scripture says, "The prayer of both was heard before the presence of the great Raphael and he was sent to heal them both,'" www.tertullian.org/fathers/origen_on_prayer_02_text.htm). He does the same with Judith; see Homily 20 on Jeremiah, 7.3 ("I want to give an example from Scripture ... Judith made an agreement ...", not available online) and On Prayer 8 ("it is open to everyone to select any number of them for himself from the Scriptures... It was, moreover, after offering holy prayer that Judith...")

[58] "...how is it that they who were captives among the Chaldæans, lost and won at play, thrown out unburied on the streets, as was prophesied of the former captivity..." Paragraph 2.

[59] When discussing Origen as proof of the New Testament canon, Kruger is quite clear that debate does not determine status: "... overplaying of disagreements over canonical books also happens in other areas. .... church fathers occasionally acknowledge that a particular book is "disputed" by

Moreover, he makes very clear his belief that the Christians have the true Scripture, not the Jews. The Jewish leaders "pretended to the Jews ... deceived the wives of their countrymen. ... hid from the knowledge of the people ... took away from the people every passage ... concealed and removed from the Scriptures..."

So sayeth Origen. Agree or disagree, it does not matter. The point is: so sayeth Origen.

According to Origen, the distinction between Christian Scripture and the Jewish canon is that the Christians had the true and complete set of the "Jewish Scriptures," while the Jews did not. And yet, Kruger listed Origen as support for the claim that "the Christian church widely adopted the Old Testament books and not the Apocrypha." He does so not only despite what Origen says about Susanna, and what Origen says about the Scriptures in general, but also despite the fact that Origen expressly says "the Churches use Tobias" even though "Tobias (as also Judith), we ought to notice, the Jews do not use. They are not even found in the Hebrew Apocrypha, as I learned from the Jews themselves."

And consider this quote from Gallagher and Meade:

> Origen's letter to Julius Africanus regarding the status of the story of Susannah —a deutero-canonical[60] addition to Daniel – seemed to suggest not only that Christians should consider Susannah an authentic element of the text of Daniel, but also that the identity of scriptural books should be decided by the church and not by Jews. (p. 29).

Seemed to suggest? Origen "seemed to suggest" that Christians "should consider" Susanna an authentic element of the text of Daniel? Origen "seemed

---

some. ... Origen is simply noting exceptions to a more broadly established trend. Thus, it is misleading to use this passage as evidence that John's letters were not regarded as canonical. That is more than this language can bear. At most, it reveals that in certain quarters of the church some disagreements over these books continued to occur (which is hardly surprising)..." (p. 265-266) and "Why cannot Origen accept a book as genuine and, at the same time, acknowledge that others had doubts about it? Kalin seems to think that if Origen admits that some have doubts about a book, then that must mean Origen himself rejects it—but this simply does not follow." (p. 285).

[60] They had previously told us that "[Deuterocanonical] refers to books that were not recognized as authoritative until a later time," but Origen is writing about Susanna's universal canonicity more than a century before several New Testament Books (Revelation and several Epistles, etc.) achieve consensus as authoritative; and Esther will still be excluded on some Old Testament canon lists more than 100 years after Origen is writing. Their definition of Deuterocanonical is a conclusory statement: it just assumes that the Books were, indeed, added later. And of course, the term "Apocrypha" is also a conclusory label as well.

to suggest" that the identity of scriptural books "should be" decided by the Church and not by Jews?

Or consider Gary Habermas, co-author of *The Case for the Resurrection of Jesus*, who tells us that the Apocrypha:

> ... are not very well attested ... in the early church (where they seldom pop up until the Fourth Century AD) ... and have nothing to do with Christianity.[61]

But Origen's letter attests that Susanna, Tobit and Judith had everything to do with Third Century Christianity and Third Century Christian Scripture. According to Origen—"the main source of information on the use of the texts that were later officially canonized"—what they have nothing to do with are the Jewish Scriptures from which they had been "concealed and removed" in the 200 years since Christ.

Having read Origen's letter, you can evaluate Habermas, Kruger, Gallagher, Meade, me, and anyone else who speaks about Origen and his beliefs. Compare the evidence to the author's description of the evidence. Judge each author by a "canon" of your own. Someone's claims about evidence (a) always say something about them and (b) occasionally say something about the evidence as well.[62]

One last thing before we dive in: It is always possible that Origen (or any Father) was overstating the case when he said that the whole Church agreed with him and always had—but in this case, there are many pieces of corroborating evidence to back him up on his claim.

Earlier in time, Hippolytus (235 AD) gave us a full commentary "On Susanna" (a typical Bible commentary, going through the Scripture line by line).[63] His comment on verse "8. And the two elders saw her" says:

> These things the rulers of the Jews wish now to expunge from the book, and assert that these things did not happen in Babylon, because they are ashamed of what was done then by the elders.

---

[61] www.garyhabermas.com/qa/qa_index.htm
[62] I am talking of bias, not bad intentions. My guesses are that Habermas did not put enough thought into the specific words he wrote on the website; Gallagher and Meade are perhaps just inconsistent (they sometimes seem more accepting of Origen's letter as clear evidence); and Kruger appears to have simply forgotten all about Susanna while writing his footnote.
[63] www.newadvent.org/fathers/0502.htm

And then there is Tertullian (Five Books against Marcion, Book V, Chapter IX, 208 AD), forty years before Origen:

> It is necessary for me to lay claim to those Scriptures which the Jews endeavour to deprive us of, and to show that they sustain my view.[64]

Going back another seventy years, we have Justin Martyr. Justin is not even 50 years removed from the writing of the last of the New Testament books, if we accept the early dates. If we accept later dates, he might even have entered the Church before the last Books were written. He is writing in 155 AD, describing a debate 20 years earlier (135 AD) with the Jew Trypho:

> your teachers... have altogether taken away many Scriptures ... but since I am aware that this is denied by all of your nation, I do not address myself to these points, but I proceed to carry on my discussions by means of those passages which are still admitted by you...[65]

But we need to go all the way back and begin at the very beginning— because none of these Fathers are the Apostles. Even Justin Martyr is writing 100 years after Christ. Perhaps the "later addition" of Apocrypha occurred during that interim. To explore that possibility, we need to start with the Bible itself.

> ...Such writers, like Matthew, feel that they as Christians understand the Jewish Scriptures better than the Jews – indeed, that the only real Jew is a Christian. "Israel" so-called is a nation of imposters for, as Paul had said, 'he is not a real Jew who is one outwardly, nor is true circumcision something external and physical. He is a Jew who is one inwardly.' (Rom. 2.28-9)[66]

It is in the New Testament, as written by the Divinely inspired Evangelists, that we read of the Jews dividing into two groups: the "real Jews" that become Christian and the "imposters" who are called Jews. Therefore, although "the Jews" of the Old Testament might be a better starting place chronologically, I believe that there are very good reasons for Christians to start with the New Testament instead.[67]

---

[64] www.newadvent.org/fathers/03125.htm
[65] Sections 71-73, at www.newadvent.org/fathers/01286.htm
[66] *The Spirit and the Letter: Studies in the Biblical Canon* by John Barton, p. 78 (SPCK, 1997).
[67] I certainly do not support any form of anti-Semitism. My only point in using such language is to convey what the ancients actually thought. I believe that trying to soften words or tone would simply exacerbate the misunderstanding of the ancients that I am trying to address.

SIDEBAR 1: SKEPTICS ARE THE OPPONENTS, NOT CATHOLICS

We will see repeatedly that whatever looks pathetically weak for Catholics and the Apocrypha will suddenly look rock solid for showing atheists that the Bible is The Truth. The point of this book is that such views are in conflict, and the claims made against Catholics would defeat the case for Christianity. The questions I am focused on are simple, factual questions, and the decisions of Catholics (modern Catholics, not anyone before 450 AD) really have nothing to do with either the questions or the answers. What is needed is an examination of all the evidence for and against the Apocrypha and consideration of how it ties into the case for Christianity.

So, take my advice: forget the Pope. Focus on the evidence, without distraction. To help, I quote from very few Catholics herein—and only when I have to.

Still, I am a believer that after reviewing the evidence, one should read the arguments from all sides, then follow the Truth wherever it leads. On that note, the leading Catholic books on the topic of late have come from Gary Michuta (*Why Catholic Bibles Are Bigger*, *The Case for the Deuterocanon*, and *15 Myths, Mistakes and Misrepresentations about the Deuterocanon*), and I heartily recommend reading them all, along with all the Protestant books on the canon that I mention herein.

Otherwise, this book is not about Catholicism. It is an attempt to: (1) be the definitive book report on possible New Testament references and "citation evidence" from the early Church, all of which I have sorted, organized and presented in the manner that makes the most sense for someone who actually wants to read them rather than read about them; (2) stress various interconnections and analytics that seem to have been missed; and (3) bring the canon debate into the context of the case for Christianity, the way I encountered it, which I believe sheds a whole new light on what the evidence is and how to honestly evaluate it.

SIDEBAR 2: SELF-AUTHENTICATION PROVES EVERYTHING

It is well-established that simply reading the Books of the true Bible with an open mind will show any reasonable person that they are the inspired word of God. Here are a small sample of famous quotes from John Calvin, Martin Luther, and other Reformers that demonstrate the many self-authenticating facets of the Bible:

Sola Scriptura

The Bible is the jewel of Christianity. The "why" of Christian belief, it is the prize of the Church and the foundation of the faith... As a Christian, my faith is built on nothing except the text of the Bible and its excellence... We regard the Bible more highly than anything else in the world. After all, we believe it is the Word of God.

The Excellence of the Bible

The excellence of the Bible is unsurpassed; it is inimitable in its literary quality. This is inherently true, because it is inspired by God. We believe that the Bible is second to none in the world according to the unanimous decision of the learned men in points of diction, style, rhetoric, thoughts and soundness of laws and regulations to shape the destinies of mankind. This, we contend, is proof positive that the Bible is the very Word of God.

The Fulfilled Prophesies

If the New Testament can be shown to contain fulfilled prophecies from the Old Testament, then we have good reason to believe that both are from God ... This is exactly what happened ... Other prophecies, more long-term in their predictions, have also come true. ... Many more prophecies confirm that the Bible is the Word of God.

The Miraculous Scientific Knowledge in the Bible

There is miraculous scientific knowledge in the Bible. Christians often argue that the Bible speaks of the big bang ... In addition to the miraculous astronomic insight, the Bible goes on to show miraculous biological insight... The best explanation of this miraculous scientific knowledge is that the Bible must have come from God.

The Mathematical Marvels of the Bible

The Bible displays mathematical marvels that could only be the result of God's inspiration. One kind of mathematical marvel is numerical parallels: the word month appears twelve times in the New Testament, the word day appears 365 times, the words man and woman appear an equal number of times, the words angels and Satan appear an equal number of times, and the words 'this world' and 'the hereafter' appear an equal number of times. Such numerical parallels could only be the result of a divine mind behind the text.

The Unity of the Bible

That the Bible has no contradictions is evidence of its divine origin: Do they [skeptics] not consider the Bible with care? Had it been from other than God, they would surely have found therein much discrepancy... the unity of the Bible is admittedly greater than that of any other sacred book. And yet how can we account for it except through the unity of God's purpose and design?

Inerrant and Eternally Correct

Of course, it would follow that since the Bible is the very Word of God, it is completely without error, since God cannot utter error.

Changed Lives

The changed lives and cultures affected by the Bible are evidence of its divine origin.

Preserved Intact from the Writing of the Original Evangelists

The text of the New Testament remains exactly as it was inspired, from God to the Evangelists and down to our day. The Bible is the eternal expression of God, so it can never change. Its immutability is also necessary because it is the foundation of Christian doctrine.

Of course, all those quotes are actually from Moslems explaining why the Qur'an is the word of God. I just changed a few words around.[68] The manifest weakness of relying on nothing but self-authentication as a basis for belief (let alone as reasoning when arguing with others) is exactly what bothered Kruger his whole life, and it is why he wrote his book. It is also why I ignore the whole topic. If you truly believe that only self-authentication is needed, and the historical case does not matter, then I would be happy to discuss sports.

Personally, I think the Buckeyes will have a good football team this year.[69]

---

[68] See *No God but One* by Nabeel Qureshi, and *Answering Islam* by Norman L. Geisler and Abdul Saleeb. (Both books provide typical Christian responses to some Moslem arguments.)

[69] Statistically, Ohio State is the most likely team in any major sport to have a good year (only six losing seasons in the last 100, two in the last 58). I would not want my book to become outdated.

SIDEBAR 3: THE EVIDENCE POINTS TO THE TRUTH

Kruger's view (part of his model, as he calls it) is that the sheep heard the Shepherd's voice as spoken through the canonical books: the sheep (the early Christians) accepted the correct books of the New Testament canon through the working of the Holy Spirit, recognizing the Divine Truth when they read it. Thus, the early Church's "corporate reception" of Apocrypha as part of its Old Testament would defeat his model by proving that the early Church accepted the "wrong" Books.

Kruger also firmly believes that his model should be used to correct errors—by which he means the errors of others: "For example, the Syriac church has a twenty-two-book canon. Those twenty-two books are sufficient for supplying the individual components of the self-authenticating model and if applied properly would show the Syriac church that they are out of step with biblical principles and have an incomplete canon." (p. 116, footnote 92)

But apparently, Kruger has no desire to follow his own model. He refers to the Old Testament canon issue as only a "potential objection" to his model—i.e., he would rather throw out the model than consider the idea that the Apocrypha should be canon. So he ever-so-humbly suggested that those foolish Syriacs should abandon their own ancient Church's history and slavishly follow the dictates of the model that he, personally, will now reject out of hand.

I believe Kruger was on to something with his model. I just think that he should consider whether the model should determine the proper Old Testament as well (i.e., the sheep heard the voice of the Shepherd through the Apocrypha too), rather than presupposing the validity of his own personal Old Testament. That is essentially what I did, although I was less formal and never called it a model. I simply thought of it as following the evidence, wherever it leads.

SIDEBAR 4: REASONABLE STANDARDS OF PROOF, PART I

Consider the Moslem view of Christianity. From Qureshi:

> ... Finally, we turn to the most common Muslim accusation against the Bible: that its text has been changed over time. It should also be clear now why Muslims accuse the Bible of having been altered: because the Quran says it teaches the same thing as the Bible, confirming the Torah and the gospel, yet the teachings of the Bible are clearly different. In the same vein, the Quran teaches that Muhammad was prophesied in the Bible, but there appears to be no such prophecy.[70]

How should we respond to such a claim? By asking Moslems to examine the evidence with an open mind, of course. I believe I could prove it to be wrong to any reasonable standard of proof. And that's the key: they have to be open to a reasonable standard, a fair standard, an honest standard. Without that, the claims that there is "no proof" will never stop until the end of time.

But it is wrong for Christians to only ask Moslems and others to be open-minded. If we ask them to test their beliefs, we should be willing to submit our own to the same test. The case for Christianity is nothing but a showing that our religion passes the same test we expect others to judge their own beliefs by. Moreover:

> Many proofs of Christianity can be shown, and proofs have been given over and over again. Evidences can be given, but is that the real issue? Do those who reject the Bible refuse to believe because the evidence is not convincing? As I said in the previous article, lack of information is not the problem. Nor is lack of evidence the problem. The reason for unbelief is simple. Unbelievers start from the presupposition that the claims of the Bible are not true.[71]

So if it is wrong for unbelievers to start with such a presupposition against Genesis, Isaiah, Psalms, Daniel, Jeremiah, and all the rest, it is also wrong for believers to start with such a presupposition against the Books of the Apocrypha. After all, as Lee Strobel's *Case for Christ* tells us:

> Judging for Yourself: Maybe you too have been basing your spiritual outlook on the evidence you've observed around you or gleaned long ago from books, college professors, family members, or friends. But is your conclusion really the best possible

---

[70] *No God But One*, Zondervan 2016, p. 117.
[71] www.everlastingtruths.com/2016/02/26/do-people-not-believe-the-bible-because-of-a-lack-of-evidence/

explanation for the evidence? If you were to dig deeper—to confront your preconceptions and systematically seek out proof—what would you find?[72]

And yet, for example, Josh McDowell, in *The New Evidence that Demands a Verdict*, builds his case upon his own biased presupposition, which seems to have blinded him to the unfair and inconsistent standards he used for judging the Apocrypha and the Protestant canon:

> Jesus and the New Testament writers never once quote the Apocrypha, although there are hundreds of quotes *and references* to almost all of the canonical books of the Old Testament. (Emphasis added).[73]

That was on page 32 of my copy, after which follow more than 700 pages of evidence without a single mention of the Apocrypha (and the hundreds of references that are claimed to have been made to them in the New Testament, including many from Jesus Himself), but with innumerable mentions of references to the Books of the Protestant canon (e.g., that Jesus was alluding to Exodus and thereby claiming to be God when he said "I AM").

However, if we are to take the case for Christianity seriously, then we must presume that (a) an opponent will object to any prejudiced double standard, and (b) a fair Judge will not allow the Christian to handwave away the opponent's evidence, i.e., all the references to the Apocrypha. In fact, that some Christians "admit" that all the references to Apocrypha are not proof is exactly the opponent's point: similar references should not be accepted as sufficient proof in the case made by such Christians either. And as we will see below, actual New Testament quotes of the Protestant canon are far fewer than is often realized, precisely because all Christians freely accept allusions, references, typology, etc. as sufficient proof without the slightest objection— unless the topic is the Apocrypha.

A related point involves all claims like these:

> No other book outside of the Hebrew canon is ever cited with the formula, "Thus says the Lord," "It is written," or "Scripture says." While some non-canonical writings may have been alluded to by the New Testament writers, these works are never quoted as

---

[72] Introduction, page 21 of the Zondervan 2016 Edition.
[73] Citing to Norman L. Geisler and William E. Nix, *A General Introduction to the Bible*.

> Scripture or as having some sort of divine authority. This is further testimony that the extent of the Hebrew canon was clear to everyone at the time of Christ.[74]

This is a simple logical error, but do not take my word for it. From Norman Geisler and Thomas Howe, *When Critics Ask: A Popular Handbook on Bible Difficulties*, discussing another instance of the same logical error:

> ... there is an infallible mathematical rule that easily explains this problem: wherever there are two, there is always one — it never fails! Matthew did not say there was only one angel. One has to add the word "only" to Matthew's account to make it contradict John's [with two angels]. But if the critic comes to the Bible in order to show it errs, then the error is not in the Bible, but in the critic.[75]

In our case, this would be a logical error even if the New Testament quoted every Book of the Protestant canon (and it does not). So the situation is even more illogical, as I try to show visually below:

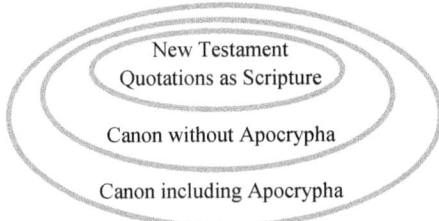

New Testament
Quotations as Scripture

Canon without Apocrypha

Canon including Apocrypha

This claim is that the existence of the innermost circle proves that the Jews accepted "only" the second circle but not the third—which is nonsense.

To actually prove which circle is correct, we need to look at other evidence beyond just those three carefully hand-picked citation formulas. That inquiry should include (even emphasize) all the other evidence the Bible gives us. That no express statement from Jesus is made about the Apocrypha is no reason to then ignore all the other Biblical evidence.[76]

---

[74] www.blueletterbible.org/Comm/stewart_don/faq/right-books-in-old-testament/question17-new-testament-quote-old-testament.cfm

[75] *When Critics Ask: A Popular Handbook on Bible Difficulties*, by Norman Geisler and Thomas Howe, SP Publications, Inc. 1996, p. 21-22.

[76] There are further arguments one could make with Stewart over his three formulae, including that one such "Scripture says" reference (James 4:5, a "quotation" not found in the Protestant canon) may be an allusion to Wisdom 2:24. See more on that in the discussion of Wisdom, below.

PART ONE

THE CHRISTIAN BIBLE

AND

THE JEWISH BIBLE

PART I: THE CHRISTIAN BIBLE AND THE JEWISH BIBLE

STATISTICAL ANALYSIS OF THE 1611 KJV CROSS-REFERENCES

The original 1611 King James Version (KJV) Bible includes cross-references that show links between the Apocrypha and the New Testament.

Of course, allusions, references, and fulfilled prophecies will be debated until the end of time—there is, in fact, an entire religion filled with "Old" Testament scholars who believe that every single Christian ever is sadly deluded when we see allusions to the coming of Jesus Christ in what we wrongly call the "Old" Testament. And of course, every single Christian on Earth believes that every single Jew on Earth reads their Old Testament scriptures incorrectly as well.

E.g., many say that when Isaac carried the wood (that Abraham would have burned to sacrifice Isaac), that was a "type" prefiguring Jesus carrying the Cross. John F. MacArthur wrote that, "Jesus fulfilled it to the very letter. This is divine inspiration... This is how verbal and typical prophecy predicted to the very tiniest point the death of Jesus Christ."[77]

Not so fast, say the Jews: "The image of Isaac's carrying the wood on which he is to be burned adds enormous power to the story. A midrash relates this to a Roman (not Jewish) method of execution that was sometimes used on Jewish martyrs: 'It is like a person who carries his cross on his own shoulder.'"[78]

No scholar can definitively answer whether Isaac is a type of Christ, a "type" of some other victim of crucifixion, or no type of anything at all. That is simply not how this works. There are Christian scholars, Jewish scholars, and skeptical scholars. Christian scholars disagree, too, on almost literally everything.[79] In the end, you must decide for yourself.[80]

---

[77] John MacArthur Sermon Archive (Panorama City, CA: Grace to You, 2014), 1972, the Crucifixion, Part 1. Cribbed from David Limbaugh's the Emmaus Code, Genesis, Isaac, FN 38.

[78] *The Jewish Study Bible*, Genesis 22:6.

[79] E.g., Revelation 9:7 ("the shapes of the locusts were like unto horses prepared unto battle.") William Barclay, *Daily Study Bible*: "It has always been noticed that the head of the locust is like the miniature head of a horse." R.C.H. Lenski: "No natural grasshopper looks like a horse..." Just two legendary scholars, each seeing whatever they wanted to see.

[80] In fact, when billions of dollars are at stake in interpreting the ambiguous language of a contract, the decision is not for scholars to make. It is left to the men and women of the Jury to make the call. You determine the answer by (a) reviewing all the evidence, including expert witnesses (who are countered by the opponent's experts and are grilled by the attorneys), then (b) listening as the

In this book, I will cite from an endless stream of Protestant authors. However, I never cite to anyone in hopes that you just take their word for it or that you concede because so-and-so said you are wrong—I cite to them to show that a reasonable person should carefully consider what they said and why. In any event, the rest of this book lays out the possible New Testament references (those from the King James Version plus hundreds of others I have collected as part of my research) so that you can judge each of them.[81]

But before we do all of that, let's look at the KJV references as a data set. Forget the specific references that the KJV saw (and those they missed): does the set of references have anything to show us with respect to the question of whether "the Jews" accepted Apocrypha as Scripture?

STATISTICAL ANALYSIS OF THE GOSPEL TO THE JEWS

There were 115 New Testament cross-references with Apocrypha in the original 1611 KJV.[82] According to the KJV, there were zero such cross-references with the Gospel of Mark, five with the Gospel of John, and 14 with Luke. According to the KJV, there were 22 cross-references between the Apocrypha and the Gospel of Matthew—more than for the other three Gospels combined.

In other words, according to the KJV, there were more cross-references between the Gospel to the Jews and the Apocrypha than for all the other three Gospels combined. After all, "[i]t is quite obvious and widely accepted that Matthew was written to the Jews."[83] *The Evangelical Biblical Theology Commentary on Matthew* (written by Charles L. Quarles, Chair of Biblical Theology at Southeastern Baptist Theological Seminary) provides more detail:

---

lawyers for both sides present their arguments, before (c) reaching an informed decision. The sequence is important—and so are the roles. It is you who decide. Experts advise the Judge and Jury; they do not make decisions for them.

My goal is simply to (a) set out all the possible references I found for you to consider, (b) push for consistency, and (c) leave final decisions up to you—but with the advice that the process (evidence, then arguments from all sides, then decision) is crucial for making correct decisions.

[81] Most references are mentioned in many sources, so to save space, I did not identify sources except for the few that seemed unique finds.

[82] I counted these things by hand. The references were mentioned in either or both of the KJV comments to the New Testament or their comments to the Apocrypha.

[83] www.blueletterbible.org/study/intros/matthew.cfm.

the Gospel was originally addressed to assemblies that still participated in temple rituals, ... observed the Sabbath ...and perhaps Jewish dietary laws..., and were in conflict with the Pharisees and their scribes ... Eusebius ... states that Matthew wrote the Gospel for the Hebrews to whom he had previously preached in order to compensate for his absence after he left to carry the gospel to other nations...[84]

Craig S. Keener, past president of the Evangelical Theological Society, notes that modern scholars believe that Matthew used Mark as a starting point (over half of Matthew seems to have been copied from Mark[85]):

Where possible, Matthew has made Mark's Jesus "more Jewish." That is ... Matthew has consistently re-Judaized Jesus for his Jewish audience... Matthew is Jewish, in dialogue with contemporary Jewish thought and skilled in traditional Jewish interpretation of the Old Testament.... Matthew's Jewish readers would have been more familiar with the traditional prophetic perspective...[86]

As part of "re-Judaizing" Jesus, he who was "skilled in traditional Jewish interpretation of the Old Testament" and was writing to "Jewish readers more familiar with the traditional prophetic perspective" may have referred to Apocrypha more than the other three Gospels combined.

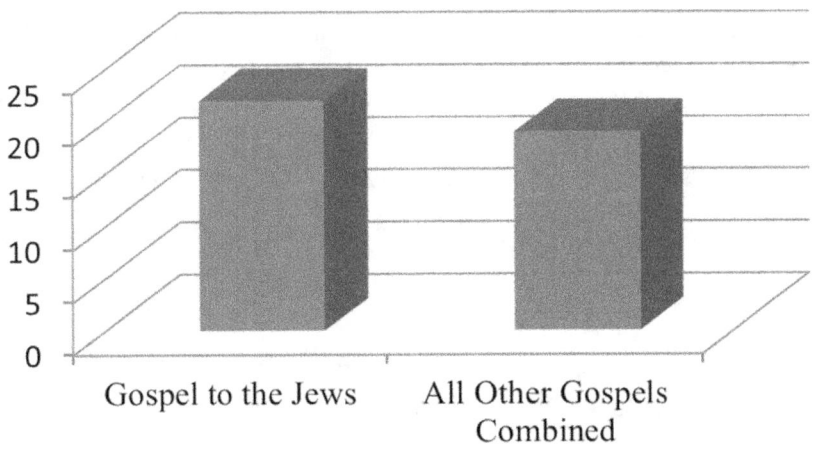

Cross References to Apocrypha

Gospel to the Jews   All Other Gospels Combined

---

[84] Lexham 2022, p. 25 and 33.
[85] wikipedia.org/wiki/Synoptic_Gospels
[86] In the IVP New Testament Commentary Series volume on Matthew 1997, p. 21-22, 32, 34.

Since a majority of Matthew parallels Mark, in essentially less than half a Gospel of additional material, Matthew has a staggering 22 KJV cross-references to Apocrypha.

All this was added to a book (the Gospel of Mark) that, according to the KJV, originally had no cross-references at all. Recall that the Gospel of Mark includes many notes to explain Judaism to its audience: "For the Pharisees, and all the Jews, except they wash their hands oft, eat not ... And many other things there be, which they have received to hold, as the washing of cups, and pots, brasen vessels, and of tables." (Mark 7:3-4). Matthew started with Mark and its notable lack of focus on Jews, then added many possible references to the Apocrypha—as part of a Gospel directed to the Jews, many of whom were converted Jewish Priests (Acts 6:7).

Edward Hindson (Dean of the Institute of Biblical Studies at Liberty University and one of the translators of the New King James Version of the Bible) and James Borland (a fellow professor at Liberty University) note that:

> The Gospel of Matthew is the most Jewish of all the Gospels. In its inspired pages ... Matthew ... writes to Jewish believers and unbelievers alike. ... It was the perfect bridge to the Old Testament and the ideal introduction to the New Testament ... it is saturated with 130 references to the Hebrew Scriptures, emphasizing that Jesus is the fulfillment of the prophecies and types of the Old Testament.[87]

It is also saturated with 22 cross-references with Apocrypha.[88] The Protestant Old Testament has 929 chapters, to which the Catholic version adds 137, for a total of 1066. The 137 extra chapters account for 12.85% of the chapters in the Catholic Old Testament. The 22 cross-references with Apocrypha added to the 130 references for the Protestant canon equal 152 references. 14.47% of the references to the "Old Testament" in the Gospel to the Jews were to the Apocrypha: by this combined metric, the Apocrypha may have been referenced even more often than the Protestant Old Testament was.

---

[87] Twenty-First Century Biblical Commentary, Matthew, AMG Publishers 2007, p. xi, 1.

[88] I own numerous KJV Bibles but none that claim to be the "New KJV" and also include references to Apocrypha. So, this comparison is of the old KJV for the Apocrypha and the new KJV for everything else. We must not make too much of the particular numbers in this comparison because it is apples to oranges, but I think it is worth discussing.

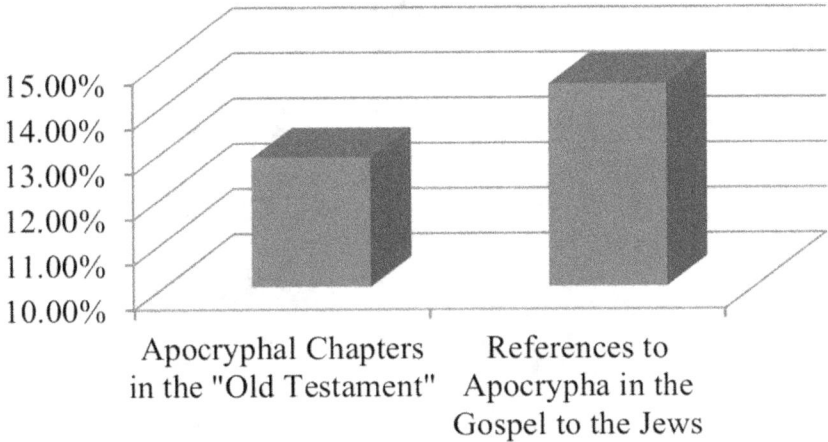

15.00%
14.00%
13.00%
12.00%
11.00%
10.00%

Apocryphal Chapters   References to
in the "Old Testament"   Apocrypha in the
                         Gospel to the Jews

I would note that not a single Apocrypha cross-reference in the 1611 KJV occurs in the genealogy of Jesus, whereas 14 cross references to the Protestant canon (in the 1611 KJV) are just references in the genealogy. So, substantively, it would seem that the focus on Apocrypha in the Gospel to the Jews is even more pronounced than the comparison initially indicates.

> ...Matthew ...quotes the fulfillment of Old Testament prophecies... Further, Matthew assumes that his readers understand Jewish prophecies, festivals, and traditions, clearly indicating his intent to persuade Jewish readers ... (p. 3).

Judging from the KJV, the Apocrypha were a key part of those Jewish prophecies and traditions. They were also a key piece of Matthew's "intent to persuade Jewish readers," when Matthew was writing the "perfect bridge to the Old Testament and the ideal introduction to the New Testament."

STATISTICAL ANALYSIS OF THE PERFECTLY TAUGHT JEW

According to the KJV, Paul accounts for almost as many possible cross references with the Apocrypha as all the other Evangelists combined. He who was "brought up in this city at the feet of Gamaliel, and taught according to the perfect manner of the law of the fathers" (Acts 22:3) has 56 references, more than two and a half times those of even the Gospel to the Jews.

Cross References

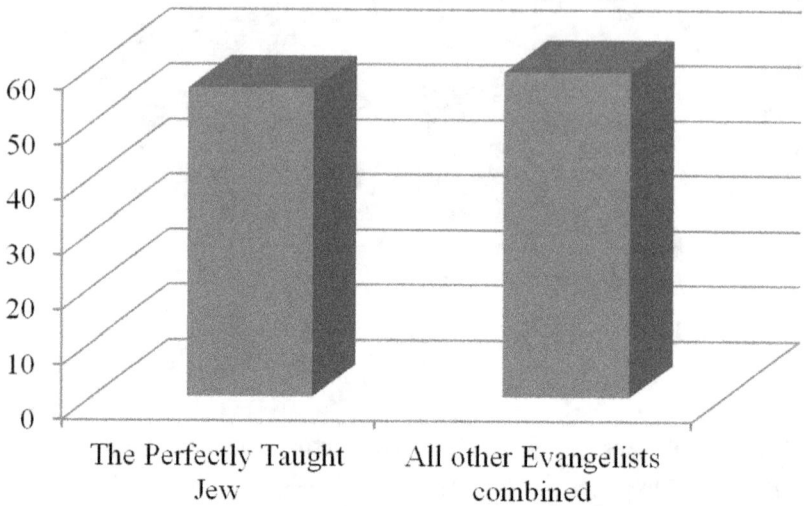

Using the original Greek word counts[89] the Epistles of Paul account for just 27% of the New Testament, yet the Perfectly Taught Jew accounts for 49% of the cross-references with Apocrypha. Cross-references to Apocrypha thus occur 2.5 times as frequently in Paul's writings than for all the other Evangelists. Apparently, cross-references with Apocrypha are a core part of the Perfectly Taught Jew's writing.

---

[89] From catholic-resources.org/Bible/NT-Statistics-Greek.htm

New Testament Word Counts

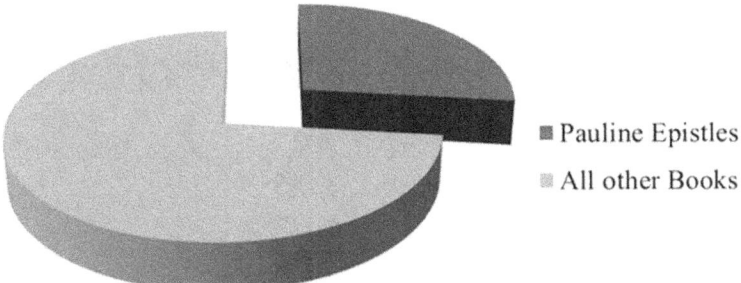

■ Pauline Epistles

▨ All other Books

Cross-References with Apocrypha

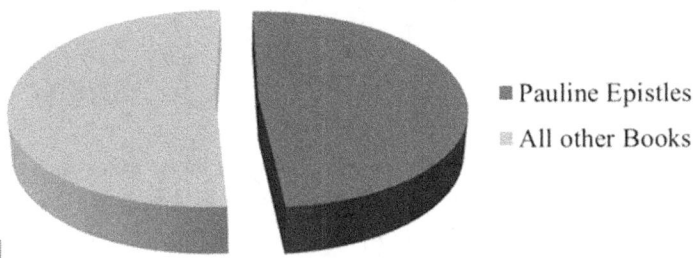

■ Pauline Epistles

▨ All other Books

One might wonder if the 'real' Paul was less focused on Apocrypha, so let's check that. Those Epistles widely seen as pseudepigraphic (1 Timothy, 2 Timothy, and Titus) account for seven cross-references to Apocrypha. Those whose authorship is widely debated (2 Thessalonians, Ephesians, and Colossians) account for six. The Epistle to the Hebrews ("who wrote the epistle, truly only God knows"—Origen), accounts for six.[90]

On the other hand, the seven Epistles that most scholars accept as written by Paul himself (Galatians, Romans, 1 Corinthians, 2 Corinthians, Philemon, Philippians, and 1 Thessalonians) account for two-thirds of the cross-references: 37 of them, twice as many as the seven whose authorship are debated.

---

[90] Using the categories described at wikipedia.org/wiki/Pauline_epistles.

Cross-references to Apocrypha

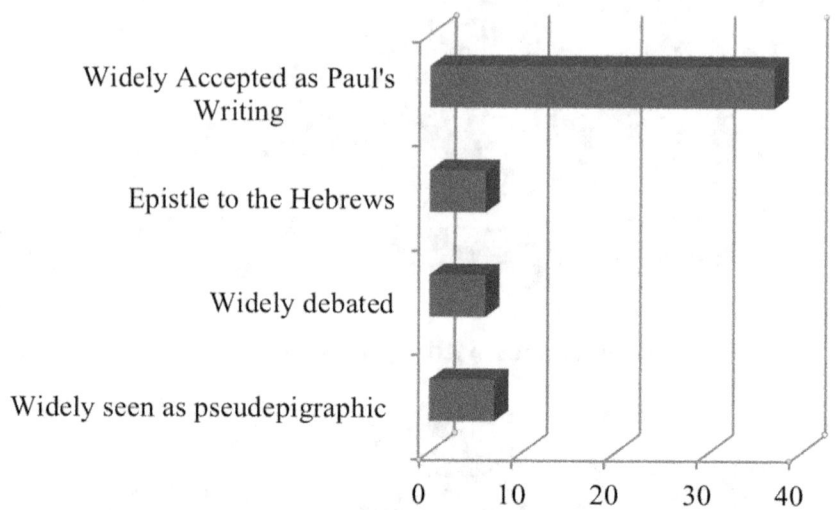

Matthew's Gospel and the Pauline Epistles have cross-references to Apocrypha at the rate of 1 per 714 words. For the rest of the New Testament, the rate is 1 per 2225 words. The Gospel to the Jews and the Perfectly Taught Jew seem to reference Apocrypha 3.1 times as often.

Rate of Cross-References to Apocrypha

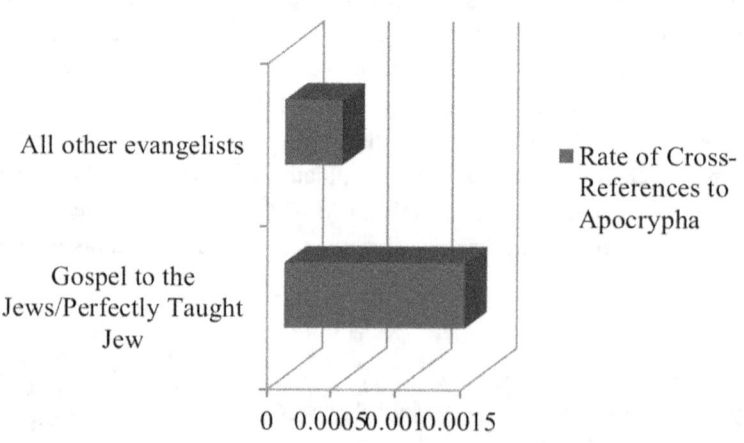

According to the KJV, between Matthew's Gospel to the Jews, Paul the Perfectly Trained Jew, and Luke (someone who learned his Christianity from Paul; and including both Luke's Gospel (which combined with Matthew accounts for 36 of 41 Gospel cross references) and Acts), we have 98 of the 115 cross-references to Apocrypha.

Cross References

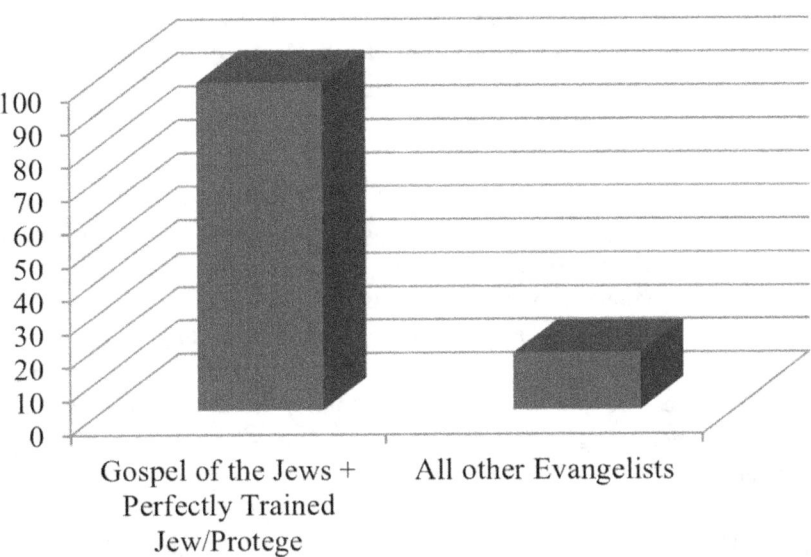

STATISTICAL ANALYSIS: OLD TESTAMENT COMPARISON

Let's also look at things from the perspective of the Old Testament. Sirach and the Book of Wisdom are part of a seven-Book division of the Bible called the Poetic Books, or Sapiential Books, or Wisdom Books (that is, they would be part of the Bible if they were not Apocrypha, of course). Accordingly, we are able to compare them to the most similar Old Testament Books:[91]

---

[91] Citations by size seems to be the main metric that the scholars use. E.g., Kruger: "… the degree to which books were used, and not just how they were cited, reveals even more about their standing in early Christian communities. When it comes to how often books were cited, proportional to their size, it quickly becomes clear that …" p. 224-225. John Barton in his book *The Spirit and the Letter: Studies in the Biblical Canon* also uses the same methodology and

Poetic Book	KJV NT Cross References	Verses	References /100 Verses
Wisdom	**40**	**436**	**9.2**
Psalms	188	2526	7.4
Proverbs	65	915	7.1
Sirach	**64**	**1372**	**4.7**
Job	34	1068	3.2
Ecclesiastes	7	222	3.2
Song of Songs	1	117	0.9

Sirach is respectably in the middle on frequency of KJV references and is very nearly the second most referenced overall (64, vs. Proverbs at 65). It is even referenced much more than the bottom three Poetic Books combined; in fact, it is referenced almost 10 times as much as Ecclesiastes and 64 times as much as the Song of Songs.[92]

But the truly shocking result is that the King James Version cross-references the Book of Wisdom with the New Testament 24% more often (per verse) than any "canonical" Poetic Book—and three times as often as two of the Books, and 10 times as often as one of the Books.

It is one thing for a non-canonical book to be referenced a time or two, but the verses of the Book of Wisdom are cross-referenced considerably more often than any comparable canonical book—and many times more often than some of them, according to the KJV.

So speaketh the King James Version data set.

THE CHURCH'S USE OF MATTHEW'S CROSS-REFERENCES

A somewhat related analysis is that of the early Church's use of the Bible. Matthew is not just the Gospel to the Jews; it was also the Gospel of the early Church. *The Evangelical Biblical Theology Commentary on Matthew* (p. 34)

---

further cites to the same methodology in a German language book (by Franz Stuhlhofer) that has not been translated into English. Barton also notes that such surveys must focus on the type of book, notably "the historical books, for example, never seem to have been in the least controversial, yet neither Jews nor Christians ever used them much in their writings ... in much the same position as Acts for early Christian writers: undoubtedly authoritative, scarcely ever used..." p. 23-24. (We will have reason to remember that historical Books are cited so much less when we discuss the Apocrypha that are historical Books: Tobit, Judith, 1 and 2 Maccabees).

[92] Song of Songs 4:7 ("Thou art all fair, my love; there is no spot in thee") is cross-referenced to Ephesians 5:27 ("That he might present it to himself a glorious church, not having spot, or wrinkle, or any such thing; but that it should be holy and without blemish"). It is not the strongest reference, and that is all the KJV considered noteworthy for the entire canonical Book.

says that "the early church cherished Matthew and quoted it more frequently than any other Gospel." This is so true that Matthew "has often been described as a kind of Christian Pentateuch."[93] In the first few centuries, the Fathers cited the Gospels as follows:[94]

Matthew	48,647
Mark	5,165
Luke	21,713
John	30,160
All Gospels	105,685

Matthew was cited more than nine times as often as Mark, even though half of Matthew parallels/copies Mark. Matthew was cited almost as much as all the other Gospels combined. And Matthew, of course, is also the Gospel that referenced Apocrypha more than all the other Gospels combined.

In fact, the early Fathers were even more inclined to cite those verses in Matthew that the KJV identified as referencing Apocrypha. They cited them almost twice as often as the average verse in Matthew:

	Chapter	Verse	Cites
Matthew	4	4	56
Matthew	5	7	66
Matthew	5	11	80
Matthew	5	25	39
Matthew	5	33	47
Matthew	5	42	41
Matthew	6	1	49

---

[93] *The Spirit and the Letter: Studies in the Biblical Canon*, John Barton, p. 25.

[94] All data is from Biblia Patristica, www.biblindex.org. Biblia Patristica is a multi-generational global work in progress that is the best source we have for collecting and indexing every single reference from the Fathers. It is the source all the scholars seem to use, without exception. But I am neither a gentleman nor a scholar, and alas, I was never able to get the updated search form (biblindex.org/en/quotations/search) to work correctly for me. So, all my searches were made using their old form (biblindex.org/citation_biblique/search), which does not result in the most up-to-date results (the database available to me has less-than-complete coverage starting in the fourth century). Accordingly, I may have missed later citations that would have been found using the new search form, or the eventual final database. However, that could only increase the amount of "citations" to the Apocrypha (compared to what I show herein), with the impact on ratios unknowable. Very notably, Augustine is not available in the database for me to search, so no Biblindex search results herein ever include him. I was able to search many of his works myself (relying of course on the footnotes the translators provide), so he does still show up in my own data, but those results are incomplete.

In addition, my review of documents found some citations (mentioned in the translations, but not indexed in Biblindex) that do not show up in my searches of their database. I believe they are all valid citations, nevertheless, just not noted and indexed correctly, etc. Such is life when you are dealing with indexes, particularly those with 300,000+ entries assembled over decades.

Matthew	6	5	42
Matthew	6	7	29
Matthew	6	20	138
Matthew	6	33	88
Matthew	7	12	53
Matthew	7	17	45
Matthew	7	19	14
Matthew	9	22	72
Matthew	11	29	327
Matthew	13	43	93
Matthew	19	28	127
Matthew	22	23	40
Matthew	25	35	139
Matthew	25	41	253
Matthew	27	43	36
Total			1874
Cites/Verse			85
Average	48,647/1071	=	45
Apocrypha/Average			189%

The 22 verses that (per the KJV) cross-reference Apocrypha were cited by the Fathers 1,874 times; the 678 verses of Mark were cited 5,165 times. The 22 cross-references to Apocrypha were cited 36% as often as the entire 678 verses of the Gospel of Mark combined, and the rates were 85 citations per verse to eight, more than 10 to one. It would appear that a key "improvement" Matthew made to the Gospel of Mark, in the eyes of the early Church Fathers, consisted of making what the KJV saw as possible references to Apocrypha.

HEBREWS: AN EPISTLE TO THOSE WHO ACCEPT APOCRYPHA?

Now let's take a deep dive into the Epistle of the Hebrews and see if that indicates anything about the Apocrypha and the Jews. After all, it is a letter to the Jews, and many of them were converted Jewish Priests (Acts 6:7).

According to the KJV, the very first reference from the Epistle to the Hebrews[95] to any "Old Testament" book is to Apocrypha, and it occurs in 1:3:

> Who [Jesus] being the brightness of his [the Father's] glory, and the express image of his person…;

---

[95] The KJV has cross references from the Epistle to the Hebrews to other Apocrypha as well, including Sirach, and 1 and 2 Maccabees. In addition, while I focus on the Epistle to the Hebrews, other Epistles from Paul seem to draw heavily from the Book of Wisdom as well. See below, especially regarding the Epistles to the Romans (see note at Wisdom 11:15 below, in the discussion of the Book of Wisdom), Ephesians (see note at Wisdom 5:20 below), 1 Corinthians (see note at Wisdom 9:17 below), and Colossians (see note at Wisdom 9:2 below).

This is seen as an allusion to Wisdom 7:26:

> For she [the Divine Wisdom] is the brightness of the everlasting light … and the image of his goodness.[96]

For context, the full quote in Hebrews is:

> 1God, who at sundry times and in divers manners spake in time past unto the fathers by the prophets, 2Hath in these last days spoken unto us by his Son, whom he hath appointed heir of all things, by whom also he made the worlds; 3Who being the brightness of his glory, and the express image of his person, and upholding all things by the word of his power, when he had by himself purged our sins, sat down on the right hand of the Majesty on high; 4Being made so much better than the angels, as he hath by inheritance obtained a more excellent name than they.

It starts with a mention of messages from the prophets in (1), ends with a claim that Jesus is higher than the angels in (4), and in between, uses words taken from the Book of Wisdom—words used to describe the Divine Wisdom—as part of establishing His status above the angels. Perhaps this is a claim that Jesus "fulfills" the description of the Divine Wisdom in the Book of Wisdom. However, that topic is beyond the scope of the present discussion, which is the Jews and their relationship to the Book of Wisdom. We will discuss the "fulfillment" piece of this reference in detail later.

As for the Jews:

> Some scholars believe [the Epistle to the Hebrews] was written for Jewish Christians who lived in Jerusalem… certain believers were considering turning back to Judaism and to the Jewish system of law … However, a growing number of scholars …posit that Hebrews was written for a Jewish audience, and is best seen as a debate between Jewish followers of Jesus and proto-rabbinical Judaism. In tone, and detail, Hebrews … attempts a more complex, nuanced, and openly adversarial definition of the relationship.[97]

According to the KJV, it is that Epistle which starts with a reference to the Book of Wisdom as part of making a claim about Jesus' divinity. Note that the Book of Wisdom declares itself to be Divinely-inspired Scripture (see Wisdom 7:15-21, so that declaration occurs shortly before the verse being referenced by the Epistle to the Hebrews).

---

[96] A second Epistle of Paul's (Colossians 1:15 "Who is the image of the invisible God") also seems to reference this exact verse (Wisdom 7:26).
[97] wikipedia.org/wiki/Epistle_to_the_Hebrews.

This possible reference to Wisdom 7:26 is not a minor part of our theology, either. It is absolutely crucial to our understanding of Christ. The First Epistle of Clement of Rome (1 Clement), a letter addressed to the Christians in the city of Corinth, is one of the earliest, if not the earliest, extra-Biblical Christian writing still extant. It may even have been written when some Disciples were still alive and before several books of the New Testament were penned.[98] Acts 18:8 tells us that in Corinth "Crispus, the chief ruler of the synagogue, believed on the Lord with all his house"—perhaps he was part of the intended audience of the Epistle. Regardless, in Chapter 36, Clement references Hebrews 1:3, the very verse that alludes to Wisdom 7:26, according to the King James Version: "Him the Lord has willed that we should taste of immortal knowledge, who, being the brightness of His majesty, is by so much greater than the angels, as He has by inheritance obtained a more excellent name than they."[99] Notice how Clement mentions immortal knowledge (Divine Wisdom?) while making this reference.

In fact, in 325 AD, the first ever ecumenical council adopted the Nicene Creed, which defines Jesus as "God from God, Light from Light, true God from true God."

> The closest New Testament reference to "light from light" is found in the Epistle to the Hebrews. ... Verse 3 describes the pre-incarnate Son's relationship to the Father: "[the Son]... is the refulgence of his [the Father's] glory, the very imprint of his being." "Refulgence," or "brightness" (Greek, apaugasma), is a very rare Greek word in the Bible. In fact, the Greek Bible only uses it twice, here in Hebrews 1:3 and in Wisdom 7:26. This is no accident. The chapter in Wisdom is a lengthy description of God's Wisdom and its relationship to God and creation. Wisdom (the Son) is the artificer of all (cf. Hebrews 1:2 and Wisdom 7:22). Wisdom (the Son) holds all things in being (cf. Hebrews 1:3 and Wisdom 4:1). But most importantly, Wisdom's relationship to God is

---

[98] Clement is thought to have been a disciple of Peter (as Luke was a disciple of Paul; plus possibly he is also the Clement mentioned as working with Paul in Philippians 4:3) and eventually became the fourth Bishop of Rome/Pope. One reason to think that the Epistle dates to before 70 AD is that it mentions the Temple and its sacrifices in the present tense (Sections 40-41: www.newadvent.org/fathers/1010.htm). One occasionally reads a claim that this background is a myth, but on the other hand, many also rely on this history when trying to prove the case for the Resurrection. Michael R. Licona, Professor at Houston Baptist University, appreciates this conflict and goes into both sides of the issue in depth in his "The Resurrection of Jesus," Section 3.2.5.1. Notably, there is no evidence of any contrary historical beliefs; e.g., the Orthodox do not recognize Clement as Pope and, yet, have always claimed the background to be true. They even sometimes include "Clementine" documents (especially 1 Clement) in their canons.

[99] Chapter 3 makes a reference to Wisdom 2:24 as well. There are also many other references to Apocrypha, e.g., explicit mention of Judith in Chapter 55, followed by a quote from the "additions" to Esther. www.newadvent.org/fathers/1010.htm

likened to the splendor of light: "the refulgence of [God's] eternal light, the spotless mirror of the power of God, the image of his goodness" (Wisdom 7:26). Since the Eternal Son is elsewhere identified as God's wisdom and power (1 Corinthians 3:24), it shouldn't surprise anyone to see the author of Hebrews using this illustration from Wisdom to describe the Son's relationship to the Father.[100]

Note the many ways that Hebrews seems to reference Wisdom in these first few verses, which strengthens the case that this is, indeed, a reference the Jewish audience was expected to understand and appreciate. More:

...The early Church fathers understood these texts to teach that both the Father and the Son existed eternally; they are co-eternal. Why? Could a flame exist without its refulgence or brightness? No, of course not. The flame and its brightness co-exist. Wisdom 7:26 likens God to an eternal light, a light with no beginning and no end. If God's Wisdom is the eternal light's brightness, than God's Wisdom is eternal as well. The Father was never without the Son, nor was the Son without the Father. The early fathers repeatedly used this text against a heresy that denied that the Son was co-eternal with the Father. St. Augustine mocked such an idea. After quoting Wisdom 7:26, Augustine wrote, "Are you seeking for a Son without a Father? Give me a light without brightness..." (Sermons on Selected N.T. Lessons, 68, 2).[101]

We will discuss Hebrews 1:3 at even more length below, but our point here is the possible Jewish acceptance of the Book of Wisdom, so let's first cover the rest of the Epistle. Because the author did not stop referring to the Book of Wisdom after verse 1:3. Anglican Divine E. H. Plumptre posited the theory that Apollos (mentioned in the Book of Acts, 1 Corinthians, and Titus) wrote the Book of Wisdom (which declares itself to be Divinely inspired Scripture) when he was a Jew; then, he wrote the Epistle to the Hebrews[102] after he had converted to Christianity. The claim of dual authorship is just an unprovable theory, but regardless, Plumptre's work is an indication of how deeply connected and similar the thinking behind the two works is.[103] Plumptre found

---

[100] *Behind the Bible*, Gary Michuta, Nikaria 2017, p. 62-64.

[101] Ibid.

[102] Martin Luther also proposed Apollos as author of Hebrews. All agree that it had to have been written by an educated Jewish Christian and that "Both Apollos and Barnabas [another possible author] were Jewish Christians with sufficient intellectual authority." wikipedia.org/wiki/Apollos

[103] He also delineates just how indebted 1 Clement (the Epistle to the Corinthians discussed above) is to the Book of Wisdom, citing two clear references and four less-clear references to the Book of Wisdom. As previously noted, Michael R. Licona's book *The Resurrection of Jesus* discusses 1 Clement at length, and he believes that "it seems more probable than not that the Clement of this letter personally knew the Apostles...[he would then be] one who had known some of those who had walked with Jesus and perhaps had been ordained by not only one of the three top leaders of the Jerusalem Church but one of Jesus' closest disciples: Peter." This is interesting both for

"words either characteristic themselves, or used in a characteristic sense... that ... tend to establish such a close affinity of thought and language as may best be explained by the hypothesis of identity of authorship" in verses 1:1, 1:3, 1:6, 2:10, 2:14, 2:15, 3:4, 3:5, 3:6, 3:13, 3:14, 4:6, 4:10, 4:12, 5:12, 5:13, 6:1, 6:6, 6:20, 7:25, 7:26, 9:1, 10:1, 10:19, 10:36, 11:1, 11:5, 12:10, 12:17, 13:7, and 13:20. That is 31 possible references to the Book of Wisdom in a 13-chapter Epistle to Jews or Jewish Christians, in every chapter except Chapter 8. They are made to 15 of the 19 chapters of the Book of Wisdom.[104]

Others—including the KJV—have found even more possible references to Apocrypha, e.g., in 1:2, 3:1, 4:13, 4:15, 8:2, 11:7, 11:35, 12:2, 13:8, and 13:21. With that reference in Chapter 8, notice that it would be a reference to Apocrypha in every single chapter of the Epistle of the Hebrews and brings us to 41 references in 13 chapters—a constant drumbeat of reference after reference, at a pace even faster than Matthew made them.

Earlier, we saw that the KJV cross-references the Book of Wisdom with the New Testament 24% more often (per verse) than any "canonical" Poetic Book (and three times as often as two of the books, and 10 times as often as one of the books). That was a stunning result—and yet, the KJV has only one cross-reference from the Epistle to the Hebrews to the Book of Wisdom. Opinions on references differ, of course, but bear in mind that the already stunning result for the Book of Wisdom in the KJV data set might actually be a massive undercount.[105]

---

proving the Resurrection (Licona's purpose) but also for our purposes, since it would also show the views held by "one who learned directly from the Apostles" about the Book of Wisdom (and the other Apocrypha (Judith, Sirach, Tobit) referenced in 1 Clement). In fact, if we accept the early date, it would show the thinking even before some of the New Testament had been written (and may still show it with the later date, if later dates are also given to New Testament Books). See the below discussion of the specific references in 1 Clement to the Apocrypha.

[104] See his paper at www.biblicalstudies.org.uk/pdf/expositor/series1/01-329.pdf. And feel free to accept his "crazy" theory that the same person wrote both Hebrews and Wisdom. Personally, I find it too convenient to really take it seriously as an explanation, and I am not aware of anyone else who actually accepted the idea. My point in bringing it up is to show how interconnected the Books are. I treat Plumptre's findings as possible references and leave them for you to judge individually; but as Plumptre notes, the point is that the "cumulative character of the evidence" is something to consider as well.

[105] And if you look at data sets beyond the KJV, you would find that the KJV missed a very large number of references from John (a Jew at the center of Judaism, known unto the high priest: John 18:15-16) and the Epistle of James the Brother of the Lord ("the Jews regarded him as one of themselves. ... He was the leader of what might be called Jewish Christianity; he was the head of that part of the Church which remained centered in Jerusalem. There must have been a time when the Church was very close to Judaism and it was more a reformed Judaism than anything else. ...The letter of James may well represent a kind of Christianity which had remained in its earliest

Also bear in mind, of course, that these references were being made for the audience of Hebrews, among whom were many converted Jewish Priests.

HEBREWS 1:3

So now, let's refocus just on Hebrews 1:3—the verse that the KJV says references Wisdom 7:26. We start with the Jimmy Swaggart Bible Commentary:

> Paul [who Swaggart believes wrote Hebrews] correlates in this Epistle as in no other, this great Finished Work with Old Testament typology ... anyone who would have written this Book would have had to have been a Scholar of unparalleled proportions of the Old Testament. It would have otherwise been impossible... to have written the Book of Hebrews, which, in effect, is an explanation of the Message of the Cross from Old Testament principles ... So here the Holy Spirit teaches that all the Divinely given Shadows, Types, Symbols, and Figures are satisfied in Christ ... It is addressed to the many thousands of Jews who believed that Jesus was the Messiah...
>
> ... Paul sees, or rather the Holy Spirit through him sees, the entirety of the Old Testament pointing to Jesus. What the ancient Writings say is fulfilled in Him. This means more than that specific Prophecies are fulfilled in Jesus. Rather the thrust of the whole Old Testament is such that it leads inescapably to Him.[106]

If we then turn to Swaggart's analysis of Hebrews 1:3 ("Who being the brightness of his glory, and the express image of his person, and upholding all things by the word of his power..."), he writes that:

> The Son is superior to the Prophets as should be obvious, because He is the brightness of God's Glory. "Brightness" in the Greek is "apaugasma," and means "a radiance, or effulgence." It is used of light beaming from a luminous body. The word, Expositors say, seems to mean, not rays of light streaming from a body in their connection with that body or as part of it, still less the reflection of these rays caused by their falling upon another body, but rather rays of light coming out from the original body and forming a similar light-body themselves. That may not be easy to understand, and in fact cannot literally be understood, but that's the best that expositors can come up with as it regards the translation of the Greek words.

The author of the Epistle chose to use phrasing taken from the Book of Wisdom "[t]hat may not be easy to understand, and in fact cannot literally be

---

form"—William Barclay, *Daily Study Bible*), etc. The comparison between Matthew's "additions" to Mark and the "original" Mark shows the focus on Apocrypha, but the other Evangelists are actually more comparable to Matthew (with his Apocrypha-focus) than to Mark (with less of one).
[106] *Hebrews*, World Evangelism Press 2001, introduction.

understood, but that's the best that expositors can come up with as it regards the translation of the Greek words."

> "Glory" spoken of here refers to the expression of the Divine attributes collectively. It is the unfolded fullness of the Divine perfections.

"Glory" was also used in Wisdom 7:25, as the lead-in to the cited section of Wisdom (7:26): God's Wisdom "...is the breath of the power of God, and a pure influence flowing from the glory of the Almighty ... For she is the brightness of the everlasting light, the unspotted mirror of the power of God, and the image of his goodness. And being but one, she can do all things: and remaining in herself, she maketh all things new..."

> The phrase, "And the express image of His person," refers to a distinctive mark or a token impressed on a person or thing, by which it is known from others, a characteristic, the character of. It refers here to an exact reproduction. Vincent says, "Here the essential Being of God is conceived as setting its distinctive stamp upon Christ, coming into definite and characteristic expression in His Person, so that the Son bears the exact impress of the Divine Nature and Character." Jesus is absolute Deity because He is the exact reproduction of the essence of God. Incidentally, the words "express image" as used here occur nowhere else in the New Testament.

There is a conception of the essential Being of God that alludes to the Book of Wisdom, using words that occur nowhere else in the New Testament; but the allusion was clear to the KJV, the author of the Epistle, and the Hebrews who were the Epistle's intended audience.

Plumptre, in his essay, gave us a fuller understanding, because it is not just that the words "express image" occur nowhere else in the New Testament—they also do not occur anywhere else in the Old:

> "the two most striking words in the opening of the Epistle to the Hebrews are to be found in the description of Wisdom in the book" of Wisdom. He also notes the parallel claim to being the brightness of his glory, and the express image of God, and that "the two words which are thus found in such close juxtaposition in the two passages are found nowhere else in the whole range of the New Testament, or the LXX version of the Old..."[107]

---

[107] Plumptre found many unique parallels in the Epistle: "Scarcely less striking is the resemblance between the language of Wisd. xviii. 22, "Thine almighty Word leaped down from heaven out of thy royal throne, ... and brought thine unfeigned commandment as a sharp sword," and that of Heb. iv. 12, "The Word of God is quick and powerful, and sharper than any two-edged sword...again the writer of the Book of Wisdom teaches that "by envy of the devil death entered

We have seen now that there are a great many parallels involved, all connecting this key concept in the Epistle to the Hebrews back to the Book of Wisdom.

But just how important is the Epistle and its allusions to the Book of Wisdom, in the grand scheme of the Bible?

> There is no book in the New Testament more important than this Epistle... Every Reader of the Old Testament needs such a guide as this Epistle, written by someone who had an intimate acquaintance from childhood with the Jewish System; who had all the advantages of the most able and faithful instruction, and who was under the influence of inspiration ...This Book of Hebrews is the true key with which to unlock the Old Testament; ... it is a treatment on Christ and the Cross as nothing else in the entirety of the Word of God. (Comment to Heb 13:25).

Still, let's get a second opinion. The Abingdon Bible Commentary (Abingdon Press 1929) gives us an old school Methodist take:

> ... Hebrews appears on the surface to be one of the most Jewish writings we possess. The argument seems to move entirely within the circle of Jewish ideas. From its commencement to its close from the string of quotations in the first chapter to the appeal to the altar and the sacrifice of beasts whose bodies were burned outside the camp in the last—the thought of the Epistle seems to be "cribb'd, cabin'd, and confin'd" within the narrow precincts of Jewish thought.... (Intro to Heb.)

Entirely within the circle of Jewish ideas, confined within the narrow precincts of Jewish thought, and a string of quotations in the first chapter—starting with a key reference to the Book of Wisdom (which declares itself to be Divinely-inspired Scripture). In addition, we learn that:

> ... If [the author] was a Jew, as he probably was (though this is incapable of absolute proof), he belonged to the more liberal school known as the Hellenists. The Bible which he used and from which he constantly quotes, is the Greek translation known as

---

into the world" (ii. 24) and the Epistle to the Hebrews names the devil as "him that hath the power of death" (ii. 14)... I note, as extending the induction, the "place of repentance" of Wisd. xii. IO, and Heb. xii. 17 (this phrase also occurring in these two passages only); ... Wisd. xvi. 21 and Heb. i. 3, iii. 14, xi. 1; the "servant" of Wisd. xvii. 21, as applied to Moses, with Heb. iii. 5 (the word does not occur elsewhere in the New Testament) ; the " maketh all things new" of Wisd. vii. 27 with Heb. vi. 6 (not elsewhere, as before); "God is witness of his reins and a true beholder of his heart" (Wisd. i. 6), and the "discerner of the thoughts and intents of the heart" of Heb. iv. 12 ; the mystic reference to the dress of the High Priest as a symbol of the universe (Wisd. xviii. 24), and the strange epithet of "the cosmic sanctuary" as applied to the Tabernacle (Heb. ix. I)."

the Septuagint (LXX), and not the original Hebrew text, with which he does not seem to have been acquainted.

So, we have a Divinely-inspired Evangelist who does not seem to even be acquainted with the Hebrew Bible. That is from a one-hundred-year-old Abingdon Bible Commentary, but The New Interpreter's Bible (the NIB, also by Abingdon Press) confirms this:

> Both the instructions and the exhortations of the letter reveal a person well educated in Greek rhetoric as well as in Judaism, especially Hellenistic Judaism formed in part by the Septuagint, a Greek translation of the Old Testament. The Greek translation and not the Hebrew text provides the major lines and the subtler nuances of the writer's argument and appeal. ... The Scripture for the writer of Hebrews is the Old Testament in Greek translation, hereafter referred to as the Septuagint (LXX)... (Intro to Heb.)

John F. MacArthur, Jr., in *The MacArthur Study Bible*, also confirms this:

> Whoever the author was, he preferred citing OT references from the Greek OT (LXX) rather than from the Hebrew text.... consistent use of the LXX...." (Intro to Heb.)

And of course, "[t]he Book of Wisdom... is a book written in Greek ... It is not part of the Hebrew Bible but is included in the Septuagint..."[108]

But it is not just the author who used the Septuagint with Hebrews as his Bible; it must have been his audience as well. William Barclay's *The Daily Study Bible* (Westminster Press) tells us more about the audience:

> [Intro]: Moreover, it was obviously written to a scholarly group. From 5:12 we can see that they had long been under instruction and were preparing themselves to become teachers of the Christian faith. Still further, Hebrews demands such a knowledge of the Old Testament that it must always have been a book written by a scholar for scholars.... The man who wrote this letter knew the scriptures; he was eloquent; and he thought and argued in the way that a cultured Alexandrian would.
>
> [Regarding verses 1:1-3]: ...The writer to the Hebrews felt that, since he was going to speak of the supreme revelation of God to men, he must clothe his thought in the noblest language that it was possible to find. ...The writer to the Hebrews uses two great pictures to describe What Jesus was. He says that he was the apaugasma of God's glory. Apaugasma can mean one of two things in Greek. It can mean effulgence, the light which shines forth, ... the writer to the Hebrews said that Jesus was the character of the being of God, he meant that he was the exact image of God. Just as when you look at the impression, you see exactly what the seal which made it is like, so when you look at Jesus you see exactly what God is like...

---

[108] wikipedia.org/wiki/Book_of_Wisdom.

He must clothe his thought in the noblest language that it was possible to find (Barclay), and what he found came from the Book of Wisdom. The language may "not be easy to understand, and in fact cannot literally be understood, but that's the best that expositors can come up with as it regards the translation of the Greek words" (Swaggart) and uses word that "can't be found anywhere else in the New Testament or in the Old Testament" (Plumptre). The Epistle to the Hebrews is not just a book written by a scholar for scholars but by a teacher for teachers of the Christian faith (Barclay). And the teacher of teachers references the Book of Wisdom (which declares itself to be Divinely-inspired Scripture) as part of that teaching of the Christian faith.

The NIB tells us still more:

> ... this letter offers the most elaborate Christian reading of the Old Testament to be found in the New Testament ... The author assumes an audience familiar enough with the Old Testament to make detailed exegesis of its texts convincing, word studies delightful, and swift allusions powerful. (Intro to Heb.)

The author also assumed an audience familiar enough with the Book of Wisdom (which declares itself to be Divinely-inspired Scripture) to make detailed exegesis of its texts convincing, its word studies delightful, and its swift allusions powerful.

> [The audience's] earlier instruction ... included extended engagement with the text of the Greek Old Testament. The author's freedom to argue from nuances of the Greek translation of the Hebrew text and to make allusions to persons and events in Israel's history certainly implies a familiarity with that material on the part of the addressees.

That would be the Greek Old Testament that included the Book of Wisdom (which declares itself to be Divinely-inspired Scripture).

But there is still far more to consider: this language from the Book of Wisdom may have been used in a Christian hymn even before being included in the Epistle:

> 1:3. ... Some scholars account for the shift by seeing this verse as all or part of an early christological hymn that has been skillfully incorporated by the writer. [Footnote: See J. T. Sanders, New Testament Christological Hymns (Cambridge: Cambridge University Press, 1971) 19-20, who follows suggestions of earlier scholars.] Certainly elements found in passages widely accepted as hymns (Phil 2:6-11; Col 1:15-20; 1 Tim 3:16) are here: the relative pronoun ὅς (hos, "who," translated here as "he"), balanced phrasing (being, sustaining, having made), and a full display of the Son's sojourn (pre-

existence, humiliation, exaltation). If the author is quoting a hymn, he has woven it well into the larger affirmation.

Others concur and explain more about these hymns:

> One of the earliest and best descriptions of early Christian behavior comes from Pliny... they "were in the habit of meeting on a certain fixed day before it was light, when they sang in alternate verses a hymn to Christ, as to a god" (Letter 10.96). ... So if this is the case, where are the hymns in the New Testament? How can they be found? ... one will likely conclude that such passages as ... Heb 1:1-3 ... may very well have had earlier literary lives as actual hymns sung by early Christian communities. ... the biblical authors use these hymns to teach the early churches the content of their confession and socialize them into a world where Jesus the Messiah reigns over all other political and supernatural powers and authorities.[109]

Sometimes, this same concept is described as a "creedal statement:"

> ... creedal passages are thought to include ... Hebrews 1:3 ... these hymns and creeds come from the earliest period of Jewish-Christian worship, which is significantly earlier than the New Testament books they appear in (likely within the first couple of decades following Jesus's death)... Blomberg says, "Such beliefs [in Christ's deity] thus emerged early in the history of the church, not at some advanced stage of the 'evolution' of Christian doctrine." He adds: "Oldest of all are passages used by Paul and Peter in their letters that scholars have identified as most likely predating the epistles in which they appear." ...
>
> 1. While the books of the New Testament take us back to the apostolic age, the primitive creeds, confessions, and hymns contained in certain New Testament books press back to the earliest period of Jewish Christianity.
>
> 2. These primitive creeds, confessions, and hymns illustrate that the earliest Christians viewed Jesus as divine (a high Christology) and serve to falsify the claim that belief in Jesus's deity went through an extended period of evolution.
>
> 3. The earliest Christians, though staunch Jewish monotheists, nevertheless almost immediately worshiped Jesus Christ as an extension of Yahweh and thus exhibited a mutation of traditional monotheism.[110]

Before the Epistle to the Hebrews was written, and perhaps before any part of the New Testament was written (not even a decade after the death and Resurrection of Jesus), there may have already been a hymn being sung by the very earliest Christians. This hymn was "Christological," meaning it explained the nature of Christ and His Divinity. In order to explain it, the hymn alluded not to any of the books of the modern Jewish canon but to the Book of

---

[109] www.bibleodyssey.org/articles/hymns-in-the-new-testament
[110] reasons.org/explore/blogs/reflections/an-early-christmas-hymn-in-the-new-testament

Wisdom, even using two crucial terms taken directly from the Book of Wisdom (the mirrored reflection (radiance) and exact imprint (representation) of God's being), an implicit claim that Jesus Christ fulfilled the statements in the Book of Wisdom (which declares itself to be Divinely-inspired Scripture). These words "may not be easy to understand, and in fact cannot literally be understood, but that's the best that expositors can come up with as it regards the translation of the Greek words"—but they made sense to the Jewish Christians, which "had long been under instruction and were preparing themselves to become teachers of the Christian faith."

Often, we are told that before there was a New Testament, the only Scripture was the Old Testament. During that time, the earliest Christians (many of whom presumably would have seen and spoken to Jesus) sang this hymn to exalt and explain the nature of Christ. Some of those earliest Christians had even been Jewish Priests; others were Jewish Christian children, singing this hymn to express a key element of faith—all while the Apostles were still alive, before they started writing and became Evangelists.

This hymn/creedal statement continues to be crucial to who we are and what we believe—so much so that it is part of the Nicene Creed (the first Creed of the Christian faith) and is read to the congregation on Christmas Day, per the Revised Common Lectionary.

Kruger: Hebrews for You

And how about this for Divinely-inspired "coincidence?" Our main man Michael J. Kruger has written just one single Bible commentary, and it happens to be on the Epistle to the Hebrews. It is called "Hebrews For You" (and is a perfectly wonderful read, if you are interested). For our purposes, here is a point to consider (emphasis added):

> [1:3]: … Our author [of Hebrews] has taken attributes which are given to the God of Israel throughout the Old Testament and ascribed them to Jesus. …
> … he is God enfleshed. Who can reveal God better than God? This is clear in the language of Hebrews 1:3: "He is the radiance of the glory of God." This word "radiance" means "brightness" or "shining." Old Testament visions of God describe him as bright and glorious (Exodus 24:10, 17; Ezekiel 1:4; Daniel 7:9).

Exactly! They certainly do. And yet, the hymn and the divinely-inspired Evangelist did not use or reference the wording from those sections of the Old

Testament to describe Jesus; they referenced the wording of the Book of Wisdom (which declares itself to be Divinely-inspired Scripture) instead.

I submit that Kruger is an example of what an author would do if the author did <u>not</u> believe that the Book of Wisdom was Scripture: they would just reference other passages from "authentic Scripture" instead. Kruger gives us three passages they could have quoted or alluded to, though they did not. Instead, they alluded to the Book of Wisdom by using the exact words used nowhere else in the Bible.

And there are two authors here—the author of the hymn, plus the author of the Epistle to the Hebrews. The Evangelist incorporated the hymn that already included the reference to the Book of Wisdom, then went on to allude to the Book of Wisdom many more times throughout the entire Epistle. He did so without ever warning anyone away from the Book (which claims to be the inspired word of God).

The hymn's creator had no desire to allude to the other Books Kruger notes, and the author of the Epistle had no desire to tie his Epistle to such other Books. They could have easily done so but did not. This choice seems strange if the Book of Wisdom (which declares itself to be Divinely-inspired Scripture) were not Scripture to the author and audience of the Epistle to the Hebrews; usually, such people are overeager to make connections to Scripture. And from the audience's perspective as well, the point would seem to be better made, and more persuasively made, by referencing "authentic" Scripture.

Before I change topics slightly, I will note a few points regarding the Book of Wisdom, each to be discussed individually later. But the problem with the Apocrypha as a topic is that everything is multifaceted and multidimensional, so it is difficult to proceed in an orderly fashion; sometimes, we have to step back and see it all together.

I have noted how tied the Book of Wisdom seems to be to the Epistle to the Hebrews, as well as to a key Christological hymn/creed that found its way into the Epistle, plus 1 Clement (perhaps written before the last books of the New Testament were written) and the 325 AD Nicene Creed, etc.

In a moment, I will turn to other possible and deeply theological uses of the Book of Wisdom in the Bible—e.g., Matthew and his Jewish audience may have seen Jesus as the fulfillment of specific prophesies made from it, etc.

Later on, we will see that biblindex.org/citation_biblique/search notes 1,798 references to the Book of Wisdom from early Fathers. We can compare that to Job, also an Old Testament "Poetic" Book, with 4552, at a rate of 4.26

references per verse (Job has 1068 verses). The Book of Wisdom has 436 verses, so it has an essentially identical rate of 4.12.

I do not have access to every such reference, and my review was not exhaustive; still, I found more than 500 references[111] in works where a Father specifically stated that the Book of Wisdom was Holy Scripture, the Word of God, Divinely-inspired, Prophecy, etc.

When we look at canon lists, we will also see that "Wisdom" appears on every Christian canon list until 350 AD. All but one of those mentions are clear references to the Book of Wisdom; the one outlier (Melito's) is just the title "Wisdom," which only might be a reference to the Book of Wisdom (but possibly it was an alternative reference to the Book of Proverbs).[112]

THE JEWISH BIBLE VS. THE PROTESTANT CANON

Let's look at the Jewish canon issue from a different perspective—in fact a different Bible, the Jewish Study Bible.[113] "Nearly forty scholars worldwide contributed ... representing the best of Jewish biblical scholarship available today. A committee of highly-respected biblical scholars and rabbis from the Orthodox, Conservative, and Reform Judaism movements..."

Of course, the Biblical books are actually the same as the Old Testament of a Protestant Bible—but my goodness, how different are the study notes.

Compare, for example, the (Christian) Apologetics Study Bible, which includes the essay "How Can We Know the Bible Includes the Correct Books?" from Norman L. Geisler. Geisler/the Apologetics Study Bible make the following factual claims:

> (2) They [the Apocrypha] were written between 250 BC and the first century AD, but according to Judaism, the Spirit of prophecy had departed from Israel before that time, by about 400 BC.[114]

---

[111] That is inarguably "a lot" in this context, by any comparison to other data I know of (many of which I will show you below). If one were to clean up the data (remove double entries in the index, etc.), then probably a third of the Books of the Protestant canon were not even vaguely alluded to 500 times in the first 450 years, let alone specifically noted as Scripture in the book doing the alluding. In the end, I gave up searching for more because if 500 does not make the point, nothing will. "Neither will they be persuaded, though one rose from the dead." Luke 16:31.

[112] And Melito's list is arguably not a Christian list. See below.

[113] www.amazon.com/Jewish-Study-Bible-Publication-Translation/dp/0195297547. My edition is Oxford University Press 2014.

[114] In case you are wondering what item (1) said: "(1) Unlike the canonical books, the apocryphal books do not have either an explicit or implicit claim to be inspired by God..." But of course the

Actually, the Jewish Study Bible says Scripture was being written long after 400 BC. The first sentence of the commentary on the Book of Daniel says that it was "probably written in its final version in 164 BCE." [p. 1635].

That is after the Book of Sirach, which had a known author and date (around 180 BC) and is roughly contemporaneous with the date ranges of all the other Apocrypha except the Book of Wisdom (50 BC is the guess I use for that one).[115]

> (3) The Jewish historian Josephus gave the names and numbers of the authentic Jewish Old Testament, which correspond exactly with the thirty nine books of our Old Testament (Against Apion 1:8).

First, no, Josephus most certainly did not do that. He does not name anything, and he just said there were 22 books, not 39. Here is the full quote from Josephus:

> For we have not an innumerable multitude of books among us ... but only twenty-two books, which contain the records of all the past times; which are justly believed to be divine; and of them five belong to Moses ... the prophets, who were after Moses, wrote down what was done in their times in thirteen books. The remaining four books contain hymns to God, and precepts for the conduct of human life.[116]

A reader has to add a lot of guesses to get from the number 22 to the modern Jewish (24 Books)/Protestant (39 Books) canon. From the Jewish Study Bible: "Josephus is often cited as evidence for the Jewish canon in the 1st c. CE, but there may have been several competing notions of canon in this period, and he should not be taken as normative for all of Judaism in his time. He is, however, apparently the earliest source to suggest a closed canon, consisting of twenty-two biblical books ... Since he does not list his twenty-two books, it is not clear if he simply had a smaller canon than the rabbinic list of twenty-four books ..." [p. 2156].

Book of Wisdom makes such claims, as already discussed. For another example, see Sirach 24: 32-33: "I will yet make doctrine to shine as the morning, and will send forth her light afar off. I will yet pour out doctrine as prophecy, and leave it to all ages for ever."

[115] Note that accepting a later date for Wisdom would have ancillary implications, given that New Testament Books seem to have relied upon it. I.e., you might not be able to accept an early date for some of the New Testament Books if Wisdom was not written well before then. Notably there are quotes of Jesus that seem to be referencing Wisdom, which means (if so) that the Book would have to be from a period well before He was talking to His audience.

[116] earlyjewishwritings.com/text/josephus/apion1.html.

Moreover, if you actually intend to follow exactly what Josephus said, then you would also need to add Josephus' books to your canon. According to the Jewish Study Bible, Josephus "understood himself to be exercising this priestly and prophetic office, carrying on the work of Scripture transmission through his own inspired interpretations" (citing Jewish Wars 3.392-408 and Antiquities 10.78-79). [p. 1850]. Indeed, the Josippon (a medieval copy, of sorts, made from the works of Josephus) has been considered canon by some Orthodox Churches.[117]

Back to Geisler/the Apologetics Study Bible:

> And [4] Judaism, which produced these books, has never accepted them into its Bible (the Hebrew Scriptures, corresponding to our Old Testament).

The Jewish Study Bible: "... the biblical scrolls found at Qumran [abandoned 68 AD, after Christ] do bear on the question of the growth of the Hebrew canon, which was, according to many scholars, fixed only at a later period. The presence at Qumran of all of the books found in the Hebrew canon (with the exception of Esth.) may support the inference that these books already had canonical status. What was not yet agreed upon was the exact boundaries of the canon as well as the final textual form of the individual works." [p. 1858].

The Jewish Study Bible: "It is important to remember that different Jewish groups from the early first millennium CE may have had different ideas of what comprised scripture..." [p. 2157].

The Jewish Study Bible: "... several points seem fairly certain. First, the process of canonization was gradual and it began long before the Rabbis. It is likely that its final stages were reached by (if not before) the 1st c. CE, perhaps as a reaction to the destruction of the Second Temple in 70 CE and its aftermath." [p. 2158].

The Jewish Study Bible: "In rabbinic literature, the Wisdom of Jesus ben Sirach ... a book in the Apocrypha but not in the Hebrew Bible, is

---

[117] There are many other potential disconnects between Josephus' number and the Books of the modern Jewish canon, including that Josephus (a) cites to the Apocryphal additions to Esther, (b) cites a lamentation from Jeremiah that does not seem to be the Book of Lamentations as we have it and he may, therefore, include a Book we do not, and (c) also says that Ezekiel wrote two Books but the modern Jews only accept one (for discussion of which the second might be, see wikipedia.org/wiki/Apocryphon_of_Ezekiel or wikipedia.org/wiki/Pseudo-Ezekiel, etc.). I discuss the first reference above; see Antiquities, X, 5 for the last two: www.gutenberg.org/files/2848/2848-h/2848-h.htm.

occasionally cited with the same formula used for introducing biblical texts[118] and was thus, in some sense, canonical for some Rabbis. Therefore, although we can probably speak of "the" canon having formed by the 1st C. CE, there was a certain amount of fluidity or variability around the fringes." [p. 2157].

The Jews completely disagree with the Catholic and Orthodox canons. And yet, the Jewish Study Bible rejects the claims made by what would seem to be their "allies" in the argument with the Catholics and the Orthodox. The Jewish Study Bible rejects the claim that the Jewish canon was firm and established by the time of Christ.

Gallagher and Meade agree with the Jewish Study Bible, as well, p. 25: "It would appear that in the era before the canon lists, there was a limited set of books that was a functional collection of authoritative texts' on which all or most Jews could agree. ... Neither can we say for sure that no other book was received as Scripture ... we might say that Josephus was half-right, or even three-quarters: while every Jew (more or less) had for so long considered the twenty-two books to be divinely authoritative, some Jews may have attributed the same status to certain other books, as well. In the period before lists, we can still be confident about the reception of the core books—the Torah, the prophets, the Psalter-but the books at the fringe of the canon remain in uncertain territory." They cite to VanderKam 2012: 55; cf. Alexander 2007: 65: 'What the Rabbis were doing was defending a canon which they had received already more or less defined (save for a little fuzziness around the edges) from the pre-70 [AD, after Christ] period.'

For a specific example, focus just on Daniel, starting with the Ancient Christian Commentary on Scripture (Volume 13: Daniel), "Both Theodotion Daniel and the Septuagint contain material that was excluded from the Jewish canon, perhaps as early as the end of the first century A.D."

The Jewish Study Bible confirms that this occurred after Christ and that "because prefigurations of Jesus and Christian resurrection were seen in Daniel by the early church, the rabbinic tradition hesitated to embrace the visions of Daniel." [p. 1637].

It is the final decision of those Rabbis—they who were hesitating to embrace a book that the Christians already considered Prophecy and

---

[118] See www.sefaria.org/Yevamot.63b.13?lang=bi – search for "Sira" and you will see two examples from the Talmud; intertextual.bible/text/sirach-13.15-bava-kamma-92b notes a third. Such citations were still being written centuries after Christ.

Scripture—that led to the modern Jewish canon. So sayeth the Jewish Study Bible.

The Rabbis were considering abandoning a book that Jews had accepted as Divinely-inspired Prophecy and Scripture for centuries ("Daniel was evidently considered a prophet at Qumran and elsewhere in early Judaism (Ant. 10.266-68 [Josephus])." [p. 1636]). But despite this, Daniel was not included in the Prophets section of the Tanakh in the Rabbis' final decision—apparently, he was demoted after Christ in such a way that he is no longer seen in quite the same light as a full "Prophet."

That the Rabbis could even conceive of not accepting Daniel is an enlightening detail. Moreover, to this day, the Jews follow the decision of those Rabbis and do not include Daniel among "the Prophets," and "the book of Daniel has not held central importance in Jewish tradition" [p. 1637]—and, of course, the Jews, following the decision of those Rabbis, excluded Susanna as well: "perhaps as early as the end of the first century A.D."

Even getting from Josephus' number (22 Books) to the modern Jewish/Protestant canon (24 Books to the Jews, 39 to the Protestants—i.e., the same books, just split up and organized differently) requires several steps of suppositions and guesses, with competing theories of how to bridge the gap. The first clear evidence of the modern arrangement (which is tripartite with 24 books) comes centuries after Josephus (who was writing almost a full century after Jesus). The only question is how many centuries. From Gallagher and Meade:

> The Hebrew Bible today consists of twenty-four books divided into three sections... This arrangement is attested by the Masoretic manuscripts from around the year 1000 CE, but we can trace the tripartite division and the number of books back much earlier than that. A passage of the Talmud ... affirming the three divisions and the twenty-four books, dates no later than the redaction of the Talmud in the sixth century, and most scholars would date it well before then, perhaps as early as the second century.... We can thus confidently date to the fourth century or earlier (depending on the date of the Talmudic list) the Jewish enumeration of the Hebrew Bible as twenty-four books divided into three major sections.[119]

Dating is always debated, and Gallagher and Meade may very well be right in picking early dates (I generally go with their dating herein), but the

---

[119] The Biblical Canon Lists from Early Christianity, p. 3.

progression from "no later" to "most scholars would date" to "confidently date" is a noteworthy example of "certainty inflation." Their final guess when they turn to the actual list is "circa 200"—the earliest date in the range.

Meanwhile, there are early Church Fathers who list variant Jewish canons. We only have two "truly Jewish" lists (meaning a list compiled by a Jew, not a Christian listing what the Jews accept) in our "early Church" time frame, one being Josephus (not really a list at all, just the number), and the other being the list Gallagher and Meade are referring to from the Babylonian Talmud (which is, indeed, a list of the modern Jewish/Protestant canon).

The lists of the alleged Jewish canon provided by the Fathers all disagree with each other and with the Talmud. Sometimes Esther is excluded (as with Melito—and note that Melito seems to have written his list before the list in the Talmud was created), the Maccabees may have had some sort of status (via Origen, writing a few years after the earliest part of the date range for this Talmud list), Baruch (and the Epistle of Jeremiah) may be included (as per Origen, Epiphanius, the Apostolic Canons, etc.), Wisdom and Sirach are disputed (and thus, some Jews did accept them—per Epiphanius), etc.

In addition, the earliest date for the Talmud's list is during Origen's lifetime, and it is he who tells us that the Jewish leaders "pretended to the Jews … deceived the wives of their countrymen. … hid from the knowledge of the people … took away from the people every passage … concealed and removed from the Scriptures…"

Moreover, the Talmud list is of 24 Books, not 22; and yet, around 391 AD, Jerome writes that the 24 enumeration is still a minority view and most Jews keep to the 22 number[120]—which would make the Talmud version a minority view to Jerome's understanding when he is living and writing in Jerusalem/Bethlehem. Jerome believes the numbers add to the same 39 Books as modern Protestants number them. However, at roughly the same time, Epiphanius gives us his 27 number, with the claim that some Apocrypha are accepted in the Jewish canon.

Even accepting the date of 200 AD for the Talmud's list, that is still two centuries after Christ and is roughly contemporaneous with other lists that disagree on the Jewish canon, plus Origen's claims of deletions that he heard of from the Jews themselves. In addition, even the 200 AD earliest date of the

---

[120] See his Preface to the Book of Kings, quoted at www.bible-researcher.com/jerome.html.

Talmud's list comes after Christians are expressly citing to all of the Apocrypha as Christian Scripture.[121]

In fact, the Talmud itself cites to Sirach as Scripture in several places (See www.sefaria.org/Yevamot.63b.13?lang=bi. Search for "Sira," and you will see two examples), evidencing that even as this first truly "Jewish" list is being developed, and for many centuries after, there are actually Jews holding to different canons.[122]

We also have a Christian Father who was writing in 385 AD and claimed that at that late date the Jews still accepted Baruch, with Sirach and Wisdom "in dispute." But in that case, that is just one Father making a claim. When judging these things, we have to look at more than the existence of evidence; the quality of the evidence matters, too.

Thus, the importance of Jerome, who clearly limits the Jewish canon to the modern Jewish list (his continued acceptance of Susanna is for Christians, not Jews). After all, Jerome lived in Bethlehem, and was a friend to the Jews—so much so that he even became fluent in Hebrew as an adult so that he could better understand the Jewish Scriptures (and, thus, become a valued translator for the Church). It is hard to be more knowledgeable about the true Jewish situation than that! Therefore, we can have certainty that Jerome knew of what he wrote and gave us accurate information.

Now, just try comparing Jerome to that other guy telling us that there was a different Jewish canon in 385 AD! Who was that clown?

He was Epiphanius, a Jewish Christian.[123] Either his parents had converted before he was born, or when he was a child.

He was born and raised just outside of Jerusalem.

He "was an extremely well-educated scholar who had deep knowledge of ancient languages."[124] He was praised by Jerome for knowing five languages—including Hebrew, of course.[125]

---

[121] Or, at the latest, they do so by 203 AD: it depends on the dating of one of Clement of Alexandria's books citing to the last few Apocrypha. Some date it as late as 203 AD, others as early as 190 AD. In any event, Gallagher and Meade's "circa 200 AD" for the Talmud is not just the early end of the date range but also not meant to be an exact number.

[122] Also, note that some of the Apocrypha "reappear" later in Judaism, such as Judith (see wikipedia.org/wiki/Book_of_Judith). Meanwhile, the Ethiopian Jews accepted all the Apocrypha—and still do. All of that might help make the case for Apocrypha as Scripture stronger, but this book will ignore those arguments.

[123] wikipedia.org/wiki/Epiphanius_of_Salamis

[124] biblecanon.org/lists/ (click on "Panarion").

He "travelled widely to combat differing beliefs." He researched and wrote a great treatise (the Panarion), which enumerated all the sects of Judaism and all those derived from Judaism.[126]

So, Epiphanius was a Jewish Christian from Judea, fluent in Hebrew. He was an expert on the ins and outs of Judaism and all its varieties and variants. And it is this expert on Jews, working on the ground in 385 AD, that is the source that says the Jews still accepted Baruch and that some of the Jews still accepted[127] Sirach and Wisdom, as late as 385 AD, and those who did accept them were still considered mainstream Jews and not some variant sect.

And there is corroborating evidence that Epiphanius is the one who was correct, not Jerome: Rabbis were still citing to Sirach as Scripture all the way until the tenth century AD, 600 years after Jerome told us that "the" Jewish canon did not include Sirach. Some of them did so in the Talmud itself. In addition, the Apostolic Constitutions of 380 AD reports that the Jews still read Baruch on the tenth day of the month Gorpiaeus, when they assembled together.[128] In other words, there are three reports at the end of the Fourth Century on what the Jews accept, and two of the three say they accept Baruch, with Jerome outvoted.

---

[125] Absolutely every detail about everything on the canon is disputed, and Epiphanius is no exception. You can find people who argue that maybe Jerome meant it as an insult or a joke, and for all I know, they are right. Regardless, a Jewish Christian from Jerusalem is a very good source, since we are not talking about a detailed understanding of nuances in Jewish thinking, just a list of Books they accept (in fact, if there had been a clear Jewish canon of only 22 Books, would that not have been exactly the sort of basic fact that every Jew would know?). His lists may have antecedents elsewhere, but even if he copied them, he would be someone with independent knowledge "authenticating" the correctness of what he copied, not a mere copyist repeating something without personal knowledge.

And bear in mind that some of Jerome's peers considered him a gullible gentile sucker being fooled by the Jews on the canon question. So, we look for corroborating evidence. The lists and other data on the Jewish canon are an inconsistent mess, which supports the claim that the Jewish canon was not settled and had "fuzzy edges." (Which, after all, is also the view of the Jewish Study Bible.)

[126] As well as the heresies derived from Christianity—and other religions, as well.

[127] Epiphanius says it is disputed, which means some accept it. That is what people tell us when the topic is the New Testament canon: e.g., "church fathers occasionally acknowledge that a particular book is "disputed" by some. ... the implications of Origen's comments [are]...that apparently most Christians do consider them genuine— including Origen himself..." – Kruger, Michael J. (p. 265-266).

[128] Book 5, 3, 20. www.newadvent.org/fathers/07155.htm.

12 NEW TESTAMENT REFERENCES TO THE APOCRYPHA

So far: (1) the Jewish Study Bible asserts (and the early Christian lists evidence) that the Jewish canon was not settled until well after the time of Christ, (2) many early Church Fathers claimed the Jewish Scriptures had become incomplete by their time, and (3) the New Testament gives us some Biblical evidence suggesting that the more Jewish the audience and the better taught the Jewish Christian writer was, the more the Evangelists focused on Apocrypha and tied them into their writings.[129]

But item (3) was a data analysis and not a discussion of the references themselves, so let's move on to that. Just what kind of references are they? They were a mixed bag, of course, just like references to the "other" Old Testament Books. There are a few that are very strong and many that are weaker but which have a cumulative effect. We start with the few.

Our standard for the canonical Old Testament has to extend to the Apocrypha: otherwise, the sorts of things we do not accept for the Apocrypha will not stand as 'proof' in the case for Christianity. Thus, we start with some baselining from Don Stewart of the Blue Letter Bible:[130]

> ...while Ezra/Nehemiah, Esther, Song of Solomon, and Ecclesiastes are not directly cited in the New Testament, this does not mean that they were not part of Scripture.

So as a preliminary matter, an authoritative citation in the New Testament is really just a "one-way" gate: it puts things in the canon but does not exclude things that are not cited.[131] The exclusion, to folks like Stewart, comes from

---

[129] The evidence operates on many levels: did the people interacting with Jesus see the Apocrypha as Scripture, did the Evangelist writing a Gospel/Epistle see it as such, did the Evangelist's audience see it as such, etc. And, of course, there is the overarching question of did Jesus, and the Holy Spirit, and the Father see it as such. Every single Biblical example has to be considered on all those levels, but I will not always mention every level.

[130] www.blueletterbible.org/Comm/stewart_don/faq/right-books-in-old-testament/question17-new-testament-quote-old-testament.cfm. First thing that came up on Google. Stewart gives us a good online summary of what the Protestant canon has going for it, which is why I am using it as my baseline here. The page I use from Stewart is part (question 17 of 21) of a much longer work on the Old Testament canon, which starts at: www.blueletterbible.org/Comm/stewart_don/faq/right-books-in-old-testament/introduction-right-books-in-old-testament.cfm

[131] Putting aside 1 Enoch, possibly cited in the Letter of Jude. It is considered noncanonical by Catholics and nearly all Protestants, while being accepted by the Ethiopian and Eritrean Orthodox. So, a full quotation is (arguably) not a perfect "one-way" gate.

the Hebrew canon: if it is not on the Hebrew list, then it is not on the Christian list, and nothing else matters.[132]

> The number of [Jewish canon] books had been long-fixed before the time of Christ.

Note he says the number of books, not the list of books by name. Note further his claim that it "had been long-fixed before the time of Christ" comes with neither a claim of exactly when that was done, nor a citation to a source 'proving' it—perhaps because Josephus (the source, I say) was not even born until several years after Christ was crucified, died, buried, rose again, and ascended into Heaven.[133]

> This list included these four works.

Note that he does not actually give us a quote showing us that the list included these four works, perhaps because there is no such list. Josephus provided a number of books, 22, which (as the Jewish Study Bible noted) might match the modern canon or might not, and does not mention what it includes or rejects.

> Indeed, at the time of Ben Sirach, two centuries before Christ, these works were cited as Holy Scripture.

With the phrase "at the time of Ben Sirach," he presumably means that this is cited in the Book of Sirach but, apparently, he does not want to mention the name of an Apocrypha that claims that it itself is Scripture, and which was canon for some Rabbis, etc. Be that as it may, let us consider what Sirach actually said.[134] I cannot just quote it all for you because it is a long list of people, books, and deeds taking up many chapters, but in summary:

> The Book of Sirach provides evidence of a collection of sacred scriptures similar to portions of the Hebrew Bible. ... a list of names of biblical figures in the same order as is found in the Torah (Law) and the Nevi'im (Prophets), and which includes the names

---

[132] Literally, nothing else matters—Stewart tells us that Books with nothing going for them New Testament-wise are still canon because they are on the Hebrew list, and (in this particular essay) Stewart does not concern himself with whatever the "Apocrypha" have going for them.

[133] Dates for when Josephus wrote the relevant book (*Against Apion*) range from 94-117 AD, 61-84 years after Christ. In the entire history of Judaism, not one single person had ever written this idea down until Josephus used it to argue that the Jews were right and the Greeks were wrong—the exact polemic use that raises the most suspicion that someone is making something up.

[134] It begins at chapter 44: www.kingjamesbibleonline.org/Ecclesiasticus-Chapter-44/

of some men mentioned in the Ketuvim (Writings). Based on this list of names, some scholars have conjectured that the author, Yeshua ben Sira, had access to, and considered authoritative, the books of Genesis, Exodus, Leviticus, Numbers, Deuteronomy, Joshua, Judges, Samuel, Kings, Job, Isaiah, Jeremiah, Ezekiel, and the Twelve Minor Prophets.[135]

Notably not mentioned in that list: the four books we were told were cited! Ezra/Nehemiah, Esther, Song of Solomon, and Ecclesiastes. Per the footnotes on Wikipedia, Esther and Ecclesiastes are simply not included in Sirach's canon, Song of Solomon might be alluded to (or might not) by a single mention of "songs," and Nehemiah the person (but not the Books Ezra/Nehemiah) is mentioned by a variant of his name in Sirach 49:13.

I bring all this up for two reasons. First, the relevant sections of Sirach are also evidence that Baruch was Jewish Scripture. The Greek translation of the Book of Jeremiah and of Baruch 1:1-3:8 show that they were translated from Hebrew into Greek by the same person. Since Sirach refers to the Law and the Prophets as a well-known and accepted collection in the Greek-speaking community of Alexandria, the Greek version of Jeremiah with Baruch must have been completed by then and part of that collection.[136]

Second, the whole reason for all this talk about Josephus and Sirach is basically a timing problem. The allegedly certain and limited canon of the Jews was not actually alleged, even in concept, until Josephus (and then only as the number of 22 books)—and he was writing no less than 61 years after the Crucifixion. It is at least 30 years after Matthew, Mark, Peter, Paul, James, and Jude were all martyred, and thus, at least 30 years after all their Gospels and Epistles were written (if, like me, you accept those attributions). John (if we use the 90's AD date) would be writing contemporaneously with the very earliest date for Josephus, but possibly well beforehand if the later dates for Josephus are correct. Polycarp (discussed below) enters the Church before Josephus writes (Justin Martyr might have, as well), and various non-Biblical works (such as 1 Clement, Clement's Epistle to the Corinthians) are also thought to have been written before Josephus was writing.

I like to think of years in modern terms. As I write this in 2025, 61 years ago was 1964. That was the year the Beatles first toured America and started

---

[135] wikipedia.org/wiki/Development_of_the_Hebrew_Bible_canon
[136] Cribbed from the New Interpreter's Bible, Introduction to Baruch, p. 931, with minor changes. The NIB's reference to the comments in Sirach is to the prologue, written by the grandson of the author of the rest of Sirach, who was translating the grandfather's Hebrew text into Greek.

the British Invasion. The Palestine Liberation Organization was founded, and the Viet Nam war began. Cassius Clay beat Sonny Liston to become World Champion, before he changed his name to Muhammad Ali. For the first time, smoking cigarettes was declared hazardous to one's health. It would be 27 years before the Soviet Union collapsed, and that was 34 years ago.

To put it mildly, 61 years is not a minor timing problem. Josephus is writing a long time after Christ, and he is the first to ever make this claim that the Jewish canon is actually limited to 22 Books. Whether any Jew agreed with him, let alone whether everyone did, is simply absent from the record. Not one scrap of paper agrees with Josephus until at least a century later (if the very earliest date of the range Gallagher and Meade discuss for the Talmud is the correct one, and obviously the range exists because many disagree with the early dating). In fact, many lists and much contrary evidence will be produced in the following centuries that counter Josephus' claim: lists with 24 books, 27 books, lists without Esther, some where Wisdom, Baruch, and Susanna are included or the Maccabees mentioned, Talmudic citations and debates over Sirach, etc.

But more importantly for us, much if not all of the Divinely-inspired Scripture of the New Testament was also produced in those 61 years. So let's look at what the New Testament references may be; they are part of the evidence about everything, including whether the Jewish canon was really as fixed and settled as Stewart believes it to have been.

Our first example from Stewart:

> While Ecclesiastes does not have any direct quotes from it in the New Testament, there are a number of passages that allude to it. For example, Paul wrote to Timothy: "For the love of money is at the root of all kinds of evil. And some people, craving money, have wandered from the faith and pierced themselves with many sorrows. (1 Timothy 6:10 NLT)" This seems to depend upon the following verse in Ecclesiastes. It reads: The lover of money will not be satisfied with money; nor the lover of wealth, with gain. This also is vanity. (Ecclesiastes 5:10 NRSV)

But the notes included with the original KJV actually say otherwise. There is no cross-reference between Ecclesiastes and 1 Timothy 6:10. Instead, it is Sirach 31:1 ("Watching for riches consumeth the flesh, and the care thereof driveth away sleep") that was cross-referenced with 1 Timothy 6:10. Thus, the website's claim that "there seems to be direct dependence upon this book in a number of places in the New Testament" should apply to Sirach (Ecclesiasticus), not Ecclesiastes, per the KJV. The KJV, in this instance, is effectively a panel of Protestant judges, dismissing the reference to Ecclesiastes and accepting this as a reference to Sirach. I submit that it is a strong indication that neutral judges would also see it that way.

A second example:

> While Judges is not directly quoted as authoritative Scripture, events that are recorded in the Book of Judges are cited in the Book of Hebrews. We read the following: "And what shall I more say? for the time would fail me to tell of Gedeon, and of Barak, and of Samson, and of Jephthae; of David also, and Samuel, and of the prophets" (Hebrews 11:32 KJV). Gideon, Barak, Samson, and Jephthah are all featured in stories in the Book of Judges. The writer to the Hebrews used them as illustrations of faith. All of the other illustrations in this portion of the Book of Hebrews, which used by the writer, were taken from characters which are found in the pages of Old Testament Scripture. These include such people as Abraham, Noah, Moses and Jacob. Placing these characters from the Book of Judges alongside the characters in the canonical books clearly testifies to the status of Judges.

Three verses later, as part of his further illustrations of faith (see 11:39), in Hebrews 11:35 ("Women received their dead raised to life again: and others were tortured, not accepting deliverance; that they might obtain a better resurrection"), the same Epistle writer references 2 Maccabees 7:7 (the Maccabean Martyrs: a woman and her seven sons, discussed at length below). Thus, 2 Maccabees meets the exact same standard as the Book of Judges (in fact, once again, the KJV actually cross references 11:35 to 2 Maccabees 7:7 but does not do so for 11:32 and Judges), and it, too, can claim that "All of the other illustrations in this portion of the Book of Hebrews, which used by the writer, were taken from characters which are found in the pages of Old Testament Scripture. .... Placing these characters from the Book of [2 Maccabees] alongside the characters in the canonical books clearly testifies to the status of [2 Maccabees]."

The story of the woman and her seven sons is the only instance in Scripture/Apocrypha that fits all three parts of the Hebrews 11:35 description (Particularly the "that they might obtain a better resurrection" piece. Recall that much of the Protestant Old Testament does not explicitly mention resurrection, whereas 2 Maccabees 7:9 does: "And when he was at the last gasp, he said, Thou like a fury takest us out of this present life, but the King of the world shall raise us up, who have died for his laws, unto everlasting life"), plus, there are Greek words connecting the description in 2 Maccabees to Hebrews (one of which is never used in the Bible except in these two places).

That the author of Hebrews is referring to 2 Maccabees 7 is acknowledged by the KJV (1611), Barnes' Notes (1843), the NIB (1998), etc.—so, this has always been acknowledged, at least by some. My personal stacks of over 100 Protestant Bible commentaries are roughly divided: one-third pass over Hebrews 11:35 without comment, one-third acknowledge it as referencing 2 Maccabees without discussing any canon implications, and one-third break the sentence into pieces so that they can point to individuals in the Protestant Bible who meet the individual sub-clauses but not all three. (Such was Kruger's approach in *Hebrews For You*.)

But this is not only a question of whether one accepts the reference as being to 2 Maccabees. Consider what would be left of references to the Old Testament if one employs a fair and consistent standard that does not accept this as a reference (even though it is the only thing that fits all the pieces; there are no other candidates that do; there are specific unique linguistic connections that link the New Testament verse to the "Old Testament" verse, etc.). E.g., compare it with the citations and quotations of authentic Scripture—in fact, the most inarguable of Old Testament Scripture, the Pentateuch.

Pentateuch Reference (from Stewart)

Genesis: Jesus cites the creation account of humanity in Genesis (Genesis 1:27): He answered, "Have you not read that the one who made them at the beginning 'made them male and female,' and said, 'For this reason a man shall leave his father and mother and be joined to his wife, and the two shall become one flesh'"? (Matthew 19:4-5 NRSV)

Exodus: The Apostle Paul quoted the Book of Exodus (Exodus 20:12): Children, obey your parents in the Lord, for this is right. Honor your father and mother-- this is the first commandment with a promise: so that it may be well with you and you may live long on the earth. (Ephesians 6:1-3 NRSV)

Leviticus: After healing a man with leprosy, Jesus told the person to go and show himself to the priest. This is according to the command written in the Law of Moses in the Book of Leviticus (Leviticus 14:2-32): Then Jesus said to him, "See that you say nothing to anyone; but go, show yourself to the priest, and offer the gift that Moses commanded, as a testimony to them." (Matthew 8:4 NRSV)

Contrarian Analysis

Jesus does not name the Book of Genesis or the author/prophet, nor does he say that it is taken from Scripture. (Recall from Sidebar 4 that Stewart gave us his three formulae for identifying Scripture: "have you not read" is not one of them.) So he could be referring to Genesis without indicating that it is Scripture, or referring to some other non-Scriptural book that makes the same point.

Not only does Paul not name a specific book or author, but he also does not actually state that this is even to be found in any book at all. Yet, we see a claim that it is a "quote" when it is merely a possible allusion and nothing more.

This is also a reference to a command, not a citation to a book and not a quote. It never says that it is to be found in a book. In addition, it does not even tell us exactly what the command was, so there is no way to prove that the command mentioned was, indeed, the command given in Leviticus.

Numbers: The faithfulness of Moses (Numbers 12:7) is cited in the Book of Hebrews: Moses was certainly faithful in God's house, but only as a servant. His work was an illustration of the truths God would reveal later. (Hebrews 3:5 NLT)	This is only a vague reference to an aspect of Moses' history and character—an aspect that might be found (explicitly or implicitly) in other books, not just Numbers. It is, therefore, not proven that Paul meant the description given in the book of Numbers.
Deuteronomy: ... Jesus quoted Deuteronomy 6:13: Jesus said to him, "Away with you, Satan! for it is written, 'Worship the Lord your God, and serve only him.'" (Matthew 4:10 NRSV)	That somewhat similar language can be found in Deuteronomy could be as accidental as Hebrews 11:35 using language from 2 Maccabees.

A standard of proof that denies that Hebrews 11:35 is a reference to 2 Maccabees 7:7 makes proving anything nearly impossible.[137]

Moreover, while not noted by the KJV, Hebrews 11:38 (they wandered in deserts, and in mountains, and in dens and caves of the earth) is also often seen as a reference to those who fled Antiochus (including Mattathias and his sons). They are described in 1 Maccabees 1:53 (And drove the Israelites into secret places, even wheresoever they could flee for succour) and 2:28-31 (28So he and his sons fled into the mountains, and left all that ever they had in the city. 29Then many that sought after justice and judgment went down into the wilderness, to dwell there: 30Both they, and their children, and their wives; and their cattle; because afflictions increased sore upon them. 31Now when it was told the king's servants, and the host that was at Jerusalem, in the city of David, that certain men, who had broken the king's commandment, were gone down into the secret places in the wilderness), as well as 2 Maccabees 5:27, 6:11, and 10:6.

In fact, the entire chapter of Hebrews 11 seems to be modeled after the list of Israel's heroes in 1 Maccabees 2:51-61.

Let's not forget that the New Testament book making these allusions to the Maccabees (per the KJV) is the Epistle to the Hebrews: "one of the most Jewish writings we possess. ... "cribb'd, cabin'd, and confin'd" within the narrow precincts of Jewish thought..." and "The Bible which he used and

---

[137] Some details about 2 Maccabees for later reference: no names are known for the mother with seven sons, neither in Scripture nor in history up until the time of Christ. They are usually labeled the Maccabean Martyrs, but that is only because they are mentioned in the Book 2 Maccabees, which is only known as that because Judas Maccabeus appears in it. The Books of the Maccabees are just Books that mention Maccabeus, and the "2" is an identifier—the Book is not a sequel and has nothing to do with 1 Maccabees. In fact, it might have been written earlier than 1 Maccabees. The Martyrs also appear in 4 Maccabees, a Book written after Christ that copied 2 Maccabees; further references to the Martyrs appear in the Josippon and Talmud, and are discussed below.

from which he constantly quotes, is the Greek translation known as the Septuagint (LXX), and not the original Hebrew text, with which he does not seem to have been acquainted." Both 1 and 2 Maccabees were, of course, part of the Septuagint.[138]

A third example, one we have considered already:

> ... while it [is] not directly cited in the New Testament, Ruth was probably attached to the Book of Judges at the time of Christ. Consequently, when the writer to the Hebrews cited these accounts of great faith from the Book of Judges, it would mean that Ruth was also recognized as Holy Scripture seeing that it was part of the Book of Judges.

The same argument applies with even greater force to Baruch as part of Jeremiah, and Susanna as part of Daniel.[139] Consider how weak in comparison is the case for Ruth as part of Judges, from Gallagher and Meade, p. 86, footnote 63: "We have no evidence that Jews ever counted Ruth as a part of the book of Judges, though Josephus may have done such. This reckoning – Ruth and Judges together as one book – became common in Christianity." In fact it is first mentioned by Origen, 200 years after Christ, and long after the references to Judges had been written.

Note, however, that it is often assumed to be true, e.g., by Don Stewart when talking of the New Testament; but even more, by authors discussing Josephus when they are trying to make his 22 books equal the 24 books equal the 27 books equal the 39 books. Thus the juxtaposition all in one sentence from Gallagher and Meade: "no evidence that Jews ever" versus "Josephus may have done such"—meaning there is no actual evidence whatsoever that Josephus really did so, there is just speculation that he "may have" done so, as part of making Josephus' statement fit the Protestant canon.

Those who accept Origen's statement about Ruth being part of Judges as sufficient evidence of Jewish beliefs and practices, usually want to reject his other claims about the Jewish canon, such as that the Jewish leaders "concealed and removed [Susanna] from the Scriptures..." But there is

---

[138] See wikipedia.org/wiki/1_Maccabees and wikipedia.org/wiki/2_Maccabees

[139] I avoid discussing much of the other evidence for Jewish acceptance of Susanna and Baruch as part of Daniel and Jeremiah, in order to just focus on comparing Origen's claim about Ruth to his claims about Susanna. But for example, there is evidence from the Greek translations that the Hebrew Jeremiah and Baruch were on the same scroll – whatever you think of it, it is inarguably better evidence (being earlier, from Jews, etc.) than Origen's claim provides for Ruth and Judges being seen as one Book by Jews at the time at Christ.

corroborating evidence from before Origen (some quoted above, including the quotes from Hippolytus in his commentary on Susanna) for the latter statements, and nothing at all for the former. By any fair standard, the statements about Susanna being removed by the Jews are better supported.

Thus, if one accepts this claim about Ruth, then all of the Biblical references to "Jeremiah" (e.g., Matthew 2:17) and "Daniel" (e.g., Matthew 24:15) would count as "recognition of Susanna and Baruch as Holy Scripture," because Susanna and Baruch are better evidenced as parts of them.[140]

A fourth example:

> It is also possible that the reference of Jesus to "living water" was referring to Song of Solomon. Jesus said the following to a Samaritan woman whom He met at a well: ... "If you only knew what God's gift is and who is asking you for a drink, you would have asked him for a drink. He would have given you living water." (John 4:10 God's Word). We read the following in the Song of Solomon: You are a garden fountain, a well of living water, as refreshing as the streams from the Lebanon mountains. (Song of Solomon 4:15 NLT). Jesus may have been referring to Song of Solomon in His illustration of living water. Therefore, He would be quoting from the Song of Solomon as Holy Scripture.

Note that this quote is (in English) just two words, "living water," and these two words alone are sufficient to be "quoting from the Song of Solomon as Holy Scripture." The same two-word phrase actually appears elsewhere in the Bible, e.g. Jeremiah 2:13: "For my people have committed two evils; they have forsaken me the fountain of living waters, and hewed them out cisterns, broken cisterns, that can hold no water;" Jeremiah 17:13: "O LORD, the hope of Israel, all that forsake thee shall be ashamed, and they that depart from me shall be written in the earth, because they have forsaken the LORD, the fountain of living waters;" Zechariah 14:8: "And it shall be in that day, that living waters shall go out from Jerusalem; half of them toward the former sea, and half of them toward the hinder sea: in summer and in winter shall it be." Thus, a reference that could be to other Books is considered acceptable evidence of a Biblical reference to one book, in this case Song of Solomon.

---

[140] In addition, of course, if one considers Origen's claims about Ruth as evidence for a Jewish practice all the way back to the time of Christ, so too would his letter's claims that the Christians accepted Susanna from the beginning also be found to go all the way back, since (a) they relate to his own Church and (b) have corroborating evidence from earlier Christian citations, etc. If, on the other hand, Origen was wrong about his own Church's practice going back to Christ, then by any fair comparison his claim about the Jewish practice with Ruth is simply worthless.

Hebrews 1:3, on the other hand, is a much more striking quotation from the Book of Wisdom. It involves more words, and they are words that appear nowhere else, words that convey a concept difficult to understand but is, nevertheless, made the focus of a Christological hymn, etc.

In addition, Plumptre's analysis of the entire Epistle to the Hebrews shows two dozen different word/phrase choices that seem to be taken from the Book of Wisdom, all of which meet this two-word standard for referencing, or even "quoting," Scripture. Those quotes are used by Plumptre to show that "a comparison of the passages thus referred to will shew, I believe, that their weight in the scale of evidence is more than numerical; that they are, for the most part, words either characteristic themselves, or used in a characteristic sense; and that they thus tend to establish such a close affinity of thought and language as may best be explained by the hypothesis of identity of authorship." Whatever you think of his crazy idea, it is immensely better proof that Wisdom is being alluded to than Song of Solomon.

Stewart's article also tells us more about Song of Solomon:

> Song of Solomon Was Read at the Passover. There is also evidence for the Song of Solomon. It was traditionally read at each Passover. This gives testimony to its importance among the people of Israel. Again, it is evidence of its divine inspiration.

Which is fascinating… and also completely irrelevant, since his topic was "Does the New Testament Quote the Old Testament as Authoritative Scripture?" Regardless, notice the elements involved: read at Passover = testimony to its importance among the people = evidence of its divine inspiration. Hebrews 1:3 is also evidence that references to the Book of Wisdom were being sung as a Christological hymn before the New Testament was even written—when the Old Testament was the only Scripture, when Christians were still going to the synagogues, etc.

In addition, Akiva (also spelled Akiba), a Rabbi of the second century, declared Sirach to be outside of the Jewish canon because it did not, in the idiom, "defile the hands." Reading it in the synagogue caused one to forfeit any participation in the next life. From wikipedia.org/wiki/Rabbi_Akiva:

> … Akiva's utterance reads, "He who reads aloud in the synagogue from books not belonging to the canon as if they were canonical," etc. But he was not opposed to a private reading of the Apocrypha, as is evident from the fact that he himself makes frequent use of Sirach.

The existence of a prohibition implies a need to prohibit, i.e., that Jews were reading Sirach aloud in the Synagogue prior to the prohibition, which comes 100 years after Christ. So Sirach, too, would seem to meet the standard for canonicity set by the Song of Solomon.

In fact, let us go back and consider John 4:10's allusion (allegedly to Song of Solomon) in full context:

> 10Jesus answered and said unto her, If thou knewest the gift of God, and who it is that saith to thee, Give me to drink; thou wouldest have asked of him, and he would have given thee living water. 11The woman saith unto him, Sir, thou hast nothing to draw with, and the well is deep: from whence then hast thou that living water? 12Art thou greater than our father Jacob, which gave us the well, and drank thereof himself, and his children, and his cattle? 13Jesus answered and said unto her, Whosoever drinketh of this water shall thirst again: 14But whosoever drinketh of the water that I shall give him shall never thirst; but the water that I shall give him shall be in him a well of water springing up into everlasting life.

When 4:10-4:14 is read in context, it seems like a reply to Wisdom's assertion in Sirach 24:19-21:

> 19Come unto me, all ye that be desirous of me, and fill yourselves with my fruits. 20For my memorial is sweeter than honey, and mine inheritance than the honeycomb. 21They that eat me shall yet be hungry, and they that drink me shall yet be thirsty.

I.e., Jesus is the completeness of God's revelation; he fulfills what could not be fulfilled before His Incarnation. That seems a much more direct reference and fulfillment than "You are a garden fountain, a well of living water, as refreshing as the streams from the Lebanon mountains" (Song of Solomon 4:15 NLT).

A fifth example:

> It should be noted that the Feast of Purim celebrated the events recorded in the Book of Esther. We read of the following command given in the Book of Esther… (Esther 9:28 NRSV)…This verse commands a continuous celebration of Purim. According to John's gospel, Jesus went to Jerusalem to celebrate a certain feast: Later, Jesus went to Jerusalem for a Jewish festival. (John 5:1 God's Word). It is possible that this refers to Purim. If so, then this indicates that the people recognized the tradition to celebrate

Purim in remembrance of their deliverance from the Persians. By doing so, it gives testimony to the authority of the Book of Esther.[141]

The exact same reasoning supports including 1 Maccabees: Jesus also attended the Feast of the Dedication (Hanukkah), as mentioned in John 10:22: "and it was at Jerusalem the feast of the dedication, and it was winter." According to the KJV notes, that is a reference to 1 Maccabees 4:59, which commands the celebration of Hanukkah just as Esther commands the celebration of Purim.[142]

Note that the Gospel of John thus clearly references Hanukkah by one of its names, whereas Purim is only possibly referenced in John 5:1 (and it might not be Purim: "It is possible that this refers to Purim"). In fact, while the KJV cross-references John 10:22 to 1 Maccabees 4:59 for the celebration of Hanukkah, there is no cross reference between John 5:1 to Esther 9:28 for the Feast of Purim.

Moreover, Jesus attended the celebration and, along the way to it, healed the man born blind and preached "As long as I am in the world, I am the light of the world." (John 9:3-5)[143] Hanukkah is the Festival of Lights, where the Jews light the Menorah candles, etc. So, the reference is not just far more certain and definite than John 5:1 is, but it is far more essential to understanding the events of the Gospel, such as why Jesus says "I am the light of the world" on His way to the Festival of Lights.

Consider just how beautiful this allusion to light and sight and blindness is (all from Chapter 9):

> [Jesus] I must work the works of him that sent me, while it is day: the night cometh, when no man can work.
> [Jesus] As long as I am in the world, I am the light of the world

---

[141] I do not devote space to the canonicity of the Apocryphal parts of Esther, but they, too, have a strong case for acceptance by the Jews, Apostles, and early Church. 1 Clement, arguably the earliest extra-Biblical Christian writing, cites to parts of Esther not found in the shorter form. See 1 Clement 55, citing the story in Esther chapters 14-16 (using the KJV numbering) www.kingjamesbibleonline.org/Additions-to-Esther-Chapter-14/. And Josephus also draws from the long form of Esther. See Antiquities of the Jews, Book 11, Chapter 6 (penelope.uchicago.edu/ josephus/ant-11.html) and compare to Esther 13:8-18 (www.kingjamesbibleonline.org/Additions-to-Esther-Chapter-13/).

[142] Strange but true: Hanukkah is only based in Scripture in Catholic/Orthodox Bibles, and not the Tanakh. There is a tie-in to 2 Maccabees here as well, but I ignore that to focus on 1 Maccabees.

[143] This is one of the Seven Signs of the Book of Signs that forms one of John's key messages (the new creation theology), and, thus, an undeniably crucial part of John's Gospel. See wikipedia .org/wiki/Book_of_Signs.

[Formerly blind man] one thing I know, that, whereas I was blind, now I see.
[Pharisees] as for this fellow [Jesus], we know not from whence he is.
[Formerly blind man] Why herein is a marvellous thing, that ye know not from whence he is, and yet he hath opened mine eyes. ... Since the world began was it not heard that any man opened the eyes of one that was born blind. If this man were not of God, he could do nothing
[Jesus] I am come into this world, that they which see not might see; and that they which see might be made blind.
And some of the Pharisees which were with him heard these words, and said unto him, Are we blind also?
Jesus said unto them, If ye were blind, ye should have no sin: but now ye say, We see; therefore your sin remaineth.

In addition, Antiochus was called "Epiphanes" (Epiphany) because he claimed that he was "God Manifest" (the meaning of the term) on Earth. (This is mocked throughout 2 Maccabees, with the true God manifestly aiding the Jews, e.g., 2:21 "And the manifest signs that came from heaven unto those that behaved themselves manfully to their honour for Judaism..."). Another allusion to 1 and 2 Maccabees is made when at Hanukkah: "John 10:22 And it was at Jerusalem the feast of the dedication, and it was winter. 23 And Jesus walked in the temple in Solomon's porch. 24 Then came the Jews round about him... If thou be the Christ, tell us plainly... 30 I and my Father are one. 31 ... the Jews took up stones again to stone him." The moment Jesus declares Himself to be the true Epiphany, the stones came out, because the Jews 'were blind' and did not recognize the true God truly Manifest in the midst of the celebration of the rededication of the very Temple He was standing in.

This is far more than just a mention of the Festival; it seems to proclaim the "fulfillment" of Hanukkah, the Festival of Lights (1 Maccabees 4:59). In fact, multiple verses in 1 Maccabees were expressly awaiting fulfillment, and then fulfilled by Jesus. For example, the rededication of the altar in 4:46 (And laid up the stones in the mountain of the temple in a convenient place, until there should come a prophet to shew what should be done with them) and the expectation of the arrival of a faithful prophet in 14:41 (Also that the Jews and priests were well pleased that Simon should be their governor and high priest forever, until there should arise a faithful prophet) are being fulfilled by Jesus.

All of these references and allusions go far beyond the "possible mention of Purim" in John 5:1. And the reason they go so far beyond it is precisely because of the meaning that Jesus and John give the allusions.

Still, there is no formal citation to the Book of 1 Maccabees. But compare that to (for example) the calming of the storm in Matthew 8:23-27 (And, behold, there arose a great tempest in the sea… And his disciples came to him, and awoke him, saying, Lord, save us: we perish. And he saith unto them, Why are ye fearful, O ye of little faith? Then he arose, and rebuked the winds and the sea; and there was a great calm. But the men marvelled, saying, What manner of man is this, that even the winds and the sea obey him!). In discussing this event, John F. MacArthur Jr. tells us that:

> The disciples knew the Psalms. Many times they had heard and repeated the words of Psalm 89: "…" They had sung, "…" (Ps. 46:1-3). They knew well the majestic and comforting words of Psalm 107: … It was a literal fulfillment of those verses that Jesus was about to accomplish on the Sea of Galilee.[144]

I submit that the Disciples, and the audience of John's Gospel, knew their Maccabees and that this is a literal fulfillment of those verses. Although we all agree that a clear citation would be inarguable, and thus infinitely more convenient for those who are just trying to resolve the canon debate, in reality, you usually expressly cite something because otherwise no one would know what you are referring to. Often, the reason you do not cite something is that everyone already knows exactly what you are referring to. Large, conceptual things that are well known are not in need of citations. It is little-known details that require citations.

Consider that Matthew, Mark, and Luke all repeat the story of the calming of the storm, and yet, not one of them ever bothered to cite to any of the Psalms. MacArthur focuses on the fact that the disciples knew the Psalms, and no doubt they did. But also, the audience of Matthew, Mark, and Luke also knew that the Psalms were being fulfilled, which is exactly why the Evangelists do not bother to say so. They certainly could have quoted Psalms, exactly as MacArthur does—they just did not need to. Perhaps John did not cite to 1 or 2 Maccabees because it was equally unnecessary to say which Scripture was being fulfilled when he shows the fulfillment of Hanukkah.

Those are five examples specifically paralleling the list from Don Stewart on the Blue Letter Bible's website; let us now consider a sixth example that is of a similar character but is not specifically set out on Stewart's list. The example is a reference to Prophecy from Matthew, a quote of the crowd that was surrounding Jesus as he hung on the cross:

---

[144] MacArthur New Testament Commentary on Matthew.

> KJV Matthew 27:43: He trusted in God; let him deliver him now, if he will have him: for he said, I am the Son of God.

The KJV cross-references this to both Psalm 22:8 (more on that later) and Wisdom 2:18, which is part of a scene which started with "the ungodly said" (Wisdom 2:1), "Let us oppress the poor righteous man" (Wisdom 2:10), "He professeth to have the knowledge of God: and he calleth himself the child of the Lord" (Wisdom 2:13), "[He] maketh his boast that God is his father. Let us see if his words be true: and let us prove what shall happen in the end of him" (Wisdom 2:16-2:17) and then:

> KJV Wisdom 2:18: For if the just man be the son of God, He will help him, and deliver him from the hand of his enemies.

Let's consult some Bible commentaries[145] for what they say about Matthew 27:43:

> Albert Barnes Notes on the New Testament (1800s, Presbyterian): ... their prophets had foretold this very scene, and when they were fulfilling the predictions of their own Scriptures. So wonderful is the way by which God causes his word to be fulfilled.

It is the fulfillment of a Prophecy.

> Ulrich Luz (Nondenominational, I believe), The Theology of the Gospel of Matthew: ... he 'fulfilled all righteousness' 3:15. Upon hearing these words, the Matthean community senses the double-edged meaning of this scene: Jesus is, of course, the Son of God, and he will save others – but not by descending from the cross. The double-edged meaning becomes even more evident in the events surrounding Jesus' death.

According to Luz, the crucial aspect is that Jesus is the Son of God, but he does not say what Prophecy is fulfilled.

> John F MacArthur, Jr. (Evangelical), MacArthur New Testament commentary: ... Nor does it seem likely that they intentionally quoted Psalm 22:8, derisively applying it to Jesus. Even to their perverse minds that would have been an irreverent treatment of Scripture. It was rather that they unwittingly fulfilled Scripture as they mocked Jesus, just as Judas, Caiaphas, Pilate, and many others had unwittingly fulfilled it.

---

[145] I am limiting myself to line-by-line Bible commentaries solely for the sake of "brevity." I could cite a thousand other non-commentary books, but to pick one: David Limbaugh, *The Emmaus Code*, lists Psalm 22:7-8 as one of the "Messianic Prophecies of the Old Testament" with its New Testament Fulfillment listed as Matthew 27:39-43, 45-49.

MacArthur says it is a quote of Psalm 22:8 that was fulfilled. We will discuss Psalm 22:8 shortly.

> Augsburg Commentary on the New Testament, Robert H. Smith (Lutheran): He trusts in God; let God deliver him now, before death, if he desires him (Ps. 22:8); for he said, I am the Son of God (26:64; cf. Wisdom of Sol. 2:12-20). Jesus will be delivered but not short of death, not before the cross.

Smith cites Psalm 22:8 directly and tells us to merely compare with Wisdom of Sol. 2:12-20. However, note that Smith's citation to Psalm 22:8 falls short—it does not cover the entire quote in Matthew, so to make it fit the full sentence in Matthew, there is a further need to compare the rest of the sentence with the Book of Wisdom.

> Matthew Henry's Commentary on the Whole Bible (from the year 1710, Presbyterian): Nay, these very words David, in that famous prophecy of Christ, mentions, as spoken by his enemies (Ps. 22:8); He trusted on the Lord that he would deliver him. Surely these priests and scribes had forgotten their psalter, or they would not have used the same words, so exactly to answer the type and prophecy: but the scriptures must be fulfilled.

Henry rules this a fulfillment of Scriptural Prophecy, by which he means Psalm 22:8, and he says it is the "same words... exactly to answer the type and prophecy" as that Psalm. We will discuss that analysis below.

> The New Interpreter's Bible (NIB; Methodist): A Commentary in Twelve Volumes: "If you are the Son of God" is added by Matthew, reflecting Wis 2:13, 18-20, itself an interpretation of Ps 22:9. Matthew adds "Son of God" because it is important to his christology (cf. his similar addition in 10:10; 20:03), and to make the challenge of the passersby correspond to 4:3, 6, where the devil issued a similar challenge using the identical words. There, too, Jesus placed himself in the category of humanity, as he does here by the most human act of all, dying a human death. The jeer of the passersby is thus more than a cruel taunt; it represents an opposing theology rejected by the canonical Gospels.

The NIB says Matthew's "Son of God" phrasing is "important to his Christology." Meanwhile, "The jeer of the passersby ... represents an opposing theology rejected by the canonical Gospels." It is a crucial point that Matthew is noting. In fact, it is a crucial point that the chief priests, scribes, and elders inadvertently make in their jeer, just as the Devil made it, too.

Just as it was also a crucial point to the Book of Wisdom, which builds the concept on top of Psalm 22:8. Psalm 22 never calls God "Father." Instead, it says "But thou art he that took me out of the womb: thou didst make me hope when I was upon my mother's breasts. I was cast upon thee from the womb: thou art my God from my mother's belly"—my God, not my Father. Psalm 22 involves no conception of the "Son of God" at all.

For comparison, here are the full quotes to compare:

> Matthew 27:43: He trusted in God; let him deliver him now, if he will have him: for he said, I am the Son of God.

That sentence fulfills either or both of the following:

1) He trusted on the LORD that he would deliver him: let him deliver him, seeing he delighted in him; or

2) For if the just man be the son of God, he will help him, and deliver him from the hand of his enemies

Wisdom 2:18 differs in a vital way from Psalm 22:8, and that difference is precisely the key to Matthew's Christology, message, and intent. Psalm 22:8 is actually a general statement that could relate to any believer in peril ("He trusted on the Lord that he would deliver him: let him deliver him"—see Acts 12:5-17 and 16:16-40, where we see such deliverances when Peter, Paul, and Silas are all rescued from prisons by God).

In fact, Jewish Rabbis consider other "Messiahs" (not Sons of God in the Christian sense) to have fulfilled Psalm 22:8. Michael L. Brown (the "foremost messianic apologist in the world," according to Dr. Barry R. Leventhal, academic dean of Southern Evangelical Seminary) notes in his argument that Psalm 22 is, indeed, a prophecy and that "...it is very interesting to see how Pesikta Rabbati, the famous eighth-century midrash [a Rabbinic homily], put some of the words of this psalm on the lips of the suffering Messiah (called Ephraim, but associated with the son of David), citing Psalm 22:8..."[146]

Wisdom 2:18, by its terms, could also apply to any believer who considers God his Father, which, of course, all believers should. E.g., Moses says God is our Father in Deuteronomy 32:6 ("is not he thy father that hath bought thee? hath he not made thee, and established thee?"), God Himself says He is our Father in Malachi 1:6 ("A son honoureth his father, and a servant his master: if

---

[146] *Answering Jewish Objections to Jesus*, Volume 3, Baker Books 2005, p. 121.

then I be a father, where is mine honour?"), and God Himself commands us to call Him Father in Jeremiah 3:19 ("Thou shalt call me, My father; and shalt not turn away from me").

But after Christ, when we look back to the Old Testament through typology and a Christological lens, then the son of God means the Son of God, and its true fulfillment can only be through Christ. It is God the Father who fulfills it and delivers Jesus the Son.

As such, it would be prophecy from the Book of Wisdom cited to and fulfilled by the Gospel to the Jews. And who shouts out this quote at the Crucifixion? "Likewise also the chief priests mocking him, with the scribes and elders, said..." Matthew goes out of his way to tell his Jewish audience that the Jewish leaders were fulfilling the words from the Book of Wisdom.

But the Lutheran Smith cites the Psalm and merely says "Cf. Wisdom" because, to him, the Psalm is Scripture, and the Book of Wisdom only Apocrypha. But when we look into why the Book of Wisdom is Apocrypha, we are told that the answer is (in part) because it is not seen as authentic Prophecy fulfilled by the New Testament. It is circular reasoning, of course.

If we break the circle, then not only is the Book of Wisdom referenced in the New Testament, but it is a Prophecy that is fulfilled in the New Testament—a key part in determining whether the book is Divinely-inspired.

The early Church Fathers did not have a circle to break. So, did they view this as Prophecy? They most certainly did. From Augustine, 400 AD:

> For among all their anointed ones the Jews looked for one who was to save them. But in the mysterious justice of God they were blinded; and thinking only of the power of the Messiah, they did not understand His weakness, in which He died for us. In the book of Wisdom it is prophesied of the Jews: "Let us condemn him to an ignominious death; for he will be proved in his words. If he is truly the Son of God, He will aid him; and deliver him from the hand of his enemies. Thus they thought, and erred; for their wickedness blinded them." Wisdom 2:18-21 These words apply also to those who, in spite of all these evidences, in spite of such a series of prophecies, and of their fulfillment, still deny that Christ is foretold in the Scriptures. As often as they repeat this denial, we can produce fresh proofs, with the help of Him who has made such provision against human perversity, that proofs already given need not be repeated. Contra Faustum, 12, 44.[147]

And Augustine was not alone. Centuries earlier, Cyprian had quoted all of Wisdom 2:12-2:20 as "the sacrament of Christ, that He has come who was

---

[147] www.newadvent.org/fathers/140612.htm

announced according to the Scriptures, and has done and perfected all those things whereby He was foretold as being able to be perceived and known."[148] In addition to Cyprian, Hippolytus and Origen also cite to it as Prophecy and do so before 250 AD.

That Christ was foretold in Prophecy is a key component of the case for Christianity. To the early Church (and moderns who accept Wisdom as Scripture) the fulfillment of Wisdom 2:18 is a key part of that case.

(This example is also subject to experiment: give friends of any and every faith, or no faith whatsoever, the verse from Matthew, along with the verses from Psalms and Wisdom. But do not identify where the verses come from and ask them which they think Matthew is alluding to.)

It is not that the Psalm does not fit, but the verse from Wisdom fits the words Matthew wrote better and addresses the key point: Matthew's Christology. Jesus is the Son of God, not just any random man who "trusted on the LORD that he would deliver him."

Not to be lost, of course, is that this possible fulfillment of Prophecy from the Book of Wisdom occurs in the Gospel to the Jews. The words alluding to the Book of Wisdom do not occur in Mark (15:31 "Likewise also the chief priests mocking said among themselves with the scribes, He saved others; himself he cannot save. 32Let Christ the King of Israel descend now from the cross, that we may see and believe. And they that were crucified with him reviled him") or Luke (23:35 "And the people stood beholding. And the rulers also with them derided him, saying, He saved others; let him save himself, if he be Christ, the chosen of God") or John (nothing is said).

It is in the Gospel to the Jews (among whom were many converted Priests) that possible reference is made to the fulfillment (via the taunts of the chief priests, scribes, and elders) of this prophecy from the Book of Wisdom (which declares itself to be Divinely-inspired Scripture).

Seventh: the Our Father, the prayer given to us by God Himself. *Manners and Customs of the Bible*, by James M. Freeman (d. 1900), breaks down the pieces of the Lord's Prayer (Matthew 6:12) and notes that:

---

[148] In his preface to Book 1, Cyprian declares that "The second book likewise contains the sacrament of Christ, that He has come who was announced according to the Scriptures ..." Book 2 is, then, a series of prophecies that Jesus fulfills, with the quote from Wisdom included in Section 14. See www.newadvent.org/fathers/050712a.htm and www.newadvent.org/fathers/050712b.htm.

The second, "Forgive us," echoes the Eighteen Benedictions, 6: "Forgive us, our Father, for we have sinned against thee; blot out our transgressions from before thine eyes. Blessed art thou, O Lord, who forgivest much." The accompanying phrase, "as we also have forgiven," reflects the Jewish teaching found in Sirach 28:2: "Forgive the wrong of your neighbor, and then your sins will be forgiven when you pray."

It is not just a quote; it is an entire concept (linking your forgiveness by God to you forgiving others) that does not appear anywhere in the Old Testament except Sirach, yet appears many times in the New Testament.

Sirach was "canonical for some Rabbis,"[149] found at Qumran, the Cairo Genizah, Masada, etc.,[150] and quoted in the Talmud as Scripture.[151] And we see here that neither Jesus nor his Divinely-inspired evangelists warned readers that while this concept had been developed and apparently popularized by Sirach, the rest of Sirach (which claims to be Scripture[152]) was not to be viewed as endorsed by Jesus. In John 4:22, for example, Jesus tells the Samaritan woman that her beliefs are wrong ("Ye worship ye know not what"), and later in Matthew, He tells the Sadducees that their beliefs are wrong (Matthew 22:29: "Ye do err, not knowing the scriptures..."). But here, He gives no warning about the book He is alluding to and taking this concept from, even as he includes the concept in the Our Father prayer.

In fact, immediately after giving us the words to pray, we have Jesus "doubling down" on the concept He is taking from Sirach:

14For if ye forgive men their trespasses, your heavenly Father will also forgive you: 15But if ye forgive not men their trespasses, neither will your Father forgive your trespasses. (Matthew Ch. 6).

Or at least, Jesus doubles down on Sirach's concept in the Gospel to the Jews. That level of additional emphasis on the concept of the prayer is not made by Luke; he merely notes it once and moves on. It is only in the Gospel to the Jews that Jesus stresses and repeats the teaching first taught in Sirach, which was "canonical for some Rabbis" and which claims to be Scripture.

---

[149] The Jewish Study Bible p. 2157
[150] wikipedia.org/wiki/Book_of_Sirach
[151] www.sefaria.org/Yevamot.63b.13?lang=bi. Search for "Sira," and you will see two examples; intertextual.bible/text/sirach-13.15-bava-kamma-92b is another.
[152] Chapter 24: 32 I will yet make doctrine to shine as the morning, and will send forth her light afar off. 33I will yet pour out doctrine as prophecy, and leave it to all ages for ever. 34Behold that I have not laboured for myself only, but for all them that seek wisdom.

But also consider the beginning of the prayer and how it strengthens the case for this reference to Sirach: the words "Our Father." We saw above that there are references in the Protestant Old Testament to God as Father, and God Himself commands us to call Him Father in Jeremiah 3:19 ("Thou shalt call me, My father; and shalt not turn away from me"). But it is in Sirach that a prayer is first addressed to God the Father: "O Lord, Father and Ruler of my life, do not abandon me to their counsel, and let me not fall because of them! ... O Lord, Father and God of my life, do not give me haughty eyes, and remove from me evil desire" (Sirach 23:14).

Here we have God Himself, varying from all "canonical" tradition by doing something first done in the Book of Sirach, as part of the opening of a prayer that incorporates a key theological concept also taken from Sirach and also not found in the Books of the Protestant canon. In the Gospel to the Jews, Jesus "doubles down" and stresses this key theological concept only found in Sirach. And neither in the Gospel to the Jews nor any other Gospel does Jesus show any concern that evoking such concepts from a book that claims to be Scripture (and that some Rabbis considered canonical, and that was found at Qumran, and is quoted in the Talmud as Scripture, etc.) would lead anyone to "wrongly" accept it as authentic Scripture.

An eighth example, from the Evangelical Biblical Theology Commentary:

> ... Wisdom of Solomon, which was probably written in Egypt in the second century BC, indicates that Solomon knew "virtues of roots" and "powers of spirits," knowledge associated with exorcism (Wis 7:20). ... Based on this evidence, a number of scholars have suggested that the title "Son of David" was part of a Solomon typology that identified Jesus as a healer and particularly as an exorcist. ... (p. 389:) By addressing Jesus as "son of David," the woman [Matthew 15:22: Have mercy on me, O Lord, thou Son of David; my daughter is grievously vexed with a devil] may have been expressing her confidence in Jesus's authority over demons. (p. 70-71).

Thus, Jesus would be the fulfillment of the "type" of Solomon—the Divine exorcist Himself, with complete power over demons. Certainly, the Jews saw Solomon as a powerful exorcist: "by the time of Christ, Solomon was recognized as the greatest of all exorcists" (p. 70). In addition, writing long after Christ, Josephus also confirmed that Solomon was a great exorcist.

The Book of Wisdom was the key basis of this Jewish worldview, according to the Evangelical Biblical Theology Commentary. And yet estimates are that 97% of Roman Palestine was illiterate (Bart Ehrman, *Forged*, p. 72-73, citing Catherine Hezser's "Literacy in Roman Palestine).[153] And that is 3% literacy in Hebrew, not Greek. But the Book of Wisdom is in Greek, not in Hebrew. Ehrman cites the most recent scholarship from Mark Chancey (*The Myth of a Gentile Galilee*) to conclude that the vast majority of Jews had no facility in even speaking Greek.

And yet somehow, the people learned these things from the Book of Wisdom. Where was that going on and why, if not at the Synagogue? The Book of Wisdom claims to be Divinely-inspired: where else would such a Greek book be read and then explained in Aramaic to the people, and why would that be occurring if it was not accepted?[154]

In fact, the verse leading to this typology occurs right in the middle of the declaration that the Book is Divinely-inspired:

> 15God hath granted me to speak as I would... 16For in his hand are both we and our words... 17For he hath given me certain knowledge of the things that are, namely, to know how the world was made, and the operation of the elements: 18The beginning, ending, and midst of the times...
> 20...the diversities of plants and the virtues of roots: ...
> 21And all such things as are either secret or manifest, them I know.

The verse which the Evangelical Biblical Theology Commentary sees as part of a "Solomon typology" occurs in the context of a declaration that the Book of Wisdom is Divinely-inspired Scripture. Matthew then describes this episode in his Gospel to the Jews, many of which were converted Priests—i.e., those who performed exorcisms and would know full well which Book provides this basis by which "Son of David" becomes a typological reference to an exorcist. Once again, it is the Gospel to the Jews that provides details that seem to be referencing Apocrypha—Mark does not note the woman's reference to the Son of David, and Luke does not describe the incident at all. Only the Gospel to the Jews stresses this typological point.

Moreover, this was a woman of Canaan, not a Jew. A gentile woman calls Jesus "Son of David" and express her faith in Him, using typology— typology!—best exemplified in the Book of Wisdom. An Apocrypha in Greek,

---

[153] HarperCollins 2011.

[154] This is a point often made regarding the New Testament, e.g., "Paul's insistence that his letters be publicly read... and his readers' understanding of what public reading would mean within a synagogue context provide good reasons to think that his letters would have been viewed as being in the same category as other "Scripture" read during times of public worship." Kruger, p. 209.

so widespread and well understood that a Gentile woman makes obscure reference to its concepts in the Gospel to the Jews.

Before this episode, in Matthew 15:19-20, Jesus had taught the Pharisees that "For out of the heart proceed evil thoughts ... these are the things which defile a man: but to eat with unwashen hands defileth not a man." Jesus then walked 100 miles out of his way (Jerusalem to Tyre) only to encounter this woman of Canaan and give this practical illustration of that teaching about the "clean" and "unclean," showing just how great was the faith existing among the "unclean" Gentiles. As part of that, the Gentile woman makes this typological reference, showing that she understands Jesus to be the fulfillment of the type of Solomon. Both immediately before the Pharisees approached him (14:35) and after this show of the woman's faith (15:30), Jews had presented to Jesus multitudes who needed healing. Matthew's point is that the Pharisees challenged Jesus immediately after the mass healings precisely because they failed to recognize him as the fulfillment of this Solomon type.

And Jesus did not just fulfill this type. He "blew it out of the water," as they say. The woman had come to Jesus, not the daughter. Before and after, the Jews brought the sick to him; but this woman came to him without the daughter or the devil that vexed her. And Jesus performed no exorcism at all. He just willed it, and it happened instantly. He showed that He is far greater than Solomon. The Gospel to the Jews makes clear to its audience, just as Jesus made it clear to His own audience on that day, that He performed an exercise of Divine power that far surpassed the Solomon typology to be found in the Book of Wisdom (and which occurs amidst a declaration that the Book of Wisdom was Divinely-inspired Scripture).

And once again, neither Jesus nor Matthew gives any warning about the key Book that this typology is derived from.[155]

---

[155] A "brief" interlude regarding Ehrman's 97% illiteracy factoid. Ehrman claims that Peter was therefore 97%+ likely to be illiterate in Hebrew (or Aramaic, which I blur together for this discussion), with far worse odds for Greek, and could not have written his Greek Epistles. (He also argues that someone else did not write them for Peter, saying there are no other examples for that practice when that someone else is not named.) Ehrman specifically claims that Peter's Epistles are forgeries because (in part) the eye witness evidence (the precise linguistic nuance of the exact words spoken by the high priest) shows that the real Peter was illiterate—the "evidence" he cites is Acts (p. 75), which he also alleges is a later fraud by someone who was not a witness (p. 208-9).

But before citing to his proof and then disproving it, Ehrman begins with his 97%+ statistic. The odds of a modern American knowing any form of Hebrew or Greek (ancient or modern) are both less than 1 in 1,000 (per Google) and yet Ehrman alleges that he himself knows both. Are the combined 1 in 1,000,000 odds (orders of magnitude worse than Peter's) evidence that Ehrman is a fraud who forged all his work? No, in fact, the odds prove that there are hundreds of such scholars and that Ehrman could easily be one of them. Whether Ehrman is a fraud actually has nothing whatsoever to do with the statistic. A court that accepted this kind of statistic as real evidence of fraud would terrify Ehrman, were he facing a prosecutor.

As it is, the living can sue for libel; but when they die, the claim dies, and speculation like Ehrman's becomes fair game. Ehrman and co. know this full well from personal experience via the Secret Gospel of Mark (which Ehrman claims is "serious evidence," p. 261). From wikipedia .org/wiki/Secret_Gospel_of_Mark: (1) "when the Swedish historian Per Beskow …wrote that there were reasons to be skeptical about the genuineness of the letter, Smith got upset and responded by threatening to sue …;" (2) "Smith … argued that … no strong argument against it had been presented…;" (3) "The allegations against Smith for having forged the Mar Saba manuscript became even more pronounced after his death in 1991." So it was a "strong argument" that no one had made allegations against Smith, who had threatened to sue the one who tried; but then he died, at which point allegations promptly became "pronounced." Funny how that happens.

However, notice the outline of this particular speculation: "Most Jews could not, therefore this Jew did not." This stereotyping technique is very effective, which is why an opponent should instantly object to it. Recognize that it is prejudicial and can lead you to misunderstand the evidence. Without the prejudicial lead-in to distract us, we have a writing (in fact, many writings) that itself (nay, themselves) may be the proof that this particular group of Jews could indeed write Greek, which in fact might explain why this group of Jews became a group in the first place.

As for the odds: Ehrman's claim is that Peter had no opportunity to learn Greek. But Peter was not a peasant (contra Ehrman, p. 75), nor a laborer: he owned the boat; Andrew the fisherman also had time to follow John the Baptist, before Christ; and Paul's tent-making is a side job; etc.

Moreover, Ehrman's statistical analysis is backwards, what he sees as barriers are actually opportunities. Frederick Douglass was a slave whose violent masters actively worked to stop him from learning how to read and write, including hiding every scrap of writing from him. A statistical study of odds and barriers might say he had no hope at all—but that is misleading. Douglass could still learn English, what he had no hope of learning was Chinese. And the reality is that his odds went from "infinitesimal" to "almost certain" the instant his goal became to read, as he wrote in his autobiography. Where there is a will, there is a way. And notice the way: in a bigoted and hateful environment, he still found help (and had time to learn it as a slave, not even a free owner of a fishing business). The barriers were two inches tall, once he formed the will.

Peter's barriers were not even two inches tall. If he truly wanted to learn to read and write Greek, there was a way, and it would be easier than Ehrman suspects (someone's brother's wife's cousin knew a guy, and Peter just needed to give him the catch of the day). E.g., Ehrman says the Gentiles (plus God-fearers, converts and Greek speaking Jews, I presume) in Galilee were almost exclusively in only two cities: Tiberias and Sepphoris. He sees that as a barrier. But Tiberias is a simple boat trip away from Peter's Capernaum (as we read in John 6:23), and that assumes no Greek ever left Tiberias. Peter could not learn Chinese, but he could learn Greek.

Regardless, work would have been involved, and we all hate that. So we are talking Ehrman-level motivation (willing to work hard for years to learn Greek), and not my level. Ehrman's presupposition is that Peter was solely focused on the Hebrew language, except for proselytizing Greeks late in life. And if we accept that, then (1) possibly Peter wanted to conduct evangelization in written Greek, but (2) what seems very far-fetched is any real desire to read anything from the Greeks. And without that desire to read Greek as the simultaneous/intermediate step, the desire to write fluent Greek is a wistful dream, not a driving motivation (given the work involved: fluency is altering entire mental concepts to fit the Greek concepts, etc.).

Ehrman concludes that the Epistles prove the forgery. But Ehrman's trust in the literal truth of Peter's résumé is not even a compelling form of skepticism. Actual revolutionary cult leaders are not open books, even in modern times with modern research (e.g., wikipedia.org/wiki/Origin_of_ Wallace_Fard_Muhammad), and it is far more likely that the chief Disciple might not have been

A ninth example, also from the Evangelical Biblical Theology Commentary, on Matthew 22:13 (and cast him into outer darkness; there shall be weeping and gnashing of teeth):

> "Outer darkness" probably connotes the deepest darkness that is so distant from any source of light that not the slightest ray pierces it. Jewish literature from the

quite what the over-literal make him out to be. And if we look at the evidence, the Epistles may prove that the real Peter (fraud or authentic) knew Greek, and Ehrman's presupposition is wrong.

Ehrman notes six passages in 1 Peter that were taken from the Septuagint and not the Hebrew. The entire New Testament was written in Greek, not Hebrew. It quotes the Greek Septuagint throughout. It includes hundreds of possible references to Greek Apocrypha. The KJV acknowledges three cross-references between 1 Peter and the Book of Wisdom (only available in Greek), three cross-references between 1 Peter and the Book of Sirach (translated into Greek by Sirach's grandson), and two cross-references between 2 Peter and the Book of Sirach. And the early Church provides further evidence of the Apostolic teaching of the Apocrypha.

The claim that Peter learned Greek in order to write a few letters is weak, but that is not my claim. My claim is that the Epistles show that he learned Greek to read all his Scriptures. Obsession with every single word of all (not just some, all) the Scriptures might make the work seem feasible and worthwhile. If Peter accepted Apocrypha to that kind of extent, literacy in Greek is a realistic goal, and introduces the possibility of learning Greek at a much younger age, depending on when his obsession formed. In a way, literacy in Greek makes more sense than Hebrew: it would let him read all the Scriptures, including those not in Hebrew. In fact, if Apocrypha were Scripture, it would seem like the leader of the Church might feel obligated to learn Greek so as to read them all (plus he might have seen the Septuagint as Divinely inspired).

I cannot fully discuss the rest of Ehrman's arguments, but if the group taught its "foremen" to read the Greek Scriptures, that explains why the leaders learned to write to them in Greek. Ehrman notes that the High Priests thought Peter was illiterate, but maybe the joke was that the "man of the people" was educated and literate, just not by the Priesthood and not in Hebrew (spoiler alert: at the end of the episode, the "simple country lawyer" (Matlock) turns out to be a Harvard grad).

And since Ehrman cites to his "later frauds"/the Scriptures, they are now admittedly evidence (the Judge decides which statements to accept from them, not Ehrman). So, Jesus of Nazareth lived within walking distance of Sepphoris (3.7 miles), the other Galilean Greektown, where his mother Mary is traditionally said to have been from. Joseph took the family to Egypt, with its large Greek speaking Jewish population who believed in the Divine inspiration of the Septuagint, and where Wisdom was written and Sirach was translated. James and Jude, possible Brothers of the Lord, wrote Greek Epistles. There is no translator between Pilate and Jesus. Jesus' mother's cousin's husband was a Priest and able to write at least Hebrew (Luke 1:63). And yet his son was named John in defiance of all Hebraic custom, and did not become a Priest, but the Herald. He formed a "cell" outside of official Judaism, and taught disciples including Andrew (and maybe Peter) before they met Jesus (the only question being what was taught). Etc. Etc. Etc.

If we do not start with Ehrman's presupposition, the best explanation of all the evidence (all, not just the single sentences that Ehrman chooses) is that the Christians themselves are reason for Peter to know or learn Greek. The group's beliefs gave its members reasons to learn Greek, and a few could (if needed) help the others. How widespread Greek and the Apocrypha were among Jews is debated, and I have changed my mind on it often, but the evidence shows that Greek was involved from the beginning, and the Apocrypha were part of that. That is enough for my beliefs, regardless of the other Jews: the seed need not be identical to the soil in which it grew.

Later I will also discuss the Greek literacy of John the Evangelist—another "poor illiterate fisherman" who was devoted to learning from the Herald, and not the Priests.

> intertestamental period taught that the plague of darkness that God used to judge the Egyptians foreshadowed eternal darkness that awaited them (Wis. 17:21). (p. 220).

Jesus Himself describes an aspect of the afterlife, the realm that no human can know of except by Divine inspiration, by referencing a description of the afterlife that had appeared in an Apocrypha (which declares itself to have received Divine inspiration as to all those things that man cannot, himself, see Wisdom 7:21: "And all such things as are either secret or manifest, them I know"). That would seem to be confirming that the Book he is alluding to had correctly envisioned the realm that no one in this world can know of except by Divine inspiration—which itself would seem to be endorsing the Book's claim that the author had "seen beyond" and saw the Truth. And all this was, again, recorded in the Divinely-inspired Gospel to the Jews, without any caveats or warnings.

The tenth example, also from the Evangelical Biblical Theology Commentary:

> Interestingly, Sirach had described the wise scribe in detail about two centuries before the ministry of Jesus. ... But, although Jesus fit these descriptions well, he had not attained this wisdom in the way Sirach thought necessary. ... The wise scribe had to "travel in foreign lands" to learn "what is good and evil in the human lot" (Sir 39:4). ... Yet, Jesus astonished those who had attended synagogue all their lives with his wisdom as an interpreter of the Hebrew Scriptures. The attendees asked the obvious question, "Where did this man get this wisdom?" His wisdom did not come from the respected rabbinic schools of Hillel or Shammai. Yet Jesus implied that he had greater wisdom than even Solomon (Matt 13:54). In fact, he not only claimed to have wisdom, but he also claimed to be Wisdom (Matt 11:19). (p. 355-56).

Again, we see that Jesus is not just fulfilling the Old Testament but surpassing it. The expected Messiah was just a man, but the true Messiah was God; and so, too, the wisest man was not just a wise man but the actual Wisdom of God.

> Although Matthew does not explicitly identify Jesus as the "Wisdom of God" like Luke 11:49-51 does, Jesus's words strongly imply this identity. The context of Matt 11:19 shows that Jesus's words, "Wisdom is vindicated by her deeds!" refer to how Jesus himself is vindicated by his deeds. Soon after this (Matt 11:25-30 [see Example Eleven, below]), Jesus's teaching makes repeated allusions to the words of personified Wisdom from an intertestamental Jewish book called the Wisdom of Ben Sira or Sirach (Sir 51:23, 26, 28). By speaking like personified Wisdom spoke, Jesus identifies himself as Wisdom. The Old Testament contains several descriptions of personified Wisdom ...Jewish literature written between the time of the Old Testament and the

New Testament further developed the concept of personified Wisdom. The most important examples appear in the Wisdom of Solomon, which describes Wisdom as "a breath of the power of God and a pure emanation of the glory of the Almighty" (Wis 7:25)... (p. 72-73).

(Wisdom 7:25-26 is of course the verse from Wisdom that is (1) referenced in the Epistle to the Hebrews 1:3 per the KJV, (2) part of a Christological hymn, (3) referenced in 1 Clement, and (4) alluded to in the Nicene Creed.)

... who can "do all things" (Wis 7:27) and is "fashioner of what exists" (Wis 8:6). The book assigns to Wisdom the mighty deeds of Yahweh from the Old Testament, such as rescuing God's people from the flood, bringing about the exodus, and parting the waters of the Red Sea (see Wis 7:25-8:5). Two important texts refer to what might fairly be described as an incarnation of Wisdom. In Wis 9:10, Wisdom is sent "from the holy heavens" and "from the throne of [Yahweh's] glory" to the earth to live with humans and show them how to live rightly. Similarly, Bar 3:36-37 says that after God granted Wisdom to Israel, "she appeared on earth and lived with humankind." This background forms a bridge between the descriptions of Wisdom in Proverbs and Jesus's identification of himself as Wisdom. The title affirms Jesus's deity and his roles in both creation (Col 1:16) and the exodus (Jude 5). (p. 72-73).

A bridge between Proverbs and Jesus. This means Proverbs, alone, is not sufficient. Apocrypha are the bridge and what Jesus' identification connects to is the bridge—His identification does not actually connect Himself to Proverbs. Jesus connects Himself to the Apocrypha.

Let's consider what Biblical Prophecy looks like. From the book *Messianic Prophecy Revealed* by Rabbi Kirt A. Schneider:

Notice the last sentence in the passage [Matthew 2:15]: "This was to fulfill what had been spoken by the Lord through the prophet: 'Out of Egypt I called My Son.'" When we go to the Hebrew Bible, we find that there is only one place where the phrase "Out of Egypt I called My Son" is used: Hosea 11:1. In its historical context, this verse doesn't seem to be written as a prophecy. Rather, Hosea just seems to be speaking on the Lord's behalf, recounting Israel's history when he says, "When Israel was a youth I loved him, and *out of Egypt I called My son*" (Hos. 11:1, emphasis added). Again, in its initial historical context, this verse does not seem to be anticipating an event that was to be fulfilled in the future. ... So how does Matthew now say that Jesus fulfilled this? ... Much of the time, the way the New Testament speaks of Jesus' fulfillment of Messianic prophecy is not in the sense that He fulfilled some type of event the Hebrew people were looking forward to coming to pass. Rather, it is pointing to the fact that

> when Yeshua came, He filled Israel's history up by repeating it in His own life. (p. 4).[156]

We often think of prophesy chronologically, i.e., moving from the Old Testament to the New. But actually, Christians see the prophecies because of Jesus, not the other way around.

> The truth of Messiah was already in the texts, but it had to be revealed … Buried deep beneath the surface of the Scriptures were prophecies that pointed to Jesus but were not immediately evident as Messianic prophecies at the time they were written.[157] (P. 36).

Bearing that 'reversal' in mind, read again what the Evangelical Biblical Theology Commentary on Matthew told us (but with emphasis added):

> Jesus's teaching makes repeated allusions to the words of personified Wisdom from an intertestamental Jewish book called the Wisdom of Ben Sira or Sirach (Sir 51:23, 26, 28). By speaking like personified Wisdom spoke, Jesus identifies himself as Wisdom. … Jewish literature written between the time of the Old Testament and the New Testament further developed the concept of personified Wisdom. The most important examples appear in the Wisdom of Solomon, … Two important texts refer to what might fairly be described as an incarnation of Wisdom [the Book of Wisdom and Baruch]. … This background forms a bridge between the descriptions of Wisdom in Proverbs and Jesus's identification of himself as Wisdom. The title affirms Jesus's deity and his roles in both creation (Col 1:16) and the exodus (Jude 5).

To add all the underlined and emphasized points up: when preaching to the Jews, Jesus Christ made repeated allusions to the words of personified Wisdom in Sirach and identified Himself as the personified Wisdom described in the Book of Wisdom, in order to show that He was the incarnation of Wisdom as described in the Books of Wisdom and Baruch. Thereby, He affirmed His deity.

All this was recorded by Matthew, in his Divinely-inspired Gospel to the Jews, among whom "a great company of the priests were obedient to the faith" (Acts 6:7).[158]

---

[156] Charisma House 2023.

[157] For a more scholarly discussion of these points, see e.g., *The Spirit and the Letter: Studies in the Biblical Canon*, Chapter 3, by John Barton.

[158] And yet of course the Evangelical Biblical Theology Commentary on Matthew uses the conclusory label "intertestamental" for these Apocrypha, with no discussion or analysis of any canon implications involved with the substance of what it is saying.

Eleventh example: A great many books and articles have been written discussing the allusions that Matthew 11:25-30 (focusing on "28Come unto me, all ye that labour and are heavy laden, and I will give you rest. 29Take my yoke upon you, and learn of me; for I am meek and lowly in heart: and ye shall find rest unto your souls. 30For my yoke is easy, and my burden is light") makes to Sirach 51:23-30 (focusing on "23Draw near unto me, ye unlearned, and dwell in the house of learning.... 26Put your neck under the yoke, and let your soul receive instruction: she is hard at hand to find. 27Behold with your eyes, how that I have but little labour, and have gotten unto me much rest. ...29Let your soul rejoice in his mercy, and be not ashamed of his praise. 30Work your work betimes, and in his time he will give you your reward").

Matthew 11:25-27 begins with another hymn—one sung even before the Gospel of Matthew was written, which was incorporated into Matthew and Luke. "Norden designated it a missionary propaganda hymn generated in hellenistic circles, while Rist considered it a hellenistic Gentile Christian baptismal hymn." (Hidden Wisdom and the Easy Yoke, by Celia Deutsch, p. 13).[159] ".... The saying about the yoke in Mt 11.28-30, however, does not appear in Luke ... Rist ... pointed out that the verbal similarities between our text and Sirach 51 'are too striking and numerous to be accidental, and indicate a definite literary dependence'... Viviano too is inclined to think that ... Luke would have omitted them on the ground that they were expressed in terms too rabbinic to be either readily intelligible or attractive to the Gentile readers at whom he aimed his gospel" (p. 25, 47-48).[160]

So, we have six verses whose similarities to Sirach 51 "are too striking and numerous to be accidental, and indicate a definite literary dependence." The verses start with a Christian hymn that predates the Bible—according to both a Methodist scholar and an Evangelical scholar, who disagree only as to what

---

[159] JSOT Press 1987. The references are to a German book by Norden, E. (*Agnostos Theos: Untersuchungen zur Formengeschichte religiöser Reden*) and an article in the Journal of Religion by Rist, M. ("Is Matt. 11.25-30 a Primitive Baptismal Hymn?" FR 15 (1935): 63-77). Martin Rist was a Professor at Iliff, the Methodist School of Theology in Denver. Eduard Norden was born a Jew, then converted and became an Evangelical.

[160] Quoting from Viviano, B.T. Study as Worship: Aboth and the New Testament. Studies in Judaism in Late Antiquity 26. Leiden: E.J. Brill, 1978.

the hymn was used for.[161] The verses end with statements perhaps too Jewish for Luke to include, since he was not writing the Gospel to the Jews.

After an exhaustive survey of other possible sources, Deutch says that:

> The apocrypha and pseudepigrapha have their clearest parallel to Mt 11.28-30 in Sir 51.23-30, through the invitation of the teacher, the imagery of the yoke, and the implied promise of refreshment. ... Only Sir 51.13-20 and 6.18-37 are true parallels to Mt 11.28-30. ... (p. 118).

Note that in Judaism, the teacher did not seek out or invite students; the disciple had to find his master.[162] This is a crucial point and was part of Deutsch's research project: to see if there were any other such references anywhere else in the Jewish literature. "The sole instance of a teacher's invitation in the so-called apocryphal and pseudepigraphical literature of Second Temple Judaism occurs in Sirach 51..." (p. 114).

Thus, this is not just a possible reference to Sirach by Jesus; Sirach is also the only possible work that Jesus could be referring to. In fact, if both Jesus' audience and Matthew's audience did not understand via Sirach that this "role-reversal" occurs with (and only with) the personified Wisdom of God, it would have made no sense in their culture for a teacher to make an invitation. But it makes sense for Jesus, not only as a matter of speaking, but also as a specific manner of claiming (via reference to Sirach) to be God. Jesus is claiming to be the fulfillment of Sirach, as if it were Scripture—and thus, as if the other Scriptures are incomplete without Sirach.

And no one objects, not even the many Priests; no explanation is needed, not even for the masses; and no warning about Sirach is given, not to the crowd nor to Matthew's readership.

> ... The presence of these motifs (invitation, yoke, promise of rest) in our passage, indicates that Matthew is presenting Jesus as Wisdom incarnate... [and] the Sage, the Teacher of wisdom." (p. 130) ...These parallels confirm that there is an explicit Wisdom Christology in the M logion [M logion means the sayings of Jesus that are in

---

[161] Since I discuss the importance of such pre-Biblical hymns for the canon question in connection with the Epistle to the Hebrews, I will focus, instead, on the second half of the passage. But this is, of course, another example of such a hymn being based on the Apocrypha.

[162] Regarding the discussion above about learning Greek: if Peter needed a teacher he would have to go get one, but we see that apparently that was normal in Jewish culture. Andrew was (and Peter may have been) involved with John the Baptist before Christ. John had disciples (Luke 7:19) too. Thus, Andrew and Peter may have sought him out to teach them.

the Gospel of Matthew but not in other Gospels, which Deutsch believes come from "M," a hypothetical source used by Matthew]... (p. 138).[163]

Again the Christology in the Gospel to the Jews uses the fulfillment of the Apocrypha as part of Matthew's Evangelization. Over two-hundred years after Sirach had been written, Jesus could assume that the "multitudes" (Matthew 11:7) fully understood the concepts of Sirach.

Recall that long after Jesus, "Akiba, the noted rabbi of the second century (d. C. 132 CE)... protested strongly against the canonicity of certain of the Apocrypha, the Wisdom of Sirach, for instance ... Akiva's utterance reads, "He who reads aloud in the synagogue from books not belonging to the canon as if they were canonical," etc. But he was not opposed to a private reading of the Apocrypha, as is evident from his own frequent use of Sirach."[164]

Akiba's statement implies a need to prohibit, i.e., that Jews were reading Sirach aloud in the Synagogue prior to the prohibition, which relates to what we are seeing here: an expectation from Jesus and Matthew that both Jesus' audience and Matthew's audience understood via Sirach that a teacher making an invitation occurs with (and only with) the personified Wisdom of God— i.e., Jesus is claiming (via reference to Sirach) to be God. We also saw above that the estimates are that 97% of Roman Palestine was illiterate (while Sirach was translated into Greek, it was perhaps still available in Hebrew).

Multiple strands of evidence point to the conclusion that Sirach was being read aloud in the Synagogues because the Jews of Jesus' initial audience and Matthew's later audience had to understand Sirach thoroughly in order to understand what Jesus was really saying to them.[165] Again, Sirach is a Book that (a) declares itself to be Scripture, (b) was "canonical for some Rabbis," (c) was found at Qumran, the Cairo Genizah, Masada, etc., and (d) is quoted in the Talmud as Scripture.

---

[163] Deutsch cites to many others in support of such parallels between Sir 51.23-30 and Mt 11.28-30, including Arvedson, T. Das Mysterium Christi: eine Studie zu Mt. 11.25-30. Leipzig: Alfred Lorentz, 1937 (p. 180-85); Christ, F. Jesus-Sophia: die Sophia-Christologie bei den Synoptikern. ATANT 57. Zürich: Zwingli, 1970 (p. 102ff.); Schweizer, E. Matthäus und seine Gemeinde. Stuttgart: KBW, 1974 (p. 177); Suggs, M.J. Wisdom Christology and Law in Matthew's Gospel. Cambridge, Mass.: Harvard University, 1970 (p. 102).

[164] wikipedia.org/wiki/Rabbi_Akiva.

[165] Again, this is a point often made re: the New Testament, e.g., "Paul's insistence that his letters be publicly read... and his readers' understanding of what public reading would mean within a synagogue context provide good reasons to think that his letters would have been viewed as being in the same category as other "Scripture" read during times of public worship." Kruger, p. 209.

Notably, Luke does not include the invitation—so the invitation is not actually needed to express the Gospel message. But Matthew chose to include this reference to Sirach as part of his explicit Christology in the Gospel to the Jews, even though it would be nonsense unless his Jewish audience can be trusted to possess a thorough knowledge of Sirach and the understanding that Jesus is claiming to be the fulfillment of the passage in Sirach.

One last example, solely to make it an even dozen and not at all because I have run out of examples (there will be hundreds more below),[166] is from Matthew 18:8-9:

> 8Wherefore if thy hand or thy foot offend thee, cut them off, and cast them from thee: it is better for thee to enter into life halt or maimed, rather than having two hands or two feet to be cast into everlasting fire. 9And if thine eye offend thee, pluck it out, and cast it from thee: it is better for thee to enter into life with one eye, rather than having two eyes to be cast into hell fire.

From the Evangelical Biblical Theology Commentary:

> The wording and meaning of [Matthew] 18:3-9 are very similar to 5:29-30, but the contexts are very different, in 5:29-30, the eye and hand are associated with temptation, particularly temptation to commit sexual sin. Here [18:3-9]... the context seems to refer to anti-Christian persecution that pressures a disciple to renounce his faith. Perhaps the hand, foot, or eye in this text causes someone to fall away in the sense that fear of dismemberment by persecutors enticed a person to renounce faith. Although such an interpretation may sound strange to the modern reader, it would not to Matthew's original Jewish-Christian readers. Antiochus Epiphanes[167] had maimed the heroes of the Maccabean era in an attempt to coerce them to renounce their Jewish faith and to worship Zeus. Second Maccabees 7:4 records that the king ordered that one young faithful Jewish man have his tongue cut out, his scalp removed, and his hands and feet cut off, all while his family was forced to watch. ... The third of the sons voluntarily stuck out his tongue and bravely extended his hands willingly offering them to the torturers and exclaiming, "I got these from Heaven, and because of his laws I disdain them, and from him I hope to get them back again" (2 Macc 7:11). Perhaps Jesus was calling his disciples to the same bold faith that characterized these Jewish martyrs since he foresaw that similar tortures awaited some of his own followers. If fear of being dismembered by persecutors prompted a disciple to renounce his faith, he would be wiser to cut off his own limbs. Suffering dismemberment was far better than being thrown into the eternal fire, the result of renouncing Jesus. Although the tortured

---

[166] And notably, all eight Apocrypha have a possible reference in at least one Gospel. See below.

[167] See the earlier discussion of John Chapters 9-10 and the references to Hanukkah, the Festival of Lights, and Antiochus Epiphanes.

believer would "enter life maimed or lame" or "with one eye," the missing limbs and organs would be restored in the resurrection. Willingness to sacrifice the limbs of one's body would ensure that the disciple fulfilled Matt 10-28: "Don't fear those who kill the body but are not able to kill the soul; rather, fear him who is able to destroy both soul and body in hell." (p. 458).

They refer us to Craig S. Keener, past president of the Evangelical Theological Society:[168]

> Here the image shifts from others as the cause of stumbling to personal responsibility. Because Judaism abhorred self-mutilation (Dalman 1929:227), this is an especially stark image of the cost one must be willing to pay to avoid spiritual death. ... The language of losing limbs was reminiscent of the price martyrs paid for their devotion to God (2 Macc 7:11; 4 Macc 10:20[169])...

According to the Evangelical Biblical Theology Commentary:

> Keener's view was influenced by William Lane, Mark, NICNT (Grand Rapids: Eerdmans, 1974), 348, who wrote, "Conversely, concern for the preservation of a hand, a leg or a foot must not lead a man to the denial of the sovereignty of God or his allegiance to Jesus. This thought found heroic exemplification in the history of Jewish martyrdom (e.g. 2 Macc. 7:2-41, where the sacrifice of limbs and life is accepted in order to be true to God and to receive life from his hand) and was to play a crucial role in the martyr Church as well."

My point with this particular example is that we need to consider how this relates to all the other evidence. So, we advance to August 1st of unknown year (around 400 AD), when Augustine gave a sermon on the feast day of the Maccabees. The sermon was devoted to explaining why Christians celebrate the Maccabean martyrs as martyrs for Christ:

> ...the Maccabees[170] really are martyrs of Christ. That's why it is not unsuitable, not in the least improper, but on the contrary absolutely right for their day and their solemnity to be celebrated especially by Christians. What do the Jews know about such a celebration? Word is going round that there is a basilica of the Holy Maccabees in Antioch; in the very city, that is to say, which is called by the name of that persecuting king...the wicked king Antiochus, and the memory of their martyrdom is celebrated in Antioch ... This basilica is owned by Christians, was built by Christians. It's we who

---

[168] InterVarsity Press New Testament Commentary Series – Matthew, 1997, p. 285.

[169] 4 Maccabees is an elaboration of the story in 2 Maccabees, written after Christ (and, thus, is not the source of any reference Jesus was making). In fact, Eusebius and Jerome thought Josephus wrote 4 Macc, but that is almost certainly not correct. wikipedia.org/wiki/4_Maccabees

[170] A colloquial reference to the Maccabean martyrs, the unnamed mother with seven sons.

keep, we who celebrate their memory; it's among us that thousands of holy martyrs throughout the world have imitated their sufferings.[171]

[From earlier in Augustine's Sermon:] Some Jew steps forward and says to us, "How can you reckon these people of ours to be your martyrs? How can you be so unwise as to celebrate their memory? Read their confessions; see whether they confessed Christ." To whom we reply, "It's true, you are one of those who did not believe in Christ, and being broken off from the olive remained withered outside, when the wild olive took your place; what are you going to say, being one of those faithless people?"

The early Christians did not just repeatedly cite to 2 Maccabees as Scripture in their writings—they read it at Mass and preached Sermons on it. Rufinus notes that the Churches read 2 Maccabees[172] and Theophilus of Alexandria, in his Festal Letter of AD 404 (in Jerome, Letter 100, 9, not available online), says that the victories of the Maccabees are praised in the churches of Christ throughout the entire world.

In addition, we have three homilies from St. John Chrysostom when he was serving in Antioch (386 AD).[173] We have sermons from others, as well, including Oration 15 from Gregory of Nazianzus.[174] The basilica in Antioch is gone, but portions of the martyrs' bodies (real or fake) were taken to churches in Istanbul, Cyprus, Rome, and Cologne.[175]

As for the Jews, we will see below that 200 years before Augustine, Origen noted that the Jews gave Maccabees some sort of status (exactly what it means we do not know, but it certainly was not completely rejected or treated as false). And it is not only the Gospel to the Jews that references 2 Maccabees.

---

[171] The Works of Saint Augustine, A Translation for the 21st Century, Part III Sermons, Volume 8: Sermons 273-305A, Sermon 300.

[172] www.bible-researcher.com/rufinus.html, 38

[173] One at www.johnsanidopoulos.com/2018/08/homily-on-holy-maccabees-and-their.html, two more in the book *Homilies on the Maccabees*, available on Amazon at https://a.co/d/be3ORon.

[174] iconandlight.wordpress.com/2021/01/24/in-praise-of-the-maccabees-saint-gregory-the-theologian-nazianzus/

[175] There are also many allusions and references to the Maccabean Martyrs in all the Martyrologies. E.g., the very first martyr document we have is for Polycarp, whose last words (d. 155 AD) before being sentenced to death include "What are you waiting for?" (2 Maccabees 7:30; Martyrdom of Polycarp 11, 2 (and see 22, where Irenaeus is alleged to have written it—Irenaeus was a disciple of Polycarp and Bishop of Lyon; both will be discussed at length below): www.newadvent.org/fathers/0102.htm). Regarding the martyrs of Lyon (177 AD; Irenaeus was in Rome delivering a letter. When he returned to Lyon, the original Bishop, Pothinus, had been martyred, so he became the second Bishop of Lyon), Eusebius records that "the blessed Blandina … having, as a noble mother, encouraged her children and sent them before her victorious to the King, endured herself all their conflicts and hastened after them, glad and rejoicing in her departure as if called to a marriage supper, rather than cast to wild beasts." (Eusebius, Church History 5, 1, 55). www.newadvent.org/fathers/250105.htm. Etc.

Earlier, we saw that the Epistle to the Hebrews also references the Maccabean Martyrs and 2 Maccabees.

The Gospel to the Jews and the Epistle to the Hebrews, I say again.

Of course, the modern Jewish canon does not include 2 Maccabees. This is used by some to claim that 2 Maccabees was never accepted by Jews or the early Christian Church as authentic Scripture.

However, I cited above to the Jewish Study Bible, which explained that their canon was finalized after Christ, e.g., after Christians had already embraced Daniel. They say that the Rabbis considered abandoning a book that many—if not all—Jews had accepted as Divinely-inspired prophecy and Scripture for centuries. They say that the Rabbis were focused on Christians and considered rejecting what Christians accept.

The early Church Fathers also repeatedly testified to such behaviors:

> "…Such writers, like Matthew, feel that … the only real Jew is a Christian. "Israel" so-called is a nation of imposters …" (The Spirit and the Letter: Studies in the Biblical Canon, by John Barton, p. 27-28).
>
> Justin Martyr (135 AD): "your teachers… have altogether taken away many Scriptures …"
>
> Tertullian (208 AD): "It is necessary for me to lay claim to those Scriptures which the Jews endeavour to deprive us of, and to show that they sustain my view."
>
> Hippolytus (235 AD): "These things the rulers of the Jews wish now to expunge from the book, and assert that these things did not happen…"
>
> Origen (248 AD): "the Jewish leaders "pretended to the Jews … deceived the wives of their countrymen. … hid from the knowledge of the people … took away from the people every passage … concealed and removed from the Scriptures…"

This leads us back to 2 Maccabees, and it is time to give you [*please use your very best Paul Harvey voice impression here:*] the rest of the story.

The Talmud, written centuries after Christ, did far more than simply exclude 2 Maccabees from the Jewish canon. It also replaced the Maccabean Martyrs with a fake copy of the story. The Rabbis who wrote the Talmud simply stole the plot and made for themselves a new story ("plagiarized it," as we would say today).

> "The Talmud tells a similar story, but with refusal to worship an idol replacing refusal to eat pork… the king is referred to as the Caesar."

> … The Josippon [sort of a copy of Josephus, with other things like the story from 2 Maccabees added to it] "probably was paraphrased from a Latin version of 2 Maccabees, and was notable as the first major exposure of medieval Jewish audiences to the story."[176]

> In rabbinic literature the story undergoes some more meaningful changes, primarily a chronological shift, which now places the story … in the second century CE…[177]

"Chronological shift" is a brilliantly dismissive way of describing it. These are two completely different stories that share a plot, one 'plagiarized' from the other. The second version is clearly a fake, given by Rabbis in their Talmud as a replacement for 2 Maccabees. And they were successful: later Jews had to be re-exposed to 2 Maccabees and their former Jewish heroes.

Both the past president of the Evangelical Theological Society and the Evangelical Biblical Theology Commentary give us the facts at the time of Christ: the Holy Maccabees were well-known heroes to the Jews. Both believe that Jesus Christ refers to 2 Maccabees Chapter 7. Above, we also saw that the KJV believes that the Epistle to the Hebrews refers to the Maccabean Martyrs in its list of sacred heroes, at 11:35.

And I repeat: these references are from (1) Jesus, (2) the Gospel to the Jews, and (3) the Epistle to the Hebrews.

Centuries later, the Rabbis created their own fake version of the story and inserted the fraud into the Talmud. They somehow eliminated the original story from Jewish memory—so much so that Jews had to be reintroduced to their ancestors' heroes in the Middle Ages.

So the timeline is that 2 Maccabees was well known at the time of Christ (33 AD) and possibly referenced by Christ Himself, the Gospel to the Jews, and the Epistle to the Hebrews; then the Books of the Maccabees had some sort of status in Origen's time (AD 240); at some point later, 2 Maccabees was completely gone—forgotten and replaced by the Talmud's fake version.[178]

---

[176] Wikipedia: wikipedia.org/wiki/Woman_with_seven_sons. The Talmud story is at www.sefaria.org/Gittin.57b.15?lang=bi. Another plagiarization appears in the Jewish Lamentations Rabbah. I compare the Talmud story with the Maccabean Martyrs in the 2 Maccabees section below.

[177] jwa.org/encyclopedia/article/hannah-mother-of-seven

[178] There is also evidence of intermediate stages in this progression. E.g., a first century Jewish author took Chapters 6-7 out of 2 Maccabees and recast them as 4 Maccabees: a standalone story. See wikipedia.org/wiki/4_Maccabees.

The Talmud is also the book which listed the modern Jewish canon—the list which excluded 2 Maccabees from the Books that the Jews claim are Scripture. Augustine, again:

> It's we who keep, we who celebrate their memory ... Some Jew steps forward ... To whom we reply... what are you going to say, being one of those faithless people?

The Bible is the evidence that the Jews of the Bible were linked to 2 Maccabees. The Talmud is the evidence that the Jews of the Talmud had changed; they were no longer linked to 2 Maccabees. The story the early Church told us has corroboration, and it comes from (1) the Bible and (2) the Talmud.

> "...Such writers, like Matthew, feel that ... the only real Jew is a Christian. "Israel" so-called is a nation of imposters ..." (The Spirit and the Letter: Studies in the Biblical Canon, by John Barton, p. 27-28).
>
> Justin Martyr (135 AD): "your teachers... have altogether taken away many Scriptures ..."
>
> Tertullian (208 AD): "It is necessary for me to lay claim to those Scriptures which the Jews endeavour to deprive us of, and to show that they sustain my view."
>
> Hippolytus (235 AD): "These things the rulers of the Jews wish now to expunge from the book, and assert that these things did not happen..."
>
> Origen (248 AD): "the Jewish leaders "pretended to the Jews ... deceived the wives of their countrymen. ... hid from the knowledge of the people ... took away from the people every passage ... concealed and removed from the Scriptures..."

The only piece in dispute is the classification of "Scripture" and whether 2 Maccabees was seen as such at the time of Christ. Evidence that it was Scripture includes references from (1) Jesus, (2) the Gospel to the Jews, and (3) the Epistle to the Hebrews.

Whereas those who claim that 2 Maccabees was not seen as Scripture at the time of Christ cite to the Talmud's list as their evidence.

SIDEBAR 5: CONTRADICTORY PROOFS

From Geisler and Saleeb, *Answering Islam*:

> Insisting that the Qur'an must be divine revelation because it is self-consistent and noncontradictory is also not convincing. Some critics raise significant questions about how totally consistent the Qur'an is. For one thing, they point out that the most blatant contradiction in Muhammad's revelations came by way of later revelations expunging former ones such as the command to stone adulterers being changed to one hundred stripes, and the so-called Satanic Verses on worshiping pagan gods being replaced with some that omit this...[179]

On the other hand, consider another book by Geisler (and Thomas Howe), called *When Critics Ask*, which argues that the Bible cannot err. The authors highlight 17 mistakes that (they claim) critics of the Bible make:

> Mistake 17: Forgetting that Later Revelation Supersedes Previous Revelation. Sometimes critics of Scripture forget the principle of progressive revelation. God does not reveal everything at once...Therefore, some of His later revelation will supersede His former statements. Bible critics sometimes confuse a change of revelation with a mistake. The mistake, however, is that of the critic. ... (page 25-26).

This is just one particular example of failing to give the other side the benefit of a rule that Christians use to defend against the alleged contradictions of the Bible and other such matters.

For purposes of determining the canon, any alleged contradiction between Apocrypha and the Bible must be determined using the same rules as those set out in Protestant apologetics. You cannot apply one set of rules to Books "inside the canon," not apply the same rules to those Books you say are "outside the canon," and then claim that you have proved that those other Books are not canon. That is circular reasoning, and the choice of what is canon would, then, determine the outcome of such analysis.

For example, let us cover the examples the Christian Apologetics and Research Ministry (CARM) gives us:[180]

> Condones the use of magic: Tobit 6:5-7. "Then the angel said to him: Take out the entrails of this fish, and lay up his heart, and his gall, and his liver for thee: for these

---

[179] Baker Books 2002, p. 201. For their part, Moslems believe that the abrogation (as they call it) of a former revelation is acceptable.

[180] Specifically Matt Slick, carm.org/roman-catholicism/errors-in-the-apocrypha/. First thing listed on Google, one of the "fair and unbiased" processes that I used to select many things in this book.

are necessary for useful medicines. And when he had done so, he roasted the flesh thereof, and they took it with them in the way: the rest they salted as much as might serve them, till they came to Rages the city of the Medes. Then Tobias asked the angel, and said to him: I beseech thee, brother Azarias, tell me what remedies are these things good for, which thou hast bid me keep of the fish? And the angel, answering, said to him: If thou put a little piece of its heart upon coals, the smoke thereof driveth away all kind of devils, either from man or from woman, so that they come no more to them."

Is it true that the smoke from a fish's heart, when burned, drives away evil spirits? Of course not. Such a superstitious teaching has no place in the word of God.

Compare this to Genesis 30: 37-43, where "Jacob ... set the rods ... in the watering troughs ... And the flocks conceived before the rods, and brought forth cattle ringstraked, speckled, and spotted"—thus does Jacob fleece Laban, using an apparently magical technique with no basis in actual science. The Apologetics Study Bible defends this: "While this passage may appear to describe a type of magic, God instructed Jacob in this through a dream." And so, too, did the angel tell Tobit to do it. Notably, he did not tell us to do it and he made no assurances that it would ever again work for anyone else.

Or consider Acts 19:12: "from his body were brought unto the sick handkerchiefs or aprons, and the diseases departed from them, and the evil spirits went out of them." The Apologetics Study Bible says that: "God's power through faith was at work in these healings, even if physical devices were a part of the process ..." Discussing Acts 5:15, it also asks: "Did God heal through talismans? Not exactly. God may heal through various devices: Peter's shadow, face cloths and aprons that touched Paul (19:12), and the hem of Jesus's robe (LK 8:44) were all mediums for healing. However, the healing power was never contained within a device; it came only from God (see Lk 8:44-46)."

There are many, many, many more examples, from Jews putting blood on their doors to ward off the wrath of God, dream interpretation, wise men using astrology to follow the star to Bethlehem, the Disciples casting lots to choose Matthias, etc. Things that look like "magic" occur many times in the Bible, and Tobit is not even remotely exceptional on that score.

Teaches that forgiveness of sins is by human effort. Salvation by works: Tobit 4:11, "For alms deliver from all sin, and from death, and will not suffer the soul to go into darkness." Tobit 12:9, "For alms delivereth from death, and the same is that which purgeth away sins, and maketh to find mercy and life everlasting."

We know from Scripture that alms (money or food given to the poor or needy as charity) does not purge our sins. The blood of Christ is what cleanses us – not money or food given to poor people. "But if we walk in the light as He Himself is in the light, we have fellowship with one another, and the blood of Jesus His Son cleanses us from all sin," (1 John 1:7).

But consider the rather famous words of James 2:14, 24: "What good is it, my brothers, if someone says he has faith but does not have works? Can that faith save him? ... Ye see then how that by works a man is justified, and not by faith only." Whatever sort of explanation you use to resolve the express contradiction involved with the words of James (and others, e.g., Luke 11:41: "41But rather give alms of such things as ye have; and, behold, all things are clean unto you") can also work to resolve any such conflict with the conceptual contradiction provided by Tobit. In fact, James 2:14-26 is often considered an allusion to Sirach 3:30-4:10, which says much the same thing ("30Water will quench a flaming fire; and alms maketh an atonement for sins..."). See below on that.

But also consider Polycarp's Epistle to the Philippians, dated 107 AD.[181] The Church in Philippi was the first Church in Europe, founded by Paul himself. Polycarp writes: "When you can do good, defer it not, because "alms delivers from death""—a quotation of exact words from Tobit, which CARM then quotes.[182] Those words may show that Polycarp and the Philippians believe that Tobit is Scripture. Regardless, the Philippians learned from Paul and yet, apparently, would be expected to see this concept as consistent with everything that they had been taught. After all, Polycarp himself instructs the Philippians to "return to the word which has been handed down to us from the beginning."[183] That is early evidence of the teaching of this concept, perhaps even the Apostolic teaching of it.

But that is not my point. There is something else to notice:

> Polycarp was a companion of Papias, another "hearer of John" ... Irenaeus regarded the memory of Polycarp as a link to the apostolic past. ... [saying] "I could tell you the place where the blessed Polycarp sat to preach the Word of God. ... I seem to hear him now relate how he conversed with John and many others who had seen Jesus Christ, the words he had heard from their mouths." In particular, he heard the account of Polycarp's discussion with John and with others who had seen Jesus. Irenaeus reports

---

[181] www.newadvent.org/fathers/0136.htm, Section 10.

[182] The Greek word for almsgiving (eleemosyne), appears more often in Tobit than any other Old Testament Book (22 times versus three in the Pentateuch) and is one of the major theological contributions of the Book of Tobit. Particularly emphasized is the charitable act of burying the dead. See New Interpreters Bible, Tobit, p. 986.

[183] www.newadvent.org/fathers/0136.htm, chapter 7.

that Polycarp was converted to Christianity by apostles, was consecrated a presbyter, and communicated with many who had seen Jesus.[184]

Depending on what dates are accepted, Polycarp may actually have been the head of the Church in Smyrna at the time that the letter to the Church in Smyrna was written down—that letter, of course, being included in the Bible as part of the Book of Revelation (2:8+), written by John.[185] We will see below that Polycarp is crucial to proving that the fourfold Gospel (including, of course, the Gospel of John) and many other writings (including the Epistles 1 John and 2 John) all "go back to the beginning" and are not just fakes made by later Christians, or frauds accepted by gullible Christians.

For example, Kruger stresses how crucial Polycarp is to authenticating the works of John, e.g., it is Polycarp's "appearing to know" 1 John in his Epistle to the Philippians that assures us that the document we call 1 John is indeed authentically Apostolic. In fact, Irenaeus (who learned from Polycarp) is the first Father to cite to 1 John (Against Heresies, 3.16.8: "Wherefore he [John] again exclaims in his Epistle, Every one that believes that Jesus is the Christ, has been born of God" (1 John 5:1)) and thereby authenticate 1 John.

Given his Epistle to the Philippians, Polycarp himself clearly believed that the doctrine that "alms delivers from death" is perfectly in-line with the authentic teaching of Jesus Christ—the teaching Polycarp personally learned at the feet of John.

Nevertheless, CARM cites to Scripture to show how this idea contradicts the clear teaching of Scripture as CARM understands and interprets the text. To prove how Tobit (and Polycarp and his Epistle to the Philippians) contradict Scripture, CARM cites to (drumroll, please...) *1 John.*[186]

---

[184] wikipedia.org/wiki/Polycarp

[185] Revelation 2:10, from the letter to Smyrna: "Fear none of those things which thou shalt suffer: behold, the devil shall cast some of you into prison, that ye may be tried; and ye shall have tribulation ten days: be thou faithful unto death, and I will give thee a crown of life."

Connections like this in the early Church are often haunting: "Polycarp is recorded as saying on the day of his death: "Eighty and six years I have served Him, and He has done me no wrong. ... How then can I blaspheme my King and Savior? You threaten me with a fire that burns for a season, and after a little while is quenched; but you are ignorant of the fire of everlasting punishment that is prepared for the wicked." Polycarp was burned at the stake and pierced with a spear for refusing to burn incense to the Roman emperor." wikipedia.org/wiki/Polycarp.

[186] Consider also that Revelation 8:2 (And I saw the seven angels which stood before God; and to them were given seven trumpets) is a possible reference to Tobit 12:15 (I am Raphael, one of the seven holy angels, which present the prayers of the saints, and which go in and out before the glory of the Holy One)—and, if so, that may be an indication that John saw Tobit as Divinely-

> Money as an offering for the sins of the dead: 2 Maccabees 12:43, "And making a gathering, he sent twelve thousand drachms of silver to Jerusalem for sacrifice to be offered for the sins of the dead, thinking well and religiously concerning the resurrection." Can anyone truly accept that money isn't offering for the sins of dead people? Such a superstitious and unbiblical concept has no place in Scripture.

Note that, this time, CARM cites no actual Scripture that is contradicted. They are seemingly asking us to start with a presupposition that such things "simply cannot be Scripture" so that we reject 2 Maccabees regardless of actual evidence. Such metaphysical arguments are beyond my scope, so that is all I will say on that.

However, there is something to note that is part of my scope: the fact is that the Jews had been praying for the dead, sacrificing for the dead, and making offerings (including money) for the sins of the dead for centuries before Christ. You want evidence of that? You just read it. It is the Book 2 Maccabees.

Ten thousand Christian claims—but to pick just one example, the massacre of the innocents at Bethlehem—involve skeptics saying "there is no evidence" that it actually occurred. Such claims are always and everywhere wrong, for the Bible itself is evidence. Christians believe the claim based on the evidence; it is the skeptic who denies the evidence, having conveniently forgotten that the Bible is a written record of events, no less than Josephus, Herodotus, etc.

So, too, is the Book of 2 Maccabees. Whether you consider it Scripture does not matter in the slightest: it provides evidence that the Jews at the time of the Maccabees, including the entire army and the priests in Jerusalem (and apparently, the Jew who later wrote the book and the even later Jews who read it), all believed in prayer, sacrifice, and offerings for the sins of the dead, including money. Since then, sacrifice and offerings may have ended in 70 AD with the fall of the Temple, but the practice of praying for the dead continues to this day, among Jews and a large majority of the world's Christians.[187]

And of course, among the Jews that became Christian were "a great company of the priests" (Acts 6:7), those whom the evidence says received the "twelve thousand drachms of silver to Jerusalem for sacrifice to be offered for the sins of the dead, thinking well and religiously concerning the resurrection."

---

inspired Scripture. It is, after all, a description of Heaven that matches what John sees in his own Divinely-inspired vision.

[187] See wikipedia.org/wiki/Prayer_for_the_dead.

Historical Errors. Wrong historical facts: Judith 1:5, "Now in the twelfth year of his reign, Nabuchodonosor, king of the Assyrians, who reigned in Ninive the great city, fought against Arphaxad and overcame him." Baruch 6:2, "And when you are come into Babylon, you shall be there many years, and for a long time, even to seven generations: and after that I will bring you away from thence with peace."

The book of Judith incorrectly says that Nebuchadnezzar was the king of the Assyrians when he was the king of the Babylonians. Baruch 6:2 says the Jews would serve in Babylon for seven generations where Jer. 25:11 says it was for 70 years. "And this whole land shall be a desolation and a horror, and these nations shall serve the king of Babylon seventy years."

The Bible contains books of many genres, and Judith may be seen as history, or allegory, or historical fiction. Her name just means "Jewess," and many details were arguably included as indications that the story was not to be taken as literal factual history (such as the nonsensical travel details, e.g., an army that marches 300 miles in three days—people who walked to everything their entire lives would not be likely to gloss over such details); meanwhile, Nabuchodonosor may be a pseudonym for another person (Artaxerses III, etc.), similar to how most interpret names in Revelation (e.g., Babylon) to be symbolic of something else. Martin Luther considered the Book of Judith a kind of poetry: "I think that the poet deliberately and painstakingly inserted the errors of time and name in order to remind the reader that the book should be taken and understood as that kind of a sacred, religious composition."[188]

Seventy years versus seven generations is merely another example of how not all prophetic numbers and references are to be taken literally (e.g., even the historicity of the 70 years in Jeremiah is debated; many claim it is a round number to make it fit). Biblical numbers often lack complete precision, e.g., 2 Chronicles 4:2: "he made a molten sea of ten cubits from brim to brim, round in compass, and ... a line of thirty cubits did compass it round about." (Diameter 10, Circumference 30, Pi = 3, not 3.14159.) Plus "even to" may not mean it will be equal to seven generations but only that it might be that long. As Tertullian advised, numbers are not to be interpreted as a math problem; sometimes, the numbers in Scripture simply do not work and must be interpreted symbolically for a deeper meaning.

Etc. Etc. Etc.

---

[188] Cribbed from the New Interpreter's Bible, which cites to Martin Luther, Luther's Works, 55 vols. (Philadelphia: Muhlenberg, 1960) 35:337-38.

The question is not whether you accept any of those explanations in this instance: it is easy to see why one might think that such things came out of the back end of a bull. Harder to understand would be alternating between thinking they are garbage and thinking that they are genius (or, at least, good enough), depending on which Book is being discussed. Ruth: genius. Judith: garbage. Esther: tell me which part of Esther, and then I can answer…

Even if you think you have a brilliant way to distinguish between all Biblical examples and these examples from the Apocrypha, you have only faced my initial arguments (since I pulled those out of the pile of Protestant arguments myself and have not even bothered to research them or ask an actual Catholic or Orthodox apologist for help), and you have yet to fairly apply all of the procedures and rules involved. E.g., the New International Encyclopedia of Bible Difficulties by Gleason L. Archer gives us a list of "Recommended Procedures in Dealing with Bible Difficulties," the first two of which are:

> 1. Be fully persuaded in your own mind that an adequate explanation exists, even though you have not yet found it. … we may have complete confidence that the divine Author preserved the human author of each book of the Bible from error or mistake as he wrote down the original manuscript of the sacred text. 2. … If the Bible is truly the Word of God, as Jesus said, then it must be treated with respect, trust, and complete obedience. Unlike all other books known to man, the Scriptures come to us from God; and in them we confront the ever-living, ever-present God (2 Tim. 3:16-17). When we are unable to understand God's ways or are unable to comprehend His words, we must bow before Him in humility and patiently wait for Him to clear up the difficulty or to deliver us from our trials as He sees fit. There is very little that God will long withhold from the surrendered heart and mind of a true believer.[189]

So, we just apply those rules fairly to the Apocrypha, as well. We persuade ourselves that there is an answer, bow our heads, and wait for some smart lawyer to come up with it.

---

[189] Zondervan 1982, p. 15.

SIDEBAR 6: REASONABLE STANDARDS OF PROOF, PART II

The case for Christianity is usually framed as a debate among scholars. This book began as the very first footnote in a different book that would have explained how ridiculous that is (in the real world, when they need to save their skins, scholars voluntarily pay very hefty fees to hire lawyers to argue the case for them—and the first, best, and most valuable advice they receive is to shut up and stop making things worse). My plan was to discuss how to proceed from start to finish with real standards of evidence and proof, and real arguments for both sides, etc. But the first thing to decide is what is the universe of possible evidence for and against, and the answer to that starts with the authentic eye witness testimony (if any). And that essentially is the Bible (maybe). So I started with a footnote trying to show what meets the standard of proof and what does not. After it had reached a thousand pages, I realized that it had started to become somewhat unwieldy, so I decided to cut the footnote in half and make it into this book instead.

Sorry: but the case would require a thousand attorneys, a million motions, a billion briefs, and no Judge could ever read them all anyway. (I decided not to trademark "If the case for Christianity were realistic, we would all be in Heaven already!" I had the idea of marketing some merchandise to skeptics, and donating the money to build a Church. But once again I was defeated by laziness, so you are free to make your own bumperstickers and tee shirts.) We each have to make our own way through the endless minefield of amateur arguments and dubious analysis. But it is a great thought experiment—if we are honest about it, and not just trying to win.

For example, human nature is always and everywhere to hold things one does not like to an unreasonable and dishonest standard of perfection, as we see with skeptics who doubt the Biblical accounts. For Christians, the Lord warns us against such errors in Matthew 7:3-5 ("thou hypocrite, first cast out the beam out of thine own eye; and then shalt thou see clearly to cast out the mote out of thy brother's eye"). So we try to look for true comparisons, and strive to avoid judging by a standard of perfection.

For instance, the canon debate is a debate about "where to draw the line." Genesis and the Psalms are not comparables—they are not on the "edge" of the canon, and comparing the Apocrypha to them is a "straw man" argument. The question is whether Tobit and 2 Maccabees should join Ruth and Nahum and Lamentations and 1 Chronicles and Song of Solomon, etc.—Books that are not alluded to in the Bible, or not frequently cited in the early Church, or disputed among the Jews, or disputed among Christians, or not found on all canon lists, or all of the above.

A similar issue of bias involves seeing bad motivations, unsupported by actual evidence. For example, Gallagher and Meade tell us (p. 5):

> Jerome knew that these books were not a part of the Jewish canon, so he thought Christians should not consider them canonical, either. Augustine also knew they were not in the Jewish canon, but he thought their usefulness for Christians granted them authority within the church.

Notice that there is no citation to prove this claim that Augustine thought their 'usefulness' mattered in the slightest, and they provide no quote from Augustine that says any such thing. Preachers quote Scripture all day long; scholars cite to articles and sources all day long; so, then, when a Bible Scholar does not cite or quote anything, alarm bells should be going off in our minds. And when someone says "X did so because…" without a quote from X showing X's reasons, everything after the word "because" is what the author thinks of the world, not necessarily what X thought.

As it is, we know Augustine learned from his mentor, Ambrose, and we can see from a simple search at biblindex.org/citation_biblique/search that Ambrose repeatedly cites every single one of the "Apocrypha" as Scripture, Prophecy, Sacred Writings, etc. In fact, total citations were: Tobit 62 times, Judith 54, 1 Maccabees 24, 2 Maccabees 90, Wisdom 183, Sirach 218, Baruch 37, and Susanna 82. That is 750 citations to Apocrypha from the man who converted Augustine to Christianity. For comparison, Ambrose cited to Ezekiel 180 times, Daniel 203, Joshua 105, Jonah 37, Ecclesiastes 174, Ruth 43, and the short form of Esther (i.e., the part canonical to Protestants) 18.

He cited to the Apocrypha even more frequently than the Books they were attached to. He cited Baruch 37 times and the rest of Jeremiah 275 times, even though Baruch is only five chapters and Jeremiah is 52 chapters. He cited to Susanna (Daniel chapter 13) 82 times even though he cited to all 14 chapters of Daniel only 203 times—in fact, a majority of his cites to "Daniel" are actually to the "Apocryphal" parts and not the canonical parts (e.g., an additional 21 cites were to Daniel chapter 14, the "Apocryphal" stories of Bel and the Dragon).

He cites to four historical Apocrypha books (Tobit 62, Judith 54, 1 Maccabees 24, 2 Maccabees 90) – compare to 4 historical canonical Books (Ruth 43, Esther 18, 1 Chronicles 43, 2 Chronicles 25). Compare Wisdom 183 and Sirach 218 to their fellow Poetic book, Ecclesiastes at 174. He even wrote a Bible Commentary on Tobit.

The evidence clearly shows that Augustine was taught that the Apocrypha were Scripture by his mentor and his Church from the very beginning of his conversion. Gallagher and Meade's claim is backwards: Augustine already accepted the books as true Christian Scripture (knowing full well (and not caring in the slightest) that they were not in the Jewish canon); therefore, he found uses for them, just as any Preacher would with any other Scripture.[190]

The kind of bias that "sees through" those who disagree, without any actual proof, and concludes that they do so out of less-than-pure motives is insurmountable. Matthew 12:24: "when the Pharisees heard it, they said, This fellow doth not cast out devils, but by Beelzebub the prince of the devils."

Lastly, recall the Moslem view of Christianity, discussed above. Qureshi:

> ... Finally, we turn to the most common Muslim accusation against the Bible: that its text has been changed over time. It should also be clear now why Muslims accuse the Bible of having been altered: because the Quran says it teaches the same thing as the Bible, confirming the Torah and the gospel, yet the teachings of the Bible are clearly different. In the same vein, the Quran teaches that Muhammad was prophesied in the Bible, but there appears to be no such prophecy.

The Moslem has a pre-supposition: the belief that the Bible and the Quran were once identical. Therefore, any difference between the Bible and the Quran can only be alterations made by Christians to the Bible. He cannot prove this but insists that his opponent must prove him wrong.

So far, we have seen that the Jewish Study Bible rejects the claim that the Jewish canon was long-settled and that any changes that Christians made to the Jewish canon can only be later additions or innovations. I believe an honest reading of the Bible raises many serious questions about that claim as well. But let's move on to discuss all the evidence from the early Church—even though we already know that not a single one of Kruger's ten witnesses and their canon lists provided evidence for the acceptance of the Jewish Old Testament canon and not the Apocrypha.

---

[190] See, for example, Augustine's extensive discussion of the canon in *On Christian Doctrine*, Book ii, Chapter 8, quoted at www.bible-researcher.com/augustine.html. His focus is entirely on whether the Churches accepted various Books, and he makes no mention at all of their usefulness.

PART TWO

THE EARLY CHURCH

PART II: THE EARLY CHURCH

INTRODUCTION: THE CERTAIN EXPLAINS THE UNCERTAIN

There is a basic rule to follow when we encounter something ambiguous in someone's writing. We are told to do it with such famous authors as Matthew, Mark, Luke, and John—consult any book on interpreting the Bible, such as *When Critics Ask* by Geisler and Howe. They list the common mistakes that critics of Christianity make, with mistake number five being:

> Neglecting to interpret difficult passages in light of clear ones.

But this rule is not unique to Christian exegesis. In any field, in fact in every field, we are all trained to leverage established facts to draw conclusions about situations where our information is incomplete or ambiguous. We use what is certain to shed light on what is uncertain.

A doctor uses the proven facts of a patient's known medical history to interpret ambiguous test results and make a diagnosis. Scientific researchers use proven facts to analyze experimental data and draw conclusions. Financial analysts use historical market data to understand the current market situation, for which they can only have incomplete data. And so on and so on.

Always and everywhere, we use the certain to judge the uncertain. Understanding the written word is no different. Ambiguous statement: "The manager wrote that the project was 'on track' but did not mention the deadline." Certain information: "The project plan clearly states the deadline is next Friday." Interpretation: "Based on the confirmed deadline, "on track" means the project is progressing as expected to meet the Friday deadline."

Using the certain to interpret the uncertain is a simple rule, well understood and universally applied—except when it arrives at an answer we do not like.

To start, how should we interpret what Origen says:

> But it is time for us to use the words of ... Susanna...which indeed those who deny the story of Susanna excise from the list of divine books...[191]

Origen indicates that Susanna was excised from the list of divine Books. Does that mean that Origen believed that the true Old Testament is the one

---

[191] 238 AD, Homilies on Leviticus, Homily 1, 3. From the Gary Wayne Barkley translation, available on Amazon at: a.co/d/1bL4LkG.

from which Susanna had been excised? That the Christian Church was wrong to consider Susanna as Scripture? That Susanna was in a separate third category and not to be relied upon?

Of course not. When viewed in light of Origen's letter on Susanna, the answer is inarguable. Origen is not distinguishing between the Jewish canon and Apocrypha because he believes the Apocrypha are false but because he thinks the Jewish canon is wrongly incomplete. (In fact, the Homily I just quoted later goes on to state Origen's view plain as day: "But we both receive it and aptly use it against them"—by which he means against the Jews).

So, then, how should we interpret what Origen also says?

> the canonical books, as the Hebrews have handed them down, are twenty-two, corresponding with the number of their letters...And outside of these there are the Maccabees...[192]

That quote is from Origen's canon list. You will find many telling you that the list is meant to be the Christian Old Testament. Because it is in "list form," it is given precedence. Because the quote from Eusebius does not say otherwise, it is taken as a given that Origen lists the Hebrew canon for the purpose of having Christians defer to it and accept it as the true Christian Old Testament. Origen's letter is dismissed as insufficient because it is not a list; e.g., a footnote which claims that it only "seems to suggest" what it says.

But it is the letter and not the list that would guide any unbiased judge. Origen gave us his own views in detail in his letter; we are not getting them third-hand and without context (as, unfortunately, we get with the list, which was "cut and pasted" by Eusebius). The views in the letter are directly on point, expressing his opinions on the exact particulars of the canon debate. Origen's letter:

1. States in plain language that he understands the Church's Scriptures do not match the books of the Jewish canon, because the Church's Scriptures are correct and the Jewish Scriptures are wrong.

2. States with approval that the Church accepts Tobit, Judith, and Susanna, while the Jews do not. That is accepting three Apocrypha,

---

[192] Eusebius, Church History, Volume VI, Chapter 25 (www.bible-researcher.com/origen.html). Not to be overlooked is that Origen knew a Hebrew name for the Books of Maccabees—"Sarbeth Sabanaiel"—so he would appear to have obtained this information from the Jews themselves. Also of note is that the Jews of his time still knew the Books of the Maccabees, but the Jews of the Middle Ages had to be reintroduced to it, as discussed above.

including two full Books. Both Books that he says the Church accepts are then not mentioned on Origen's list of "the Books the Hebrews accept."

3. Utilizes Tobit (which the Jews do not even consider Apocrypha) to confirm that Susanna—part of Daniel—should be Christian Scripture.

4. Explains his view that the reason that the differences exist between Christian and Jewish Scriptures is because the Jewish leaders "pretended to the Jews ... deceived the wives of their countrymen. ... hid from the knowledge of the people ... took away from the people every passage ... concealed and removed from the Scriptures..."

Origen's letter is certain; the list is ambiguous. The answer is to look to Origen's letter to explain the ambiguities on the list. If we do so, we then know from Origen's own words that he did not believe that the Christian Old Testament should match a list of "books of the Hebrews." In particular, we know that it can only be the Christian list if it includes Tobit and Judith because Origen told us "Tobias (as also Judith), we ought to notice, the Jews do not use. They are not even found in the Hebrew Apocrypha, as I learned from the Jews themselves. However, since the Churches use Tobias..." In this case, the list did not include them, so this is the Jewish list. Thus, it is incomplete for Christians. It is only a list of what the Hebrews accept.

Is Origen saying that the Maccabees are Scripture to the Jews or not? No one knows. But, when read in light of the letter on Susanna, it is clear that Origen would never be saying that being "outside of these [the Jewish list he had given]" means that they are, therefore, not Christian Scripture—whatever the Jews think is separate from what Christians think. Instead, he seems to indicate that the Jews of his acquaintance "sort of" acknowledge the Books of the Maccabees, somehow, in a way that they do not acknowledge Tobit or Judith. Perhaps they at least call them Apocrypha, or maybe different Jewish groups have different opinions on them.[193]

---

[193] Origen states his own view (and evidences the Christian view) on the Maccabees on other occasions, e.g., Against Celsus 8, 46: "What need is there to quote all the princes and private persons in Scripture history who fared well or ill according as they obeyed or despised the words of the prophets? ... And the books of the Maccabees relate what punishments were inflicted upon those who dared to profane the Jewish service in the temple at Jerusalem." www.newadvent .org/fathers/04168.htm.

As we move on, the point is that at least some in the early Church rejected the idea that they should accept only the Jewish canon as the "Old Testament." They believed that the Church possessed the true Old Testament, not the Jews. The question is not whether that view existed, it is how far it extended. What to make of it all is ultimately for you to decide, but at a minimum, the existence of this view is a crucial key to understanding the evidence:

(1) A quote from an early Church Father identifying the Jewish canon, or distinguishing between the Jewish canon and the Christian Old Testament, is not itself evidence that the Apocrypha are not accepted, lower, less trustworthy, less central to the faith, or not to be relied on. If we look at what else the Father tells us, we may see that all the Father is really saying is that (in his view) the Jews were wrong to reject them.

(2) Similarly, that people in the Church also disagree about accepting Apocrypha meant nothing to Origen. People like Africanus are just wrong (to Origen). That Origen acknowledges the existence of Africanus' opinions does not alter the status of Apocrypha in Origen's mind—it does not become inferior just because Africanus has concerns. Thus, that a Father notes that a writing is disputed within the Church is not, by itself, a reason to conclude that (to that Father) it is of a different stature—which, again, often becomes clear as we look at other quotes from that Father.[194]

But also (3), we will find Fathers saying that there are tiers of Scripture and "only Ecclesiastical" books or denying any authority at all to certain Apocrypha. Such people also exist—we just have to be careful not to automatically impose their views on other Fathers (or vice versa).

Sorting sheep from goats is the goal here: we just want to find out what people were really thinking, doing, and saying.

---

[194] Kruger agrees—when discussing the New Testament canon. "Throughout early Patristic testimony about the canon, the church fathers occasionally acknowledge that a particular book is "disputed" by some. A well-known example is Origen's comments on 2 and 3 John in which he acknowledges that "not all say that these are genuine." Although Hahneman uses this comment to point out that universal agreement on these epistles has not yet been achieved, he entirely overlooks the implications of Origen's comments in the other direction, namely, that apparently most Christians do consider them genuine— including Origen himself. The phrase "not all say" indicates that Origen is simply noting exceptions to a more broadly established trend. Thus, it is misleading to use this passage as evidence that John's letters were not regarded as canonical. That is more than this language can bear. At most, it reveals that in certain quarters of the church some disagreements over these books continued to occur (which is hardly surprising)." (P. 265-266).

33 AD

TO

200 AD

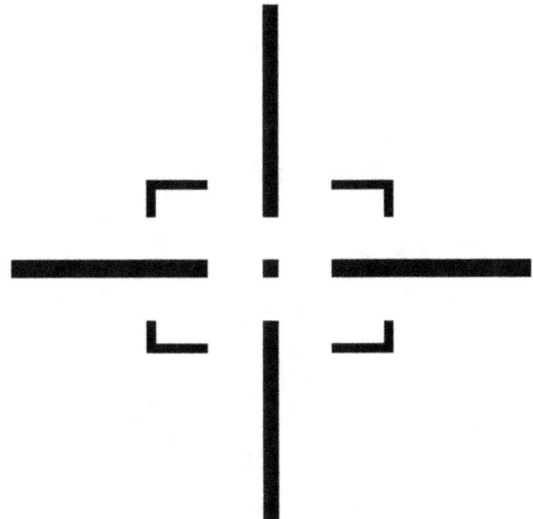

33 AD-200 AD

We begin with canon lists, where a Father from the early Church may have provided a list of the Books of the Bible. From Gallagher and Meade (p. 27):

> The Greek canon lists from the first four centuries attest a very stable collection that consistently mirrored the Jewish canon.[195]

Well there we go, debate settled. But then they give us a footnote that says:

> For a possible exception, see ... the Latin list in the Codex Claromontanus, which scholars sometimes interpret as a translation from an early fourth-century Greek list.

The Codex lists the Book of Wisdom (and all the other Apocrypha). So, that is a possible exception to the idea that the lists consistently mirrored the Jewish canon, addressed in a footnote. Now, back to the main text:

> Of course, such a statement oversimplifies the reality, as chapter 3 shows. But chapter 3 will also show that the early Greek lists always have the same core books-constituting nearly the entire Jewish canon-with, perhaps, an additional book or two. ... It is possible that Melito of Sardis includes the Wisdom of Solomon, but his statement is open to varying interpretations, and neither the Wisdom of Solomon nor any of the other deuterocanonicals is included in any of the other early Greek lists, with one exception: the Apostolic Canons...

It is possible that the Book of Wisdom was included on Melito's list. They tell us that, otherwise, it is not included on any other list, with one exception: the Apostolic Canons list. Well, there is also the Codex Claromontanus list, alluded to only in a footnote, without mentioning that it, too, lists the Book of Wisdom. This arrangement conveniently allows this powerful "only one exception" statement to be made.

Regardless, we are now up to three possible mentions on Greek lists. Is three a lot?

---

[195] For the sake of simplifying discussion, authors write as if the Jewish canon was continuously identical to the Protestant canon, but that is disputed, both as to what Books were named in the canon (until long after Christ) and what texts the names actually referred to. For example, Josephus does not actually identify the Books of his "canon," although it is generally assumed that he included Esther; but then, he uses the long form of Esther (the Apocrypha portion) in Antiquities 11, 6, not the shorter Masoretic/modern Jewish/Protestant version. Thus the definition is conclusory and can cause problems, as we have seen with "Apocrypha." Regardless, the modern Jewish canon is almost always what people mean by the term "Jewish canon," unless they say otherwise, even when speaking of Josephus and his era.

Well, they do not define "early Greek lists," but their book's table of contents for Greek lists has 11 lists mentioned. One of those, however, is Eusebius, whose list is of the New Testament Books, not the Old (so, only ten lists for our purposes). Plus, there is the Claromontanus list (not in Greek but thought to be a copy of a Greek list) that they have relegated to an earlier footnote, which would bring it up to 11 again.

Meanwhile, another one of their Greek lists is from Epiphanius, who clearly lists the Book of Wisdom on his Christian list and states that it is "in dispute" among the Jews on his Jewish lists (and for there to be a dispute, some Jews must accept it). You can debate what to do with that if you want, but the point is that it says the Book of Wisdom right there on the Christian list. Yet, it is not even mentioned, presumably by simple mistake.[196]

So that is now four out of 11 that may include the Book of Wisdom— again, much of it is debatable, like everything in this context always is. But my point is just that Wisdom may be pretty well attested on the Greek lists if you (a) count up lists yourself, (b) track through each of the dismissive references to the Book of Wisdom in Gallagher and Meade's paragraph, (c) correct for some strange omissions, and (d) remember several things that Gallagher and Meade do not explain or highlight for you.

That is also before we point out problems with many of the Greek lists that do not include the Book of Wisdom. E.g., Origen's canon list is for the Jews and not Christians; one list (Bryennios, discussed below) has since been debunked after Gallagher and Meade published their book; and the evidence for the list from the Council of Laodicea is much debated.

The Book of Wisdom may well be on half of the Greek lists.

And that is just Greek lists. Five of the eight Latin lists include the Book of Wisdom, as does the one Syriac List.

Then add additional possible lists (like the contents of the four surviving Bibles from the early Church, all of which include the Book of Wisdom). Next, consider the debated dating of some of the lists (which may not be as early as Gallagher and Meade believe they are). Etc.

All of this ends with the Book of Wisdom on a healthy majority of the lists. In fact, the word "Wisdom" is inarguably included on every single Christian list until 350 AD, and all but one of those references is definitely to the Book

---

[196] Epiphanius' lists in his Panarion are dated before the Apostolic Canons (per Gallagher and Meade), so the dates given the lists do not explain why Gallagher and Meade fail to mention them.

of Wisdom. That is a claim that, for example, the canonical book of Esther cannot make.[197]

It honestly should not take so much work for a reader to understand that the lists give us a pretty good prima facie ("on the face of it") case for the Book of Wisdom. Whether the case stands up to scrutiny, or is enough to include the Book of Wisdom in the canon, is for us to decide once we see all the evidence, but my point is that even works like that of Gallagher and Meade—works on the scholarly end of the spectrum, and by no means a partisan sectarian screed—are not stressing the point that there is a very good case that might be made for the Book of Wisdom from nothing but the canon lists. Instead, they are (1) explaining away references as they appear and not giving a reader the big picture and (2) focusing on Apocrypha, not specific books like the Book of Wisdom.

But that is not the only problem. There are two Apocrypha with a canon list case to be made that is even better than the case for the Book of Wisdom:

> The book of Jeremiah would not only be the short Greek version of the book (as opposed to the longer Masoretic Text version) but would usually include additional, brief compositions, such as Lamentations, Baruch, and the Epistle of Jeremiah. The books of Esther and Daniel would feature the expansions known in the Septuagint versions of these books. (p. 27)[198]

Gallagher and Meade told us that the Greek lists "consistently mirrored the Jewish canon"—but, actually, they always differed from it. Even when they shared the same nominal table of contents, two Apocrypha were always included on Christian lists.

This is an absolutely crucial point, which is why I keep repeating it: the names on the lists are the same, but they refer to different things, and the names on the Greek lists include Apocrypha. If you ask an Englishman to list his three favorite sports, that he says "football" does not mean that he agrees with an American whose list also says "football." The eight consecutive matching letters that spell out the word "football" would seem to imply that

---

[197] And arguably a few other Books cannot make, since Wisdom is not the only debatable reference on Melito's List (and other lists). But in this book, I will generally ignore debates over what Esdras meant, whether Lamentations was included (except to note that Baruch has the same claim to be included), who the 12 Minor Prophets were, etc.

[198] Note, again, that this is what all the canon experts say—it is not an argument. They merely try to dismiss the facts, which means that people miss the implications.

they share an interest in the same sport, but that is an optical illusion. If you look at what they truly meant, their lists are not identical at all.

And once again, we read a little farther and immediately see the importance of keeping this straight:

> The different versions of ... Daniel, and even the additional compositions included with Jeremiah ... were probably all considered to be issues of the textual form of these books, rather than matters of the canonicity of books. So, whereas we might say that such elements distinguish the Christian canon from the Jewish canon, probably most early Christians would not have thought about the matter in these terms, but rather would have seen the two canons as equivalent, though Christians and Jews use different versions of some of the books.

This is simply not the hypothetical that Gallagher and Meade are making it out to be. These exact facts still exist today. A substantial majority of Christians (Catholics and Orthodox) consider those "alternate versions" as canon, while Jews do not. Nothing has changed, and those groups do not think that their canons are equivalent. Nor do Catholics and Protestants, which is, after all, the exact same dispute. The table of contents of a Catholic Bible says "Daniel;" the table of contents of a Jewish or Protestant Bible says "Daniel;" but the books differ, and neither side accepts the other's version as equivalent.

In fact, the New Testament is 7,957 verses, while the Old (without Apocrypha) is 23,145—so, the Christian Bible is 26% "additional material." The Catholic Daniel has 173 "additional verses" compared to the 357 verses of the Protestant/Jewish version. The Catholic Daniel has 33% additional material, considerably more than the "additional material" added to the Jewish Bible. So do we see the Christian Bible as mere "textual variation" of the Jewish Bible? Why not, if even more variation within Daniel was allegedly seen that way?[199]

Regardless, the names have two meanings. One meaning includes Apocrypha, while the other one does not. That Jews and Christians agreed upon the non-Apocrypha portion of Daniel is irrelevant when discussing

---

[199] Whether I would say Protestants and Catholics have the same Daniel depends on context. An outsider asking whether all Christians accept Daniel? Sure, all Christians accept Daniel. I.e., Daniel and not Susanna is the focus of the question and the answer. But what of someone converting to Christianity asking if all Christians accept Daniel? We have completely different versions of Daniel; it is important to read the right one. I.e., Susanna or lack thereof is the focus of the question and answer. There is not one answer to these questions, or one mindset; it varies by context. Why not expect it to vary long ago as well?

Apocrypha: we take the canonicity of that part of Daniel as a given. For our purposes, the Christian and Jewish lists are not the same, because the words did not have the same meaning to the original authors on the relevant point.

No one should confuse themselves about this. In a better world, an ancient Christian list that says Daniel should have "[and Susanna]" added in brackets by the modern author; an ancient Christian list that says Jeremiah should have "[and Baruch]" added. Because that is what the ancient list actually said to its author and to its audience: to them, the word Daniel included Susanna. What he meant is the same as "and Susanna;" he just did not think in modern (Protestant) linguistic terms.

Recall that, earlier, we saw Gallagher and Meade say that "It is possible that Melito of Sardis includes the Wisdom of Solomon, but his statement is open to varying interpretations." In that context, they certainly seem to understand that disparate meanings for the word "Wisdom" should matter to how you read a list! But now, they have switched sides and are emphasizing the name being the same, while soft pedaling the different meanings.

Moreover, they are doing so as part of making broad "next level" claims. On the first level, yes, they note the basic facts about Wisdom, Daniel, and Jeremiah being effectively on the lists (albeit, often dismissively).

Then, they go up another level and generalize about the data. At that level, they are claiming that "The Greek canon lists ... consistently mirrored the Jewish canon" and "early Christians ... would have seen the two canons as equivalent." In the context of the Apocrypha, those are not accurate conclusions that can be relied upon. Two additional books are clearly on the Christian lists, and a third is on them a majority of the time.

So, what happens is:

> Level One: "The book of Jeremiah ... would usually include additional, brief compositions, such as ... Baruch... The books of Esther and Daniel would feature the expansions known in the Septuagint versions of these books." Gallagher and Meade, above.

> Level Two: "The Greek canon lists ... consistently mirrored the Jewish canon" and "early Christians ... would have seen the two canons as equivalent." Gallagher and Meade, above.

> Level Three: "the dominant position ... was an acceptance of the Jewish Old Testament canon and not the Apocrypha...both the Jewish "church" and the first centuries of the Christian church widely adopted the Old Testament books and not the Apocrypha." Kruger Ch. 6 FN11.

Focus on the evidence (Level One) so that you can avoid the "not entirely accurate" abstractions and generalizations (Level Two) that others mistakenly rely on (Level Three). Abstractions and generalizations are not facts and should not be the foundation of your arguments and beliefs.

Notice also, that Kruger et al. actually try to claim that (on the Apocrypha) the Protestant canon is supported by <u>both</u> the early Church and the Jews. But that is manifestly impossible because the two groups inarguably disagreed on Susanna and Baruch. Similarly, Gallagher and Meade say the canons were mirrored and equivalent: the words were identical, but with respect to Apocrypha, the meanings were diametrically opposed.

The reason to keep focusing on this is that Gallagher and Meade go on to say that (p. 28-29):

> One might interpret this evidence from the canon lists in different ways. Sundberg and those of a similar mindset acknowledge that some Christians began to limit their Old Testament to the books of the Jewish canon, but they believe this reflects a development in Christian thinking, that earlier Christians would have generally considered the deuterocanonical books as canonical. Sundberg thinks the fourth-century lists innovate in their advocacy of the Jewish canon for the church. ...Other scholars believe that ... the Christian Old Testament canon began in conscious accord with the Jewish canon, and only later-especially in the Latin West-did the religious value and liturgical use of the deuterocanonical books secure them a place in canonical lists. ...

We will discuss the evidence and arguments at length, with respect to each book separately. But consider, before we even get into it, that on two Books, you already know for certain who wins the debate. Two Apocrypha (Deuterocanonical) books were considered canonical by the early Church and can only have been eliminated later. That is not my opinion, nor is it a "Catholic" belief—it was Gallagher and Meade who already told us the facts one single page earlier. On page 27 (see the two previous quotes above the one just quoted), they tell us that two Deuterocanonical Books were textual variants from the "Septuagint versions," which were being used by the Christians, including the Fathers making the canon lists.

Yet on pages 28-29 (the ones just quoted) they tell us that the Deuterocanonical books were "only later" added to the canon.[200] Even though they know the facts, they keep confusing the issue, all while referring to Susanna and Baruch dismissively—and, thus, they get general statements wrong and confuse readers. And they are not alone! Nearly every book discussing the Apocrypha and the canon confuses things.

With that as background, let us refocus on the case for Christianity. For example, when discussing the Apocrypha, Gallagher and Meade note the lack of mentions on canon lists (a topic which I will ignore for a moment and return to shortly) and lack of early citations (their use of "early" in this context means before the canon lists). From page 19:

> ... judging an ancient author's canon from the citations found in his work is a precarious methodology, which is part of the reason the biblical canon lists presented later in this book serve such a valuable purpose. When investigating the period before the lists, we have no choice but to look at citations, but we should acknowledge their limited value in establishing the boundaries of an ancient scriptural collection. After all, apparently no Dead Sea Scroll cites the Book of Genesis.

First off: "we have no choice but to look at citations." That is a mighty interesting sentiment regarding the examination of evidence. It is almost enough to make one suspect that the citation evidence is not in favor of Gallagher and Meade's deeply cherished beliefs.

But the real point for the moment is that last sentence: "no Dead Sea Scroll cites the Book of Genesis." That is also mighty interesting to consider, particularly when encountering claims that "we have found no cites from the Jews to X," or that "the early Church did not cite a Book until Y year," or that "the Apostles did not cite to Z Book of the Old Testament." It is possible they saw the other books as Scripture but never had a need to cite to them, just as the authors of the Dead Sea Scrolls never had a need to cite to Genesis.

But also, that is just an example of <u>not</u> citing to something. What about the opposite? Does referring to something repeatedly as the Divinely-inspired

---

[200] Remember that to argue that Susanna and Baruch were not canonical would be to argue against Daniel and Jeremiah as canon. If Daniel and Jeremiah were canon, then so were Susanna and Baruch. If Susanna and Baruch were not canon, then neither were Daniel and Jeremiah. E.g., Origen is the very first person to separate Baruch and Jeremiah. Until then, every single person in the early Church saw them as one united whole. For Susanna, the first separation occurs after Jerome, due to Jerome's influence.

word of God truly have "limited value?" In fact, some of the citations are entire Sermons on the Apocrypha delivered by Bishops (not just individual Priests, and we find Bishops with 800 local parishes under them). The passage from Scripture was read to the congregation, and then they preached upon it, using the Scripture to make their point for that Sunday. Does that really have "limited value" in showing what the Church accepted as Scripture?

Even more so: some citations are full-blown Scriptural commentaries, going through the Bible line by line and analyzing it, just with the Scripture in question being an Apocrypha. That would certainly seem to have some value in determining what was Scripture to those writing/reading the commentary.

Some citations are, indeed, found in an ancient author's works and are the usual "as it is written" citation to a sentence in the Apocrypha, quoted as support for an argument or discourse on a subject that is not really about the Apocrypha. But not all: others are enormously more indicative of whether a Book was seen as Scripture and are pretty solid evidence all by themselves.[201] The only way to notice such things is to look at the evidence, see what it is, then decide afterwards.

Specifically, Gallagher and Meade are concerned with the lack of citations from the first two centuries (p. 29):

> The lack of formal citation [to the Apocrypha] continues for the first couple of centuries of Christian history: according to Oskar Skarsaune, until Clement of Alexandria at the end of the second century, Greek Christian writers formally cite the deuterocanonical books only twice, both of which are quotations by Irenaeus of Baruch, which would have formed part of the book of Jeremiah at that time. Such evidence suggests to some scholars that the Christian Old Testament canon began in conscious accord with the Jewish canon, and only later-especially in the Latin West-did the religious value and liturgical use of the deuterocanonical books secure them a place in canonical lists.

To repeat, we have citations only from Irenaeus and Clement of Alexandria.[202] That is it—just those two guys. Two and only two.

---

[201] Such as the ten-page letter from Origen discussing the canonicity of Susanna in detail, of course.

[202] Clement cited to at least Baruch, Judith, Tobit, the Maccabees, Wisdom, and Sirach; Irenaeus at least to Baruch and Susanna. (Irenaeus also alludes to the Book of Wisdom (Against Heresies 4, 38, 3), but it is not a full citation. The Martyrology of Polycarp may also have been written by Irenaeus and alludes to 2 Maccabees.) Those are full citations; allusions and references to Apocrypha go back to 1 Clement, the Epistle to the Corinthians written by the other Clement (Clement of Rome), possibly while Disciples were still alive and before some of the New

It is absolutely amazing that there are fools out there who actually think the Apocrypha were Scripture to the earliest Christians, when in the first two centuries of Christianity, they were only cited by a measly two Fathers!

That is, unless we consider the equally foolish fools who think that the Bible should include the four Gospels (all four Gospels, and only those four: the Fourfold Gospel, an absolutely crucial point for Bible-based Christians, and quite possibly the single most crucial point, in terms of the canon):

> The Fourfold Gospel was widely – not universally – accepted from the end of the second century. Irenaeus of Lyon in Gaul, about 180 CE, provides the pre-eminent testimony, to which we will give attention in a moment. Shortly after Irenaeus and on the other side of the Roman empire, Clement of Alexandria notes incidentally in a discussion of the Gospel according to the Egyptians that this latter work is not among the four Gospels passed down to us... (p. 32).

The exact same two fellows—Irenaeus and Clement of Alexandria—who first assured us that Apocrypha were Apostolic teaching are also the very ones who first assure us that the Fourfold Gospel is Apostolic teaching.

Suddenly, the "pre-eminent testimony" of Irenaeus seems like a pretty good thing. Note the emphasis on the books being "widely" accepted "on the other side of the Roman empire" during the same timeframe and how persuasive that makes the case sound. It is, of course, the exact same basis for making the exact same case for the books of the Apocrypha.

> Some scholars consider these statements by Irenaeus demonstrating the authority of the four Gospels to be a weak attempt to establish a new opinion, while others, on the contrary, think his statements reveal an attempt to explain what Irenaeus had received as the church's traditional view. In other words, some scholars think this passage from Irenaeus demonstrates the novelty of the idea of the fourfold Gospel, others think it demonstrates its antiquity. This debate is a symptom of the difficulty of interpreting the evidence earlier than Irenaeus. (p. 33).

Here, we have the same dispute as with the Apocrypha. The earliest certain written support for the Fourfold Gospel comes at the exact same time from the exact same people, and some of that came in the exact same Books.

But of course, that is just the Fourfold Gospel; surely, we have endless citations to each individual Gospel that clearly prove beyond a shadow of a

---

Testament had even been written. He included references to Judith, the "additions to Esther," Wisdom, Sirach, and Tobit.

doubt that each and every single Father before Irenaeus and Clement of Alexandria accepted at least one of the canonical Gospels, right?

No, of course not. Page 34:

> As for early comments on the Gospels, we have very uncertain evidence in the collection of early Christian writings now known as the Apostolic Fathers, mostly from the late first or second century. These documents perhaps feature some interaction with written Gospels, but on this point scholars disagree. For the most part, when these writings cite the words of Jesus, we cannot be sure whether they have access to one of our Gospels, to some other written source, or to oral tradition.

And that is the case for the Gospels, let alone the Apocrypha. To set a standard that demands specific and inarguable citations from the very early Church is unreasonable to the point of being utterly irrational—yet, of course, we find people arguing against the Apocrypha on that basis, such as the scholars Gallagher and Meade cited precisely five pages earlier.

There are allusions and references to the Apocrypha going back to 1 Clement (Clement of Rome, not Alexandria) and the Didache, the earliest non-Biblical Christian writings still extant. 1 Clement references Wisdom (Ch. 27), Sirach (Ch. 59), Tobit (Ch. 61), Judith (Ch. 55), and the additions to Esther (Ch. 55); the Didache references Sirach (Ch. 4) and Tobit (Ch. 1). (See below for more detail on the specific references.)

When you combine those (and other such evidence, like Polycarp), with the clear citations from Irenaeus and Clement of Alexandria and others before 200 AD, you end up with an argument for acceptance "back to the Apostles" comparable to what every Christian considers persuasive when arguing for the Gospels and the other books of the New Testament.

The evidence is also the same, or even better, when compared to the Old Testament. Psalms (by far the most referenced Old Testament book) is "perhaps referenced" by 15 Fathers before 200 AD, per biblindex.org/citation_biblique/search, but one source is Jewish (Philo), one gnostic, and another is just a category for "anonymous" scraps of paper. Ignatius, Clement of Rome, Melito, Justin Martyr, the Shepherd of Hermas, and others from the "only allusions/not full citations" era are most of the rest (and they all appear to make allusions to Apocrypha, as well—or in the case of Melito, appear to put Apocrypha on his canon list). Then, we get to Irenaeus and the full-citation era—exactly the same as the Apocrypha and the Gospels.

But that is for Psalms, which was referenced 686 times as often as Nahum (so far more in one single average year than Nahum was referenced in 400 years). Clement of Alexandria is the first to make even the slightest allusion to Nahum. Before then, it had been ignored entirely for 200 years.[203] He is also the first full citation for many other books, including Esther. Not all canonical Books are cited by 200: the earliest citation to the Song of Songs was from Tertullian in 207-213 AD.[204] Song of Songs is a "Poetic" Book, the same category as Sirach and Wisdom, and we find clear citations to both Sirach and Wisdom (from Clement) before we find clear citations to Songs (which neither Irenaeus nor Clement ever cite, per biblindex.org/citation_biblique/search.)

So, by any fair, comparable standard, the clear citations to the Apocrypha come early, not late.

> Our survey has shown that the second century was the decisive time for the formation of the fourfold Gospel ... The end of the century witnessed the solidification of the fourfold Gospel in the writings of Irenaeus, followed not long after by less enthusiastic but no less definitive testimony from Clement of Alexandria, Tertullian, and Origen. (p. 39).

All of those named also cited to multiple Apocrypha as Scripture, of course. But more to the point: Gallagher and Meade sure love citation evidence when the topic is the Gospels! Suddenly, the writings of Irenaeus, Clement of Alexandria, Tertullian, and Origen are "definitive testimony" that "witnesses" to the "solidification" of the Bible. Judging an ancient author's canon from the citations found in his work is no longer "a precarious methodology." Forgotten are all directives to "acknowledge their limited value in establishing the boundaries of an ancient scriptural collection."

But why should we believe that these "late" witnesses are passing on authentic knowledge of the true Scriptures that they had received from those they succeeded? Let's focus on Irenaeus and quote from Kruger this time:

> One of the most influential voices in the early church was Irenaeus, bishop of Lyons and disciple of Polycarp. Writing soon after Justin Martyr (c. 170-180), Irenaeus quotes

---

[203] Of course, despite never being cited even once by the early Christians, Nahum was still clearly accepted as canon by the early Christian Church because they considered it to be part of the book of the Twelve Minor Prophets – just like they thought that Susanna was part of Daniel, Baruch was part of Jeremiah, etc.

[204] There are much earlier allusions and such in the Odes of Solomon (gnosis.org/library/odes.htm; per Wikipedia, a "majority of scholars believe it to have been written by a Jewish Christian... between AD 70 and 125"), just as there are such early allusions to the Apocrypha as well (see e.g., discussions of 1 Clement, Polycarp's possible references to Tobit, etc.). In fact, the Odes of Solomon themselves allude to the Book of Wisdom many times (e.g. 6, 10 re: Wisdom 1:7).

New Testament books extensively... There is no indication that he rejects the unmentioned New Testament books (2 Peter, 3 John, and Jude); the extant writings of Irenaeus simply do not refer to them. .... Irenaeus's defense of the fourfold Gospel... appears to draw upon tradition that has been entrenched within the church for quite some time....Given that Irenaeus appears to have known Justin's works (and maybe Justin himself), and certainly knew Polycarp, it is possible that he received this tradition from them. ... [from a footnote:] Irenaeus also affirms that Polycarp knew Papias ... which suggests that he may also be a source of this fourfold Gospel tradition... (p. 228-229).

We should apply all of that to the Apocrypha:

"There is no indication that he rejects the unmentioned Apocrypha; the extant writings of Irenaeus simply do not refer to them."

"Irenaeus's defense of the Apocrypha... appears to draw upon tradition that has been entrenched within the church for quite some time...."

"Given that Irenaeus appears to have known Justin's works (and maybe Justin himself), and certainly knew Polycarp, it is possible that he received this tradition from them. ... Irenaeus also affirms that Polycarp knew Papias ... which suggests that he may also be a source of the tradition of accepting the Apocrypha."

And Polycarp and Papias learned at the feet of John, so they take us directly back to the Apostles, the Evangelists, and the teachings of Jesus Christ Himself. (Much more on this aspect of Irenaeus, Polycarp and Papias below.)

Kruger goes on to say that (p. 201):

... we should also remember that disagreements and debates among early Christians were not necessarily detrimental to the church or its ability to recognize the canonical books. Indeed, such debates would have encouraged critical thinking about these texts, deeper reflection on their content, and more vigorous historical investigation into their origins. Robert Grant argues that a number of early church fathers— Papias, Justin, Irenaeus, Clement of Alexandria, and others – were astute "literary critics" who carefully analyzed the literary merits and historical origins of canonical and noncanonical books... As a result, they took the task of distinguishing between canonical and apocryphal books very seriously, giving us reason for greater confidence in their final conclusions.

And p. 263:

The ability of Patristic writers to distinguish between scriptural books and merely useful books is particularly evident in the writings of Clement of Alexandria and Origen. Both of these men were intellectual giants, widely read and familiar with vast amounts of literature beyond the Scriptures— which they often put to use in their various theological treatises. ...

And from p. 286:

> The above examples are merely a sampling of pre-fourth-century attitudes toward the extent of the canon. They reveal that the early stages of the canon were not a wide-open affair where newly produced apocryphal literature could have easily found a welcome home, but were marked by concern to affirm only books from the apostolic time period.

No doubt about it: he makes a mighty persuasive case for both the New Testament, and the inclusion of the Apocrypha in the canon.

Our focus is on what the earliest Church (before 200 AD) actually accepted. The evidence is from books dedicated to fighting heresy and manuals to instruct Christians; they were written by the giants of their era, authors of "fundamental importance" (Gallagher and Meade, p. xv), located in widely dispersed locations across the Empire. The authors had learned of Christian tradition from the lines back to the Apostles—lines as short as Polycarp learning from John, Papias learning from John, and Justin Martyr, who may well have entered the Church before some books of the New Testament were even written. They and their audience "took the task of distinguishing between canonical and apocryphal books very seriously, giving us reason for greater confidence in their final conclusions." They were all "marked by concern to affirm only books from the apostolic time period."

That is what people say about this evidence when the topic is the case for Christianity, the Gospels, or the New Testament. It is a powerful, compelling case—right up until they deny it all when asked about the Apocrypha instead.

The Mistaken Bryennios List: 20/20 Hindsight

Gallagher and Meade are the best resource I have found for all the early canon lists.[205] So we start with their first Christian entry, the Bryennios List, allegedly the earliest canon list. They date it from 100-150 AD.[206]

---

[205] Although their 405 AD cutoff date is problematic, since it keeps the 419 Council of Carthage (attended by 217 Bishops who voted to accept all of the Apocrypha) out of the discussion. I think my choice of 450 is a much better date to end it.

[206] I generally do not provide copies of the entire lists in this book. You should buy Gallagher and Meade's book, or I offer links to the lists online. On my end, I break the information from the lists

In fact, Gallagher and Meade (writing in 2017) tell us that "392 [the date of Epiphanius' list, to be discussed below] is the terminus ad quem [latest possible date] for the source of [the Bryennios List]" because "All scholars agree that Epiphanius' list [and the Bryennios List] share a common source."

Three years later, Luke J. Stevens[207] proved that the Bryennios List was actually a copy made in 1056 AD from a medieval book (written around 700 AD) that, itself, was a collection of extracts/copies, including an extract of the 392 AD list from Epiphanius. The medieval book includes many of the same differences as the Bryennios List has when compared to Epiphanius, with the Bryennios List having some additional scribal errors that its own scribe must have made. In addition, the medieval book was clearly a copy of Epiphanius (because it copied more of Epiphanius than just what appears in the Bryennios List). So, that chain of evidence and reasoning seems very solid to me—a slam dunk, in fact. Still, judge it for yourself, even though I now move on.[208]

Gallagher and Meade (and many others) were misled. Every single piece of scholarly speculation about the list was wrong. All of it—even the claims that its "latest possible date" was 392 AD. Every part of it was bunk.

Of course, to some extent, that is just how science works. All we can do is learn from it and move on. On one level, we could learn that this is not a fair and equal situation. It was those who wanted to believe in the early dating of the Bryennios List who were most accepting of the early date—and most likely to make wide and sweeping claims of what the list proved. For example:

> If the usual dating of BL can be accepted, then we have an early-second-century Jewish list of books received among Christians, comprising the twenty-seven books of the Old Testament. (p. 78).

They make it a point to tell us that their beloved dating was the "usual" date. The "most scholars agree" trick is usually the weakest part of someone's proof of something. We all rely on it because we have to. But science is not a democracy, and majority vote is actually not as meaningful as we writers attempt to make it when trying to win the debate—because every single day,

---

out by the specific Apocrypha, which I believe is really much more useful for this purpose. Focus on individual books; it will help a lot.

[207] "The Bryennios List and its Origin" (The Journal of Theological Studies, October 2020—free copies for non-scholars are available at www.academia.edu)

[208] I did not find any critique of it to read. Perhaps there is none to be made, or perhaps it will be published tomorrow, or perhaps Google is not the right method for finding such things.

lone scientists prove everyone else wrong. That is what science is all about, and Stevens was such a lone scientist in this case. The real distinction should be between honest and dishonest debate. If it is honest, then ideally, we should see it as debated and leave it at that. (Good luck with that…)

Meanwhile, the phrase "comprising the Old Testament" is not actually what the list says. The list actually says, "Names of the Books among the Hebrews." It took a lot of guessing to get from that statement to the conclusion that because it is a list of the Hebrew books it is, therefore, meant to "comprise" the complete and entire Christian Old Testament. And the guessing was dead wrong. The "true author," Epiphanius, was just listing the Hebrew books. Elsewhere, he makes it clear that Christians have (and to his mind, should have) a different list.

Guessing is dangerous, especially if you are already making guesses before you have seen all the evidence. Hence, for my purposes, a list of that sort is always a "Jewish List" for the canon debate—if, at the end of the process, you decide a Jewish list is to also be your Christian list, that is your decision. But make it at the end, not along the way.

> … The different orthographies [used in the Bryennios List and Epiphanius' List] resulted from the long textual transmission of the list, in all probability. Also, Epiphanius's list has much fuller Greek titles than BL. The agreements and differences probably demonstrate that these lists descend from a common source and that Epiphanius's list has undergone more revision or correction than BL. This contrast may be observed in the different ordering of the books as well… (p. 73).
>
> [footnote 16]: … Epiphanius's version of the list is usually viewed as a later revision of the common source from which [his list] and BL descended … BL was probably a more faithful copy of the source than [Epiphanius], since the latter shows a greater conformity to the other lists of the fourth century. … [Emphasis added.]

All wrong. Note the multiple assessments of "probably" that were not probable at all. (The medieval book simplified the spelling in Epiphanius, and the Bryennios List simplified the spelling in the medieval book.)

Still, many scholars convinced themselves that there was an original document: a source document called "Q." They believed that they could tell what a later copyist (who actually turned out to be the original author—funny how that happened) had changed from this Q. They alleged what they were doing to be "science," even though no one had ever found a fragment of Q, or even a single ancient mention of the existence of this alleged document. But the important thing is that they were able to publish an endless stream of books and articles showing what they claimed were the "original words" to be found in Q. Turns out, they were all just writing their own fantasies, while gullible simpletons believed only the actual, documented evidence. Somewhere in there is a lesson, if only we are wise enough to seek it.[209]

> ... The language of the list and its unusual order of the books suggested to Audet an early second century date (ca. 100-50). Not all subsequent research agreed with Audet's conclusions regarding the language of the titles. (p. 74).

Note that Audet's dating analysis would turn out to be wrong. Whatever he saw in the language was never really there.

> ...The identification of the list's source language [Hebrew or Aramaic] has had a considerable influence on whether the list is interpreted as Jewish or Jewish-Christian. ...Audet [seeing it as Aramaic] considered either a Jewish or Jewish-Christian community as the ultimate origin of the list. ... Goodblatt, on the other hand, concluded that nothing in the titles (including the Aramaic prefixes) prevents attributing those titles to a strict Jewish milieu. ... (p. 74).

In this case, we know the answer: it was in Greek, not Hebrew, and not Aramaic, and is a Jewish list written by a Jewish Christian.[210]

> Assuming the Jewish origin of the list based on its original language, the questions still to be answered are: (1) when did Christians receive it; and (2) how did they adapt it? We will see later that Melito's list provides a plausible context for BL and might show that it was received by Christians before the end of the second century. (p. 74).

Melito's list was not at all a plausible context. And we see how scholars used the Bryennios List as a data point when they made judgments and claims about the other Lists (and vice versa). All of it was wrong.

> ... If the list comprises primarily Hebrew titles in Middle/Mishnaic Hebrew, the evidence of the list's language dates it before the fifth century. Other considerations such as the ordering of the books, its relation to other lists, and the reception history of individual books, provide a more precise basis for dating the list. Most scholars have dated this list to some time during the first or second centuries. (p. 74-75).

---

[209] A sarcastic reference to the "Q" source, the alleged document(s) from which folks like the Jesus Seminar claim the Gospels derive. Here we have a test case, where such methods pointed to a document that never existed, without even alerting the practitioners of such techniques that they might be completely and entirely wrong. That there was no separate source document, and some Evangelists may have copied the other(s), has always been one of the arguments against Q.

[210] Gallagher and Meade say he gave both the Hebrew names and the Greek names on his list, but I believe they mean transliterations of the Hebrew into the Greek alphabet, judging by their depiction of the actual text (which looks all Greek to me).

So, the allegedly more precise methods were actually less precise. That, to me, is the key lesson here: what "most scholars" thought was more precise was actually less precise, and that is what led them astray. Those methods were focused on the order of the Books, the names of the Books, the history of the Books, and how all of that relates in comparison to other lists.

Whereas the linguists (or at least some of them) were right that the Hebrew went back to before the fifth century because Epiphanius' list (the one it was copied from) was from the fourth century. But linguistics did not work for determining the actual order of which document came first and which was the copy—which, itself, often matters for dating things.

> ...The second century attests both very few canonical lists and documented confusion on the number and order of the biblical books (cf. Melito, discussed above and also the section on Melito below), so it seems to provide a more likely context for BL than the fourth century, when canonical lists become much more numerous, reflecting more awareness of the issues and more stability. (p. 77-78).

Actually, it turns out that the second century attests just one single list, Melito's. All others depended on debatable datings, and this one was way off. We should use certainties to judge ambiguities, not use ambiguities to judge certainties. And we really did not know that the other lists were from the second century. The dating and all the speculation about Bryennios were dead wrong. It might well be wrong for others, too.

Meanwhile, note exactly what happened: a list that fits perfectly in the fourth century (since that is what it was copied from) was pushed into the second century because it fit someone's preconceived notions of where it ought to go. Worse, it was pushed despite evidence to the contrary. I am particularly dubious of claims about dates that rely on where something "fits" because, over and over, people push the lists they like to an early date.

Melito's List

The earliest certain date for a list is Melito's, which is dated at 170 AD.[211] The main issue with this list is a debate as to whether it is just a list of the Jewish canon or intended as the list for Christians as well. We do not actually

---

[211] Available at www.bible-researcher.com/melito.html

have Melito's full writing, just a portion of the cover letter, as copied by Eusebius, with some slight commentary by Eusebius. I will discuss the issues with Eusebius later and focus, now, only on the words of Melito. But bear in mind what we have already seen with the Bryennios List: a lack of context is a really bad basis for guessing.

Melito was a Bishop in modern Turkey who traveled to the East (Judea, presumably) and sent back to "brother" Onesimus (presumably a fellow Bishop) the following:

> Melito to his brother Onesimus, greeting! Since you have often, in your zeal for the Word, expressed a wish to have extracts made from the Law and the Prophets concerning the Saviour, and concerning our entire Faith, and have also desired to have an accurate statement of the ancient books, as regards their number and their order, I have endeavored to perform the task, knowing your zeal for the faith, and your desire to gain information in regard to the Word, and knowing that you, in your yearning after God, esteem these things above all else, struggling to attain eternal salvation. Accordingly when I went to the East and reached the place where these things were preached and done, I learned accurately the books of the Old Testament, and I send them to you as written below. These are their names: Of Moses five, Genesis, Exodus, Numbers, Leviticus, Deuteronomy; Joshua the son of Nun, Judges, Ruth, four of Kingdoms, two of Chronicles, the Psalms of David, Solomon's Proverbs or Wisdom, Ecclesiastes, Song of Songs, Job; of the Prophets: Isaiah, Jeremiah, the Twelve [minor prophets] in one book, Daniel, Ezekiel, Esdras. From which also I have made the extracts, dividing them into six books.

People have asked many questions about this whole situation, including why a Bishop would go in search of the Books he has long been preaching; why go to Judea rather than just ask the local Jews (in his Bishopric of Sardis, a city in Turkey); why make "extracts" from the Books; etc.

Some believe Onesimus must have wanted to know the Jewish version of the Books so that he could argue with Jews, not so that he could use them as his own Bible, which he and Melito already had. Others believe this is evidence that the Jews of Asia Minor may have kept a different canon, so Melito went to Judea to get the Judean Jewish canon. To others, still, it was a mission to confirm that the Christians had the right Books (i.e., Books that match the Jewish books), and their order and number, etc. Who Melito speaks for is also an open question: does his view represent others or not?

Melito, incidentally, was "Jewish by birth," which makes some of these questions and possible answers even stranger to think about. In fact, there are people who doubt he even traveled to the East—the ancients might say such things without meaning them literally. And at least one scholar is dubious that

Melito was actually a Bishop.[212] The possibility that he asked the wrong people for the canon also cannot be dismissed: i.e., he asked the Jews without realizing they would give him a canon different from his Church's canon.

If you are thinking of answers to any of those questions, you are already lost. "Facts are truth; explanations of facts are lies," as we say. Make speculative decisions after you see all the evidence, not piece by piece. For my purposes, the letter says what it says; otherwise, it is ambiguous. And bear in mind that our actual goal is not to decide anything about Melito; it is to decide about the canon. The letter is a piece of that, not the whole, and the answers to the Melito Mystery may not even matter to the final conclusion on the canon.

One part that makes the letter ambiguous is that Melito expressly says "Books of the Old Testament"—but that is the first known reference to such a thing; for all we know, Melito invented the phrase.[213] We know what it means to later writers, but we must be careful about guessing from later evidence (E.g., Gallagher and Meade tell us that "the later LXX codices do not necessarily provide insight into the nature of the title 'Of Jeremiah'").[214] While Melito clearly sees the phrase Old Testament to mean Scripture (for Jews or Christians), there is nothing in the letter to indicate that the list is exclusive (so that not being on this list constitutes a Christian rejection of a book) or that his concept of how to divide the Old/New Testament would match ours. He may have considered Apocrypha part of the New Testament and seen the Old Testament as nothing but those Books the Jews accept.[215]

Eusebius (writing 150 years later) calls Melito's List "a catalog of the acknowledged books of the Old Testament"—but that is Eusebius' view of Melito's view, which is not necessarily Melito's view (nor Eusebius' personal view either).[216]

---

[212] Eusebius says he was, but Eusebius is not as reliable as historians wish he had been. I, personally, accept Melito's Bishop-ness and see no real reason to speculate about it, but I point it out to show the extent of our ignorance.

[213] Paul in 2 Corinthians 3:14 uses the phrase "old covenant," and there are those who think the terms are virtually synonymous, but with Melito there is no way to know for sure that he is using it that way. The real question is whether he thought of the New in a way that a failure to mention Apocrypha as part of the Old excludes any possibility of their being part of his Bible.

[214] When discussing the Bryennios list, p. 72.

[215] Wisdom and other Books are in the New Testament sometimes, and Esther considered to be with the Apocrypha, etc. See below. The first reference to the Books of the New Testament comes in 190 AD—the New Testament is technically the covenant sealed by the sacrifice, not the Books.

[216] There's an extra layer to this, as well, because it was apparently also Rufinus' view when he translated Eusebius' translation of Melito. Each link in that chain is separated by a long time period, so their views on how to read an old writing are interesting but not necessarily correct.

Regardless, the actual contents of the letter raise several issues:

1. Esther is missing. That could be a mistake (by the Jews, Melito, or Eusebius), but there are lists that do not include Esther, and lists that note that it is disputed, plus we know that objections to Esther were raised among the Jews until they settled on their canon. When there are reasons to think that it might have been intentional, then the burden of proof is on those claiming it was an unintentional mistake; and in this case, there is no evidence that it was a mistake.[217] What Melito thought of things that are not on the list is ambiguous (as it also is for the Apocrypha).[218]

2. Five Apocrypha are not mentioned (Tobit, Judith, Sirach, and 1 and 2 Maccabees). If it is a Christian list (i.e., intended by Melito to list the books for Christians as well), that would be some negative evidence against them, although not conclusive (they could be part of Melito's idea of the "New" Testament, for example). If it is just a Jewish list, then by itself it would not be meaningful regarding the question of what the early Church accepted.

3. Two Apocrypha (Susanna and Baruch) are implicitly included because of the Septuagint names for Daniel and Jeremiah. That is the evidentiary view. Alternative speculation exists, varying by whether (a) the list (and Books from which the extracts were made) came from Christians,[219] in which case they probably were included or (b) it came from Jews, in which case, perhaps, they were not, except that (c) from the titles it seems that the Jews (if Jews they were) gave Melito the Septuagint Books (which, then, would probably include these Apocrypha). Perhaps the Jews he got them from accepted the Septuagint; perhaps these were the only

---

In addition, Eusebius might intend for 'acknowledged' to mean all agree; e.g., Eusebius has a "disputed" category in his own list, as we will discuss later. Notably, to Eusebius, disputed is still accepted. (But yet another complication is that Eusebius' disputed category might have been meant to apply only to the New Testament; it is not clear.)

More than anything, understand that Eusebius wrote prolifically, and we still are not entirely certain what exactly he meant to say on this and much else. Melito left us practically nothing, so speculation is particularly dangerous.

[217] We will see that one scholar once claimed that the word 'not' must have been accidentally left out of a sentence. Imagine how dangerous that could be without an evidentiary hurdle.

[218] There may also have been a different way to treat it than just complete rejection. Athanasius, for example, lumps in Esther with Apocrypha in his "third category" of "not canon but to be read by catechumens" before they even read the Bible.

[219] Nothing in the letter says that he went East to talk to the Jews. He may have gotten his answers and his Books from Christians there.

Greek translations they had; or perhaps they wanted to sell the "wrong" books that no Jew wanted; etc. Who knows.

4. One Apocrypha (Wisdom) may be mentioned—the wording is unclear; in fact, the ancient manuscripts themselves can differ on the key words. It could be a reference to Proverbs, which was sometimes called "Wisdom," but it might not.[220] More on that below.

5. Several "canonical" Books are missing, but the guess is they were included as parts of other works (Nehemiah as part of Esdras, Lamentations as part of Jeremiah, etc.). Such presumptions are fine, and we may agree with them (I do, and all these combined Books are seen in the Septuagint), but the same presumptions should be applied to Susanna and Baruch.

6. On the other hand, Melito lists Ruth separate from Judges. This is interesting, since so much is made of Judges and Ruth being combined when Josephus' numbering is discussed, etc. But between the time of Josephus' list and Origen's explanation (he is the first to claim that they were combined into one Book, and he comes later), we have this list separating the books. This is one more aspect of how weak the claim is that Judges and Ruth were one Book, when compared to Jeremiah and Baruch, or Daniel and Susanna.

Let's discuss Wisdom a bit first. As evidence that the word might mean Proverbs in this case, Gallagher and Meade note that (per Eusebius) Irenaeus ("and the whole company of the ancients") referred to Proverbs as Wisdom.[221] Irenaeus is contemporaneous with this use of the word Wisdom, so that has real evidentiary value.

---

[220] Something that we non-translators can see for ourselves from the list is that if this reference does mean Proverbs, it would be the one and only Book given two names on the list. No other canon list ever refers to Proverbs as Wisdom either.

[221] "Irenaeus and the whole company of the ancients called the Proverbs of Solomon All-virtuous Wisdom." *Church History*, 4, 22, 8. www.newadvent.org/fathers/250104.htm. You can also read linguistic discussions on this issue. I have read enough to conclude that it is ambiguous and leave it at that. Gallagher and Meade say that "the titles in Melitos list are all anarthrous, suggesting that the Greek eta in the phrase ... might not be an article but could be either a relative pronoun ... or a conjunction [or]." But they support their linguistic argument with only a citation to a personal communication with Adam McCollum (a perfectly legitimate scholar who may be expressing ironclad proof, for all I know, but he did not do so in a published work). I view the lack of publication and the probability that such things are known to other scholars who have managed to disagree about the translation for the past 1700 years as signs that staring at the words will not achieve any additional clarity; it is just ambiguous.

But Gallagher and Meade conveniently forgot to mention Irenaeus (who calls the Book of Baruch "Jeremiah") when discussing the meaning "Of Jeremiah" on this exact same list. If you accept one, you should accept the other, and we have Irenaeus, in his own words, referring to Baruch as Jeremiah. We seem to only have Eusebius telling us that Irenaeus said that Wisdom could mean Proverbs (mere hearsay, to a lawyer).

And since Gallagher and Meade are now encouraging the use of citation evidence to determine the meaning of the word Wisdom on this list, what other citations should we consider?

First, they also tell us with characteristic understatement that the Book of Wisdom was "certainly an important book in early Christianity."[222] Putting aside Biblical allusions for the moment, the earliest allusions to the Book of Wisdom occur in the earliest non-Biblical work we have, Clement of Rome's Epistle to the Corinthians (1 Clement, dating back to perhaps before 70 AD, when Disciples were still alive and many New Testament Books had yet to be written—it even shows up in ancient Bibles and on canon lists as part of the New Testament). There is an allusion to Wisdom 2:24 in Section 3, and to 12:10 in Section 7, but the clearest allusion comes in Section 27.[223]

Justin Martyr, in 155 AD, alludes to the Book of Wisdom as Scripture and Prophecy in his Dialogue with Trypho (describing the debate which had occurred in 135 AD (Sections 137-138)).[224]

Irenaeus, then, alludes to Wisdom 6:18-19 (And love is the keeping of her [Divine Wisdom's] laws; and the giving heed unto her laws is the assurance of incorruption; And incorruption maketh us near unto God) in Against Heresies 4, 38, 3 "...the beholding of God is productive of immortality, but immortality renders one near unto God."[225] Irenaeus (from Smyrna, on the coast 50 miles

---

[222] For example, when speaking for himself in his treatise *The Preparation of the Gospel*, Eusebius cites to the Book of Wisdom more than a dozen times as one of the "Oracles of the Hebrews" and asserts that it is Divine prophecy fulfilled by Christ.

[223] "Who shall say unto Him, What have you done? Or, Who shall resist the power of His strength?" which seems to allude to Wisdom 12:12: "For who shall say, What hast thou done? or who shall withstand thy judgment?" www.newadvent.org/fathers/1010.htm

[224] "My friends I now refer to the Scriptures as the Seventy have interpreted them; ... Accordingly, when the prophet says, 'I saved you in the times of Noah,' ... he addresses the people who are equally faithful to God, and possess the same signs. ... I mean, that by water, faith, and wood, those who are afore-prepared, and who repent of the sins which they have committed, shall escape from the impending judgment of God." The allusion appears to be to Wisdom 10:4: "For whose cause the earth being drowned with the flood, wisdom again preserved it, and directed the course of the righteous in a piece of wood of small value." www.newadvent.org/fathers/01289.htm.

[225] www.newadvent.org/fathers/0103438.htm.

by road from Melito's inland Sardis) is writing around 180 AD, a few years after Melito wrote, and it is Irenaeus that Gallagher and Meade are using to confirm that the ancients sometimes called Proverbs "Wisdom."

Otherwise, it is unclear who the "whole company of ancients" are when Eusebius is writing 150 years later.[226] Clement of Alexandria, Tertullian, and Origen were, perhaps, all "ancient" to Eusebius, and all of them quote from the Book of Wisdom repeatedly, sometimes describing it as Solomon,[227] sometimes as Wisdom, and sometimes as both (the Wisdom of Solomon). We also know that there are many possible Biblical allusions to the Book of Wisdom, and some of them are quite strong. The point is not that such allusions and citations prove that Melito's reference is to the Book of Wisdom, let alone that the Book is Scripture: the point is that the Book has a good case for being what Melito meant, just as Proverbs does.

But there is more evidence for Melito's possible meaning from other canon lists as well. Gallagher and Meade go on to say:

> The Muratorian Fragment contains a reference to the Wisdom of Solomon, and the book is also found along with the other deuterocanonical books in the Mommsen Catalogue, Augustine's canon list, and the canon list contained in the Breviarium Hipponense, all from the later fourth century … (Footnote 40).

When we turn to their discussion on the Muratorian Fragment, we see that its dating is debated, and it could be contemporaneous with Melito. Obviously, authors are entitled to pick whatever dates they want to use whenever things are this debated, but I would point out that a different author could have chosen to present only two lists from the second century (i.e., rejecting an early date for the Bryennios List—let alone its authenticity—and accepting one for the Muratorian Fragment). Both Melito and the Muratorian Fragment include "Wisdom," with one of them being a clear reference to the Book of

---

[226] The quote is in the context of a discussion about something written by Hegesippus, d. 180, but we do not know when Hegesippus would have been writing (although since his now lost works were called "memoirs," it may have also been late in life around 170).

[227] As noted elsewhere, "of Solomon" is sometimes just an idiom meaning something like "a book full of wisdom like Solomon's" (which is how Sirach gets included as one of the five Books "of Solomon" by some ancients, even though Solomon clearly did not write it), but some people took it literally and thought the author of all the Books of Solomon was Solomon himself (even saying that about Sirach, which was written by Sirach and says so). The Wisdom of Solomon/Book of Wisdom alludes to the idea that Solomon is speaking (7:1-14; 8:17 - 9:18) but never actually says that it was written by Solomon and, in fact, includes other parts that would rule out Solomon as the author.

Wisdom. That would put a very different "spin" on the question of whether Melito meant the Book of Wisdom.

In addition, as mentioned earlier, if you page through all the lists in Gallagher and Meade, you would notice that, between these three possible second century lists (Bryennios (erroneously), Melito, and the Muratorian Fragment) and the year 300, there is just one single list: Origen's, which is a list of the Jewish canon, not the Christian canon. I.e., while those other references to the Book of Wisdom do, indeed, come in the fourth century as Gallagher and Meade note, there is also zero possibility that any references on Christian canon lists could have come before then.

Moreover, they say all the lists including the Book of Wisdom are from the "later" fourth century—but that is not true, even using their own dating. Putting aside the list from Eusebius (which, as a New Testament list, does not matter for our purposes), there is still one single fourth-century list dated before 350 AD: the Codex Claromontanus, which they claim is from the first half of the fourth century. And it lists the Book of Wisdom. (And all the other Apocrypha, too.)

As mentioned previously, the list-based case for the Book of Wisdom is no joke; you just have to look for it. Everything is debated, as it always is, but the point is that it has a good case that no one seems to be laying out. And with respect to Melito's list, the evidence that he might have meant the Book of Wisdom is pretty strong and dovetails into the Christian lists that are closest to his in time (the Muratorian Fragment and the Codex Claromontanus).

I am not interested in guessing or assigning probabilities, but I think it is fairly considered a tossup between Melito meaning the Book of Wisdom versus the Book of Proverbs.

Another issue is that Esther is missing from Melito's list, which means, firstly, that the earliest certain Christian list of certain date to include Esther comes in the early fourth century. Of course, it is arguable that the first certain Christian list of any kind comes in the early fourth century, since Melito's list might be a Jewish list, and the Bryennios List was misdated—in which case, the first Christian list is the Codex Claromontanus. It includes Esther and all the Apocrypha.

Secondly, that Esther is missing, ultimately, means nothing to anyone. Esther ends up on everyone's modern canon list, regardless.

Thirdly, that Ether is missing simultaneously means everything to the canon debate, because if Esther can be canon regardless of its absence on Melito's list, then so can unmentioned Apocrypha. The point is that, in both cases, it is really a discussion of other evidence, not Melito, that is determinative.

One last thing, not to be forgotten: what tiny little possibility there is even for debate over the inclusion of Baruch and Susanna on canon lists begins and ends with Melito. From now on, we have quotes from the actual authors of the individual lists. We will still have a few anonymous lists and Council lists, where we do not have direct proof, but we have indirect evidence that every single person we do have evidence on was including them, without evidence of a single person who disagreed (until Jerome, and only on Baruch).

The Muratorian Fragment

The Muratorian Fragment[228] is our last (allegedly) second-century canon list. I include it here because Professor Bart Ehrman once gave implicit support for this dating,[229] and (as a frequent opponent of Christianity) I consider him neutral enough to arbitrate this one, since I do not see why he would care how it helps or hurts arguments over the canon. Gallagher and Meade say "second, third, or fourth century," which is true enough, but that wording is itself evidence that they slant things when they want. They determined that the Bryennios List was "100-150 AD" when it was equally disputed (and rightly so, as it turns out). Accordingly, I go with Ehrman.

Gallagher and Meade give us more detail:

> The traditional dating and provenance were challenged by Albert Sundberg, who proposed a fourth-century Eastern provenance. The movement to revise the Fragment's date gained momentum due to Geoffrey Mark Hahneman's elaboration of Sundberg's thesis; their arguments have gained a significant following. ... (p. 176).

So, we went from "most scholars" and the "usual dating" as being a reason to accept the second century for the Bryennios List, to now pushing for a later date on the Muratorian Fragment because a minority view has gained a significant following. I think we can assume, with great confidence, that this list will not be favorable to Gallagher and Meade's deeply cherished beliefs. A footnote (10) goes on to tell us that:

---

[228] www.bible-researcher.com/muratorian.html
[229] *After The New Testament, A Reader in Early Christianity*, p. 311

"On the influence of Hahneman 1992, see Schnabel 2014..."[230]

We have reached the point where they have started telling us to go read articles about the influence of their favored minority view.

> ...Whereas Sundberg and Hahneman insist that the Fragment has its most exact parallels with the fourth-century canon lists, other scholars... (p. 177).

Just a reminder that Sundberg's and Hahneman's basis for arguing for the later dating of the Muratorian Fragment is the (allegedly) more precise method that failed so spectacularly to correctly date the Bryennios List.

> ...A recent assessment asserts that the older consensus (i.e. on an earlier date) has now been widely restored. Perhaps widely, but not universally... (p. 177).

The view that supports their preferred dating must be badly outnumbered—and the fragment must be really, really bad for their deeply cherished beliefs.

> ...Clare Rothschild takes another mediating position, arguing that the Fragment is a forgery designed to legitimate later views of the canon by representing them as earlier, second-century views. (p. 177).

(You will have to figure out their intended meaning of "mediating," as calling it a forgery does not sound like mediating to me!)

Here, we have the opposite situation than with the Bryennios List: this time, it is Gallagher and Meade who are promoting the idea that the Muratorian Fragment is not really what it seems. Their citation (written in 2017) is to "See Rothschild forthcoming," and since then, a book is now available for a steep price ($125),[231] and an article is available for an amazingly steep price ($40 for just one article?).[232]

On the other hand, a critique of her book by Christophe Guignard is available for free.[233] This is the part I particularly focused on:

> 10. ... Even more surprising is what Rothschild writes in the following lines: "Church leaders such as Chromatius of Aquileia, Jerome, and Isidore of Seville—whose

---

[230] Ehrman wrote his book in 1998, after Hahneman 1992's influence had occurred but before Schnabel 2014 had been written—so, for all I know, he has now changed his mind.
[231] www.amazon.com/Muratorian-Fragment-Translation-Commentary-Christianity/dp/3161611748
[232] brill.com/view/journals/nt/60/1/article-p55_55.xml
[233] journals.openedition.org/rsr/6220

writings are often considered dependent on the Fragment—were present at the Council of 381. Together with Ambrose, bishop in Milan at the time, they could have drafted the Fragment as evidence in a case against heresies" (p. 81).

So now you have Ambrose, Chromatius, Isidore, and Jerome faking evidence. The idea that Jerome might have been proven to be a lying fraud producing fake canon lists would certainly change the discussion around the canon forever! Still, that is a level of conspiracy theorizing that I do not want to spend $165 to read. But to each their own.[234]

I searched for responses to Guignard's critique and found people saying that it was mean and that he is Catholic. Otherwise, the closest to a real defense were statements that, despite his critique, Rothschild's views still "merited debate"—which sounds like damning with faint praise to me. (So says an author who is literally begging for even such faint praise in Amazon reviews, social media, etc. *Hint, hint…*).

But enough about the dating; what exactly is the Muratorian Fragment? It is a scrap of paper that lists a New Testament canon and says:

> … Moreover, the Epistle of Jude and two of the above-mentioned (or, bearing the name of) John are counted (or, used) in the catholic [Church]; and [the book of] Wisdom, written by the friends of Solomon in his honor. We receive only the apocalypses of John and Peter, though some of us are not willing that the latter be read in church. But Hermas wrote the Shepherd very recently, in our times, in the city of Rome, while bishop Pius, his brother, was occupying the [episcopal] chair of the church of the city of Rome. And therefore it ought indeed to be read; but it cannot be read publicly to the people in church either among the prophets, whose number is complete, or among[235]

And there it ends—it is just a fragment. The key thing for our purposes is that the Book of Wisdom is listed, as if it is part of the New Testament. Gallagher and Meade tell us that:

---

[234] I have no idea how much of Rothschild's claim was known when Gallagher and Meade cited to it. I have no reason to question the sanity of their scholarship, or even hers—I would still have bought and considered her arguments, if they were available at a reasonable price. As it is, I am not going to rely on her claims. Gallagher maintains a blog devoted to "Saint Jerome" (sanctushieronymus.blogspot.com), but I found no mention of Rothschild or her paper.

[235] www.bible-researcher.com/muratorian.html. Since it is an incomplete fragment covering only the New Testament, lack of mention of other Apocrypha (or other Old Testament canonical Books) is presumably irrelevant; the only reason to mention this list for our purposes is to discuss the mention of the Book of Wisdom.

> The presence of the Wisdom of Solomon-usually considered a part of the Old Testament, even if apocryphal or deuterocanonical-in a discussion of NT books is strange and often remarked upon. Zahn (1888-92: 2.66) conjectured that a negative had fallen out of the text. (Footnote 33).

No one I have read actually endorses Zahn's idea. Without strong evidence, it is pure speculation of the most extreme sort, obviously.

> Proponents of a fourth-century date point to the parallels in Eusebius, Hist. eccl. 5.8.1-8 (discussing Irenaeus) and Epiphanius, Pan. 76.22.5... (Footnote 33).

Allow me to remind you, yet again, that relying on such parallels was the (allegedly) more precise method that failed so spectacularly to correctly date the Bryennios List. Perhaps the Fragment is itself evidence of an earlier practice that continued into the later period.

> Horbury (1994) has suggested that the Fragment's reference to the Wisdom of Solomon coheres with a wider patristic practice of placing at the end of the entire canon the useful non-canonical books for each Testament. (Footnote 33).

The reason one can see such a "wider patristic practice" in other writings is that those other authors (Jerome, Rufinus, Athanasius, etc.) specifically state that they mean certain works to be "useful non-canonical books." The claim that someone just named some extra books at the end of the list and expected the reader to intuitively understand that those books are, therefore, merely "useful non-canonical books" is contrary to the plain meaning of the text. The Muratorian Fragment's author actually identifies and discusses Books that do not quite fit in the canon—and yet does not say such things about the Book of Wisdom.

By any fair reading, the list identifies the Book of Wisdom as canon.

Clement of Alexandria's List

There is one other list—which is only considered a list when it is useful. It is another reference in Eusebius, that Clement of Alexandria (writing 190-203 AD, so right at the end of our timeframe here) "has not only treated extensively of the Divine Scripture, but ... makes use also in these works of testimonies from the disputed Scriptures, the so-called Wisdom of Solomon, and of Jesus, the son of Sirach...”[236]

Here, we have a list of Scriptures that Clement used, which are disputed by others. In this case, we have Clement's book, which you can read for yourself if you wish[237]—he does not use “disputed Scriptures” in the sense that Clement disputes them, nor does Clement refer to them as disputed.[238] He is using Scripture, as he sees it, and says so many times (see below for the citations themselves). In other words, it is Eusebius who notes them as disputed, which is (a) not Eusebius' personal view (as noted above, he refers to Wisdom as Scripture many times) but (b) would, therefore, seem to indicate a dispute occurring with someone else.

Clement also does not assemble the list—Eusebius does. It is a list of only the items Eusebius knows to be disputed (Clement considered many other Books to be Scripture, but Eusebius did not see them as disputed; notably, Clement cited to other Apocrypha as Scripture, including at least Baruch, Judith, Tobit, and 2 Maccabees, plus the aforementioned Wisdom and Sirach).

So, Eusebius layers his own views on top of Clement's. In this case, we have Clement's writing to see for ourselves, so it is clear to us what Eusebius is doing. Wisdom and Sirach were Scripture to Clement; Eusebius knew that but also knows that others (who?) dispute them (at least in Eusebius' time, which is more than a century after Clement was writing). But note, also, that in other cases where we do not have the underlying writing, we must be careful not to assume that what Eusebius says about something is what the underlying Father's writing itself actually said.

Lastly, when interpreting Melito's reference to Wisdom, this list (if we call it that) or citation evidence (even if it does not qualify as a list) reinforces the claim that a reference to the Book of Wisdom in the second century would actually be fitting for a Christian canon list. That Clement's “list” includes the Book of Wisdom is not in doubt any more than the Muratorian canon.

---

[236] *Eusebius Church History*, Book 6, Chapter 13, 4-6 (www.newadvent.org/fathers/250106.htm).
[237] www.newadvent.org/fathers/0210.htm
[238] That I found, anyway. “Nevers” are scary, it only takes one such reference to prove me wrong, and Clement's works are not short. Still, I did not find one.

THE CANON, AS OF 200 AD

Let's pause to consider the status of the Apocrypha in the second century. After all, what date we use to end our inquiry into the "early Church" is arbitrary. I end at 450, Gallagher and Meade at 400, but we could just as easily pick 200. If we did, then what would the canon be?

As of the year 200, all the evidence shows that Susanna and Baruch were accepted as Scripture, with no evidence to dispute it.[239] Melito's canon list would seem to include them both.

Meanwhile, Wisdom may be on canon lists, possibly even all of them, depending on the dating of lists, whether they are Christian lists, and whether the word Wisdom on Melito's list really means the Book of Wisdom.

The other five Apocrypha do not show up on lists, which might be meaningful or might not, depending on the nature of Melito's list; in addition they may show up on a list if we accept Clement's list as a list (since it includes Sirach) or expand it to add the Apocrypha that Clement considered Scripture but that Eusebius did not list as "disputed" (I found such cites to at least Baruch, Judith, Tobit, and 2 Maccabees; he also cites to 1 Maccabees but not expressly as Scripture).

Regardless, Apocrypha had been referenced in the New Testament (using Stewart's standards), and in the earliest extra-Biblical writings of the earliest Christians. They had all been clearly cited by the year 200 (or 203). Citations from Irenaeus, Clement of Alexandria, etc. are the same people we rely on for acceptance of the fourfold Gospel and numerous Epistles. The evidence for the acceptance of the Apocrypha comes from different geographies; the Fathers are known to have direct connections to the even more distant past, and their testimony is corroborated by earlier allusions. All these are considered good reasons to trust that they are passing on truths and documents that were passed down to them—or so it is said, when the topic is the Gospels.

We can compare the Apocrypha to other canonical Books. Melito leaves Esther out, which is a "bad fact" for Esther, as it is for the Apocrypha not

---

[239] In addition to the evidence discussed earlier, before 200 AD, Athenagoras cites to Baruch, and Tertullian to Susanna. There is another line of evidence relating to the Church's use of the Septuagint. Also remember the possible Biblical argument about Baruch as part of Jeremiah earlier, although that is debatable. On the other hand, there is no evidence of any Christian denying or rejecting these Books until Jerome. The closest we come is Africanus, well after the year 200, but even he only asks for instruction on Susanna.

mentioned on Melito's list (but which is a relatively "good fact" for Wisdom, Susanna, and Baruch, since they were/may have been included when Esther was not). Otherwise, it is unclear whether Lamentations is considered part of Jeremiah or what he means by "Esdras" (and other such quibbles). These involve issues comparable with the claims made for Baruch and Susanna.

Not all the canonical Books have been cited by Christians—some take until after the year 200. In fact, a few have not even been alluded to yet, let alone cited.

We can also compare with the canon of the Jews at 200. There is some Jewish citation evidence for the canonical Books.[240] The Christian citation evidence also supports Jewish acceptance of some of the Books of the Jewish canon. But the Jews also provide citation evidence for the Apocrypha (see Sirach below; Josephus references the longer parts of Esther; etc.), and there is physical evidence from Qumran and other sites supporting the acceptance of both the modern Jewish canon and Apocrypha (see Sirach and Tobit below, etc.). Josephus provides the number (22) of Books but not the names he means to include. Melito's list is either direct or indirect evidence of what (he claims) the Jews accepted. It supports some of their canon, but not Esther, and may indicate that the Jews accepted Wisdom, Susanna, and Baruch. The Talmud's list may also be evidence, if truly written by 200 AD. But Melito's list and the Talmud conflict—as do Melito and Josephus. Melito's list does not equal the "from 22 to 39" logic that is so often attributed to Josephus' number (given at least Esther, Ruth, Wisdom, Susanna, and Baruch).

New Testament Comparison

But let's compare against the New Testament Books in more detail. The only New Testament canon list that could be from this period (given Gallagher and Meade's dating ranges and list selection) is the Muratorian Fragment. Whatever support it provides would simultaneously apply to the Book of Wisdom, as discussed above. In fact, list-wise, the Book of Wisdom is in even better shape than some of the Gospels, as of the year 200—the Book of Wisdom is included on the same Muratorian list as Luke and John (Matthew

---

[240] I have no idea what it is specifically, but I presume it exists. I know Josephus, Philo, the Dead Sea Scrolls, etc. refer to a lot of the Books, but whether they (and others) mention all of them would be the question.

and Mark are missing and only presumed to be listed) and also could have been included on Melito's list as well. (And if we elevate Clement to the exalted status of "Canon List," then Wisdom gets a mention there, along with many of the New Testament Books).

Susanna and Baruch are comparable to much of the New Testament, since they all have arguments (strong arguments, for all of these) to be implicitly on either Melito's list or the Muratorian Fragment, respectively. In fact, the case for Susanna and Baruch is superior to the list-based case for Hebrews, James, 1-2 Peter, etc. (which Books are definitely not on the Fragment's list).

The rest of the Apocrypha are, arguably, at the exact same point list-wise as Hebrews, James, 1-2 Peter, etc.—none of them were mentioned on any list prior to 200.

But these are just lists. Kruger (p. 269-273) details all the evidence we have for New Testament Books. Let's see how a few of them stack up when compared to the Apocrypha:

> The book of James ... clearly did not enjoy the same popularity in the early church as the core New Testament books (like Paul's epistles), as is evidenced by the paucity of explicit Patristic citations of the book. However, its impact can be seen more indirectly as it appears to have influenced a number of other early Christian writings, such as 1 Clement and the Shepherd of Hermas. In addition, James is cited by Irenaeus, Clement of Alexandria wrote a commentary on it which is now lost, and it was recognized as canonical Scripture by Origen, who cites it frequently ... Eusebius acknowledges that some had doubts about it, but counts it among the canonical books "known to most," and the letter is fully received by Jerome, Augustine, and the councils of Hippo and Carthage. ...

A "paucity of explicit Patristic citations of the book;" so, "influence" without actual citation is considered valid evidence of "impact" (and, thus, early acceptance). The writings of the Fathers showing such influence are 1 Clement and the Shepherd of Hermas, both of which show such influence from Apocrypha as well. 1 Clement references Wisdom, Sirach, Judith and Tobit. The Shepherd references Tobit and 2 Maccabees.[241]

---

[241] I discuss 1 Clement elsewhere; the Shepherd references (1) the idea of a good angel on one shoulder and a bad angel on the other, which comes from Tobit 3:8-3:17 etc.; see The Shepherd Bk 2, Commandment 6, Chapter 2 ("Hear now, said he, in regard to faith. There are two angels with a man — one of righteousness, and the other of iniquity." www.newadvent.org/fathers/02012.htm); and (2) the belief "that there is one God who created and finished all things, and made all things out of nothing" (The Shepherd Bk2, First Commandment, www.newadvent.org/fathers/02012.htm) which alludes to 2 Maccabees 7:28 (look upon the

Later, the first clear citations to the Book of James are from Irenaeus and Clement, exactly the same as for the Apocrypha. Irenaeus authenticated the Sacred Scriptures, as he had learned them from Polycarp, who learned them from John: the Fourfold Gospel, the Epistle of James, Susanna, Baruch, and Wisdom. Clement authenticated the Sacred Scriptures, as he had learned them from Tatian, who learned them from Justin Martyr: the Fourfold Gospel, the Epistle of James, Wisdom, Sirach, Baruch, Tobit, Judith, 1 and 2 Maccabees.

Everything else is in the "future" (meaning beyond our current reference date of 200 AD). But note the importance given to being "recognized as canonical Scripture by Origen, who cites it frequently." That would be the same Origen who wrote a long letter explaining (in extensive detail) why Susanna was recognized by "every Church of Christ" as canonical Scripture.

In fact, the evidence for Susanna and Baruch surpass James in the early Church, since Eusebius acknowledges that some doubt the Epistle of James. Still, he accepts James as canonical because it is "known [as such] to most" (not all, just most)—a crucial standard to apply when we see that some Apocrypha are also doubted.

Note the importance that is attached to being received by Augustine and the councils of Hippo and Carthage, all of which accepted every single Apocrypha. On the other hand, Jerome only evidences the acceptance of Susanna and (sort of) Judith—but note that mention of Jerome is made in the exact same sentence that stresses that the acknowledgement that some had doubts is not what matters; what matters is that it is "known to most."

Kruger says that the "impact [of James] can be seen more indirectly as it appears to have influenced ..."—but, of course, opinions differ and not everyone will see such influence. In fact, it seems that Gallagher and Meade do not agree. They say that "There is little evidence for the use of James in the second century. Origen is the first early theologian to make clear use of the letter of James" (p. 272). So, the first clear use is by Origen, a third-century writer, and he would be making this first use of the Epistle of James a generation after the first citations were made to each of the Apocrypha.

---

heaven and the earth, and all that is therein, and consider that God made them of things that were not). wikipedia.org/wiki/Creatio_ex_nihilo discusses the latter concept and where it comes from in more detail (it is not actually clear just from Genesis, and for what it is worth, the Jewish Study Bible interprets the beginning of Genesis as "When God began to create heaven and earth - the earth being unformed and void, with darkness over the surface of the deep and a wind from God sweeping over the water - "God said, "Let there be light"...").

> Jude... we have good reason to think that this letter stems from apostolic circles and would therefore contain apostolic teaching. Like the book of James, Jude was also largely overlooked by many Patristic authors. Of course, as with many of these "disputed" books, the small size of the writing becomes a significant factor in why these books have received less attention. ... Nevertheless, Jude's reception is remarkably positive: it was included in our earliest canonical list (the Muratorian canon), Tertullian acknowledged it as apostolic Scripture, Clement of Alexandria clearly cited it and wrote a commentary on it, Origen received it as fully canonical, and Eusebius placed it firmly in the canonical Catholic Epistles as a book "used publicly with the rest in most churches."

Notice that Irenaeus is not included; thus the earliest citations come later than some of the Apocrypha (Irenaeus is a little before Tertullian and Clement) and lack the short and direct line back to the Apostles that we get from Irenaeus (John to Polycarp to Irenaeus). Nevertheless, "we have good reason to think that this letter stems from apostolic circles and would therefore contain apostolic teaching."

One 'good reason' presented by Kruger is that it is mentioned by the Muratorian Fragment—which lists the Book of Wisdom. Once again, we see the importance of citations from Clement, Origen's views, and that "most churches" use it (which implies that some do not, but that is not by itself a reason for it to be excluded from the canon). New is Tertullian, who also cited to Tobit, Judith, Susanna, Wisdom, Sirach, Baruch, and 1 Maccabees.

> Perhaps no book has had a more difficult journey into the canon than 2 Peter. ... a number of early sources that may have known and used 2 Peter, such as 1 Clement (c. 96), which has several places of overlap (e.g., 23.3 [2 Pet. 3:41; 9.2 [2 Pet. 1:17); ... In addition, Justin Martyr makes a striking allusion to 2 Peter 2:1 in his Dialogue with Trypho, Irenaeus appears to cite it, and Hippolytus also seems to show knowledge of it. Clement of Alexandria wrote a now-lost commentary on 2 Peter, Origen cited it six times and clearly received it as canonical Scripture, and Eusebius considered it to be part of the "disputed" books in the canon that were nevertheless known to most of the church. ... Thus, even with its slow start, it is important to remember that 2 Peter still has significantly more support for its inclusion in the canon than the best of those [potential New Testament] books that have been rejected.

"Places of overlap," "allusion," "appears to cite to it," and "shows knowledge of it"—i.e., comparable (and in some cases inferior) to the Apocrypha. We again see the importance of citation evidence (Origen cited to it six times (biblindex.org/citation_biblique/search says 42, including allusions), whereas Biblindex notes Origen as citing to Apocrypha 626 times. 1 Maccabees received the fewest (eight), Wisdom received 270, Sirach 130, etc.). And we see, again, that "disputes" are no blocker to canonicity. The importance of commentaries is again noted, and the exact same Hippolytus wrote one on Susanna, as did Origen, and (outside of our second-century focus) so will Jerome; others will write commentaries on Tobit, Baruch, Wisdom, etc.[242]

But note that last sentence: "2 Peter still has significantly more support for its inclusion in the canon than the best of those [potential New Testament] books that have been rejected." Whereas we find the Apocrypha are comparable to 2 Peter and, in many respects, have a superior case to be made.

> As would be expected, 2 and 3 John are cited less frequently than 1 John, no doubt owing (in part) to their very small size. However, these two little letters have still left their mark on the historical record. Polycarp appears to know both 1 and 2 John,[243] and there are also reasons to think that Ignatius knew 2 John. By the end of the second century, our first canonical list, the Muratorian fragment, mentions at least two of the epistles of John (and possibly all three). Irenaeus received at least the first and second epistle, and Clement of Alexandria cited from 2 John and wrote commentaries on 2 and

---

[242] The comparison with Apocrypha regarding commentaries is, perhaps, weaker for the New Testament Epistles than Kruger has been indicating. Several times now, he has relied on a Greek word that he takes to mean that Clement wrote a now-lost "commentary"—but two translations of Eusebius available online translate the same word as "abridged accounts" and "concise explanations". See 6, 14, 1 at www.newadvent.org/fathers/250106.htm and at archive.org/details/eusebius-ecclesiastical-history-loeb/page/47/mode/2up. So, these may not be real "line-by-line" Scripture commentaries—just summaries, which may not clearly indicate Scripture. No modern has ever seen them, and it depends on an apparently ambiguous translation, so who knows?

Whereas the commentaries on Susanna and Baruch are line-by-line/section-by-section Scripture commentaries, exactly as we moderns expect. The one by Hippolytus is online (www.newadvent .org/fathers/0502.htm), as are the commentaries by Origen and Jerome (www.tertullian.org/ fathers/jerome_daniel_02_text.htm—Jerome translates Origen's and adds his comments on top of it). The commentary on Baruch (by Theodoret) is available at Amazon (a.co/d/1xe1eFf).

Ambrose's commentary on Tobit (*On Tobias*) is a strange one to our way of thinking. Of its 91 sections, the first seven and last four discuss Tobit the most. The middle 80 consist of a long discussion of usury and related issues, since part of the story of Tobit involves money committed to others (See Tobit 4:1 etc.). It is available online at babel.hathitrust.org/cgi/pt?id=ucl.$b109460 &seq=1. A reader writing a review would describe it as a treatise on usury, but I viewed the beginning and the end as sufficiently commentary-esque to at least note it for our purposes.

Lastly, Cassiodorus (writing around 550 AD) says that the "priest Bellator stated that he himself undertook a commentary on this volume [the Book of Wisdom] in eight books and we keep this work together with his other shorter works." The eight-book commentary is lost, and I am unsure of Bellator's exact dates, but there was a Basilica built and named after someone of that name in "the late fourth or early fifth century," so the commentary seems to have been written before 400 AD. If so, at eight volumes it would also seem to have been a line-by-line commentary. faculty.georgetown.edu/jod/inst-trans.html; wikipedia.org/wiki/Archaeological_site_of_Sbeitla.

[243] Polycarp "appears to know" 1 John, says Kruger, and that is crucial to the proof that 1 John is actually authentic Scripture. Of course, 1 John was also the Epistle quoted by CARM to argue that Polycarp's/Tobit's claim that "alms delivers from death" is contrary to Scripture (carm.org/roman-catholicism/errors-in-the-apocrypha/). In any event, Polycarp also "appears to know" Tobit as well, since he uses the exact same language and concept.

3 John that are now lost. Hippolytus accepted at least 1 and 2 John (but is silent about 3 John), Cyprian was familiar with 2 John, and Dionysius of Alexandria mentions 2 and 3 John quite confidently as canonical Scripture. Although Origen recognized that some had doubts about 2 and 3 John, it appears most in his day regarded the two letters as genuine-including Origen himself. By the time we reach Eusebius in the fourth century, as noted above, 2 and 3 John have found a firm home as part of the seven "Catholic Epistles."

So there is an ambiguous possible mention in the Muratorian Fragment that clearly mentions the Book of Wisdom; Irenaeus and Clement; and—after 200, not before—Hippolytus (who also accepted Tobit, 1 and 2 Maccabees, Baruch, and Wisdom, and wrote a full commentary on Susanna), Cyprian (accepted Tobit, Wisdom, Sirach, Baruch, Susanna, 1 and 2 Maccabees), and Dionysius of Alexandria (accepted Susanna and Tobit); Origen acknowledges doubts but regards it as canonical—and he saw all of the Apocrypha as canon as well.

For earlier Fathers, we see the importance of "appears to know" and "reasons to think he knew." But also, we see Kruger noting individual Fathers who are citing to some of the Books but not others. Lack of citations by an individual Father does not imply that they did not accept a Book, though. They may have had other reasons for not citing to them (such as never having a need). In fact, an earlier footnote (#46) by Kruger discusses lack of citations:

> The reasons a book was infrequently cited can be quite complex and are not always historically accessible to us. ... The book should not be guilty until proven innocent. ... simply because we do not know why it was rarely employed by early Christians.

Another footnote (#47) supports Gallagher and Meade's rejection of Irenaeus' alleged citation to James:

> Bruce, The Canon of Scripture, 176, calls this a "fairly clear quotation of James." Likewise, Metzger includes James in the books that Irenaeus knew (The Canon of the New Testament, 154). In disagreement is Nienhuis, Not by Paul Alone, 36.

Irenaeus is the first to give even a debatable citation to James, while simultaneously giving an extremely certain citation to Baruch—which leads us into the real canon debate, as it relates to the case for Christianity.

Irenaeus Testifies that Baruch was Apostolic Preaching

It is time to refocus on Baruch and the question we originally passed over: was Baruch wrongfully accepted in the period before the canon lists, or was it true teaching from the Apostles? Personally, I think Baruch is the key to everything, and it is precisely at this point, the end of the second century, that the canon debate reaches the real crux of the issue.

Recall that Gallagher and Meade have told us that:

> The lack of formal citation [to the Apocrypha] continues for the first couple of centuries of Christian history: according to Oskar Skarsaune, until Clement of Alexandria at the end of the second century, Greek Christian writers formally cite the deuterocanonical books only twice, both of which are quotations by Irenaeus of Baruch, which would have formed part of the book of Jeremiah at that time.[244] Such evidence suggests to some scholars that the Christian Old Testament canon began in conscious accord with the Jewish canon, and only later-especially in the Latin West-did the religious value and liturgical use of the deuterocanonical books secure them a place in canonical lists. (p. 29).

(Skarsaune/Gallagher and Meade somehow miss that Athenagoras also cites to Baruch at the same time, as noted below.)

Baruch "formed part of the book of Jeremiah at that time"—which means that it was Scripture to Irenaeus, just like the rest of Jeremiah, and just like Genesis, the Fourfold Gospel, the Epistles of James, 1 John, and 2 John. If Irenaeus can be trusted, then the Churches already preached Susanna and Baruch (Daniel and Jeremiah were Scripture and, therefore, were preached; Susanna and Baruch were part of Daniel and Jeremiah and were preached, too). Thus, this "citation evidence" speaks to the early Church's belief that Baruch was Scripture.

But actually, all that is missing the real point when it comes to this citation from Irenaeus. The point that matters most is that Irenaeus is one step removed from the Apostles, and he says Baruch is Apostolic preaching—not just

---

[244] Irenaeus also cites to Susanna: Irenaeus *Against Heresy* IV, 26, 3: "hear those words, to be found in Daniel the prophet: 'O you seed of Canaan, and not of Judah, beauty has deceived you, and lust perverted your heart. You that are waxen old in wicked days, now your sins which you have committed aforetime have come to light; for you have pronounced false judgments, and have been accustomed to condemn the innocent, and to let the guilty go free, albeit the Lord says, The innocent and the righteous shall you not slay.'" (Quoting from Susanna 53-56; www.newadvent .org/fathers/0103426.htm; presumably, Gallagher and Meade do not mention this citation to Apocrypha since Susanna is not a full "Book").

Scripture, mind you, but Apostolic preaching, from John to Polycarp to Irenaeus.

Let us begin by first reading Irenaeus, in his own words, from sections 97-98 of the work entitled "Demonstration of the Apostolic Preaching." In fact, read that title again, and focus on what it is saying: Demonstration of the Apostolic Preaching. Irenaeus wrote this as an instruction manual for new converts on how to learn and preach the true Apostolic faith when Gnostics and others were out there preaching false teachings. Emphasis added:

> Wherefore also Jeremiah saith concerning her (i. e. wisdom): "Who hath gone up into heaven, and taken her, and brought her down from the clouds? Who hath gone over the sea, found her, and will bring her for choice gold? There is none that hath found her way, nor any that comprehendeth her path. But he that knoweth all things knoweth her by his understanding: he that prepareth the earth for evermore, hath filled it with four-footed beasts: he that sendeth forth the light and it goeth; he called it, and it obeyed him with fear: and the stars shined in their watches, and were glad: he called them, and they said Here we be; they shined with gladness unto him that made them. This is our God: there shall none other be accounted of in comparison with him. He hath found out every way by knowledge, and hath given it unto Jacob his servant, and to Israel that is beloved of him. Afterward did he appear upon earth, and was conversant with men. This is the book of the commandments of God, and of the law which endureth for ever. All they that hold it fast (are appointed) to life: but such as leave it shall die." [Baruch 3:28-4:1, i.e., 3:28-3:37 plus 4:1.] Now by "Jacob" and "Israel" he means the Son of God, who received power from the Father over our life, and after having received this brought it down to us who were far off from Him, when He "appeared on earth and was conversant with men," mingling and mixing the Spirit of God the Father with the creature formed by God, that man might be "after the image and likeness of God."
> This, beloved, is the preaching of the truth, and this is the manner of our redemption, and this is the way of life, which the prophets proclaimed, and Christ established, and the apostles delivered, and the Church in all the world hands on to her children. This must we keep with all certainty, with a sound will and pleasing to God, with good works and right-willed disposition.[245]

(a) Irenaeus quotes ten straight verses direct from the Book of Baruch, finishing with Baruch 4:1: "This is the book of the commandments of God,

---

[245]www.ccel.org/ccel/irenaeus/demonstr.preaching_the_demonstration_of_the_apostolic_ preaching.html. Numbering for the verses in Baruch is a mess (as to which verses are assigned which numbers). KJV verse 3:37 will show up as 3:35, 3:36, or 3:38 in other citations. I generally copied the numbers in the source I was using at that moment. Fortunately, citations to Baruch are overwhelmingly to the last three verses of Baruch Chapter 3 (3:35-3:37 in the KJV), so no matter what number a cite uses, you can easily find it at the end of Baruch Chapter 3.

and of the law which endureth for ever. All they that hold it fast (are appointed) to life: but such as leave it shall die,"

(b) Irenaeus identifies this as a crucial prophecy that is fulfilled by Jesus Christ. He does so a few sentences before ending this Demonstration of the Apostolic Preaching with "… error has strayed widely from the truth. … they reject prophecy. And of all such must we beware, and shun their ways,"

and (c) Irenaeus tells his audience that this is "the preaching of the truth, … which the prophets proclaimed, and Christ established, and the apostles delivered, and the Church in all the world hands on to her children. This must we keep with all certainty …"

Irenaeus—who learned from Polycarp, who learned from John[246]—says in very clear terms that Baruch is Apostolic preaching. That is not nearly the same thing as a writer two hundred years later listing Baruch on a canon list, or referencing Baruch as "Scripture," or even also stating that it was "Apostolic preaching." Irenaeus does not just think that Baruch was part of Jeremiah, he is saying that it was part of Jeremiah as preached by John and Polycarp. It is "Jeremiah" as he was taught it, as it was read to him at Church, as it was preached to him as a disciple of Polycarp, and as it was preached to Polycarp as a disciple of John.

So saith the man who provides the pre-eminent testimony as to what John and Polycarp said and taught and preached—and is cited as such endlessly in the case for Christianity, the case for the historicity of the Gospels, and the case for the New Testament as the authentic Christian Scripture.

Irenaeus authenticates that John passed the text of what we call the Gospel of John on to Polycarp, who then authenticated, taught, and preached from that text—and Irenaeus authenticates the exact same thing for the Book of Baruch. The importance of Irenaeus is precisely this "one step removed" linkage between the Apostle's teaching and the words on the page, which assure us that we have the right documents: the texts that are authentically Apostolic.

---

[246] Of course, he also learned from Papias and other "elders" who learned from the Apostles. I do not think that identifying the source as Polycarp is unfair or unreasonable. E.g., Richard Bauckham's *Jesus and the Eyewitnesses* (Chapter 17, footnote 62, p. 455) notes that, although Irenaeus drew from three sources for his knowledge of John (he even includes a chart as Table 17, diagramming their influence), Polycarp "clearly takes pride of place." And, if it was someone else, it does not really alter the analysis: Irenaeus is the one who authenticates and "mistakenly" broadcasts Baruch to the Church, regardless of whether he got it from someone else or introduced it on his own (exactly as Irenaeus does for numerous Gospels, Epistles, etc.) Whether he was a fool or had bad motives, the result is the same: his testimony is impeached.

The implications for what Irenaeus is saying about Baruch are enormous.[247]

Jeremiah Saith

Still, Irenaeus says that the prophesy is what "Jeremiah saith," and people claim that this "misunderstanding" is why Irenaeus "mistakenly" believes it is Scripture—i.e., that Irenaeus has the "wrong" Book of Jeremiah and believes Baruch is Scripture only because he thinks it is part of the Book of Jeremiah (or the words of Jeremiah), and not because John preached from Baruch.

But first, this is the case for Christianity. Whether something is seen as Scripture is certainly part of the canon debate, but in the case for Christianity the part that matters is whether it is Apostolic preaching. That a Father accepts something as "Divinely inspired Scripture" implies his belief that it was Apostolic preaching, but the concepts are not always identical.

And Irenaeus does not say that Baruch is Scripture. What he says is that it is "the preaching of the truth ... which the prophets proclaimed, and Christ established, and the apostles delivered, and the Church in all the world hands on to her children." We have a precise, mechanical question presented: Did Irenaeus speak the truth when he stated that "the apostles delivered" the verses from the Book of Baruch? "No" is an answer that will have profound consequences in the case for Christianity, because Irenaeus is the pre-eminent testimony of Apostolic preaching upon which claims for being Scripture are based—claims for the Gospels, the Epistles, and all the documents that allegedly prove that the Apostles saw the risen Christ.

Furthermore, we must be mindful of the context here and shift gears away from "list-thinking." On a list that says Jeremiah, the point is that the label Jeremiah as mentioned on the list references the physical Book of Baruch. Thus, for that list, the Book of Baruch is canon because it was part of the object the writer called Jeremiah.

---

[247] Note also that Irenaeus further evidences his teaching of Baruch 3:35-37 by alluding to it in his other surviving work, where he, again, ties it to the teaching of John: "this is His Word, our Lord Jesus Christ, who in the last times was made a man among men, that He might join the end to the beginning, that is, man to God. Wherefore the prophets, receiving the prophetic gift from the same Word, announced His advent according to the flesh, ... the Word of God foretelling from the beginning that God should be seen by men, and hold converse with them upon earth, should confer with them." Against Heresies 4, 20, 4. www.newadvent.org/fathers/0103420.htm.

But here is the reverse situation: Jeremiah is now a label that Irenaeus uses for the Book of Baruch. It is the Book of Baruch—the physical Book itself, the words on the page, the words of the prophet—that he is quoting, not the "rest of" the Book of Jeremiah. Irenaeus is speaking of the words he has just quoted, taken from the Book of Baruch. The words of the Book of Baruch are the preaching that "Christ established, and the apostles delivered, and the Church in all the world hands on to her children." It is the words found in the Book of Baruch that we must keep with all certainty, and such as leave it shall die.[248]

The "rest of" Jeremiah has nothing to do with what he is saying, nor is Jeremiah (the person) the subject that he is discussing. At no point does Irenaeus argue that a reader is to accept the words of the Book because it is part of Jeremiah; to the contrary, he expressly states that the reader is to accept the words precisely because they are Apostolic preaching (unlike the words of all the false documents and preaching he counters). That is literally the entire point of Irenaeus' book, *Demonstration of the Apostolic Preaching*: he is telling his readers that the words of the Book of Baruch are what the Apostles preached. He is not providing a canon list declaring that "Jeremiah" is canon and whatever is labeled "Jeremiah saith" is to be accepted as canon.

There were many other fake Books,[249] including several claiming to be by Baruch, which moderns call 2 Baruch, 3 Baruch, and 4 Baruch.[250] There were also fake Books claiming to be from Jeremiah, such as the Ethiopic Lamentations of Jeremiah.[251] Irenaeus did not accept any of them because "Jeremiah saith," he accepted this particular one because (he says) this one was part of the Apostolic preaching he had learned. He says this as part of warning his own disciples against all the false teaching that was being offered, including false books of "Jeremiah saith" and "Baruch saith."

Nor is Irenaeus confused about who wrote the Book of Baruch and the Book of Jeremiah. Having read both Books, he undoubtedly knew full well (and better than many who just throw this claim out there) that Baruch wrote both of them. Jeremiah may have written nothing at all. He dictated parts (not

---

[248] Baruch 1:1 ("And these are the words of the book, which Baruch ... wrote in Babylon") forms the foundation for the statement in 4:1 that Irenaeus quotes ("This is the book of the commandments of God, and of the law which endureth for ever. All they that hold it fast (are appointed) to life: but such as leave it shall die").

[249] "Fake books" from the perspective of Catholics and Protestants. The Orthodox say otherwise on some of these, and I mean no disparagement to their claims.

[250] wikipedia.org/wiki/2_Baruch, wikipedia.org/wiki/3_Baruch, wikipedia.org/wiki/4_Baruch

[251] wikipedia.org/wiki/Rest_of_the_Words_of_Baruch

all) of the Book of Jeremiah to Baruch, who wrote it down while also writing all the rest of the Book of Jeremiah—and all of it is Scripture, not just the parts Jeremiah dictated.[252]

The Book of Baruch is not "fake Jeremiah"—it is either an honest Book of Baruch or a fake Book of Baruch. That the ancients thought Jeremiah was the one speaking in the Book of Baruch is not really the story; the story is that the ancients knew that the writer of the Book of Jeremiah was Baruch. And the Book of Baruch says in its very first verse (1:1) that "these are the words of the book, which Baruch the son of Nerias ... wrote in Babylon..." The Book of Baruch never even mentions Jeremiah at all.[253]

Origen will later separate the Book of Baruch from the Book of Jeremiah, but he did not "expose the Book of Baruch as a fraud" or anything of the sort; he merely splits a collection of Books into some of its component pieces (exactly like splitting Lamentations from Jeremiah, Ruth from Judges, and Nehemiah from Ezra). After that, Origen calls Baruch a prophet; Athanasius (a successor of Origen's in Alexandria) specifically lists the Book of Baruch as canon by name, as does Cyril of Jerusalem; Epiphanius and the Apostolic Canons/Constitutions both specifically note that (some?) Jews accept the Book of Baruch as well as the Book of Jeremiah. Some Fathers, like Chrysostom, quote it as "Baruch in the book of Jeremiah..." Augustine says, "Some attribute this testimony not to Jeremiah, but to his secretary, who was called Baruch, but it is more commonly ascribed to Jeremiah."[254] At no point before Jerome does anyone claim that the Book of Baruch is not true or not Scripture.

This situation has other Biblical parallels: earlier, I quoted Jimmy Swaggart telling us Hebrews came from Paul and noted that Martin Luther told us it was from Apollos, but neither really cared. They had their opinions, and were no doubt attached to them, but not so attached that it makes any real difference to whether the actual Book is Scripture.

---

[252] E.g., see Jeremiah 51:64: "... and they shall be weary. Thus far are the words of Jeremiah." There is still another chapter of the Book of Jeremiah following the "thus far are the words of Jeremiah."

[253] The first mention of Jeremiah occurs in Baruch Chapter 6, which is actually not part of the Book of Baruch (at least as I am discussing it herein). It is the Epistle of Jeremiah, which Catholics add at the back of the original Book of Baruch as Chapter 6; but it is a separate work with its own history, although tied in many ways to Baruch, Lamentations, and Jeremiah.

[254] www.newadvent.org/fathers/04122.htm (Ch 3, 6), www.bible-researcher.com/athanasius.html, www.bible-researcher.com/cyril.html, www.bible-researcher.com/epiphanius.html, www.newadvent.org/fathers/07155.htm, www.newadvent.org/fathers/1910.htm

Jewish tradition claimed that Jeremiah was also the author of 1 and 2 Kings, though few believe that now, with no one claiming the books are not Scripture on that account. In fact, whether one person (that person being Baruch, not Jeremiah) actually wrote even the Book of Jeremiah is debated. Chapters 27-29 use different spellings of names, for example, implying multiple authors. The KJV changes some of the transliterations to match, so you can compare 27:6 (Nebuchadnezzar, the king of Babylon) to 25:1 (Nebuchadrezzar, king of Babylon). The NIB commentary says that even the spelling of "Jeremiah" changes (Overview 26:1, p. 768), but that change does not seem to transliterate in the KJV (at least that I could find).

Another rather notable comparable is Ezra/Nehemiah. This situation is far too confusing to go into detail herein, but consider that "Mid-16th century Reformed Protestant Bible translations produced in Geneva were the first to introduce the name 'Book of Nehemiah' for the text formerly called the 'Second Book of Ezra'."[255] Earlier citations to the Book of Nehemiah actually say Ezra/Esdras. Not infrequently, people confuse which of the two is writing (e.g., Nehemiah Chapters 8-10 are actually part of the "Ezra Memoir," and Ezra Chapter 10 changes from speaking in the first person to speaking in the third person). In addition, the attributions to the person Ezra are far from certain: "it is possible that Ezra was responsible for the final text. However ... a definitive answer to the question of the authorship of Ezra and Nehemiah cannot be given." (Apologetics Study Bible, introduction to Ezra). Moreover, there were many other books attributed to Ezra—some are still accepted by all Christians, even though few now believe Ezra wrote them (1 and 2 Chronicles); others are only accepted by Orthodox Churches, and others still are not accepted by anyone.

So it is that Cyprian, in his treatise *Ad Quirinum*, quotes as Scripture "In Ezra also: They have fallen away from You, and have cast Your law behind their backs, and have killed Your prophets which testified against them that they should return to You." The quote is now Nehemiah 9:26. Cyprian, too, "thought it was Ezra"—but the fact that we eventually decided to separate the Book of Nehemiah from the Book of Ezra does not alter what he said: the

---

[255] wikipedia.org/wiki/Book_of_Nehemiah. Previously, there had been two Books of Ezra, which before that were combined as the Book of Ezra, which before that was called the Second Book of Esdras because there is another Book of Esdras, which was meant when early Church Fathers cited to Esdras. The combined Book was/is also known as Ezra-Nehemiah, Esdras B, and 1 Ezra, but sometimes the parts are called 1 Esdras and 2 Esdras. wikipedia.org/wiki/Esdras.

words of the Book of Nehemiah were clearly Scripture to Cyprian and, clearly the point of what he was saying, not the label Ezra.

In fact, consider all the other references to Jeremiah made by Irenaeus in the same book, the Demonstration of the Apostolic Preaching:

Section	Quote	Notes
43	This Jeremiah the prophet also testified, saying thus: ...	The footnotes say that this is a "composite quotation from the Psalms, here attributed to Jeremiah." I believe it is taken from Psalm 110:3 plus 72:17 plus 33:6.
43	And again the same says: Blessed is he who was, before he became man	This quote does not seem to be anywhere in the Scriptures, although there is similar wording in the false Gospel of Thomas, Section 19: Jesus said, "Blessed is he who came into being before he came into being."[256]
68	And Jeremiah the prophet says the same, thus: ...	This is not a quote from the Book of Jeremiah; it is a quote from the Book of Lamentations 3:30. The ancients saw it as part of the Book called "Jeremiah"—exactly as they did with the Book of Baruch.
71	And in another place Jeremiah says: The Spirit of our face, the Lord Christ	Also Lamentations (4:20), not Jeremiah. This is something that had been previously cited by Justin Martyr (see next note), but Lamentations does not actually say this; it is a combination of the text and the interpretation of the text, presented as if it were a quote from the text.
78	And in Jeremiah He thus declares His death and descent into hell, saying:...	Footnote: "This is one of the prophecies which Justin [Martyr] declared the Jews had erased from their Scriptures (Dial. 72). It is quoted several times by Irenaeus [in his other book Against Heresy]: III, xxii. 1 (as from Isaiah); IV, xxxvi. 1 (as from Jeremiah, to whom Justin had attributed it); l. 1 (an allusion only); lv. 3 ("alii autem dicentes: Rememoratus . . . causam reddiderunt propter quam passus est hæc omnia"); V, xxxi. 1 (with variations, and no name of author)."
80	And again Jeremiah the prophet says: And they took the thirty pieces of silver, the price of him that was sold, whom they bought from the children of Israel; and they gave them for the potter's field, as the Lord commanded me.	A quote mostly from Zachariah 11:13 but attributed to Jeremiah.

---

[256] See www.marquette.edu/maqom/Gospel%20of%20Thomas%20Lambdin.pdf. The date range for the false Gospel of Thomas could be after Irenaeus (i.e., it might have taken the concept from him), it could be contemporaneous, or it could be earlier (but it seems unlikely that Irenaeus would be intentionally quoting from it, since he is the preacher of the Fourfold Gospel). In any event, regardless of where he got it, Irenaeus seems to be misattributing this to Jeremiah.

| 90 | even as Jeremiah prophesied: ... | Jeremiah 31:31-34. This language was cited repeatedly in the New Testament: Heb 8:8-12; Heb 10:16-17; Rom 11:26. |
| 97 | the quote from Baruch 3:29-4:1 | |

That is eight quotes from Jeremiah, but seven of them are not in the modern Book of Jeremiah. Three are definitely from someone who was not Jeremiah; one was allegedly erased from the Book of Jeremiah or the Book of Isaiah—Irenaeus is not consistent on which; two are included in what we now call Lamentations, which may not be correctly attributed to "Jeremiah;" the one under discussion is included in what we now call Baruch.

Two are found nowhere in the Scriptures anyone accepts today. Five quotes are in Books that some have considered to be part of the Book of Jeremiah. Only one is from what is still Jeremiah, two are from Lamentations (separated but considered canon), one is from Baruch (separated and considered canon by some and Apocrypha by others), and one was allegedly erased by the Jews before the time of Irenaeus.

The quotes from Lamentations are one short verse, then half of a longer verse. The only lengthy quotations are the one from the Book of Jeremiah (four verses out of the 1,364 verses of Jeremiah (0.3% of the book)), and the one from the Book of Baruch which is ten verses long (10 out of 140; the Catholic Book of Baruch is 213 verses, but 73 are from the Epistle of Jeremiah, a different book that is included with their version of the historical Book of Baruch) - 7.1% of the Book of Baruch is quoted by Irenaeus). Irenaeus quotes many more verses from Baruch than Jeremiah, and as a percentage of the books it is a landslide.

(In his other surviving work, Against Heresies, Irenaeus will also quote another 300 words from Baruch 4:36-5:9. That is the two final verses of Chapter 4 and every single word of Chapter 5, and makes a total of 500 words and 21 out of 140 verses that Irenaeus testifies to: 15.0% of the entire Book of Baruch. Recall that Kruger tells us Irenaeus "appeared" to cite a verse of 2 Peter and discusses the debate over whether he may have alluded to a verse of James. Vague possible mentions of a single verse from Irenaeus are crucial to the case for the New Testament, whereas Irenaeus quoted 500 words and 15% of the entire Book of Baruch as part of his Demonstration of the Apostolic Preaching and his fight Against Heresies.)

Irenaeus also wrote that it was Jeremiah who spoke the words of the Book of Psalms, the Book of Zechariah, the Book of Lamentations, the Book of Baruch, and possibly the Book of Isaiah—but that is not why he believed

Psalms, Zechariah, Lamentations, Baruch, and Isaiah are Scripture. He believed them to be Scripture because he believed them to be Apostolic preaching. In fact, the words of Zechariah that Irenaeus says were spoken by Jeremiah were inarguably what "the apostles delivered, and the Church in all the world hands on to her children" (the words Irenaeus used for Baruch). Inarguably, because Irenaeus is not actually quoting Jeremiah, he is actually quoting Matthew, who quotes Jeremiah. Matthew:

> Then was fulfilled that which was spoken by Jeremy the prophet, saying, And they took the thirty pieces of silver, the price of him that was valued, whom they of the children of Israel did value; And gave them for the potter's field, as the Lord appointed me. (27:9-10).

Here is the quote from Zechariah (11:9-13):

> And I took my staff ... If ye think good, give me my price; and if not, forbear. So they weighed for my price thirty pieces of silver. And the LORD said unto me, Cast it unto the potter: a goodly price that I was prised at of them. And I took the thirty pieces of silver, and cast them to the potter in the house of the LORD.

So, that is the sale of a staff with proceeds cast to the potter, and there is no field involved, but it is 30 pieces of silver. Here is the quote from Jeremiah that seems to also be involved:

> And Jeremiah said, The word of the LORD came unto me, saying, Behold, Hanameel the son of Shallum thine uncle shall come unto thee, saying, Buy thee my field that is in Anathoth: for the right of redemption is thine to buy it. ... And I bought the field of Hanameel my uncle's son, that was in Anathoth, and weighed him the money, even seventeen shekels of silver. (32:8-9).

That is a field, no potter, and 17 shekels, not 30 pieces of silver. In the Gospel to the Jews (many of whom were former Jewish Priests), Matthew cites to the name Jeremiah while quoting Zechariah. See, e.g., David Limbaugh's *The Emmaus Code*, p. 324, which evaluates it as the fulfillment of a prophecy from Zechariah—without even mentioning that Matthew actually said that it was from Jeremiah.

How is this explained? From Gleason L. Archer and *The Encyclopedia of Bible Difficulties*:

> ... since Jeremiah is the more prominent of the two prophets, he mentions Jeremiah's name by preference to that of the minor prophet. ... Since that was the normal literary practice of the first century A.D., when the Gospels were written, the authors can scarcely be faulted for not following the modern practice of precise identification and

footnoting (which could never have become feasible until after the transition had been made from the scroll to the codex and the invention of the printing press).

Jeremiah was, of course, also more prominent than Baruch his scribe, and people already included the Book of Baruch as part of the Book of Jeremiah. Perhaps that explains why Irenaeus "mentions Jeremiah's name by preference to that of the minor prophet."

R.C.H. Lenski gives us a different possible explanation:

> ... One of the older ways of dividing the Scriptures was to begin with the law and to call this part "The Law." Next the section commencing with the Psalms was called "The Psalms" although it contained other writings. The third part began with Jeremiah and included all the other prophets, and yet the whole was called "Jeremiah." Lightfoot cites the Baba Bathra and Rabbi David Kimchi's Preface to the prophet Jeremiah as his authorities. Horn, Introduction, 7th ed. II, 290. Thus any passage taken from this third section of the Old Testament would be quoted as coming from "Jeremiah."

Lenski and Lightfoot give us evidence that any other prophet at all—let alone Baruch, his scribe and the one he was indeed partnered with in actual fact—could sometimes be referred to as Jeremiah. Human nature would, then, say that Jeremiah was the "lazy" answer, used by someone who for whatever reason is not looking it up to be certain—just say Jeremiah and move on. That might also explain Irenaeus' references to the Psalms, Isaiah, and the parallel found in the Gospel of Thomas. It did not really matter who exactly said it, or even where—just say Jeremiah and move on.

In addition, consider Lamentations, once attached to Jeremiah and quoted as "Jeremiah saith," as well. The Hebrew/Masoretic text of Lamentations does not name any author; it is the later Greek Septuagint translation that adds an interpretive opening line claiming Jeremiah as the author.[257] But (1) the author of Lamentations writes as an eyewitness in Jerusalem following its destruction by the Babylonians, when Jeremiah was never in the city of Jerusalem after it was destroyed, (2) the first four chapters are four poems whose lines begin with the letters of the Hebrew alphabet, yet they differ in the order of the letters (most likely indicating different authors; it is thought that two different

---

[257] Note also that the Greek translation of the Book of Jeremiah and the Greek translation of Baruch 1:1-3:8 show that they were translated from Hebrew into Greek by the same person and were, thus, on the same scroll—and the Septuagint sometimes has the Books in the order of Jeremiah, then Baruch, then Lamentations (per the NIB, Introduction to Lamentations, p. 1016), which is mighty odd if (as some claim) the Jews never accepted Baruch as Scripture.

sequences were used by the Jews, but that means used by different groups of people, not used by the same person); and (3) "many positions in Lamentations appear to contradict Jeremiah's prophecies."[258]

The NIB explains all this:

> Jeremiah is the author of Lamentations in a symbolic sense but probably not in a literal sense. Authorship in the ancient world did not follow modern customs. In order to bring books under the aura of heroes and their moral authority, writings were often ascribed to them. (Intro to Lam.)

The point is this: exactly why Irenaeus refers to the Book of Baruch as "Jeremiah saith" can be debated, as with Lamentations, Psalms, Zachariah, Isaiah, etc., and it can be explained in many different ways. But what is inarguable is that the reasons Irenaeus himself states for believing that the Book of Baruch is authentic Scripture is that "This, beloved, is the preaching of the truth, ... which the prophets proclaimed, and Christ established, and the apostles delivered, and the Church in all the world hands on to her children." That is the part that matters, not the attribution to Jeremiah.

The idea that "Irenaeus just thought Baruch was part of Jeremiah" sounds like an answer, but it is simply not good enough in the case for Christianity. Irenaeus shows no sign of basing his beliefs (or asking his audience to base their beliefs) on the actual identity of the author or the name of the book. To the contrary, he expressly says that the 200 words that "Jeremiah saith" are Apostolic teaching – something he himself was taught, and that his teacher said came direct from the Apostles (presumably John). That is exactly the point he is making in his Demonstration of the Apostolic Preaching.

Chain of Custody

Either what Irenaeus said is true, or it is not. If not, who exactly introduced this allegedly false Scripture into Christianity? Or, put another way, how does Irenaeus come to claim that Baruch is Apostolic teaching, when (for the sake of argument) the Jews, Jesus, and the Apostles did not preach it as true Scripture? By the time of Irenaeus, it has already arrived as "fake" Apostolic

---

[258] New Interpreter's Bible, Introduction to Lamentations, p. 1016, citing Delbert Hillers, *Lamentations*, AB 7A (Garden City, N.I.: Doubleday, 1972) xxi-xxii. I repeat (3) because they say it, but of course, such claims are no more than someone's opinion.

preaching—Baruch was now, for the first time, being promoted as if it were Apostolic preaching when it was not.

There are five links in the Baruch chain, and only five links: the Jews to Jesus to John to Polycarp to Irenaeus. There are no other links, and thus, no other possible suspects:

THE JEWS -> JESUS -> JOHN -> POLYCARP -> IRENAEUS

The Jews? The entire argument is over the claim that Baruch is not Scripture because it was not considered Scripture by the Jews. So, for purposes of the question, the Jews could not have thought Baruch was Scripture.

Jesus? That would be even more nonsensical.

Was it John (when not being Divinely inspired, of course)? John was the Beloved Disciple, a Jew himself, "known unto the High Priest" (John 18:16), and the Evangelist who wrote five books of Scripture. In reality, John is almost as nonsensical a suspect as Jesus, at least if Christianity is true (John 21:24: "This is the disciple which testifieth of these things, and wrote these things: and we know that his testimony is true."). Still, let us imagine the almost unimaginable. Even if we assume some bizarre motivation to add an existing book that was not Scripture to the authentic Jewish Scriptures (rather than just write whatever he wanted in his own new Scriptures), it is difficult to imagine he could do this, just as a matter of mechanics. While we could assume he does it after the other Apostles have died, there would still be all the Jews who had converted, among whom were many Priests, which would seem to make it impossible to "quietly" introduce Baruch as Scripture to people who had been taught it was not part of the (allegedly) certain 22 Book canon.

Or was it Polycarp, "O Polycarp, most blessed in God" (as he is addressed in the Epistle of Ignatius to Polycarp, shortly before Ignatius (a fellow disciple of John's) was martyred)?[259] Polycarp learned at the feet of John, "appears to know both 1 John and 2 John," and authenticates multiple Books of the Bible alleged to be from John and others. He may have received the letter to Smyrna in the Book of Revelation and was thought to be the last alive to have known an Apostle personally. Polycarp was taught from the Old Testament—meaning only Jeremiah, not Baruch(?)—while sitting at the feet of John with all the other students, including all those former Priests and converted Jews. And yet

---

[259] www.newadvent.org/fathers/0110.htm, ch. 7.

Polycarp would have listened to all that teaching and still decided later to add Baruch by his own initiative.

Polycarp is the second Christian whose martyrdom we have a genuine written account of (the first was Stephen). He would have ignored the words of the Letter to Smyrna (Revelation 2:10: "be thou faithful unto death, and I will give thee a crown of life"), and then been unfaithful to the teaching of John and the authentic Scriptures, all in order to start preaching Baruch.

There were, indeed, false preachers at this time, so it is not unimaginable. Still, the timing would be difficult—e.g., Kruger says that "Campenhausen's well-known claim that the Pastoral Epistles derive from the time of Polycarp has not been widely accepted and places the letters too late to be so readily received by Irenaeus and the Muratorian fragment just a short time later."[260] But actually, the timing means it might have to be Polycarp. Fathers who were not disciples of Polycarp's will be quoting Baruch at the same time as Irenaeus, and in far-off geographies. Somehow, that spread occurs before we have written record of it.

If it was Polycarp, he took the authentic teaching of John and added Baruch to the Scriptures (and perhaps also Tobit, which he himself references in the one single writing of his that we have,[261] and 2 Maccabees if his recorded last words are correct[262]). It is hard to say more about Polycarp, however, because Baruch is not cited in his own writing. So, while it might have been him, I will mostly focus on Irenaeus. If we decide it was not Irenaeus who did it, then Polycarp is implicated by process of elimination and is, then, virtually certain to be the one who defrauded Christianity by introducing this fake Apostolic teaching.

---

[260] Kruger cites to: "(H. von Campenhausen, *The Formation of the Christian Bible* [London: A&C Black, 19721, 181). See critiques of Campenhausen in L. T. Johnson, The First and Second Letters to Timothy (New York: Doubleday, 2001), 85; and Kümmel, Introduction to the New Testament, 386-87."

[261] The one writing that I personally accept as Polycarp's, anyway. Others have other ideas: "Some scholars attribute the pastoral epistles—the biblical Books 1 Timothy, 2 Timothy, and the Epistle to Titus—to Polycarp." wikipedia.org/wiki/Polycarp.

[262] According to the Martyrdom of Polycarp (www.newadvent.org/fathers/0102.htm, Chapter 11), his last words before being sentenced to death include, "You threaten me with fire which burns for an hour, and after a little is extinguished, but are ignorant of the fire of the coming judgment and of eternal punishment, reserved for the ungodly. But why do you tarry?..." which may be an allusion to the last words of the last of the seven sons in 2 Maccabees 7:30: "Whom wait ye for? I will not obey the king's commandment: but I will obey the commandment of the law that was given unto our fathers by Moses."

If not for the timing of the simultaneous citations, then the obvious suspect would be Irenaeus, who learned from Polycarp ("I could tell you the place where the blessed Polycarp sat to preach the Word of God. ... I seem to hear him now relate how he conversed with John and many others who had seen Jesus Christ, the words he had heard from their mouths"). He is of course the one who provides the pre-eminent testimony that the Fourfold Gospel is authentic Apostolic teaching; and he was the first to authenticate the Epistles of James, 1 John, 2 John, and others, all on the basis of what he claimed he had been taught directly from Polycarp.

But there are only five links in the chain, and it must be one of them.

The Teachings of Each Link in the Chain

THE JEWS -> JESUS -> JOHN -> POLYCARP -> IRENAEUS

Let's go over the chain again, focusing now on the teachings of each link. John says in his Gospel that "And the Word was made flesh, and dwelt among us ..." John 1:14. The KJV cross-references John 1:14 and Baruch 3:37. So, John himself may have actually been alluding to the section of Baruch quoted by Irenaeus, per the KJV.

John's first Epistle says that: "every spirit that confesseth not that Jesus Christ is come in the flesh is not of God: and this is that spirit of antichrist..." (1 John 4:3). Thus, John's first Epistle stresses the point John made in his Gospel at verse 1:14 (the verse that may allude to Baruch) and says that anyone who denies it is the antichrist. 1 John is the Epistle that "advises Christians on how to discern true teachers."[263] It says that "... even now are there many antichrists... They went out from us, but they were not of us" (2:19). I.e., the antichrists are teachers who do not teach that the Word/Jesus came in the flesh. In other words, the antichrists are those who do not teach the teaching of John 1:14—the verse that may allude to Baruch, per the KJV.

The entire focus of the Epistle is distinguishing authentic Apostolic preaching from the false teaching, on exactly the point that Irenaeus is discussing. So, how to distinguish the true from the false? "Let that therefore abide in you, which ye have heard from the beginning. If that which ye have heard from the beginning shall remain in you, ye also shall continue in the

---

[263] wikipedia.org/wiki/First_Epistle_of_John

Son, and in the Father." (2:24). "We are of God: he that knoweth God heareth us; he that is not of God heareth not us. Hereby know we the spirit of truth, and the spirit of error." (4:6). "If there come any unto you, and bring not this doctrine, receive him not into your house, neither bid him God speed." (2:10).

John's second Epistle says that "…many deceivers are entered into the world, who confess not that Jesus Christ is come in the flesh. This is a deceiver and an antichrist." (2 John 7). John doubles down on the concept, saying exactly the same thing in his second Epistle as in his first.

1 John and 2 John are the Epistles that Polycarp "appears to know," according to Kruger. Thus, the Epistles were (in part) communications from one link in our chain to another, from John the writer to Polycarp the reader. And Polycarp "appears to know" 1 John because he seems to quote it in Chapter 7 of his own Epistle:[264]

> For whosoever does not confess that Jesus Christ has come in the flesh, is antichrist; (1 John 4:3) …Wherefore, forsaking the vanity of many, and their false doctrines, let us return to the word which has been handed down to us from the beginning; …

Note that the quote by Polycarp could just as easily come from 2 John 7; it is hard to tell because it is really the same point made in 1 John, 2 John, and Polycarp's Epistle to the Philippians. All three make the same point using the same language (at a time when "same language" quotation is very rare). All three allude to John 1:14, which itself may allude to Baruch 3:37, per the KJV.

Baruch 3:37 ("Afterward did he shew himself upon earth, and conversed with men") is not just at the heart of the prophecy that Irenaeus quotes but is alluded to by Irenaeus on other occasions as well—just not as a formal citation/quotation. Against Heresies 4, 20, 4: "Wherefore the prophets, receiving the prophetic gift from the same Word, announced His advent according to the flesh... the Word of God foretelling from the beginning that God should be seen by men, and hold converse with them upon earth, should confer with them ..." (In 5.35.1 of the same work, he quotes almost 300 words from Baruch 4:36-5:9, including every word of Chapter 5.)[265]

Here, Irenaeus also provides the interpretation for this verse from Baruch, saying that it "…means the Son of God…He "appeared on earth and was conversant with men," mingling and mixing the Spirit of God the Father with

---

[264] www.newadvent.org/fathers/0136.htm
[265] www.newadvent.org/fathers/0103420.htm

the creature formed by God, that man might be "after the image and likeness of God."" Then, of course, he claims that "This, beloved, is the preaching of the truth, and this is the manner of our redemption, and this is the way of life, which the prophets proclaimed, and Christ established, and the apostles delivered..."

Irenaeus ends this "Demonstration of the Apostolic Preaching" with the note that "others again reject the coming of the Son of God and the dispensation of His incarnation, which the apostles delivered and the prophets declared beforehand... they accept not the Son and speak against the dispensation of His incarnation; or else they ... reject prophecy. And of all such must we beware, and shun their ways..."

We see that Irenaeus is saying the exact same thing as Polycarp and John. The issue in dispute flows from link to link to link; and also, the method of determining authentic doctrine (only that which goes back to original preaching is authentic) is the same for every person in the link.

In addition, the substance of the matter is inarguably something John stressed and taught repeatedly, since he does so in multiple Epistles. It is inarguably a point that Polycarp taught (since he, too, is teaching it in his Epistle), and we have clear indications that Polycarp's teaching "appears to know" the two Epistles of John that stress and teach this point, since he effectively quotes it from either or both of them.

The only development in the chain is that Baruch's prophecy now appears as the "prophetic forerunner" of this teaching. This occurs in Irenaeus' manual, written (see Section 1): "to show ... the preaching of the truth for the confirmation of your faith. We send you as it were a manual of essentials... So shall it be fruitful to your own salvation, and you shall put to shame all who inculcate falsehood..." This manual is, of course, a much longer document than the Epistles (to my eyes, it is about four times as long as all three Epistles (1 John, 2 John, and the Epistle from Polycarp) combined). It provides the fuller teaching if, indeed, Irenaeus can be trusted—so, the appearance of an additional element makes perfect sense.

Irenaeus has already quoted John's Gospel as New Testament proof of the point in question, in Section 94: "...He was made flesh and tabernacled with men; as also His disciple John says: And his Word was made flesh and dwelt among us." That is citing John 1:14, the verse that the KJV sees as a cross-reference to Baruch 3:37, and doing so three paragraphs before citing Baruch 3:37.

In fact, Irenaeus references John 1:14 nine separate times in this particular work, as part of this Demonstration of the Apostolic Preaching (per biblindex.org/citation_biblique/search he makes reference to it in sections 6, 12, 30, 31, 37, 39, 53, 92, 94). That is nine times that he references John 1:14 before he mentions this Old Testament precursor from Baruch. He mentions John 1:14, the verse that the KJV sees as a cross-reference to Baruch 3:37, in the beginning, the middle, and the end of this treatise on Apostolic Preaching.

The Question of Why?

The words quoted from Baruch are not actually all that notable—certainly not in the sense that one would be tempted to introduce a fake prophecy to prove that the Incarnation of Christ was foretold. There are many other prophecies that could be cited instead, such as Isaiah 9:6: "<u>For unto us a child is born</u>, unto us a son is given: and the government shall be upon his shoulder: and his name shall be called Wonderful, Counsellor, <u>The mighty God</u>, The everlasting Father, The Prince of Peace." David Limbaugh's *Emmaus Code* (p. 286) says that this is an "explicit" prophecy that "God would literally be born in human flesh and live with us."

Indeed, Irenaeus quotes Isaiah 9:6 in his Demonstration of Apostolic Preaching and discusses it over three paragraphs (54-56). Irenaeus had no need or motive to introduce a fake prophecy into the discussion and declare that it was what "Christ established, and the apostles delivered, and the Church in all the world hands on to her children."

Irenaeus had been taught that the Incarnation had fulfilled prophecies, and the original teachings of true prophecies must have been working just fine (in fact, we are often told how explosive the growth of early Christianity was).[266]

---

[266] E.g.: "We are but of yesterday, and we have filled every place among you — cities, islands, fortresses, towns, market-places, the very camp, tribes, companies, palace, senate, forum — we have left nothing to you but the temples of your gods. ... For now it is the immense number of Christians which makes your enemies so few — almost all the inhabitants of your various cities being followers of Christ..." (Tertullian's Apology, Chapter 37 (197 A.D). www.newadvent .org/fathers/0301.htm); "... consider how in the space of a short time the Word of God has run through all the world that was possessed of false beliefs, and has recalled it to the knowledge of the true faith..." (Origen Commentary on the Song of Songs, Book 3, 11 (240 AD). Not available online.); "... the Roman Senate, and the princes of the time, and the soldiery, and the people, and the relatives of those who had become converts to the faith, made war upon [Christianity], and would have prevented (its progress), overcoming it by a confederacy of so powerful a nature, had

And bear in mind that this false teaching would be easily disproven. Irenaeus is literally daring a reader to go ask the Churches and verify the facts:

> Polycarp …always taught the things which he had learned from the apostles, and which the Church has handed down, and which alone are true. To these things all the Asiatic Churches testify, as do also those men who have succeeded Polycarp down to the present time…[267]

From Wikipedia:

> [Irenaeus] offered three pillars of orthodoxy: the scriptures, the tradition said to be handed down from the apostles, and the teaching of the apostles' successors. … In his writing against the Gnostics, who claimed to possess a secret oral tradition from Jesus himself, Irenaeus claimed that the bishops in different cities are known as far back as the Apostles and that the oral tradition he lists from the Apostles is a safe guide to the interpretation of Scripture. … Irenaeus's point … was that all of the Apostolic churches had preserved the same traditions and teachings in many independent streams. It was the unanimous agreement between these many independent streams of transmission that proved the orthodox faith, current in those churches, to be true.[268]

Polycarp's death was not that long beforehand (155 AD, so 22-25ish years), so there would be others still alive who had also learned from Polycarp. In addition, disciples whose training "descended from" other Apostles were teaching all over the world. Irenaeus would risk everything by teaching this false Scripture that no Christian had ever been taught. It was not just the Jews who would object, because any authentic Christian would refute the lie. All had been taught to "return to the word which has been handed down to us from the beginning" (Polycarp), and "If there come any unto you, and bring not this doctrine, receive him not into your house..." (1 John 2:10).

Or Why Not, If It Was This Easy?

Or, at least, that is the way it would have happened, if the claims of Christians are true. Here we have a test case that shows how well all the safeguards actually worked. From "Is The New Testament Trustworthy?" by Darrell L. Bock, an essay in the Apologetics Study Bible:

---

it not, by the help of God, escaped the danger, and risen above it, so as (finally) to defeat the whole world in its conspiracy against it." (Origen Against Celsus 1.3 (248 AD)).

[267] www.newadvent.org/fathers/0103303.htm

[268] wikipedia.org/wiki/Irenaeus

> The NT is based on reliable sources carefully used and faithfully transmitted. ... The texts surrounding Jesus stress the role of eyewitnesses as the root of the tradition (see Lk 1:2). An apostolic association ensured the account's credibility. The distance between event and recording is not great-less than a lifetime, a small distance of time by ancient standards. ... Judaism depended on the ability to pass things on with care from one generation to the next, recounting events with care. ... Judaism, and the Christianity that grew out of it, was a culture of memory...

If any of that is actually true, and Baruch is not authentic Apostolic teaching, then we should have evidence of criticism against Irenaeus for introducing the false Scripture. Not only is there no record of any challenge (or even questions), but to the contrary, we know that Athenagoras (over in Alexandria) also quotes the words of Baruch 3:35 ("The Lord is our God; no other can be compared with Him") as the words of a prophet in his letter to the Roman Emperor Marcus Aurelius in 177 AD.[269] That is a citation to some of the exact same words Irenaeus is citing to—at almost the exact same time.

A few years later, Clement of Alexandria, in his treatise *The Instructor,* quotes three different sections of Baruch as Jeremiah.[270] The three verses come from the same chapters (3 and 4) that Irenaeus and Athenagoras cite. That is three Fathers, roughly contemporaneous, all evidencing that Baruch had been taught as Scripture—and especially this part of Baruch.

Recall that Gallagher and Meade told us that:

> the second century was the decisive time for the formation of the fourfold Gospel ... The end of the century witnessed the solidification of the fourfold Gospel in the writings of Irenaeus, followed not long after by less enthusiastic but no less definitive testimony from Clement of Alexandria, Tertullian, and Origen. (p. 39).

---

[269] See www.newadvent.org/fathers/0205.htm Chapter 9: "the voices of the prophets confirm our arguments... the writings either of Moses or of Isaiah and Jeremiah, and the other prophets, ... what, then, do these men say? The Lord is our God; no other can be compared with Him." FYI, the KJV of Baruch 3:35 is "This is our God, and there shall none other be accounted of in comparison of him"—which seems like the exact word for word quote to me.

Perhaps the issue that quibblers see with that as a full citation may be that it does not precisely state that the line is taken from Jeremiah. Otherwise, I cannot see why it does not qualify as a solid citation and show up in biblindex.org/citation_biblique/search, or Skarsaune/Gallagher and Meade. Note also that I am not sure how certain the date is for Athenagoras; Irenaeus cites to Baruch in the other work of his we still have (*Against Heresies*), which also gets a date of 177. The Demonstration of Apostolic Preaching comes a few years later; the common guess is 180 AD.

[270] www.newadvent.org/fathers/02091.htm, Chapter 10.

Irenaeus, Clement, and Origen cited Baruch as Scripture. Tertullian made an allusion. In fact, as far as we have evidence, Baruch was universally accepted—unlike the Fourfold Gospel. The three second century Fathers cite to Baruch when fighting heresy (Irenaeus), when pleading for justice from the Roman Emperor (Athenagoras), and when creating a manual for living as a Christian (Clement). The early date, contemporaneous timing, geographical spread, and crucial doctrinal context of all these references point to a practice that extends back in time to the Apostles.

Or not. But if not, then such indicia of credibility have been proven to fail within the early Church, and those indicia are what support the alleged authenticity of the Fourfold Gospel and much else.

In addition, it is also time to stop kidding ourselves about "mere" citation evidence. Starting in the second century, there is not just the widespread "citation" to Baruch—there is widespread preaching of Baruch. Baruch 3:36-38 was preached as a Prophecy, as Scripture, as handed down by the Apostles, and as fulfilled by Christ, and it was so taught by all the Churches in all the world. It was not cited in some esoteric or academic manner; it was preached, just as Irenaeus preached it in the Demonstration of the Apostolic Preaching.

Not only is there no record whatsoever of anyone objecting to Baruch before Jerome, but to the contrary, there is an astonishingly full and voluminous record of its consistent and repetitive preaching. Baruch was preached by Epiphanius, Eusebius, Athanasius, Cyril of Jerusalem, Gregory of Nazianzus, Hilary of Poitiers, Rufinus, and Origen. That is eight of Kruger's ten Fathers, all preaching the same preaching as Irenaeus. Missing are Melito (as always, since we have little of Melito's writings) and Jerome.

Otherwise, eight of Kruger's ten Fathers expressly declare that particular verse from the Book of Baruch to be Prophecy, Scripture, the Word of God, etc.—just as did Irenaeus.[271] They preach it as fulfilled by Jesus Christ and as a reason—frankly, not infrequently as *the* reason—to believe in Christ. We can have confidence that Jesus Christ is truly Divine because His coming was foretold. Who foretold His coming? According to Irenaeus and the early Church, it was Baruch. When the early Church claimed that God fulfilled the prophecies and became man, they cited to Baruch.

In the entire history of the early Church, Isaiah 9:6 ("For unto us a child is born ... The mighty God"—the verse that David Limbaugh's Emmaus Code

---

[271] Whereas three of those ten left the Book of Esther off their Old Testament canon lists.

(p. 286) says is an "explicit" prophecy that "God would literally be born in human flesh and live with us") was cited only 58 times. Baruch 3:36-38 was cited 158 times (per biblindex.org/citation_biblique/search—three times as often, per the same data set) and essentially always as Prophecy, Scripture, etc.

Wednesdayintheword.com/jeremiah-in-the-new-testament/ provides a list of every quote/allusion to Jeremiah in the New Testament. Here is a chart noting the number of times early Church Fathers cited to all the passages of Jeremiah that are quoted/alluded to in the New Testament:

Jeremiah	New Testament	Cites
Jer 5:21	Mark 8:18	7
Jer 6:16	Matt 11:29	30
Jer 7:11	Matt 21:13; Mark 11:17; Luke 19:46	9
Jer 9:23-24	1Co 1:31; 2Co 10:17	42
Jer 10:7	Rev 15:3-4	5
Jer 12:3	Jas 5:5	5
Jer 12:15	Acts 15:16	4
Jer 22:24	Rom 14:11	20
Jer 31:15	Matt 2:18	18
Jer 31:31-34[272]	Heb 8:8-12; Heb 10:16-17; Rom 11:26	214

All or part of the passage from Baruch quoted by Irenaeus (Baruch 3:28-4:1) is cited by Fathers 188 times, more than nine of the 10 prophecies from the Book of Jeremiah combined. Those other prophecies are quoted in the New Testament—which certainly certifies them as being of crucial importance to authentic Apostolic preaching—but the prophecy of Baruch was preached vastly more often by the early Church.

The lead-in to Matthew 2:18 (i.e., 2:17) says, "Then was fulfilled that which was spoken by Jeremy the prophet"—so Matthew 2:18 is expressly declaring Jeremiah 31:15 to be authentic Prophecy spoken by Jeremiah and fulfilled by Jesus Christ. And the early Church preached the fulfillment of the Prophecy of Baruch quoted by Irenaeus more than 10 times as often as it preached the fulfillment of Jeremiah 31:15.

In fact, Jeremiah is quoted by name twice in the New Testament, each time as giving a Prophecy fulfilled by Christ. The other named citation is in Matthew 27:9-10, which (as discussed above) says Jeremiah is the prophet

---

[272] "Behold, days are coming," declares the Lord, "when I will make a new covenant with the house of Israel ... I will put My law within them and on their heart I will write it; and I will be their God, and they shall be My people..." It is the longest passage of the Old Testament quoted in the New (Hebrews 8:8-12).

being quoted but, then, quotes mostly from Zechariah. So, it could be seen as referencing both Jeremiah 32:6-9 and Zechariah 11:12-13 (per the Apologetics Study Bible). I presume it is not included on the website's list for that reason. Regardless, Jeremiah 32:6-9 was cited 15 times (and Zechariah 11:12-13 59 times).[273]

The alleged safeguards that work to ensure Apostolicity not only would have failed, but they would have failed spectacularly.

The Importance of Irenaeus and His Pre-Eminent Testimony

In the end, we either have a chain of custody we can trust, or we do not. And it is from this chain (Jesus to John to Polycarp to Irenaeus) that we first receive the Gospels, plural—not just one Gospel, but all four, and not any of the other false Gospels that existed:

> Before Irenaeus, Christians differed as to which gospel they preferred. The Christians of Asia Minor preferred the Gospel of John. The Gospel of Matthew was the most popular overall. ... Irenaeus acknowledged that many heterodox Christians used only one gospel and that some use more than four.[274]
>
> ...Irenaeus asserted that all four of the Gospels, John, Luke, Matthew, and Mark ... were canonical scripture. Thus Irenaeus provides the earliest witness to the assertion of the four canonical Gospels, possibly in reaction to Marcion's edited version of the Gospel of Luke, which Marcion asserted was the one and only true gospel.[275]

Irenaeus is the true key to the canon. He provides the crucial link for the Apostolicity of the Gospel of John:

---

[273] I refer to all the verses cited by Irenaeus for simplicity's sake, but actually, Baruch 4:1 is only cited by Theodoret (in a line-by-line commentary that commented on almost every verse of the Book), and Baruch 3:28-3:34 are cited by four Fathers: Eusebius, Didymus, Methodius, and Theodoret again. In other words, seven of the 10 verses Irenaeus quotes from Baruch are almost uncited, and the "usual three verses" of Baruch are what is really quoted by those who came after Irenaeus—and they are essentially always quoted for the purpose of preaching Baruch as Prophecy fulfilled by Christ.

[274] E.g., "For the Ebionites, who use Matthew's Gospel only... Marcion, mutilating that according to Luke, ... Those, again, who separate Jesus from Christ... preferring the Gospel by Mark, ...Those, moreover, who follow Valentinus, making copious use of that according to John..." *Against Heresies*, III 11, 7-8 www.newadvent.org/fathers/0103311.htm.

[275] wikipedia.org/wiki/Irenaeus. Note, incidentally, that the version of Jeremiah with Baruch was essentially the "long form" of Jeremiah, and it is Irenaeus who gives us the pre-eminent testimony that the long forms of both Luke and Jeremiah are the true versions.

Early Christian tradition, first found in Irenaeus (c. 130 – c. 202 AD), identified this disciple with John the Apostle, but most scholars have abandoned this hypothesis or hold it only tenuously; there are multiple reasons for this conclusion, including, for example, the fact that the gospel is written in good Greek and displays sophisticated theology, and is therefore unlikely to have been the work of a simple fisherman.[276]

Not all believed Irenaeus, however:

Marcion … is said to have rejected all other gospels, including those of Matthew, Mark and especially John, which he alleged had been forged by Irenaeus.[277]

The conclusion that the Gospel of John was not forged, that it is truly and authentically Apostolic, depends on the "pre-eminent" testimony of Irenaeus, in the words of Gallagher and Meade.[278] Consider all the inconsistencies between Gospels, and especially those between John and the other three Gospels (the Synoptic Gospels, which have more in common with each other and less in common with John). Craig L. Blomberg, the Historical Reliability of the Gospels:

The conviction that apostles or close associates of the apostles penned the four Gospels already in the first century led Christians throughout most of church history to believe

---

[276] wikipedia.org/wiki/Gospel_of_John. But John was not a simple fisherman, he is the son of a man who owned a fishing business (Mark 1:19-20). James and John (and presumably their father) were partners with Simon Peter (Luke 5:10), and presumably Andrew; they also employ servants (Mark 1:20). Boats needed 5 to 16 men, and sometimes two boats were needed to handle the nets. This was not a small operation, even if it was only a few boats (and we do not know that; it could have been many). John is also known unto the high priest (John 18:15-16), including the damsel that kept the door, presumably because he was the one who supplied them with fish—a lucrative gig. The Bible also notes that he was a spoiled momma's boy—momma literally begged in order to advance John's career (Matthew 20:20-21: Then came to him the mother of Zebedee's children with her sons, worshipping him, and desiring a certain thing of him…). The idea that such a family arranged for John to be tutored in Greek is not nearly as inconceivable as skeptics contend.

Note, however, that I have proved my point by using Matthew, Mark, Luke, and John: the Fourfold Gospel, four Books that interconnect and supplement each other. Allegedly.

I am also leaving out many other possible explanations for the evangelists' perfect Greek, such as that their linguistic skills derived from Pentecost (Acts 2:8: And how hear we every man in our own tongue, wherein we were born?). Of course, a skeptic like Ehrman would never accept that explanation, in part because he believes Acts was just a forgery, authenticated by Irenaeus—who, among other things, is the Father who first named the Book of Acts.

[277] wikipedia.org/wiki/Gospel#Canonical_gospels

[278] In fact, Kruger's entire thesis for why we can trust the New Testament is based on John 10:27: "Jesus's statement that "my sheep hear my voice... and they follow me" (John 10:27) is not evidence for the authority of the sheep's decision to follow, but evidence for the authority and efficacy of the Shepherd's voice to call." The problem, of course, is that the sheep accepted Baruch, says Irenaeus, who was taught by Polycarp, who was taught by John, who was taught by the Shepherd Himself.

that they recorded historically reliable as well as theologically authoritative material. Thus they regularly attempted to reconcile apparent contradictions, confident that plausible solutions would emerge.[279]

Recall that CARM rejects Baruch as Apocrypha, and thus showed us what happens when one does not reconcile seeming conflicts.[280] But because CARM accepts the Fourfold Gospel, they (like all Christians) reconcile when the text in seeming conflict is the Gospel of John. In other situations, the inability of multiple alleged witnesses to get basic facts straight is a sign that they were not really there, and things did not happen the way they say.[281]

In essence, evidence of Apostolicity for the Gospel of John (based in substantial part on the pre-eminent testimony of Irenaeus) is held to be so trustworthy that it overrides the potential inconsistencies that could otherwise be used as a basis to "prove" that the Gospel of John is inauthentic. But in the case for Christianity, the question would be why a judge would trust the pre-eminent testimony of Irenaeus regarding the Gospel of John being authentic Apostolic teaching, when the Christian admits that Irenaeus gave false testimony about Baruch being Apostolic teaching.

But it is not just the Gospel of John, either. Irenaeus is really at the heart of it all. It was Irenaeus who first said that the longer form of Luke's Gospel (not the shorter form then promoted by Marcion) and the Book of Acts (which Irenaeus is the first to name) are authentic, descend from a disciple of an Apostle, and are, thus, true Scripture. Of course, not all believe him:

> According to a Church tradition beginning with Irenaeus (c. 130 – c. 202 AD) he was the Luke named as a companion of Paul in three of the Pauline letters, but "a critical consensus emphasizes the countless contradictions between the account in Acts and the authentic Pauline letters"... he does not represent Paul's views accurately. ... Luke-Acts contains differences in theology and historical narrative which are irreconcilable[282] with the authentic letters of Paul the Apostle. ... The eclipse of the traditional attribution to Luke the companion of Paul has meant that an early date for the gospel is now rarely put forward.[283]
>
> According to Bart D. Ehrman, the "we" passages are written by someone falsely claiming to have been a travelling companion of Paul, in order to present the untrue

---

[279] InterVarsity Press 2007, p. 27-28.
[280] carm.org/roman-catholicism/errors-in-the-apocrypha/
[281] The plot of the Apocrypha Susanna, incidentally.
[282] Says who? Read the arguments from both sides, then decide for yourself whether they are actually irreconcilable.
[283] wikipedia.org/wiki/Gospel_of_Luke

idea that the author had firsthand knowledge of Paul's views and activities. Ehrman holds that The Acts of the Apostles is thereby shown to be a forgery.[284]

According to Marcion, Irenaeus forged the Gospel of John and falsely authenticated the "long form" of the Gospel of Luke; according to Ehrman, Irenaeus falsely attributed Acts to Luke. But do not forget Matthew either: Matthew is basically a copy of Mark, with "additions" having been made. Because of Irenaeus, we accept Matthew as authentic and supplementary to Mark, an entirely separate "witness," rather than as a fake, inauthentic "addition" to or "long form" of a copy of the "original Gospel, the true Gospel, that of Mark"—just as Irenaeus accepts Baruch as an authentic supplement to the Book of Jeremiah, rather than as an inauthentic "addition" to the version of Jeremiah that the Jews accept. Papias, one of Irenaeus' teachers, had earlier identified the Gospels of Matthew and Mark by name, but Irenaeus is, again, the crucial witness, because it is through him that the names get attached to the specific documents we possess. In fact, Ehrman claims that Papias' information does not match the documents we have.

Nor is Irenaeus only crucial for the Gospels, either, but for very nearly every single word of the New Testament. Acts is, in many ways, an apologetic for Paul, explaining to the unconvinced why a former oppressor who was not one of the original 12 became a valid Disciple. Irenaeus' pre-eminent testimony for Luke and Acts is thus crucial to proving that Paul was an authentic Apostle. There was a group called the Ebionites who denied this, and therefore, denied all of Paul's Epistles. But they were refuted by Irenaeus and

---

[284] wikipedia.org/wiki/Authorship_of_Luke-Acts (citing Ehrman's Book *Forged* (2011)). I just looked up something in connection with Ehrman's book and encountered a review that said, "I have no doubt that apologists are feverishly working on books rebutting Forged, just as they have with Ehrman's last two mass-market books. But I fail to see why anyone who can think for themselves would find those necessary." And that foolishness was the top review on the list, the one that got the most "up" votes.

I submit that the correct decision-making process is critical to making correct decisions, even for people who actually are as smart as the reviewer mistakenly thinks he is. Look at the evidence; then read the arguments for both sides (or all sides); then decide what is truth and what is not. Even for a $50 jaywalking ticket, you would be horrified to find that a Judge simply declared you guilty after the prosecutor finished speaking and refused to hear what you had to say—and yet people will risk the fate of their immortal soul by reading only the side they want to hear.

What I looked up, incidentally, was confirmation that Ehrman said what I had remembered Ehrman said. Wikipedia is wrong; that is the title of the book (and applies to some things (he claims), but not the Gospels and Acts. He actually specifically says that the Gospels and Acts are false attributions and not forgeries (p. 228). I.e., the man who wrote Acts did not write out a claim that he was Luke, and the writer of John never claimed to be John, etc. It was Irenaeus who claimed that they were Luke and John.

disappeared from history (only to be reborn in modern times, where there has been "a resurgence of Ebionitism, specifically the problem of Israeli Messianic leaders apostatizing from the belief in the divinity of Jesus").[285]

In fact, Ehrman's choice to attack Acts is probably no accident. A generation ago, J.P. Moreland (*Scaling the Secular City: A Defense of Christianity*) made:

> ...a strong case ... for dating Acts at 62 to 64. ... Luke should be dated just prior to that. Further, Matthew and Mark should be dated even earlier, perhaps from the mid-40s to mid-50s. The picture of Jesus presented in the Synoptics is one that is only twelve to twenty-nine years removed from the events themselves. And they incorporate sources which are even earlier. ...
>
> Six arguments, taken together, provide a powerful case for dating Acts at 62 to 64. First, Acts has no mention of the fall of Jerusalem in 70... [which] makes sense if Luke-Acts was written prior to the event itself. Second, no mention is made of Nero's persecutions in the mid-60s ... Third, the martyrdoms of James (61), Paul (64), and Peter (65) are not mentioned in Acts. ... Fourth, the subject matter of Acts deals with issues of importance prior to the fall of Jerusalem in 70. ... Fifth, several of the expressions in Acts are very early and primitive. ... Sixth, the Jewish war against the Romans (from 66 onward) is not mentioned in Acts. ...[286]

Of course, Ehrman has a very simple counterargument that simultaneously deals with all six of Moreland's arguments at once: Acts was not authentic; it was a fake that was wrongly authenticated by Irenaeus. A fake would not mention things that came later than the time period it purports to be from. If one were to fake a newspaper article set in the 1930s, one would carefully avoid mentioning World War II. It is the testimony of Irenaeus that counters Ehrman's speculation. Ehrman shows us what happens without Irenaeus' pre-eminent testimony:

> It is not difficult to see why orthodox writers like Irenaeus wanted to stress the point. ... The authority of a Gospel resided in the person of its author. ... it came to be seen as necessary to assign authors' names to the four Gospels that were being most widely used in orthodox circles, to differentiate them from the "false" Gospels used by heretics... It does not appear, however, that any of these books was written by an eyewitness to the life of Jesus or by companions of his two great apostles. For my purposes here it is enough to reemphasize that the books do not claim to be written by these people and early on they were not assumed to be written by these people. The authors of these books never speak in the first person (the First Gospel never says,

---

[285] wikipedia.org/wiki/Ebionites
[286] Baker Book 1993, p. 154, 152-3.

"One day, Jesus and I went to Jerusalem ..."). They never claim to be personally connected with any of the events they narrate or the persons about whom they tell their stories. The books are thoroughly, ineluctably, and invariably anonymous. At the same time, later Christians had very good reasons to assign the books to people who had not written them. As a result, the authors of these books are not themselves making false authorial claims. Later readers are making these claims about them. They are therefore not forgeries, but false attributions.[287]

That's the view of Irenaeus' importance from the skeptical side. From the Christian side, I quoted much of Kruger's analysis in pieces already, but here it is at length to make sure we all have the full context:

One of the most influential voices in the early church was Irenaeus, bishop of Lyons and disciple of Polycarp... Irenaeus's defense of the fourfold Gospel... appears to draw upon tradition that has been entrenched within the church for quite some time....Given that Irenaeus appears to have known Justin's works (and maybe Justin himself), and certainly knew Polycarp, it is possible that he received this tradition from them. ... [from Footnote 17:] Irenaeus also affirms that Polycarp knew Papias ... which suggests that he may also be a source of this fourfold Gospel tradition... (p. 228-229).

... debates would have encouraged critical thinking about these texts, deeper reflection on their content, and more vigorous historical investigation into their origins. Robert Grant argues that a number of early church fathers— Papias, Justin, Irenaeus, Clement of Alexandria, and others – were astute "literary critics" who carefully analyzed the literary merits and historical origins of canonical and noncanonical books... As a result, they took the task of distinguishing between canonical and apocryphal books very seriously, giving us reason for greater confidence in their final conclusions. (p. 201).

The above examples ... reveal that the early stages of the canon were not a wide-open affair where newly produced apocryphal literature could have easily found a welcome home, but were marked by concern to affirm only books from the apostolic time period. (p. 286).

In case anyone needs to hear it, Kruger also stresses the importance of the New Testament canon to the case for Christianity:

This book is about a very specific problem confronting the Christian faith. It is certainly not a new problem ... but is perhaps one of the oldest. ... It is what D. F. Strauss has called the "Achilles' heel of Protestant Christianity." It is what many still consider to be, as Herman Ridderbos has observed, the "hidden, dragging illness of the Church." It is the ... fundamental question of how we, as Christians, can know that we have the right twenty-seven books in our New Testament. ... Certainly, there can be no New Testament theology if there is no such thing as a New Testament in the first place. ... Unless a coherent response can be offered to such questions, then Strauss may be all

---

[287] *Forged*, p. 226-228

too right-the canon issue could become the single thread that unravels the entire garment of the Christian faith. (p. 15-16).

I completely agree, of course. And Kruger did a great job of showing all the evidence that supports the authenticity of the New Testament. But the Apocrypha are also part of this discussion. Either the absence of clear evidence in the first two centuries is devastating to the case for both the Apocrypha and the New Testament Books, or it is not. Either citations are valid and meaningful evidence of support, or they are not. Either the Fathers give solid and trustworthy testimony of what had been handed down by the Apostles, or they do not. And in particular, either Irenaeus can be trusted when he claims something is Apostolic preaching, or he cannot.

I also pulled three books off the top of a pile devoted to Christian Apologetics to see what they have to say about Irenaeus. *Evidence for Christianity*, by Josh McDowell (an update, of sorts, to his more famous *Evidence that Demands a Verdict*), states:

> Concerning the significance of Irenaeus (A.D. 180), F. F. Bruce writes "The importance of evidence lies in his [Irenaeus's] link with the apostolic age and in his ecumenical associations. ... His writings attest the canonical recognition of the fourfold Gospel and Acts, of Romans, 1 and 2 Corinthians, Galatians, Ephesians, Philippians, Colossians, 1 and 2 Thessalonians, 1 and 2 Timothy, and Titus, of 1 Peter and 1 John and of the Revelation..."[288]

That is 20 of the 27 books of the New Testament, some of which do not need Irenaeus' testimony as much as others. Still, he is important for all of them and is absolutely critical for many, including all four Gospels.

The second book up is *The Case for the Resurrection of Jesus* by Gary R. Habermas and Michael R. Licona: the index gives us five mentions of Irenaeus. The first is a quote from Irenaeus. The second follows the quote: "If Irenaeus and Tertullian are correct..." Big if. The third: "As with Clement, if Irenaeus and Tertullian are correct..." Big if. The fourth: "If Irenaeus is correct in claiming..." Big if. The fifth: "Hippolytus was a disciple of Irenaeus and a leader in the church of the late second and early third century..." Three "big ifs" and a reminder that Irenaeus influenced everyone who came after him, either for good or ill. (Clement and Hippolytus both cite to Baruch as Scripture, while Tertullian makes an allusion.)

---

[288] Thomas Nelson, Inc. 2006, p. 47.

The third book is Lee Strobel's *The Case for Christ*.[289] He mentions Irenaeus only once, in a discussion with Craig Blomberg, but it is worth quoting in full:

> Blomberg: "Then Irenaeus, writing about AD 180, confirmed the traditional authorship. In fact, here—," he said, reaching for a book. He flipped it open and read Irenaeus' words.
>
>> Matthew published his own Gospel among the Hebrews in their own tongue, when Peter and Paul were preaching the Gospel in Rome and founding the church there. After their departure, Mark, the disciple and interpreter of Peter, himself handed down to us in writing the substance of Peter's preaching. Luke, the follower of Paul, set down in a book the Gospel preached by his teacher. Then John, the disciple of the Lord, who also leaned on his breast, himself produced his Gospel while he was living at Ephesus in Asia.
>
> Strobel: I looked up from the notes I was taking. "OK, let me clarify this," I said. "If we can have confidence that the gospels were written by the disciples Matthew and John, by Mark, the companion of the disciple Peter, and by Luke, the historian, companion of Paul, and sort of a first-century journalist, we can be assured that the events they record are based on either direct or indirect eyewitness testimony." As I was speaking, Blomberg was mentally sifting my words. When I finished, he nodded.
>
> "Exactly," he said crisply.

Exactly, I say crisply. If we can have confidence. If, and only if. If, if, if. Christianity may not have four eyewitness accounts of the Resurrection. What it does have is one crucial man at the heart of it all, authenticating four separate alleged eyewitness accounts.

A chain is only as strong as its weakest link. Irenaeus is either a strong link or a weak link.

THE JEWS -> JESUS -> JOHN -> POLYCARP -> IRENAEUS

Irenaeus is either the pre-eminent testimony proving the teachings of the Apostles, or he is the pre-eminent testimony of just how easy it was for fraudulent Scripture to be introduced in the early Church.

The Skeptical Case Against Christianity

---

[289] Zondervan 2006, p. 35-36.

There are simple, easy explanations of how this happened—but only for the skeptic. Perhaps Irenaeus was only lying about Baruch, or was just a fool, or made a mistake (and Irenaeus made plenty of mistakes). But first off, this would consist of more than a false number or name or detail. Irenaeus quoted 200 words from the Book of Baruch as a Prophecy fulfilled by Christ, the preaching of which "the apostles delivered, and the Church in all the world hands on to her children." Irenaeus authenticated Baruch as Apostolic preaching and Scripture—the exact matters for which we depend upon Irenaeus the most.

In addition, the case is not about Baruch but about Christianity. Baruch also becomes proof: proof that the processes that allegedly ensure historicity, authenticity, and Apostolicity do not work. I discussed a few already, but there are more, of course. Kruger:

> In their role as guardians of the oral tradition, not only would the apostles have passed it along themselves in their own preaching and teaching, but, as Bauckham has argued, they would have entrusted that oral tradition to key leaders and disciples "with the skills and gifts necessary for preserving the tradition." (p. 177).

The key leader and disciple that John passed the oral tradition on to was Polycarp. He is (in part because of the link with Irenaeus) truly the single most crucial leader that Christians claim had "the skills and gifts necessary for preserving the tradition."

J.P. Moreland:

> When they refer to the way they handled the material about Jesus, they say that they "delivered over" to others exactly what they "received." These terms are the ones used in Jewish oral tradition to describe the way such tradition was passed on." (p. 143-144).

Those are the same terms John used, Polycarp used, and Irenaeus used. "The apostles delivered," sayeth Irenaeus. In point of fact, nearly all the data people cite to prove these sorts of claims about reliability and trustworthiness comes from the Rabbis after the time of Irenaeus, combined with an argument that we can, therefore, assume it went back in time to Christ.

Richard Bauckham's *Jesus and the Eyewitnesses* relies on contemporaneous sources to "confirm" testimony and evidence an earlier tradition:

> What Irenaeus tells us about John of Ephesus is what was known in the churches of the province of Asia where Irenaeus resided. From more than one local source of such knowledge, including Polycarp, who had known John personally, he knew that this John

was the Beloved Disciple, lived in Ephesus, wrote the Gospel there, and survived until around the end of the first century. Most of this is also independently confirmed by Polycrates of Ephesus, writing at about the same time as Irenaeus. We would need very good grounds for doubting the basic accuracy of this account of the authorship of the Gospel of John. (p. 457-458).

But if the Christian admits that Irenaeus' testimony about Baruch is false, then that provides the "very good grounds for doubting the basic accuracy of this account." In fact, Irenaeus would not evidence "more than one local source." He would evidence having zero sources. Even more, however, independent confirmation (by Athenagoras, for Baruch) would be shown to be worthless to establish either earlier teaching or credibility.

We have also seen the claim that "In questions that are not answered by Scripture itself, we inquire into the earliest available evidence for the teachings and practices of the churches, and have little regard for traditions that cannot be traced back to the generation that immediately followed the Apostles."[290] That generation is literally Polycarp's, and includes the teachings of Polycarp that Irenaeus evidences. In a very real sense, it is not all that much else. The period between the Apostles and Irenaeus is a dark age of vague references and debatable allusions, and everyone else (not from the line of Polycarp) is actually several generations removed from the Apostles—even by the second half of the second century, the time of Irenaeus. The claim that it is even possible to trace the evidentiary trail back to that generation to prove the authenticity of anything would be almost completely untenable.

And that is all looking back in time. Looking forward, all the evidence after Irenaeus would be tainted. All of it. No matter how much there seems to be, it can all be dismissed as passing on false information. No one opposed Baruch, so their own inaction shows that they could be fooled (by Irenaeus or someone else). There is no reason to trust the later Fathers, who may have simply trusted Irenaeus' false testimony.

And bear in mind that Professor Ehrman is not really the skeptical opponent in a case for Christianity. He is only an expert witness, an egghead scholar who lives in a quaint, genteel world where a man of honor actually wastes his time trying to prove that Irenaeus was a fraud and a forger. The case for Christianity is not such a world, it is a world of wolves, sharks, and blood-thirsty parasites—i.e., lawyers. For lawyers, no actual evidence is needed, no

---

[290] www.bible-researcher.com/canon1.html.

"means, motive, and opportunity" need ever be discussed. The skeptical lawyer need only ask the Christian opponent a question: "Was Baruch authentic Apostolic teaching, yes or no?" If the answer is "no," then Irenaeus falsely authenticated something that was not Apostolic. The details do not matter to anyone, and no one cares how or why or even if such false authentication actually happened. It is the Christian who admits that Irenaeus gave false testimony, and that is all that the skeptic needs to win the case.

With that answer, the Christian tears down all the evidence they had built up for Christianity, and everything Irenaeus authenticates is called into question—if Irenaeus' dramatic quote of 200 words in the Demonstration of the Apostolic Preaching is not trustworthy, what is? Why would a judge accept his references to other scrolls as persuasive evidence that those particular scrolls were authentic and were indeed handed down to him by the Apostles?

But it is even worse than just that. "The earliest testimony is more likely to be true." "Simultaneous references across a vast geography evidence an earlier history." "Lack of contradiction shows that people must have believed it long before it was written down." All the claims that Christians make to show the strength of the evidence for Christianity are admitted by the Christian not to have worked in the context of Irenaeus, Scripture, and Apostolic teaching. All the safeguards failed, and all the citations, all the canon lists, all the codices, and all the rest of the later evidence is tainted.

After that answer, winning the case for Christianity requires an explanation of what happened that is so wonderful that it would lead a competent neutral judge to turn around and trust the rest of the evidence from the early Church— including Irenaeus' pre-eminent testimony to the Fourfold Gospel.

I do not believe that it is possible. But that is just my opinion.[291]

---

[291] Many apologists show deep concern about this concept in other contexts, over inconsistencies that are far less central than the authenticity of the Fourfold Gospel. E.g., Gleason L. Archer, in his Encyclopedia of Bible Difficulties: "In any court of law, whether in a civil or criminal case, the trustworthiness of a witness who takes a stand is necessarily an important point at issue if his testimony is to be received. Therefore, the attorney for the opposing side will make every effort in his cross-examination of the witness to demonstrate that he is not a consistently truthful person. If the attorney can trap the opposing witness into statements that contradict what he has said previously or furnish evidence that in his own community the man has a reputation for untruthfulness, then the jury may be led to doubt the accuracy of the witness's testimony that bears directly on the case itself. This is true even though such untruthfulness relates to other matters having no relationship to the present litigation. While the witness on the stand may indeed be giving a true report on this particular case, the judge and jury have no way of being sure. Therefore, they are logically compelled to discount this man's testimony." (p. 23). Emphasis added: in this case, Irenaeus would be shown to be untruthful on the matter of Apostolic preaching and authentic Scripture.

THE JEWS -> JESUS -> JOHN -> POLYCARP -> IRENAEUS

Before you decide for yourself, let us first look at the chain from the opposite perspective. Every single other piece of evidence that proves the historicity of the Gospels (and other Books of the Bible) corroborates Irenaeus' story and reinforces his credibility. We believe that the evidence proves that he told the truth when talking about some Apostolically-preached Scriptures (like the Gospels), which is some indication that he was also telling the truth about other Apostolically-preached Scriptures, like Baruch.

The importance of the Fourfold Gospel actually strengthens all the indicia of credibility for Baruch. At the time Irenaeus was writing, some groups accepted only one Gospel as authentic and viewed the others as worthless or heretical. It is the pre-eminent testimony of Irenaeus, on behalf of the Fourfold Gospel, that responds to those views. To those groups, a false claim that Baruch was authentic Apostolic preaching should have been the end of any hope for convincing them that the "additional" Gospels were authentically Apostolic. If there was, indeed, a canon received from the Jews and known to all, then introducing Baruch should have been the end of Irenaeus' credibility and the Fourfold Gospel. Those groups would know from their own history that Baruch could not be authentic, and therefore, they would not accept that Irenaeus was correct that the "other" Gospels were Apostolic teaching as well.

That the other 'orthodox' Churches did not denounce Irenaeus over Baruch in fear that this would happen, and that the heterodox groups merged into orthodox Christianity without denouncing Irenaeus' testimony about Baruch, would seem to be assurance that his testimony was true.

The Easy Solution to the Mystery

So just for the sake of argument, let us consider the crazy idea that the weak link is the first link in the chain instead of the last. To begin, I mislabeled it: the Jews (meaning the Jews of today) actually deny that the Jews of old are part of this chain at all. A more precise name for the link is "the Jewish canon, as a fraction of Christians now claim it was."

After all, the Jewish Study Bible told us that Daniel was "probably written in its final version in 164 BCE." It was Geisler and the Apologetics Study Bible who told us that "according to Judaism, the Spirit of prophecy had departed from Israel before that time, by about 400 BC."

And it was not the Jews who told us that "the Jewish historian Josephus gave the names and numbers of the authentic Jewish Old Testament, which correspond exactly with the thirty nine books of our Old Testament" (that was Geisler and the Apologetics Study Bible). Nor is it the Jews who say that "the extent of the Hebrew canon was clear to everyone at the time of Christ" (that comes from Don Stewart and the Blue Letter Bible). To the contrary, the Jewish Study Bible said that "there may have been several competing notions of canon in this period, and he [Josephus, writing long after Christ] should not be taken as normative for all of Judaism in his time … it is not clear if he simply had a smaller canon than the rabbinic list …"

Recall, also, that in making his claims Stewart cited to sections of Sirach which also evidence that Baruch was Jewish Scripture.[292] Not a minor point in this context. After all, it is folks like Geisler and the Apologetics Study Bible who say that "Judaism, which produced these books, has never accepted them into its Bible (the Hebrew Scriptures, corresponding to our Old Testament)." The Jewish Study Bible, on the other hand, says "… the biblical scrolls found at Qumran [abandoned 68 AD, after Christ] do bear on the question …. What was not yet agreed upon was the exact boundaries of the canon as well as the final textual form of the individual works." It also says that "different Jewish groups from the early first millennium CE may have had different ideas of what comprised scripture…" and that "…It is likely that its [the process of canonization's] final stages were reached by (if not before) the 1st c. CE, perhaps as a reaction to the destruction of the Second Temple in 70 CE and its aftermath." Finally, "the Wisdom of Jesus ben Sirach … was thus, in some sense, canonical for some Rabbis. Therefore, although we can probably speak of "the" canon having formed by the 1st C. CE, there was a certain amount of fluidity or variability around the fringes."

Bear in mind that Polycarp's discipleship not only takes us back to John but before Josephus had written that the Jews had 22 Books (which occurred no earlier than 94 AD). It would be long after Polycarp's death that a Jew first writes a list of the names of all their Books and inserts it into the Talmud. Hundreds of years after Polycarp, others were still claiming that Apocrypha were accepted by the Jews. Notably, the Book of Baruch was still being so

---

[292] The Books of Jeremiah and Baruch 1:1-3:8 were apparently translated from Hebrew into Greek by the same person. Since Sirach refers to the Law and the Prophets as a well-known and accepted collection in the Greek-speaking community of Alexandria, the Greek version of Jeremiah/Baruch 1:1-3:8 must have been completed before 110 B.C.

identified on lists of the Books Jews accept in 385 AD—a list from Epiphanius, himself a Jewish Christian. In addition, the Apostolic Constitutions of 380 AD reports that the Jews still read Baruch on the tenth day of the month Gorpiaeus, when they assembled together.[293]

The Jews are not the first link in the chain. They claim that their limited and exclusive canon was finalized later, after Christ. They also claim that there was diversity in Judaism, not unity. It is claims being made by certain Christians that form the first link in the chain.

In fact, if we go back and read it again, and read it carefully, we can see that what Irenaeus says is that Christ established the preaching of Baruch— Christ, not the Jews. The Jewish prophets proclaimed it, but then Christ established it. Irenaeus then tells us that the Apostles delivered it, not the Jews, and that the Church hands it on, not the Jews.

For Irenaeus himself, the first link in the chain is Christ. It is what Christ established that anchors everything. There were many prophets proclaiming Prophecy, and many false prophets proclaiming false Prophecy. In fact, there were many Books of "Baruch" and many Books of "Jeremiah." There were factions and groups within Judaism. So, how do we know what was true? The Truth is what Christ established.

And remember that Irenaeus is not our only chain. We have other chains: corroborating evidence descending from Jesus to the Apostles to the predecessors of each Father writing—for example to Athenagoras and to Clement, both of whom also contemporaneously claimed Baruch is Scripture. Each chain attaches to Christ and reinforces and corroborates the others.

We even have some corroboration from Melito, with his admittedly ambiguous list. Recall that his list uses the Septuagint names for the Books, implying Susanna and Baruch, and has a mention of Wisdom that might mean the Book of Wisdom. Those happen to be the exact three Apocrypha that Irenaeus references in his own works. Perhaps that corroborates that they received the same teaching: Melito was Bishop of Sardis, 50 miles inland from Smyrna—and, thus, near where Polycarp was Bishop, and where Irenaeus was from, and where Irenaeus learned from Polycarp. Melito wrote his list in 170, while Irenaeus' writings are dated around 177 or 180. "Though Melito's extant writings never quote directly from the New Testament corpus, it is thought

---

[293] Book 5, 3, 20. www.newadvent.org/fathers/07155.htm.

that his orientation represents the Johannine tradition, and that his theological understanding of Christ often mirrored that of John."[294]

Notice, by the way, that the view that Melito's list is a Christian list directly supports Irenaeus' pre-eminent testimony that Baruch is Scripture and authentic Apostolic preaching. If, on the other hand, Melito's list is a Jewish list, then it is an indication that Jews of that time and place (the time and place of Melito and Irenaeus, and before them Polycarp and John) may have accepted Baruch—which indirectly supports Irenaeus' pre-eminent testimony that Baruch is Scripture and authentic Apostolic preaching. The ambiguity does not matter much and supports Irenaeus' claim either way.

In fact, Baruch might actually be a perfect demonstration of Kruger's model in action: the true sheep recognized the true Shepherd speaking via Baruch. Perhaps they heard the Shepherd's voice over the voices of some Jews disclaiming Baruch. "A stranger will they not follow, but will flee from him: for they know not the voice of strangers." (John 10:5). Perhaps there were different Jewish groups, some accepting Baruch and some not.[295] "And other sheep I have, which are not of this fold: them also I must bring, and they shall hear my voice; and there shall be one fold, and one shepherd." (John 10:16). Or perhaps, the Jews at the time of Christ still heard his voice through Baruch, then distanced themselves from Baruch after Christ—as may have happened with 2 Maccabees.

Last, and certainly not least, let us finally turn to where we should always begin: the Bible. Per the notes included with the original King James Bible, John 1:14 (the verse referenced by Irenaeus nine times before he cited to Baruch) is cross-referenced to Baruch 3:37. So, "And the Word was made flesh, and dwelt among us, (and we beheld his glory, the glory as of the only begotten of the Father), full of grace and truth" (John 1:14) is possibly referencing "Afterward did he shew himself upon earth, and conversed with men" (Baruch 3:37), per the KJV. This is, of course, Irenaeus' point—that

---

[294] wikipedia.org/wiki/Melito_of_Sardis
[295] The Jewish Study Bible: "It is important to remember that different Jewish groups from the early first millennium CE may have had different ideas of what comprised scripture..." (p. 2157). In the Bible, there are Sadducees and Pharisees and Samaritans, and then John the Baptist is essentially the founder of a popular movement completely outside the official Jewish hierarchy. Outside of the Bible were the Essenes, and there still are the Mandaeans (who follow the teachings of John the Baptist (as they claim them to have been) and not Christ: wikipedia.org/wiki/ Mandaeans). Epiphanius' Panarion (385 AD) also details other Jewish groups, heretics, etc. and all their histories.

Jesus fulfills this Prophecy from Baruch. We see that the KJV notes it as seemingly fulfilled by John 1:14, as well. But of course, references are always debatable; that is just the KJV's opinion, and we have no certainty.

Still, things may become more certain if we note that John 1:17 says "For the law was given through Moses, grace and truth came through Jesus." Combine that with John 1:14, "the Word of God became flesh," and we see that first the law had been given, then the grace and truth of God became flesh through Jesus. Baruch is connecting the initial giving of the commandments of the Torah to the later coming of God to Earth: "36He hath found out all the way of knowledge, and hath given it unto Jacob his servant, and to Israel his beloved. 37Afterward did he shew himself upon earth, and conversed with men." This is, thus, a conceptual parallel to John 1:14-17, and if we broaden our perspective beyond John 1:14 to see the context, we see a possible corroborating second reference to the Book of Baruch.

And certainty might be increased further. The word for "only-begotten" (monogenes) appears in John 1:14 and also the Book of Wisdom, 7:22: "For wisdom, which is the worker of all things, taught me: for in her is an understanding spirit holy, one only [monogenes]..." So, that could be another reference to a different Apocrypha in the same verse of the Gospel of John.

Combine that with the word "glory:" R.C.H. Lenski (Lutheran) in his Commentary on John, 1:14 says:

> The phrase "from the Father" 'is coordinate with "as of the Only-begotten," both equally modifying "glory." What these witnesses beheld was "glory from the Father," a glory so great, so truly divine, resulting from the eternal relation of the Logos to the Father and thus shining forth in the Incarnate Son. This was the kabod Yaweh revealed in the Old Testament in a variety of ways, because of which also the Son is called "the effulgence of his glory, and the very image (impress) of his substance," Heb. 1:3.

If that sounds familiar, it is because the language that Lenski references from Hebrews 1:3 is the language we have discussed previously, taken from Wisdom 7:26 (recall that effulgence or "brightness" (Greek, *apaugasma*) is only used in Hebrews 1:3 and in Wisdom 7:26. The same reference is made in the Nicene creed, part of a Christological hymn before the Epistle to the Hebrews was written, etc.).

Two possible references to the Book of Baruch and another two to the Book of Wisdom, all within the context of John 1:14. So, John may be referencing (in just one single passage of his Gospel) two of the three

Apocrypha that both Irenaeus and Melito—both intellectual descendants of John—evidence accepting as Scripture.

Nor is that all. Recall that Irenaeus began his long quote with Baruch 3:29 (Who hath gone up into heaven, and taken her [the Divine Wisdom], and brought her down from the clouds?). Many see allusions to Baruch 3:29 from John 3:13: "And no man hath ascended up to heaven, but he that came down from heaven, even the Son of man which is in heaven"—yet another possible reference from John, who taught Polycarp, who taught Irenaeus.

And another Evangelist may have alluded to the same verse, Paul in Romans 10:6: "But the righteousness which is of faith speaketh on this wise, Say not in thine heart, Who shall ascend into heaven? (that is, to bring Christ down from above:)."[296]

Those are possible allusions at the beginning of the long quote extracted by Irenaeus. In the middle is the Prophecy. Then, Irenaeus ended his long quote with the next verse after the Prophecy in 3:37, i.e., 4:1: "This is the book of the commandments of God, and the law that endureth for ever: all they that keep it shall come to life; but such as leave it shall die." Some see Matthew 5:18 as alluding to "the law that endureth for ever" in Baruch 4:1: "For verily I say unto you, Till heaven and earth pass, one jot or one tittle shall in no wise pass from the law, till all be fulfilled."

In addition to specific verse-by-verse parallels, there are more general parallels. From the NIB commentary:

> Baruch 3:29-4:4 also speaks of wisdom in a way parallel to the Gospel of John's discourse about Jesus the son of God in John 3:13-21 and 31-36. In both Baruch and John humans cannot ascend to heaven to get wisdom, but rather wisdom in Baruch and the son of the Father in John descend from heaven to humans as a divine gift. In Baruch, wisdom is associated with life, light, and salvation, as is Jesus in John. Wisdom understood as the law dwells with Israel in Baruch just as Jesus dwells with humans as the truth, the word, and the way in John.[297]

---

[296] Paul may also reference another verse of the Book of Baruch in 1 Corinthians, per the notes included with the original King James Bible. See below for that citation.

[297] Volume VI, Introduction to Baruch, p. 935. Note that their way of saying it in the first sentence does not draw attention to what they are really saying, which is that the later John parallels the earlier Baruch. My KJV analysis involves cross-references for exactly this reason: the choice to put the note in the Apocrypha section is editorial, and can easily cause a reader to miss the possible implication of what is being noted. Whether you accept something as a reference is up to you, but the point is that any reference comes only from the later author; and a reader might easily miss the fact that they have a decision to make when people note these things in reverse order.

"Baruch 3:29-4:4 also speaks of wisdom in a way parallel to the Gospel of John's discourse" is one way of saying it, another is that "the Gospel of John's discourse speaks of wisdom in a way parallel to Baruch 3:29-4:4"—and Irenaeus then quoted Baruch 3:28-4:1. A few of the parallels, in table form:

Baruch Chapters 3-4	John Chapter 3
29Who hath gone up into heaven, and taken her, and brought her down from the clouds?	13And no man hath ascended up to heaven, but he that came down from heaven, even the Son of man which is in heaven.
33He that sendeth forth light, and it goeth, calleth it again, and it obeyeth him with fear. 34The stars shined in their watches, and rejoiced: when he calleth them, they say, Here we be; and so with cheerfulness they shewed light unto him that made them.	19And this is the condemnation, that light is come into the world, and men loved darkness rather than light, because their deeds were evil. 20For every one that doeth evil hateth the light, neither cometh to the light, lest his deeds should be reproved. 21But he that doeth truth cometh to the light, that his deeds may be made manifest, that they are wrought in God.
35This is our God, and there shall none other be accounted of in comparison of him 36He hath found out all the way of knowledge, and hath given it unto Jacob his servant, and to Israel his beloved. 37Afterward did he shew himself upon earth, and conversed with men.	31He that cometh from above is above all: he that is of the earth is earthly, and speaketh of the earth: he that cometh from heaven is above all. 32And what he hath seen and heard, that he testifieth; and no man receiveth his testimony. 33He that hath received his testimony hath set to his seal that God is true. 34For he whom God hath sent speaketh the words of God: for God giveth not the Spirit by measure unto him.
1This is the book of the commandments of God, and the law that endureth for ever: all they that keep it shall come to life; but such as leave it shall die.	36He that believeth on the Son hath everlasting life: and he that believeth not the Son shall not see life; but the wrath of God abideth on him.

John is thought by some to have made even more references to Baruch in his other writings as well (such as Revelations—see below).

All these possible Biblical references provide support to Irenaeus' claim to have learned the Apostolic preaching of Baruch from Polycarp, who learned at the feet of John.[298]

---

[298] Bear in mind that similar issues exist with essentially all of the very earliest evidence used to establish Apostolicity. The problem (that the evidence also points to the Apocrypha) is not limited to Irenaeus and Baruch, though it is best exemplified by them.

Hebraica Veritas

The year 393 AD is 216 years after Irenaeus first wrote about Baruch. Two hundred and sixteen years ago would be 1809, as I write this: the year of the birth of Abraham Lincoln. It is also 360 years after the Crucifixion and Resurrection of Christ—360 years ago, young student Isaac Newton abandoned his formal studies and fled Cambridge University to avoid the Great Plague. Finally having some free time, he would go on to conduct a few scientific experiments that changed the world forever.

In the year 393 AD, after every canon list and every Father on Kruger's list has unanimously accepted Baruch as Scripture, and after the Fathers of the Church have been preaching Baruch for centuries, Jerome will omit the Book of Baruch from his translation of Jeremiah. Whether that constitutes rejection of Baruch can be debated, but for the purposes of this book, I treat it as such. If so, for the first time in history, a Christian claims that Irenaeus' testimony that Baruch is authentic Apostolic preaching was false.

Of course, Jerome never says it that way specifically. But Hebraica Veritas (the idea that only the Hebrew language Books accepted by the modern Jews are authentic Scripture, and Baruch, therefore, cannot have been authentic Apostolic preaching) is only possible if there was a break in the chain between John to Polycarp to Irenaeus.

We do not even have to wonder what Irenaeus would have said about that view, he already quoted it for us from the Book of Baruch: "All they that hold it fast (are appointed) to life: but such as leave it shall die."[299]

So saith Irenaeus.

Interpretations A Judge Might Buy

One way to deal with Baruch is to carefully "interpret" what Irenaeus wrote, so as to dismiss it. To save time and simplify things, I hereby concede

---

[299] Of possible interest: Irenaeus' *Against Heresies* includes extensive arguments about what is authentic Scripture and the heresy of not accepting it. His main opponents were those (Marcion, the Ebionites, etc.) who had cut up the Gospel of Luke, or rejected the writings of Paul, etc. He even lists everything that would be lost from Christianity if Luke's Gospel were not authentic: see *Against Heresies* 3.14.3.

that whatever explanation you have thought up is, indeed, an explanation, and no doubt, there are people born every minute who will accept it as gospel.

No one can ever stop lawyers and would be lawyers from trying such things, if only because judges are born every minute, too. Karl Llewellyn wrote a famous paper (since handed out to generations of law school students) explaining how "rules of statutory interpretation" are contradictory, allowing lawyers to argue that the text says absolutely anything. His first example: "Thrust: 1. A statute cannot go beyond its text. But Parry: 1. To effect its purpose a statute may be implemented beyond its text."[300] Those are two citations from two actual courts making two actual interpretations.[301] Depending on what their client needs, lawyers will cite to one, or they will cite to the other. The lawyer will cite one at 8am for one client, the other at 9am for a different client, and then alternate all day long without the slightest care in the world. Whatever you need the text to say, we can argue it says that (if you pay us enough, of course).

For example, in 2014, Professor Michael Sinclair set out to prove himself superior to the average bloodsucking legal parasite, so he lawyered Llewellyn's own claims. He "shows that Llewellyn's justificatory list contains no real contradictions, nor even inconsistencies of significance" and claims that in order to prove this merely "requires exploration of the function of statutes in society, the foundational conditions of governing communication, and the role of policy, intuition, and linguistic theory in statutory interpretation."[302] Let Sinclair talk his gibberish unopposed for an hour or two, and you will find yourself agreeing that the blatantly obvious conflicts do, indeed, unite into a beautiful, holistic unity. This is no criticism: that is extremely excellent lawyering, the sort of achievement that would get me to hire him at $1000 an hour if I ever need help that badly.

However, a good judge would, first, just read the document without all the arguments attached. Then they would hear arguments and determine whether Irenaeus identified the quote from Baruch as Apostolic preaching. So, try to read it calmly yourself. Then construct the best argument you can from your

---

[300] scholarship.law.vanderbilt.edu/vlr/vol3/iss3/4/

[301] For the first: First National Bank v. DeBerriz, 87 W. Va. 477, 105 S.E. 900 (1921) ; Sutherland, Statutory Construction § 388 (2d ed. 1904) ; 59 C.J., Statutes, § 575 (1932). For the second: Dooley v. Penn. R.R., 250 Fed. 142 (D. Minn. 1918); 59 C.J., Statutes § 57S (1932).

[302] Amazon.com/Karl-Llewellyns-Dueling-Canons-Perspective/dp/1600421857. When standing on dubious ground, useth thine own vocabulary to overwhelm thine own opponent.

perspective. Then get a good night's sleep. Then wake up tomorrow and construct the best argument you can that proves that yesterday you were young and foolish. When you can do no better for either side, be the judge.

I was such a judge once—I started this as an atheist and did not care whether Irenaeus was for or against Baruch. While I can see other ways to read it, I do not believe these ways represent what Irenaeus was actually saying or what his readers would take from it. So, while "a" judge might buy anything anyone has to say to the contrary, in an honest thought experiment I believe the answer is that the judge would read it as a declaration (be it true or false) that Baruch was taught and preached by the Apostles.

I particularly believe this in light of all the other corroborating evidence, such as the contemporaneous citations elsewhere in the Empire. But there are also things within the "four corners" of the document that would lead one to this conclusion, such as the fact that Irenaeus says something similar earlier in the document, in section 86:

> If then the prophets prophesied that the Son of God was to appear upon the earth, and prophesied also where on the earth and how and in what manner He should make known His appearance, and all these prophecies the Lord took upon Himself; our faith in Him was well-founded, and the tradition of the preaching (is) true: that is to say, the testimony of the apostles...
>
> And this was declared by the prophets in the words: How beautiful are the feet of them that bring tidings of peace, and of them that bring tidings of good things. (Isa. lii. 7) And that these were to go forth from Judaea and from Jerusalem, to declare to us the word of God, which is the law for us, Isaiah says thus: For from Sion shall come forth the law, and the word of the Lord from Jerusalem. And that in all the earth they were to preach, David says: Into all the earth went forth their speech, and their words to the ends of the world.

Section 86 is the lead-in, where Irenaeus begins stressing what the preaching and testimony was: that God would come to Earth. He begins citing prophecy after prophecy to make his point; he supports it with testimony from the New Testament (e.g., he alludes to John 1:14 twice); and he then ended with the Prophecy from Baruch in order to emphasize it. The build-up shows that the Prophecy from Baruch was the culmination of his list of Prophecies, the crescendo, the epitome, the top step of Prophecy that connects to Jesus as the fulfillment of them all:

> By the invocation of the name of Jesus Christ, crucified under Pontius Pilate, there is a separation and division among mankind; and wheresoever any of those who believe on Him shall invoke and call upon Him and do His will, He is near and present, fulfilling the requests of those who with pure hearts call upon Him. Whereby receiving salvation, we

continually give thanks to God, who by His great, inscrutable and unsearchable wisdom delivered us, and proclaimed the salvation from heaven—to wit, the visible coming of our Lord, that is, His living as man to which we by ourselves could not attain: for the things which are impossible with men are possible with God. Wherefore also Jeremiah saith concerning her (i. e. wisdom): "Who hath gone up into heaven, and taken her, and brought her down from the clouds? Who hath gone over the sea, found her, and will bring her for choice gold? There is none that hath found her way, nor any that comprehendeth her path. But he that knoweth all things knoweth her by his understanding: he that prepareth the earth for evermore, hath filled it with four-footed beasts: he that sendeth forth the light and it goeth; he called it, and it obeyed him with fear: and the stars shined in their watches, and were glad: he called them, and they said Here we be; they shined with gladness unto him that made them. This is our God: there shall none other be accounted of in comparison with him. He hath found out every way by knowledge, and hath given it unto Jacob his servant, and to Israel that is beloved of him. Afterward did he appear upon earth, and was conversant with men. This is the book of the commandments of God, and of the law which endureth for ever. All they that hold it fast (are appointed) to life: but such as leave it shall die." [Baruch 3:28-4:1, i.e., 3:28-3:37 plus 4:1.] ... This, beloved, is the preaching of the truth, and this is the manner of our redemption, and this is the way of life, which the prophets proclaimed, and Christ established, and the apostles delivered, and the Church in all the world hands on to her children. This must we keep with all certainty, with a sound will and pleasing to God, with good works and right-willed disposition.

Baruch's prophecy was the jewel in the crown, according to Irenaeus.

Irenaeus references John 1:14 nine separate times in his Demonstration of the Apostolic Preaching (per biblindex.org/citation_biblique/search: sections 6, 12, 30, 31, 37, 39, 53, 92, 94). He references John 1:14 more times than any other verse in the Gospel of John. He references it more times than any other verse in any of the four Gospels. He references it more than any other verse in the New Testament. He mentions it in the beginning, the middle, and the end of his treatise on Apostolic Preaching. He references it twice right before he quotes Baruch as the Prophecy that he claims the Apostles preached as being fulfilled.

The evidence also shows that Irenaeus' actual readers, the Fathers of the early Church, saw John 1:14 as the fulfillment of the Prophecy in Baruch, and preached Baruch far more often than comparable prophecies. Even the team of Protestant "Judges" who created the King James Version saw John 1:14 as a cross-reference to Baruch 3:37.

While "a" Judge might believe anything, I believe an honest thought experiment would involve a Judge who sees Irenaeus as preaching that the Apostles preached Baruch's Prophecy.

Comparing the Evidence

The ultimate task remains proving that we have "good reasons" to believe that the Books of the New Testament are the "written embodiment of apostolic tradition" (Kruger's phrasing; emphasis added to his claims below):

2 Peter, via Kruger (p. 271-2)	Baruch, via me
Perhaps no book has had a more difficult journey into the canon than 2 Peter. ... a number of early sources that may have known and used 2 Peter, such as 1 Clement (c. 96), which has several places of overlap ... and the Apocalypse of Peter (c. 110), which also seems to have known the letter. Bauckham considers the connections to the Apocalypse of Peter to be "very good" and "sufficient to rule out a late date for 2 Peter."	E.g., Kruger cites to 1 Clement 9:2: Let us steadfastly contemplate those who have perfectly ministered to his excellent glory, "which overlaps" 2 Peter 1:17: For he received from God the Father honour and glory, when there came such a voice to him from the excellent glory, This is my beloved Son, in whom I am well pleased. There are eleven possible allusions to Baruch from the New Testament itself, two are referenced in the KJV. John 1:14 plus 1 Corinthians 10:20: But I say, that the things which the Gentiles sacrifice, they sacrifice to devils, and not to God: and I would not that ye should have fellowship with devils. Baruch 4:7: For ye provoked him that made you by sacrificing unto devils, and not to God.
In addition, Justin Martyr makes a striking allusion to 2 Peter 2:1 in his Dialogue with Trypho, 5.	Per Kruger's footnote, the striking allusion to 2 Peter uses one word found nowhere else in Scripture except 2 Peter. Polycarp taught Baruch, per Irenaeus, and he quotes 500 words (15% of the entire Book) as that teaching.
Irenaeus appears to cite it	Kruger's footnote cites to Against Heresies 5.23.2: "For it is said, There was made in the evening, and there was made in the morning, one day" which appears to cite 2 Peter 3:8 "But, beloved, be not ignorant of this one thing, that one day is with the Lord as a thousand years, and a thousand years as one day." In the same book (4, 20, 4), Irenaeus quotes 300 words from Baruch 4:36-5:9. That is the two final verses of Chapter 4 and every single word of Chapter 5.
Hippolytus also seems to show knowledge of it.	Hippolytus expressly accepts Baruch in Against Noetus 2 and 5. In addition, Athenagoras is an earlier express acceptance of Baruch; Hippolytus is later and only "seems to show knowledge of" 2 Peter.

Clement of Alexandria wrote a now-lost commentary on 2 Peter

It is not clear what that commentary really was, and in fact Eusebius does not say it was on 2 Peter. The reference is to commentaries on "disputed writings" and Kruger feels that such label would include 2 Peter.

Theodoret wrote a full commentary on Baruch. Clement cites to Baruch repeatedly as "Divine Scripture."

Origen cited it six times and clearly received it as canonical Scripture

Biblindex.org/citation_biblique/search lists 42 cites from Origen to 2 Peter and 15 to Baruch. These numbers include allusions.

Eusebius considered it to be part of the "disputed" books in the canon that were nevertheless known to most of the church.

Regarding Baruch, Eusebius wrote: "It is prophesied that the God of the Prophets…will some Day afterwards be seen on Earth, and mingle among Men. I need add nothing to these inspired words, which so clearly support my argument."

Despite some initial hesitancy toward 2 Peter from some quarters of the church, in the end it was widely received by such figures as Jerome, Athanasius, Gregory of Nazianzus, and Augustine.

Baruch was expressly accepted on Athanasius' and Augustine's lists; Gregory of Nazianzus lists Jeremiah as canon and quotes from Baruch (without naming a Book), e.g.: "Since I have …solved in the mass the objections and oppositions drawn from Holy Scripture, … yet we have not yet gone through the passages in detail, because of the haste of our argument. ... In what passage? Why, in this: This is your God; … after this did He show Himself upon earth, and conversed with men."

Thus, even with its slow start, it is important to remember that 2 Peter still has significantly more support for its inclusion in the canon than the best of those books that have been rejected.

Through 450 AD every Father except Jerome accepted Baruch. The 'clear citation' start for Baruch begins earlier than for 2 Peter, and the allusions from the Gospels are of course earlier and seem stronger than the early allusions to 2 Peter.

Biblindex lists 369 citations to 2 Peter, 549 to Baruch. Eight of Kruger's ten Fathers expressly declare Baruch to be Prophecy, Scripture, the Word of God, etc. Baruch 3:36-38 was cited 158 times and was cited essentially always as Prophecy, Scripture, etc.

I believe that by any fair metric, Baruch is better evidenced as Apostolic teaching than some Books of the New Testament (as well as some of the Old, as discussed below). Any comparison with the evidence for the core Books of the New Testament (the four Gospels, etc.) is more subjective, because there is so much more evidence for the Gospels (many more scraps of paper and citations from Fathers, etc.). But more is not more trustworthy when it all seems to relate back to and rely upon one initial witness, and for Christians trying to prove the Apostolicity of the Four Gospels and most of the New Testament, Irenaeus (who learned from Polycarp, who learned from John) is that witness—just as he is for Baruch as well.

SIDEBAR 7: REASONABLE STANDARDS OF PROOF, PART III

As we start to move beyond Irenaeus, let us consider some advice from Kruger's treatise regarding issues we will see in the remaining evidence:

> … overplaying of disagreements over canonical books also happens in other areas. Throughout early Patristic testimony about the canon, the church fathers occasionally acknowledge that a particular book is "disputed" by some. A well-known example is Origen's comments on 2 and 3 John in which he acknowledges that "not all say that these are genuine." Although Hahneman uses this comment to point out that universal agreement on these epistles has not yet been achieved, he entirely overlooks the implications of Origen's comments in the other direction, namely, that apparently most Christians do consider them genuine-including Origen himself. The phrase "not all say" indicates that Origen is simply noting exceptions to a more broadly established trend. Thus, it is misleading to use this passage as evidence that John's letters were not regarded as canonical. That is more than this language can bear. At most, it reveals that in certain quarters of the church some disagreements over these books continued to occur (which is hardly surprising). (p. 265-266).
>
> This cannot be true, argues Kalin, because elsewhere Origen acknowledges that some had doubts about these books. However, it is unclear how these two facts are incompatible. Why cannot Origen accept a book as genuine and, at the same time, acknowledge that others had doubts about it? Kalin seems to think that if Origen admits that some have doubts about a book, then that must mean Origen himself rejects it—but this simply does not follow. (P. 285).

Exactly correct! Now, apply such reasoning to the Apocrypha. This is a common error when discussing the "third category" that a handful of early Fathers mention—but not all Fathers. The others who do not mention it cannot be presumed to agree with the idea of a category for 'disputed Books' purely because they acknowledge that something is disputed by someone else. By simply noting that someone disagrees with it being Scripture, a father is not "putting a Book in a lesser category" or denying full canonicity. He only noted disagreement. And like everyone else, he may well see those who disagree with him as just plain stupid.

> … it took a while for the church to reach a consensus about all of these books. … there was no formal, official declaration of the church that closed the canon. We can agree with Ehrman that "the canon of the New Testament was ratified by widespread consensus rather than by official proclamation." There are numerous examples of this consensus, most notably the Festal Letter of Athanasius in 367, where he affirms precise twenty-seven books of our current New Testament. In agreement are also Eusebius, Codex Claromontanus, Rufinus, Jerome, Augustine, the African Canons, and the Synods of Hippo and Carthage. Although there was not absolute uniformity (which

is true still today), after this period the church coalesced around these twenty-seven books with remarkable unity. (p. 286-287).

Every single one of those lists and Fathers that Kruger specifically mentions as examples of the consensus for the New Testament is also evidence of the acceptance of Susanna. Every single one except Jerome is evidence of the acceptance of Baruch. We have other evidence that, in fact, those Books were unanimously Scripture from "time immemorial"—in that as far as we know, every Christian church and Father had always accepted them (until Jerome, in the case of Baruch).

This means that a consensus—in fact, a unanimity, or nearly so—for some Apocrypha as canon is actually of far earlier date than the consensus Kruger is relying upon as proof of many of the Books of the New Testament canon.

On the other Apocrypha, we are reviewing the evidence as we go, and you should judge when and whether a consensus may have existed to accept those Apocrypha.

However, note the way Kruger assigns each of these "witnesses" equal importance. Jerome gives us a list, and the Codex Claromontanus gives us a list, and multiple synods voted on lists. All lists are equal, right? But they are not equal at all. We are looking for a consensus within the Church, a consensus of people, not a "consensus of lists."

E.g., 217 bishops attended the Council of Carthage in 419. The list from that Council is really 217 lists, unanimously agreeing with each other in every single detail. (Bear in mind, they need not have entered the Council in agreement and need not have voted 217-0. The point is that (a) at least a majority apparently did feel that way, and (b) after the vote, all 217 went forth and followed the collective will).[303] We are concerned with what the Church accepted, and the evidence from that one list is that 217 Bishops agreed to accept the canon list of the Council (all of the Apocrypha). For the purposes of trying to figure out whether a consensus existed, it is 217 lists, not one.

And 217 is a staggeringly large number in this context. There are only two dozen-ish lists (depending on how you count them). Only 127 Fathers have

---

[303] At least in those 217 Bishoprics. It may have had greater scope in terms of number of Bishoprics (perhaps other Bishops who did not attend were within the geography covered), but it was also limited (it was only a "North Africa" council, not a full council from Europe or Asia, and it does not seem like Alexandria/Egypt were included either). Alas, I could not find how many Bishops there were globally in 419 AD—it would be nice to know what percentage of the world's Christians were covered, etc. In any event, lacking other information, I just say 217 Bishoprics.

left source material to be referenced biblindex.org/citation_biblique/search, which is part of Biblia Patristica). Wikipedia.org/wiki/List_of_Church_Fathers lists 137 Fathers that might fit my timeframe (up until 450 AD) but it is not clear that all left writings.

On the other hand, the individual lists of Fathers who were authors may have been 'followed' by many or only a few. To determine such things, we need to look outside the list for evidence. Some of the lists are scraps of paper found in monasteries a thousand years later. Melito's letter may have been known to no one but the recipient until Eusebius found it in a box and copied it into his book. Or the writings of a Father could go on to have vast impact via changing minds, educating people, etc.—just like Eusebius' book would. We are looking for evidence that shows the impact of a list, and needless to say, citation evidence is the key to that analysis. Jerome's canon list, in particular, had considerable influence in the Middle Ages, but for our purposes, we are looking for what his influence was by 450 (a generation after his death).

Only with Synods and Councils can the list alone tell us what a group really thought. Other lists could just be one man's opinion, or they could have a massive impact far beyond the region (North Africa) of the Councils (that could have the same impact too), but only citation evidence can tell us which.

> ... one gets the impression that it would require an extremely high (if not unanimous) amount of agreement about a book before Hahneman would regard its canonical status as decided. .... With this sort of standard in place, we would never be able to say that we have a canon, even in the modern day. ... [even] in the twenty-first century because the Syrian church continues to have a different list.... it seems that Hahneman has applied an unreasonably strict standard for the level of agreement required for a book to count as canon. (P. 265).

Of note: without a standard of "consensus," there can be no canon even today. Also, even if some Books are more disputed than others (e.g., the Books the Syrians do not accept), all are still canon.

My focus here is not to argue whether to have a canon or what standard is appropriate; my point is that such decisions have to be made consistently. Still, I use Kruger's standard as the standard for the purposes of my discussion. Because bear in mind that Kruger was writing his book to show that Christians have "good reasons" for accepting the 27-Book New Testament as the authentic Apostolic Books.

That is it. That is all he was trying to prove, but it is not easy to do so. He had spent his entire life up to that point worrying about the "Achilles' heel of Protestant Christianity," the "hidden, dragging illness of the Church," "the single thread that unravels the entire garment of the Christian faith." He fought the good fight, consulted a thousand books, and penned his magnum opus. And he believes "consensus" has to be the standard to prove "good reasons."

On that basis, then, the question is whether the early Church had a consensus on the Apocrypha (besides Susanna and Baruch, which clearly meet any fair standard of consensus), and whether they, too, were canon.[304]

> Moreover, when drawing upon the Gospels, Justin [Martyr] sometimes uses "it is written," the *formula citandi* for introducing scriptural books. (P. 228).

The question is what to make of such a reference (and similar things, of which there are many, such as a mention of the "blessed Judith" without a mention of the Book of Judith). The words do not say "Scripture" or "Canon", but everyone agrees it may mean "Scripture"... but it might not... and even "Scripture" does not quite mean "Canon"...

My point, as you would expect, is just that this sort of wording is accepted as 'proof enough' when people want it to be and quibbled over when they do not. So, whatever you decide, you then have to be consistent. The evidence consists of mostly the same authors, the same Books, etc.

In addition, these quibbles have more value the fewer the citations, because once there are more than a few, the concept becomes arguing for the sake of arguing. Once you have a couple citations to the Book of Wisdom, you have more than enough contextual evidence to see whether the Father thought the Book of Wisdom was Scripture. I cannot really convey that sort of context easily in a "short" book like this, but it is there in the background, nonetheless,

---

[304] Some people claim that the early Church never "decided" to consider Apocrypha as Scripture, because there was no ecumenical council (or some such). But that amounts to a requirement for a particular parliamentary procedure, and only for the Apocrypha. Substantively, "the churches choose to read Daniel in the version of Theodotion," as Jerome says—to them, they chose, somehow, some way. My question is what choices did they make, as evidenced by what they were actually doing? I am less concerned with what procedure they did or should have followed. I would also note that if you look at many of my quotes from Kruger, Geisler, Gallagher and Meade, etc., you will find claims that the early Church accepted Books of the New Testament, or the Protestant canon, etc. Whatever standard they (or you) have for the acceptance of such things has to be consistent—you cannot use consensus for the acceptance of the Gospels and demand unanimity or an ecumenical council for the Apocrypha.

Also, I have no concern whatsoever for whether or how a canon decision might be eternal, or whether the canon was "closed" as of a certain date. If the Church had one canon and later changed it (by adding or by removing), that is something I want to know. For my purposes, I talk of a canon at 200 AD (etc.). What that means to "The" canon is for you to figure out.

because if I did not truly think someone meant a reference to be Scripture, then it is never included herein (or at least is expressly noted otherwise).

Even so, I think there are very few debatable instances below, and I honestly feel a lot more was kept out that should have been put in. Had I used Don Stewart's standards for judging New Testament references, there would be a great many more citations below. That is not a criticism of Stewart, just a comparison to show that I set out to be conservative to avoid arguing over such things. If the individual citation was not a clear acceptance of the Apocrypha as Scripture, then either (a) I found somewhere else in the same work that the author described it as Sacred Scripture or Prophecy or some such, and identify that with the quote,[305] or (b) I note that I am including it on some other basis (e.g., a few notable mentions are included where they are just cited along with canonical Scripture without any distinction being made by the Father, etc.—the vast majority of that category I did not add to my data; they just are not worth the effort given how many of category (a) I found).[306]

In general, even if you wish to argue that a fraction of what I found is mistaken, or mistranslated, or whatever, it actually makes no great difference. I believe that it is "plenty" by any reasonable comparative standard. The specific numbers are useful but not really the point, which is that the Protestant admits that "plenty" is not enough to prove authentic Apostolicity—and yet still has to somehow prove that Books with comparable evidence are authentic.

---

[305] Example: In Treatise 8, 20 Cyprian writes "Be rather such a father to your children as was Tobias. ...command your children what he also commanded his son, saying: [Tobit 14:10-11] And again: [Tobit 4:5-11]..." (www.newadvent.org/fathers/050708.htm). So, he does not clearly identify it as Scripture, and he could be quoting a mere example. It is a very good point...

... Except it is not. Because (1) in other works, he quotes the exact same lengthy passage using the wording "Holy Scripture," e.g., in Treatise 12,3,1 www.newadvent.org/fathers/050712c.htm, and (2) even in the same work, he quotes other sections of Tobit in other places (section 5) as "the words of God Himself; the divine instructions."

When looked at holistically, there is no doubt that Cyprian was citing Scripture when he quoted Tobit in Treatise 8, 20, even if the language used was vague. And yet, even something that met the standard of item (1) (a reference as "Holy Scripture" for even the exact same long quote in another work) was excluded; it had to be said in the same work (item (2).

[306] Such citations are noted by "cited along with Scripture without qualification..." and similar notations. I took all the lingo from Gary Michuta's *The Case for the Deuterocanon*.

200 AD

TO

350 AD

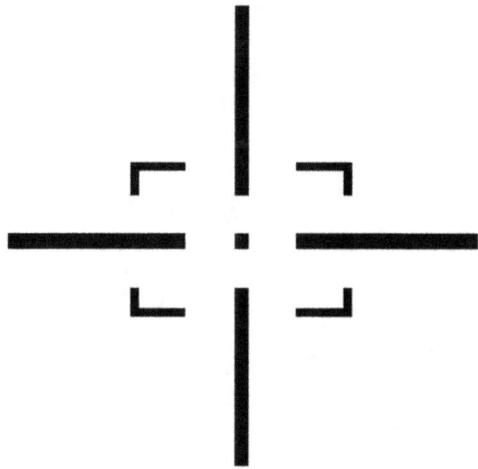

200-350 AD

This is the middle period of the early Church, for our purposes. By the end of this period, with the conversion of Constantine, and the Edict of Milan finally granting freedom from persecution, the early Church will enter a new phase, which will include the vast majority of the canon lists.

But unfortunately, with so few canon lists during this middle period, there is almost no evidence to understand what people thought about the canon. It is 150 years of utter and complete blankness, during which no one cared at all about what Books were being read and preached every Sunday.

Of course, that is not remotely true. We actually have plenty of evidence to discuss, and in fact clear documented evidence starts to grow rapidly—it is just not assembled in list form. But anyone who focuses only on lists is, indeed, skipping over a vast swath of history. And there is no good reason at all to pass over the evidence that comes outside of lists.

After 200, citation evidence starts to grow enormously for all the New Testament, Old Testament, and Apocryphal Books, and we will be able to make comparisons among them. But also, this is the era when the types of writings we find begin to diversify—some citations are sermons and homilies on the Apocrypha themselves, some citations are Scriptural commentaries on the Apocrypha, some (like the letter from Origen) are treatises on what is Scripture, why it is Scripture, and how the decision is being made.

Citation evidence also helps us understand the lists we will see in the later era (350 AD+). We will know what was going on before the lists, which will be useful information when Fathers in later years give us conflicting versions of what they claim "was handed down from the beginning."

THE GREAT UNCIAL CODICES

But before we cover all that, let's first begin with a different kind of "canon list": entire manuscript copies of the Apocrypha, and specifically the manuscript copies that appear in the four "Great Uncial Codices." These are the four Bibles of the fourth and fifth century that have survived for us to examine. The latter two (Codex Alexandrinus and Codex Ephraemi Rescriptus) are from the fifth century and, thus, outside of this 200-350 timeframe. Nevertheless, I shall discuss all the codex evidence as one unit.

The earlier ones are Codex Vaticanus (the earliest[307]) and Codex Sinaiticus (dated to sometime after 325).

Each of these ancient manuscript Bibles included Apocrypha, as we see in the table below. That is not, however, the end of the inquiry. It is a little like the Melito List discussion—we simply do not know what went into creating these Bibles and whether the contents were all seen as Scripture. There are, sometimes, other Books contained in Bibles that are not seen as Scripture (just as most modern Bibles have introductions and essays in them). These Great Uncial Codices include a couple Books that no one today considers canon, and it is unclear if anyone at the time thought they were canon either.

Still, as with Melito, while we are not certain what to make of the evidence, the evidence is what it is:[308]

Codex Vaticanus	Codex Sinaiticus	Codex Alexandrinus	Codex Ephraemi R.
Wisdom	Wisdom	Wisdom	Wisdom
Sirach	Sirach	Sirach	Sirach
Judith	Judith	Judith	?
Tobit	Tobit	Tobit	?
Baruch (after but separated from Jeremiah)	Baruch (but whether it was part of Jeremiah cannot be determined)	Baruch (position and lack of numbers imply it is part of Jeremiah)	?
Susanna (as Daniel Ch 1)	Susanna? [all of Daniel is missing]	Susanna (as Daniel Ch 1)	?
~~Not included: 1 Maccabees~~	1 Maccabees	1 Maccabees	?
~~Not included: 2 Maccabees~~	2 Maccabees?	2 Maccabees	?

As with inclusion, so with exclusion: it is hard to know what to make of it. The Old Testament of the Codex Ephraemi Rescriptus is mostly lost (with no idea what, in fact, is lost), so no conclusions at all should be made from the absence of some Apocrypha in that one. Codex Sinaiticus was broken into pieces, with pieces still being discovered in the 21st century. While pieces of 1 and 4 Maccabees have been found, nothing from 2 Maccabees has been found.[309] I have found no scholarship on why 2 Maccabees is specifically

---

[307] Although not everyone agrees, as with everything else on this topic. There are even some who would claim that all four codices fall outside the 350 end date for my time frame.

[308] The table is assembled from data in Gallagher and Meade, p. 244-251.

[309] The Books of the Maccabees are largely unrelated. So, 2 does not "follow" 1 in sequence, as 2 Kings follows 1 Kings. The inclusion of 1 and 4 does not mean that 2 and 3 were also present, nor do they need to occur in between 1 and 4. Still, everything I have read indicates that they were thought to be included, although no one gets specific as to why. See, e.g., wikipedia.org/wiki/Codex_Sinaiticus, which says "the entire Deuterocanonical books" were included.

thought to have been included, but there are general references to the thought that "all" the Deuterocanonical Books and/or "1-4" Maccabees were included, so that would seem to be the expectation. Codex Vaticanus (while missing a few pages) is essentially complete and did not include any of the Maccabees (1, 2, 3 or 4). For comparison, Vaticanus also does not include several canonical New Testament Epistles (which may have been originally included) or Revelation (highly debated as to whether it was originally included).[310]

With respect to the Maccabees, inclusion in two of the codices seems to help their case; exclusion in one seems to hurt their case. In either event, the evidence is not, by itself, determinative. The codices are just data points.

Other than the Maccabees, all the other Apocrypha were always included in all these ancient manuscript Bibles. We are often told how much work went into making a book, how expensive they were, etc. If nothing else, we see that the creators of these codices in the 300s and 400s always went to the trouble and expense of including those Apocrypha.

In addition, the Apocrypha are spread throughout the Bible—they are not segregated in one section nor identified any differently from the inarguably canonical Books, which seems to go against the idea of a "third category."

However, while we are being so careful to avoid undue speculation, consider the differences from the Melito situation: we have multiple samples, not just one, and the samples have definite points of agreement. We have at least the outline of a definite Christian context: preparation of a full Bible codex. That is a context with clear application to the Christian canon question, even if it is not fully identical to the canon question. We have a definite level of importance (these would have been expensive and labor intensive creations for the early Church), even if we cannot conclude that either of the early ones were one of the fifty Bibles Eusebius prepared for the Emperor Constantine in 331 AD.[311] My point is not that any of these contextual facts makes this evidence conclusive, but that Melito's List has far less going for it, and yet everyone devotes so much paper to speculating on it.

Also, I personally think it noteworthy (because there is no reason that it had to be done the way it was done) that the Church produced its own Old Testament and included it in its own Book, the Bible. It seems like it was

---

[310] Later manuscript copies of them were added to Vaticanus in the Middle Ages. The question is whether they were replacements or new additions.

[311] See wikipedia.org/wiki/Fifty_Bibles_of_Constantine. Some have made such a guess, but it does not seem like they are doing anything more than guessing.

important to the Church to maintain control of their own set of what the Old Testament was supposed to be. I.e., they did not acquire Jewish sets to use for Christians, they gave Christians a Christian set.

CANON LISTS

One last thing before we start discussing citation evidence: a brief review of the three alleged lists in this 200-350 AD time frame.

Origen's Jewish List

The first is the list from Origen.[312] It is a Jewish list. On the face of it, it is merely telling us what the Books of the Hebrews are. Whether that meant (to Origen) that the list was also an exclusive list of the Books of the Old Testament for Christians, is not stated in the excerpt from Origen that Eusebius gives us. Eusebius himself may think so, but that is his opinion, not Origen's.[313] And why Eusebius may have thought that is unknown.

To me, Origen's views are not in doubt, thanks to the letter on Susanna. The list says absolutely nothing about the Church at all—not one single word of Origen's mentions the early Church or the Christian Bible. The list is missing the "from there to the Christian Old Testament" logic that is crucial to the canon debate, whereas the letter addresses the debate head on.

---

[312] Discussed earlier, and available at www.bible-researcher.com/origen.html. Origen also begins a divergence in canon lists: there are New Testament lists that will make no mention of the Old Testament/the Jews/the Apocrypha at all. So for my purposes, there is rarely a reason to mention them, although books discussing the entire canon do so in detail. That people sometimes blend these New and Old Testament canon discussions together in their own mind may help explain why Eusebius often appears as a separate item in discussion of lists, even when the topic is confined to the Old Testament/Apocrypha – for which he himself produced no such list.

[313] Gallagher and Meade say it is clear that Eusebius thought so, citing to a different book by Gallagher, which I have not read. No English translation I have read of Eusebius' works really convinces me on that point, but I do not view it as important enough to make a big deal out of it (or to learn Greek, for that matter). If Eusebius actually thought so, he was wrong, based on all the actual writings of Origen I have seen (and part of the reason I am dubious about Gallagher's view of Eusebius' thoughts is that Eusebius himself saw the letter to Africanus and gave it his approval; at most Eusebius seems inconsistent or (my vote) not a stickler for detail). In legal terms the writings of Origen are evidence, Eusebius' opinions are "hearsay" and not admissible into evidence, particularly when there is direct evidence available from Origen himself that contradicts Eusebius' opinion. This is not a legal matter, of course, but there are very good reasons why that is the rule when your money, property, and freedom are at stake.

By now, you either agree or you do not. However, there is also one more thing to consider: this list of Books of the Hebrews is a different list. It does not match Melito's list or the Talmud's list.[314] This matters not only as direct differences in the Christian canon (for anyone who takes the lists as meant to be the Christian canon, it is a different canon from both Melito's and the modern Jewish/Protestant canon) but also an indirect difference. For anyone who thinks the Christian canon should match the Jewish canon, Melito and Origen are evidence that the Jews either have changed their canon several times or disagree about their canon. By this 250 AD-ish period, we have three different "Hebrew canons" from Melito, Origen, and the Talmud.[315] There is a conceptual problem that the early Christians cannot be matching "the" Jewish canon because there seem to be variations in that canon; and there is a practical problem for the case because there is also no actual proof that there was "a" canon at all. The evidence shows Jewish canons, plural, not the canon.

We will find the same thing with later lists, as well—a frequently changed list of Books accepted as canon by the "Jews" themselves.

Eusebius' "Lists"

The next "list" is Eusebius. However, he never gives his own Old Testament list. Instead, he copied lists he read from others. And unfortunately, Eusebius is not as reliable as moderns wish he had been.

Far too much nonsense is written about Eusebius for several reasons. One, while he only provided his own New Testament canon lists, people often include his opinions and comments about the Old Testament in a discussion of canon lists. But that is not treating the evidence fairly. Eusebius' comments are not in list form. One should not exclude everyone else's comments on the

---

[314] Origen includes Esther, Melito does not. Origen did not include the "Twelve Minor Prophets," but everyone agrees that was a mistake (his or Eusebius') since no one else ever left them out (so not at all like Melito leaving out Esther). Origen expressly includes the Epistle of Jeremiah (but does not mention Baruch). Melito uses the Septuagint term for Jeremiah and so probably includes both. There are also possible issues with their mutual references to Esdras, which I will ignore, as I always do in this discussion (it just complicates things and does not really matter to the Apocrypha (meaning the Catholic Apocrypha) discussion). And there are the Maccabees, unmentioned by Melito but mentioned by Origen, even if the meaning of the mention is debatable and uncertain. (Note that for this purpose I treat Melito's as a Jewish list.)

[315] In addition to other Christian lists (discussed elsewhere), there is also physical evidence of alternative canons that continued for centuries. Jerome obtained Hebrew texts of Sirach, Tobit, Judith (Aramaic), and 1 Maccabees. Nachmanides (ca. 1194-1270 AD) also used an Aramaic text of Wisdom in his Commentary on the Pentateuch (the "Introduction," and in 1:7, 8, 11).

grounds that they are not in list form, yet include Eusebius' comments. It really should be all or none—and, of course, I say it should be all.

Secondly, way too many authors confuse what Eusebius says and what he is quoting from. For example, my chosen canon list website quotes an old passage from Westcott (1896) where Westcott confuses Eusebius quoting Origen for Eusebius' own words.[316]

Thirdly, the canons that Eusebius cites differ. From Gallagher and Meade:

> In his Ecclesiastical History, Eusebius recorded three lists of OT books, those of Josephus (3.10.1-5), Melito of Sardis (4.26.12-14), and Origen (6.25.1-2), all more or less agreeing in content. (p. 99).

"Agreeing in content" is their view (their spin, their bias), and in one sense, they are right (the lists agree on most of the 39 Books of the Protestant canon, which are accepted by Catholics as well). However, obsessed as we are with only the Apocrypha, the real point is that the lists still differ, and nowhere does Eusebius discuss that aspect or clearly express what that means.

> He apparently intended readers to understand that these lists, despite their minor disagreements, represented the OT canon of the church. ... his introduction to Melito's list describes it as a list of the recognized scriptures of the Old Testament' (4.26.12), and before quoting Origen's list he says that it is the catalogue of the sacred Scriptures of the Old Testament (6.25.1). Eusebius seems to have thought that the OT canon was settled. (p. 99).

Settled yes, but how, exactly? One could see it to be that the points of agreement are all canon, or that anything mentioned on any list is canon. The core is settled either way, but the edges are what we are concerned with here.

Eusebius never expresses any personal judgment against the individual Books of the Apocrypha. The worst thing he ever says about the Apocrypha is that they are disputed, which he himself seems to indicate might mean that something is still accepted as canon.

And I think it could be argued that Eusebius is giving his support to lists (and Origen's letter) that would include Susanna, Baruch, Wisdom, Sirach, Tobit, Judith, 1 Maccabees and 2 Maccabees (i.e., all the Apocrypha). If we

---

[316] www.bible-researcher.com/eusebius.html. At least that is my view, as well as Gallagher and Meade's view. There are also people who think Eusebius made the list up and attributed it to Origen (see above re: Eusebius' unreliability...). In which case, Origen's list really is Eusebius' list, meaning Westcott would not be confused.

are just going to guess about what "he really meant," then I think that is a fair reading of every time Eusebius shows his approval for Origen's letter, Origen's list, Clement's list, Melito's list, etc.

Of course, such a guess is also directly 100% contrary to the usual guesses made (that he only approved of the 39 Protestant Books, which is the Gallagher and Meade view). That is what happens when we are only guessing. But if someone quotes many things with approval, it is just as fair to accept all the differences as to exclude all the differences.

But actually, my guess for Wisdom, Baruch, and Susanna is not much of a guess at all. I am the one abiding by what Eusebius himself clearly said; it is others who believe that the lists he copied override his own words about his own view:

When clearly speaking for himself, in his treatise "The Preparation of the Gospel," Eusebius cites to the Book of Wisdom more than a dozen times as one of the "Oracles of the Hebrews" and asserts that it is Divine prophecy fulfilled by Christ.[317]

In addition, Eusebius cites to Baruch as inspired prophecy, e.g.: "It is prophesied that the God of the Prophets...will some Day afterwards be seen on Earth, and mingle among Men. I need add nothing to these inspired words, which so clearly support my argument." (Baruch 3:29-37).[318]

Moreover, Eusebius noted that: "There is extant an epistle [from Africanus] to Origen, expressing doubts of the story of Susannah in Daniel, as being spurious and fictitious. Origen answered this very fully."[319]

(And I note, by the way, that Wisdom, Baruch, and Susanna are the same three Books that Irenaeus and Melito may also accept, and this reinforces Irenaeus' claim that Baruch was, indeed, Apostolic preaching.)

Lastly, Eusebius articulated a system of categories for considering New Testament Books: (1) unanimously agreed, (2) disputed (as long as "most" accept them) and (3) heretical works, with category (2) divided between "spurious" works (those which were not universally recognized as written by a particular author, e.g., Revelations and Hebrews) and those which are not

---

[317] See www.tertullian.org/fathers/eusebius_pe_01_book1.htm et seq. Oracles of the Hebrews is the same term that he uses for all the Scriptures, such as 1 Chronicles. (See the discussion of 1 Maccabees, below).
[318] Demonstratio Evangelica, 6.19 www.ccel.org/ccel/pearse/morefathers/files/eusebius_de_08_book6.htm.
[319] Church History 6, 31, 1: www.newadvent.org/fathers/250106.htm

spurious (the named author was accepted as the true author) but still disputed. One can spend a lot of pages discussing such things (as Gallagher and Meade do, since they have a wider scope for their work), but the point for us is that none of that was applied by Eusebius himself to the Old Testament. Hence, it is just a distraction when discussing the Apocrypha.[320]

The Codex Claromontanus

The last of our lists before 350, and our first inarguably Christian canon list, is the Codex Claromontanus.[321] Gallagher and Meade tell us that scholars generally date it to the fourth century, or even earlier (with the inevitable disagreement noted), and they give it a date of "early fourth century," which is the date I use as well (but note that they picked a late date for this one: want to guess whether it contradicts their own deeply cherished beliefs?). Thus, it is the one list that would come before 350.

The list includes all the Apocrypha (and Esther, which makes it the first inclusion of Esther on a list that is clearly Christian). Jeremiah is listed, without Baruch being mentioned. However, if you look at the numbers (it is a stichometric list, with line counts for all the Books), I believe it is clear enough that it is included (Gallagher and Meade just say it is probably included), and I believe the same line counting information shows that Susanna is part of Daniel (Gallagher and Meade do not mention that aspect). The Apocrypha are interspersed among the Books of the Protestant canon and are not set off separately or noted differently—again, evidence against a "third category."

The early fourth century dating for the list is, essentially, contemporaneous with Eusebius. The list could be seen as conflicting with Eusebius on some points and agreeing with Eusebius on others (Susanna, Baruch, Wisdom, maybe the other Apocrypha). It is also contemporaneous with Codex Vaticanus and Codex Sinaiticus. And it is in agreement with them on

---

[320] In particular, although he refers to some of the Apocrypha as "disputed," it is not clear that he is using the word to mean the same thing as his New Testament category (he is using the words in passing when talking about the Apocrypha); and then, he also does not detail what happens with an Old Testament Book that is disputed. New Testament Books that are disputed but recognized by many/most are still considered canon (both to Eusebius and to us moderns). In addition, he does not say that he personally disputes them. Read his own words on the matter at www.newadvent.org/fathers/250103.htm, Book 3, Ch 25, Sec 3.
[321] www.bible-researcher.com/claromontanus.html

including most of the Apocrypha, parting ways only on the Maccabees (in part, since the Codices disagree, too).

Perhaps all these lines of evidence match up quite well. After all, there are also those who guess that the Codices were part of the 50 "Eusebian" Bibles that Eusebius produced at Constantine's order, and here we have a list counting up all the lines of the Books of the Bible, which would seem useful for such an enterprise. Still, the list, the Bibles, and what we read of Eusebius' own views in his writings do not match perfectly.

One can speculate from these data points in any direction one wants; the real key is to distinguish the facts from the speculation. And the fact is that the Claromontanus List includes all the Apocrypha as canon.

With that, let's finally move on to the citation evidence.

CITATION EVIDENCE

It is virtually impossible to avoid confusion when discussing the Apocrypha as a set. There is nothing that really unites them, except that they are the additional Books in Catholic Bibles that are either not in the Protestant Bible at all or separated out as a third category. Otherwise, they are each independent and should be thought of separately to avoid error.

They each have their own data: not every Book is on all the lists like Susanna; not every Book is cited as Scripture in the Jewish Talmud like Sirach; and not every Book has claims to be a Prophecy fulfilled by Christ like the Book of Wisdom. Accordingly, I break each Book out separately.

On the other hand, I will cover all citation evidence[322] for each Book at once, rather than break them out by era. There is sparse evidence for anything before 200, and biblindex.org/citation_biblique/search is not complete after 350, so 200-350 is the key era for citation evidence. However, at the end of each section, I include a chart with chronological information for that particular Book, which may be helpful. I also provide a chart of "canon list" data for each of the Apocrypha[323]—I believe that breaking it out by Book for that analysis is vital.

Apocrypha had been cited 2,313 times (biblindex.org/citation_biblique /search) before 350 AD, the date by which the first inarguably Christian "canon list" was written. That is as many times as Proverbs and twice as many as Job—both much-quoted core Old Testament Books. The 8 Apocrypha were cited more than 13 canonical Books combined (Ruth, Nehemiah, Zephaniah, Esther, Nahum, Haggai, Habakkuk, Obadiah, Ezra, Amos, Jonah, Lamentations, and 1 Chronicles). As we will see below, they each individually also meet standards set by other comparable Scriptures. From 350-450 AD they were cited an additional 4,404 times.

In addition, what is weak in one instance (a "mere citation") may be quite strong by the 400th instance of "layering it on." And there are at least 400 citations to every Apocrypha except Tobit and Judith (which, as historical

---

[322] I am utterly and completely indebted to all those who found and pointed out the citations in the translations, indexes, websites, etc. I quote herein. My own work is just a book report on theirs.
[323] The charts for Susanna and Baruch were already provided earlier. As for the canon lists, some of them have been discussed already, and I will discuss the others later.

works, would not be expected to be cited often). As such citations grew in number, (a) the implication becomes much stronger that a writer who does not specifically say (one way or the other) that something is Scripture did so precisely because he and his readership already saw the particular Book as Scripture, and (b) anyone who felt otherwise would have had every reason to be crystal clear about that view and to argue for it, given how many of his readers and peers were simultaneously calling the Book Scripture, etc.

My search for the Fathers' comments on Apocrypha was as complete as I believe necessary. The various citations that I did not go find to read for myself (and thus present to you) were not worth it, in my opinion. In any event, I give you, by far, the best starting point I know of for your own research into what these citations actually said.

I have searched many books and websites trying to find every piece of evidence there is for the claim that the Fathers supported only the Protestant/Jewish canon and rejected these Apocrypha. When I checked citations and looked for actual sources among the Fathers, I always ended up with the same handful of names, books, and quotes. I simply did not find anything more to it than what I show herein.

I originally did this work to see who said what and when, then use that data to evaluate claims. One thing that stood out was that the Fathers who cited Apocrypha cited to verses throughout the Books, on many issues; and individuals with a large body of works quoted them repeatedly throughout their lives and throughout their discourses, letters, teachings, and sermons. It seems that they knew these Books "cover-to-cover" and used them just like they used the Protestant canon. And the Fathers expected their audience to also know them cover-to-cover. One can argue of course that people have also done such with Plato, Shakespeare, and the Simpsons. But my point is that if I did not find the evidence to be used that way, that might have been a problem.

In addition, the Apocrypha are repeatedly cited in theological treatises and in arguments over heresy. I found no evidence for a "third category" until mentions of the concept (but not really use of the concept) as part of the canon lists (350 AD+), and I never found it for Baruch or Susanna (although maybe Jerome's obelus with Susanna implicitly creates a third category).

Moreover, not all evidence is equal. A sentence quoting Apocrypha in a book interpreting Paul's Epistle to the Philippians is one thing—and, sometimes, a thing easily dismissed—but it is not the same thing as an entire Biblical Commentary on the Apocrypha. Bishops were preaching sermons on that day's readings of Apocrypha, which is more of a commitment to them as

Scripture than a citation in a book.[324] Similarly, there was a Feast Day set aside for the Maccabean Martyrs, and a Basilica of the Holy Maccabees. "Put your money where your mouth is," they say. Well, some folks in "the cradle of Christianity" (Antioch[325]) must have tithed a lot of money for that Basilica dedicated to an Apocrypha.

I present the evidence for the first four Apocrypha (Susanna, Tobit, Judith, and Baruch) by annotating the Books using the KJV as my translation. The first layer of annotations includes every New Testament cross-reference to or from the Apocrypha, as noted in the original 1611 KJV, including possible quotations, fulfilled Prophesies, etc. Also included are additional possible New Testament references to Apocrypha from other sources.[326]

The second layer of annotations are (a) each and every citation where someone in the early Church specifically identified an Apocrypha as <u>not</u> being Christian canon, Scripture, etc., as well as (b) a selection of citations I found and read from all the works of the Church Fathers through 450 AD that cite the relevant Book from the Apocrypha as Sacred Scripture (or similar wording).[327] I stopped my searches (into ever more obscure and hard to find works of the Fathers) after finding over 1500 citations to all the Apocrypha as "Scripture"—and specifically after finding 500 to Wisdom, 500 to Sirach, and over 500 for the others.[328] I also give you website links to find many original sources online so that you can read the context.

---

[324] Again, this is a point often made re: the New Testament, e.g., "Paul's insistence that his letters be publicly read… and his readers' understanding of what public reading would mean within a synagogue context provide good reasons to think that his letters would have been viewed as being in the same category as other "Scripture" read during times of public worship." Kruger, p. 209. And compare to www.blueletterbible.org/Comm/stewart_don/faq/right-books-in-old-testament/question17-new-testament-quote-old-testament.cfm: "There is also evidence for the Song of Solomon. It was traditionally read at each Passover. This gives testimony to its importance among the people of Israel. Again, it is evidence of its divine inspiration."

[325] wikipedia.org/wiki/Antioch

[326] In a few cases, I also note Old Testament cross-references. There were about 700 OT-Apocrypha cross references in the KJV, but it would have been too much clutter to note them all.

[327] However, I do not always include comments that are part of the canon list data set, whether for or against Apocrypha. See the list discussions for that data.

[328] Give or take. I stopped actively counting once my personal spreadsheet reached these numbers, from which I then created this part of the book, double checking everything, deleting some mistakes and duplicates as I went, yet also stumbling on new sources—so I am not sure of the exact final tallies.

In addition, I also identify some citations that confirm doctrine[329] and "citations along with books of the Protestant canon without any qualification,"[330] Consider those a very small sampling; there are thousands more out there that just were not worth the trouble of noting them.[331]

My system for annotation is as follows:

Possible references made in the New Testament are bolded and highlighted. [332]

All text from an Apocrypha referred to in a work of the early Church Fathers is underlined.

All citations countering the claim that the Apocrypha are Sacred Scripture are in italics.

All citations supporting the claim that the Apocrypha are Sacred Scripture are bolded.

---

[329] I only looked at this piece comprehensively for the Book of Tobit; after that, it just takes too much work and is clearly superfluous. See the discussion under Tobit below.

[330] E.g., quoting Sirach with the Gospels ("as Mark says… and as Sirach says…") and adding nothing to say that Sirach is not actually Scripture (or only "Ecclesiastical" or only "to be read" but not relied upon to confirm doctrine, etc.). These citations are far too numerous to bother tracking, and I only include a few I thought were notable. As it is, my judgment after reading through a great many of them is that the vast majority of such debatable citations are obviously intended to be to the Apocrypha "as Scripture," even if they did not say so. But I still did not include them herein, except as mentioned.

[331] Gary G. Michuta, in his book *The Case for the Deuterocanon*, discusses these categories (which I have stolen/am paying homage to) and the reasons for using them. He gives 100 to 200 citations (for all the books, not for each book) in each such category, presenting them in list form, and then (in that book and his other books) goes into the Catholic theology he believes one should derive from the data. One of the questions I had from Michuta's book was "Is that a lot?"—not sarcastically, but seriously. Is a measly one or two hundred citations to all the Books over 400 years really a lot, especially when so many come from the same few Fathers? The answer is (a) he did not come close to presenting them all, (b) therefore, his lists by themselves are probably not "a lot," but (c) yes, I looked into how many there are in total, for each book, and made fair comparisons, and there are definitely a lot by any fair metric.

[332] Note that quotes almost never match the KJV exactly, thanks to translation choices, etc. Also, a few KJV cross-references between the Old Testament Books and Apocrypha are footnoted.

SUSANNA

What, precisely, is the evidence against the acceptance of Susanna as authentic Scripture by the early Church? Precisely nothing. Not a single Father wrote against it. The only evidences I found against Susanna are the letter from Africanus (asking for instruction) and the comments from Jerome (who does not argue for its exclusion).

Every canon list includes it. One cannot use canon lists to prove that the early Church accepted only the Jewish canon and not Susanna. Even if (despite the Jewish Study Bible's view) one could prove beyond a shadow of a doubt that the Jewish canon was entirely fixed and certain at the time of Christ, there is still no evidence that the early Christians held to only that canon. All the evidence there is shows they accepted Susanna as well.

Of course, translations of canon lists say Daniel. Earlier, I noted the evidence for translating Daniel as "Daniel [and Susanna]" for all the canon lists. And given that all the Fathers we know of supported Susanna (without a single exception) there is also no evidence that anonymous lists and groups were not referencing the Daniel that included Susanna.

There are also two canon lists that are specific about the size of Daniel:

> From 349 AD, a "Stichometric list" in the Codex Claromontanus: "Verses of the Holy Scriptures......Daniel 1600." [333] Sixteen hundred verses (in Latin) is the same as Job on the same list, yet in Protestant Bibles, Daniel is much shorter than Job (16 vs. 30 pages in my 1611 KJV). So, while I cannot myself count up Latin verses, I have to believe that this listing is of the Catholic version of Daniel and, thus, Susanna.
>
> From 360 AD, the Cheltenham (or Mommsen) List: "Daniel 1350 lines."[334] Those 1350 lines (in Latin) make up almost 80% the size of Job on the same list (1700 lines), yet in Protestant Bibles, Daniel is much shorter than Job (16 vs. 30 pages in my 1611 KJV). This indicates the Catholic version of Daniel, and thus, Susanna.

Meanwhile, the Fathers wrote so much about Susanna that it overwhelms the one short chapter of text. Multiple sermons and ancient Biblical commentaries discuss it line-by-line. To save space, I just give the sermons and commentaries a single mention here at the beginning, which is unfortunately misleading but it cannot be helped:

---

[333] www.bible-researcher.com/claromontanus.html
[334] www.bible-researcher.com/cheltenham.html

A full sermon from Pseudo-Chrysostom (i.e., an authentic homily from 400 AD, originally thought to have been given by John Chrysostom, but no one knows who actually gave it).[335]

Chromatius' Sermon 35 (407 AD)—I will give you this one (we only have pieces of it) as a Postscript immediately after Susanna.

Hippolytus (235 AD), a full, line-by-line commentary.[336] As noted above, he tells us in his comments on Verse 8 that "These things the rulers of the Jews wish now to expunge from the book, and assert that these things did not happen in Babylon, because they are ashamed of what was done then by the elders." In his later comments he adds: "12…For up to the present time both the Gentiles and the Jews of the circumcision watch and busy themselves with the dealings of the Church, desiring to suborn false witnesses against us" and "22. …Now it is in our power also to apprehend the real meaning of all that befell Susannah. For you may find this also fulfilled in the present condition of the Church. For when the two peoples conspire to destroy any of the saints, they watch for a fit time, and enter the house of God while all there are praying and praising God, and seize some of them, and carry them off, and keep hold of them, saying, Come, consent with us, and worship our Gods; and if not, we will bear witness against you. And when they refuse, they drag them before the court and accuse them of acting contrary to the decrees of Caesar, and condemn them to death."[337]

Origen wrote a Bible commentary on Susanna.

---

[335] www.roger-pearse.com/weblog/wp-content/uploads/2018/01/alcock-ps-chrysostom-de-susanna-2018.pdf

[336] www.newadvent.org/fathers/0502.htm

[337] In addition, Hippolytus's commentary also ties Susanna's story in with another Apocrypha, Tobit: Verse 55, ("For even now the angel of God…."): Hippolytus says: "He shows also, that when Susannah prayed to God, and was heard, the angel was sent then to help her, just as was the case in the instance of Tobias and Sara. For when they prayed, the supplication of both of them was heard in the same day and the same hour, and the angel Raphael was sent to heal them both."

Jerome translated Origen and layered his own comments on top.[338] Again Jerome acknowledges it as Scripture, but with plenty of indications that he probably wanted to get rid of it. In fact, the English translation of the last sentence of verse 54 seems to read as if Jerome wants proof before he accepts it as Scripture, but his earlier comments (and the wording of his response to Rufinus) indicate that he accepts it. Even his wording ("if ... then we too are of necessity forced to agree") seems to indicate that he wants some other folks to be the "cover" he could hide behind—i.e., he has elected to not go out on a limb over Susanna. In any event, here are his key statements, for canonical purposes:

> Verse 3. ... This verse should be used as a testimony
> Verse 8. ... For the sake of pleasing those people who seek out Scriptural precedent for everything we do, it would not be inappropriate to seize upon this passage ...
> Verse 24. ... And so for this reason the Scripture did not attribute a great voice to the outcry of the elders,
> Verse 45. ... By this language it is shown that the Holy Spirit did not then enter into Daniel, but rather that He was already within him,
> Verse 46. ... the Holy Spirit was roused up within him and dictated to the boy what he should say ... And if there is any place in Holy Scripture where the voice of a sinner is called great, it has (yet) to be noted.
> Verses 54 ff. ... Since the Hebrews reject the story of Susanna, asserting that it is not contained in the Book of Daniel, we ought to investigate carefully the names of the trees ... But if no such derivation can be found, then we too are of necessity forced to agree with the verdict of those who claim that this chapter was originally composed in Greek, because it contains Greek etymology not found in Hebrew. But if anyone can show that the derivation ... is valid in Hebrew, then we may accept this scripture also as canonical.

Earlier, I quoted what Rufinus, Jerome, Origen, and Africanus had to say in their discussions about Susanna; in addition, Eusebius cites Origen's letter on Susanna with approval but without actually citing to Susanna itself.

And even though only a few sermons and homilies were preserved for us to read, Susanna was read as Scripture and preached upon innumerable times in every single Christian Church for at least 400 years after Christ. We know that occurred because it was Daniel. The churches read Daniel and preached upon it, so they did on Susanna, as well.

---

[338] www.tertullian.org/fathers/jerome_daniel_02_text.htm (Susanna being Chapter 13).

Even without all the forgoing, you will still see plenty of references to Susanna as full Scripture below, although only a small fraction of the 499 citations from early Fathers noted at biblindex.org/citation_biblique/search.

So how do the 499 citations compare to "canonical" Daniel? Susanna is the fifth-most cited chapter of the 14 chapters of Daniel (including the other "additional" Apocrypha chapter of Daniel). Susanna is cited twice as much as five chapters, and very nearly twice as much as a sixth. Susanna holds up very well, and even more so given the contents of the chapters cited more (and how important they are to Christian beliefs). Of course, that is no surprise, since everyone accepted it as part of Daniel and thus full canonical Scripture.

Chapter	Cites	Content
3	1071	Nebuchadnezzar's dream
7	761	4 beasts; "one like the Son of man came with the clouds of heaven..."
9	708	prophecy of the 70 weeks
2	609	Nebuchadnezzar's dream
13	**499**	**Susanna**
6	329	Daniel in the lions' den
1	322	The Jews in the exile
4	278	Nebuchadnezzar's dream, continued
10	254	A theology of history
11	241	A theology of history, continued
12	226	A theology of history, continued
8	225	The ram and the he-goat
14	225	Bel and the Dragon
5	198	The writing on the wall

The first full citation to Susanna is from Irenaeus in 180 AD (70 years before Origen wrote his letter): "hear those words, to be found in Daniel the prophet: O you seed of Canaan, and not of Judah, beauty has deceived you, and lust perverted your heart. You that are waxen old in wicked days, now your sins which you have committed aforetime have come to light; for you have pronounced false judgments, and have been accustomed to condemn the innocent, and to let the guilty go free, albeit the Lord says, The innocent and the righteous shall you not slay."[339]

At the other end of the time scale, 450 AD is 200 years after Africanus sent his letter to Origen touching off that exchange. And what has happened in the 200 intervening years?

---

[339] *Against Heresy* IV, 26, 3 (www.newadvent.org/fathers/0103426.htm), quoting from Susanna (Daniel Ch. 13) 48-53.

Nothing. In 450, Susanna is still canonical Scripture to everyone. It has even been 50 years since Jerome and Rufinus feuded over Rufinus' mistaken belief that Jerome had removed Susanna—and still, everyone accepts Susanna.

As noted above, I have never been able to determine who first called for Susanna to be removed, which canon list first excludes it, which Bibles exclude it, etc. From my research, it was not before 450 AD. As I write this, our man Gallagher has announced an upcoming book: *The Apocrypha through History: The Canonical Reception of the Deuterocanonical Literature*, which I will probably buy and read with interest, even at the $130 price tag. It might answer my question (it is focused on the entire 2000-year history), but at only 288 pages (Seriously? For $130?), it probably will not.[340]

Otherwise, I know my own personal Gutenberg Bible has Susanna as part of Daniel, and that was printed (1454) before the Reformation began.[341]

Finally, there is a significant swath of literature on the canonicity of Susanna that I do not address: whether the Rabbis excluded it because it is the story of a woman fighting off sexual abuse from two Jewish leaders. Other than the preceding mention, that is just not part of my topic, interesting as it is.

However, there is also a related issue: whether the Rabbis excluded it because it is a story of the (alleged) rot and corruption within the Jewish leadership. Susanna resists the oppression of her own people and shows considerable spiritual tenacity against corrupt Elders who wield all the power and attempt to inflict injustice—and even martyrdom—upon her. That parallel to the early Christians as they suffered persecution was not lost on the early Fathers and was, perhaps, not lost on the Rabbis either. As Origen wrote:

> ... they hid from the knowledge of the people as many of the passages which contained any scandal against the elders, rulers, and judges, as they could, some of which have been preserved in uncanonical writings (Apocrypha). ... they who had the reputation of wisdom, and the rulers and elders, took away from the people every passage which might bring them into discredit among the people. We need not wonder, then, if this history of the evil device of the licentious elders against Susanna is true, but was concealed and removed from the Scriptures by men themselves not very far removed from the counsel of these elders.[342]

---

[340] Amazon says that the book will be available in late July 2025: a.co/d/ccF36Lh.
[341] Some people claim that my Gutenberg is not an original but only a modern copy. But by using the time-honored technique of never double checking things I want to believe, it remains my deeply cherished belief that I own a true Gutenberg.
[342] www.newadvent.org/fathers/0414.htm

The Jewish Study Bible notes other aspects of the discussion, which may have reinforced this concern over respect for the Jewish leaders and their decisions: "because prefigurations of Jesus and Christian resurrection were seen in Daniel by the early church, the rabbinic tradition hesitated to embrace the visions of Daniel." p. 1637.

Susanna: Annotated

1:1 There dwelt a man in Babylon, called Joacim: 1:2 And he took a wife, whose name was Susanna, the daughter of Chelcias, a very fair woman, and <u>one that feared the Lord</u>.

Cyprian 249 AD Ad Quirinum Bk 3 Intro, Ch. 20: ...you asked me to gather out for your instruction from the Holy Scriptures ... I have done what you wished. ...I have collected certain precepts of the Lord, and divine teachings ... Also in Daniel: There was a man dwelling in Babylon whose name was Joachim; and he took a wife by name Susanna, the daughter of Helchias, a very beautiful woman, and one that feared the Lord. And her parents were righteous, and taught their daughter according to the law of Moses.... www.newadvent.org/fathers/050712c.htm

Chromatius 407 AD Sermon 24.2.6: In the church there are three models of chastity that everybody must imitate: Joseph, Susanna and Mary. May men imitate Joseph, women Susanna and the virgin Mary. [Per Ancient Christian Commentary on Scripture] Not online.

Augustine 430 AD Sermon 196, 2 All the models of salvation have been set before our eyes;... If you are looking for an example of married chastity, you have Susanna; if of widowed, you have Anna; if of virginal, you have Mary. [Per The Works of Saint Augustine, A Translation for the 21st Century] Not available online.

Augustine 430 AD Sermon 96, 10: After all, it's not the case that Anna will be there and Susanna won't be there [in Heaven]. [Per The Works of Saint Augustine, A Translation for the 21st Century] Not available online.

1:3 Her parents also were righteous, and taught their daughter according to the law of Moses.

Augustine 430 AD On Holy Virginity 19: whereby, both by sure reason and authority of holy Scriptures, we both discover that marriage is not a sin, and yet equal it not to the good either of virginal or even of widowed chastity. Some forsooth by aiming at virginity, have thought marriage hateful even as adultery: but others, by defending marriage, would have the excellence of perpetual continence to deserve nothing more than married chastity; as though either the good of Susanna be the lowering of Mary: or the greater good of Mary ought to be the condemnation of Susanna. www.newadvent. org/fathers/1310.htm

1:4 Now Joacim was a great rich man, and had a fair garden joining unto his house: and to him resorted the Jews; because he was more honourable than all others. 1:5 The same year were appointed two of the ancients of the people to be judges, such as the Lord spake of, that wickedness came from Babylon from ancient judges, who seemed to govern the people.

Gregory of Nazianzus 362 AD Oration 2, 64: Passing by the elders in the book of Daniel; for it is better to pass them by, together with the Lord's righteous sentence and declaration concerning them, that wickedness came from Babylon from ancient judges. www.newadvent.org/fathers /310202.htm.

1:6 These kept much at Joacim's house: and all that had any suits in law came unto them. 1:7 Now when the people departed away at noon, <u>Susanna went into her husband's garden to walk</u>.

Ambrose 398 AD On Widows 4, 24: Let us remember then how Mary, how Anna, and how Susanna are spoken of. But since not only must we celebrate their praises but also follow their manner of life, let us remember where Susanna, and Anna, and Mary are found, and observe how each is spoken of with her special commendation, and where each is mentioned, she that is married in the garden, the widow in the temple, the virgin in her secret chamber. www.newadvent.org/fathers/3408.htm.

Ambrose 397 AD On Virgins, Book 1, 9, 45 ....Take, then, O Virgin, the wings of the Spirit, ...if you wish to attain to Christ: ...His appearance is as that of a cedar of Lebanon, ... For its beginning is from heaven, its ending on earth, and it produces fruit very close to heaven. Search diligently for so precious a flower, ... 45. It loves to grow in gardens, in which Susanna, while walking, found it, and was ready to die rather than it should be violated. www.newadvent.org/fathers/34071.htm.

1:8 And the two elders saw her going in every day, and walking; so that their lust was inflamed toward her. 1:9 And they perverted their own mind, and turned away their eyes, that they might not look unto heaven, nor remember just judgments.

Origen 253 AD Commentary on John 28.32.34: we will quote the words of Daniel about the lawless elders who lusted after Susanna. The words are as follows: "And they perverted their own mind and turned their eyes away that they might not look to heaven or remember just judgments."... [Per Ancient Christian Commentary on Scripture] Not available online.

1:10 And albeit they both were wounded with her love, yet durst not one shew another his grief. 1:11 For they were ashamed to declare their lust, that they desired to have to do with her. 1:12 Yet they watched diligently from day to day to see her. 1:13 And the one said to the other, Let us now go home: for it is dinner time. 1:14 So when they were gone out, they parted the one from the other, and turning back again they came to the same place; and after that they had asked one another the cause, they acknowledged their lust: then appointed they a time both together, when they might find her alone. 1:15 And it fell out, as they watched a fit time, she went in as before with two maids only, and she was desirous to wash herself in the garden: for it was hot. 1:16 And there was no body there save the two elders, that had hid themselves, and watched her. 1:17 Then she said to her maids, Bring me oil and washing

balls, and shut the garden doors, that I may wash me. 1:18 And they did as she bade them, and shut the garden doors, and went out themselves at privy doors to fetch the things that she had commanded them: but they saw not the elders, because they were hid. 1:19 Now when the maids were gone forth, the two elders rose up, and ran unto her, saying, 1:20 Behold, the garden doors are shut, that no man can see us, and we are in love with thee; therefore consent unto us, and lie with us. 1:21 If thou wilt not, we will bear witness against thee, that a young man was with thee: and therefore thou didst send away thy maids from thee.

Augustine 430 AD Homilies on the Gospel of John, Homily 36, 10: The chaste Susanna was harried by two false witnesses. ... Thus, to prove the point, when Susanna, a chaste woman and faithful wife, was being harried by two false witnesses, the Trinity sustained her in her conscience, in secret; in secret the Trinity raised up for her one witness, Daniel, and he confounded the two witnesses. [Per The Works of Saint Augustine, A Translation for the 21st Century] Not available online.

1:22 Then Susanna sighed, and said, I am straitened on every side: for if I do this thing, it is death unto me: and if I do it not I cannot escape your hands.

Methodius 311 AD Banquet of the Ten Virgins, 11, 2: Cited along with Genesis (Japheth) without qualification: Seeing the great beauty of Susanna, the two Judges, maddened with desire, said, O dear lady, we have come desiring secret intercourse with you; but she with tremulous cries said:— www.newadvent.org/fathers/062311.htm.

Augustine 430 AD On the Sermon on the Mount, Book 2, 9, 32: ...the heretics who are opposed to the Old Testament, not understanding this, think that the brand of ignorance, as it were, is to be placed upon Him of whom it is said, The Lord your God tempts you: ... 32. Here, therefore, the prayer is not, that we should not be tempted, but that we should not be brought into temptation: ... Susanna was tempted, but she was not led or brought into temptation; and many others of both sexes: but Job most of all, ... www.newadvent.org/fathers/16012.htm.

1:23 It is better for me to fall into your hands, and not do it, than to sin in the sight of the Lord.

Origen 253 AD Commentary on Leviticus, Homily 1, 1: But it is time for us to use the words of the holy Susanna against these wicked presbyters, which indeed those who deny the story of Susanna excise from the list of divine books. But we both receive it and aptly use it against them when it says, "Everywhere there is distress for me." For if I shall agree with you to follow the letter of the law, "it will mean death for me"; but if I will not agree, "I will not escape from your hands. But it is better for me to fall into your hands without resistance than to sin in the sight of the Lord." Not online.

1:24 With that Susanna cried with a loud voice: and the two elders cried out against her. 1:25 Then ran the one, and opened the garden door. 1:26 So when the servants of the house heard the cry in the garden, they rushed in at the privy door, to see what was done unto her. 1:27 But when the elders had declared their matter, the servants were greatly ashamed: for there was never such a report made of Susanna.

Augustine 430 AD On Holy Virginity 20: And now so often as married chastity is by truth of holy Scripture justified against such as bring calumnies and charges against marriage, so often is Susanna by the Holy Spirit defended against false witnesses,... Is it not now a milder charge, to charge Susanna, not with marriage, but with adultery itself, than to charge the doctrine of the Apostle with falsehood? What in so great peril could we do, were it not as sure and plain that chaste marriage ought not to be condemned, as it is sure and plain that

holy Scripture cannot lie? www.newadvent.org/fathers/1310.htm.

1:28 And it came to pass the next day, when the people were assembled to her husband Joacim, the two elders came also full of mischievous imagination against Susanna to put her to death; 1:29 And said before the people, Send for Susanna, the daughter of Chelcias, Joacim's wife. And so they sent. 1:30 So she came with her father and mother, her children, and all her kindred. 1:31 Now Susanna was a very delicate woman, and beauteous to behold. 1:32 And these wicked men commanded to uncover her face, (for she was covered) that they might be filled with her beauty.

Tertullian 201 AD The Chaplet, 4: If, for these and other such rules, you insist upon having positive Scripture injunction, you will find none. ... If Susanna also, who was subjected to unveiling on her trial, furnishes an argument for the veiling of women, I can say here also, the veil was a voluntary thing... www.newadvent.org/fathers/0304.htm.

1:33 Therefore her friends and all that saw her wept. 1:34 Then the two elders stood up in the midst of the people, and laid their hands upon her head. 1:35 And she weeping looked up toward heaven: for her heart trusted in the Lord.

Origen 253 AD Commentary on John 28.32.34: we will quote the words of Daniel about the lawless elders who lusted after Susanna. ... These words should be taken along with the following remarks made about Susanna, "But she, weeping, looked up to heaven, for her heart trusted in the Lord." [Per Ancient Christian Commentary on Scripture] Not online.

Ambrose 397 AD Duty of the Clergy 1, 18, 68: [teaching of Sacred writings, per 1, 1, 3] Susanna was silent in danger, and thought the loss of modesty was worse than loss of life.... www.newadvent.org/fathers/34011.htm.

Ambrose 397 AD Duty of the Clergy 1, 3, 9: [teaching of Sacred writings, per 1, 1, 3] For there is also an active silence, such as Susanna's was, who did more by keeping silence than if she had spoken. ...Yea, the Lord Himself in the Gospel worked out in silence the salvation of men. www. newadvent.org/fathers/34011.htm.

Ambrose 397 AD Duty of the Clergy 3, 14, 90: [teaching of Sacred writings, per 1, 1, 3] Holy Susanna, too, when threatened with the fear of false witness, seeing herself hard pressed on one side by danger, on the other by disgrace, preferred to avoid disgrace by a virtuous death rather than to endure and live a shameful life in the desire to save herself. www.newadvent.org/ fathers/34013.htm.

Augustine 430 AD Sermon 156, 15: Cited along with Romans, Matthew, etc. without qualification: This is a cry of the heart, not of the mouth, not of the lips; it makes itself heard inside, it makes itself heard in God's ears. Her mouth closed, her lips not moving, Susanna cried out with these words...[Dn 13:35].... [Per The Works of Saint Augustine, A Translation for the 21st Century] Not available online.

1:36 And the elders said, As we walked in the garden alone, this woman came in with two maids, and shut the garden doors, and sent the maids away. 1:37 Then a young man, who there was hid, came unto her, and lay with her. 1:38 Then we that stood in a corner of the garden, seeing this wickedness, ran unto them. 1:39 And when we saw them together, the man we could not hold: for he was stronger than we, and opened the door, and leaped out. 1:40 But having taken this woman, we asked who the young man was, but she would not tell us: these things do we testify. 1:41 Then the assembly believed them as those that were the elders and judges of the people: so they condemned her to death.

Cyril of Jerusalem 386 AD Catechetical Lecture 16, 31: ...29 And if further a man peruse all the books of the Prophets, both of the Twelve, and of the others, he will find many testimonies concerning the Holy Ghost... 31. The chaste Susanna was condemned as a wanton; ...We bring this forward as a testimony; for this is not the season for expounding. ... 32. And indeed it were easy to collect very many texts out of the Old Testament, and to discourse more largely concerning the Holy Ghost. www.newadvent.org/fathers/310116.htm

1:42 Then Susanna cried out with a loud voice, and said, O everlasting God, that knowest the secrets, and knowest all things before they be:

Athanasius 373 AD Four Discourses against the Arians 1, 12 ...where the sacred writers say, 'Who exists before the ages,' and 'By whom He made the ages,' they thereby as clearly preach the eternal and everlasting being of the Son, even while they are designating God Himself. Thus, if ... Susanna said, 'O Everlasting God' ... who has so little sense as to doubt of the eternity of the Son? www.newadvent.org/fathers /28161.htm.

Athanasius 373 AD Four Discourses against the Arians 1, 13 ... it is equally plain from what follows that the Arian phrases 'He was not,' and 'before' and 'when,' are in the same Scriptures predicated of creatures. ... And in Daniel, 'Susanna cried out with a loud voice and said, O everlasting God, that know the secrets, and know all things before they be.' www.newadvent.org/ fathers/28161.htm.

Augustine 430 AD Exposition of Psalm 35, 16 And My prayer shall return into Mine Own Bosom. In the bosom of this verse is plainly a great depth ...where Susanna prayed, and her voice, though it was not heard by men, yet by God was heard... www.newadvent.org/fathers/ 1801035.htm.

Augustine 430 AD Exposition on Psalm 3, 4: With my voice have I cried unto the Lord; that is, not with the voice of the body, which is drawn out with the sound of the reverberation of the air; but with the voice of the heart, which to men speaks not, but with God sounds as a cry. By this voice Susanna was heard...www.newadvent.org/fathers/1801003.htm.

Augustine 430 AD Letter 140, 28: Moses from the Egyptians, Rahab from the destruction of the city, Susanna from the false witnesses,... and other fathers who cried out, and they were saved... [Per The Works of Saint Augustine, A Translation for the 21st Century] Not available online.

Epiphanius 403 AD Panarion, Section 2, Heresy 30, Ebionites 9, 2: "God knoweth all things before they be," as scripture says. Not available online.

Hilary of Poitiers 368 AD On the Trinity Book 4, 8: ...7. ...refute their vain and pestilent teaching by the witness of the evangelists and apostles. ... 8. ... They say that the Father has prescience of all things, as the blessed Susanna says, O eternal God, that know secrets, and know all things before they be ... www.newadvent.org/fathers/330204.htm.

Origen 253 AD Homilies on Genesis 8.8 ... God knew, and it was not hidden from him, since it is he "who has known all things before they come to pass."' But these things are written on account of you, because you too indeed have believed in God... [Per Ancient Christian Commentary on Scripture] Not available online.

1:43 Thou knowest that they have borne false witness against me, and, behold, I must die; whereas I never did such things as these men have maliciously invented against me.

Origen 253 AD Commentary on Genesis, in Eusebius Preparation of the Gospel, Book 6, 11: But if it is necessary to prove this from Scripture also, the prophecies are full of examples of this kind, and so also is the description by Susanna of God as knowing all things before they come to pass, where she speaks as follows: "O God, the Eternal, the discerner of secrets, that knowest all things before they be, Thou understandest that these have borne false

witness against me." www.tertullian.org/fathers/eusebius_pe_06_book6.htm .

1:44 And the Lord heard her voice. 1:45 Therefore when she was led to be put to death, the Lord raised up the holy spirit of a young youth whose name was Daniel:

Ambrose 397 AD On the Holy Spirit, Book 3, 6, 39: [God] judges in a prophet... 39. Daniel also, unless he had received the Spirit of God, would never have been able to discover that lustful adultery, that fraudulent lie. For when Susanna, assailed by the conspiracy of the elders, saw that the mind of the people was moved by consideration for the old men, and destitute of all help, alone among men, conscious of her chastity she prayed God to judge; it is written: The Lord heard her voice, when she was being led to be put to death, and the Lord raised up the Holy Spirit of a young youth, whose name was Daniel. And so according to the grace of the Holy Spirit received by him, he discovered the varying evidence of the treacherous, for it was none other than the operation of divine power, that his voice should make them whose inward feelings were concealed to be known....
www.newadvent.org/fathers/34023.htm.

1:46 Who cried with a loud voice, **I am clear from the blood of this woman.**

Matthew 27:24 (When Pilate saw that he could prevail nothing, but that rather a tumult was made, he took water, and washed his hands before the multitude, saying, I am innocent of the blood of this just person: see ye to it.)

"A judge declares himself innocent of this one's blood. Finding the people insistent upon crucifixion, Pilate publicly declared his innocence: "I am innocent of the blood of this one". Daniel had made the same declaration: "I am innocent of the blood of this one". In the entire Bible only two persons, Daniel and Pilate, uttered this statement, and they did so publicly, immediately after a trial in which a falsely

accused innocent had been condemned to death. It is the typological likeness between the persons being judged, Susanna and Christ, that made it fitting for Matthew to report Pilate's words as echoing Daniel's: Daniel's words: Ἀθῷός ἐγὼ ἀπὸ τοῦ αἵματος ταύτης. Pilate's words: Ἀθῷός εἰμι ἀπὸ τοῦ αἵματος τούτου. As far as I have seen, no modern vernacular translation of the Bible conveys Matthew's quotation from Daniel: only in the Greek is this parallel made ..." Tkacz, Catherine Brown: Susanna as a Type of Christ, Studies in Iconography 20 (pp. 101-153) Western Michigan University, 1999

Augustine 430 AD Sermon 318, 2: You all know how Susanna struggled against sin to the point of shedding her blood... [Per The Works of Saint Augustine, A Translation for the 21st Century] Not available online.

1:47 Then all the people turned them toward him, and said, What mean these words that thou hast spoken? 1:48 So he standing in the midst of them said, Are ye such fools, ye sons of Israel, that without examination or knowledge of the truth ye have condemned a daughter of Israel? 1:49 Return again to the place of judgment: for they have borne false witness against her.

Apostolic Constitutions 400 AD Book 2, 51: For the Lord by Daniel delivered Susanna from the hand of the ungodly, but condemned to the fire those elders who were guilty of her blood, and reproaches you by him, saying: Are you so foolish, you children of Israel? Without examination, and without knowing the truth, have you condemned a daughter of Israel? Return again to the place of judgment, for these men have borne false witness against her." www.newadvent.org/fathers/07152.htm.

1:50 Wherefore all the people turned again in haste, and the elders said unto him, Come, sit down among us, and shew it us, seeing God hath given thee the honour of an elder. 1:51 Then said Daniel unto them, Put these two

aside one far from another, and I will examine them. 1:52 So when they were put asunder one from another, he called one of them, and said unto him, O thou that art waxen old in wickedness, now thy sins which thou hast committed aforetime are come to light. 1:53 For thou hast pronounced false judgment and hast condemned the innocent and hast let the guilty go free; albeit the Lord saith, The innocent and righteous shalt thou not slay.

Irenaeus 180 AD Against Heresy IV, 26, 3 ...they shall hear those words, to be found in Daniel the prophet: ... You that are waxen old in wicked days, now your sins which you have committed aforetime have come to light; for you have pronounced false judgments, and have been accustomed to condemn the innocent, and to let the guilty go free, albeit the Lord says, The innocent and the righteous shall you not slay. www.newadvent.org/fathers/0103426.htm

Ambrose 397 AD On Virgins, Book 2, 4, 27 Listen, you holy virgins, to the miracles of the martyr....28. ... she did not forget what she had read. Daniel, said she, had gone to see the punishment of Susanna, and alone pronounced her guiltless, whom the people had condemned... www.newadvent.org/fathers/34072.htm.

1:54 Now then, if thou hast seen her, tell me, Under what tree sawest thou them companying together? Who answered, Under a mastick tree. 1:55 And Daniel said, Very well; thou hast lied against thine own head; for even now the angel of God hath received the sentence of God to cut thee in two.

Augustine 430 AD Tractate on the Gospel of John 36, 10 (John 8:15-18): Have two or three witnesses, — the Father, Son, and Holy Ghost. In short, when Susanna, the chaste woman and faithful wife, was pressed by two false witnesses, the Trinity supported her in her conscience and in secret: that Trinity raised up from secrecy one witness, Daniel, and convicted the two. www.newadvent.org/fathers/1701036.htm

1:56 So he put him aside, and commanded to bring the other, and said unto him, <u>O thou seed of Chanaan, and not of Juda, beauty hath deceived thee, and lust hath perverted thine heart.</u>

Irenaeus 180 AD Against Heresy IV, 26, 3 ...they shall hear those words, to be found in Daniel the prophet: O you seed of Canaan, and not of Judah, beauty has deceived you, and lust perverted your heart. www.newadvent.org/fathers/0103426.htm

Origen 253 AD Commentary on the Gospel of John 20.32-33, 41, 43, 45 ...But just as some are seed of Abraham, so others are really "seed of Canaan, not of Judah," as Daniel says... [Per Ancient Christian Commentary on Scripture] Not online.

1:57 Thus have ye dealt with the daughters of Israel, and they for fear companied with you: but the daughter of Juda would not abide your wickedness. 1:58 Now therefore tell me, Under what tree didst thou take them companying together? Who answered, Under an holm tree. 1:59 Then said Daniel unto him, Well; thou hast also lied against thine own head: for the angel of God waiteth with the sword to cut thee in two, that he may destroy you. 1:60 With that all the assembly cried out with a loud voice, and praised <u>God, who saveth them that trust in him.</u>

Augustine 430 AD Sermon 46 on the New Testament, 10: Let not the virgin say, I shall alone be there [Heaven]. For Mary shall not be there alone but the widow Anna shall be there also. Let not the woman which has an husband say, The widow will be there, not I; for it is not that Anna will be there, and Susanna not be there. www.newadvent.org/fathers/160346.htm

1:61 And they arose against the two elders, for Daniel had convicted them of false witness by their own mouth: 1:62 And according to the law of Moses they did unto them in such sort as they maliciously intended to do to their neighbour: and they put them to death. Thus the innocent blood was saved the same day. 1:63 Therefore Chelcias and his wife praised God for their daughter Susanna, with Joacim her husband, and all the kindred, because there was no dishonesty found in her. 1:64 From that day forth was Daniel had in great reputation in the sight of the people.

Sulpitius Severus 420 AD Sacred History 2, 1: (Ch 1, 1:) I address myself to give a condensed account of those things which are set forth in the sacred Scriptures from the beginning of the world ... (Ch 2,1:) The times of the captivity have been rendered illustrious by the predictions and deeds of the prophets, and especially by the remarkable persistency of Daniel in upholding the law, and by the deliverance of Susanna through the divine wisdom, as well as by the other things which it accomplished, and which we shall now relate in their order... About the same time, Susanna, the wife of a certain man called Joachis... Susanna was acquitted; and the elders, who had brought the innocent into danger, were condemned to death. www.newadvent.org/fathers/35052.htm.

Postscript to Susanna: A Sermon from Chromatius of Aquileia

Chromatius of Aquileia: Sermons and Tractates on Matthew, a translation from Thomas P. Scheck, explains how important Chromatius (Bishop of Aquileia) was to Jerome, Rufinus, and the canon:

> Several of Jerome's translations of Scripture … and commentaries … are indebted to Chromatius's insistence and monetary support. A number of contemporary figures, including Augustine and Rufinus, were disturbed by Jerome's interest in Hebrew philology and his translation work based on the Hebrew text of the Old Testament. They tried to dissuade him from Hebrew studies and even accused him of Judaizing … In striking contrast with these critics, Chromatius belonged to the limited circle of Jerome's friends who understood his motives, applauded his principles, and encouraged his efforts in translating and expounding the Hebrew text of the Old Testament.
>
> Yet, simultaneously, the magnanimous and scholarly Chromatius was also a lifelong friend and supporter of Rufinus … when the friendship between Rufinus and Jerome was ruptured … Chromatius maintained his friendship with both men and did his best to reconcile them. It is noteworthy that a number of Chromatius's Sermons and Tractates emphasize the importance of fraternal charity and unanimity! Additionally, Chromatius even commissioned Rufinus with the task of translating … and he became the dedicatee of these works. … Rufinus says further that he defers entirely to Chromatius's judgment in assessing the quality of Origen's offering. …

His Sermon 35 was dedicated to that day's Scripture reading—Susanna:

> In today's reading that you have heard [dearly beloved], the story of the most noble woman Susanna was read to us, who has offered to us a model of chastity and an example of purity. To be sure, she was lovely in appearance, but lovelier in character. For with her the beauty of soul surpassed that of body; for the body's beauty is temporary, but the soul's beauty is eternal. For she was not adorned with bodily necklaces, nor did she have earrings on her body, nor rings, nor pearls, but she was filled within with every ornament of the virtues. For in place of earrings she had the divine words, in place of a ring she had comely faith, in place of pearls she had the precious works by which daily she beautified the appearance of her mind and soul.
>
> Using this example among others, the blessed apostle Paul exhorts the women and says, "Finally, let women be holy, adorning themselves not with plaited hair, or gold, or pearls, or costly attire, but preserving chastity with good works" [1 Tim 2:9-10; cf. 1 Pet 3:3- 5]. …Therefore if you desire to please God, follow the example of Susanna: be chaste, be modest, be of virtuous character, be a worker of justice, and you will be sufficiently beautiful, and not only to God but also precious to men. For this beauty usually pleases faithful husbands as well, if he finds in his wife beautiful actions and comeliness of mind….
>
> Susanna, then, for the sake of purity, even despised death. For she is denounced by two ruined elders, she is accused as if guilty and condemned as an adulteress [see Dan 13:41]. But the holy and admirable woman preferred to submit to death with her purity

intact than to live with a bad conscience. But when she was being led to death, God stirred up the holy spirit of the boy Daniel, who is called "desirable to God" [see Dan 9:23; 10:11], who both made known Susanna's innocence and revealed the false accusation of her accusers [see Dan 13:44-59]. Whence it came about that the innocent Susanna was set free before the just judgment of God and the elderly falsely accusing adulterers perished by a deserved death. The king of Babylon roasted them in fire on account of the iniquity that they committed in Israel, and because they were committing adultery with the wives of their own citizens [see Dan 13:62].

Therefore Susanna has prefigured the church, namely by the example of purity and modesty, since she remained in the paradise of Christ by faith and by the manner of her life [see Dan 13:4, 7], just as all the faithful in the church strive to please Christ, their God and head, by the purity of their character, the holiness of good works, right faith, firm hope, and perfect love. Finally, chastity and modesty are aided by fasting. For we fast to this end, not merely to abstain from food, but to separate ourselves from all the vices of the flesh, namely, from bodily lust, from concupiscence of soul, from depraved thoughts, from hatred and ill will, from detraction and murmuring, from fury and wrath, from all vices and sins together. But merely to abstain from food is not fasting. That is why, when we fast, we ought especially to abstain from vices, lest it be said to us by the Lord through the prophet, "That is not the sort of fast I have chosen, says the Lord..." [Isa 58:5].

Postscript: Chromatius as Data

Chromatius is an interesting data point, since he was something of a bridge between Rufinus and Jerome (friends who became nasty enemies[343]), as well as between Jerome's view of the Hebrew canon and the view of the rest of the Church. So the book itself is another data set that I decided to analyze.

In the midst of commenting on Matthew, Chromatius referred to Apocrypha 64 times.[344] Fifty-nine times (more than 90%) he specifically calls them Scripture, Prophecy, the inspiration of the Holy Spirit, etc. He never refers to any Apocrypha as "Ecclesiastical" or "only to be read" or any such. He clearly had no problem citing to Apocrypha to confirm doctrine. He sees the Apocrypha as prophecies fulfilled by the Gospel, and he explains much of the Gospel by reference to the Apocrypha. He cites to Susanna, Judith,[345]

---

[343] Rufinus and Jerome were rather prickly fellows, to put it mildly. See their mutual attacks on each other, and many other Fathers, at www.newadvent.org/fathers/2709.htm and www.newadvent.org/fathers/2710.htm.

[344] Counting his entire sermon on Susanna as only one citation. Many of the other citations will appear below.

[345] The reference to Judith is personal to her and not the book: "...prefigured in saints of past times. For the most holy Judith, ..." I view that as sufficient to say Chromatius saw Judith as Scripture, but for the data set on the Book of Judith, I considered it only a citation to Judith made

Baruch, Tobit, 2 Maccabees, Sirach, and Wisdom—all the Apocrypha except 1 Maccabees.

Of the 59 Tractates (each covering a piece of Matthew Chapters 1-18, but several chapters of that sequence from Matthew are missing from the Tractates we still have), 26 of them cite to Apocrypha, involving 11 of the 15 chapters of Matthew that Chromatius covers. Only a handful of the citations are to duplicate passages of Apocrypha. Sirach is, by far, the most-cited Book, with 38 citations (all full quotations). Of those 38, they come from 18 different chapters of Sirach and represent 36 different pieces of Sirach, since only two are duplicates of other quotations he also used elsewhere.

He would seem to have been a man who knew the Apocrypha well and saw them as full Scripture (and we know from Rufinus that the Apocrypha were read as part of the liturgy in Chromatius' Episcopal See of Aquileia).[346] He used them often and at a considerable rate, selecting quotes from all over the texts, etc.

Backing that up is the fact that it was he who insisted upon (and even paid for) Jerome's translation of Tobit. Otherwise, it is not clear why he would waste Jerome's time and talent (and Chromatius' own money) on "books that are not Scripture" when there was still more Scripture to cover.

And Chromatius was one of the Bishops who supported Jerome, although even they would come to have a falling out.

---

along with other citations to Scripture without qualifying that Judith was, somehow, different from the Scriptures. As always, make up your own mind about such things.

[346] Commentary on the Apostles' Creed 38 www.newadvent.org/fathers/2711.htm

TOBIT

"Four Aramaic and one Hebrew fragment [of Tobit] were found among the Dead Sea Scrolls, indicating an authoritative status among some sects."[347] Bear in mind that, to us, such a find is more than just an indication of the status of Tobit before 68 AD, interesting and relevant as that factoid is.

We know that, by Origen's time, "Tobias (as also Judith) ...the Jews do not use. They are not even found in the Hebrew Apocrypha, as I learned from the Jews themselves. ..." Origen tells us that the Jewish leaders "pretended to the Jews ... deceived the wives of their countrymen. ... hid from the knowledge of the people ... took away from the people every passage ... concealed and removed from the Scriptures..." Thus, from the Dead Sea Scrolls, we have evidence that Tobit had been seen as authoritative by some by 68 AD, only to cease being accepted even as Hebrew Apocrypha by Origen's time. In less than 200 years, it may have gone from authoritative (at least to some) to nothing, exactly as Origen and others claimed.

The New Testament makes 16 possible cross-references to Tobit, which I set out for you to judge. For example, elements of a question asked of Jesus (the woman with seven husbands) occur in Tobit 3:8; there are seven angels in Revelation, and Raphael says in Tobit 12:15 that he is "one of the seven holy angels, which present the prayers of the saints, and which go in and out before the glory of the Holy One;" the Greek word in John 1:14 for "[the Word] made His dwelling" is literally "tabernacled" which parallels the language in Tobit 13:10. Those could be multiple references from John in multiple works, which, as noted previously, dovetails into the references to Tobit in the Epistle written by Polycarp, the disciple who learned at the feet of John.

In addition, Mary's "Magnificat" in Luke 1:48 says that all generations shall call her blessed, while Tobit 13:11 says "all generations shall praise thee with great joy." Matthew's tale of the Magi seems to have many parallels to Tobit 13:11 as well, e.g. "Many nations shall come from far to the name of the Lord God with gifts in their hands, even gifts to the King of heaven." Moreover, in modern Bibles that include Tobit (but not in the KJV), there is

---

[347] wikipedia.org/wiki/Book_of_Tobit, citing Klawans, Jonathan (2020): The Jewish Annotated Apocrypha; Oxford University Press. p. 149–151

another sentence to Tobit 13:11: "A bright light will shine forth into the farthest corners of the earth,"[348] which is evocative of the Star of Bethlehem.

Biblindex.org/citation_biblique/search lists 235 citations to Tobit by the Fathers. For comparison, Tobit, Judith, and the two Books of the Maccabees are considered historical Books.[349] That category includes 12 Books of the Protestant canon for a total of 16 comparable Books.[350] Tobit would rank 10th, comfortably ahead of three Books of the Protestant canon (1 Chronicles, Nehemiah, and Esther), as well as ranking highest among the historical Books of the Apocrypha.

	Book	Verses	Cites	Rate
1	2 Kings	719	4358	6.06
2	1 Samuel	810	4780	5.90
3	Joshua	658	3475	5.28
4	1 Kings	817	4120	5.04
5	2 Samuel	695	2804	4.03
6	Judges	618	2201	3.56
7	2 Chronicles	821	2172	2.65
8	Ruth	85	201	2.36
9	Ezra[351]	280	592	2.11
10	**Tobit**	**245**	**235**	**0.96**
11	**2 Maccabees**	**556**	**488**	**0.88**
12	1 Chronicles	943	787	0.83
13	**1 Maccabees**	**922**	**596**	**0.65**
14	Nehemiah	405	256	0.63
15	Esther	272	143	0.53
16	**Judith**	**340**	**120**	**0.35**

---

[348] See, for example, www.biblegateway.com/verse/en/Tobit%2013%3A11

[349] John Barton, in his book *The Spirit and the Letter: Studies in the Biblical Canon*, uses the same citations per verse methodology and notes that such surveys have to focus on the type of book. See, e.g., p. 23-24, where he notes that "The historical books, for example, never seem to have been in the least controversial, yet neither Jews nor Christians ever used them much in their writings … in much the same position as Acts for early Christian writers: undoubtedly authoritative, scarcely ever used…" Susanna, for example, is cited almost eight times as often by this metric, but it is (to the early Church) part of a prophetic work, and thus, we find that it gets quoted at a rate comparable to the rest of Daniel—not at all comparable to Tobit.

[350] Esther straddles the Protestant canon and the Apocrypha, as there are substantial changes in the Catholic version. The Biblindex database seems to use only the Protestant version, not including any citations to the Catholic verses (which is part of the reason I analyze Susanna herein and not Esther). I am not certain if the Catholic portion would change the data significantly, but it might— some of the most notable early citations to Esther (from Josephus, 1 Clement, etc.) are to the Apocrypha portion (and of course, the Protestant version never explicitly mentions God either).

[351] We will see that Judith's ranking at the bottom is more a testament to how many times Eusebius cites Nehemiah than an indictment on Judith, and he has the same effect on Tobit when compared to Ezra (Ezra-Nehemiah having been one book to the early Church): a majority (53%) of all of the cites to Ezra are just from Eusebius; if we count everyone except Eusebius, then Tobit would be very nearly equal to Ezra.

Noted below for your review are 132 of the citations to Tobit by Fathers of the early Church (these are the ones I could personally find and read for myself). The citations I note come from 79 different works of 29 Fathers[352]— i.e., the works I could access online or in my own library.

If the small numbers initially surprise you, bear in mind that there are not all that many Fathers whose writings have survived. Only 127 Fathers have left source material to be referenced in biblindex.org/citation_biblique /search.[353] Of the 127, 16 are "pseudo" attributions (they are real writings but definitely not written by the name given), 26 are dubious attributions to a name (could be his but probably not). Six are "anonymous" categories for unknown authors. At least 11 are (to my mind) opponents of Christianity, not Christians. Many of the remaining 68 entries include just a work or two (which may have no application to our inquiry). Most of the Fathers who show up in any search I ran for Apocrypha or canonical Books are the same big names/usual suspects among the Fathers.

Wikipedia lists 137 Fathers that might fit my timeframe (up until 450 AD) but it is not clear that all left writings.[354] And by my count, fewer than two dozen of those could have written a single word before 200.

Habermas and Licona report that the total of all authors who simply mention Jesus within 150 years of his life (183 AD) is 42 (*The Case for the Resurrection of Jesus*, p.127)—which they do as part of claiming how much evidence there is for Jesus, not how little. 9 of those mentions were the Evangelists in the Bible, only 20 came from the early Church.

So, the fact that I found citations as Scripture from dozens of Fathers, even for Tobit and Judith (the two least-cited Apocrypha in the database, by total citations), is actually a very meaningful result. Basically, every single Father

---

[352] My numbers on specific details like this (how many Fathers cite to something, etc.) can differ a bit compared to Biblindex, since I found some things that are not included in the portion of the database I am able to access. For Tobit, I counted the Fathers listed by Biblindex by hand and came up with a slightly different set of 29 Fathers citing Tobit per Biblindex, of whom three are anonymous categories. So, their total number is not hugely different than my data set; both just have "fuzzy edges."

[353] The database is a work in progress (the part I can search does not yet reach Augustine, etc.). But it is said to be comprehensive until some point in the 300s AD, so all I would have missed would be later citations. I also supplemented with many searches elsewhere, so I believe that my research, while not perfectly complete, is reasonably complete coverage through 450 AD.

[354] wikipedia.org/wiki/List_of_Church_Fathers.

for whom we have substantial writings cited to some Apocrypha as Scripture, and a high percentage of them included cites to Tobit, in particular.

We also see that one Father (Athanasius) created a canon list that put Tobit in the "not canon, only to be read" category but is arguably contradictory: in three separate works, (1) he cites Tobit as Prophesy (See 14:6), (2) he cites Tobit as providing a command that his accusers violated (See 12:7),[355] and (3) he implies that Tobit is on an equal footing with Isaiah (See 4:18).

Hilary of Poitiers noted that "some accept" Tobit on his list, and in his own works, he refers to Tobit to confirm doctrine and cites to it with other Scripture without qualification. Clement of Alexandria (who gave us a partial list recorded by Eusebius, which noted that he used Wisdom and Sirach but did not mention Tobit either way) also cites to Tobit as Scripture several times in his Stromata. (Why Eusebius does not note that is unclear, but maybe he saw Tobit as undisputed Scripture.)

Of the 132 citations, 81 citations (a clear majority) specifically refer to Tobit as Scripture (or some other such word: at least five Fathers (Africanus, Ambrose, Augustine, Chrysostom, and Athanasius) specifically cite to Tobit as Prophecy, for example).

Of the other 51 citations, 49 reference[356] Tobit along with other Scripture without qualification. Of the two remaining citations, one I took from the Ancient Christian Commentary on Scripture,[357] and the quotation extracted by ACCS does not include any reference to other Scriptures (and is unavailable online for me to see its context). The quote is a long instruction to fast and give alms, and the citation is used to confirm the doctrine that fasting with prayer mitigates the Lord's indignation. The other is from *The Life and Passion of Cyprian* by his deacon, Pontius, in which (as far as I can tell) the only citation to Scripture/Apocrypha that he makes in the entire obituary is to Tobit (a Book which Cyprian himself repeatedly declared to be Scripture).

---

[355] Technically, the words had once been stated by Bishops ruling in Athanasius' favor, and he quotes them (obviously with approval) as part of his defense on a later charge (he made and faced charges all the time—his nickname was Athanasius Contra Mundum, Athanasius Against the World). Even if Athanasius would not agree with the precise wording as a technical matter (perhaps he was just using it to save his own skin), the Bishops' letter is evidence that the ancient Church cited it as a command without qualification.

[356] Some instances of this category are allusions—a mixed bag of obvious allusions that cannot realistically be to anything else, as well as some that might also be allusions to other Scriptures, and a few that, arguably, might not be intentional allusions at all. Note that such things may be more or less obvious in Greek (etc.) than in translation.

[357] Gaudentius of Brescia, Sermon 13, 21, citing Tobit 12:8.

By my count, 102 of the 132 citations (a clear majority) are used specifically to confirm doctrine,[358] and of the remaining 30, 18 of the citations are specifically calling Tobit Scripture (or some such term) for some other purpose (e.g., discussing historical events from sacred history, etc.). Those two categories—referring to it as Scripture and using it to confirm doctrine, i.e., the categories directly contrary to the claims of Jerome and Rufinus (and to some extent Athanasius)—combine to account for 120 of 132 citations. The overlap of those two categories (62 instances where Tobit is specifically referred to as Scripture and also used to confirm doctrine) is a majority of each such category—and more than half of both categories combined.

The remaining citations are to things like "be rather such a father to your children as was Tobias" (from Cyprian, see Tobit 14:11).

Fifty-eight of the 132 citations occurred before 350 AD, and the first certain council or clearly-Christian canon list—notably including cites from 1 Clement (listed as 96 AD, but arguably, it was written before 70 AD since 1 Clement speaks of the Temple as still in existence; either way, it may have been written before the last Books of the New Testament), the Didache (100 AD), Polycarp (107 AD), Tertullian (192 AD), Clement of Alexandria (198 AD), and Origen (230 AD).

No Father (when citing to Tobit) ever distinguished it with warnings or labels or claimed it was in a third category of Books that should only be read, etc. Such concepts only appear on canon lists.

Biblindex.org/citation_biblique/search notes citations to 88 verses out of 245, or 36% of verses, which seems pretty normal for a historical Book—they often have significant gaps in what people want to cite to (e.g., only two of the 22 verses of 2 Chronicles Chapter 4 were ever cited in the first 450 years of Christianity, both (4:8 and 4:19) by Hilary, in a single Sermon).[359]

Notable individual pieces of evidence include a treatise on Tobit (On Tobias) written by Ambrose of Milan in 377 AD. It is mostly a long discussion of usury and related issues, since part of the story of Tobit involves money

---

[358] But defining doctrine and what confirms it is a fuzzy parameter, so be your own judge.

[359] Perhaps there was a vast conspiracy to avoid drawing attention to the mathematical discrepancy in 2 Chronicles 4:2 ("Also he made a molten sea of ten cubits from brim to brim, round in compass, and five cubits the height thereof; and a line of thirty cubits did compass it round about." I.e., Pi = 3, not 3.14159…).

committed to others (See Tobit 4:1, etc.), but included with that is some Scriptural commentary on Tobit itself.[360]

In addition, in 2:1, we will see explicit mention by Augustine of Tobit being read at a memorial service at the shrine of a Saint, and we know that Tobit was read as part of the liturgy in the early Churches.[361]

Tobit is the only work for which my data can be used to calculate percentages for "confirming doctrine," because only for Tobit did I collect all citations I could, including those that were not explicitly as Scripture. Some citations for confirming doctrine are still included for other Apocrypha (I had already found them before I stopped), but definitely not all. Thus, these sorts of percentage calculations would not be accurate and will no longer be made.

I stopped gathering them because there is no point: anyone claiming that the Apocrypha were not used to confirm doctrine would appear to be relying on claims from Athanasius, Rufinus, and Jerome rather than actual research into original sources.[362] I try to show this by using the percentage data on Tobit; otherwise, it should be quickly obvious to anyone who looks into the matter that a huge fraction of citations are to confirm doctrine.

Putting the Maccabees aside,[363] the majority of citations from the ancient Fathers are (explicitly or implicitly) to the Apocrypha in support of doctrine. In many—if not most—cases, one quotes Scripture as the exact doctrine one is "confirming." E.g., Augustine Letter 140, 69: "For scripture says where an angel speaks to human beings, "I presented the record of your prayer" (Tobit 12: 12)." What doctrine is he confirming with that quote from Scripture? The doctrine that is exactly what the Scripture says it is: angels present our prayers to God.[364] You can plainly see from just the partial language quotes given herein that most of the cites are confirming doctrines.

---

[360] It is available online at babel.hathitrust.org/cgi/pt?id=uc1.$b109460&seq=1.

[361] See, e.g., Rufinus on the Apostles' Creed 38 at www.newadvent.org/fathers/2711.htm.

[362] In fact the original sources would also show Athanasius' own extensive use of the Apocrypha to confirm doctrine. Of course he had not mentioned that concept (his own wording was "only to be read"), so maybe that is no surprise. See below.

[363] The majority of cites to the Maccabees are only as historical events; but even for them, there are still many cites used to confirm doctrine, especially for 2 Maccabees. See the discussion below, where I go into all the cites to those books.

[364] Augustine's point is, of course, only a piece of an even larger point he is making. At higher levels this analysis becomes very subjective, since there is no guidance from the "only to confirm doctrine" claimants to define what level qualifies as a doctrine. That quickly became part of my annoyance with this attempted research.

Tobit: Annotated

1:1 <u>The book of the words of Tobit</u>, son of Tobiel, the son of Ananiel, the son of Aduel, the son of Gabael, of the seed of Asael, of the tribe of Nephthali;

Pseudo-Ambrose 390 AD Quaestiones Veteris et Noui Testamenti 119, 2: p. 359: God's holy rites, therefore, were given to us by Tobias as an example of the law. And, if temptations come, do not depart from the fear of God... archive.org/details/ pseudoaugustini00soutgoog/page/358/mode/ 2up. Used to confirm the doctrine that God allows us to suffer and be tempted in order to strengthen us.

1:2 Who in the time of Enemessar king of the Assyrians was led captive out of Thisbe, which is at the right hand of that city, which is called properly Nephthali in Galilee above Aser. 1:3 I Tobit have walked all the days of my life in the ways of truth and justice, and I did many almsdeeds to my brethren, and my nation, who came with me to Nineve, into the land of the Assyrians. 1:4 And when I was in mine own country, in the land of Israel being but young, all the tribe of Nephthali my father fell from the house of Jerusalem, which was chosen out of all the tribes of Israel, that all the tribes should sacrifice there, where the temple of the habitation of the most High was consecrated and built for all ages. 1:5 Now all the tribes which together revolted, and the house of my father Nephthali, sacrificed unto the heifer Baal. 1:6 But I alone went often to Jerusalem at the feasts, as it was ordained unto all the people of Israel by an everlasting decree, having the firstfruits and tenths of increase, with that which was first shorn; and them gave I at the altar to the priests the children of Aaron. 1:7 The first tenth part of all increase I gave to the sons of Aaron, who ministered at Jerusalem: another tenth part I sold away, and went, and spent it every year at Jerusalem: 1:8 And the third I gave unto them to whom it was meet, as Debora my father's mother had commanded me, because I was left an orphan by my father. 1:9 Furthermore, when I was come to the age of a man, I married Anna of mine own kindred, and of her I begat Tobias. 1:10 And when <u>we were carried away captives to Nineve</u>, all my brethren and those that were of my kindred did eat of the bread of the Gentiles.

Sulpitius Severus 420 AD Sacred History 1, 49 (Ch 1, 1:) I address myself to give a condensed account of those things which are set forth in the sacred Scriptures... (Ch 1, 49:) ... in this war, Tobias was carried into captivity.... www.newadvent.org/fathers/35051.htm

1:11 But I kept myself from eating; <u>1:12 Because I remembered God with all my heart. 1:13 And the most High gave me grace and favour before Enemessar, so that I was his purveyor. 1:14 And I went into Media, and left in trust with Gabael, the brother of Gabrias, at Rages a city of Media ten talents of silver.</u>

Origen (248 AD), Letter to Africanus 13 [Referred to Tobit as Scripture the Churches use in 13] Tobias ... the Jews do not use. They are not even found in the Hebrew Apocrypha, as I learned from the Jews themselves. However, since the Churches use Tobias, ... Tobias himself says, [Tobit 1:12-1:14]. www.newadvent. org/fathers/0414.htm. Used as Scripture to confirm other books as Scripture.

1:15 Now when Enemessar was dead, Sennacherib his son reigned in his stead; whose estate was troubled, that I could not go into Media. 1:16 <u>And in the time of Enemessar I gave many alms to my brethren, and gave my bread to the hungry, 1:17 And my clothes to the naked: and if I saw any of my nation dead, or cast about the walls of Nineve, I buried him. 1:18 And if the king Sennacherib had slain any, when he was come, and fled from Judea, I buried them privily; for in his wrath he killed many;</u> but the bodies were not found, when they were sought for of the king.

Origen (248 AD), Letter to Africanus 13 [Referred to Tobit as Scripture the Churches use, see Tobit 1:14] And he adds,

as if he were a rich man, [Tobit 1:15-1:18]. www.newadvent.org/fathers/0414.htm. Used as Scripture to confirm other books as Scripture.

Pontius 258 AD The Life and Passion of Cyprian, Bishop and Martyr, 10: Something more was done than is recorded of the incomparable benevolence of Tobias. ... although very much might be done before Christ, yet that something more might be done after Christ, since to His times all fulness is attributed. Tobias collected together those who were slain by the king and cast out, of his own race only. www.newadvent.org/fathers/0505.htm. Used to confirm the doctrine that more is expected of Christians.

Chromatius 407 AD Tractate on Matthew 41, 9: Here, then, in the words that the Lord speaks, "Let the dead bury their own dead" [Matt 8:22], he has not inhibited the obligations of religious piety, by which we know that many saints have pleased God [see Tob 1:17], ... Surely we notice that this was said not about the burial of a body but about works of the flesh, dead in transgressions.... [Per Chromatius of Aquileia, Sermons and Tractates on Matthew]. Not available online. Used to confirm the doctrine that burying the dead is pleasing to God.

1:19 And when one of the Ninevites went and complained of me to the king, that I buried them, and hid myself; understanding that I was sought for to be put to death, I withdrew myself for fear. 1:20 Then all my goods were forcibly taken away, neither was there any thing left me, beside my wife Anna and my son Tobias.

Origen (248 AD), Letter to Africanus 13 [Referred to Tobit as Scripture the Churches use, see Tobit 1:14] Think whether this great catalogue of Tobias's good deeds does not betoken great wealth and much property, especially when he adds, [Tobit 1:19-1:20]. www.newadvent. org/fathers/0414.htm. Used as Scripture to confirm other books as Scripture.

1:21 And there passed not five and fifty days, before two of his sons killed him, and they fled into the mountains of Ararath; and Sarchedonus his son reigned in his stead; who appointed over his father's accounts, and over all his affairs, Achiacharus my brother Anael's son. 1:22 And Achiacharus intreating for me, I returned to Nineve. Now Achiacharus was cupbearer, and keeper of the signet, and steward, and overseer of the accounts: and Sarchedonus appointed him next unto him: and he was my brother's son.

Origen (248 AD), Letter to Africanus 13 [Referred to Tobit as Scripture the Churches use, see Tobit 1:14] cited Tobit 1:21-1:22. www.newadvent.org/fathers/0414 .htm. Used as Scripture to confirm other books as Scripture.

2:1 Now when I was come home again, and my wife Anna was restored unto me, with my son Tobias, in the feast of Pentecost, which is the holy feast of the seven weeks, there was a good dinner prepared me, in the which I sat down to eat.

Augustine 400 AD Reply to Faustus 22, 35:[Referred to as Scripture in 22, 35: See Tobit 8:9] We learn also from the book of Tobit, that Pentecost was the feast of seven weeks. www.newadvent.org/fathers/140622 .htm

Augustine 430 AD Sermon 272B, 2: Refers to Tobit being read at the memorial shrine of a Saint: Cited along with Acts, etc. without qualification: You 'You heard earlier this morning, those of you who were paying attention, when the reading from Tobit was being read at the memorial shrine (memoria) of the blessed Theogenes, how on the day of Pentecost he made a dinner for himself, intending to invite others of his people who would be worthy to share his table, seeing that they had in them the fear of the Lord.' portal.sds.ox. ac.uk/articles/online_resource/E02217_Aug ustine_of_Hippo_refers_to_his_sermon_pre ached_at_the_memorial_shrine_memoria_o f_Theogenes_bishop_and_martyr_of_Hippo _S01133_Sermon_272B_delivered_in_Hipp o_North_Africa_in_AD_417_/13818152/1

Augustine 430 AD Sermon 270, 6: The law, then, is fulfilled through the grace of the Holy Spirit; so now observe how the number ten was to be both drawn to our attention and impressed upon us, as we have already shown, and also the number seven, on account of this very grace of the Holy Spirit... So where, in this connection, shall we find the number seven impressed on us, above all because of the Holy Spirit himself? In the book of Tobit you have this very festival, that is Pentecost, consisting of seven-day weeks... [Per The Works of Saint Augustine, A Translation for the 21st Century] Not available online.

2:2 And when I saw abundance of meat, I said to my son, Go and bring what poor man soever thou shalt find out of our brethren, who is mindful of the Lord; and, lo, I tarry for thee.

Luke 14:13 (But when thou makest a feast, call the poor, the maimed, the lame, the blind) (cf. 4:7 which is a KJV cross reference; 2:2 calls for inviting any poor man soever thou shalt find out of our brethren to a meal).

Cyprian258 AD Treatise 12, 3, 1 [Referred to as Holy Scriptures in 12, 3, Introduction: ... you asked me to gather out for your instruction from the Holy Scriptures ...] Of this same matter in Tobit: [Tobit 2:2] www.newadvent.org/fathers/ 050712c.htm. Used to confirm the doctrine of the benefits of good works and mercy.

2:3 But he came again, and said, Father, one of our nation is strangled, and is cast out in the marketplace.

Africanus 248 AD Letter to Origen 2: [In arguing that Susannah is not Scripture, Africanus cites to Tobit as prophesy:] Moreover, how is it that they who were captives among the Chaldæans, lost and won at play, thrown out unburied on the streets, as was prophesied of the former captivity,... www.newadvent.org/ fathers/ 0413.htm. Used as Scripture to dispute the claim that another books is Scripture.

2:4 Then before I had tasted of any meat, I started up, and took him up into a room until the going down of the sun.

Ambrose 397 AD Duties of the Clergy 3, 96: Cited along with Moses without qualification: Tobit also clearly portrayed in his life true virtue, when he left the feast and buried the dead, and invited the needy to the meals at his own poor table. www.newadvent.org/fathers/34013.htm. Used to confirm the doctrine that burying the dead is pleasing to God

Maximus of Turin 450 AD Sermons 41.2 Cited along with Matthew, etc. without qualification: ...Tobit is justified because he abandons his meal for the sake of a burial...Thus, ... in consideration of Christ we owe burial to everyone.... [Per Ancient Christian Commentary on Scripture]. Not available online. Used to confirm the doctrine that we owe burial to everyone.

2:5 Then I returned, and washed myself, and ate my meat in heaviness,

Ambrose 397 AD On Paradise 15.75: Cited with Exodus w/o qualification: Hence the Hebrews, who groaned in the works of Egypt, attained the grace of the just, and those "who ate bread with mourning and fear" were supplied with spiritual good. [Per Ancient Christian Commentary on Scripture]. Not available online.

2:6 Remembering that prophecy of Amos, as he said, Your feasts shall be turned into mourning, and all your mirth into lamentation.

2:7 Therefore I wept: and after the going down of the sun I went and made a grave, and buried him.

Augustine 422 AD On the Care of the Dead 5: Cited along with Matthew, etc. without qualification. www.newadvent.org/ fathers/1316.htm. Used to confirm the doctrine that burying the dead pleases God

2:8 But my neighbours mocked me, and said, This man is not yet afraid to be put to death for this matter: who fled away; and yet, lo, he burieth the dead again. 2:9 The same night also I returned from the burial, and slept by the wall of my courtyard, being polluted and my face was uncovered: 2:10 And I knew not that there were sparrows in the wall, and mine eyes being open, the sparrows muted warm dung into mine eyes, and a whiteness came in mine eyes: and I went to the physicians, but they helped me not: moreover Achiacharus did nourish me, until I went into Elymais.

Cyprian 258 AD Treatise 9: 10. Finally, we find that both patriarchs and prophets ... preserve patience with a strong and steadfast equanimity..... 17. ...the righteous is proved by his patience, as it is written: ... 18. Thus Job ... Tobias also, who, after the sublime works of his justice and mercy, was tried with the loss of his eyes, in proportion as he patiently endured his blindness, in that proportion deserved greatly of God by the praise of patience. www.newadvent.org/ fathers/050709.htm. Used to confirm the doctrine that the righteous is proved by his patience.

Augustine 430 AD Tractate 35 (John 8:13-14) 3: The Lord Jesus Christ, then, had the witness of prophets sent before Him, of the heralds that preceded the judge: ... Now Tobias had the eyes in his face closed, and the son gave his hand to the father; and yet the father, by his instruction, pointed out the way to the son. www.newadvent.org/fathers/1701035.htm

Augustine 430 AD Homilies on the Gospel of John, Homily 13, 3: Cited along with Psalms, John etc. without qualification: Tobit, you remember, had the eyes in his face blinded, and his son gave a hand to his father; but the father, with his instructions, showed his son the way. [Per The Works of Saint Augustine, A Translation for the 21st Century]. Not available online. Used to confirm the doctrine that there is an inner eye.

Augustine 421 AD On the Soul and its Origin 2, 3: Cited along with John, etc. without qualification: that faculty by which white and black are distinguished, which sparrows even see as well as ourselves, ... which Tobit also perceived even after he lost the sight of his eyes. www.newadvent .org/fathers/15082.htm.

2:11 And my wife Anna did take women's works to do. 2:12 And when she had sent them home to the owners, they paid her wages, and gave her also besides a kid. 2:13 And when it was in my house, and began to cry, I said unto her, From whence is this kid? is it not stolen? render it to the owners; for it is not lawful to eat any thing that is stolen. 2:14 But she replied upon me, It was given for a gift more than the wages. Howbeit I did not believe her, but bade her render it to the owners: and I was abashed at her. But she replied upon me, Where are thine alms and thy righteous deeds? behold, thou and all thy works are known.

Cyprian 258 AD Treatise 12, 3, 6 [Referred to as Holy Scriptures in 12, 3, Introduction; see Tobit 2:2] Of this same thing in Tobias: Where are your righteousnesses? Behold what you suffer www.newadvent.org/fathers/050712c.htm. Used to confirm the doctrine that righteous men suffer more, but ought to endure

Cyprian 258 AD Treatise 7, 10: Holy Scripture teaches and forewarns... And Tobias, after his excellent works, after the many and glorious illustrations of his merciful spirit, having suffered the loss of his sight, fearing and blessing God in his adversity, by his very bodily affliction increased in praise; and even him also his wife tried to pervert, saying... [Tobit 2:14]. www.newadvent.org/fathers/050707.htm. Used to confirm the doctrine that suffering must be expected

Augustine 430 AD Sermon 38, 15: Cited along with Matthew, Paul, etc. without qualification: So said Tobias' wife to her husband ... [Tobit 2:13-2:14] www. newadvent.org/fathers/160338.htm. Used to

confirm the doctrine that good and righteous men suffer, but ought to see the light of God regardless.

Augustine 430 AD Sermon 88, 15: Cited along with Luke without qualification: she answered scornfully, Where are your acts of justice? [Per The Works of Saint Augustine, A Translation for the 21st Century]. Not available online.

3:1 Then I being grieved did weep, and in my sorrow prayed, saying,

Origen 230 AD On Prayer 6 [the angels] pray along with those who genuinely pray...Raphael offers their service to God for Tobit and Sarah. After both had prayed, After both had prayed, the scripture says... www.tertullian.org/fathers/origen_on _prayer_02_text.htm. Used to confirm the doctrine of the intercession of angels

3:2 O Lord, thou art just, and all thy works and all thy ways are mercy and truth, and thou judgest truly and justly for ever.

Origen 230 AD On Prayer 9 [Referred to as Scripture in 6; See Tobit 3:1] ... and in Tobit: "And with anguish I prayed saying, 'Righteous art you, O Lord, and all your works; all your ways are mercy and truth, and judgment true and righteous dost you judge forever.'" www.tertullian.org/ fathers/origen_on_prayer_02_text.htm.

3:3 Remember me, and look on me, punish me not for my sins and ignorances, and the sins of my fathers, who have sinned before thee: 3:4 For they obeyed not thy commandments: wherefore thou hast delivered us for a spoil, and unto captivity, and unto death, and for a proverb of reproach to all the nations among whom we are dispersed. 3:5 And now thy judgments are many and true: deal with me according to my sins and my fathers': because we have not kept thy commandments, neither have walked in truth before thee. 3:6 Now therefore deal with me as seemeth best unto thee, and command my spirit to be taken from me, that I may be dissolved, and become earth: for it is profitable for me to die rather than to live, because I have heard false reproaches,

and have much sorrow: command therefore that I may now be delivered out of this distress, and go into the everlasting place: turn not thy face away from me. 3:7 It came to pass the same day, that in Ecbatane a city of Media Sara the daughter of Raguel was also reproached by her father's maids; 3:8 **Because that she had been married to seven husbands, whom Asmodeus the evil spirit had killed, before they had lain with her**. Dost thou not know, said they, that thou hast strangled thine husbands? thou hast had already seven husbands, neither wast thou named after any of them.

Luke 20:31 (Saying, Master, Moses wrote unto us, If any man's brother die, having a wife, and he die without children, that his brother should take his wife, and raise up seed unto his brother. There were therefore seven brethren: and the first took a wife, and died without children. And the second took her to wife, and he died childless. And the third took her; and in like manner the seven also: and they left no children, and died.)

Mark 12:22 (Master, Moses wrote unto us, If a man's brother die, and leave his wife behind him, and leave no children, that his brother should take his wife, and raise up seed unto his brother. Now there were seven brethren: and the first took a wife, and dying left no seed. And the second took her, and died, neither left he any seed: and the third likewise. And the seven had her, and left no seed: last of all the woman died also.)

Matthew 22:26 (Master, Moses said, If a man die, having no children, his brother shall marry his wife, and raise up seed unto his brother. Now there were with us seven brethren: and the first, when he had married a wife, deceased, and, having no issue, left his wife unto his brother: Likewise the second also, and the third, unto the seventh.)

The Shepherd of Hermas 150 AD Bk 2, Commandment 6: Cited along with Matthew, Luke, etc. without qualification:

Commandment 6 ... Chapter 2: Hear now, said he, in regard to faith. There are two angels with a man — one of righteousness [see Tobit 3:17], and the other of iniquity. www.newadvent.org/fathers/02012.htm.
Used to confirm the doctrine that angels accompany us

3:9 Wherefore dost thou beat us for them? if they be dead, go thy ways after them, let us never see of thee either son or daughter. 3:10 When she heard these things, she was very sorrowful, so that she thought to have strangled herself; and she said, I am the only daughter of my father, and if I do this, it shall be a reproach unto him, and I shall bring his old age with sorrow unto the grave. 3:11 Then she prayed toward the window, and said, Blessed art thou, O Lord my God, and thine holy and glorious name is blessed and honourable for ever: let all thy works praise thee for ever.

Origen 230 AD On Prayer 6: [the angels] pray along with those who genuinely pray...Raphael offers their service to God for Tobit and Sarah. After both had prayed, the scripture says... www.tertullian.org/fathers/origen_on_prayer_02_text.htm.
Used to confirm the doctrine of the intercession of angels.

3:12 And now, O Lord, I set mine eyes and my face toward thee,

Augustine 400 AD Confessions 5, 1: Cited [see Tobit 3:11 as well] along with many Psalms without qualification: every spirit praises you through the mouth that is turned to you... www.newadvent.org/fathers/110105.htm

3:13 And say, Take me out of the earth, that I may hear no more the reproach.

Augustine 400 AD Confessions 4, 9, 14 Cited along with John, Genesis, etc. without qualification: Blessed be he who loves You, and his friend in You, and his enemy for Your sake. For he alone loses none dear to him to whom all are dear in Him who

cannot be lost.[365] www.newadvent.org/fathers/110104.htm

3:14 Thou knowest, Lord, that I am pure from all sin with man, 3:15 And that I never polluted my name, nor the name of my father, in the land of my captivity: I am the only daughter of my father, neither hath he any child to be his heir, neither any near kinsman, nor any son of his alive, to whom I may keep myself for a wife: my seven husbands are already dead; and why should I live? but if it please not thee that I should die, command some regard to be had of me, and pity taken of me, that I hear no more reproach. 3:16 So the prayers of them both were heard before the majesty of the great God. 3:17 And Raphael was sent to heal them both, that is, to scale away the whiteness of Tobit's eyes, and to give Sara the daughter of Raguel for a wife to Tobias the son of Tobit; and to bind Asmodeus the evil spirit; because she belonged to Tobias by right of inheritance. The selfsame time came Tobit home, and entered into his house, and Sara the daughter of Raguel came down from her upper chamber.

Origen 230 AD On Prayer 6: The scripture says, "The prayer of both was heard before the presence of the great Raphael and he was sent to heal them both," www.tertullian.org/fathers/origen_on_prayer_02_text.htm. Used to confirm the doctrine of the intercession of angels.

Hippolytus of Rome 235 AD On Susanna: cited along with Susannah/Daniel without qualification: "'For even now the angel of God.'" He shows also, that when Susannah prayed to God, and was heard, the angel was sent then to help her, just as was the case in the instance of Tobias and Sara...[Tobit 3:17]... www.newadvent.org/fathers/0502.htm. Used to confirm the doctrine of the intercession of angels.

---

[365] This one is opaque, but I think maybe the reference is that if taken out of the earth she would still exist and thus "cannot be lost"?

The Shepherd of Hermas 150 AD Bk 2, Commandment 6: Cited along with Matthew, Luke, etc. without qualification: Commandment 6 ... Chapter 2 Hear now, said he, in regard to faith. There are two angels with a man — one of righteousness, and the other of iniquity. www.newadvent. org/fathers/02012.htm. Used to confirm the doctrine that angels accompany us.

Origen 253 AD On Prayer 11: For the Scripture says that after they had prayed, the prayers of them both were heard in the sight of the glory of the great Raphael, and he was sent to heal them both. www.tertullian.org/fathers/origen_on_praye r_02_text.htm. Used to confirm the doctrine of the intercession of angels.

4:1 In that day Tobit remembered the money which he had committed to Gabael in Rages of Media,

Origen 230 AD First Principles 3, 2, 4: ... such a statement will perhaps appear incredible, unless it be confirmed by the testimony of holy Scripture. ...That certain thoughts are suggested to men's hearts either by good or evil angels, is shown both by the angel that accompanied Tobias... www.newadvent.org/fathers/04123.htm. Used to confirm the doctrine that thoughts sometimes proceed from ourselves, and sometimes devils, angels or God

4:2 And said with himself, I have wished for death; wherefore do I not call for my son Tobias that I may signify to him of the money before I die?

Augustine 430 AD Exposition on Psalm 58, 15 [Referred to as truth written by our Maker in 58, 1; See Tobit 4:15] Did Tobias by any means have fleshly eyes? His own son had, and he had not [See Tob 4:3-19]... www.newadvent.org/fathers/1801058.htm.

4:3 And when he had called him, he said, My son, when I am dead, bury me; and despise not thy mother, but honour her all the days of thy life, and do that which shall please her, and grieve her not. 4:4 Remember, my son, that she saw many dangers for thee, when thou

wast in her womb: and when she is dead, bury her by me in one grave. 4:5 My son, be mindful of the Lord our God all thy days, and let not thy will be set to sin, or to transgress his commandments: do uprightly all thy life long, and follow not the ways of unrighteousness. 4:6 For if thou deal truly, thy doings shall prosperously succeed to thee, and to all them that live justly.

Augustine 421 AD On the Soul and its Origin 2, 3: Cited along with John, Ephesians, etc. without qualification: "the difference between the bodily senses and the sensibilities of the soul; ...[the difference between] that faculty by which white and black are distinguished, which sparrows even see as well as ourselves [cf. Tobit 2:8], and that by which justice and injustice are discriminated, which Tobit also perceived even after he lost the sight of his eyes." www.newadvent.org/fathers/15082.htm

4:7 Give alms of thy substance; and when thou givest alms, let not thine eye be envious, neither turn thy face from any poor, and the face of God shall not be turned away from thee.

Luke 11:41 (But rather give alms of such things as ye have; and, behold, all things are clean unto you) -per the notes included with the original King James Bible.

Luke 14:13 (But when thou makest a feast, call the poor, the maimed, the lame, the blind) – per the notes included with the original King James Bible.

Leo the Great 450 AD Sermon 10, 4 Cited along with Proverbs, James, etc. without qualification: For almsgiving wipes out sin, kills death, and extinguishes the punishment of perpetual fire. But he who has not been fruitful therein, shall have no indulgence from the great Recompenser, ... hence Tobias also, while instructing his son in the precepts of godliness, says, "Give alms of thy substance, and turn not thy face from any poor man: so shall it come to pass that the face of God shall not be turned from thee. www.newadvent.org/fathers/360310.htm Used to confirm the doctrine that almsgiving wipes out sin, kills death, and extinguishes the punishment of perpetual fire.

Augustine 430 AD Exposition on Psalm 97, 15: Cited along with Matthew, Isaiah, etc. without qualification: Tobit was blind, but ... Tobit warned his son, and said to him, Son, give alms of your substance; because that alms suffer not to come into darkness. www.newadvent.org/fathers/1801097.htm Used to confirm the doctrine that alms suffer not to come into darkness
4:8 If thou hast abundance give alms accordingly: if thou have but a little, be not afraid to give according to that little: 4:9 For thou layest up a good treasure for thyself against the day of necessity. 4:10 Because that alms do deliver from death, and suffereth not to come into darkness.

Polycarp 107 AD Epistle to the Philippians, 10: Cited along with 1 Peter, Isaiah, etc. without qualification: When you can do good, defer it not, because alms delivers from death. www.newadvent.org/fathers/0136.htm. Used to confirm the doctrine that alms can save one from death

Origen 230 AD On First Principles 1.2.13: [Referred to as Holy Scripture in 3, 2, 4] ...And if there be any other things which in Scripture are called good, whether ... treasure... all these are so termed catachrestically, having in them an accidental, not an essential goodness. ... www.newadvent.org/fathers/04121.htm. Used to confirm the doctrine that God alone is truly good.

Cyprian 258 AD Letter 51: whom the Lord exhorts to rise up again by his works, because it is written, Alms do deliver from death. www.newadvent.org/fathers/050651.htm. Used to confirm the doctrine that the Lord exhorts us to rise up again by works.

Cyprian 258 AD Letter 55 (to Antonian) 22: This is certainly said to him who, it is ascertained, has fallen and whom

the Lord exhorts to rise again through works since is it written, "Alms deliver ... from death." [Per Ancient Christian Commentary on Scripture]. Not available online. Used to confirm the doctrine that alms deliver from death.

Augustine 430 AD Sermon 125A, 4: So carry out, and be astonished at the words of scripture. A blind father was talking to a son who could see, and advising him to give alms; among other things, he had this to say: For almsgiving delivers from death. ... What follows, though, is astonishing. After saying about almsgiving that it delivers from death, he added, and does not permit you to go into darkness. ... There is another sort of darkness, into which almsgiving does not permit those to go who love practicing it... [Per The Works of Saint Augustine, A Translation for the 21st Century] Not available online. Used to confirm the doctrine that there is an inner eye.

Augustine 430 AD Sermon 125A, 4: On this matter of charitable giving, you have heard the advice Saint Tobit gave his son Tobias: As you have the means, so do; if you have much, do much; if little, share this little amount. [Per The Works of Saint Augustine, A Translation for the 21st Century]. Not available online. Used to confirm the doctrine that alms deliver from death

Augustine 430 AD Exposition on Psalm 97, 15: Cited along with Matthew, Isaiah, etc. without qualification: Tobit was blind, but he used to teach his son the way of God. You know this, that Tobit warned his son, and said to him, Son, give alms of your substance; because that alms suffer not to come into darkness. www.newadvent.org/fathers/1801097.htm Used to confirm the doctrine that alms suffer not to come into darkness.

Augustine 430 AD Sermon 38, 16 Cited along with Matthew, Paul, etc. without qualification: The same Tobias in giving advice to his son, instructed him to this, to cry out; that is, he instructed him to good works. He told him to give to the poor, charged him to give alms to the needy, and taught him, saying, My son, alms suffers not to come into darkness. www.newadvent.org/fathers/160338.htm. Used to confirm the doctrine that good works and almsgiving can save one from death.

Augustine 430 AD Sermon 88, 16: Cited along with Luke without qualification: Our friend Tobit, giving instructions to his son, instructed him precisely in this matter of crying out; that is, he instructed him in the good works he should perform; he told him to give to the poor, he ordered him to distribute alms to the needy, and he taught him this lesson: Son, almsgiving does not allow you to go into the dark. [Per The Works of Saint Augustine, A Translation for the 21st Century]. Not available online. Used to confirm the doctrine that almsgiving is pleasing to God.

Augustine 430 AD Sermon 125A, 5: So this man Tobit had blindness in the flesh, but bright light in his heart. ... What light was he seeing by, when he said that? Certainly, his eyes were darkened, and yet he said, Son, give alms; almsgiving delivers you from death. Was the person who said this really unable to see anything? Indeed he was able to see, not white and black, but just and unjust realities; ... even if he hadn't got his eyesight back in the flesh, wouldn't his eyes have been closed sooner or later in death? All the saints, you see, when they depart from here, come to the light; the light of this sun is worth nothing to those who are seeing God... [Per The Works of Saint Augustine, A Translation for the 21st Century] Not available online. Used to confirm the doctrine that there is an inner eye.

4:11 For alms is a good gift unto all that give it in the sight of the most High.

Cyprian 258 AD Treatise 12, 3, 1: [Referred to as Holy Scriptures in 12, 3, Introduction; see Tobit 2:2]: Also in the

same place: [quotes all of Tobit 4:5-4:11]. www.newadvent.org/fathers/050712c.htm. Used to confirm the doctrine of the efficacy of alms and other good works before God

Cyprian 258 AD Treatise 8, 20: cited along with Proverbs, Acts, etc. without qualification: And again: [quotes all of Tobit 4:5-4:11]. www.newadvent.org/fathers/050708.htm. Used to confirm the doctrine that alms are a good gift to all that give it, in the sight of the most high God.

4:12 **Beware of all whoredom, my son,** and chiefly take a wife of the seed of thy fathers, and take not a strange woman to wife, which is not of thy father's tribe: for we are the children of the prophets, Noe, Abraham, Isaac, and Jacob: remember, my son, that our fathers from the beginning, even that they all married wives of their own kindred, and were blessed in their children, and their seed shall inherit the land.

1 Thessalonians 4:3 (For this is the will of God, even your sanctification, that ye should abstain from fornication), per the notes included with the original King James Bible.

Cyprian 258 AD Treatise 12, 3, 62: [Referred to as Holy Scriptures in 12, 3, Introduction; see Tobit 2:2] In Tobias: Take a wife from the seed of your parents, and take not a strange woman who is not of the tribe of your parents. www.newadvent.org/fathers/050712c.htm. Used to confirm the doctrine that marriage is not to be contracted with Gentiles

4:13 Now therefore, my son, love thy brethren, and despise not in thy heart thy brethren, the sons and daughters of thy people, in not taking a wife of them: for in pride is destruction and much trouble, and in lewdness is decay and great want: for lewdness is the mother of famine. 4:14 Let not the wages of any man, which hath wrought for thee, tarry with thee, but give him it out of hand: for if thou serve God, he will also repay thee: be circumspect my son, in all things thou doest, and be wise in all thy conversation. 4:15 **Do that to no man** which thou hatest: drink not wine to make thee drunken: neither let drunkenness go with thee in thy journey.

Luke 6:31 (And as ye would that men should do to you, do ye also to them likewise), per the notes included with the original King James Bible.

Matthew 7:12 (Therefore all things whatsoever ye would that men should do to you, do ye even so to them: for this is the law and the prophets), per the notes included with the original King James Bible.

Didache 100 AD Didache 1: Cited along with Matthew, Luke, etc. without qualification: and all things whatsoever you would should not occur to you, do not also do to another. www.newadvent.org/fathers/0714.htm. Used as a direct commandment.

Clement of Alexandria 198 AD Stromata 2, 23: [Referred to as Scripture in 6, 12] This Scripture has briefly showed, when it says, What you hate you shall not do to another. www.newadvent.org/fathers/02102.htm. Used to confirm the sanctity of marriage.

Augustine 430 AD Exposition on Psalm 58, 1: The hand of our Maker in our very hearts has written this truth, That which to yourself you would not have done, do not do to another. www.newadvent.org/fathers/1801058.htm. Used as a direct command.

Augustine 430 AD On Psalm 51/52: If they will only obey Scripture's injunction, "You shall love your neighbor as yourself," and "Whatever good you want people to do for you, do the same yourselves for them," they will have within themselves evidence that they must not treat others as they would not wish to be treated themselves. [Ancient Christian Commentary on Scripture – whose translation differs from that at New Advent] www.newadvent.org/fathers/1801052.htm.

Didymus the Blind 386 AD Commentary on Zechariah 9:14-15: calls Tobit 4:15 a "commandment" that is

transgressed per Gary G. Michuta in The Case of the Deuterocanon.   Not online.

John Chrysostom 407 AD Homily 13 on the Statues: Cited along with Matthew, Jeremiah, etc. without qualification: Do not to another what you hate. www.newadvent.org/fathers/190113.htm. Used as a direct commandment.

Augustine 430 AD Sermon 130A: Cited along with John etc. without qualification: Does anyone fail to approve, fail to say, "It's true," when I say, Do not do to others what you do not want done to you? "It's true," you shout, and "Nothing truer," you cry. [Per The Works of Saint Augustine, A Translation for the 21st Century]. Not available online. Used to confirm the doctrine that you should not do to another what you do not want anyone to do to you.

The Apostolic Constitutions 400 AD Book 1, 1: But as to those who are obedient to God, there is one law of God, [simple,] true, living, which is this: "Do not that to another which you hate another should do to you." www.newadvent.org/fathers/07151.htm. Used to confirm the doctrine that you should not do to another what you would not want anyone to do to you.

The Apostolic Constitutions 400 AD Book 7, 1-2: ... the law also does appoint: ...And whatsoever you would not should be done to you, do not do to another. www.newadvent.org/fathers/07157.htm. Used to confirm the doctrine that you should not do to another what you would not want anyone to do to you.

The Apostolic Constitutions 400 AD Book 3, 15: Wherefore he that avoids a curse, let him not curse another; for what you hate should be done to you, do not do to another. www.newadvent.org/fathers/07153.htm. Used to confirm the doctrine that you should not do to another what you would not want anyone to do to you.

Augustine 430 AD Exposition on Psalm 35, 1: does anyone really have to make an effort to understand the injunction, Do not do to another what you would not want anyone to do to you? [Per The Works of Saint Augustine, A Translation for the 21st Century]. Not available online. Used to confirm the doctrine that you should not do to another what you would not want anyone to do to you.

Augustine 430 AD Exposition on Psalm 57, 1: And this is not surprising, for by the hand of our Fashioner truth has written in our very hearts the precept, Do not do to another what you would not want anyone to do to you. [Per The Works of Saint Augustine, A Translation for the 21st Century]. Not available online. Used to confirm the doctrine that you should not do to another what you would not want anyone to do to you.

4:16 Give of thy bread to the hungry, and of thy garments to them that are naked; and according to thine abundance give alms; and let not thine eye be envious, when thou givest alms.

Luke 14:13 (But when thou makest a feast, call the poor, the maimed, the lame, the blind), per the notes included with the original King James Bible.

Matthew 6:1 (Take heed that ye do not your alms before men, to be seen of them: otherwise ye have no reward of your Father which is in heaven), per the notes included with the original King James Bible.

Commodianus 250 AD Instructions, LXI, to Him Who Wishes for Martyrdom: He who commands us to give food even to our enemies. Look forward to thy meals from that Tobias who always on every day shared them entirely with the poor man. Thou seekest to feed him, O fool, who feedeth thee again. www.newadvent.org/fathers/0411.htm. Used to confirm the doctrine that we should feed everyone and count on God to feed ourselves.

4:17 Pour out thy bread on the burial of the just, but give nothing to the wicked.

Augustine 430 AD Sermon 361, 6 as for the objection some people bring from the scriptures: Break your bread and pour out your wine on the tombs of the just, but do not hand it over to the unjust, this is not the occasion, indeed, to expatiate on it; but still I will say that the faithful can understand what is being said. [Per The Works of Saint Augustine, A Translation for the 21st Century]. Not available online. Used to confirm the doctrine of offering Mass for the dead

Augustine 426 AD On Christian Doctrine: [3, 16, 1:] let him proceed to the examination and solution of the ambiguities of Scripture... [3, 16, 24:] It is written: Give to the godly man, and help not a sinner. The latter clause of this sentence seems to forbid benevolence; for it says, help not a sinner. Understand, therefore, that sinner is put figuratively for sin, so that it is his sin you are not to help. www.newadvent.org/fathers/12023.htm. Used as an example of how to interpret Scripture.

4:18 Ask counsel of all that are wise, and despise not any counsel that is profitable.

Athanasius 361 AD Apologia ad Constantium 17: Cited along with Matthew and Daniel without qualification: what will all prudent and true Christians say? ...for it is written of the other, 'The foolish person will speak foolishness (Is. 32:6 LXX)' but of these, 'Ask counsel of all that are wise'. www.newadvent.org/fathers/2813.htm.

4:19 Bless the Lord thy God alway, and desire of him that thy ways may be directed, and that all thy paths and counsels may prosper: for every nation hath not counsel; but the Lord himself giveth all good things, and he humbleth whom he will, as he will; now therefore, my son, remember my commandments, neither let them be put out of thy mind. 4:20 And now I signify this to they that I committed ten talents to Gabael the son of Gabrias at Rages in Media. 4:21 And fear not, my son, that we are made poor: for thou hast much wealth, if thou fear God, and depart from all sin, and do that which is pleasing in his sight.

Chromatius 407 AD Sermon 5, 5: listen to what the prophet Tobit says to his son: "We endure a poor man's life, son, to be sure; but you have great wealth if you fear God". Not available online. Used to confirm the doctrine that you have great wealth if you fear God.

Augustine 430 AD Tractate 13 (John 3:22-3:29) 3: [Referred to as prophecy of Christ in Tractate 35, 3; see Tobit 2:10] There is another eye, there is an inner eye. Tobias, for example, was not without eyes, when, blind in his bodily eyes, he was giving precepts of life to his son. Tobit iv The son was holding the father's hand, that the father might walk with his feet, while the father was giving the son counsel to walk in the way of righteousness. www.newadvent. org/fathers/1701013.htm. Used to confirm the doctrine that there is an inner eye.

Augustine 416 AD On Man's Perfection in Righteousness, 13: Augustine's opponent adds: "Holy Tobit also said, 'Fear not, my son, that we have to endure poverty; we shall have many blessings if we fear God, and depart from all sin, and do that which is good.'" Augustine accepts this as a valid Scriptural principle derived from Tobit: "Most true indeed it is, that man shall have many blessings when he shall have departed from all sin." www.newadvent.org/fathers/ 1504.htm. Used to confirm the doctrine that perfection is in the next world, in this world we progress towards it.

Augustine 430 AD Homilies on the Gospel of John, Homily 13, 3 : Cited along with Psalms, John etc. without qualification: After all, even Tobit can be said to have had no eyes when, blind in the eyes of his body, he was giving his son rules of life. Tobit was holding his father's hand, that he might walk with his feet; the father was giving his son advice, that he might stay on the way of justice. [Per The Works of Saint Augustine, A Translation for the 21st Century]. Not available online.

Augustine 400 AD Confessions 10, 51: Cited along with Genesis without qualification: O Thou Light, which Tobias saw, when, his eyes being closed, he taught his son the way of life; himself going before with the feet of charity, never going astray. Or that which Isaac saw... www.newadvent. org/fathers/110110.htm.

5:1 Tobias then answered and said, Father, I will do all things which thou hast commanded me: 5:2 But how can I receive the money, seeing I know him not? 5:3 Then he gave him the handwriting, and said unto him, Seek thee a man which may go with thee, whiles I yet live, and I will give him wages: and go and receive the money. 5:4 Therefore when he went to seek a man, he found Raphael that was an angel. 5:5 But he knew not; and he said unto him, Canst thou go with me to Rages? and knowest thou those places well? 5:6 To whom the angel said, I will go with thee, and I know the way well: for I have lodged with our brother Gabael. 5:7 Then Tobias said unto him, Tarry for me, till I tell my father. 5:8 Then he said unto him, Go and tarry not. So he went in and said to his father, Behold, I have found one which will go with me. Then he said, Call him unto me, that I may know of what tribe he is, and whether he be a trusty man to go with thee. 5:9 So he called him, and he came in, and they saluted one another. 5:10 Then Tobit said unto him, Brother, shew me of what tribe and family thou art. 5:11 To whom he said, Dost thou seek for a tribe or family, or an hired man to go with thy son? Then Tobit said unto him, I would know, brother, thy kindred and name. 5:12 Then he said, I am Azarias, the son of Ananias the great, and of thy brethren. 5:13 Then Tobit said, Thou art welcome, brother; be not now angry with me, because I have enquired to know thy tribe and thy family; for thou art my brother, of an honest and good stock: for I know Ananias and Jonathas, sons of that great Samaias, as we went together to Jerusalem to worship, and offered the firstborn, and the tenths of the fruits; and they were not seduced with the error of our brethren: my brother, thou art of a good stock. 5:14 But tell me, what wages shall I give thee? wilt thou a drachm a day, and things necessary, as to mine own son? 5:15 Yea, moreover, if ye return safe, I will add something to thy wages. 5:16 So they were well pleased. Then said he to Tobias, Prepare thyself for the journey, and God send you a good journey. And when his son had prepared all things for the journey, his father said, Go thou with this man, and God, which dwelleth in heaven, prosper your journey, and the angel of God keep you company. So they went forth both, and the young man's dog with them.

Ambrose 397 AD Hexameron 6, 4, 17: Not without reason did Raphael in the prophetic book cause this dog to accompany the son of Tobias when he went on a journey, in order to drive out Asmodeus and thereby confirm the marriage. The demon is driven out as the result of a grateful recognition and the union is stabilized. archive.org/stream/fathersofthe chur027571mbp/fathersofthechur027571mb p_djvu.txt

5:17 But Anna his mother wept, and said to Tobit, Why hast thou sent away our son? is he not the staff of our hand, in going in and out before us? 5:18 Be not greedy to add money to money: but let it be as refuse in respect of our child. 5:19 For that which the Lord hath given us to live with doth suffice us. 5:20 Then said Tobit to her, Take no care, my sister; he shall return in safety, and thine eyes shall see him. 5:21 For the good angel will keep him company, and his journey shall be prosperous, and he shall return safe.

Origen 230 AD On First Principles 1.2.13: [Referred to as Holy Scripture in 3, 2, 4] ...And if there be any other things which in Scripture are called good, whether angel, ... all these are so termed catachrestically, having in them an accidental, not an essential goodness. ...www.newadvent.org/fathers/04121.htm. Used to confirm the doctrine that God alone is truly good.

5:22 Then she made an end of weeping.
6:1 And as they went on their journey, they came in the evening to the river Tigris, and they lodged there. 6:2 And when the young man went down to wash himself, a fish leaped out of the river, and would have devoured him. 6:3 Then the angel said unto him, Take the fish. And the young man laid hold of the fish, and drew it to land. 6:4 To whom the angel said, Open the fish, and take the heart and the liver and the gall, and put them up safely. 6:5 So the young man did as the angel commanded him; and when they had roasted the fish, they did eat it: then they both went on their way, till they drew near to Ecbatane. 6:6 Then the young man said to the angel, Brother Azarias, to what use is the heart and the liver and the gal of the fish? 6:7 And he said unto him, Touching the heart and the liver, if a devil or an evil spirit trouble any, we must make a smoke thereof before the man or the woman, and the party shall be no more vexed. 6:8 As for the gall, it is good to anoint a man that hath whiteness in his eyes, and he shall be healed. 6:9 And when they were come near to Rages, 6:10 The angel said to the young man, Brother, today we shall lodge with Raguel, who is thy cousin; he also hath one only daughter, named Sara; I will speak for her, that she may be given thee for a wife. 6:11 For to thee doth the right of her appertain, seeing thou only art of her kindred. 6:12 And the maid is fair and wise: now therefore hear me, and I will speak to her father; and when we return from Rages we will celebrate the marriage: for I know that Raguel cannot marry her to another according to the law of Moses, but he shall be guilty of death, because the right of inheritance doth rather appertain to thee than to any other. 6:13 Then the young man answered the angel, I have heard, brother Azarias that this maid hath been given to seven men, who all died in the marriage chamber. 6:14 And now I am the only son of my father, and I am afraid, lest if I go in unto her, I die, as the other before: for a wicked spirit loveth her, which hurteth no body, but those which come unto her;

wherefore I also fear lest I die, and bring my father's and my mother's life because of me to the grave with sorrow: for they have no other son to bury them. 6:15 Then the angel said unto him, Dost thou not remember the precepts which thy father gave thee, that thou shouldest marry a wife of thine own kindred? wherefore hear me, O my brother; for she shall be given thee to wife; and make thou no reckoning of the evil spirit; for this same night shall she be given thee in marriage. 6:16 And when thou shalt come into the marriage chamber, thou shalt take the ashes of perfume, and shalt lay upon them some of the heart and liver of the fish, and shalt make a smoke with it: 6:17 And the devil shall smell it, and flee away, and never come again any more: but when thou shalt come to her, rise up both of you, and pray to God which is merciful, who will have pity on you, and save you: fear not, for she is appointed unto thee from the beginning; and thou shalt preserve her, and she shall go with thee. Moreover I suppose that she shall bear thee children. Now when Tobias had heard these things, he loved her, and his heart was effectually joined to her.

7:1 And when they were come to Ecbatane, they came to the house of Raguel, and Sara met them: and after they had saluted one another, she brought them into the house. 7:2 Then said Raguel to Edna his wife, How like is this young man to Tobit my cousin! 7:3 And Raguel asked them, From whence are ye, brethren? To whom they said, We are of the sons of Nephthalim, which are captives in Nineve. 7:4 Then he said to them, Do ye know Tobit our kinsman? And they said, We know him. Then said he, Is he in good health? 7:5 And they said, He is both alive, and in good health: and Tobias said, He is my father. 7:6 Then Raguel leaped up, and kissed him, and wept, 7:7 And blessed him, and said unto him, Thou art the son of an honest and good man. But when he had heard that Tobit was blind, he was sorrowful, and wept. 7:8 And likewise Edna his wife and Sara his daughter wept. Moreover they entertained them cheerfully;

and after that they had killed a ram of the flock, they set store of meat on the table. Then said Tobias to Raphael, Brother Azarias, speak of those things of which thou didst talk in the way, and let this business be dispatched. 7:9 So he communicated the matter with Raguel: and Raguel said to Tobias, Eat and drink, and make merry: 7:10 For it is meet that thou shouldest marry my daughter: nevertheless I will declare unto thee the truth. 7:11 I have given my daughter in marriage to seven men, who died that night they came in unto her: nevertheless for the present be merry. But Tobias said, I will eat nothing here, till we agree and swear one to another.

Ambrose 397 AD Duties of the Clergy 3, 96: Cited along with Moses without qualification: And Raguel is a still brighter example. For he, in his regard for virtue, when asked to give his daughter in marriage, was not silent regarding his daughter's faults, for fear of seeming to get the better of the suitor by silence. So when Tobit the son of Tobias asked that his daughter might be given him, he answered that, according to the law, she ought to be given him as near of kin, but that he had already given her to six men, and all of them were dead. This just man, then, ... www.newadvent.org/fathers/34013.htm. Used to confirm the doctrine that we should fear more for others than for ourselves.

7:12 Raguel said, Then take her from henceforth according to the manner, for thou art her cousin, and she is thine, and the merciful God give you good success in all things. 7:13 Then he called his daughter Sara, and she came to her father, and he took her by the hand, and gave her to be wife to Tobias, saying, Behold, take her after the law of Moses, and lead her away to thy father. And he blessed them; 7:14 And called Edna his wife, and took paper, and did write an instrument of covenants, and sealed it. 7:15 Then they began to eat. 7:16 After Raguel called his wife Edna, and said unto her, Sister, prepare another chamber, and bring her in thither. 7:17 Which when she had done as he had bidden her, she brought her thither: and she wept, and she received the tears of her daughter, and said unto her, 7:18 Be of good comfort, my daughter; the Lord of heaven and earth give thee joy for this thy sorrow: be of good comfort, my daughter.

8:1 And when they had supped, they brought Tobias in unto her. 8:2 And as he went, he remembered the words of Raphael, and took the ashes of the perfumes, and put the heart and the liver of the fish thereupon, and made a smoke therewith. 8:3 The which smell when the evil spirit had smelled, he fled into the utmost parts of Egypt, and the angel bound him.

Ambrose 397 AD Hexameron 6, 4, 17: Not without reason did Raphael in the prophetic book ... drive out Asmodeus and thereby confirm the marriage. The demon is driven out as the result of a grateful recognition and the union is stabilized. archive.org/stream/fathersofthechur027571 mbp/fathersofthechur027571mbp_djvu.txt

8:4 And after that they were both shut in together, Tobias rose out of the bed, and said, Sister, arise, and let us pray that God would have pity on us. 8:5 Then began Tobias to say, Blessed art thou, O God of our fathers, and blessed is thy holy and glorious name for ever; let the heavens bless thee, and all thy creatures. 8:6 Thou madest Adam, and gavest him Eve his wife for an helper and stay: of them came mankind: thou hast said, It is not good that man should be alone; let us make unto him an aid like unto himself. 8:7 And now, O Lord, I take not this my sister for lust but uprightly: therefore mercifully ordain that we may become aged together.

Augustine 400 AD Reply to Faustus 22, 35 We learn from Scripture that, among the ancients, it was customary to call cousins brothers and sisters. Thus Tobias says in his prayer to God, before having intercourse with his wife, "And now, O Lord, You know that not in wantonness I take to wife my sister;" though she was not sprung immediately from the same father or the same mother, but only belonged to the same family. And Lot is called the brother of Abraham, though Abraham was his uncle. And, by the same use of the word, those called in the Gospel the Lord's brothers are certainly not children of the Virgin Mary, but all the blood relations of the Lord. www.newadvent.org/fathers/140622.htm. Used to confirm that Scripture calls cousins "brothers" and "sisters."

Augustine 426 AD On Christian Doctrine 3, 18, 27 [Referred to as canon in 2, 8, 13: see the beginning of Tobit] ... as is proved by Tobit's prayer when he was married to his wife. For he says: Blessed are You, O God of our fathers, and blessed is Your holy and glorious name for ever; let the heavens bless You, and all Your creatures. You made Adam, and gave him Eve his wife for an helper and stay. . . . And now, O Lord, You know that I take not this my sister for lust, but uprightly: therefore have pity on us, O Lord. www.newadvent.org/fathers/12023.htm. Used to confirm the doctrine that wantonness even in regard to wives is abuse and intemperance.

8:8 And she said with him, Amen. 8:9 So they slept both that night. And Raguel arose, and went and made a grave,

Augustine 430 AD Sermon 60, 6: Cited along with other Scriptures without qualification: There is also the heaven of heavens (Dt 10: 14, 1 Kgs 8:27), like the holy of holies (Ex 26:34, 1 Kgs 6:16), like ages of ages (Tob 8:9). Lay up for yourselves treasure in heaven... Matthew 6:20. [Per The Works of Saint Augustine, A Translation for the 21st Century – a footnote states that this is "in the Latin text only. But it is the conventional liturgical phrase for concluding prayers, the English equivalent being "for ever and ever.""]. Not available online. Used to confirm the doctrine that there is an age of ages yet to come.

8:10 Saying, I fear lest he also be dead. 8:11 But when Raguel was come into his house, 8:12 He said unto his wife Edna. Send one of the maids, and let her see whether he be alive: if he be not, that we may bury him, and no man know it. 8:13 So the maid opened the door, and went in, and found them both asleep, 8:14 And came forth, and told them that he was alive. 8:15 Then Raguel praised God, and said, O God, thou art worthy to be praised with all pure and holy praise; therefore let thy saints praise thee with all thy creatures; and let all thine angels and thine elect praise thee for ever. 8:16 Thou art to be praised, for thou hast made me joyful; and that is not come to me which I suspected; but thou hast dealt with us according to thy great mercy. 8:17 Thou art to be praised because thou hast had mercy of two that were the only begotten children of their fathers: grant them mercy, O Lord, and finish their life in health with joy and mercy. 8:18 Then Raguel bade his servants to fill the grave. 8:19 And he kept the wedding feast fourteen days. 8:20 For before the days of the marriage were finished, Raguel had said unto him by an oath, that he should not depart till the fourteen days of the marriage were expired; 8:21 And then he should take the half of his goods, and go in safety to his father; and should have the rest when I and my wife be dead.

9:1 Then Tobias called Raphael, and said unto him, 9:2 Brother Azarias, take with thee a servant, and two camels, and go to Rages of Media to Gabael, and bring me the money, and bring him to the wedding. 9:3 For Raguel hath sworn that I shall not depart. 9:4 But my father counteth the days; and if I tarry long, he will be very sorry.

Ambrose 397 AD Exposition of the Christian Faith, Book V, 7, 94: But if you do not accept the truth of His mission according to the flesh, as the Apostle spoke of it, ... what answer will you give to the fact that the Son was sent to men? For ... superiors have been sent to inferiors. For Tobias sent Raphael the archangel, ... www.newadvent.org/fathers/34045.htm.

Used to confirm the doctrine that God the superior came to save man, the inferior.

9:5 So Raphael went out, and lodged with Gabael, and gave him the handwriting: who brought forth bags which were sealed up, and gave them to him. 9:6 And early in the morning they went forth both together, and came to the wedding: and Tobias blessed his wife.

10:1 Now Tobit his father counted every day: and when the days of the journey were expired, and they came not, 10:2 Then Tobit said, Are they detained? or is Gabael dead, and there is no man to give him the money? 10:3 Therefore he was very sorry. 10:4 Then his wife said unto him, My son is dead, seeing he stayeth long; and she began to wail him, and said, 10:5 Now I care for nothing, my son, since I have let thee go, the light of mine eyes. 10:6 To whom Tobit said, Hold thy peace, take no care, for he is safe. 10:7 But she said, Hold thy peace, and deceive me not; my son is dead. And she went out every day into the way which they went, and did eat no meat on the daytime, and ceased not whole nights to bewail her son Tobias, until the fourteen days of the wedding were expired, which Raguel had sworn that he should spend there. Then Tobias said to Raguel, Let me go, for my father and my mother look no more to see me. 10:8 But his father in law said unto him, Tarry with me, and I will send to thy father, and they shall declare unto him how things go with thee. 10:9 But Tobias said, No; but let me go to my father. 10:10 Then Raguel arose, and gave him Sara his wife, and half his goods, servants, and cattle, and money: 10:11 And he blessed them, and sent them away, saying, The God of heaven give you a prosperous journey, my children. 10:12 And he said to his daughter, Honour thy father and thy mother in law, which are now thy parents, that I may hear good report of thee. And he kissed her. Edna also said to Tobias, The Lord of heaven restore thee, my dear brother, and grant that I may see thy children of my daughter Sara before I die, that I may rejoice before the Lord:

behold, I commit my daughter unto thee of special trust; where are do not entreat her evil. 11:1 After these things Tobias went his way, praising God that he had given him a prosperous journey, and blessed Raguel and Edna his wife, and went on his way till they drew near unto Nineve. 11:2 Then Raphael said to Tobias, Thou knowest, brother, how thou didst leave thy father: 11:3 Let us haste before thy wife, and prepare the house. 11:4 And take in thine hand the gall of the fish. So they went their way, and the dog went after them. 11:5 Now Anna sat looking about toward the way for her son. 11:6 And when she espied him coming, she said to his father, Behold, thy son cometh, and the man that went with him. 11:7 Then said Raphael, I know, Tobias, that thy father will open his eyes. 11:8 Therefore anoint thou his eyes with the gall, and being pricked therewith, he shall rub, and the whiteness shall fall away, and he shall see thee. 11:9 Then Anna ran forth, and fell upon the neck of her son, and said unto him, Seeing I have seen thee, my son, from henceforth I am content to die. And they wept both. 11:10 Tobit also went forth toward the door, and stumbled: but his son ran unto him, 11:11 And took hold of his father: and he strake of the gall on his fathers' eyes, saying, Be of good hope, my father. 11:12 And when his eyes began to smart, he rubbed them; 11:13 And the whiteness pilled away from the corners of his eyes: and when he saw his son, he fell upon his neck.

Origen 253 AD Commentary on John, Fragment 66.16: Cited along with the Gospel of John without qualification:...We will be able to find the difference between the expressions from Tobit. When white patches had formed over his eyes, it is not written that his eyes were later opened but that he saw. Of the rest, you will be able to observe one or the other aspect in the course of the entire episode related concerning the blind person, where one person asserts one thing and another that, with quite a bit of dissent from each other.

[Per Ancient Christian Commentary on Scripture]. Not available online.

11:14 And he wept, and said, Blessed art thou, O God, and blessed is thy name for ever; and blessed are all thine holy angels: 11:15 For thou hast scourged, and hast taken pity on me: for, behold, I see my son Tobias. And his son went in rejoicing, and told his father the great things that had happened to him in Media. 11:16 Then Tobit went out to meet his daughter in law at the gate of Nineve, rejoicing and praising God: and they which saw him go marvelled, because he had received his sight. 11:17 But Tobias gave thanks before them, because God had mercy on him. And when he came near to Sara his daughter in law, he blessed her, saying, Thou art welcome, daughter: God be blessed, which hath brought thee unto us, and blessed be thy father and thy mother. And there was joy among all his brethren which were at Nineve. 11:18 And Achiacharus, and Nasbas his brother's son, came: 11:19 And Tobias' wedding was kept seven days with great joy.

12:1 Then Tobit called his son Tobias, and said unto him, My son, see that the man have his wages, which went with thee, and thou must give him more. 12:2 And Tobias said unto him, O father, it is no harm to me to give him half of those things which I have brought: 12:3 For he hath brought me again to thee in safety, and made whole my wife, and brought me the money, and likewise healed thee. 12:4 Then the old man said, It is due unto him. 12:5 So he called the angel, and he said unto him, Take half of all that ye have brought and go away in safety. 12:6 Then he took them both apart, and said unto them, Bless God, praise him, and magnify him, and praise him for the things which he hath done unto you in the sight of all that live. It is good to praise God, and exalt his name, and honourably to shew forth the works of God; therefore be not slack to praise him. 12:7 It is good to keep close the secret of a king, but it is honourable to reveal the works of God. Do that which is good, and no evil shall touch you.

Athanasius 335 AD Defense against Arius 1, 11: Cited along with Matthew without qualification: And they are not ashamed to parade the sacred mysteries before Catechumens, and worse than that, even before heathens: whereas, they ought to attend to what is written, 'It is good to keep close the secret of a king;' [technically stated by Bishops ruling in Athanasius' favor, but he quotes them, obviously with approval, as part of his defense on a later charge] www.newadvent.org/fathers/28081 .htm. Used to confirm the doctrine of keeping the sacred mysteries secret.

Hilary of Poitiers 367 AD Homily on Psalm 118, 6: Cited along with Matthew, Psalms, etc. without qualification: Recall that something similar is often read, where it says, "It is good to hide the mystery of the king." We thus understand that some things are enclosed in the secret of our hearts. If they were to be divulged, it would imply the guilt of an unpardonable sin. [Per Ancient Christian Commentary on Scripture]. Not available online. Used to confirm the doctrine of keeping sacred mysteries secret.

Dionysius 265 AD Against Germanus 4. Cited along with Acts without qualification: Since, however, as one says, it is good to keep close the secret of a king, but it is honourable to reveal the works of God... www.newadvent.org/fathers/0632.htm. Used to confirm the doctrine that it is honourable to reveal the works of God.

Origen 248 AD Against Celsus 5, 19: cited along with Genesis, Deuteronomy, etc. without qualification: as is written in the book of Tobit: It is good to keep close the secret of a king, but honourable to reveal the works of God, in a way consistent with truth and God's glory, and so as to be to the advantage of the multitude. www. newadvent.org/fathers/04165.htm. Used to confirm the doctrine that matters of a profounder and more mystical nature are fittingly concealed from the multitude until properly revealed.

Origen 248 AD Against Celsus 5, 29: Cited along with Wisdom and Genesis without qualification: But on these subjects much, and that of a mystical kind, might be said; in keeping with which is the following: It is good to keep close the secret of a king... www.newadvent.org/fathers/04165.htm. Used to confirm the doctrine that matters of a profounder and more mystical nature are fittingly concealed from the multitude.

Origen 253 AD Commentary on Romans, 2.4.4.5: Naturally some people will ask why this day, concerning which we have, in the foregoing, deployed the library of the prophet, is appointed at the end of the world, so that all those who have died from the beginning of the world until its end are reserved for the last day of judgment. The interior cause of this matter are certainly veiled in deep mysteries. And indeed "it is good to conceal the mystery of the kings." vivacatholic.wordpress.com/2007/08/14/orig en-and-canon-of-old-testament/. Used to confirm the doctrine that it is good to conceal the secret of the king.

Augustine 430 AD Letter 237, 8: Suppose that what it says in this [heretical] hymn, "You who see what I do, be silent about my works," signifies what is written in the Book of Tobit, It is good to conceal the secret of the king. Why, then, is this hymn said [by the heretics] not to be in the canon precisely in order that the secret of the king may be hidden from those who are carnal? After all, those ideas that are set forth in this hymn are also found in the canon, and they are found to be so clear in the canon that those obscure ideas are explained by them. [Per The Works of Saint Augustine, A Translation for the 21st Century]. Not available online. Used to confirm the doctrine that it is good to conceal the secret of the king.

Augustine 430 AD Letter 237, 4: [Referred to as canon in 237, 8; See Tobit 12:7]: The Priscillianists used Tobit 12:7 ("For this reason scripture says, It is good to conceal the secret of the king, but it is honorable to reveal the works of God") to argue for their doctrine that some secrets of Christ were not written down in Scripture, which Augustine refutes without challenging Tobit as Scripture. The Works of Saint Augustine, A Translation for the 21st Century. Not available online. Used to argue for the doctrine that Christ kept secrets[366] and the doctrine that it is honorable to reveal the works of God.

12:8 Prayer is good with fasting and alms and righteousness. A little with righteousness is better than much with unrighteousness. It is better to give alms than to lay up gold:

Clement of Alexandria 198 AD Stromata 6, 12: [Referred to as Scripture in 6, 12; see Tobit 4:15] ...having heard the Scripture which says, Fasting with prayer is a good thing. www.newadvent.org/fathers/02106.htm. Used to confirm the doctrine that fasting with prayer is a good thing.

Cyprian 258 AD Treatise 4, 32: And thus Holy Scripture instructs us, saying, Prayer is good with fasting and almsgiving. www.newadvent.org/fathers/050704.htm. Used to confirm the doctrine that Prayer is good with fasting and almsgiving.

Gaudentius of Brescia 410 AD Sermon 13, 21: It is written that fasting with almsgiving is a good thing. It was necessary to do both, to mitigate the Lord's indignation. [Per Ancient Christian Commentary on Scripture]. Not available online. Used to confirm the doctrine that fasting with prayer mitigates the Lord's indignation.

Clement of Rome 140 AD "Second Epistle" 16 (Attribution to Clement is

considered spurious): cited along with 1 Timothy, Isaiah, etc. without qualification: Good, then, is alms as repentance from sin; better is fasting than prayer, and alms than both. www.newadvent.org/fathers/1011.htm. Used to confirm the doctrine that alms lightens the burden of sin.

Augustine 430 AD Letter 130, 31: Cited along with 1 Thessalonians, etc. without qualification: By fasting, by vigils, and all mortification of the body, prayer is greatly helped. www.newadvent.org/fathers/1102130.htm. Used to confirm the doctrine that prayer is greatly helped by fasting, vigils, and mortification.

Augustine 430 AD Letter 36, 8, 18: Then he adds that testimony of the angel saying, Prayer along with fasting and almsgiving is good. [Per The Works of Saint Augustine, A Translation for the 21st Century]. Not available online. Used to confirm the doctrine that prayer along with fasting and almsgiving is good.

12:9 For alms doth deliver from death, and shall purge away all sin. Those that exercise alms and righteousness shall be filled with life:

Polycarp 107 AD Epistle to the Philippians, 10: Cited along with 1 Peter, Isaiah, etc. without qualification: When you can do good, defer it not, because alms delivers from death. www.newadvent.org/fathers/0136.htm. Used to confirm the doctrine that alms can save one from death.

Gaudentius of Brescia 410 AD To Benivolus, 21-27.15: Cited along with Luke without qualification: He intended that through your works of mercy you would again find medicine to treat the wounds of your sins. "Certainly alms freely given preserve one from death and purify from every sin." [Per Ancient Christian Commentary on Scripture]. Not available online. Used to confirm the doctrine that alms freely given preserve one from death and purify from every sin.

John Chrysostom 407 AD Homily 4 on Philippians: ... says the Prophet... Much

---

[366] That the heretics were arguing for this doctrine is not relevant to us. What matters for the present discussion is that both parties considered Tobit to be Scriptural evidence when arguing about doctrine.

mention does Paul, too, make ... Listen to a certain other one who says, Alms do deliver from death. www.newadvent.org/fathers/230204.htm. Used to confirm the doctrine that almsgiving can save one from death.

Ambrose 397 AD Letter 63, 16 And what safety can there be for us unless we wash away our sins by fasting, since Scripture says that fasting and alms do away sin? www.newadvent.org/fathers/340963.htm. Used to confirm the doctrine that fasting can wash away sins.

Ambrose 397 AD Exposition on the Gospel of Luke 7.100-101: Not only in this passage but also in others you have revealed how great grace is. "Alms delivers from death." [Per Ancient Christian Commentary on Scripture]. Not available online. Used to confirm the doctrine that alms deliver from death

Cyprian 258 AD Treatise 8, 5: Cited along with Proverbs, Acts, etc. without qualification: Raphael the angel also witnesses ... Prayer is good, with fasting and alms; because alms does deliver from death, and it purges away sins. He shows that our prayers and fastings are of less avail, unless they are aided by almsgiving; that entreaties alone are of little force to obtain what they seek, unless they be made sufficient by the addition of deeds and good works. The angel ... certifies that our petitions become efficacious by almsgiving, that life is redeemed from dangers by almsgiving, that souls are delivered from death by almsgiving. www.newadvent.org/fathers/050708.htm. Used to confirm the doctrine that good works and alms can save one from death and deliver one's soul.

Didymus the Blind 386 AD Commentary on Zechariah 7:5-7: quotes Tobit 12:8-9 as a reference from "the divinely- inspired Scripture" per Gary G. Michuta in The Case of the Deuterocanon. Not available online.

12:10 But they that sin are enemies to their own life. 12:11 Surely I will keep close

nothing from you. For I said, It was good to keep close the secret of a king, but that it was honourable to reveal the works of God. 12:12 Now therefore, when thou didst pray, and Sara thy daughter in law, I did bring the remembrance of your prayers before the Holy One; and when thou didst bury the dead, I was with thee likewise.

Tertullian 192 AD On Prayer 16: Cited along with 2 Timothy, Luke, etc. without qualification: ...it is irreverent to sit under the eye... of the living God, while the angel of prayer is still standing by unless we are upbraiding God that prayer has wearied us! www.newadvent.org/fathers/0322.htm. Used to confirm the doctrine that angels accompany us.

Origen 230 AD On Prayer 20: [Referred to as Scripture in 6; See Tobit 3:1] there is a twofold church, the one of men the other of angels. ... the prayer of Tobit, and after him of Sarah who later became his daughter-in-law owing to her marriage to Tobias, that Raphael says he has offered up as a memorial... www.tertullian.org/fathers/origen_on_prayer_02_text.htm. Used to confirm the doctrine of the intercession of angels.

Origen 230 AD On Prayer 6: the scripture says, ... Raphael himself, when explaining his angelic commission at God's command to help them, says: "Even now when you prayed, and Sarah your daughter-in-law, I brought the memorial of your prayer before the Holy One,"... www.tertullian.org/fathers/origen_on_prayer_02_text.htm. Used to confirm the doctrine of the intercession of angels.

Hilary of Poitiers 367 AD Tractate in Psalm 129, 7: [per Gary G. Michuta in The Case of the Deuterocanon]. Not available online and no English translation given. Used to confirm the doctrine that angels have their own proper work and stations.

Augustine 430 AD Letter 140, 69: ... as the angels announce not only to us the gifts of God but also our prayers to him. For scripture says where an angel speaks to human beings, I presented the record of your prayer... [Per The Works of Saint Augustine, A Translation for the 21st Century]. Not available online. Used to confirm the doctrine of the intercession of angels.

Augustine 430 AD Letter 130, 9: Cited along with 1 Thessalonians, etc. without qualification: for the angel said to Tobias: Now, therefore, when you prayed, and Sara your daughter-in-law, I brought the remembrance of your prayers before the Holy One. www.newadvent.org/fathers/1102130.htm. Used to confirm the doctrine of the intercession of angels.

Anonymous 450 AD Opus Imperfectum in Matthaeum, Homily 13.5: Cited along with Revelation without qualification: Do you want to know how precious prayer is? ... Do you wish to know its dignity? As soon as it issues from the mouth, the angels take it up in their hands and bring it before God, just as the archangel said to Tobias: "I am he who has brought your prayer before God." [Per Ancient Christian Commentary on Scripture]. Not online. Used to confirm the doctrine of the intercession of angels.

Chromatius 407 AD Tractate on Matthew 57.1.12: Cited along with Matthew without qualification: Finally, the angels carry their prayers to heaven. Hence the word of Raphael to Tobias: "When you prayed along with your daughter-in-law Sara, I offered the memory of your prayer in the sight of God." [Per Ancient Christian Commentary on Scripture]. Not available online. Used to confirm the doctrine of the intercession of angels.

Augustine 426 AD City of God 1, 13: And Tobit, according to the angel's testimony, is commended, and is said to have pleased God by burying the dead. www.newadvent.org/fathers/120101.htm. Used to confirm the doctrine that burying the dead is pleasing to God.

Augustine 422 AD On the Care of the Dead 5: Cited along with Matthew, John, etc. without qualification: Tobias also, to have by burying of the dead obtained favor with God, is by witness of an Angel commended. www.newadvent.org/fathers/1316.htm. Used to confirm the doctrine that burying the dead is pleasing to God.

Augustine 430 AD Sermon 198, 48: Cited along with Hebrews, Acts, etc. without qualification: The angel says to the man, I offered your petition in the presence of the glory of God; and yet the man wasn't pleading with the angel but with God; the attendant offered his prayer. [Per The Works of Saint Augustine, A Translation for the 21st Century]. Not available online. Used to confirm the doctrine that good angels demand no compensation.

12:13 And when thou didst not delay to rise up, and leave thy dinner, to go and cover the dead, thy good deed was not hid from me: but I was with thee. 12:14 And now God hath sent me to heal thee and Sara thy daughter in law. 12:15 I am Raphael, one of the seven holy angels, which present the prayers of the saints, and which go in and out before the glory of the Holy One.

Revelation 8:2-4 (And I saw the seven angels which stood before God; and to them were given seven trumpets. And another angel came and stood at the altar, having a golden censer; and there was given unto him much incense, that he should offer it with the prayers of all saints upon the golden altar which was before the throne. And the smoke of the incense, which came with the prayers of the saints, ascended up before God out of the angel's hand.)

Cyprian 258 AD Treatise 12, 1, 20: [Referred to as divine teachings/Holy Scriptures in 12, 1, Introduction] ...as the seven angels who stand and go in and out before the face of God, as Raphael the angel says in Tobit... www.newadvent.org/fathers/050712a.htm. Used to confirm the doctrine of angelic intercession in prayer.

Cyprian 258 AD Treatise 4, 33: [Referred to as Holy Scripture in 4, 32; See Tobit 12:8] Thus also Raphael the angel was a witness to the constant prayer and the constant good works of Tobias, saying, [Tobit 12:11-15]... www.newadvent.org/fathers/050704.htm. Used to confirm the doctrine of angelic intercession in prayer.

Origen 230 AD On Prayer 6: the scripture says... "I am Raphael, one of the Seven angels who present the prayers of saints and enter in before the glory of the Holy One. www.tertullian.org/fathers/origen_on_prayer_02_text.htm. Used to confirm doctrine of intercession of angels.

Cyprian 258 AD Treatise 7, 10: Holy Scripture teaches and forewarns... Thus Job... And Tobias... afterwards Raphael the angel praises him, saying, [Tobit 12:11-15]... www.newadvent.org/fathers/050707.htm. Used to confirm the doctrine that suffering must be expected.

Chromatius 407 AD Tractate on Matthew 41, 9: Here, then, in the words that the Lord speaks, "Let the dead bury their own dead" he has not inhibited the obligations of religious piety, by which we know that many saints have pleased God [Tob 12:12-13] ... [Per Chromatius of Aquileia, Sermons and Tractates on Matthew]. Not available online. Used to confirm the doctrine that burying the dead is pleasing to God.

12:16 Then they were both troubled, and fell upon their faces: for they feared.

Evodius 430 AD Letter (to Augustine) 158, 6: ... I do not feel myself called upon to give to a sentence in apocryphal writings a preference over the definite statements quoted above. We must therefore give attention to this, and search out, by the help ... of the authority of revelation ... the angels, who are like our souls invisible, have at times desired to appear in bodily forms and be seen, and ... they have appeared, for example, to Abraham Genesis 18:6 and to Tobias. www.newadvent.org/fathers/

1102130.htm. Used to confirm the doctrine that souls may have bodies after death.

12:17 But he said unto them, Fear not, for it shall go well with you; praise God therefore. 12:18 For not of any favour of mine, but by the will of our God I came; wherefore praise him for ever. 12:19 All these days I did appear unto you; but I did neither eat nor drink, but ye did see a vision.

Augustine 426 AD City of God 13, 22: For neither are we to suppose, when men receive them as guests, that the angels eat only in appearance, though to any who did not know them to be angels they might seem to eat from the same necessity as ourselves. So these words spoken in the Book of Tobit, You saw me eat, but you saw it but in vision; that is, you thought I took food as you do for the sake of refreshing my body. www.newadvent.org/fathers/120113.htm. Used to confirm the doctrine that angels are spiritual but can appear to be material.

12:20 Now therefore give God thanks: for I go up to him that sent me; but write all things which are done in a book. 12:21 And when they arose, they saw him no more. 12:22 Then they confessed the great and wonderful works of God, and how the angel of the Lord had appeared unto them.

13:1 Then Tobit wrote a prayer of rejoicing, and said, Blessed be God that liveth for ever, and blessed be his kingdom. 13:2 For he doth scourge, and hath mercy: he leadeth down to hell, and bringeth up again: neither is there any that can avoid his hand. 13:3 Confess him before the Gentiles, ye children of Israel: for he hath scattered us among them.

Saint Patrick 450 AD Confession 1.1: Cited along with Isaiah without qualification: The Lord brought over us the wrath of his anger and scattered us among many nations... [Per Ancient Christian Commentary on Scripture] Not online.

13:4 There declare his greatness, and extol him before all the living: for he is our Lord, and he is the God our Father for ever. 13:5 And he will scourge us for our iniquities, and will have mercy again, and will gather us out of all nations, among whom he hath scattered us. 13:6 If ye turn to him with your whole heart, and with your whole mind, and deal uprightly before him, then will he turn unto you, and will not hide his face from you. Therefore see what he will do with you, and confess him with your whole mouth, and praise the Lord of might, and extol the everlasting King. In the land of my captivity do I praise him, and declare his might and majesty to a sinful nation. O ye sinners, turn and do justice before him: who can tell if he will accept you, and have mercy on you?

Clement of Rome 96 AD 1 Clement, 61: Cited along with Genesis, Deuteronomy, etc. without qualification: For it is you, Master, the heavenly "King of eternity," ... www.newadvent.org/fathers/1010.htm.

Cyprian 258 AD Treatise 11, 11: [Referred to as Sacred Scripture in 11, 1: you have desired... I would collect from the sacred Scriptures ...] Tobias ... sublimely announces both the divine power and majesty, saying: In the land of my captivity I confess to Him, and I show forth His power in a sinful nation. www.newadvent .org/fathers/050711.htm.

13:7 I will extol my God, and my soul shall praise the King of heaven, and shall rejoice in his greatness. 13:8 Let all men speak, and let all praise him for his righteousness. 13:9 O Jerusalem, the holy city, he will scourge thee for thy children's works, and will have mercy again on the sons of the righteous. 13:10 Give praise to the Lord, for he is good: and praise the everlasting King, **that his tabernacle may be builded in thee again with joy**, and let him make joyful there in thee those that are captives, and love in thee for ever those that are miserable.

John 1:14 (And the Word was made flesh, and dwelt among us, and we beheld his glory, the glory as of the only begotten of the Father, full of grace and truth. (The Greek word for "made His dwelling" is

literally "tabernacled", per Gary G. Michuta in the Case for the Deuterocanon)).

Clement of Rome 96 AD 1 Clement, 61: Cited along with Genesis, Deuteronomy, etc. without qualification: For it is you, Master, the heavenly "King of eternity," ... www.newadvent.org/fathers/1010.htm.

13:11 <u>Many nations shall come from far to the name of the Lord God with gifts in their hands, even gifts to the King of heaven; all generations shall praise thee with great joy</u>.

Matthew 2:1 (Now when Jesus was born in Bethlehem of Judaea in the days of Herod the king, behold, there came wise men from the east to Jerusalem).

Matthew 2:11 (And when they were come into the house, they saw the young child with Mary his mother, and fell down, and worshipped him: and when they had opened their treasures, they presented unto him gifts; gold, and frankincense, and myrrh).

Matthew 2:2 (Saying, Where is he that is born King of the Jews? for we have seen his star in the east, and are come to worship him. The King James Version of Tobit 13:11 is missing a sentence found in many modern Bibles: "A bright light will shine forth into the farthest corners of the earth" – see www.biblegateway.com/verse/en/Tobit %2013%3A11).

Luke 1:48 (For he hath regarded the low estate of his handmaiden: for, behold, from henceforth all generations shall call me blessed).

Tertullian 220 AD On Modesty 7: Cited along with John etc. without qualification: In that case, you make the Lord to have given no answer to the Pharisees' muttering ... Tell me, is not all mankind one flock of God? Is not the same God both Lord and Shepherd of the universal nations? www.newadvent.org/fathers/0407.htm. Used to confirm doctrine that God is Lord of all.

13:12 Cursed are all they which hate thee, and blessed shall all be which love thee for ever. 13:13 Rejoice and be glad for the children of the just: for they shall be gathered together, and shall bless the Lord of the just. 13:14 O blessed are they which love thee, for they shall rejoice in thy peace: blessed are they which have been sorrowful for all thy scourges; for they shall rejoice for thee, when they have seen all thy glory, and shall be glad for ever. 13:15 Let my soul bless God the great King. 13:16 For Jerusalem shall be built up with sapphires and emeralds, and precious stone: thy walls and towers and battlements with pure gold. 13:17 And the streets of Jerusalem shall be paved with beryl and carbuncle and stones of Ophir. 13:18 And all her streets shall say, Alleluia; and they shall praise him, saying, Blessed be God, which hath extolled it for ever.

14:1 So Tobit made an end of praising God. 14:2 And he was eight and fifty years old when he lost his sight, which was restored to him after eight years: and he gave alms, and he increased in the fear of the Lord God, and praised him.

Clement of Alexandria 198 AD Stromata 1, 21: [Referred to as Scripture in 6, 12; see Tobit 4:15] At this period, too, occurred the sign of Jona; and Tobias, through the assistance of the angel Raphael, married Sarah, the demon having killed her seven first suitors; and after the marriage of Tobias, his father Tobit recovered his sight. www.newadvent.org/fathers/02091.htm.

14:3 And when he was very aged he called his son, and the sons of his son, and said to him, My son, take thy children; for, behold, I am aged, and am ready to depart out of this life. 14:4 Go into Media my son, for I surely believe those things which Jonas the prophet spake of Nineve, that it shall be overthrown; and that for a time peace shall rather be in Media; and that our brethren shall lie scattered in the earth from that good land: and Jerusalem shall be desolate, and the house of God in it shall be burned, and shall be desolate for a time; 14:5 And that again God will have mercy on them, and bring them again into the land, where they shall build a temple, but not like to

the first, until the time of that age be fulfilled; and afterward they shall return from all places of their captivity, and build up Jerusalem gloriously, and the house of God shall be built in it for ever with a glorious building, as the prophets have spoken thereof. 14:6 And all nations shall turn, and fear the Lord God truly, and shall bury their idols.

Athanasius 335 AD Discourses against the Arians 1, 43: Cited along with John and Philippians without qualification: No longer Israel alone, but from this time forward all the nations, as the prophet has foretold, abandon their idols and acknowledge the true God, the Father of Christ. www.newadvent.org/fathers/28161.htm. Considered prophesy fulfilled by Christ.

14:7 So shall all nations praise the Lord, and his people shall confess God, and the Lord shall exalt his people; and all those which love the Lord God in truth and justice shall rejoice, shewing mercy to our brethren.

Tertullian 220 AD On Modesty 7: Cited along with John etc. without qualification:... Tell me, is not all mankind one flock of God? Is not the same God both Lord and Shepherd of the universal nations? www.newadvent.org/fathers/0407.htm. Used to confirm the doctrine that God is Lord of all.

14:8 And now, my son, depart out of Nineve, because that those things which the prophet Jonas spake shall surely come to pass. 14:9 But keep thou the law and the commandments, and shew thyself merciful and just, that it may go well with thee.

14:10 And bury me decently, and thy mother with me; but tarry no longer at Nineve. Remember, my son, how Aman handled Achiacharus that brought him up, how out of light he brought him into darkness, and how he rewarded him again: yet Achiacharus was saved, but the other had his reward: for he went down into darkness. Manasses gave alms, and escaped the snares of death which they had set for him: but Aman fell into the snare, and perished. 14:11 Wherefore now, my son, consider what alms doeth, and how righteousness doth deliver. When he had said these things, he gave up the ghost in the bed, being an hundred and eight and fifty years old; and he buried him honourably.

Cyprian 258 AD Treatise 8, 20: cited along with Acts, etc. without qualification: Be rather such a father to your children as was Tobias. Give useful and saving precepts to your pledges, such as he gave to his son; command your children what he also commanded his son, saying: And now, my son, I command you, serve God in truth, and do before Him that which pleases Him; and command your sons, that they exercise righteousness and alms, and be mindful of God, and bless His name always. www.newadvent.org/fathers/050708.htm
14:12 And when Anna his mother was dead, he buried her with his father. But Tobias departed with his wife and children to Ecbatane to Raguel his father in law, 14:13 Where he became old with honour, and he buried his father and mother in law honourably, and he inherited their substance, and his father Tobit's. 14:14 And he died at Ecbatane in Media, being an hundred and seven and twenty years old. 14:15 But before he died he heard of the destruction of Nineve, which was taken by Nabuchodonosor and Assuerus: and before his death he rejoiced over Nineve.

Postscript to Tobit: Summarizing the Data

The following is a chronological chart of all these citations from the Fathers, plus all canon lists and Councils and codices (which are in ALL CAPS, in **BOLD IF A COUNCIL,** and in *ITALICS IF A CODEX*). In the "Work" column, I either cite to the mention in a Book or use a shorthand reference for where the List/Council/Codex stood on Tobit.

NOTE! These lists are just quick and dirty, and deficient in several ways (in particular, I am mostly using the date of death of the Father rather than the actual date of publication, so the dates of individual works on this list are mostly <u>later</u> than they ought to be).[367]

Afterwards, I will break out the canon lists and Councils and codices separately, including explanatory notes.

Ch	V	Father	Year?	Work
13	6	Clement of Rome	96	1 Clement, 61
13	10	Clement of Rome	96	1 Clement, 61
4	15	Didache	100	Didache 1
4	10	Polycarp	107	Epistle to the Philippians, 10
12	9	Polycarp	107	Epistle to the Philippians, 10
12	8	Clement of Rome	140	"Second Epistle" 16
3	8	Hermas	150	The Shepherd Bk 2, Commandment 6
3	17	Hermas	150	The Shepherd Bk 2, Commandment 6
		MELITO OF SARDIS	170	NOT CANONICAL (FOR JEWS?)
		MURATORIAN (NT LIST)	170	UNKNOWN
12	12	Tertullian	192	On Prayer 16
14	2	Clement of Alexandria	198	Stromata 1, 21
4	15	Clement of Alexandria	198	Stromata 2, 23
12	8	Clement of Alexandria	198	Stromata 6, 12
		CLEMENT ALEX. (EUSEB.)	203	UNKNOWN
13	11	Tertullian	220	On Modesty 7
14	7	Tertullian	220	On Modesty 7
		ORIGEN (JEWISH LIST)	220	NOT CANONICAL FOR JEWS
4	1	Origen	230	First Principles 3, 2, 4
5	21	Origen	230	On First Principles 1.2.13
4	9	Origen	230	On First Principles 1.2.13
12	12	Origen	230	On Prayer 20
3	1	Origen	230	On Prayer 6
3	11	Origen	230	On Prayer 6
3	17	Origen	230	On Prayer 6
12	12	Origen	230	On Prayer 6
12	15	Origen	230	On Prayer 6

---

[367] More exact dates are hard to find and debated anyway, so I did not see getting more precise as worth the trouble. In addition, these are just the quotes I myself read and organized, which are only a fraction of what Biblindex reports (but those may be vague allusions, not as Scripture, etc.).

3	1	Origen	230	On Prayer 9
3	17	Hippolytus of Rome	235	On Susanna
2	3	Africanus	240	Letter to Origen 2
1	14	Origen	248	Letter to Africanus 13
1	18	Origen	248	Letter to Africanus 13
1	20	Origen	248	Letter to Africanus 13
1	22	Origen	248	Letter to Africanus 13
12	7	Origen	248	Against Celsus 5, 19
12	7	Origen	248	Against Celsus 5, 29
		ORIGEN (LETTER)	248	CANON
4	16	Commodianus	250	Instructions, LXI, for Martyrdom
		ORIGEN (CITATIONS)	250	CANON
12	7	Origen	253	Commentary on Romans, 2.4.4.5
3	17	Origen	253	on Prayer 11
11	13	Origen	253	Comm. on John, Fragment 66.16
4	10	Cyprian	258	Letter 51
4	10	Cyprian	258	Letter 55 (to Antonian) 22,
13	6	Cyprian	258	Treatise 11, 11
12	15	Cyprian	258	Treatise 12, 1, 20
2	2	Cyprian	258	Treatise 12, 3, 1
4	11	Cyprian	258	Treatise 12, 3, 1
2	14	Cyprian	258	Treatise 12, 3, 6
4	12	Cyprian	258	Treatise 12, 3, 62
12	8	Cyprian	258	Treatise 4, 32
12	15	Cyprian	258	Treatise 4, 33
2	14	Cyprian	258	Treatise 7, 10
12	15	Cyprian	258	Treatise 7, 10
2	10	Cyprian	258	Treatise 9
12	9	Cyprian	258	Treatise 8, 5
4	11	Cyprian	258	Treatise 8, 20
14	11	Cyprian	258	Treatise 8, 20
1	16	Pontius	258	The Life of Cyprian, 10
12	7	Dionysius	265	Against Germanus 4
		EUSEBIUS (APPROVAL)	324	CANON
		~~THE NICENE COUNCIL~~	325	~~UNKNOWN~~
12	7	Athanasius	335	Defense against Arius 1, 11
14	6	Athanasius	335	Discourses against the Arians 1, 43
		CLAROMONTANUS	349	CANON
		CODEX VATICANUS	*350*	*CANON*
		CODEX SINAITICUS	*350*	*CANON*
		CYRIL OF JERUSALEM	350	NOT CANONICAL
		ST CATHERINE'S SYRIAC	350	NOT CANONICAL
		CHELTENHAM LIST	360	CANON
4	18	Athanasius	361	Apologia ad Constantium 17
		~~COUNCIL AT LAODICEA~~	363	~~NOT CANONICAL~~
12	7	Hilary of Poitiers	367	Homily on Psalm 118, 6
12	12	Hilary of Poitiers	367	Tractate in Psalm 129, 7
		ATHANASIUS	367	VERSION 3.1
		HILARY OF POITIERS	367	CANON FOR SOME
		GREGORY OF NAZIANZUS	380	NOT CANONICAL
		AMPHILOCHIUS	380	NOT CANONICAL
		THE APOSTOLIC CANONS	380	CANON
		~~THE COUNCIL OF ROME~~	382	~~CANON~~
		EPIPHANIUS PAN. 8.6.1-4	385	NOT CANONICAL FOR JEWS

		EPIPHANIUS PAN. 76.22.5	385	NOT CANONICAL
12	9	Didymus the Blind	386	Commentary on Zechariah 7:5-7
4	15	Didymus the Blind	386	Commentary on Zechariah 9:14-15
1	1	Pseudo-Ambrose	390	Quaestiones Veteris 119, 2: p. 359
		JEROME (HELMETED)	390	NOT CANONICAL
		EPIPHANIUS DE MENS. 4-5	392	NOT CANONICAL FOR JEWS
		THE COUNCIL OF HIPPO – 70 BISHOPS	**393**	**CANON**
9	3	Ambrose	397	Christian Faith, Book V, 7, 94
12	9	Ambrose	397	Exposition on Luke 7.100-101
3	8	Ambrose	397	Hexameron 6, 4, 17
5	16	Ambrose	397	Hexameron 6, 4, 17
8	3	Ambrose	397	Hexameron 6, 4, 17
12	9	Ambrose	397	Letter 63, 16
2	4	Ambrose	397	Duties of the Clergy 3, 96
7	11	Ambrose	397	Duties of the Clergy 3, 96
2	5	Ambrose	397	On Paradise 15.75
4	**1**	**Ambrose**	**397**	**On Tobias – Scriptural Commentary**
		AUGUSTINE	397	CANON
		COUNCIL OF CARTHAGE – 44-48 BISHOPS	**397**	**CANON**
		JEROME (SOLOMON)	398	VERSION 3.2
2	1	Augustine	400	Reply to Faustus 22, 35
8	7	Augustine	400	Reply to Faustus 22, 35
4		Augustine	400	Confessions 10, 51
3	14	Augustine	400	Confessions 4, 9, 14
3	12	Augustine	400	Confessions 5, 1
4	15	The Apostolic Constitutions	400	Book 1, 1
4	15	The Apostolic Constitutions	400	Book 3, 15
4	15	The Apostolic Constitutions	400	Book 7, 1-2
		RUFINUS	400	VERSION 3.3
		JEROME (TOBIT/JUDITH)	404	CANON
		POPE INNOCENT I	405	CANON
4	23	Chromatius	407	Sermon 5, 5
1	17	Chromatius	407	Tractate on Matthew 41, 9
12	13	Chromatius	407	Tractate on Matthew 41, 9
12	12	Chromatius	407	Tractate on Matthew 57.1.12
12	9	John Chrysostom	407	Homily 4 on Philippians
4	15	John Chrysostom	407	Homily 13 on the Statues
12	8	Gaudentius of Brescia	410	Sermon 13, 21
12	8	Gaudentius of Brescia	410	To Benivolus, 21-27.15
4	21	Augustine	416	Man's Perfection in Righteousness, 13
		COUNCIL OF CARTHAGE – 217 BISHOPS	**419**	**CANON**
1	10	Sulpitius Severus	420	Sacred History 1, 49
2	10	Augustine	421	On the Soul and its Origin 2, 3
4	6	Augustine	421	On the Soul and its Origin 2, 3
2	7	Augustine	422	On the Care of the Dead 5
12	12	Augustine	422	On the Care of the Dead 5
12	12	Augustine	426	City of God 1, 13
12	19	Augustine	426	City of God 13, 22
4	17	Augustine	426	On Christian Doctrine 3, 16, 24
8	7	Augustine	426	On Christian Doctrine 3, 18, 27
4	15	Augustine	430	Exposition on Psalm 35, 1

4	15	Augustine	430	Exposition on Psalm 57, 1
4	15	Augustine	430	Exposition on Psalm 58, 1
4	19	Augustine	430	Exposition on Psalm 58, 15
12	12	Augustine	430	Letter 140, 69
12	7	Augustine	430	Letter 237, 4
12	7	Augustine	430	Letter 237, 8
12	8	Augustine	430	Letter 36, 8, 18
4	15	Augustine	430	On Psalm 51/52
4	9	Augustine	430	Sermon 125A, 4
4	10	Augustine	430	Sermon 125A, 4
4	10	Augustine	430	Sermon 125A, 5
1	2	Augustine	430	Sermon 270, 6
2	1	Augustine	430	Sermon 272B
4	17	Augustine	430	Sermon 361, 6
8	9	Augustine	430	Sermon 60, 6
4		Augustine	430	Tractate 13 (John 3:22-3:29) 3
2	10	Augustine	430	Tractate 35 (John 8:13-14) 3
12	12	Augustine	430	Sermon 198, 48
4	7	Augustine	430	Exposition on Psalm 97, 15
4	10	Augustine	430	Exposition on Psalm 97, 15
2	10	Augustine	430	Homilies on John, Homily 13, 3
4		Augustine	430	Homilies on John, Homily 13, 3
12	8	Augustine	430	Letter 130, 31
12	12	Augustine	430	Letter 130, 9
4	15	Augustine	430	Sermon 130A
2	14	Augustine	430	Sermon 38, 15
4	10	Augustine	430	Sermon 38, 16
2	14	Augustine	430	Sermon 88, 15
4	10	Augustine	430	Sermon 88, 16
12	16	Evodius	430	Letter (to Augustine) 158, 6
12	12	Anonymous	450	Opus Imperfectum in Matthaeum, 13.5
4	7	Leo the Great	450	Sermon 10, 4
2	4	Maximus of Turin	450	Sermons 41.2
13	3	Saint Patrick	450	Confession 1.1
		CODEX ALEXANDRINUS	*450*	*CANON*
		CODEX EPHRAEMI R.	*450*	*UNKNOWN*

The following chart is a subset consisting of all the canon lists given by Fathers and Councils through 450 AD (the end date for this book, but it is really a complete chart through 550 AD, since there were no more lists until 550) and what they had to say about Tobit. As noted previously, I believe focusing on such things by each individual Apocrypha is a much better approach.

On the chart, the Councils are in bold because any one council would involve many more Bishops voting on the canon than the entire collection of individual authors of canon lists combined. E.g., there were 217 bishops at the 419 AD Council of Carthage—that is enormous when "counting" Fathers. That is ten times as many "voices" as the mere two dozen individual entries listed separately on the chart. The crossed-out councils are disputed, in that there is no certainty that they voted on the canon, as will be discussed later.

Another element to consider is the timeframe: until 350 AD, there are no certain Councils that voted on the canon, and there are no certain Christian canon lists either. And 350 is 317 years after Christ, who was as far back in time to those of 350 as the year 1708 is to us (Sweden invaded Russia; the British East India Company was founded; the father of Thomas Jefferson was born). From 350 until 420, there is suddenly a 70-year interest in producing conflicting canon lists and Council votes, which then dies down.

The "Other Citations" column notes how that particular Father cited to Tobit in his works, and I give example language (sometimes, I merely note "cites" as indicated by the biblindex.org/citation_biblique/search database because I had no access to the source material; note that those may well be only allusions). Part of what I take from those other citations is how inconsistent the Fathers who created restrictive lists were in their application of the concepts they express in their lists. I personally think the lists should be viewed as aspirational ideas they had, not the rules they were taught and followed all along (otherwise, would they not be complying with them?). I believe that view is consistent with all the many variations we find across all the lists, the conflicting claims of what had been handed down from the beginning, the Fathers' personal usage, the lack of real heated controversy, the lack of allegations of heresy directed at those who accepted any of the Apocrypha (whereas such things are charged with other Books), etc.

FATHER/LIST/BOOK	Year	**TOBIT** CANONICAL?	OTHER CITATIONS
MELITO OF SARDIS	170	NOT FOR JEWS?	NONE
MURATORIAN CANON	170	UNKNOWN	NOT APPLICABLE
CLEMENT ALEXANDRIA	203	UNKNOWN	AS SCRIPTURE
ORIGEN (JEWISH LIST)	220	NOT FOR JEWS	NOT APPLICABLE
ORIGEN (LETTER)	248	CANON	AS HOLY SCRIPTURE
ORIGEN (CITATIONS)	250	CANON	AS HOLY SCRIPTURE
EUSEBIUS (CITES WITH APPROVAL)	324	CANON	QUOTES CITATIONS MADE BY OTHERS
~~THE NICENE COUNCIL~~	**325**	~~UNKNOWN~~	~~NOT APPLICABLE~~
C. CLAROMONTANUS	349	CANON	NOT APPLICABLE
CODEX VATICANUS	*350*	*CANON*	*NOT APPLICABLE*
CODEX SINAITICUS	*350*	*CANON*	*NOT APPLICABLE*
CYRIL OF JERUSALEM	350	NOT CANONICAL	NONE
ST CATHERINE'S SYRIAC	350	NOT CANONICAL	NOT APPLICABLE
CHELTENHAM LIST	360	CANON	NOT APPLICABLE
~~COUNCIL AT LAODICEA~~	**363**	~~NOT CANONICAL~~	~~NOT APPLICABLE~~
ATHANASIUS	367	VERSION 3.1	PROPHECY
HILARY OF POITIERS	367	CANON FOR SOME	CONFIRMED DOCTRINE

			W/O QUALIFICATION
GREGORY NAZIANZUS	380	NOT CANONICAL	ALLUSIONS ONLY
AMPHILOCHIUS	380	NOT CANONICAL	2 CITES (NOT ONLINE)
THE APOSTOLIC CANONS	380	CANON	AS THE LAW OF GOD
~~THE COUNCIL OF ROME~~	~~382~~	~~CANON~~	~~NOT APPLICABLE~~
EPIPHANIUS PAN. 8.6.1-4	385	NOT FOR JEWS	NONE
EPIPHANIUS PAN. 76.22.5	385	NOT CANONICAL	NONE
JEROME (HELMETED)	390	NOT CANONICAL	IF ONE CARES TO ACCEPT
EPIPHANIUS DE MENS. 4-5	392	NOT FOR JEWS	NONE
THE COUNCIL OF HIPPO - 70 BISHOPS	**393**	**CANON**	**NOT APPLICABLE**
AUGUSTINE	397	CANON	AS HOLY SCRIPTURE
COUNCIL CARTHAGE - 44-48 BISHOPS	**397**	**CANON**	**NOT APPLICABLE**
JEROME (SOLOMON)	398	VERSION 3.2	IF ONE CARES TO ACCEPT
RUFINUS	400	VERSION 3.3	NONE
JEROME (TOBIT/JUDITH)	404	CANON	IF ONE CARES TO ACCEPT
POPE INNOCENT I	405	CANON	NONE
COUNCIL CARTHAGE - 217 BISHOPS	**419**	**CANON**	**NOT APPLICABLE**
CODEX ALEXANDRINUS	*450*	*CANON*	*NOT APPLICABLE*
CODEX EPHRAEMI R.	*450*	*UNKNOWN*	*NOT APPLICABLE*

Version 3.1: Tobit (and Esther (but not Baruch, which is canon)) not canonical but to be read by those learning the faith.

Version 3.2: Tobit (unlike Esther (which is canon) or Baruch (which is not canon)) read for strengthening but not canonical or for confirming the authority of ecclesiastical dogmas.

Version 3.3: Tobit (unlike Esther or Baruch (both of which are canon)) not canonical but "Ecclesiastical."

Notes:

MELITO OF SARDIS (JEWISH LIST?): www.bible-researcher.com/melito.html

MURATORIAN CANON (NEW TESTAMENT LIST): www.bible-researcher.com/muratorian.html

CLEMENT OF ALEXANDRIA (MADE BY EUSEBIUS): www.newadvent.org/fathers/250106.htm; Eusebius gives an incomplete canon list for Clement, and it is a list assembled by Eusebius, not Clement.

ORIGEN (JEWISH LIST): www.newadvent.org/fathers/250106.htm

ORIGEN (LETTER TO AFRICANUS): www.newadvent.org/fathers/0414.htm; the letter discussing the canonicity of Susanna

ORIGEN (CITATIONS): First Principles 3, 2, 4: www.newadvent.org/fathers/04123.htm; not a list but since everyone discusses Origen's list, I provide his citations for comparison to the Jewish list quoted by Eusebius.

EUSEBIUS (CITES CANONICITY WITH APPROVAL): "There is extant an epistle of [Africanus'] to Origen, expressing doubts of the story of Susannah in Daniel, as being spurious and fictitious. Origen answered this very fully." Church History 6, 31, 1: www.newadvent.org/fathers/250106.htm. In the letter Origen confirms that the Churches accept Tobit. As with Origen,

Eusebius does not provide an actual list—but since even "canon list" discussions go into Eusebius' views, I include this for comparison.

THE NICENE COUNCIL: www.tertullian.org/fathers/jerome_preface_judith_e.htm

CODEX CLAROMONTANUS: www.bible-researcher.com/claromontanus.html

CODEX VATICANUS: wikipedia.org/wiki/Codex_Vaticanus

CODEX SINAITICUS: wikipedia.org/wiki/Codex_Sinaiticus

CYRIL OF JERUSALEM: www.bible-researcher.com/cyril.html

ST CATHERINE'S SYRIAC LIST MS 10: 4marksofthechurch.com/biblical-canon-of-st-catherines-monastery/

CHELTENHAM LIST: www.bible-researcher.com/cheltenham.html

THE COUNCIL AT LAODICEA: www.bible-researcher.com/laodicea.html

ATHANASIUS: www.bible-researcher.com/athanasius.html; Athanasius' references outside of his list are discussed above.

HILARY OF POITIERS: www.bible-researcher.com/hilary.html; Hilary of Poitiers gives a list of the modern Jewish/Protestant canon that says "and some add Tobit;" in other works, he refers to Tobit with Scripture without qualification and to confirm doctrine.

GREGORY OF NAZIANZUS: www.bible-researcher.com/gregory.html, see biblindex.org/citation_biblique/search for citations to the allusions.

AMPHILOCHIUS OF ICONIUM: www.bible-researcher.com/amphilocius.html; two citations are listed at Biblindex, but I could not find the actual books to see what he said.

THE APOSTOLIC CANONS/CONSTITUTIONS: www.bible-researcher.com/apostolic.html

THE COUNCIL OF ROME: wikipedia.org/wiki/Council_of_Rome and www.bible-researcher.com/gelasius.html

EPIPHANIUS PANARION 8.6.1-4 (JEWISH LIST): www.bible-researcher.com/epiphanius.html

EPIPHANIUS PANARION 76.22.5 (CHRISTIAN LIST): www.bible-researcher.com/epiphanius.html

JEROME (KINGS/HELMETED PREFACE): www.bible-researcher.com/jerome.html; citation is from www.tertullian.org/fathers/jerome_daniel_02_text.htm: "whenever it is medicine or healing that is needed, it is Raphael who is sent, for his name is rendered as "the healing of," or "the medicine of God" ---- that is, if one cares to accept the authority of the Book of Tobias."

EPIPHANIUS DE MENSURIS 4-5 (JEWISH LIST): isac.uchicago.edu/sites/default/files/uploads/shared/docs/saoc11.pdf; see 22-3 for a second Jewish list in the same work, which does not mention Wisdom, Sirach, or Baruch; that section is discussing the number/numerology of Books (22 or 27), which perhaps explains why he restates the names of the Books that make up that number without mentioning the ancillary Books that he discusses in 4-5.

THE COUNCIL OF HIPPO—70 BISHOPS: wikipedia.org/wiki/Synod_of_Hippo

AUGUSTINE: www.bible-researcher.com/augustine.html

THE COUNCIL OF CARTHAGE—44-48 BISHOPS: wikipedia.org/wiki/Councils_of_Carthage

JEROME (PREFACE TO SOLOMON): www.tertullian.org/fathers/jerome_preface_solomon.htm; see above for the citation.

RUFINUS: www.bible-researcher.com/rufinus.html

JEROME (PREFACE TO TOBIT/JUDITH): www.tertullian.org/fathers/jerome_preface_judith_e.htm and www.tertullian.org/fathers/jerome_preface_tobit.htm; see above for the citation.

POPE INNOCENT I: www.bible-researcher.com/innocent.html

THE COUNCIL OF CARTHAGE—217 BISHOPS: wikipedia.org/wiki/Councils_of_Carthage

CODEX ALEXANDRINUS: wikipedia.org/wiki/Codex_Alexandrinus

CODEX EPHRAEMI RESCRIPTUS: wikipedia.org/wiki/Codex_Ephraemi_Rescriptus

JUDITH

The issues Irenaeus evinces for Baruch (and Susanna, etc.) are but a piece of the problem that the earliest Fathers present. Clement of Rome's Epistle (1 Clement) is a letter addressed to the Christians in the city of Corinth and is one of the earliest, if not the earliest, extra-Biblical Christian writing still extant. It may, in fact, have been written when disciples were still alive and before several Books of the New Testament were completed. Its audience included people who were alive when Paul preached in Corinth.

Clement is thought to have been a disciple of Peter (as Luke was a disciple of Paul); and possibly, he is also the Clement mentioned as working with Paul in Philippians 4:3. One reason to think that Clement's Epistle dates to before 70 AD is that it mentions the Temple and its sacrifices in the present tense.[368]

The Epistle references Wisdom (Chapters 3 and 27), Sirach (Chapter 59), and Tobit (Chapter 61)—but those are allusions and not citations. So, let's focus on the ladies, as it mentions by name both Judith and the Apocryphal additions to Esther (Chapter 55):

> To bring forward some examples from among the heathen: Many kings and princes, in times of pestilence, when they had been instructed by an oracle, have given themselves up to death, in order that by their own blood they might deliver their fellow citizens [from destruction]. Many have gone forth from their own cities, that so sedition might be brought to an end within them.
>
> We know many among ourselves who have given themselves up to bonds, in order that they might ransom others. Many, too, have surrendered themselves to slavery, that with the price which they received for themselves, they might provide food for others. Many women also, being strengthened by the grace of God, have performed numerous manly exploits. The blessed Judith, when her city was besieged, asked of the elders permission to go forth into the camp of the strangers; and, exposing herself to danger, she went out for the love which she bare to her country and people then besieged; and the Lord delivered Holofernes into the hands of a woman. Esther also, being perfect in faith, exposed herself to no less danger, in order to deliver the twelve tribes of Israel from impending destruction. For with fasting and humiliation she entreated the everlasting God, who sees all things; and He, perceiving the humility of her spirit, delivered the people for whose sake she had encountered peril.

These are references to Judith and Esther as people, and no mention is made of the Books. However, we often see such references counted as

---

[368] Sections 40-41: www.newadvent.org/fathers/1010.htm

references to Scripture. Recall the discussion of New Testament references from Don Stewart of the Blue Letter Bible,[369] in which three of the five alleged references to Books of the Pentateuch actually do not mention a Book at all. In the case of Nehemiah, he accepts a reference to something mentioned in several other Books, as well.[370]

Consider also the audience of the Epistle. In Corinth, Paul had "reasoned in the synagogue every Sabbath, and persuaded the Jews and the Greeks" (Acts 18:4) and "was pressed in the spirit, and testified to the Jews that Jesus was Christ: (Acts 18:5) and "Then spake the Lord to Paul in the night by a vision, Be not afraid...for I have much people in this city." Acts 18:9-10. In fact, "Crispus, the chief ruler of the synagogue, believed on the Lord with all his house"—he may well have been one of the recipients. Clement and this audience in Corinth must have both believed that Judith was blessed and that "the Lord delivered Holofernes into her hands."

There are also five possible New Testament references to Judith, and two of the five come in Paul's own Epistle to that same audience in Corinth.

> 1 Corinthians 1:27: "But God hath chosen the foolish things of the world to confound the wise; and God hath chosen the weak things of the world to confound the things which are mighty;"
> Judith 16:7: "For the mighty one did not fall by the young men, neither did the sons of the Titans smite him, nor high giants set upon him: but Judith the daughter of Merari weakened him with the beauty of her countenance."
> And:
> 1 Corinthians 2:11: "But God hath revealed them unto us by his Spirit: for the Spirit searcheth all things, yea, the deep things of God. 11For what man knoweth the things of a man, save the spirit of man which is in him? even so the things of God knoweth no man, but the Spirit of God."
> Judith 8:14: "For ye cannot find the depth of the heart of man, neither can ye perceive the things that he thinketh: then how can ye search out God, that hath made all these things, and know his mind, or comprehend his purpose?"

Those are two possible references to the Book of Judith in the span of 16 verses, in an Epistle to the same audience that would soon (before 70 AD?)

---

[369] www.blueletterbible.org/Comm/stewart_don/faq/right-books-in-old-testament/question17-new-testament-quote-old-testament.cfm
[370] An oddity to bear in mind is that if Judith is considered a sort of historical fiction, then any reference to Judith is to the Book (since she did not exist outside of the Book); but if it is actual history, then the reference need not be to the Book.

receive the Epistle from Clement, which specifically names the blessed Judith and discussed the story set forth in the Book of Judith.

An additional two references come from Paul's disciple Luke. The "we" passages of Acts begin in Acts Chapter 16, and Paul arrives in Corinth in Chapter 18, which would seem to indicate that Luke was with Paul in Corinth.

Elizabeth honors Mary with the words, "Blessed art thou among women," (Luke 1:42) which may be referring to Judith 13:18 "O daughter, blessed art thou of the most high God above all the women upon the earth." Judith was seen as an Old Testament "type" of the New Testament's Mary and the Church in other ways. In fact, we will see Jerome using such typology below.

That possible reference might be paired with another: Mary replies in Luke 1:48 "behold, from henceforth all generations shall call me blessed." Judith 8:32 says that "Then said Judith unto them, Hear me, and I will do a thing, which shall go throughout all generations to the children of our nation."

So, within seven verses, we have two possible references to Judith in the Gospel written by a disciple of Paul. Both of them may have worked in Corinth together. Paul himself may also make two references to Judith in his own Epistle to the Corinthians. And Clement, who may also have worked with Paul, clearly references the Blessed Judith in his Epistle to the Corinthians. All this may have come before the fall of Jerusalem, and a generation before Josephus claims the 22 Book canon of the Jews.[371]

The evidence that the Christians in Corinth accepted Judith as Scripture is pretty strong.[372] And they would have been taught it was Scripture by Paul, Luke, and Clement, in which case Judith was Scripture, period.[373]

The fifth possible New Testament reference is from Mark 9:46: "And if thy hand offend thee, cut it off: it is better for thee to enter into life maimed, than having two hands to go into hell, into the fire that never shall be quenched: 44Where their worm dieth not, and the fire is not quenched. 45And if thy foot offend thee, cut it off: it is better for thee to enter halt into life, than having

---

[371] Or 1 Clement is at the latest contemporary with Josephus' writing.

[372] Historians would conclude that a Greek city worshipped a Pagan goddess on similar evidence.

[373] Note that Elizabeth (whose husband was a Priest) and Mary are the ones speaking in Luke's possible references. That two women would know and reference Judith the heroine would seem to be exactly what one would expect. In addition, these two references plus another to Tobit are indications that both Mary (traditionally from Sepphoris, one of the two Greektowns in Galilee per Ehrman) and her cousin Elizabeth (wife of a Priest who could write, who raises the Herald instead of a Priest) may come from a bilingual cultural background (the oldest copies of Judith are in Greek), which is further evidence that their menfolk may have been literate in Greek as well. See the discussion of Peter's literacy above.

two feet to be cast into hell, into the fire that never shall be quenched: 46Where their worm dieth not, and the fire is not quenched."

The references to worms and fire are from Judith 16:17: "Woe to the nations that rise up against my kindred! the Lord Almighty will take vengeance of them in the day of judgment, in putting fire and worms in their flesh; and they shall feel them, and weep for ever."

Otherwise, I hate to come off as sexist, but there are pretty good reasons to note how comparable Judith is to Esther in the canon debate. They are both "historical" Books, with relatively few citations from the Fathers (biblindex.org/citation_biblique/search gives 143 for Esther, 120 for Judith).[374] But then many of the references to the higher ranking books are allusions, whereas (because the ladies themselves are often specifically named) we actually have remarkably clear references to Esther and Judith (at least as people) very early on, from 1 Clement (96 AD at the latest, possibly before some of the New Testament had been written) and, in the case of Judith, also from Ignatius (117 AD: Letter to the Philadelphians (Long Version) IV).[375]

Other comparables include the canon lists, because inclusion is neither unanimous nor free from disagreement for either of them. Neither Book is listed in the first two centuries because Melito does not mention them. In the middle period, Origen notes in his letter that the Churches use Judith (while knowing that the Jews do not accept it), and Eusebius then mentions that letter with approval; and Jerome tells us that the Nicene Council accepted Judith (if we believe that, but we probably should not).

When we get to the main era of lists after 350 AD, we find that (as with Melito's list) Esther gets treatment more comparable to Judith than other canonical Books would be. So, Athanasius denies both Books' canonicity and places them in his third category; Hilary of Poitiers accepts Esther and says "some" accept Judith (and that appears to include himself, judging from his citations to it); Gregory of Nazianzus rejects both, while Amphilochius of Iconium rejects Judith and says only "some" include Esther.

Later, no matter what we think of Jerome's personal view or his mistake about Nicea, we see that he clearly evidences that the Church accepted Judith.

---

[374] Speaking of sexism, the three least-cited historical Books for the Fathers are Ruth (201), Esther, and Judith.

[375] And recall that a reference to Judith would be to the Book if she did not exist outside of it.

In fact, in Letter 79, 10,[376] Jerome would write that "Judith renowned in Hebrew story ... was a type of the Church which cuts off the head of the devil (referring to Genesis 3:15, the proto-Evangelium)..." This was in 400 AD (if the dating is correct), between saying "the Church also reads the books of Judith... but does not receive them among the canonical Scriptures..." and later saying that "this book is found by the Nicene Council to have been counted among the number of the Sacred Scriptures." Referring to Judith as a "type" might be evidence that he had already softened his personal view and accepted Judith as Scripture by 400 AD.[377]

We know that Judith was used in the Churches long before 248 AD (as mentioned by Origen in his letter), with later confirmations that Judith remained part of the liturgy until the end of our inquiry in 450 AD (e.g., the sermons from Chromatius, Rufinus notes that it is read in the Churches, etc.). Judith also gets mention in sermons on monogamy, virginity, widowhood, etc.

Meanwhile, Jerome obtained texts of Judith in Aramaic/Chaldee, which he presumably obtained from the Jews in or around Bethlehem, and says that Judith had a status ("hagiographa," which has a debatable meaning) among the Jews that is higher than Tobit (which he says is not hagiographa). Origen had already told us that the Jews did not accept either, even as Apocrypha. But between the different words, centuries, and geography, it is hard to compare that to what Jerome says with any certainty. Jews living in the Diaspora seem to have considered Judith scriptural, since it is found in the Greek Septuagint, and perhaps the connections with Corinth evidence that as well.

Also, while beyond my scope, although Judith would disappear from Judaism, it then returned to prominence among Jews in the Middle Ages.[378]

---

[376] www.newadvent.org/fathers/3001079.htm

[377] Which would make sense to me due to my guess that he meant to refer to not Nicea but the African councils (they had voted, and he accepts their decision). But that is just my guess and not a particularly well-informed one. There is no real discussion in the early Church of exactly what is meant by the "third category" of Books that the handful of Fathers like Jerome claim are only read but not received as canonical. Perhaps typology could apply to them, and as far as I know, no Father ever says otherwise. Meanwhile, Gallagher wrote a paper on Jerome's motivations for making the translations of Judith and Tobit, concluding that Jerome had a more favorable view of them than the other Apocrypha—but not so favorable a view that Jerome thought they were Scripture. www.academia.edu/14345165

[378] wikipedia.org/wiki/Book_of_Judith, which also notes that Rabbi "Nachmanides (Ramban) [d. 1270] quoted several passages from a Peshitta (Syriac version) of Judith in support of his rendering of Deuteronomy 21:14..."

When discussing Tobit, I gave a chart of citations to all historical books, which placed Judith dead last. However, the bottom of that chart is somewhat overwhelmed by one man: Eusebius. He wrote the great Church History and several related books (e.g., the Chronicon/Chronicle) to which we owe so much of our knowledge of the early Church. However, Eusebius distorts the data for the little-cited historical Books, and in fact, 54%—a majority of all citations, 138 of 256—to Nehemiah are actually just from Eusebius. Without Eusebius (effectively, "cites by everyone else"), Judith is not at the bottom. It is cited 120 times, more than Nehemiah (118) and Esther (111), and was cited more per verse (0.35) than Nehemiah (0.29) and almost as often as Esther (0.41). (All data is from biblindex.org/citation_biblique/search).

I was able to review 63 citations to Judith from 19 Fathers (including four of the ten on Kruger's list) and 30 of their works. (19 Fathers cited to Nehemiah as well, per Biblindex; 16 cited to Esther.)

Twenty of 63 citations occurred before 350 AD—and the first certain council or clearly Christian canon list—notably including cites from 1 Clement (Listed as written in 96 AD, but arguably, it was written before 70 AD since 1 Clement speaks of the Temple as still in existence. Either way, it may have been written before the last books of the New Testament were, and before Josephus claimed there were 22 Books in the Jewish canon). Additional early citations are from Clement of Alexandria and Origen.

Forty-eight citations (a large majority) specifically refer to Judith as Scripture, and a majority of the remainder refer to her as a saint, "blessed," etc.

Only one Father, when citing to Judith, ever distinguished it with warnings or labels or claimed it was in a third category of books that should only be read: Jerome's Letter 54, where he says "In the book of Judith—if any one is of opinion that it should be received as canonical—we read ..." That occurs in 394 AD, which is right in the middle of the eight-year period where Jerome claimed Judith, et al., "are not in the canon" and before he claimed "the Church ... does not receive them among the canonical Scriptures, so also one may read ... for the strengthening of the people, (but) not for confirming the authority of ecclesiastical dogmas," and before he finally said that "this book is found by the Nicene Council to have been counted among the number of the Sacred Scriptures." (Jerome and his three views on Judith will be discussed in the section on 350 AD-450 AD Canon Lists below.)

Judith: Annotated

Augustine 426 AD City of God 18, 26: During the same time also those things were done which are written in the book of Judith, which, indeed, the Jews are said not to have received into the canon of the Scriptures. [Refers to the Jewish canon, not the Christian. His canon list in "On Christian Doctrine," identified Judith as Christian Scripture 30 years earlier.] www.newadvent.org/fathers/120118.htm

1:1 In the twelfth year of the reign of Nabuchodonosor, who reigned in Nineve, the great city; in the days of Arphaxad, which reigned over the Medes in Ecbatane,

Sulpitius Severus 420 AD Sacred History 2, 14: ... the sacred history is opposed to this opinion; for Judith is described as having lived in the twelfth year of the king in question. www.newadvent. org/fathers/35052.htm

1:2 And built in Ecbatane walls round about of stones hewn three cubits broad and six cubits long, and made the height of the wall seventy cubits, and the breadth thereof fifty cubits: 1:3 And set the towers thereof upon the gates of it an hundred cubits high, and the breadth thereof in the foundation threescore cubits: 1:4 And he made the gates thereof, even gates that were raised to the height of seventy cubits, and the breadth of them was forty cubits, for the going forth of his mighty armies, and for the setting in array of his footmen: 1:5 Even in those days king Nabuchodonosor made war with king Arphaxad in the great plain, which is the plain in the borders of Ragau. 1:6 And there came unto him all they that dwelt in the hill country, and all that dwelt by Euphrates, and Tigris and Hydaspes, and the plain of Arioch the king of the Elymeans, and very many nations of the sons of Chelod, assembled themselves to the battle. 1:7 Then Nabuchodonosor king of the Assyrians sent unto all that dwelt in Persia, and to all that dwelt westward, and to those that dwelt in Cilicia, and Damascus, and Libanus, and Antilibanus, and to all that dwelt upon the sea coast, 1:8 And to those among the nations that were of Carmel, and Galaad, and the higher Galilee, and the great plain of Esdrelom, 1:9 And to all that were in Samaria and the cities thereof, and beyond Jordan unto Jerusalem, and Betane, and Chelus, and Kades, and the river of Egypt, and Taphnes, and Ramesse, and all the land of Gesem, 1:10 Until ye come beyond Tanis and Memphis, and to all the inhabitants of Egypt, until ye come to the borders of Ethiopia. 1:11 But all the inhabitants of the land made light of the commandment of Nabuchodonosor king of the Assyrians, neither went they with him to the battle; for they were not afraid of him: yea, he was before them as one man, and they sent away his ambassadors from them without effect, and with disgrace. 1:12 Therefore Nabuchodonosor was very angry with all this country, and sware by his throne and kingdom, that he would surely be avenged upon all those coasts of Cilicia, and Damascus, and Syria, and that he would slay with the sword all the inhabitants of the land of Moab, and the children of Ammon, and all Judea, and all that were in Egypt, till ye come to the borders of the two seas. 1:13 Then he marched in battle array with his power against king Arphaxad in the seventeenth year, and he prevailed in his battle: for he overthrew all the power of Arphaxad, and all his horsemen, and all his chariots, 1:14 And became lord of his cities, and came unto Ecbatane, and took the towers, and spoiled the streets thereof, and turned the beauty thereof into shame. 1:15 <u>He took also Arphaxad in the mountains of Ragau, and smote him through with his darts, and destroyed him utterly that day</u>.

Sulpitius Severus 420 AD Sacred History 2, 15: [Referred to as "recorded in the sacred writings. The spirit of God thus took care that the histories..." in 2, 14]: The Jews, then, having returned, as we have narrated above, to their native land, ... the king of the Persians made war on the Medes, and engaged in a successful battle against their king, who was named

Arphaxad. That monarch being slain, he added the nation to his empire. www.newadvent.org/fathers/35052.htm
1:16 So he returned afterward to Nineve, both he and all his company of sundry nations being a very great multitude of men of war, and there he took his ease, and banqueted, both he and his army, an hundred and twenty days.
2:1 And in the eighteenth year, the two and twentieth day of the first month, there was talk in the house of Nabuchodonosor king of the Assyrians that he should, as he said, avenge himself on all the earth. 2:2 So he called unto him all his officers, and all his nobles, and communicated with them his secret counsel, and concluded the afflicting of the whole earth out of his own mouth. 2:3 Then they decreed to destroy all flesh, that did not obey the commandment of his mouth. 2:4 And when he had ended his counsel, Nabuchodonosor king of the Assyrians called Holofernes the chief captain of his army, which was next unto him, and said unto him.

Origen 231 AD On Prayer 11: [Referred to as Scripture in 8] wisely does He will, even though we are unable to describe a cause and reason worthy of the Giver for each of His gifts....Mightier was the prince that sought to ruin her soul, whose power Judith had cut through than he whom she met in Holophermes. www.tertullian.org/fathers/origen_on_prayer_02_text.htm
2:5 Thus saith the great king, the lord of the whole earth, Behold, thou shalt go forth from my presence, and take with thee men that trust in their own strength, of footmen an hundred and twenty thousand; and the number of horses with their riders twelve thousand. 2:6 And thou shalt go against all the west country, because they disobeyed my commandment. 2:7 And thou shalt declare unto that they prepare for me earth and water: for I will go forth in my wrath against them and will cover the whole face of the earth with the feet of mine army, and I will give them for a spoil unto them: 2:8 So that their slain shall fill their valleys and brooks and the river shall be filled with their dead, till it overflow: 2:9 And I will lead them captives to the utmost parts of all the earth. 2:10 Thou therefore shalt go forth. and take beforehand for me all their coasts: and if they will yield themselves unto thee, thou shalt reserve them for me till the day of their punishment. 2:11 But concerning them that rebel, let not thine eye spare them; but put them to the slaughter, and spoil them wheresoever thou goest. 2:12 For as I live, and by the power of my kingdom, whatsoever I have spoken, that will I do by mine hand. 2:13 And take thou heed that thou transgress none of the commandments of thy lord, but accomplish them fully, as I have commanded thee, and defer not to do them. 2:14 Then Holofernes went forth from the presence of his lord, and called all the governors and captains, and the officers of the army of Assur; 2:15 And he mustered the chosen men for the battle, as his lord had commanded him, unto an hundred and twenty thousand, and twelve thousand archers on horseback;

Sulpitius Severus 420 AD Sacred History 2, 15: [Referred to as "recorded in the sacred writings. The spirit of God thus took care that the histories..." in 2, 14]: He did the same to other nations, having sent before him Holofernes whom he had appointed master of his host, with a hundred and twenty thousand foot-soldiers, and twelve thousand cavalry. www.newadvent.org/fathers/35052.htm
2:16 And he ranged them, as a great army is ordered for the war. 2:17 And he took camels and asses for their carriages, a very great number; and sheep and oxen and goats without number for their provision: 2:18 And plenty of victual for every man of the army, and very much gold and silver out of the king's house. 2:19 Then he went forth and all his power to go before king Nabuchodonosor in the voyage, and to cover all the face of the earth westward with their chariots, and horsemen, and their chosen footmen. 2:20 A great number also sundry countries came with them like locusts,

and like the sand of the earth: for the multitude was without number. 2:21 And they went forth of Nineve three days' journey toward the plain of Bectileth, and pitched from Bectileth near the mountain which is at the left hand of the upper Cilicia. 2:22 Then he took all his army, his footmen, and horsemen and chariots, and went from thence into the hill country; 2:23 And destroyed Phud and Lud, and spoiled all the children of Rasses, and the children of Israel, which were toward the wilderness at the south of the land of the Chellians. 2:24 Then he went over Euphrates, and went through Mesopotamia, and destroyed all the high cities that were upon the river Arbonai, till ye come to the sea. 2:25 And he took the borders of Cilicia, and killed all that resisted him, and came to the borders of Japheth, which were toward the south, over against Arabia. 2:26 He compassed also all the children of Madian, and burned up their tabernacles, and spoiled their sheepcotes. 2:27 Then he went down into the plain of Damascus in the time of wheat harvest, and burnt up all their fields, and destroyed their flocks and herds, also he spoiled their cities, and utterly wasted their countries, and smote all their young men with the edge of the sword. 2:28 Therefore the fear and dread of him fell upon all the inhabitants of the sea coasts, which were in Sidon and Tyrus, and them that dwelt in Sur and Ocina, and all that dwelt in Jemnaan; and they that dwelt in Azotus and Ascalon feared him greatly.

3:1 So they sent ambassadors unto him to treat of peace, saying, 3:2 Behold, we the servants of Nabuchodonosor the great king lie before thee; use us as shall be good in thy sight. 3:3 Behold, our houses, and all our places, and all our fields of wheat, and flocks, and herds, and all the lodges of our tents lie before thy face; use them as it pleaseth thee. 3:4 Behold, even our cities and the inhabitants thereof are thy servants; come and deal with them as seemeth good unto thee. 3:5 So the men came to Holofernes, and declared unto him after this manner. 3:6 Then came he down toward the sea coast, both he and his army, and set garrisons in the high cities, and took out of them chosen men for aid. 3:7 So they and all the country round about received them with garlands, with dances, and with timbrels. 3:8 Yet he did cast down their frontiers, and cut down their groves: for he had decreed to destroy all the gods of the land, that all nations should worship Nabuchodonosor only, and that all tongues and tribes should call upon him as god. 3:9 Also he came over against Esdraelon near unto Judea, over against the great strait of Judea. 3:10 And he pitched between Geba and Scythopolis, and there he tarried a whole month, that he might gather together all the carriages of his army.

Origen 231 AD On Prayer 8: ... from the Scriptures... that we may ... like ... Judith be delivered from plotting enemies... www.tertullian.org/fathers/origen_on_praye r_02_text.htm

4:1 Now the children of Israel, that dwelt in Judea, heard all that Holofernes the chief captain of Nabuchodonosor king of the Assyrians had done to the nations, and after what manner he had spoiled all their temples, and brought them to nought. 4:2 Therefore they were exceedingly afraid of him, and were troubled for Jerusalem, and for the temple of the Lord their God: 4:3 For they were newly returned from the captivity, and all the people of Judea were lately gathered together: and the vessels, and the altar, and the house, were sanctified after the profanation. 4:4 Therefore they sent into all the coasts of Samaria, and the villages and to Bethoron, and Belmen, and Jericho, and to Choba, and Esora, and to the valley of Salem: 4:5 And possessed themselves beforehand of all the tops of the high mountains, and fortified the villages that were in them, and laid up victuals for the provision of war: for their fields were of late reaped. 4:6 Also Joacim the high priest, which was in those days in Jerusalem, wrote to them that dwelt in Bethulia, and Betomestham, which is over against Esdraelon toward the open country, near to Dothaim, 4:7 Charging them to keep the passages of the hill country: for by them there was an entrance into Judea, and it was easy to stop them that would come up, because the passage was straight, for two men at the most. 4:8 And the children of Israel did as Joacim the high priest had commanded them, with the ancients of all the people of Israel, which dwelt at Jerusalem. 4:9 Then every man of Israel cried to God with great fervency, and with great vehemency did they humble their souls: 4:10 Both they, and their wives and their children, and their cattle, and every stranger and hireling, and their servants bought with money, put sackcloth upon their loins. 4:11 <u>Thus every man and women, and the little children, and the inhabitants of Jerusalem, fell before the temple</u>, and cast ashes upon their heads, and spread out their sackcloth before the face of the Lord: also they put sackcloth about the altar, 4:12 And cried to the God of Israel all with one consent earnestly, that he would not give their children for a prey, and their wives for a spoil, and the cities of their inheritance to destruction, and the sanctuary to profanation and reproach, and for the nations to rejoice at.

Sulpitius Severus 420 AD Sacred History 2, 15: [Referred to as "recorded in the sacred writings. The spirit of God thus took care that the histories..." in 2, 14]: ... since they had previously known from experience the miseries of slavery, they betook themselves in crowds to the temple. There ... they implored the divine assistance; ... begging him to spare the remnant of them who had recently been delivered from slavery. www.newadvent. org/fathers/35052.htm

4:13 So God heard their prayers, and looked upon their afflictions: for the people fasted many days in all Judea and Jerusalem before the sanctuary of the Lord Almighty. 4:14 And Joacim the high priest, and all the priests that stood before the Lord, and they which ministered unto the Lord, had their loins girt with sackcloth, and offered the daily burnt offerings, with the vows and free gifts of the people, 4:15 And had ashes on their mitres, and cried unto the Lord with all their power, that he would look upon all the house of Israel graciously.

5:1 Then was it declared to Holofernes, the chief captain of the army of Assur, that the children of Israel had prepared for war, and had shut up the passages of the hill country, and had fortified all the tops of the high hills and had laid impediments in the champaign countries: 5:2 Wherewith he was very angry, and called all the princes of Moab, and the captains of Ammon, and all the governors of the sea coast, 5:3 And he said unto them, Tell me now, ye sons of Chanaan, who this people is, that dwelleth in the hill country, and what are the cities that they inhabit, and what is the multitude of their army, and wherein is their power and strength, and what king is set over them, or captain of their army; 5:4 And why have they determined not to come and meet me, more than all the inhabitants of the west. 5:5 Then said Achior, the captain of all the sons of Ammon, <u>Let my lord now hear a word from the mouth of thy servant, and I will declare unto thee the truth concerning this people, which dwelleth near thee, and inhabiteth the hill countries: and there shall no lie come out of the mouth of thy servant. 5:6 This people are descended of the Chaldeans:</u>

Gregory of Nazianzus 389 AD Orations 45, 15: ... which are also called in the Scripture the Seed of the Chaldeans... www.newadvent.org/fathers/310245.htm.

<u>5:7 And they sojourned heretofore in Mesopotamia, because they would not follow the gods of their fathers, which were in the land of Chaldea. 5:8 For they left the way of their ancestors, and worshipped the God of heaven, the God whom they knew: so they cast them out from the face of their gods, and they fled into Mesopotamia, and sojourned there many days. 5:9 Then their God commanded them to depart from the place where they sojourned, and to go into the land of Chanaan: where they dwelt, and were increased with gold and silver, and with very much cattle.</u>

Augustine 426 AD City of God 16, 13: Why, then, did the Scripture [Genesis] not mention [Nahor, Abraham's brother] ... The only reason we can think of is, that perhaps he had lapsed from the piety of his father and brother, and adhered to the superstition of the Chaldeans... For in the book called Judith, when Holofernes, the enemy of the Israelites, inquired what kind of nation that might be, and whether war should be made against them, Achior, the leader of the Ammonites, answered him thus: Let our lord now hear a word from the mouth of your servant, ... and go into the land of Canaan; and they dwelt, etc., as Achior the Ammonite narrates. www.newadvent.org/fathers/120116.htm.

5:10 But when a famine covered all the land of Chanaan, they went down into Egypt, and sojourned there, while they were nourished, and became there a great multitude, so that one could not number their nation. 5:11 Therefore the king of Egypt rose up against them, and dealt subtilly with them, and brought them low with labouring in brick, and made them slaves. 5:12 Then they cried unto their God, and he smote all the land of Egypt with incurable plagues: so the Egyptians cast them out of their sight. 5:13 And God dried the Red sea before them, 5:14 And brought them to mount Sina, and Cades-Barne, and cast forth all that dwelt in the wilderness. 5:15 So they dwelt in the land of the Amorites, and they destroyed by their strength all them of Esebon, and passing over Jordan they possessed all the hill country. 5:16 And they cast forth before them the Chanaanite, the Pherezite, the Jebusite, and the Sychemite, and all the Gergesites, and they dwelt in that country many days. 5:17 And whilst they sinned not before their God, they prospered, because the God that hateth iniquity was with them.

Sulpitius Severus 420 AD Sacred History 2, 15: [Referred to as "recorded in the sacred writings. The spirit of God thus took care that the histories..." in 2, 14]: ...when they sinned, they were chastised by

the attacks of enemies or by being sent into captivity, but were always unconquerable when they enjoyed the divine favor. www.newadvent.org/fathers/35052.htm

5:18 But when they departed from the way which he appointed them, they were destroyed in many battles very sore, and were led captives into a land that was not their's, and the temple of their God was cast to the ground, and their cities were taken by the enemies. 5:19 But now are they returned to their God, and are come up from the places where they were scattered, and have possessed Jerusalem, where their sanctuary is, and are seated in the hill country; for it was desolate. 5:20 Now therefore, my lord and governor, if there be any error against this people, and they sin against their God, let us consider that this shall be their ruin, and let us go up, and we shall overcome them. 5:21 But if there be no iniquity in their nation, let my lord now pass by, lest their Lord defend them, and their God be for them, and we become a reproach before all the world.

Augustine 417 AD On Nature and Grace 42 His opponent lists Judith among the biblical examples of those who (he says) lived justly without sin. Augustine disagrees (they were holy yet stilled sinned), and notes the inquiry as "why has not the Scripture mentioned any sins in the persons to whom reference has been made, especially when it has carefully recorded the eminent goodness of their faith?" www.newadvent.org/fathers/1503.htm.

5:22 And when Achior had finished these sayings, all the people standing round about the tent murmured, and the chief men of Holofernes, and all that dwelt by the sea side, and in Moab, spake that he should kill him. 5:23 For, say they, we will not be afraid of the face of the children of Israel: for, lo, it is a people that have no strength nor power for a strong battle 5:24 Now therefore, lord Holofernes, we will go up, and they shall be a prey to be devoured of all thine army.

6:1 And when the tumult of men that were about the council was ceased, Holofernes the chief captain of the army of Assur said unto Achior and all the Moabites before all the company of other nations, 6:2 And who art thou, Achior, and the hirelings of Ephraim, that thou hast prophesied against us as to day, and hast said, that we should not make war with the people of Israel, because their God will defend them? and who is God but Nabuchodonosor? 6:3 He will send his power, and will destroy them from the face of the earth, and their God shall not deliver them: but we his servants will destroy them as one man; for they are not able to sustain the power of our horses. 6:4 For with them we will tread them under foot, and their mountains shall be drunken with their blood, and their fields shall be filled with their dead bodies, and their footsteps shall not be able to stand before us, for they shall utterly perish, saith king Nabuchodonosor, lord of all the earth: for he said, None of my words shall be in vain. 6:5 And thou, Achior, an hireling of Ammon, which hast spoken these words in the day of thine iniquity, shalt see my face no more from this day, until I take vengeance of this nation that came out of Egypt. 6:6 And then shall the sword of mine army, and the multitude of them that serve me, pass through thy sides, and thou shalt fall among their slain, when I return.

Sulpitius Severus 420 AD Sacred History 2, 15: [Referred to as "recorded in the sacred writings. The spirit of God thus took care that the histories…" in 2, 14]: Upon this, Holofernes, flushed with many victories, and thinking that everything must give way before him, was roused to wrath, because victory on his part was regarded as principally depending on the sin of the Jews, and ordered Achior to be pushed forward into the camp of the Hebrews, that he might perish in company with those who he had affirmed could not be conquered. www.newadvent.org/fathers/35052.htm

6:7 Now therefore my servants shall bring thee back into the hill country, and shall set thee in one of the cities of the passages: 6:8 And thou shalt not perish, till thou be destroyed with them. 6:9 And if thou persuade thyself in thy mind that they shall be taken, let not thy countenance fall: I have spoken it, and none of my words shall be in vain. 6:10 Then Holofernes commanded his servants, that waited in his tent, to take Achior, and bring him to Bethulia, and deliver him into the hands of the children of Israel. 6:11 So his servants took him, and brought him out of the camp into the plain, and they went from the midst of the plain into the hill country, and came unto the fountains that were under Bethulia. 6:12 And when the men of the city saw them, they took up their weapons, and went out of the city to the top of the hill: and every man that used a sling kept them from coming up by casting of stones against them. 6:13 Nevertheless having gotten privily under the hill, they bound Achior, and cast him down, and left him at the foot of the hill, and returned to their lord. 6:14 But the Israelites descended from their city, and came unto him, and loosed him, and brought him to Bethulia, and presented him to the governors of the city: 6:15 Which were in those days Ozias the son of Micha, of the tribe of Simeon, and Chabris the son of Gothoniel, and Charmis the son of Melchiel. 6:16 And they called together all the ancients of the city, and all their youth ran together, and their women, to the assembly, and they set Achior in the midst of all their people. Then Ozias asked him of that which was done. 6:17 And he answered and declared unto them the words of the council of Holofernes, and all the words that he had spoken in the midst of the princes of Assur, and whatsoever Holofernes had spoken proudly against the house of Israel. 6:18 Then the people fell down and worshipped God, and cried unto God. saying, 6:19 O Lord God of heaven, behold their pride, and pity the low estate of our nation, and look upon the face of those that are sanctified unto thee this day. 6:20 Then they comforted Achior, and praised him greatly. 6:21 And Ozias took him out of the assembly unto his house, and made a feast to the elders; and they called on the God of Israel all that night for help.

7:1 The next day Holofernes commanded all his army, and all his people which were come to take his part, that they should remove their camp against Bethulia, to take aforehand the ascents of the hill country, and to make war against the children of Israel.

John Chrysostom 407 AD Homilies on John, 61, 4: Cited along with Judges, etc. without qualification: Women have preserved whole nations; for Deborah and Judith exhibited successes worthy of men; so also do ten thousand other women. www.newadvent.org/fathers/240161.htm

7:2 Then their strong men removed their camps in that day, and the army of the men of war was an hundred and seventy thousand footmen, and twelve thousand horsemen, beside the baggage, and other men that were afoot among them, a very great multitude. 7:3 And they camped in the valley near unto Bethulia, by the fountain, and they spread themselves in breadth over Dothaim even to Belmaim, and in length from Bethulia unto Cynamon, which is over against Esdraelon. 7:4 Now the children of Israel, when they saw the multitude of them, were greatly troubled, and said every one to his neighbour, Now will these men lick up the face of the earth; for neither the high mountains, nor the valleys, nor the hills, are able to bear their weight. 7:5 Then every man took up his weapons of war, and when they had kindled fires upon their towers, they remained and watched all that night. 7:6 But in the second day Holofernes brought forth all his horsemen in the sight of the children of Israel which were in Bethulia, 7:7 And viewed the passages up to the city, and came to the fountains of their waters, and took them, and set garrisons of men of war over them, and he himself removed toward his people. 7:8 Then came unto him all the chief of the children of Esau, and all the governors of the people of Moab, and the captains of the sea coast, and said, 7:9 Let our lord now hear a

word, that there be not an overthrow in thine army. 7:10 For this people of the children of Israel do not trust in their spears, but in the height of the mountains wherein they dwell, because it is not easy to come up to the tops of their mountains. 7:11 Now therefore, my lord, fight not against them in battle array, and there shall not so much as one man of thy people perish. 7:12 Remain in thy camp, and keep all the men of thine army, and let thy servants get into their hands the fountain of water, which issueth forth of the foot of the mountain: 7:13 For all the inhabitants of Bethulia have their water thence; so shall thirst kill them, and they shall give up their city, and we and our people shall go up to the tops of the mountains that are near, and will camp upon them, to watch that none go out of the city.

Sulpitius Severus 420 AD Sacred History 2, 15: [Referred to as "recorded in the sacred writings. The spirit of God thus took care that the histories…" in 2, 14]: Well, Holofernes, perceiving the difficulty of the localities, because he could not reach the heights, surrounded the mountains with soldiers, and took the greatest pains to cut off the Hebrews from all water supplies. www.newadvent.org/fathers/35052.htm

7:14 So they and their wives and their children shall be consumed with fire, and before the sword come against them, they shall be overthrown in the streets where they dwell. 7:15 Thus shalt thou render them an evil reward; because they rebelled, and met not thy person peaceably. 7:16 And these words pleased Holofernes and all his servants, and he appointed to do as they had spoken. 7:17 So the camp of the children of Ammon departed, and with them five thousand of the Assyrians, and they pitched in the valley, and took the waters, and the fountains of the waters of the children of Israel. 7:18 Then the children of Esau went up with the children of Ammon, and camped in the hill country over against Dothaim: and they sent some of them toward the south, and toward the east over against Ekrebel, which is near unto Chusi, that is upon the brook Mochmur; and the rest of the army of the Assyrians camped in the plain, and covered the face of the whole land; and their tents and carriages were pitched to a very great multitude. 7:19 Then the children of Israel cried unto the Lord their God, because their heart failed, for all their enemies had compassed them round about, and there was no way to escape out from among them. 7:20 Thus all the company of Assur remained about them, both their footmen, chariots, and horsemen, four and thirty days, so that all their vessels of water failed all the inhabitants of Bethulia. 7:21 And the cisterns were emptied, and they had not water to drink their fill for one day; for they gave them drink by measure. 7:22 Therefore their young children were out of heart, and their women and young men fainted for thirst, and fell down in the streets of the city, and by the passages of the gates, and there was no longer any strength in them. 7:23 Then all the people assembled to Ozias, and to the chief of the city, both young men, and women, and children, and cried with a loud voice, and said before all the elders, 7:24 God be judge between us and you: for ye have done us great injury, in that ye have not required peace of the children of Assur. 7:25 For now we have no helper: but God hath sold us into their hands, that we should be thrown down before them with thirst and great destruction. 7:26 Now therefore call them unto you, and deliver the whole city for a spoil to the people of Holofernes, and to all his army. 7:27 For it is better for us to be made a spoil unto them, than to die for thirst: for we will be his servants, that our souls may live, and not see the death of our infants before our eyes, nor our wives nor our children to die.

Ambrose 397 AD Duty of the Clergy 3, 13, 82-85; 88: [teaching of Sacred writings, per 1, 1, 3] Judith then followed the call of virtue, and as she follows that, she wins great benefits. It was virtuous to prevent the people of the Lord ... from betraying their native rites and mysteries ... It was virtuous for her to be willing to encounter danger on behalf of all, so as to deliver all from danger... www.newadvent.org/fathers/34013 .htm

7:28 We take to witness against you the heaven and the earth, and our God and Lord of our fathers, which punisheth us according to our sins and the sins of our fathers, that he do not according as we have said this day. 7:29 Then there was great weeping with one consent in the midst of the assembly; and they cried unto the Lord God with a loud voice. 7:30 Then said Ozias to them, Brethren, be of good courage, let us yet endure five days, in the which space the Lord our God may turn his mercy toward us; for he will not forsake us utterly. 7:31 And if these days pass, and there come no help unto us, I will do according to your word. 7:32 And he dispersed the people, every one to their own charge; and they went unto the walls and towers of their city, and sent the women and children into their houses: and they were very low brought in the city.

8:1 Now at that time Judith heard thereof, which was the daughter of Merari, the son of Ox, the son of Joseph, the son of Ozel, the son of Elcia, the son of Ananias, the son of Gedeon, the son of Raphaim, the son of Acitho, the son of Eliu, the son of Eliab, the son of Nathanael, the son of Samael, the son of Salasadal, the son of Israel.

Tertullian 240 AD On Monogamy 17: cited without qualification: ... or a John, a noted voluntary celibate of Christ's; or a Judith, daughter of Merari; or so many other examples of saints. www.newadvent.org/fathers/0406.htm.

8:2 And Manasses was her husband, of her tribe and kindred, who died in the barley harvest. 8:3 For as he stood overseeing them that bound sheaves in the field, the heat came upon his head, and he fell on his bed, and died in the city of Bethulia: and they buried him with his fathers in the field between Dothaim and Balamo.

Ambrose 397 AD Concerning Widows 7, 37-42: ... such as was in her who was named Judith, ... But in order to learn the

dispositions of ripe widowhood, run through the course of the Scriptures. From the time when her husband died she... www.newadvent.org/fathers/3408.htm.

8:4 So Judith was a widow in her house three years and four months. 8:5 And she made her a tent upon the top of her house, and put on sackcloth upon her loins and ware her widow's apparel.

Ignatius 117 AD Letter to the Philadelphians (Long Version) IV Cited along with Luke, etc. without qualification: Let not the widows be wanderers about, nor fond of dainties, nor gadders from house to house; but let them be like Judith, noted for her seriousness; and like Anna ... www.earlychristianwritings.com/ text/ignatius-philadelphians-longer.html

8:6 And she fasted all the days of her widowhood, save the eves of the Sabbaths, and the Sabbaths, and the eves of the new moons, and the new moons and the feasts and solemn days of the house of Israel.

Ambrose 397 AD Concerning Widows 7, 38: ... run through the course of the Scriptures. From the time when her husband died she laid aside the garments of mirth, and took those of mourning. Every day she was intent on fasting .... So then, holy Judith, strengthened by lengthened mourning and by daily fasting... www.newadvent.org/fathers/3408.htm

The Apostolic Constitutions 400 AD Book V, 3, XX [Defined as Scripture in Book VIII, 5, XLVII 85]: Him therefore do we [the "Apostles"] also preach to you, ... Therefore, after you have kept the festival of Pentecost, keep one week more festival, and after that fast; for it is reasonable ... And Esther, and Mordecai, and Judith, by fasting, escaped the insurrection of the ungodly Holofernes and Haman. ... www.newadvent.org/fathers/07155.htm

Ambrose 397 AD Letter 58, 29 [Citing Scriptural proof for the practice of fasting]: And why should I speak of men? Judith, in no way moved by the luxurious banquet of

Holophernes... A clear proof both that his luxury had enervated that warrior, terrible to the nations, and that temperance made this woman stronger than men. In this case it was not in her sex that nature was surpassed, but she overcame by her diet. ... Not available online

8:7 She was also of a goodly countenance, and very beautiful to behold: and her husband Manasses had left her gold, and silver, and menservants and maidservants, and cattle, and lands; and she remained upon them. 8:8 And there was none that gave her an ill word; as she feared God greatly.

Didymus the Blind 386 AD Commentary on Zechariah 8:4-5: points to Judith as an "Old Testament" example of chaste widowhood per Gary G. Michuta in The Case of the Deuterocanon. Not available online

Didymus the Blind: 398 AD Commentary on Zechariah 12:1-3: [referred to as "Old Testament" in 8:4-5] uses Judith as an example in demonstrating a triecomus anthropology [I have absolutely no idea what that means, but include it in case you do] per Gary G. Michuta in The Case of the Deuterocanon. Not available online

8:9 Now when she heard the evil words of the people against the governor, that they fainted for lack of water; for Judith had heard all the words that Ozias had spoken unto them, and that he had sworn to deliver the city unto the Assyrians after five days; 8:10 Then she sent her waitingwoman, that had the government of all things that she had, to call Ozias and Chabris and Charmis, the ancients of the city. 8:11 And they came unto her, and she said unto them, Hear me now, O ye governors of the inhabitants of Bethulia: for your words that ye have spoken before the people this day are not right, touching this oath which ye made and pronounced between God and you, and have promised to deliver the city to our enemies, unless within these days the Lord turn to help you.

Ambrose 397 AD Duty of the Clergy 3, 13, 82-85; 88: [teaching of Sacred writings, per 1, 1, 3] How great must have been the power of her virtue, that she, a woman, should claim to give counsel on the chiefest matters and not leave it in the hands of the leaders of the people! How great, again, the power of her virtue to reckon for certain upon God to help her! How great her grace to find His help!... www.newadvent.org/fathers/34013.htm

8:12 And now who are ye that have tempted God this day, and stand instead of God among the children of men? 8:13 And now try the Lord Almighty, but ye shall never know any thing. 8:14 <u>For ye cannot find the depth of the heart of man, neither can ye perceive the things that he thinketh: then how can ye search out God, that hath made all these things, and know his mind, or comprehend his purpose?</u> Nay, my brethren, provoke not the Lord our God to anger.

1 Corinthians 2:10-11 (But God hath revealed them unto us by his Spirit: for the Spirit searcheth all things, yea, the deep things of God. For what man knoweth the things of a man, save the spirit of man which is in him? even so the things of God knoweth no man, but the Spirit of God.)

8:15 For if he will not help us within these five days, he hath power to defend us when he will, even every day, or to destroy us before our enemies. 8:16 Do not bind the counsels of the Lord our God: <u>for God is not as man</u>, that he may be threatened; neither is he as the son of man, that he should be wavering.

Athanasius 335 AD Four Discourses against the Arians 2, 35: But God is not as man, as Scripture has said;... www.newadvent.org/fathers/28162.htm

8:17 Therefore let us wait for salvation of him, and call upon him to help us, and he will hear our voice, if it please him. 8:18 For there arose none in our age, neither is there any now in these days neither tribe, nor family, nor people, nor city among us, which worship gods made with hands, as hath been aforetime.

8:19 For the which cause our fathers were given to the sword, and for a spoil, and had a great fall before our enemies. 8:20 But we know none other god, therefore we trust that he will not despise us, nor any of our nation. 8:21 For if we be taken so, all Judea shall lie waste, and our sanctuary shall be spoiled; and he will require the profanation thereof at our mouth. 8:22 And the slaughter of our brethren, and the captivity of the country, and the desolation of our inheritance, will he turn upon our heads among the Gentiles, wheresoever we shall be in bondage; and we shall be an offence and a reproach to all them that possess us. 8:23 For our servitude shall not be directed to favour: but the Lord our God shall turn it to dishonour. 8:24 Now therefore, O brethren, let us shew an example to our brethren, because their hearts depend upon us, and the sanctuary, and the house, and the altar, rest upon us. 8:25 Moreover let us give thanks to the Lord our God, which trieth us, even as he did our fathers. 8:26 Remember what things he did to Abraham, and how he tried Isaac, and what happened to Jacob in Mesopotamia of Syria, when he kept the sheep of Laban his mother's brother. 8:27 For he hath not tried us in the fire, as he did them, for the examination of their hearts, neither hath he taken vengeance on us: but <u>the Lord doth scourge them that come near unto him, to admonish them.</u>

Clement of Alexandria 198 AD The Stromata, Bk II, Ch 7: Referred to as having heard from God in Bk IV, Ch 19: Now the commandment works repentance; inasmuch as it deters from what ought not to be done, and enjoins good deeds. ... And he that is near the Lord is full of stripes. www.newadvent.org/fathers/02102.htm

8:28 Then said Ozias to her, All that thou hast spoken hast thou spoken <u>with a good heart</u>, and there is none that may gainsay thy words.

Origen 230 AD On First Principles 1.2.13: ...And if there be any other things which in Scripture are called good, whether ... a good heart, ... all these are so termed catachrestically, having in them an

accidental, not an essential goodness. ... [possible reference, as Origen considered Judith to be Scripture in other works. Other references to a person having a good heart (Wisdom 1:1, Sirach 26:4, Luke 8:15) are generic and not to a specific person.] www.newadvent.org/fathers/04121.htm.
Used to confirm the doctrine that God alone is truly good
8:29 For this is not the first day wherein thy wisdom is manifested; but from the beginning of thy days all the people have known thy understanding, because the disposition of thine heart is good. 8:30 But the people were very thirsty, and compelled us to do unto them as we have spoken, and to bring an oath upon ourselves, which we will not break. 8:31 Therefore now pray thou for us, because thou art a godly woman, and the Lord will send us rain to fill our cisterns, and we shall faint no more. 8:32 Then said Judith unto them, Hear me, and **I will do a thing, which shall go throughout all generations to the children of our nation**.
Luke 1:48: (For he hath regarded the low estate of his handmaiden: for, behold, from henceforth all generations shall call me blessed).
8:33 Ye shall stand this night in the gate, and I will go forth with my waitingwoman: and within the days that ye have promised to deliver the city to our enemies the Lord will visit Israel by mine hand. 8:34 But enquire not ye of mine act: for I will not declare it unto you, till the things be finished that I do.
Clement of Rome 96 AD, 1 Clement 55:2-6: Cited along with Esther, etc. without qualification: The blessed Judith, when her city was besieged, asked of the elders permission to go forth into the camp of the strangers; and, exposing herself to danger, she went out for the love which she bare to her country and people then besieged; and the Lord delivered Holofernes into the hands of a woman. www.newadvent.org/fathers/1010.htm.

The Apostolic Constitutions 400 AD Book VIII, 2, III [Defined as Scripture in Book VIII, 5, XLVII 85]: ... women prophesied also. Of old, ... Judith... www.newadvent.org/fathers/07158.htm.
8:35 Then said Ozias and the princes unto her, Go in peace, and the Lord God be before thee, to take vengeance on our enemies. 8:36 So they returned from the tent, and went to their wards.
9:1 Judith fell upon her face, and put ashes upon her head, and uncovered the sackcloth wherewith she was clothed; and about the time that the incense of that evening was offered in Jerusalem in the house of the Lord Judith cried with a loud voice, and said, 9:2 O Lord God of my father Simeon, to whom thou gavest a sword to take vengeance of the strangers, who loosened the girdle of a maid to defile her, and discovered the thigh to her shame, and polluted her virginity to her reproach; for thou saidst, It shall not be so; and yet they did so:
Origen 253 AD Commentary on John 2, 16: ... He is also the God of Elijah, 2 Kings 2:14 and, as Judith says, of her father Simeon, and the God of the Hebrews. By analogy of reasoning, then, if nothing prevents Him from being the God of others, nothing prevents the light of men from being the light of others besides men. www.newadvent.org/fathers/101502.htm.
9:3 Wherefore thou gavest their rulers to be slain, so that they dyed their bed in blood, being deceived, and smotest the servants with their lords, and the lords upon their thrones; 9:4 And hast given their wives for a prey, and their daughters to be captives, and all their spoils to be divided among thy dear children; which were moved with thy zeal, and abhorred the pollution of their blood, and called upon thee for aid: O God, O my God, hear me also a widow. 9:5 For thou hast wrought not only those things, but also the things which fell out before, and which ensued after; thou hast thought upon the things which are now, and which are to come.

Basil the Great 379 AD On the Holy Spirit, 18: Cited along with Hebrews and John without qualification: So as Judith says, "You have thought, and what things you determined were ready at hand." www.newadvent.org/fathers/3203.htm.
9:6 Yea, what things thou didst determine were ready at hand, and said, Lo, we are here: for all thy ways are prepared, and thy judgments are in thy foreknowledge. 9:7 For, behold, the Assyrians are multiplied in their power; they are exalted with horse and man; they glory in the strength of their footmen; they trust in shield, and spear, and bow, and sling; and know not that thou art the Lord that breakest the battles: the Lord is thy name. 9:8 Throw down their strength in thy power, and bring down their force in thy wrath: for they have purposed to defile thy sanctuary, and to pollute the tabernacle where thy glorious name resteth and to cast down with sword the horn of thy altar. 9:9 Behold their pride, and send thy wrath upon their heads: give into mine hand, which am a widow, the power that I have conceived. 9:10 Smite by the deceit of my lips the servant with the prince, and the prince with the servant: break down their stateliness by the hand of a woman. 9:11 For thy power standeth not in multitude nor thy might in strong men: for thou art a God of the afflicted, an helper of the oppressed, an upholder of the weak, a protector of the forlorn, a saviour of them that are without hope.

Clement of Rome 96 AD, 1 Clement, 59: Cited along with Genesis, Deuteronomy, etc. without qualification: ...You ... who layest low the insolence of the haughty, Isaiah 13:11 ... who settest the low on high and bringest low the exalted; who makest rich and makest poor, 1 Samuel 2:7 who killest and makest to live, Deuteronomy 32:39 ... who beholdest the depths, the eye-witness of human works, the help of those in danger, the Saviour of those in despair... www.newadvent.org/fathers/1010.htm.

Origen 253 AD Commentary on the Gospel of John 13.167-68: Cited along with Genesis, Psalms, etc. without qualification: We forget that the words "Let us make man according to our image and according to our likeness" apply to each person. ... God is a helper of those who are lowly and inferior, a protector of the weak, a provider of shelter of those who have been given up in despair and Savior of those who have been given up as hopeless. [Per Ancient Christian Commentary on Scripture]. Not available online.
9:12 I pray thee, I pray thee, O God of my father, and God of the inheritance of Israel, Lord of the heavens and earth, Creator of the waters, king of every creature, hear thou my prayer: 9:13 And make my speech and deceit to be their wound and stripe, who have purposed cruel things against thy covenant, and thy hallowed house, and against the top of Sion, and against the house of the possession of thy children. 9:14 And make every nation and tribe to acknowledge that thou art the God of all power and might, and that there is none other that protecteth the people of Israel but thou.

Origen 253 AD Commentary on John 2, 16: ...He, then, who infers from the saying, The life was the light of men, that the light is for no other than for men, ought also to conclude that the God of Abraham and the God of Isaac and the God of Jacob is the God of no one else but these three patriarchs. But He is also the God of Elijah, 2 Kings 2:14 and, as Judith says, of her father Simeon, and the God of the Hebrews. By analogy of reasoning, then, if nothing prevents Him from being the God of others, nothing prevents the light of men from being the light of others besides men. www.newadvent.org/fathers/101502.htm
10:1 Now after that she had ceased to cry unto the God of Israel, and had made an end of all these words. 10:2 She rose where she had fallen down, and called her maid, and went down into the house in the which she abode in

the Sabbath days, and in her feast days, 10:3 And pulled off the sackcloth which she had on, and put off the garments of her widowhood, and washed her body all over with water, and anointed herself with precious ointment, and braided the hair of her head, and put on a tire upon it, and put on her garments of gladness, wherewith she was clad during the life of Manasses her husband. 10:4 And she took sandals upon her feet, and put about her bracelets, and her chains, and her rings, and her earrings, and all her ornaments, and decked herself bravely, to allure the eyes of all men that should see her.

Chromatius 407 AD Tractate on Matthew 29, II, 2: Cited along with Esther, Matthew, etc. without qualification: We read examples of this matter, even according to history, prefigured in saints of past times. For the most holy Judith, when she was afflicted with great grief on behalf of the people, after the solemnity of a three-day fast, so covered up the sadness of her internal affliction by anointing her head and washing her face, that she seemed to delight her enemies by her feigned joy. And what is more, when she covered up her fasting by her glad countenance, she brought back a triumph of victory over the enemy. [Per Chromatius of Aquileia, Sermons and Tractates on Matthew]. Not available online

Ambrose 397 AD Concerning Widows 7, 37 [Referred to as Scripture in 7, 38]: But bravery ... such as was in her who was named Judith... For she, as we read, when Holofernes, dreaded after his success in so many battles, had driven countless thousands of men within the walls; when the armed men were afraid, and were already treating about the final surrender, went forth outside the wall, both excelling that army which she delivered, and braver than that which she put to flight. www.newadvent.org/fathers/3408.htm

10:5 Then she gave her maid a bottle of wine, and a cruse of oil, and filled a bag with parched corn, and lumps of figs, and with fine bread; so she folded all these things together, and laid them upon her. 10:6 Thus they went forth to the gate of the city of Bethulia, and found standing there Ozias and the ancients of the city, Chabris and Charmis. 10:7 And when they saw her, that her countenance was altered, and her apparel was changed, they wondered at her beauty very greatly, and said unto her. 10:8 The God, the God of our fathers give thee favour, and accomplish thine enterprizes to the glory of the children of Israel, and to the exaltation of Jerusalem. Then they worshipped God. 10:9 And she said unto them, Command the gates of the city to be opened unto me, that I may go forth to accomplish the things whereof ye have spoken with me. So they commanded the young men to open unto her, as she had spoken. 10:10 And when they had done so, Judith went out, she, and her maid with her; and the men of the city looked after her, until she was gone down the mountain, and till she had passed the valley, and could see her no more. 10:11 Thus they went straight forth in the valley: and the first watch of the Assyrians met her, 10:12 And took her, and asked her, Of what people art thou? and whence comest thou? and whither goest thou? And she said, I am a woman of the Hebrews, and am fled from them: for they shall be given you to be consumed:

Ambrose 397 AD Duty of the Clergy 3, 13, 82-85; 88: [teaching of Sacred writings, per 1, 1, 3] See! Judith presents herself to you as worthy of admiration. ... The Persians were terrified at her daring. And so what is admired in the case of those two Pythagoreans deserves also in her case our admiration, for she trembled not at the danger of death, nor even at the danger her modesty was in, which is a matter of greater concern to good women. She feared not the blow of one scoundrel, nor even the weapons of a whole army. She, a woman, stood between the lines of the combatants — right amidst victorious arms — heedless of death. As one looks at her overwhelming

danger, one would say she went out to die; as one looks at her faith, one says she went but out to fight.... www.newadvent.org/ fathers/34013.htm

10:13 And I am coming before Holofernes the chief captain of your army, to declare words of truth; and I will shew him a way, whereby he shall go, and win all the hill country, without losing the body or life of any one of his men. 10:14 Now when the men heard her words, and beheld her countenance, they wondered greatly at her beauty, and said unto her, 10:15 Thou hast saved thy life, in that thou hast hasted to come down to the presence of our lord: now therefore come to his tent, and some of us shall conduct thee, until they have delivered thee to his hands. 10:16 And when thou standest before him, be not afraid in thine heart, but shew unto him according to thy word; and he will entreat thee well. 10:17 Then they chose out of them an hundred men to accompany her and her maid; and they brought her to the tent of Holofernes.

Sulpitius Severus 420 AD Sacred History 2, 16: [Referred to as "recorded in the sacred writings. The spirit of God thus took care that the histories…" in 2, 14]: She was immediately conducted to Holofernes, and tells him that the affairs of her countrymen were desperate, so that she had taken precautions for her life by flight. www.newadvent.org/fathers/35052.htm

10:18 Then was there a concourse throughout all the camp: for her coming was noised among the tents, and they came about her, as she stood without the tent of Holofernes, till they told him of her. 10:19 And they wondered at her beauty, and admired the children of Israel because of her, and every one said to his neighbour, Who would despise this people, that have among them such women? surely it is not good that one man of them be left who being let go might deceive the whole earth. 10:20 And they that lay near Holofernes went out, and all his servants and they brought her into the tent. 10:21 Now Holofernes rested upon his bed under a canopy, which was woven with purple, and gold, and emeralds, and precious stones. 10:22 So they shewed him of her; and he came out before his tent with silver lamps going before him. 10:23 And when Judith was come before him and his servants they all marvelled at the beauty of her countenance; and she fell down upon her face, and did reverence unto him: and his servants took her up.

11:1 Then said Holofernes unto her, Woman, be of good comfort, fear not in thine heart: for I never hurt any that was willing to serve Nabuchodonosor, the king of all the earth. 11:2 Now therefore, if thy people that dwelleth in the mountains had not set light by me, I would not have lifted up my spear against them: but they have done these things to themselves. 11:3 But now tell me wherefore thou art fled from them, and art come unto us: for thou art come for safeguard; be of good comfort, thou shalt live this night, and hereafter: 11:4 For none shall hurt thee, but entreat thee well, as they do the servants of king Nabuchodonosor my lord. 11:5 Then Judith said unto him, Receive the words of thy servant, and suffer thine handmaid to speak in thy presence, and I will declare no lie to my lord this night. 11:6 And if thou wilt follow the words of thine handmaid, God will bring the thing perfectly to pass by thee; and my lord shall not fail of his purposes. 11:7 As Nabuchodonosor king of all the earth liveth, and as his power liveth, who hath sent thee for the upholding of every living thing: for not only men shall serve him by thee, but also the beasts of the field, and the cattle, and the fowls of the air, shall live by thy power under Nabuchodonosor and all his house. 11:8 For we have heard of thy wisdom and thy policies, and it is reported in all the earth, that thou only art excellent in all the kingdom, and mighty in knowledge, and wonderful in feats of war. 11:9 Now as concerning the matter, which Achior did speak in thy council, we have heard his words; for the men of Bethulia saved him, and he declared unto them all that he had spoken unto thee. 11:10 Therefore, O lord and governor, respect not his word; but lay it up in thine heart, for it is true: for our nation shall not be punished, neither can sword prevail against them, except they sin against their God. 11:11 And now, that my lord be not defeated and frustrate of his purpose, even death is now fallen upon them, and their sin hath overtaken them, wherewith they will provoke their God to anger whensoever they shall do that which is not fit to be done: 11:12 For their victuals fail them, and all their water is scant, and they have determined to lay hands upon their cattle, and purposed to consume all those things, that God hath forbidden them to eat by his laws: 11:13 And are resolved to spend the firstfruits of the tenths of wine and oil, which they had sanctified, and reserved for the priests that serve in Jerusalem before the face of our God; the which things it is not lawful for any of the people so much as to touch with their hands. 11:14 For they have sent some to Jerusalem, because they also that dwell there have done the like, to bring them a licence from the senate. 11:15 Now when they shall bring them word, they will forthwith do it, and they shall be given to thee to be destroyed the same day. 11:16 Wherefore I thine handmaid, knowing all this, am fled from their presence; and God hath sent me to work things with thee, whereat all the earth shall be astonished, and whosoever shall hear it. 11:17 For thy servant is religious, and serveth the God of heaven day and night: now therefore, my lord, I will remain with thee, and thy servant will go out by night into the valley, and I will pray unto God, and he will tell me when they have committed their sins:

Origen 253 AD Homily 20 on Jeremiah, 7.3: I want to give an example from Scripture of righteous lack of faith in an agreement in order to demonstrate that man can call upon faithlessness in act. Judith made an agreement with Holophernes that though she would leave for certain number of days to pray to God, she also would present herself after these days at the marriage bed of Holophernes.

vivacatholic.wordpress.com/2007/08/14/origen-and-canon-of-old-testament/

**The Apostolic Constitutions 400 AD Book III, Ch VII [Defined as Scripture in Book VIII, 5, XLVII 85]: As therefore Judith, most famous for her wisdom, and of a good report for her modesty, "prayed to God night and day for Israel;" so also the widow who is like to her ....
www.newadvent.org/fathers/07153.htm**

11:18 And I will come and shew it unto thee: then thou shalt go forth with all thine army, and there shall be none of them that shall resist thee. 11:19 And I will lead thee through the midst of Judea, until thou come before Jerusalem; and I will set thy throne in the midst thereof; and thou shalt drive them as sheep that have no shepherd, and a dog shall not so much as open his mouth at thee: for these things were told me according to my foreknowledge, and they were declared unto me, and I am sent to tell thee. 11:20 Then her words pleased Holofernes and all his servants; and they marvelled at her wisdom, and said, 11:21 There is not such a woman from one end of the earth to the other, both for beauty of face, and wisdom of words.

Ambrose 397 AD Duty of the Clergy 3, 13, 82-85; 88: [teaching of Sacred writings, per 1, 1, 3] ...She approaches Holophernes, a man feared by the people, and surrounded by the victorious troops of the Assyrians. At first she makes an impression on him by the grace of her form and the beauty of her countenance. Then she entraps him by the refinement of her speech. ... www.newadvent.org/fathers/34013.htm

11:22 Likewise Holofernes said unto her. God hath done well to send thee before the people, that strength might be in our hands and destruction upon them that lightly regard my lord. 11:23 And now thou art both beautiful in thy countenance, and witty in thy words: surely if thou do as thou hast spoken thy God shall be my God, and thou shalt dwell in the house of king Nabuchodonosor, and shalt be renowned through the whole earth.

12:1 Then he commanded to bring her in where his plate was set; and bade that they should prepare for her of his own meats, and that she should drink of his own wine. 12:2 And Judith said, I will not eat thereof, lest there be an offence: but provision shall be made for me of the things that I have brought.

Ambrose 397 AD Concerning Widows 7, 39 [Referred to as Scripture in 7, 38]: ... How she among thousands of enemies, remained chaste. Why speak of her wisdom... unpolluted, as we read, either by food or by adultery, she gained no less a triumph over the enemy by preserving her chastity than by delivering her country. www.newadvent.org/fathers/3408.htm

12:3 Then Holofernes said unto her, If thy provision should fail, how should we give thee the like? for there be none with us of thy nation. 12:4 Then said Judith unto him As thy soul liveth, my lord, thine handmaid shall not spend those things that I have, before the Lord work by mine hand the things that he hath determined. 12:5 Then the servants of Holofernes brought her into the tent, and she slept till midnight, and she arose when it was toward the morning watch, 12:6 And sent to Holofernes, saying, Let my lord now command that thine handmaid may go forth unto prayer. 12:7 Then Holofernes commanded his guard that they should not stay her: thus she abode in the camp three days, and went out in the night into the valley of Bethulia, and washed herself in a fountain of water by the camp. 12:8 And when she came out, she besought the Lord God of Israel to direct her way to the raising up of the children of her people.

Origen 231 AD On Prayer 8: ... from the Scriptures... after offering holy prayer that Judith with God's help overcame Holophernes....many a time indeed does he whose trust is in praise to God—for Judith means praise... www.tertullian.org/fathers/origen_on_prayer_02_text.htm

12:9 So she came in clean, and remained in the tent, until she did eat her meat at evening.

12:10 And in the fourth day Holofernes made a feast to his own servants only, and called none of the officers to the banquet. 12:11 Then said he to Bagoas the eunuch, who had charge over all that he had, Go now, and persuade this Hebrew woman which is with thee, that she come unto us, and eat and drink with us.

Sulpitius Severus 420 AD Sacred History 2, 14: ...Now, the inspired history makes mention of this Baguas; for, when Holofernes by the order of the king led an army against the Jews, it has related that Baguas was among the host. www.newadvent.org/fathers/35052.htm.

12:12 For, lo, it will be a shame for our person, if we shall let such a woman go, not having had her company; for if we draw her not unto us, she will laugh us to scorn. 12:13 Then went Bagoas from the presence of Holofernes, and came to her, and he said, Let not this fair damsel fear to come to my lord, and to be honoured in his presence, and drink wine, and be merry with us and be made this day as one of the daughters of the Assyrians, which serve in the house of Nabuchodonosor. 12:14 Then said Judith unto him, Who am I now, that I should gainsay my lord? surely whatsoever pleaseth him I will do speedily, and it shall be my joy unto the day of my death. 12:15 So she arose, and decked herself with her apparel and all her woman's attire, and her maid went and laid soft skins on the ground for her over against Holofernes, which she had received of Bagoas for her daily use, that she might sit and eat upon them. 12:16 Now when Judith came in and sat down, Holofernes his heart was ravished with her, and his mind was moved, and he desired greatly her company; for he waited a time to deceive her, from the day that he had seen her. 12:17 Then said Holofernes unto her, Drink now, and be merry with us. 12:18 So Judith said, I will drink now, my lord, because my life is magnified in me this day more than all the days since I was born. 12:19 Then she took and ate and drank before him what her maid had prepared.

Ambrose 397 AD Concerning Widows 7, 40 [Referred to as Scripture in 7, 38]: Temperance, indeed, is the virtue of women. When the men were intoxicated with wine and buried in sleep, the widow took the sword, put forth her hand, cut off the warrior's head, and passed unharmed through the midst of the ranks of the enemy. ... if Judith had drunk she would have slept with the adulterer. But because she drank not, the sobriety of one without difficulty was able both to overcome and to escape from a drunken army. www. newadvent.org/fathers/3408.htm

12:20 And Holofernes took great delight in her, and drank more wine than he had drunk at any time in one day since he was born.

13:1 Now when the evening was come, his servants made haste to depart, and Bagoas shut his tent without, and dismissed the waiters from the presence of his lord; and they went to their beds: for they were all weary, because the feast had been long.

Sulpitius Severus 420 AD Sacred History 2, 14: ... Wherefore, not without reason may I bring it forward in proof of the opinion I have expressed that that king who was named Nebuchadnezzar was really Ochus, since profane historians have related that Baguas lived in his reign. But this ought not to be felt at all remarkable by any one, that mere worldly writers have not touched on any of those points which are recorded in the sacred writings. ... www.newadvent.org/fathers/35052.htm

13:2 And Judith was left alone in the tent, and Holofernes lying alone upon his bed: for he was filled with wine. 13:3 Now Judith had commanded her maid to stand without her bedchamber, and to wait for her. coming forth, as she did daily: for she said she would go forth to her prayers, and she spake to Bagoas according to the same purpose. 13:4 So all went forth and none was left in the bedchamber, neither little nor great. Then Judith, standing by his bed, said in her heart, O Lord God of all power, look at this present

upon the works of mine hands for the exaltation of Jerusalem. 13:5 For now is the time to help thine inheritance, and to execute thine enterprizes to the destruction of the enemies which are risen against us. 13:6 Then she came to the pillar of the bed, which was at Holofernes' head, and took down his fauchion from thence, 13:7 And approached to his bed, and took hold of the hair of his head, and said, Strengthen me, O Lord God of Israel, this day. 13:8 **And she smote twice upon his neck with all her might, and she took away his head from him**.

Jerome 400 AD Letter 72, 10: Judith renowned in Hebrew story ... was a type of the Church which cuts off the head of the devil (Genesis 3:15, the proto-evangelium). www.newadvent.org/fathers/3001079.htm

Athanasius 373 AD Festal Letter 4, 2: For by these means we shall have strength to overcome our adversaries, like blessed Judith, when having first exercised herself in fastings and prayers, she overcame the enemies, and killed Olophernes. And blessed Esther... www.newadvent.org/ fathers/2806004.htm

13:9 And tumbled his body down from the bed, and pulled down the canopy from the pillars; and anon after she went forth, and gave Holofernes his head to her maid; 13:10 And she put it in her bag of meat: so they twain went together according to their custom unto prayer: and when they passed the camp, they compassed the valley, and went up the mountain of Bethulia, and came to the gates thereof. 13:11 Then said Judith afar off, to the watchmen at the gate, Open, open now the gate: God, even our God, is with us, to shew his power yet in Jerusalem, and his forces against the enemy, as he hath even done this day.

Methodius 311 AD Banquet of the Ten Virgins, 11, 2: Cited along with Genesis (Japheth) without qualification: Daring Judith, by clever wiles having cut off the head of the leader of the foreign hosts, whom previously she had allured by her

beautiful form, without polluting the limbs of her body, with a victor's shout said:—
www.newadvent.org/fathers/062311.htm
13:12 Now when the men of her city heard her voice, they made haste to go down to the gate of their city, and they called the elders of the city. 13:13 And then they ran all together, both small and great, for it was strange unto them that she was come: so they opened the gate, and received them, and made a fire for a light, and stood round about them. 13:14 Then she said to them with a loud voice, Praise, praise God, praise God, I say, for he hath not taken away his mercy from the house of Israel, but hath destroyed our enemies by mine hands this night. 13:15 So she took the head out of the bag, and shewed it, and said unto them, behold the head of Holofernes, the chief captain of the army of Assur, and behold the canopy, wherein he did lie in his drunkenness; and the Lord hath smitten him by the hand of a woman.

Clement of Alexandria 198 AD The Stromata, Bk IV, Ch 19 It is not only Moses, then, that heard from God,... But Judith too, who became perfect among women, ... and straightway she obtained the reward of her faith — though a woman, prevailing over the enemy of her faith, and gaining possession of the head of Holofernes.
www.newadvent.org/fathers/02104.htm
13:16 As the Lord liveth, who hath kept me in my way that I went, my countenance hath deceived him to his destruction, and yet hath he not committed sin with me, to defile and shame me.

Ambrose 397 AD Duty of the Clergy 3, 13, 82-85; 88: [teaching of Sacred writings, per 1, 1, 3] Judith['s] ... first triumph was that she returned from the tent of the enemy with her purity unspotted.
www.newadvent.org/fathers/34013.htm
13:17 Then all the people were wonderfully astonished, and bowed themselves and worshipped God, and said with one accord, Blessed be thou, O our God, which hast this day brought to nought the enemies of thy people. 13:18 Then said Ozias unto her, **O daughter, blessed art thou of the most high God above all the women upon the earth**; and blessed be the Lord God, which hath created the heavens and the earth, which hath directed thee to the cutting off of the head of the chief of our enemies.

Luke 1:42 (And she spake out with a loud voice, and said, Blessed art thou among women, and blessed is the fruit of thy womb).
13:19 For this thy confidence shall not depart from the heart of men, which remember the power of God for ever. 13:20 And God turn these things to thee for a perpetual praise, to visit thee in good things because thou hast not spared thy life for the affliction of our nation, but hast revenged our ruin, walking a straight way before our God. And all the people said; So be it, so be it.

Jerome 420 AD Letter 54, 16: In the book of Judith — if any one is of opinion that it should be received as canonical — we read of a widow wasted with fasting and wearing the sombre garb of a mourner, whose outward squalor indicated not so much the regret which she felt for her dead husband as the temper in which she looked forward to the coming of the Bridegroom. I see her hand armed with the sword and stained with blood. I recognize the head of Holofernes which she has carried away from the camp of the enemy. Here a woman vanquishes men, and chastity beheads lust. Quickly changing her garb, she puts on once more in the hour of victory her own mean dress finer than all the splendours of the world. www.newadvent.org/fathers/3001054.htm

14:1 Then said Judith unto them, Hear me now, my brethren, and take this head, and hang it upon the highest place of your walls. 14:2 And so soon as the morning shall appear, and the sun shall come forth upon the earth, take ye every one his weapons, and go forth every valiant man out of the city, and set ye a captain over them, as though ye would go down into the field toward the watch of the

Assyrians; but go not down. 14:3 Then they shall take their armour, and shall go into their camp, and raise up the captains of the army of Assur, and shall run to the tent of Holofernes, but shall not find him: then fear shall fall upon them, and they shall flee before your face. 14:4 So ye, and all that inhabit the coast of Israel, shall pursue them, and overthrow them as they go. 14:5 But before ye do these things, call me Achior the Ammonite, that he may see and know him that despised the house of Israel, and that sent him to us as it were to his death. 14:6 Then they called Achior out of the house of Ozias; and when he was come, and saw the head of Holofernes in a man's hand in the assembly of the people, he fell down on his face, and his spirit failed. 14:7 But when they had recovered him, he fell at Judith's feet, and reverenced her, and said, Blessed art thou in all the tabernacles of Juda, and in all nations, which hearing thy name shall be astonished. 14:8 Now therefore tell me all the things that thou hast done in these days. Then Judith declared unto him in the midst of the people all that she had done, from the day that she went forth until that hour she spake unto them. 14:9 And when she had left off speaking, the people shouted with a loud voice, and made a joyful noise in their city. 14:10 <u>And when Achior had seen all that the God of Israel had done, he believed in God greatly, and circumcised the flesh of his foreskin, and was joined unto the house of Israel unto this day</u>.

Africanus 240 AD The Epistle to Aristides, V Cited along with Ruth, etc. without qualification: ... those, too, which were traced back to the proselytes --as, for example, to Achior the Ammanite, and Ruth the Moabitess, ... bkv.unifr.ch/en/ works/cpg-1693/versions/the-epistle-to-aristides/divisions/6

Sulpitius Severus 420 AD Sacred History 2, 15: [Referred to as "recorded in the sacred writings. The spirit of God thus took care that the histories..." in 2, 14]: ...those to whom the business had been assigned, proceeded to the foot of the

mountains, and there left Achior in chains. ... I may add that, after the victory, he was circumcised and became a Jew. www.newadvent.org/fathers/35052.htm

14:11 And as soon as the morning arose, they hanged the head of Holofernes upon the wall, and every man took his weapons, and they went forth by bands unto the straits of the mountain. 14:12 But when the Assyrians saw them, they sent to their leaders, which came to their captains and tribunes, and to every one of their rulers. 14:13 So they came to Holofernes' tent, and said to him that had the charge of all his things, Waken now our lord: for the slaves have been bold to come down against us to battle, that they may be utterly destroyed. 14:14 Then went in Bagoas, and knocked at the door of the tent; for he thought that he had slept with Judith. 14:15 But because none answered, he opened it, and went into the bedchamber, and found him cast upon the floor dead, and his head was taken from him. 14:16 Therefore he cried with a loud voice, with weeping, and sighing, and a mighty cry, and rent his garments. 14:17 After he went into the tent where Judith lodged: and when he found her not, he leaped out to the people, and cried, 14:18 These slaves have dealt treacherously; one woman of the Hebrews hath brought shame upon the house of king Nabuchodonosor: for, behold, Holofernes lieth upon the ground without a head. 14:19 When the captains of the Assyrians' army heard these words, they rent their coats and their minds were wonderfully troubled, and there was a cry and a very great noise throughout the camp.

15:1 And when they that were in the tents heard, they were astonished at the thing that was done. 15:2 <u>And fear and trembling fell upon them, so that there was no man that durst abide in the sight of his neighbour, but rushing out all together, they fled into every way of the plain, and of the hill country. 15:3 They also that had camped in the mountains round about Bethulia fled away.</u> Then the children of

Israel, every one that was a warrior among them, rushed out upon them.

Ambrose 397 AD Duty of the Clergy 3, 13, 82-85; 88: [teaching of Sacred writings, per 1, 1, 3] ... she gained a victory over a man, and put to flight the people by her counsel.... www.newadvent.org/fathers/34013.htm

15:4 Then sent Ozias to Betomasthem, and to Bebai, and Chobai, and Cola and to all the coasts of Israel, such as should tell the things that were done, and that all should rush forth upon their enemies to destroy them. 15:5 Now when the children of Israel heard it, they all fell upon them with one consent, and slew them unto Chobai: likewise also they that came from Jerusalem, and from all the hill country, (for men had told them what things were done in the camp of their enemies) and they that were in Galaad, and in Galilee, chased them with a great slaughter, until they were past Damascus and the borders thereof. 15:6 And the residue that dwelt at Bethulia, fell upon the camp of Assur, and spoiled them, and were greatly enriched. 15:7 And the children of Israel that returned from the slaughter had that which remained; and the villages and the cities, that were in the mountains and in the plain, gat many spoils: for the multitude was very great. 15:8 Then Joacim the high priest, and the ancients of the children of Israel that dwelt in Jerusalem, came to behold the good things that God had shewed to Israel, and to see Judith, and to salute her. 15:9 And when they came unto her, they blessed her with one accord, and said unto her, Thou art the exaltation of Jerusalem, thou art the great glory of Israel, thou art the great rejoicing of our nation:

Origen 253 AD Homilies on Judges 9, 1: After talking about Deborah (Judges 4:4) says, "should I recount about Judith, that admirable and most noble of all women?" per Gary G. Michuta in The Case of the Deuterocanon. Not available online

15:10 Thou hast done all these things by thine hand: thou hast done much good to Israel, and

God is pleased therewith: blessed be thou of the Almighty Lord for evermore. And all the people said, So be it.

Ambrose 397 AD Duty of the Clergy 3, 13, 82-85; 88: [teaching of Sacred writings, per 1, 1, 3] ... whatever is seemly is always useful. For holy Judith by seemly disregard for her own safety put an end to the dangers of the siege, and by her own virtue won what was useful to all in common. www.newadvent.org/fathers/34013.htm

15:11 And the people spoiled the camp the space of thirty days: and they gave unto Judith Holofernes his tent, and all his plate, and beds, and vessels, and all his stuff: and she took it and laid it on her mule; and made ready her carts, and laid them thereon. 15:12 Then all the women of Israel ran together to see her, and blessed her, and made a dance among them for her: and she took branches in her hand, and gave also to the women that were with her. 15:13 And they put a garland of olive upon her and her maid that was with her, and she went before all the people in the dance, leading all the women: and all the men of Israel followed in their armour with garlands, and with songs in their mouths.

16:1 Then Judith began to sing this thanksgiving in all Israel, and all the people sang after her this song of praise. 16:2 And Judith said, Begin unto my God with timbrels, sing unto my Lord with cymbals: tune unto him a new psalm: exalt him, and call upon his name. 16:3 For God breaketh the battles: for among the camps in the midst of the people he hath delivered me out of the hands of them that persecuted me.

Hilary of Poitiers 368 AD Tractate on Psalm 125, 6: quoted Judith 16:3 as being among the "Law and the prophets" per Gary G. Michuta in The Case of the Deuterocanon. Not available online

16:4 Assur came out of the mountains from the north, he came with ten thousands of his army, the multitude whereof stopped the torrents, and their horsemen have covered the hills. 16:5 He bragged that he would burn up my borders, and kill my young men with the sword, and dash the sucking children against the ground, and make mine infants as a prey, and my virgins as a spoil. 16:6 But the Almighty Lord hath disappointed them by the hand of a woman.

Origen 230 AD On Prayer 8: ... it is open to everyone to select any number of them for himself from the Scriptures... It was, moreover, after offering holy prayer that Judith with God's help overcame Holophernes, and thus a single woman of the Hebrews wrought shame upon the house of Nebuchadnezzar.... www.tertullian.org/ fathers/origen_on_prayer_02_text.htm

16:7 For the mighty one did not fall by the young men, neither did the sons of the Titans smite him, nor high giants set upon him: but Judith the daughter of Merari weakened him with the beauty of her countenance.

1 Corinthians 1:27 (But God hath chosen the foolish things of the world to confound the wise; and God hath chosen the weak things of the world to confound the things which are mighty).

16:8 For she put off the garment of her widowhood for the exaltation of those that were oppressed in Israel, and anointed her face with ointment, and bound her hair in a tire, and took a linen garment to deceive him. 16:9 Her sandals ravished his eyes, her beauty took his mind prisoner, and the fauchion passed through his neck. 16:10 The Persians quaked at her boldness, and the Medes were daunted at her hardiness. 16:11 Then my afflicted shouted for joy, and my weak ones cried aloud; but they were astonished: these lifted up their voices, but they were overthrown. 16:12 The sons of the damsels have pierced them through, and wounded them as fugitives' children: they perished by the battle of the Lord. 16:13 I will sing unto the Lord a new song: O Lord, thou art great and glorious, wonderful in strength, and invincible.

Augustine 430 AD Letter 227: What shall I say, but, Let us sing a hymn [Judith

16:13] to the Lord, and highly exalt Him for ever! Amen. www.newadvent.org/fathers/ 1102227.htm

16:14 Let all creatures serve thee: for thou spakest, and they were made, thou didst send forth thy spirit, and it created them, and there is none that can resist thy voice. 16:15 For the mountains shall be moved from their foundations with the waters, the rocks shall melt as wax at thy presence: yet thou art merciful to them that fear thee. 16:16 For all sacrifice is too little for a sweet savour unto thee, and all the fat is not sufficient for thy burnt offering: but he that feareth the Lord is great at all times. 16:17 Woe to the nations that rise up against my kindred! the Lord Almighty will take vengeance of them in the day of judgment, in putting fire and worms in their flesh; and they shall feel them, and weep for ever.

Mark 9:43-46 (And if thy hand offend thee, cut it off: it is better for thee to enter into life maimed, than having two hands to go into hell, into the fire that never shall be quenched: 44Where their worm dieth not, and the fire is not quenched. 45And if thy foot offend thee, cut it off: it is better for thee to enter halt into life, than having two feet to be cast into hell, into the fire that never shall be quenched: 46Where their worm dieth not, and the fire is not quenched). (Often cross referenced with Isaiah 66:24, however that is an earthly, temporal punishment: "And they shall go forth, and look upon the carcases of the men that have transgressed against me: for their worm shall not die, neither shall their fire be quenched; and they shall be an abhorring unto all flesh." Only Judith and Sirach 7:17 (both Apocrypha) identify this as eternal punishment).

The Apostolic Constitutions 400 AD Book VII, 2, XXXVIII [Defined as Scripture in Book VIII, 5, XLVII 85]: We give You thanks for all things, O Lord Almighty,... for You assisted in the days of Enos and

Enoch, ... in the days of Judith, ...
www.newadvent.org/fathers/07157.htm
16:18 Now as soon as they entered into Jerusalem, they worshipped the Lord; and as soon as the people were purified, they offered their burnt offerings, and their free offerings, and their gifts. 16:19 Judith also dedicated all the stuff of Holofernes, which the people had given her, and gave the canopy, which she had taken out of his bedchamber, for a gift unto the Lord. 16:20 So the people continued feasting in Jerusalem before the sanctuary for the space of three months and Judith remained with them. 16:21 After this time every one returned to his own inheritance, and Judith went to Bethulia, and remained in her own possession, and was in her time honourable in all the country. 16:22 And many desired her, but none knew her all the days of her life, after that Manasses her husband was dead, and was gathered to his people. 16:23 But she increased more and more in honour, and waxed old in her husband's house, being an hundred and five years old, and made her maid free; so she died in Bethulia: and they buried her in the cave of her husband Manasses.

The Apostolic Constitutions 400 AD Book VIII, 3, XV [Defined as Scripture in Book VIII, 5, XLVII 85]: And I Lebbæus, surnamed Thaddæus [in some manuscripts: Judas the Zealot], make this constitution in regard to widows: ... if she has lived soberly and unblameably, and has taken extraordinary care of her family, as Judith and Anna — those women of great reputation— let her be chosen into the order of widows. www.newadvent.org/ fathers/07158.htm
16:24 And the house of Israel lamented her seven days: and before she died, she did distribute her goods to all them that were nearest of kindred to Manasses her husband, and to them that were the nearest of her kindred. 16:25 And there was none that made the children of Israel any more afraid in the days of Judith, nor a long time after her death.

Origen 231 AD On Prayer 19: [Referred to as Scripture in 8] In what sense then does the Savior bid us pray not to enter into temptation, when God in some sense tempts all men? Think you, says Judith, not only to the elders of that day but also to all readers of her writing, ... www.tertullian.org/fathers/origen_on_praye r_02_text.htm

Postscript to Judith: Summarizing the Data

The following is a chronological chart of all these citations from the Fathers, plus all canon lists and Councils and codices (which are in ALL CAPS, and in **BOLD IF A COUNCIL** and in *ITALICS IF A CODEX*).

Ch	V	Father	Year?	Work
8	34	Clement of Rome	96	1 Clement 55:2-6
9	11	Clement of Rome	96	1 Clement, 59
8	5	Ignatius	117	Philadelphians (Long V.) IV
		MELITO OF SARDIS	170	NOT CANON (FOR JEWS?)
		MURATORIAN CANON NT	170	UNKNOWN
8	27	Clement of Alexandria	198	The Stromata, Bk II, Ch 7
13	15	Clement of Alexandria	198	The Stromata, Bk IV, Ch 19
		CLEMENT OF ALEX.	203	CANON
		ORIGEN (JEWISH LIST)	220	NOT CANON FOR JEWS
8	28	Origen	230	On First Principles 1.2.13
16	6	Origen	230	On Prayer 8
2	4	Origen	231	On Prayer 11
16	25	Origen	231	On Prayer 19
12	8	Origen	231	On Prayer 8
3	10	Origen	231	On Prayer 8
14	10	Africanus	240	The Epistle to Aristides, V
8	1	Tertullian	240	On Monogamy 17
		ORIGEN (TO AFRICANUS)	248	CANON
		ORIGEN (CITATIONS)	250	CANON
9	2	Origen	253	Commentary on John 2, 16
9	14	Origen	253	Commentary on John 2, 16
9	11	Origen	253	Comm. on John 13.167-68
15	9	Origen	253	Homilies on Judges 9, 1
11	17	Origen	253	Homily 20 on Jeremiah, 7.3
13	11	Methodius	311	Banquet of Ten Virgins, 11, 2
		EUSEBIUS (APPROVAL)	324	CANON
		~~THE NICENE COUNCIL~~	~~325~~	~~UNKNOWN~~
8	16	Athanasius	335	4 Discourses Arians 2, 35
		CLAROMONTANUS	349	CANON
		CODEX VATICANUS	*350*	*CANON*
		CODEX SINAITICUS	*350*	*CANON*
		CYRIL OF JERUSALEM	350	NOT CANON
		ST CATHERINE'S SYRIAC	350	CANON
		CHELTENHAM LIST	360	CANON
		~~COUNCIL AT LAODICEA~~	~~363~~	~~NOT CANONICAL~~
		ATHANASIUS	367	VERSION 3.1
		HILARY OF POITIERS	367	SOME ADD
16	3	Hilary of Poitiers	368	Tractate on Psalm 125, 6
13	8	Athanasius	373	Festal Letter 4, 2
9	5	Basil the Great	379	On the Holy Spirit, 18
		GREGORY NAZIANZUS	380	NOT CANON
		AMPHILOCHIUS	380	NOT CANON
		THE APOSTOLIC CANONS	380	CANON
		~~THE COUNCIL OF ROME~~	~~382~~	~~CANON~~
		EPIPHANIUS PAN. 8.6.1-4	385	NOT CANON FOR JEWS

		EPIPHANIUS PAN. 76.22.5 (	385	NOT CANON
8	8	Didymus the Blind	386	Commentary on Zech. 8:4-5
5	6	Gregory of Nazianzus	389	Orations 45, 15
		JEROME (HELMETED)	390	NOT CANON
		EPIPHANIUS DE MENS 4-5	392	NOT CANON FOR JEWS
		THE COUNCIL OF HIPPO - 70 BISHOPS	**393**	**CANON**
10	4	Ambrose	397	Concerning Widows 7, 37
8	3	Ambrose	397	Concerning Widows 7, 37-42
8	6	Ambrose	397	Concerning Widows 7, 38
12	1	Ambrose	397	Concerning Widows 7, 39
		Ambrose	397	Concerning Widows 7, 40
13	16	Ambrose	397	Duty of the Clergy 3, 13
11	21	Ambrose	397	Duty of the Clergy 3, 82
15	3	Ambrose	397	Duty of the Clergy 3, 82
10	12	Ambrose	397	Duty of the Clergy 3, 82-83
7	27	Ambrose	397	Duty of the Clergy 3, 84
8	11	Ambrose	397	Duty of the Clergy 3, 85
15	10	Ambrose	397	Duty of the Clergy 3, 88
8	6	Ambrose	397	Letter 58, 29
		AUGUSTINE	397	CANON
		COUNCIL CARTHAGE: 44-48 BISHOPS	**397**	**CANON**
8	8	Didymus the Blind	398	Comm. on Zechariah 12:1-3
		JEROME (SOLOMON)	398	VERSION 3.2
13	8	Jerome	400	Letter 72, 10
11	17	The Apostolic Constitutions	400	Book III, Ch VII
8	6	The Apostolic Constitutions	400	Book V, 3, XX
16	17	The Apostolic Constitutions	400	Book VII, 2, XXXVIII
8	32	The Apostolic Constitutions	400	Book VIII, 2, III
16	23	The Apostolic Constitutions	400	Book VIII, 3, XV
		RUFINUS	400	VERSION 3.3
		JEROME (TOBIT/JUDITH)	404	CANON
		POPE INNOCENT I	405	CANON
12+		Chromatius	407	Tractate on Matthew 29, II, 2
7	1	John Chrysostom	407	Homilies on John, 61, 4
5	21	Augustine	417	On Nature and Grace 42
		THE COUNCIL OF CARTHAGE:217 BISHOPS	**419**	**CANON**
13	20	Jerome	420	Letter 54, 16
1	1	Sulpitius Severus	420	Sacred History 2, 14
12	11	Sulpitius Severus	420	Sacred History 2, 14
13	1	Sulpitius Severus	420	Sacred History 2, 14
1	15	Sulpitius Severus	420	Sacred History 2, 15
2	15	Sulpitius Severus	420	Sacred History 2, 15
4	12	Sulpitius Severus	420	Sacred History 2, 15
5	17	Sulpitius Severus	420	Sacred History 2, 15
6	6	Sulpitius Severus	420	Sacred History 2, 15
7	13	Sulpitius Severus	420	Sacred History 2, 15
14	10	Sulpitius Severus	420	Sacred History 2, 15
10	17	Sulpitius Severus	420	Sacred History 2, 16
5	9	Augustine	426	City of God 16, 13
1	1	Augustine	426	City of God 18, 26
16	13	Augustine	430	Letter 227

CODEX ALEXANDRINUS	*450*	*CANON*	
CODEX EPHRAEMI R.	*450*	*UNKNOWN*	

CANON LISTS

FATHER/LIST/BOOK	Year	JUDITH CANONICAL?	OTHER CITATIONS
MELITO OF SARDIS	170	NOT FOR JEWS?	NONE
MURATORIAN CANON	170	UNKNOWN	NOT APPLICABLE
CLEMENT OF ALEXANDRIA	203	CANON	HEARD FROM GOD
ORIGEN (JEWISH LIST)	220	NOT FOR JEWS	NOT APPLICABLE
ORIGEN (LETTER)	248	CANON	SCRIPTURE
ORIGEN (CITATIONS)	250	CANON	SCRIPTURE
EUSEBIUS (APPROVAL)	324	CANON	ORIGEN LETTER
~~THE NICENE COUNCIL~~	~~325~~	~~CANON~~	~~NOT APPLICABLE~~
CODEX CLAROMONTANUS	349	CANON	NOT APPLICABLE
CODEX VATICANUS	*350*	*CANON*	*NOT APPLICABLE*
CODEX SINAITICUS	*350*	*CANON*	*NOT APPLICABLE*
CYRIL OF JERUSALEM	350	NOT CANON	NONE
ST CATHERINE'S SYRIAC	350	CANON	NOT APPLICABLE
CHELTENHAM LIST	360	CANON	NOT APPLICABLE
~~COUNCIL AT LAODICEA~~	~~363~~	~~NOT CANON~~	~~NOT APPLICABLE~~
ATHANASIUS	367	VERSION 3.1	SCRIPTURE
HILARY OF POITIERS	367	SOME ADD	AMONG THE LAW AND THE PROPHETS
GREGORY OF NAZIANZUS	380	NOT CANON	ONCE (NOT ONLINE)
AMPHILOCHIUS	380	NOT CANON	NONE
THE APOSTOLIC CANONS	380	CANON	SCRIPTURE
~~THE COUNCIL OF ROME~~	~~382~~	~~CANON~~	~~NOT APPLICABLE~~
EPIPHANIUS PAN. 8.6.1-4	385	NOT FOR JEWS	NONE
EPIPHANIUS PAN. 76.22.5	385	NOT CANON	NONE
JEROME (HELMETED)	390	NOT CANON	TYPE OF THE CHURCH
EPIPHANIUS DE MENS. 4-5	392	NOT FOR JEWS	NONE
THE COUNCIL OF HIPPO – 70 BISHOPS	**393**	**CANON**	**NOT APPLICABLE**
AUGUSTINE	397	CANON	SCRIPTURE
COUNCIL OF CARTHAGE - 44-48 BISHOPS	**397**	**CANON**	**NOT APPLICABLE**
JEROME (SOLOMON)	398	VERSION 3.2	TYPE OF THE CHURCH
RUFINUS	400	VERSION 3.3	NONE
JEROME (TOBIT/JUDITH)	404	CANON	TYPE OF THE CHURCH
POPE INNOCENT I	405	CANON	NONE
COUNCIL OF CARTHAGE - 217 BISHOPS	**419**	**CANON**	**NOT APPLICABLE**
CODEX ALEXANDRINUS	*450*	*CANON*	*NOT APPLICABLE*
CODEX EPHRAEMI R.	*450*	*UNKNOWN*	*NOT APPLICABLE*

Version 3.1: Judith (and Esther (but not Baruch, which is canon)) not canonical but to be read.

Version 3.2: Judith (unlike Esther (which is canon) or Baruch (which is not canon)) read for strengthening but not canonical or for confirming the authority of ecclesiastical dogmas.

Version 3.3: Judith (unlike Esther or Baruch (both of which are canon)) not canonical but "Ecclesiastical."

BARUCH

I view Irenaeus as, by far, the most important piece of evidence for Baruch: "the commandments of God, and of the law which endureth for ever. All they that hold it fast (are appointed) to life: but such as leave it shall die… This, beloved, is the preaching of the truth, and this is the manner of our redemption, and this is the way of life, which the prophets proclaimed, and Christ established, and the apostles delivered, and the Church in all the world hands on to her children. This must we keep with all certainty…"

But it is also important to consider comparables—i.e., what the data for "canonical" Scripture looks like. With Baruch, that is easy, since we can just compare it to the other pieces of what was Jeremiah, including Lamentations.

Baruch Chapter 3 (its most-cited chapter) was cited by the early Church more than any chapter in Lamentations and more than 46 of the 52 chapters of Jeremiah, per Biblindex.org/citation_biblique/search. Baruch Chapter 5 is the least-cited chapter of Baruch (no surprise: it is only nine verses long). It is cited more than the least-cited chapters of both Lamentations and Jeremiah. In fact, it received 20 cites over 9 verses, while Lamentations Chapter 5 received just 4 cites over 22 verses. There are also 14 "five-chapter stretches" of Jeremiah with fewer citations than the five chapters of Baruch, and even a nine-chapter stretch (39-47).

Book	Ch.	Cites	Book	Ch.	Cites	Book	Ch.	Cites
Jer	2	467	Jer	29	211	Jer	44	77
Jer	31	457	Jer	22	210	Jer	39	75
Jer	1	453	Lam	1	191	Jer	24	72
Jer	23	363	Lam	4	186	Jer	33	71
Jer	25	350	Jer	8	184	Jer	43	68
Jer	17	321	Jer	50	181	Bar	2	67
Bar	3	310	Jer	12	179	Jer	36	67
Jer	3	301	Jer	13	177	Jer	35	64
Jer	5	297	Jer	32	166	Jer	21	59
Lam	3	293	Jer	49	150	Jer	42	55
Jer	4	283	Jer	16	135	Jer	37	54
Jer	9	247	Jer	52	130	Jer	19	46
Jer	7	243	Jer	38	127	Jer	40	43
Jer	51	242	Jer	30	117	Bar	1	41
Jer	10	228	Jer	14	112	Jer	34	37
Jer	15	226	Lam	2	105	Jer	41	35
Jer	18	226	Bar	4	104	Bar	5	20
Jer	6	220	Jer	26	98	Jer	47	20
Jer	20	212	Jer	27	84	Jer	45	19
Jer	48	212	Jer	46	80	Lam	5	4
Jer	11	211	Jer	28	78			

So Baruch holds up well by any fair comparison, which is no surprise. We also know that Baruch was read as Scripture and preached upon innumerable times in every single Christian Church for at least 400 years after Christ. The Churches read Jeremiah and preached upon it like all other Scripture, which means they did so on Baruch as well.

As for canon lists, Baruch can be considered a separate Book (itself sometimes united with the Epistle of Jeremiah and sometimes not) or as part of Jeremiah (itself sometimes united with Lamentations and sometimes not). It was never excluded from any Christian canon lists until Jerome.[379] And that was by Jerome alone: both Rufinus and Athanasius consider Baruch canon (either separately or as part of Jeremiah). Note that, therefore, no one before 450 AD considered it "Ecclesiastical" or "only to be read."

Origen is the first Father to separate Baruch from Jeremiah—but he did so to distinguish it from the Jewish version of Jeremiah, and never indicates that he excludes it from the Christian canon. In fact, the Fathers either explicitly include Baruch on their canon lists or continue to cite to Baruch as Jeremiah. That was something I looked for: what happened after Origen separated Baruch out? Very little. A fraction called it Baruch, but many did not. Baruch remained canon to everyone except Jerome, regardless of what they called it.

Epiphanius (a Jewish Christian) and the book called the Apostolic Constitutions not only accept Baruch for Christians, but both indicate that some Jews accept Baruch, even in the late fourth century (385 and 380 AD). There is also much earlier evidence for the Jewish acceptance of Baruch: the Greek of both the Book of Jeremiah and Baruch 1:1-3:8 show that they were translated from Hebrew into Greek by the same person (i.e., on the same scroll). Since Sirach refers to the Law and the Prophets as a well-known and accepted collection in the Greek-speaking community of Alexandria, the Greek version of Jeremiah/Baruch 1:1-3:8 must have been completed before 110 BC and accepted by the Jews.[380] (Recall that as part of his proof of the acceptance of the Old Testament, Don Stewart at the Blue Letter Bible cited to the same sections of Sirach which evidence that Baruch was Jewish

---

[379] Who never expressly says so, and is actually inconsistent about it. However, for the purposes of this book, I treat him as the lone Father rejecting Baruch.

[380] See NIB Introduction to Baruch, p. 931. The reference to the comments in Sirach is to the prologue, written by the grandson of the author of the rest of Sirach, who was translating the grandfather's Hebrew text into Greek.

Scripture.)[381] In addition, the Greek (Septuagint) scrolls of Jeremiah sometimes have the Books in the order of Jeremiah, then Baruch, then Lamentations, which indicates that the Jews accepted Baruch as Scripture.[382]

Eventually, we arrive at Jerome, who does not translate Baruch into Latin and does not mention Baruch on his canon lists.[383] But no one else agrees.

Later lists are from Councils, so we do not have direct citation evidence to define the reference to Jeremiah. However, that is a "pedantic point" and not a real point, since aside from Jerome, I found zero evidence that any Father or Bishop at such time actually rejected Baruch. Instead, we have plenty of evidence that the practice of considering Baruch part of Jeremiah continued long after this period, such as Theodoret's commentary on Jeremiah written around 448 AD, a generation after Jerome had died. It includes Baruch and makes no mention of Jerome, his ideas, or the slightest controversy. Theodoret was wealthy and well educated (in Antioch, the Cradle of Christianity), and his Bishopric in Syria (not far from Bethlehem, from where Jerome had been writing) included 800 parishes[384]—so, he would seem likely to be well-informed. The fact that he does not even mention Jerome's idea would seem to be some indication that it had not found traction as of 448 AD.

As for citation evidence in general, most citations to Baruch reference all or part of the final three verses of Chapter 3:

> 35This is our God, and there shall none other be accounted of in comparison of him
> 36He hath found out all the way of knowledge, and hath given it unto Jacob his servant, and to Israel his beloved.
> 37Afterward did he shew himself upon earth, and conversed with men.

That creates a bit of a problem for secondary sources on Baruch. E.g., the Ancient Christian Commentary on Scripture (ACCS) is a masterpiece, as respectable as any publication could possibly be, and a multi-denominational

---

[381] www.blueletterbible.org/Comm/stewart_don/faq/right-books-in-old-testament/question17-new-testament-quote-old-testament.cfm.

[382] The NIB Introduction to Lamentations, p. 1016.

[383] Note that the Greek Septuagint version (based on a now-lost Hebrew version) of Jeremiah is considerably older than the more recent Hebrew version (which became the Masoretic text) that Jerome used and mistakenly thought was older. See wikipedia.org/wiki/Book_of_Jeremiah. Baruch is found in Greek but is thought by some to also be based (at least in part) on a now-lost earlier Hebrew/Aramaic version.

[384] wikipedia.org/wiki/Theodoret.

effort "(scholars from Eastern Orthodoxy, Roman Catholicism, and Protestantism as well as Jewish participation). ...The ACCS was first conceived of in 1993 and inspired by Joseph Cardinal Ratzinger [the man who would become Pope Benedict XVI]. The Methodist scholar Thomas C. Oden, one of the leading paleo-orthodox theologians of the twentieth and twenty-first centuries, served as the overall ACCS series editor."[385]

However, it is close to worthless for our present purposes. For its purposes, ACCS wants to spread the quotes around, rather than give an impression of the Fathers' actual citations to Baruch. So, they provide eight quotations citing to Baruch Chapter 1 and just five quotations of citations to Baruch 3:35-37. But a search of biblindex.org/citation_biblique/search shows 41 for all of Chapter 1 (less than two citations per verse, 30 of which are from one single Father: Theodoret, simply as part of his line-by-line commentary on all of Baruch) and 160 for the three verses at the end of Chapter 3. Thus ACCS gives a reader the exact opposite impression of what part of Baruch the Fathers were focused on.

But it also distorts how important Baruch was, as shown by a footnote: "The citation [to Baruch 3:36-37 (3:37-38 xx)] we have included from Quodvultdeus is only one example among many others; they are, however, very repetitive, and usually do not go beyond stating the prophecy." Very repetitive—as in, too many to keep reading, so the ACCS does not give them to us. And the Fathers "state the prophecy"—they state it because they state that it is a Scriptural Prophecy fulfilled by Jesus Christ. For us, repetition is exactly what we are concerned with, and each individual example is data showing us what the early Church thought. The Fathers thought it was a key Scriptural Prophecy fulfilled by Christ, and said so very, very repetitively.

As mentioned, Theodoret wrote a commentary on Baruch that was completed around 448 AD, a full generation after Jerome had died. It is part of his commentary on Jeremiah. He knows, of course, that both the Book of Jeremiah and the Book of Baruch were written by Baruch, not Jeremiah; yet he, too, considers all the writings as part of one collection known as Jeremiah.

Several things stand out when looking at the distribution of citations across the Book of Baruch. First, Theodoret comments on everything, so I could easily cite him for almost every verse (but I only do so a few times). Second, 3:35-3:37 is quoted so "repetitively" by the ancients that it completely overwhelms the text of the actual Book of Baruch. And yet third, the

---

[385] wikipedia.org/wiki/Ancient_Christian_Commentary_on_Scripture

distribution of citations to Baruch is comparable with other such prophetic works: certain things are, indeed, cited repetitively, and other things (the not very prophetic parts) are almost ignored completely. E.g., Ezekiel Chapter 15 is cited by exactly two people in the first 400 years of the early Church: Theodoret and Origen. Jeremiah Chapter 45: only Theodoret and Origen. Jeremiah Chapter 47: only Theodoret and Didymus. Lamentations Chapter 5: four cites in 450 years. Etc.

Similarly, for Baruch Chapter 1, we have the commentary from Theodoret citing basically every verse, but we also have citations from Eusebius, Hippolytus, and Origen. Chapter 2 is Theodoret again, plus Didymus, Gregory of Nazianzus, Origen, Athanasius, Cyril of Jerusalem and Augustine; Chapter 4 has Theodoret, as always, plus Irenaeus, Origen, Methodius, Ambrose, Athanasius, Cyril of Jerusalem, Clement of Alexandria, and various anonymous works; Chapter 5 has Theodoret, plus Ambrose, Jerome, and Basil the Great.[386]

Comparatively, the "rest of" Baruch holds up well. But it is still not a lot, and the fact remains that citations to Baruch are largely to Chapter 3. These are mostly the last three verses, but the first 34 are still cited by Theodoret, Ambrose, Athanasius, Didymus, Chrysostom, Basil, Origen, Dionysius, Jerome, Gregory of Nyssa, Methodius, Clement of Alexandria, Eusebius, Saint Patrick, Pachomius, Chromatius, John Cassian, and Augustine.

In order to save space, I do not show the exact wording of every citation to Baruch 3:35-38 as Scripture—actually reading them is, indeed, very repetitive. I discussed the exact language from Irenaeus in exhaustive detail above; below, I have only noted those that I feel qualify as full citations as Scripture (and ignored a few that were not crystal clear), quoting several fully. I also give you links to the others, where available. That will have to suffice. There are 65 of them below, and still more that I could not double check (and so, they are not included in my data set below; as mentioned above, the total comes to 160 at biblindex.org/citation_biblique/search).

Noted below are eleven possible references to Baruch in the New Testament.[387] Most of those have already been discussed at length, but one

---

[386] All the data comes from biblindex.org/citation_biblique/search. I was unable to find some of the citations to read, so not all of them are included below.

[387] As noted previously, there is a piece of possible Old Testament evidence as well: in Daniel 9:2, Daniel explicitly mentions Jeremiah, then in 9:5 and 9:8 may have quoted from Baruch (i.e., the

more is that John may have made another reference to Baruch via Revelation 18:2 (And he cried mightily with a strong voice, saying, Babylon the great is fallen, is fallen, and is become the habitation of devils, and the hold of every foul spirit, and a cage of every unclean and hateful bird). Compare this to Baruch 4:35, which says of the cities which thy children served (i.e., Babylon, etc.) "fire shall come upon her from the Everlasting, long to endure; and she shall be inhabited of devils for a great time." That would make multiple references to Baruch from multiple works by John, who taught Polycarp, who taught Irenaeus, who wrote that Baruch was Apostolic preaching.

I was able to review 349 citations to Baruch. Biblindex.org /citation_biblique/search lists 549, so the information below is missing a great many I could not access. My data set includes 32 Fathers (nine of which were on Kruger's list of ten Fathers) and 62 of their works. Almost every Father who cited to Baruch 3:35+ expressly stated that it was Prophecy or Scripture, etc. While I do not go into the exact wording for each of those, here are a few notables:

First, from a dispute over John's teaching. Hippolytus of Rome was writing in 220 AD against Noetus (excommunicated as a heretic). Noetus "accepted the fourth Gospel, but regarded its statements about the Logos as allegorical"[388]—the very issue that Irenaeus cited as Apostolic preaching, that the Word became flesh. Baruch is accepted as Scripture by both sides:

> For whenever they wish to attempt anything underhand, they mutilate the Scriptures. But let him [Noetus] quote the passage as a whole, and he will discover the reason kept in view in writing it. ... But what is meant, says he [Noetus], in the other passage: This is God, and there shall none other be accounted of in comparison of Him? ... But he [the Scripture writer] says: This is our God; there shall none other be accounted of in comparison of Him. He has found out all the way of knowledge, and has given it unto Jacob His servant, and to Israel His beloved. Baruch 3:35-36.[389]

Later, we find Gregory of Nazianzus (one of the Fathers on Kruger's list) showing us that John and Baruch are still tied theologically, in yet another dispute over orthodoxy:

Baruch part of Jeremiah) in his prayers. Daniel 9:15 may also be quoting from Baruch 2:11-12; and there may be an allusion to Baruch 2:19 in Daniel 9:20.

[388] wikipedia.org/wiki/Noetus

[389] www.newadvent.org/fathers/0521.htm

They play the same trick with the word that describes the Incarnation, viz.: ... "He knew what was in man" (John 2:25) but teaching that it means, He consorted and conversed with men, and taking refuge in the expression which says that He was seen on Earth and conversed with Men. (Baruch 3:37) ... for it is from hence that they have derived their second Judaism and ... bring in His flesh as a phantom rather than a reality, ... and use for this purpose the apostolic expression, understood and spoken in a sense which is not apostolic...Since then these expressions, rightly understood, make for orthodoxy, but wrongly interpreted are heretical...[390]

Here is another example of the Baruch-John connection, from Athanasius (another Father on Kruger's list) arguing against the Arians:

If then henceforward openly adopting Caiaphas's way, they have determined on judaizing, and are ignorant of the text, that verily God shall dwell upon the earth (see Baruch 3:37), let them not inquire into the Apostolical sayings; for this is not the manner of Jews. But if, mixing themselves up with the godless Manichees, they deny that 'the Word was made flesh,' (John 1:14) ....[391]

Ambrose also quotes from Baruch in support of authentic Christian belief—in this case, in support of Paul:

Scripture speaks, in the Book of Jeremiah, of One God, and yet acknowledges both Father and Son. Thus we read: He is our God ... He appeared upon earth, and conversed with men. (Baruch 3:35-37). The prophet speaks of the Son, for it was the Son Himself Who conversed with men ... Shall we believe the wise of this world, if we believe not the prophets? ... Are we to believe the Jews? For God was once known in Jewry. Nay, but they deny that very thing, which is the foundation of our belief, seeing that they know not the Father, who have denied the Son.[392]

Those are just four examples of Baruch being used to confirm doctrine, incidentally. And three of them make clear that the Prophecy of Baruch is a key support for a doctrine opposed by a "second Judaism," "Judaizing," and "Jewry." The fourth, Hippolytus, uses Baruch to condemn heretics who would mutilate the Christian Scriptures—including Baruch.

---

[390] 390 AD Against Apollinarius: www.newadvent.org/fathers/3103a.htm
[391] 335 AD Four Discourses against the Arians 1, 13, 53: www.newadvent.org/fathers/28161.htm
[392] 397 AD Exposition of the Christian Faith 1, 3, 30: www.newadvent.org/fathers/34041.htm

Baruch: Annotated

1:1 And these are the words of the book, which Baruch the son of Nerias, the son of Maasias, the son of Sedecias, the son of Asadias, the son of Chelcias, wrote in Babylon, 1:2 In the fifth year, and in the seventh day of the month, what time as the Chaldeans took Jerusalem, and burnt it with fire. 1:3 And Baruch did read the words of this book in the hearing of Jechonias the son of Joachim king of Juda, and in the ears of all the people that came to hear the book,

Theodoret 448 AD cited this section as part of his Commentary on Jeremiah [Not available online].

1:4 And in the hearing of the nobles, and of the king's sons, and in the hearing of the elders, and of all the people, from the lowest unto the highest, even of all them that dwelt at Babylon by the river Sud. 1:5 Whereupon they wept, fasted, and prayed before the Lord. 1:6 They made also a collection of money according to every man's power: 1:7 And they sent it to Jerusalem unto Joachim the high priest, the son of Chelcias, son of Salom, and to the priests, and to all the people which were found with him at Jerusalem,

Theodoret 448 AD cited this section as part of his Commentary on Jeremiah [Not available online].

1:8 At the same time when he received the vessels of the house of the Lord, that were carried out of the temple, to return them into the land of Juda, the tenth day of the month Sivan, namely, silver vessels, which Sedecias the son of Josias king of Juda had made, 1:9 After that Nabuchodonosor king of Babylon had carried away Jechonias, and the princes, and the captives, and the mighty men, and the people of the land, from Jerusalem, and brought them unto Babylon. 1:10 And they said, Behold, we have sent you money to buy you burnt offerings, and sin offerings, and incense, and prepare ye manna, and offer upon the altar of the Lord our God; 1:11 And pray for the life of Nabuchodonosor king of Babylon, and for the life of Balthasar his son, that their days may be upon earth as the days of heaven:

Theodoret 448 AD cited this section as part of his Commentary on Jeremiah [Not available online]. (Balthasar (referenced in Daniel as well) had been unknown to history until evidence was found in the late 19th century proving his existence.)

1:12 And the Lord will give us strength, and lighten our eyes, and we shall live under the shadow of Nabuchodonosor king of Babylon, and under the shadow of Balthasar his son, and we shall serve them many days, and find favour in their sight. 1:13 Pray for us also unto the Lord our God, for we have sinned against the Lord our God; and unto this day the fury of the Lord and his wrath is not turned from us. 1:14 And ye shall read this book which we have sent unto you, to make confession in the house of the Lord, upon the feasts and solemn days.

Theodoret 448 AD cited this section as part of his Commentary on Jeremiah [Not available online].

1:15 **And ye shall say, To the Lord our God belongeth righteousness, but unto us the confusion of faces, as it is come to pass this day, unto them of Juda, and to the inhabitants of Jerusalem,**[393]

1:16 And to our kings, and to our princes, and to our priests, and to our prophets, and to our fathers:

Theodoret 448 AD cited this section as part of his Commentary on Jeremiah [Not available online].

1:17 **For we have sinned before the Lord, 1:18 And disobeyed him, and have not**

---

[393] In Daniel 9:2, Daniel explicitly mentions Jeremiah, and then in 9:5 and 9:8 ,he may have quoted from Baruch in his prayers: Daniel 9:8 (O Lord, to us belongeth confusion of face, to our kings, to our princes, and to our fathers, because we have sinned against thee).

hearkened unto the voice of the Lord our God, to walk in the commandments that he gave us openly:[394]

Theodoret 448 AD cited this section as part of his Commentary on Jeremiah [Not available online].

1:19 Since the day that the Lord brought our forefathers out of the land of Egypt, unto this present day, we have been disobedient unto the Lord our God, and we have been negligent in not hearing his voice.

Theodoret 448 AD cited this section as part of his Commentary on Jeremiah [Not available online].

1:20 Wherefore the evils cleaved unto us, and the curse, which the Lord appointed by Moses his servant at the time that he brought our fathers out of the land of Egypt, to give us a land that floweth with milk and honey, like as it is to see this day.

Theodoret 448 AD cited this section as part of his Commentary on Jeremiah [Not available online].

1:21 Nevertheless we have not hearkened unto the voice of the Lord our God, according unto all the words of the prophets, whom he sent unto us: 1:22 But every man followed the imagination of his own wicked heart, to serve strange gods, and to do evil in the sight of the Lord our God.

2:1 Therefore the Lord hath made good his word, which he pronounced against us, and against our judges that judged Israel, and against our kings, and against our princes, and against the men of Israel and Juda, 2:2 To bring upon us great plagues, such as never happened under the whole heaven, as it came to pass in Jerusalem, according to the things that were written in the law of Moses; 2:3 That a man should eat the flesh of his own son, and the flesh of his own daughter. 2:4 Moreover he hath delivered them to be in subjection to all the kingdoms that are round about us, to be as a reproach and desolation among all the people round about, where the Lord hath scattered them. 2:5 Thus we were cast down, and not exalted, because we have sinned against the Lord our God, and have not been obedient unto his voice.

Theodoret 448 AD cited this section as part of his Commentary on Jeremiah [Not available online].

2:6 To the Lord our God appertaineth righteousness: but unto us and to our fathers open shame, as appeareth this day. 2:7 For all these plagues are come upon us, which the Lord hath pronounced against us 2:8 Yet have we not prayed before the Lord, that we might turn every one from the imaginations of his wicked heart. 2:9 Wherefore the Lord watched over us for evil, and the Lord hath brought it upon us: for the Lord is righteous in all his works which he hath commanded us. 2:10 Yet we have not hearkened unto his voice, to walk in the commandments of the Lord, that he hath set before us. 2:11 **And now, O Lord God of Israel, that hast brought thy people out of the land of Egypt with a mighty hand, and high arm, and with signs, and with wonders, and with great power, and hast gotten thyself a name, as appeareth this day:**[395]

2:12 O Lord our God, we have sinned, we have done ungodly, we have dealt unrighteously in all thine ordinances.

---

[394] **In Daniel 9:2, Daniel explicitly mentions Jeremiah, and then in 9:5 and 9:8, he may have quoted from Baruch in his prayers: Daniel 9:5 (We have sinned, and have committed iniquity, and have done wickedly, and have rebelled, even by departing from thy precepts and from thy judgments).**

[395] **In Daniel 9:2, Daniel explicitly mentions Jeremiah, and then in 9:5 and 9:8, he may have quoted from Baruch in his prayers; and Daniel 9:15 may be quoting from Baruch 2:11-12: And now, O Lord our God, that hast brought thy people forth out of the land of Egypt with a mighty hand, and hast gotten thee renown, as at this day; we have sinned, we have done wickedly.**

Gregory of Nazianzus 390 AD Oration 16, 12 Cited along with Isaiah without qualification: We have sinned, we have done amiss, and have dealt wickedly, for we have forgotten Your commandments. www. newadvent.org/fathers/310216.htm

2:13 Let thy wrath turn from us: for we are but a few left among the heathen, where thou hast scattered us. 2:14 Hear our prayers, O Lord, and our petitions, and deliver us for thine own sake, and give us favour in the sight of them which have led us away: 2:15 That all the earth may know that thou art the Lord our God, because Israel and his posterity is called by thy name. 2:16 O Lord, look down from thine holy house, and consider us: bow down thine ear, O Lord, to hear us. 2:17 Open thine eyes, and behold; for the dead that are in the graves, whose souls are taken from their bodies, will give unto the Lord neither praise nor righteousness: 2:18 But the soul that is greatly vexed, which goeth stooping and feeble, and the eyes that fail, and the hungry soul, will give thee praise and righteousness, O Lord. 2:19 **Therefore we do not make our humble supplication before thee, O Lord our God, for the righteousness of our fathers, and of our kings.**[396]

2:20 For thou hast sent out thy wrath and indignation upon us, as thou hast spoken by thy servants the prophets, saying, 2:21 Thus saith the Lord, <u>Bow down your shoulders to serve the king of Babylon</u>: so shall ye remain in the land that I gave unto your fathers.

---

[396] **In Daniel 9:2, Daniel explicitly mentions Jeremiah, and then in 9:5 and 9:8, he may have quoted from Baruch in his prayers; Daniel 9:15 may be quoting from Baruch 2:11-12; and there may be an allusion to Baruch 2:19 in Daniel 9:20 (And whiles I was speaking, and praying, and confessing my sin and the sin of my people Israel, and presenting my supplication before the LORD my God for the holy mountain of my God).**

Athanasius 373 AD Letter 13, 6 Cited along with James without qualification: we also, when the enemies are arrayed against us, should... bow the shoulder www. newadvent.org/fathers/2806013.htm

2:22 But if ye will not hear the voice of the Lord, to serve the king of Babylon, 2:23 I will cause to cease out of the cites of Judah, and from without Jerusalem, the voice of mirth, and the voice of joy, the voice of the bridegroom, and the voice of the bride: and the whole land shall be desolate of inhabitants. 2:24 But we would not hearken unto thy voice, <u>to serve the king of Babylon: therefore hast thou made good the words that thou spakest by thy servants the prophets, namely, that the bones of our kings, and the bones of our fathers, should be taken out of their place.</u>

Cyril of Jerusalem 386 AD Catechetical Lecture 2, 17 What do you think of Nebuchadnezzar? Have you not heard out of the Scriptures that he was bloodthirsty, fierce, lion-like in disposition? Have you not heard that he brought out the bones of the kings from their graves into the light? www.newadvent.org/fathers/310102.htm

2:25 And, lo, they are cast out to the heat of the day, and to the frost of the night, and they died in great miseries by famine, by sword, and by pestilence. 2:26 And the house which is called by thy name hast thou laid waste, as it is to be seen this day, for the wickedness of the house of Israel and the house of Juda. 2:27 O Lord our God, thou hast dealt with us after all thy goodness, and according to all that great mercy of thine, 2:28 As thou spakest by thy servant Moses in the day when thou didst command him to write the law before the children of Israel, saying, 2:29 If ye will not hear my voice, surely this very great multitude shall be turned into a small number among the nations, where I will scatter them. 2:30 For I knew that they would not hear me, because it is a stiffnecked people: but in the land of their captivities they shall remember themselves. 2:31 And shall know that I am the Lord their

God: <u>for I will give them an heart, and ears to hear</u>:

Augustine 430 AD Letter 217, 7, 26: You surely do not, do you, forbid the Church to pray for non-believers in order that they may become believers ... in order that God may give them what he promised through the prophet: a heart for knowing him and ears for hearing? [Per The Works of Saint Augustine, A Translation for the 21st Century, not available online.

Augustine 430 AD On the Gift of Perseverance, 51 It must absolutely be preached, so that he who has ears to hear, may hear. And who has them if he has not received them from Him who says, 'I will give them a heart to know me, and ears to hear"? newadvent.org/fathers/15122.htm

Augustine 430 AD Treatise on the Predestination of the Saints, 42 ...it is in vain that objectors have alleged, that what we have proved by Scripture testimony from the books of Kings and Chronicles is not pertinent to the subject of which we are discoursing: ...do they not think that these instances are appropriate to this subject...? But I think that it was in reference to the kingdom of heaven, and not to an earthly kingdom, that it was said, ... I will give them a heart to know me, and ears that hear; Baruch 2:31 or ... Let them hear these passages, and whatever others of the kind I have not mentioned... www.newadvent.org/fathers/15121.htm

2:32 And they shall praise me in the land of their captivity, and think upon my name, 2:33 And return from their stiff neck, and from their wicked deeds: for they shall remember the way of their fathers, which sinned before the Lord. 2:34 And I will bring them again into the land which I promised with an oath unto their fathers, Abraham, Isaac, and Jacob, and they shall be lords of it: and I will increase them, and they shall not be diminished. 2:35 And I will make an everlasting covenant with them to be their God, and they shall be my people:

and I will no more drive my people of Israel out of the land that I have given them.

3:1 <u>O Lord Almighty, God of Israel, the soul in anguish the troubled spirit, crieth unto thee</u>.

Athanasius 335 AD Letter to Serapion I.7.1 The Scripture, in fact, also speaks of the "spirit of man [a person]," as David sings, "I spoke with my heart by night, and my spirit was afflicted! And Baruch prays, saying, "An anguished soul and a saddened spirit raises its cry to you." Not available online.

3:2 <u>Hear, O Lord, and have mercy</u>; for thou art merciful: and have pity upon us, because we have sinned before thee.

Ambrose 397 AD On Repentance 1, 9, 43 For at the intercession of the prophet, and the entreaty of so great a seer, the Lord was moved and said to Jerusalem, which had meanwhile repented for its sins, and had said: O Almighty Lord God of Israel, the soul in anguish, and the troubled spirit cries unto You, hear, O Lord, and have mercy. 3:1-3:2. www.newadvent.org/fathers/34061.htm

3:3 <u>For thou endurest for ever, and we perish utterly</u>.

Basil the Great 379 AD On the Holy Spirit, 6, 15: We have only touched cursorily on these proofs,... when the Father says, Sit on my right hand; when the Holy Spirit bears witness that he has sat down on the right hand of the majesty Hebrews 8:1 of God; we attempt to degrade him who shares the honour and the throne, from his condition of equality, to a lower state? Standing and sitting, I apprehend, indicate the fixity and entire stability of the nature, as Baruch, when he wishes to exhibit the immutability and immobility of the Divine mode of existence, says, For you sit for ever and we perish utterly.... www.newadvent.org/fathers/3203.htm

3:4 O Lord Almighty, thou God of Israel, hear now the prayers of the dead Israelites, and of their children, which have sinned before thee, and not hearkened unto the voice of thee their

God: for the which cause these plagues cleave unto us. 3:5 Remember not the iniquities of our forefathers: but think upon thy power and thy name now at this time. 3:6 For thou art the Lord our God, and thee, O Lord, will we praise. 3:7 And for this cause thou hast put thy fear in our hearts, to the intent that we should call upon thy name, and praise thee in our captivity: for we have called to mind all the iniquity of our forefathers, that sinned before thee. 3:8 Behold, we are yet this day in our captivity, where thou hast scattered us, for a reproach and a curse, and to be subject to payments, according to all the iniquities of our fathers, which departed from the Lord our God.

Saint Patrick 450 AD Confession 1.1: Cited along with Isaiah without qualification: I was taken as a captive to Ireland with many thousands of people, and deservedly so, because we had turned away from God... [Per Ancient Christian Commentary on Scripture]. Not available online

3:9 Hear, Israel, the commandments of life: give ear to understand wisdom.

Clement of Alexandria 198 AD The Instructor 1, 10 [Referred to as the word of a prophet in 1, 10] For wisdom and knowledge are mentioned by the same prophet, when he says, Hear, O Israel, the commandments of life, and give ear to know understanding. www.newadvent. org/fathers/02091.htm

3:10 How happeneth it Israel, that thou art in thine enemies' land, that thou art waxen old in a strange country, that thou art defiled with the dead,

Pachomius 348 AD Instructions 16.23: O man, what are you doing in Babylon? "You have grown old in an alien land" because you did not submit to the test and because your relations with God are not proper. [Per Ancient Christian Commentary on Scripture] Not available online

Chromatius 407 AD Tractate on Matthew 41, 9 Whence long ago the law had shown the same thing figuratively, that anyone who had touched a dead body is defiled. [Per Chromatius of Aquileia, Sermons and Tractates on Matthew] Not available online.

John Cassian 435 AD Conferences 1, 7, 5 hear the words of the prophet: Why are you grown old in a strange country? www.newadvent.org/fathers/350807.htm

3:11 That thou art counted with them that go down into the grave? 3:12 Thou hast forsaken the fountain of wisdom.

Athanasius 335 AD 4 Discourses against the Arians 1, 19 [Referred to as from the sacred writers in 1, 12] in the book of Baruch it is written, 'You have forsaken the Fountain of wisdom' www.newadvent.org/fathers/28161.htm

Athanasius 335 AD Four Discourses against the Arians 2, 42 [Referred to as from the sacred writers in 1, 12] Whence the Jews, as denying the Son as well as they, have not the Father either; for, as having left the 'Fountain of Wisdom,' as Baruch reproaches them. www.newadvent.org/fathers/28162.htm

Athanasius 356 AD De Decretis, 3, 12 when the Word ... says, 'You have forsaken the Fountain of wisdom;' www.newadvent.org/fathers/2809.htm

Jerome 419 AD Homily 92: On Psalm 41 (42): quotes Baruch 3:12 to establish the Trinitarian nature of Baptism, per Gary G. Michuta in The Case of the Deuterocanon. Not available online.

3:13 For if thou hadst walked in the way of God, thou shouldest have dwelled in peace for ever.

Clement of Alexandria 198 AD The Instructor 1, 10 [Referred to as the word of a prophet in 1, 10] He says by Jeremiah, Had you walked in the way of God, you would have dwelt for ever in peace... www.newadvent.org/fathers/02091.htm

Origen 253 AD Origen, Homily 7 on Jeremiah, 3.3 ... about which it is written: Hear Israel. "Why is it that you are in the land of enemies, that you are counted among those in Hades? You have forsaken the fountain of life, the Lord. If you have walked in the way of God, you would have dwelt in peace forever." [3:9-13] vivacatholic.wordpress.com/2007/08/14/origen-and-canon-of-old-testament/

3:14 Learn where is wisdom, where is strength, where is understanding; that thou mayest know also where is length of days, and life, where is the light of the eyes, and peace.

Athanasius 359 AD De Synodis, 41-42 the opponents of Nicaea used Baruch 3:14 to describe the Son. Athanasius counters with an orthodox understanding, per Gary G. Michuta in The Case of the Deuterocanon. www.newadvent.org/fathers/2817.htm

3:15 Who hath found out her place? or who hath come into her treasures?

Methodius 311 AD Banquet of the Ten Virgins, 8, 3 Cited along with Exodus, Revelation, etc. without qualification: Now Jeremiah ... says: Learn where is wisdom, where is strength, where is understanding; that you may know also where is length of days, and life, where is the light of the eyes, and peace. Who has found out her place? Or who has come into her treasures? www.newadvent.org/fathers/062308.htm

3:16 Where are the princes of the heathen become, and such as ruled the beasts upon the earth; 3:17 They that had their pastime with the fowls of the air, and they that hoarded up silver and gold, wherein men trust, and made no end of their getting? 3:18 For they that wrought in silver, and were so careful, and whose works are unsearchable, 3:19 They are vanished and gone down to the grave, and others are come up in their steads.

Clement of Alexandria 198 AD The Instructor 2, 3: the Divine Scripture ... says, Where are the rulers of the nations, and the lords of the wild beasts of the earth, who sport among the birds of heaven, who treasured up silver and gold, in whom men trusted, and there was no end of their substance, who fashioned silver and gold, and were full of care? There is no finding of their works. They have vanished, and gone down to Hades. www.newadvent.org/fathers/02092.htm

3:20 Young men have seen light, and dwelt upon the earth: but the way of knowledge have they not known, 3:21 Nor understood the paths thereof, nor laid hold of it: their children were far off from that way. 3:22 It hath not been heard of in Chanaan, neither hath it been seen in Theman. 3:23 The Agarenes that seek wisdom upon earth, the merchants of Meran and of Theman, the authors of fables, and searchers out of understanding; none of these have known the way of wisdom, or remember her paths. 3:24 O Israel, how great is the house of God! and how large is the place of his possession!

Eusebius 325 AD Church History 10, 4, 8 Cited along with Job, Daniel, Luke, etc. without qualification: And let us ... honor him and cry aloud, saying, 'Great is the Lord and greatly to be praised in the city of our God, in his holy mountain.' For he is truly great, and great is his house, lofty and spacious and 'comely in beauty above the sons of men.' www.newadvent.org/fathers/250110.htm

3:25 Great, and hath none end; high, and unmeasurable.

Methodius 311 AD Oration Concerning Simeon and Anna, X ...even as somewhere the illustrious prophet says, teaching us how incomprehensible thou art. ccel.org/ccel/schaff/anf06.xi.viii.html

Ambrose 397 AD Hexameron 6, 8, 52 ... said the Prophet, 'how great is the house of God and how vast is the place of his possession ! It is great and hath no end : it is high and immense. archive.org/stream/fathersofthechur027571mbp/fathersofthechur027571mbp_djvu.txt

3:26 There were the giants famous from the beginning, that were of so great stature, and so expert in war. 3:27 Those did not the Lord choose, neither gave he the way of knowledge unto them: 3:28 But they were destroyed, because they had no wisdom, and perished through their own foolishness.

Augustine 426 AD City of God 15, 23: ... There is therefore no doubt that, according to the Hebrew and Christian canonical Scriptures, there were many giants before the deluge ... It is this which another prophet confirms when he says, These were the giants, famous from the beginning, that were of so great stature, and so expert in war. Those did not the Lord choose, neither gave He the way of knowledge unto them; but they were destroyed because they had no wisdom, and perished through their own foolishness. www.newadvent.org/fathers/120115.htm
3:29 Who hath gone up into heaven, and taken her, and brought her down from the clouds?

John 3:13 And no man hath ascended up to heaven, but he that came down from heaven, even the Son of man which is in heaven.

Romans 10:6 But the righteousness which is of faith speaketh on this wise, Say not in thine heart, Who shall ascend into heaven? (that is, to bring Christ down from above:) – see below
3:30 Who hath gone over the sea, and found her, and will bring her for pure gold?

Romans 10:7 Or, Who shall descend into the deep? (that is, to bring up Christ again from the dead.) – see above
3:31 No man knoweth her way, nor thinketh of her path. 3:32 But he that knoweth all things knoweth her, and hath found her out with his understanding: he that prepared the earth for evermore hath filled it with fourfooted beasts: 3:33 He that sendeth forth light, and it goeth, calleth it again, and it obeyeth him with fear. 3:34 The stars shined in their watches, and rejoiced: when he calleth them, they say, Here we be; and so with cheerfulness they shewed light unto him that made them. 3:35 This is our God, and there shall none other be accounted of in comparison of him 3:36 He hath found out all the way of knowledge, and hath given it unto Jacob his servant, and to Israel his beloved. 3:37 Afterward did he shew himself upon earth, and conversed with men.

John 1:14 (And the Word was made flesh, and dwelt among us, (and we beheld his glory, the glory as of the only begotten of the Father,) full of grace and truth), per the notes included with the original King James Bible
Note that this would be a prophecy, fulfilled by Jesus.

See also John 1:17 (For the law was given through Moses, grace and truth came through Jesus); Baruch means that God came and lived among men via the commandments of the Torah (see 3:27-28, etc.) - thus the parallel to the Word of God who came in John 1:14.
[Citations by early Church Fathers to 3:35-3:37 as Prophecy, Scripture, etc. are shown in the attached chart]
4:1 This is the book of the commandments of God, and the law that endureth for ever: all they that keep it shall come to life; but such as leave it shall die.

Matthew 5:18: For verily I say unto you, Till heaven and earth pass, one jot or one tittle shall in no wise pass from the law, till all be fulfilled.

Irenaeus of Lyon 180 AD Demonstration of Apostolic Teaching, 97: "Wherefore also Jeremiah saith ... This is the book of the commandments of God, and of the law which endureth for ever. All they that hold it fast (are appointed) to life: but such as leave it shall die."... This, beloved, is the preaching of the truth ... which the prophets proclaimed, and Christ established, and the apostles delivered, and the Church in all the world hands on to her children." www.tertullian.org/fathers/irenaeus_02_proof.htm

Father	Year	Work citing Baruch 3:35-37 as Scripture, etc.
Athenagoras	177	Plea for Christians, 9
Athenagoras	177	Plea for Christians 9
Irenaeus	177	Against Heresies 4, 20, 4
Irenaeus	180	Demonstration of Apostolic Teaching, 97
Hippolytus	220	Against Noetus 5
Hippolytus	220	Against Noetus 2
Cyprian	258	Treatise 12, 2, 6
Lactantius	311	The Divine Institutes, 4, 8
Lactantius	311	The Epitome of the Divine Institutes, 44
Athanasius	335	Four Discourses against the Arians 2, 49
Athanasius	335	Four Discourses against the Arians 1, 13, 53
Eusebius	339	Demonstratio Evangelica, 6.19
Hilary	367	On the Trinity, 4, 42
Hilary	367	On the Trinity, 5, 39
Cyril Jeru.	386	Catechetical Lectures, 11, 15
Didymus	386	Commentary on Zechariah 3:6-7
Didymus	386	Commentary on Zechariah 8:23
Greg. Nyssa	386	Against Eunomius 2, 1
Greg. Nyssa	386	Against Eunomius 5, 3
Greg. Nyssa	386	Against Eunomius 6, 4
Gregory Naz.	390	Against Apollinarius (2nd Letter to Cledonius)
Gregory Naz.	390	Oration 30, 13 (Fourth Theological Oration)
Ambrose	397	Exposition of the Christian Faith 1, 28
Ambrose	397	Exposition of the Christian Faith 2, 9, 80
Ambrose	397	Exposition of the Christian Faith 1, 3, 30
Ap. Const.	400	Book 5, 3, 20
Augustine	400	Reply to Faustus 12, 43
Amphilochius	403	Oration I, 2
Epiphanius	403	Panarion, Section 3, Heresy 37, 9, 1 Noetus
Epiphanius	403	Panarion, Section 4, Heresy 49, Arians, 31, 1
Epiphanius	403	Panarion, Section 4, Heresy 49, Arians, 53, 7
Epiphanius	403	Panarion, Section 4, Heresy 51, Photinians, 3, 5
Epiphanius	403	Panarion Section 3, Heresy 37, 2, 1 Noetus
Epiphanius	403	Panarion Section 7, De Fide, 16, 2
Epiphanius	403	Panarion, Section 4, Heresy 49, Arians, 31, 1
Epiphanius	403	Panarion, Section 4, Heresy 49, Arians, 55, 6
Chrysostom	407	Homilies on Matthew, 2, 2
Chrysostom	407	Homilies on Matthew, 19, 12
Chrysostom	407	Homilies on Matthew, 26, 19
Chrysostom	407	Demonstration Against the Jews 8, 6
Chrysostom	407	On the Incomprehensible Nature of God 5, 14-16
Rufinus	409	Commentary on the Apostles' Creed, 5
Cyril of Alex.	418	Commentary on John 5, IV
Cyril of Alex.	418	Commentary on John 1, Introduction
Cyril of Alex.	418	Commentary on John 1, IX
Cyril of Alex.	418	Letter 31
Cyril of Alex.	418	Festal Letter 4
Cyril of Alex.	418	Festal Letter 10
Augustine	426	City of God 18, 33
Augustine	430	Sermon 277, 16
Augustine	430	Reply to Faustus the Manichean, 12, 43
Augustine	430	Letter 147, 5, 16
Augustine	430	Letter 164, 6, 17

Augustine	430	Exposition on Psalm 47, 15
Augustine	430	Letter 164, 6, 17
Theodoret	430	Commentary on Psalm 67
John Cassian	435	On the Incarnation 5, 5
John Cassian	435	On the Incarnation, 4, 13
John Cassian	435	On the Incarnation, 4, 9
Cyril of Alex.	444	Festal Letter 18
Cyril of Alex.	444	Festal Letter 28
Theodoret	448	Commentary on Baruch
Theodoret	448	Eranistes or the Polymorph, 1
Theodoret	448	Letter to the Monks of the Euphratensian, etc.
Peter Chrysologus	450	Sermon 88

4:2 Turn thee, O Jacob, and take hold of it: walk in the presence of the light thereof, that thou mayest be illuminated. 4:3 Give not thine honour to another, nor the things that are profitable unto thee to a strange nation. 4:4 O Israel, happy are we: for things that are pleasing to God are made known unto us.

Clement of Alexandria 198 AD The Instructor 1, 10: [Referred to as the word of a prophet in 1, 10] For the good is found by him who seeks it, and is wont to be seen by him who has found it. By Jeremiah, too, He sets forth prudence, when he says, Blessed are we, Israel; for what is pleasing to God is known by us — and it is known by the Word, by whom we are blessed and wise. www.newadvent.org/fathers/02091.htm

Apostolic Constitutions 400 AD Book 6, 4, 23 And again: Blessed are we, O Israel, because those things that are pleasing to God are known to us. www.newadvent.org/fathers/07156.htm

Baruch 3:29-4:4 also speaks of wisdom in a way parallel to the Gospel of John's discourse about Jesus the son of God in John 3:13-21 and 31-36. In both Baruch and John humans cannot ascend to heaven to get wisdom, but rather wisdom in Baruch and the son of the Father in John descend from heaven to humans as a divine gift. In Baruch, wisdom is associated with life, light, and salvation, as is Jesus in John. Wisdom understood as the law dwells with Israel in Baruch just as Jesus dwells with humans as the truth, the word, and the way in John. (I did not specifically mark these general parallels in the text above).

4:5 Be of good cheer, my people, the memorial of Israel. 4:6 Ye were sold to the nations, not for [your] destruction: but because ye moved God to wrath, ye were delivered unto the enemies. 4:7 For ye provoked him that made you by sacrificing unto devils, and not to God.

1 Corinthians 10:20: (But I say, that the things which the Gentiles sacrifice, they sacrifice to devils, and not to God: and I would not that ye should have fellowship with devils), per the notes included with the original King James Bible.

4:8 Ye have forgotten the everlasting God, that brought you up; and ye have grieved Jerusalem, that nursed you. 4:9 For when she saw the wrath of God coming upon you, she said, Hearken, O ye that dwell about Sion: God hath brought upon me great mourning; 4:10 For I saw the captivity of my sons and daughters, which the Everlasting brought upon them. 4:11 With joy did I nourish them; but sent them away with weeping and mourning. 4:12 Let no man rejoice over me, a widow, and forsaken of many, who for the sins of my children am left desolate; because they departed from the law of God. 4:13 They knew not his statutes, nor walked in the ways of his commandments, nor trod in the paths of discipline in his righteousness. 4:14 Let them that dwell about Sion come, and remember ye the captivity of my sons and daughters, which the Everlasting hath brought upon them. 4:15 For he hath brought a nation upon them from far, a shameless nation, and of a strange language, who neither reverenced old man, nor pitied child. 4:16 These have carried away the dear beloved children of the widow, and left her that was alone desolate without daughters. 4:17 But what can I help you? 4:18 For he that brought these plagues upon you will deliver you from the hands of your enemies. 4:19 Go your way, O my children, go your way: for I am left desolate. 4:20 I have put off the clothing of peace, and put upon me the sackcloth of my prayer: I will cry unto the Everlasting in my days.

Athanasius 335 AD Four Discourses against the Arians 1, 12 "...where the sacred writers say, 'Who exists before the ages,' and 'By whom He made the ages,' they thereby as clearly preach the eternal and everlasting being of the Son, even while they are designating God Himself. ... and Baruch wrote, 'I will cry unto the Everlasting in my days,' ... www.newadvent.org/fathers/28161.htm

4:21 Be of good cheer, O my children, cry unto the Lord, and he will deliver you from the power and hand of the enemies. 4:22 For my hope is in the Everlasting, that he will save you; and joy is come unto me from the Holy One, because of the mercy which shall soon come unto you from the Everlasting our Saviour.

Athanasius 335 AD Four Discourses against the Arians 1, 12 "...where the sacred writers say... and Baruch wrote... shortly after, 'My hope is in the Everlasting, that He will save you, and joy has come unto me from the Holy One ;' ... who has so little sense as to doubt of the eternity of the Son? www. newadvent.org/fathers/28161.htm

4:23 For I sent you out with mourning and weeping: but God will give you to me again with joy and gladness for ever. 4:24 Like as now the neighbours of Sion have seen your captivity: so shall they see shortly your salvation from our God which shall come upon you with great glory, and brightness of the Everlasting. 4:25 My children, suffer patiently the wrath that is come upon you from God: for thine enemy hath persecuted thee; but shortly thou shalt see his destruction, and shalt tread upon his neck. 4:26 My delicate ones have gone rough ways, and were taken away as a flock caught of the enemies. 4:27 Be of good comfort, O my children, and cry unto God: for ye shall be remembered of him that brought these things upon you. 4:28 For as it was your mind to go astray from God: so, being returned, seek him ten times more. 4:29 For he that hath brought these plagues upon you shall bring you everlasting joy with your salvation. 4:30 Take a good heart, O Jerusalem: for he that gave thee that name will comfort thee.

Cyril of Jerusalem 386 AD Catechetical Lecture 3, 16: cited along with Isaiah, Ezekiel, etc. without qualification: Be of good courage, O Jerusalem; the Lord will take away all your iniquities. www.newadvent.org/ fathers/310103.htm

4:31 Miserable are they that afflicted thee, and rejoiced at thy fall. 4:32 Miserable are **the cities which thy children served:** miserable is she that received thy sons. 4:33 For as she rejoiced at thy ruin, and was glad of thy fall: so shall she be grieved for her own desolation. 4:34 For I will take away the rejoicing of her great multitude, and her pride shall be turned into mourning. 4:35 **For fire shall come upon her from the Everlasting, long to endure; and she shall be inhabited of devils for a great time.**

Revelation 18:2 (And he cried mightily with a strong voice, saying, Babylon the great is fallen, is fallen, and is become the habitation of devils, and

the hold of every foul spirit, and a cage of every unclean and hateful bird.) 4:36 <u>O Jerusalem, look about thee toward the east, and behold the joy that cometh unto thee from God. 4:37 Lo, thy sons come, whom thou sentest away, they come gathered together from the east to the west by the word of the Holy One, rejoicing in the glory of God.</u>

Matthew 8:11 (And I say unto you, That many shall come from the east and west, and shall sit down with Abraham, and Isaac, and Jacob, in the kingdom of heaven.)

Luke 13:29 (And they shall come from the east, and from the west, and from the north, and from the south, and shall sit down in the kingdom of God.)

5:1 <u>Put off, O Jerusalem, the garment of mourning and affliction, and put on the comeliness of the glory that cometh from God for ever.</u>

Ambrose 394 AD Concerning Repentance 1, 9, 43 And the Lord bids them lay aside the garments of mourning, and to cease the groanings of repentance, saying: Put off, O Jerusalem, the garment of your mourning and affliction. and clothe yourself in beauty, the glory which God has given you forever. www.newadvent. org/fathers/34061.htm

5:2 <u>Cast about thee a double garment of the righteousness which cometh from God; and set a diadem on thine head of the glory of the Everlasting. 5:3 For God will shew thy brightness unto every country under heaven. 5:4 For thy name shall be called of God for ever The peace of righteousness, and The glory of God's worship. 5:5 Arise, O Jerusalem, and stand on high, and look about toward the east, and behold thy children gathered from the west unto the east by the word of the Holy One, rejoicing in the remembrance of God.</u>

Jerome 419 AD Letter 77, 4 I would cite the words of the psalmist: the

sacrifices of God are a broken spirit, and those of Ezekiel I prefer the repentance of a sinner rather than his death, Ezekiel 18:23 and those of Baruch, Arise, arise, O Jerusalem, and many other proclamations made by the trumpets of the prophets. www.newadvent.org/ fathers/3001077.htm

5:6 <u>For they departed from thee on foot, and were led away of their enemies: but God bringeth them unto thee exalted with glory, as children of the kingdom. 5:7 For God hath appointed that every high hill, and banks of long continuance, should be cast down, and valleys filled up, to make even the ground, that Israel may go safely in the glory of God. 5:8 Moreover even the woods and every sweetsmelling tree shall overshadow Israel by the commandment of God. 5:9 For God shall lead Israel with joy in the light of his glory with the mercy and righteousness that cometh from him.</u>

Irenaeus of Lyon 180 AD Against Heresies 5.35: And Jeremiah the prophet has pointed out, that as many believers as God has prepared for this purpose, to multiply those left upon earth, should both be under the rule of the saints to minister to this Jerusalem, and that [His] kingdom shall be in it, saying, Look around Jerusalem towards the east... For God shall go before with joy in the light of His splendour, with the pity and righteousness which proceeds from Him. 4:36-5:9. www.newadvent.org/fathers/ 0103535.htm

Postscript To Baruch: True Churches

My focus ends at 450 AD. But Baruch is a big part of the debate about the Medieval Church, and our experts speak to that. Gallagher translates parts of an article from Pierre-Maurice Bogaert:[397]

> Eventually Jerome's translation overtook the Old Latin Jeremiah, which had included Baruch ... so that [it] virtually disappear[s] in Latin literature for a while.[398] Gregory the Great (d. 600),[399] Isidore (d. 636), and Bede (d. 735 AD)[400] never--or hardly ever-- cite or mention Baruch. Jerome's omission of Baruch ... became a more decisive rejection ... than, for example, his rejection of the Additions to Daniel and Esther, which he condemned in his prefaces but included in his translations. ... The Roman liturgy features Bar 3:9–38 in the Easter Vigil, while other traditions read the same passage on the Saturday before Pentecost. According to Bogaert, "all ancient books cite this reading under the name of Jeremiah," and he then lists 16 examples, up to the fifteenth century. This liturgical use will contribute toward the reintegration of Baruch into Latin Bibles, though it had disappeared from many (due to Jerome's influence), such as the Amiatinus [a Codex produced around 700 AD].

Note that this continuing liturgical use is of the part of Baruch that Irenaeus quoted at length, then said: "This, beloved, is the preaching of the truth ...which the prophets proclaimed, and Christ established, and the apostles delivered, and the Church in all the world hands on to her children. This must we keep with all certainty..." Make of that what you will.

Otherwise, I am in no position to determine what "many" means on a relative basis, but just from the Bibles specifically noted in Gallagher's posts, I counted a lot more Bibles that include Baruch than do not. That may be misleading, however, since he is summarizing a French work for us, and maybe neither his posts nor his source are all inclusive. But it is noteworthy, all the same: clearly there is disagreement, not unanimity, in the Middle Ages.

---

[397] "Le livre de Baruch dans les manuscrits de la Bible latine. Disparition et réintégration," Revue bénédictine 115 (2005): 286–342 at sanctushieronymus.blogspot.com/search/label/Baruch

[398] I am dubious of this claim, though only as an initial matter, since I have not researched it. But I would insist on comparing the data to references we have for comparable books. I presume that they do not call them the "Dark Ages" for nothing, and I suspect there may actually be little evidence for other comparables in that timeframe (just as I found for the years before 200 AD).

[399] Cites to Tobit, Wisdom, and Sirach (not a complete list: I only noticed these by mistake, since it was often hard to sort out which "Gregory" was of Nyssa, of Nazianzus, the Great, etc.).

[400] Notably, he wrote a complete, line-by-line Scriptural commentary on Tobit.

> The most ancient witnesses to the grouping of Jerome's translations are a palimpsest from León (VL 67)[401] and the Amiatinus[402] ... Neither of these contains Baruch. There are several manuscripts--though fragmentary--that date before 800 and contain Jerome's Jeremiah. Bogaert lists 11.

So, that is two Bibles plus 11 fragments. The Bibles are "evidence of absence," but the fragments are not—we really cannot know either way from just a fragment. (We know there are Bibles that have Jerome's Jeremiah and yet also included the Old Latin Baruch, such as the Codex Cavensis (or Biblia de Danila)—see Gallagher and Meade, p. 256.)

In any event, it is clear that Baruch is included in "many" Bibles in the Middle Ages and not included in "many" other Bibles. I have no way to measure which is the majority and which the minority, but in either case, we see that some are now rejecting Baruch, not including it in the canon, and that this is a development of the Middle Ages, not the early Church.[403]

Which should be no surprise to anyone. Gallagher says outright: "it had disappeared from many (due to Jerome's influence)." Before Jerome, we find Baruch; after Jerome, it is absent from "many." But of course, that is somehow a surprise to many.

And that is exactly why I bring it up: what should we make of the actual situation, where it is in the Middle Ages that some start to reject Baruch? Let us turn back to Professor Kruger. Recall that as he is writing, he has forgotten that Baruch et al. were canon to the early Church and only started to disappear in the Middle Ages. So you will have to "translate" from his mention of "adding books" to the actual situation: that of "subtracting books," but he gives us reasons to distrust decisions made by the Church of the Middle Ages:

> ... we must explain how the church in the Middle Ages, and ultimately at the Council of Trent, could divert from this clear foundation and affirm additional books that were not canonical. We noted above that there can be, in principle, "a situation where the

---

[401] Which is incomplete, so not all of its contents are known, but it included Wisdom, Sirach, Tobit, Judith, and 1 and 2 Maccabees. I found no mention of whether or not Daniel included Susanna. That is six—and possibly all seven—of the other Apocrypha. textus-receptus.com/wiki/Le%C3%B3n_palimpsest

[402] Contains Susanna, Tobit, Judith, Wisdom, Sirach, and 1 and 2 Maccabees (i.e., every Apocrypha except Baruch). wikipedia.org/wiki/Codex_Amiatinus

[403] Note that the existence of diversity and disagreement during the Middle Ages is not an argument for the exclusion of Baruch. Kruger himself makes the point many times that unanimity is not an honest criterion. "For many modern scholars, the validity of the church's final consensus on the canon is disproved simply by showing that at some point early Christians disagreed over its boundaries. The mere existence of diversity itself has become the argument..." (p. 197).

Spirit's testimony was so obscured by the church's sin and rebellion that the church reached consensus on books that are not canonical." No doubt we have good reasons to think that the extensive moral and doctrinal corruption of the church in the Middle Ages— which stood in opposition to the consensus of the Jewish believers, as well as the teachings of Jesus and the New Testament-would constitute just such a situation. The apocryphal books would have been attractive to the church during this time since they were used to justify doctrines, like purgatory and prayers for the dead, that were at the heart of the ecclesiastical abuse of power. Indeed, so substantial was this corruption, especially in regard to the gospel message, that legitimate questions can be raised about whether the Roman Catholic Church continued to be the true church of Jesus Christ—and therefore a place where the Spirit was actively working (and if, lacking the Spirit, it is not the true church, then its affirmation of the apocryphal books is not relevant). But even if one accepts Roman Catholicism as a true church, the fact remains that we have good grounds for believing that, in this instance, the Spirit's witness was widely obscured by the church's sin and rebellion. Of course, at this point one might raise the following objection: If the church was mistaken about the Old Testament books, how can we be sure that it was not mistaken about the New Testament books? But it is here that we must remember our model: we have warrant for thinking that the church's consensus is a reliable indicator of canonicity, unless we have good reasons to think the contrary. In regard to the very specific situation of the Roman Catholic Church's acceptance of the Apocrypha at the Council of Trent, we do have good reasons to think the contrary. But in regard to the New Testament canon, we have no reasons to think that the [early] church was mistaken in this regard. ...[404]

I submit that, once again, Kruger makes an argument for why Baruch, Susanna, and perhaps the other Apocrypha should be Scripture: we cannot trust the Church of the Middle Ages.

Less sarcastically, Kruger does not imagine that it may have worked in reverse; maybe the decision makers in the Church already believed the books were Scripture, which is why they developed the doctrines, which were then taken too far in later years. There are two different theories of what happened, and there is evidence to show which is correct, i.e., which came first: belief that the books were Scripture and therefore a desire to implement doctrines, or a desire to implement doctrines that led to adding the books to the existing Scripture? When we look at the evidence, Baruch itself shows us that the second view (Kruger's view) is the one that is wrong (at least in part), and that at least some Apocrypha were accepted as Scripture long before the doctrines of the Middle Ages. The only question is whether Kruger's view is wrong on all the Apocrypha or just some.

---

[404] Chapter 6, Footnote 11, p. 201.

Overall, Kruger's argument for the truth and authenticity of the New Testament is not really a problem for those who accept the Apocrypha. If we accept the Apocrypha, his model works just fine.

But I have already made that point. My new point here is that the early Church Fathers also provide us with evidence of what the early Church was actually like. Since I did the reading, here is my book report. (You're welcome.) The following are just a few chapter titles from Rufinus' Apology Against Jerome and Jerome's Apology Against Rufinus:[405]

The Apology of Rufinus
- I am no heretic, but declare my faith, that of my baptism.
- Eusebius, if acting honestly, should have shown me what he thought dangerous.
- Jerome's complaint of new doctrines may be retorted on himself.
- Jerome says that the defenders of Origen are united in a federation of perjury.
- Jerome has not only allowed perjury but has practised it.
- His treatise on Virginity defames all orders of Christians.
- Jerome at Bethlehem had heathen books copied and taught them to boys.
- A Synod, if called on to condemn Origen, must condemn Jerome also.

Jerome's Apology Against Rufinus
- I had praised Eusebius [and] Origen … and was forced to condemn them as heretics…
- The story of Hilary's being condemned through his writings having been falsified has no foundation.
- The attack on Epiphanius as a plagiarist of Origen is an outrage …
- Why do you, by threats of death, compel me to answer?
- Had you translated honestly, you would not have had Origen's heresies imputed to you.
- You swear that you did not write my pretended retractation. Your style betrays you, and I have given a full answer about my translations already.
- You bid me beware of falsification and treachery. You warn me against yourself.
- It was not I who first disclosed your heresies, but Epiphanius long ago …

In just this handful of headlines, we have allegations made against six of the 10 Fathers Kruger cites to as proof that the sheep heard the Shepherd's voice. They are accused of heresy, dishonesty, plagiarism, perjury, forgery, defaming all Christians, corrupting minors, falsification, treachery, outrage on the church leaders, etc. And those are the Church Fathers: the leaders, the teachers, the best and the brightest, those worth reading and learning from. So what was the rest of the church like...?

---

[405] www.newadvent.org/fathers/2705.htm and www.newadvent.org/fathers/2710.htm; there are hundreds of chapter titles of this stuff, let alone hundreds of pages of detailed allegations to read.

At an even earlier date, Acts and the Epistles are full of false preaching (2 Peter 3:14-18, 1 John 4:1-6, Titus 1:10-16, 2 Peter 2, Acts 13:5-12, Acts 15:1-27, Acts 20:29, etc.). 1 John 2:19 notes that the Apostles themselves sent out false preachers: "They went out from us, but they were not of us...." In Revelation, the church of Ephesus had to deal with false Apostles; Pergamos had people who held the doctrine of the Nicolaitans, "which thing I hate;" Thyatira had Jezebel, "which calleth herself a prophetess." Five of the seven churches in Revelation deal with false teaching.

How did Jesus handle that situation at Thyatira?

> And I gave her [Jezebel] space to repent of her fornication; and she repented not.

He gave her space. He allowed her to continue. A true Church had a cancer in it, one preaching false Prophecy, and Jesus Christ let her continue.

> Behold, I will cast her into a bed, and them that commit adultery with her into great tribulation, except they repent of their deeds. And I will kill her children with death; and all the churches shall know that I am he which searcheth the reins and hearts: and I will give unto every one of you according to your works.

He allows the heresy to continue within His church, and allows it to continue to draw people to their doom.

And so, too, with the disciples: Jesus knew Judas would not be a believer from the very beginning (John 6:64: "Jesus knew from the beginning who they were that believed not, and who should betray him."). Yet He sent Judas out to preach (Matthew Ch. 10, Mark 6:7+, Luke Ch. 9). He sends the betrayer, a man He knows does not actually believe, out to preach—the seeming definition of a wolf among the sheep, and it is Jesus Himself who grants the wolf His authority to preach.

Even the good disciples were not able to fully process and preach Jesus' message. Luke 9:54-56: "And when his disciples James and John saw this, they said, Lord, wilt thou that we command fire to come down from heaven... But he turned, and rebuked them, and said, Ye know not what manner of spirit ye are of." In Galatians 2:11+, we read that "when Peter was come to Antioch, I withstood him to the face, because he was to be blamed. ... And the other Jews dissembled likewise with him; insomuch that Barnabas also was carried away with their dissimulation. But when I saw that they walked not uprightly according to the truth of the gospel, I said unto Peter ..."

That they dissembled and "walked not uprightly according to the truth of the gospel" would seem to meet the definition of Kruger's "corruption, especially in regard to the gospel message"—and that was done by the chief Disciple (installed as such by Jesus Christ Himself, empowered by Pentecost, Divinely-inspired to write his own Sacred Scriptures, etc.) and many other leaders of the very earliest Church.

Biblically, a true Church always has false preaching going on within it, and we all should know full well that it has always been so and (according to Revelations) will always be so. The disciples had to watch heresy infect their own Church and faithless preachers go out from them to preach lies. They told us not to lose faith but to hold fast: the gates of Hell shall not prevail.

The existence of sin, rebellion, and "corruption, especially in regard to the Gospel message" sounds like a slam dunk argument against a Church—as it surely would be against every single Church ever, were it to be compared to purity. But the only purity is God; the Church was not pure, even in its earliest days. If we want to apply Kruger's idea, then the Church of the Middle Ages should be compared to the Church of the Bible, and the early Church, and their sin, rebellion, and corruption. Based on my readings into the early Church, I confidently predict that the Church of the Middle Ages would hold up just fine.

After all, for the Church of the Middle Ages to be "a situation where the Spirit's testimony was so obscured by the church's sin and rebellion that the church reached consensus on books that are not canonical," then it would have to be a whole lot worse than Basil the Great's authentic eye witness testimony from right in the middle of the "canon list era" (the 370s):

> ... all is in a weak state; the Church has given way before the continuous attacks of her foes ... The doctrines of the Fathers are despised; apostolic traditions are set at nought; the devices of innovators are in vogue in the Churches; now men are rather contrivers of cunning systems...[406]

---

[406] newadvent.org/fathers/3202090.htm. Basil of course accepted Apocrypha as doctrine of the Fathers and authentic Apostolic tradition, e.g., Letter 8, 10: "Now let us examine, and to the best of our ability explain, the meaning of the words of Holy Scripture, which our opponents seize and wrest to their own sense, and urge against us for the destruction of the glory of the Only-begotten....How then can the two following passages stand? The Spirit of the Lord fills the world..." (Citing Wisdom 1:7 For the Spirit of the Lord filleth the world: and that which containeth all things hath knowledge of the voice) www.newadvent.org/fathers/3202008.htm.

THE WISDOM OF SOLOMON

The Book of Wisdom is, of course, oddly named. It is confused with the Book of Sirach, which is technically named the Book of the Wisdom of Jesus the Son of Sirach. And other books (such as Proverbs, as might be the case with Melito's list) could sometimes be called "Wisdom" as well.

Second, the Book's author is unknown, so there is no other name attached to it. There are all sorts of guesses about the author, including "the friends of Solomon." In fact, Sirach is sometimes thought to be the author, which makes things doubly confusing.

And third, the reference "of Solomon" is both confusing yet appropriate. The phrase "of Solomon" was sometimes an idiom, meaning "a Book containing wisdom like Solomon's" (e.g., Sirach was sometimes called one of the Books "of Solomon" when, clearly, Solomon did not write it). Plus, there was a literary convention of adopting the name of a famous man of old to "father" one's work. Thus, David was said to have authored all the psalms; the name "Mosaic" law could be applied to laws and rulings that came long after Moses; and "Jeremiah is the author of Lamentations in a symbolic sense but probably not in a literal sense. Authorship in the ancient world did not follow modern customs. In order to bring Books under the aura of heroes and their moral authority, writings were often ascribed to them."[407] Thus, Solomon was the father of all wisdom, not just his own. Such might explain why the Muratorian Fragment identifies the authors as "the friends of Solomon"— lovers of wisdom, perhaps.

But also, the Book of Wisdom does have passages that (a) do not name Solomon and yet (b) imply that Solomon is speaking (see, e.g., 7:1+). That could be a literary device—the Bible is filled with quotes, conversations and even entire speeches that the authors did not witness (and no one could possibly think they had, except via Divine inspiration, of course).[408] And yet the Book of Wisdom also includes passages that clearly distinguish the author

---

[407] New Interpreter's Bible, Introduction to Lamentations, p. 1016.
[408] Examples include the author of Genesis quoting the words of Adam, or Luke quoting the words of the angel that visited Zacharias, who was already "well stricken in years" and had to be long dead by the time Luke was writing. All the usual explanations and defenses Christians give (including literary device, memories passed down and memorized word-for-word, Divine inspiration, etc.) could, of course, apply to the Book of Wisdom as well.

from Solomon, such as Wisdom 8:15: "I shall be found good among the multitude, and valiant in war" (cf. 1 Chronicles 22:9: ... for his name shall be Solomon, and I will give peace and quietness unto Israel in his days).

The dating of the Book of Wisdom is late (it would be the youngest Book of the Old Testament), and the latest possible date actually depends on the New Testament, since the Evangelists' evident familiarity with it means that it had to have been written some years before the New Testament. If, like me, you believe in the actual truthful historicity of the New Testament, then we would also say that Jesus' evident familiarity with it means that it had to be written well before He spoke and made His allusions to the Book (since His audience had to have learned it, etc.).[409]

Meanwhile, Gallagher and Meade, with characteristic understatement, note that Wisdom "was certainly an important book in early Christianity." (p. 81). The KJV cross-references the Wisdom with the New Testament 24% more often (per verse) than any "canonical" Poetic Book (and three times as often as two of the Books, and 10 times as often as one of the Books).

I have listed over 200 possible references to the Book of Wisdom in the New Testament. On average, every other verse of the Book has a possible New Testament reference.

We have also seen that the Book of Wisdom appears to be tied to the Epistle to the Hebrews and the Gospel to the Jews. But the Epistle to the Hebrews and the Gospel to the Jews are not unique. Pretty much everything in the New Testament seems to reference Wisdom; for example, other Epistles from Paul the Perfectly Taught Jew (in particular Romans (see note at 11:15 below), Ephesians (see note at 5:20 below), 1 Corinthians (see e.g. note at 9:17 below), and Colossians (see note at 9:2 below), etc.) all seem to devote considerable attention to the Book of Wisdom.

As for the early Church, Biblindex.org/citation_biblique/search notes 1,798 references to Wisdom from early Fathers. Compare to Job, also a Poetic Book, with 4552, at a rate of 4.262 references per verse (Job has 1068 verses). The Book of Wisdom has 436 verses, so an essentially identical rate of 4.124.

---

[409] This applies regardless of whether the allusions amount to a showing that the Book is Scripture, since the mere existence of any such allusion means that the dating for the Book would have to be well before Jesus is speaking. Of course what allusions you recognize are up to you, but Wisdom is another case where not recognizing at least some of them sets a standard that would prevent you from ever proving much of anything yourself.

The Book of Wisdom is cited by the early Church more times than 17 of the 39 canonical Old Testament Books. In fact, it is cited by the early Church more times than nine canonical Old Testament Books combined: Obadiah, Nahum, Zephaniah, Esther, Ruth, Haggai, Nehemiah, Habakkuk, and Joel. And those nine Books combine for 1050 verses; Wisdom only has 436.

I found more citations as full Scripture (well over 500, from over 50 Fathers) than there are total citations (including a great many debatable and vague "allusions") for nine Books.[410] And from 1 Clement to Justin Martyr to Irenaeus to Clement of Alexandria, we find references as early as any Book— and full citations as early as most. By 350 AD (the date of the earliest certain Christian list that specifically excludes Wisdom), it had been cited 758 times (per Biblindex), of which it was expressly stated to be Scripture at least 150 times (solely that I could find, so that is a substantial undercount). We also know that Wisdom was read as part of the Liturgy in the early Churches.[411]

Cassiodorus (circa 550 AD) says that the "priest Bellator stated that he himself undertook a commentary on this volume in eight books and we keep this work together with his other shorter works."[412] The commentary is lost, but there was a Basilica built and named after Bellator in "the late fourth or early fifth century,"[413] it was probably written by the mid-300s AD.

When we looked at canon lists, we saw that the title "Wisdom" appears on every single Christian canon list until 350 AD. All but one of those are clear references to the Book of Wisdom; the one (Melito's) is just the word Wisdom, which may be a reference to the Book (or an alternative name for Proverbs). Ultimately, the Book of Wisdom appears on a majority of all lists— just counting lists. If you give the Council votes more weight for the numbers of Fathers participating, it is then, of course, overwhelmingly supported by the lists.[414] And all four surviving Bible codices also include the Book of Wisdom.

---

[410] I stopped looking for them once I had reached 500. How many there really are, I do not know.

[411] See, e.g., Rufinus Commentary on the Apostles' Creed 38 at newadvent.org/fathers/2711.htm.

[412] faculty.georgetown.edu/jod/inst-trans.html, 5.5.

[413] wikipedia.org/wiki/Archaeological_site_of_Sbeitla

[414] Even lists that place Wisdom in a "third category" are not dismissing it. In fact, they intend for it to be read <u>before</u> one moves on to the Bible. *The Spirit and the Letter: Studies in the Biblical Canon* by John Barton (p. 55-56) tells us that: "For catechumens, as we know from even so late a writer as Athanasius, non-canonical Christian books were probably deemed more useful reading [than the Books of the canonical Bible]... For the beginner... the effective 'canon' would be the New Testament and wisdom books. Perhaps we have here the explanation for the Muratorian Fragment's inclusion of the Wisdom of Solomon with the books of the New Testament."

All in all, the case for the Book of Wisdom as canon is about as strong as it could be (given that we have something to argue about) with respect to the early Church and the Bible. Thus, I will focus on our third prong: the Jews.

Wisdom seems to have been written in Greek—and after the Septuagint Greek translations of Hebrew Scriptures had been made (it quotes the Septuagint Isaiah, Job, etc.). Therefore, for Jerome, the later Jews, and others who subscribe to "Hebraica Veritas," Wisdom could not be Scripture. By the rule they have chosen to follow, it simply cannot be, and nothing else matters.

Whether that is the correct rule and why, I leave to you. But for our purposes, Wisdom appears to have been included with the Greek Jewish Scriptures (it is considered part of the Septuagint), and Nachmanides cited to it in his 1270 AD Commentary on the Torah (per Sundberg in the Canon Debate, p. 88). Recall that the scholars say the author of the Epistle to the Hebrews (among whom would be the many Priests that had converted (Acts 6:7)):

> ... "belonged to the more liberal school known as the Hellenists. The Bible which he used and from which he constantly quotes, is the Greek translation known as the Septuagint (LXX), and not the original Hebrew text, with which he does not seem to have been acquainted." Abingdon Bible Commentary.
>
> "a person well educated in Greek rhetoric as well as in Judaism, especially Hellenistic Judaism formed in part by the Septuagint, a Greek translation of the Old Testament. The Greek translation and not the Hebrew text provides the major lines and the subtler nuances of the writer's argument and appeal. ... The Scripture for the writer of Hebrews is the Old Testament in Greek translation... the Septuagint (LXX)..." NIB.
>
> "Whoever the author was, he preferred citing OT references from the Greek OT (LXX) rather than from the Hebrew text...." John F. MacArthur Study Bible.

In fact, the Epistle to the Hebrews is so intertwined with the Book of Wisdom that Plumptre proposed that they were both written by Apollos. It also includes an even earlier Christological hymn that explained the nature of Christ and His Divinity by alluding to the Book of Wisdom, using two crucial terms taken directly from the Book of Wisdom, thereby making an implicit claim that Jesus Christ fulfilled the statements in the Book of Wisdom.

Basically, one theory of history is that the Jews reinvented themselves after 70 AD (the old religion of the Temple was gone forever), and they "circled the wagons." They distanced themselves from things not "purely Jewish" and tried to get back to their roots (no Books that were not written in Hebrew, older Books rather than newer ones, etc.) to protect their cultural identity.

That is just a polite way of saying that bigotry reigned supreme (on all sides, as always), and the attitude that triumphed was that which we glimpse in the Bible: "Can there any good thing come out of Nazareth?" (John 1:46), "But some said, Shall Christ come out of Galilee?" (John 7:41), "saying one to another, Behold, are not all these which speak Galilaeans?" (Acts 2:7), etc.

The theory goes that they pressured everyone who disagreed until, eventually, the non-Hebrew Scriptures were found only among Christians.

But countering that theory, we have Kruger, Geisler, the Apologetics Study Bible, Don Stewart and the Blue Letter Bible website, etc.—all of whom claim that the Jewish canon was firmly established and always had been.

So, let's look at the evidence to see whether it supports the claim that the Hebrew canon was established at the time of Christ.

One: the modern Jews say otherwise. The Jewish Study Bible says that the firm canon came later. Until then, it had fuzzy edges and was in flux.

Two: the KJV and other Biblical evidence (the Apocrypha-focus of the Epistle to the Hebrews, the Gospel to the Jews, etc.) seems to show that Jesus and the Evangelists allude to the Book of Wisdom many times, in deep and meaningful ways—even though they could have easily referenced many other Scriptures instead, if their audience preferred those Books.

Three: the Fathers of the early Church repeatedly disagree, saying that the Jewish canon was in flux (e.g., their lists for the Jews kept changing), and Epiphanius the Jewish Christian from Jerusalem tells us that the Jews were still disputing the Book of Wisdom in 385 AD. The Fathers also note that the Jewish leaders "hid from the knowledge of the people ... took away from the people every passage ... concealed and removed from the Scriptures..."

Four: Greek scrolls were found at Qumran, which have never been found in their "original" Hebrew. One example is the Epistle of Jeremiah (Baruch Chapter 6 in Catholic Bibles), and whether it was originally written in Hebrew is unknown and debated. But it is notable that it was not stored with a Hebrew version, which would seem to indicate that it was accepted in Greek, not in Hebrew, by a group that did not insist on reading Hebrew in their services.[415]

Five: the Rabbis had the means, motive, and opportunity to reject Books that some (or all) Jews had once accepted, and to do so because Christians had accepted them. The Jewish Study Bible: "because prefigurations of Jesus and Christian resurrection were seen in Daniel by the early church, the rabbinic tradition hesitated to embrace the visions of Daniel." The Rabbis were considering abandoning a Book that many (if not all) Jews had accepted as

---

[415] wikipedia.org/wiki/Letter_of_Jeremiah

Divinely-inspired Prophecy and Scripture for centuries. They did not do so with such a "core" Book, but they still minimized Daniel by not including it among the Prophets. They clearly had a focus on Christians and a desire to reject what Christians accept. The Jewish Study Bible: "the Septuagint ... material [i.e., Susanna, at a minimum] ... was excluded from the Jewish canon, perhaps as early as the end of the first century A.D." And perhaps, so were the other Apocrypha.

Six: there is evidence that the Jews did exactly what they were accused of: "The Talmud tells a similar story [to the Maccabean Martyrs], but with refusal to worship an idol replacing refusal to eat pork... the king is referred to as the "Caesar"..." and then, later, the Josippon "was notable as the first major exposure of medieval Jewish audiences to the story." That Talmud also identifies the modern Jewish/Protestant canon.

In any event, the Jewish canon is only a "blocker"—it is raised as a way to keep the Apocrypha out. If the Apocrypha are not blocked by the Jewish canon, then the focus returns to the early Church's view of them.

Let's move on to that, then. Below is the Book of Wisdom, annotated to show possible Biblical references.[416] Non-KJV sources note a great many references to Wisdom missed by the KJV (even though the KJV still cross-references Wisdom with the New Testament 24% more often (per verse) than any "canonical" Poetic Book (and three times as often as two of the Books, and 10 times as often as one of the Books)).

Recall that Plumptre's analysis of the Epistle to the Hebrews showed two dozen different word/phrase choices that seem to be taken from the Book of Wisdom, such that he states that "their weight in the scale of evidence is more than numerical; that they are, for the most part, words either characteristic themselves, or used in a characteristic sense; and that they thus tend to establish such a close affinity of thought and language as may best be explained by the hypothesis of identity of authorship." We do not need to accept his conclusion, but perhaps the quantity and quality of the evidence points to the acceptance of the Book of Wisdom by Jesus, the Evangelists, and their audience of Jews, including Priests. It is, otherwise, hard to explain why

---

[416] In addition to KJV references, many others were noted in Gary G. Michuta's book, *The Case for the Deuterocanon*, and Plumptre's article. Note that Plumptre's parallels may be linguistic and difficult to see in the English translation.

the New Testament (and in particular, the Books directed toward Jews) share such a "close affinity of thought and language" with a Book that claims to be Scripture.

Many of the New Testament references are quite notable, including those already discussed above. In addition, let's consider three more. The first is from the Evangelical Biblical Theology Commentary, discussing Matthew 16:19 ("And I say also unto thee, That thou art Peter, and upon this rock I will build my church; and the gates of hell shall not prevail against it"):

> Hades was the realm of the dead. The purpose of the gates of Hades was to prevent its inhabitants from escaping and reentering the realm of the living. The gates were intended not to keep people out but to keep them in. Yet Hades would not be able to keep the followers of Jesus incarcerated. They would smash the gates, escape Hades' grip, and enjoy life again. Thus Jesus's statement is a promise of resurrection. The phrase "gates of Hades" appears five times in the LXX (3 Macc 5:51; Ode 11:10; Wisdom 16:13; Pss. Sol. 16:2; Isa 38:10) and is equivalent to the phrase "gates of death" (núai Cavátov; cf. Job 38:17; Ps 9:14). Wisdom 16:13 described God as having the power to rescue his people from the gates of Hades: "You have the power of life and of death; you bring down to the gates of Hades and you bring up again." God will exercise that power for the sake of Jesus's followers.

Second, Wisdom 2:24 (through envy of the devil came death into the world) is the first time in Scripture/Apocrypha that the serpent of Genesis 3:1-15 is openly identified with the Devil. We then find that reference throughout the New Testament (John 8:44; Revelation 12:9; Paul alludes to this verse many times: Romans 5:12, 16:20, Hebrews 2:14). In fact, the Greek word for "envy" is phthonos, which never appears in the Protestant Old Testament. In the Book of Wisdom, envy is directly opposed to wisdom (Wis 6:23 "Neither will I go with consuming envy; for such a man shall have no fellowship with wisdom") and is depicted as the evil behind the Devil's actions in Genesis (Wis 2:24). In the New Testament, envy was the motivation behind the Crucifixion (Matthew 27:18, Mark 15:10), and a linkage is noted between envy/phthonos, murder, and the Devil (e.g., John 8:44 "Ye are of your father the devil, and the lusts of your father ye will do. He was a murderer from the beginning..."), which may explain some word choices and orderings in the New Testament (Romans 1:29: ... full of envy, murder; Galatians 5:21: Envyings, murders...). It may also explain what James is paraphrasing in James 4:5, a "quotation" from Scripture that is not found in Scripture: "Do ye think that the scripture saith in vain, "The spirit that dwelleth in us lusteth to envy?" ... 7Submit yourselves therefore to God. Resist the devil..."[417]

Third, Chapters 13-15 of Wisdom parallel many other Scriptural condemnations of idolatry. But Paul, in his Epistle to the Romans, will adopt many specific elements of the Book of Wisdom's approach. The KJV noted three such references, but there are many more, as we will see below.

As for the early Fathers, there are so many references to the Book of Wisdom as Scripture that it would take far too many pages to give you the wording for all of them (it would be more citations than the preceding four Books combined). So, all I provide is a chronological chart.

But recall that we are often told of the power of the Fourfold Gospel to prove the Truth of Christianity. We have four varying eyewitness accounts, from four different perspectives, giving us the same, consistent story—all relatively shortly after the Resurrection. So, consider just four of the citations to the status of the Book of Wisdom within the Church before 200 AD:

> Justin Martyr (Rome, Italy) 155 AD, describing a debate twenty years earlier (135 AD): I now refer to the Scriptures as the Seventy have interpreted them ... when the prophet says, 'I saved you in the times of Noah,' ... by water, faith, and wood, those who are afore-prepared, and who repent of the sins which they have committed, shall escape from the impending judgment of God. (Wisdom 10:4)[418]
>
> Irenaeus of Lyon (France) 177 AD: cited along with 1 Corinthians etc. without qualification: ...the beholding of God is productive of immortality, but immortality renders one near unto God. (Wisdom 6:19)[419]
>
> Tertullian (Carthage, Tunisia) 198 AD: We are taught by God concerning both these questions — viz. that there is a ruling power in the soul, and that it is enshrined in one particular recess of the body. For, when one reads of God as being the searcher and witness of the heart... (Wisdom 1:6)[420]
>
> Clement of Alexandria (Egypt) 198 AD: The divine Wisdom says of the martyrs, They seemed in the eyes of the foolish to die, and their departure was reckoned a calamity, and their migration from us an affliction. ... For though in the sight of men they were punished, their hope was full of immortality. (Wisdom 3:2-4)[421]

---

[417] And "Irenaeus was the first Christian to understand Genesis 3:15 as a prophecy about Christ (and Mary)..." Evidence for Christianity, Josh McDowell, citing Claus Westermann. Furthermore, one could see this allusion from James 4:5 to Wisdom 2:24 as meeting Don Stewart's three formulae (specifically "Scripture says")—see the discussion in Sidebar 4 above.

[418] Dialogue with Trypho 137-138: www.newadvent.org/fathers/01289.htm

[419] 180 AD *Against Heresies* 4, 38, 3: www.newadvent.org/fathers/0103438.htm. Eusebius confirms this citation for us: 324 AD, Church History 5, 8, 8: [Re: Irenaeus] "And he uses almost the precise words of the Wisdom of Solomon, saying: The vision of God produces immortality..."

[420] On the Soul 15: www.newadvent.org/fathers/0310.htm

[421] Stromata 4, 16: www.newadvent.org/fathers/02104.htm

Before 200 AD, Justin in Rome alludes to the Book of Wisdom as Scripture and Prophecy, Irenaeus in Lyon apparently agrees, Tertullian in Carthage calls it the teaching of God, and Clement in Egypt calls it the Divine Wisdom. Those are four witnesses of widely different upbringings, backgrounds, geographies, and languages. Justin may have entered the Church before the last Books of the New Testament were written. Irenaeus is one step removed from John. Tertullian was the first theologian to write in Latin.

Clement has been called "the first Christian scholar" (Shelley), "the first systematic teacher of Christian doctrine" (Patrick), "the first great teacher of philosophical Christianity" (Hatch), "the first self-conscious theologian and ethicist" (Backhouse), "the first great Christian teacher in Alexandria" (Needham), "the founder of Christian philosophical theology" (Bray), "the true creator of ecclesiastical theology" (DeFaye), "the first major commentator on the Bible" (Bray), "the founder of Christian literature" (ANF), "the great founder of the Alexandrian School" (Coxe), a "pioneer of Christian scholarship" (ACCS), "an intellectual giant in the early church" (Kruger), and "that man of genius who introduced Christianity to itself" (Coxe).[422]

Four eyewitnesses from the earliest days give us evidence that Wisdom had long been accepted as Scripture.[423] And so, once again, we have the problem: how did four pillars of the very earliest Church all end up preaching that the Book of Wisdom is authentic Scripture, Prophecy, teaching of God, and Divine Wisdom, given that we are told that the Jews, Jesus and the Apostles never accepted the Book of Wisdom as such?

In fact, that foursome is not even our first Fourfold testimony to the Book of Wisdom. We could construct an even earlier one: Clement of Rome alluded to it four times before 96 AD (and possibly before 70 AD); the Epistle of Barnabas also does so (latest date 135 AD, but the range goes back to 40 AD); Polycarp (107 AD), in Section 6 of his Epistle, may make an allusion to Wisdom 6:7; and the Odes of Solomon (per Wikipedia, a "majority of scholars believe it to have been written by a Jewish Christian... between AD 70 and 125") allude to it many times (e.g. 6, 10 re: Wisdom 1:7).[424]

---

[422] Mostly taken from wikipedia.org/wiki/Clement_of_Alexandria.
[423] And do not forget the canon lists: the Muratorian Canon includes the Book of Wisdom (170 AD?), and Melito's list says Wisdom (170 AD).
[424] www.gnosis.org/library/odes.htm

That would be four writings contemporaneous with the New Testament or shortly after. Nor are they alone—there are many fragmentary and anonymous writings from the period that also evidence the acceptance of Wisdom, such as the Didache, the Shepherd of Hermas, the Epistle of the Gallican churches, Lugdunum and Vienna (177 AD),[425] and other early writings.

Chapter 1 was cited 250 times per biblindex.org/citation_biblique/search (more citations from the early Church than for five entire canonical Old Testament Books). Here are the dates for the earliest possible citations to just the first few verses, with a comparison to another Poetic Book, Ecclesiastes:

Wis.	First Cite	Year	Eccl.	First Cite	Year
1:1	Tertullian	198 AD	1:1	Origen	245 AD
1:2	Origen	239 AD	1:2	Clement	190 AD
1:3	Origen	222 AD	1:3	Dionysius(?)	250 AD
1:4	Ps-Clement	201 AD	1:4	Origen	222 AD
1:5	Origen	222 AD	1:5	Victorinus	250 AD
1:6	Clement	190 AD	1:6	Origen	248 AD
1:7	Odes of Solomon	75 AD	1:7	Methodius	280 AD

Hardly the greatest statistical analysis ever done, but I think it is enough to show that the Book of Wisdom was cited both early and thoroughly.

Just in citations to Chapter 1, we have a couple interesting explanations of who is speaking in the Book of Wisdom. Chromatius says it is "what Solomon says in the persona of wisdom," and Tertullian says that it is "the teaching of God." I.e., it does not appear that they base their determinations of its status as Scripture on the identity of the person holding the pen (as with Hebrews).

Eusebius (who cites to the Book of Wisdom as Christian Scripture many times) tells us in his Preparation of the Gospel that Wisdom is part of the "Hebrew Scripture" and that Wisdom 1:13 is "a doctrine of the Hebrews." That testimony of what the Jews believed is written 300 years after Christ.[426]

Jerome shows inconsistency again, using the Book of Wisdom as Scripture to prove authentic Christian doctrine when arguing against the Pelagians, who

---

[425] Preserved in the Church History of Eusebius, Bk V. Ch. 1-3, which alludes to Wisdom several times (e.g., Ch 1, Section 63 re: Wisdom 2:17): www.newadvent.org/fathers/250105.htm

[426] And he continues to do so throughout his work. E.g., Book 7, 12 "Let us therefore look also at the oracles of the Hebrews...." before quoting Wisdom 8:1; and Book 12, 52 "The meaning of this, if not the actual words, has been previously set down very briefly in the oracles of the Hebrews, the thought being comprised in few words..." before quoting Wisdom 8:5. Note that he cannot recognize anything resembling "Hebraica Veritas," since Wisdom is a Greek book, not Hebrew.

may have denied the authority of the Book. But at other times, Jerome declared Wisdom to be "not in the canon" and "read for the strengthening of the people, (but) not for confirming the authority of ecclesiastical dogmas." Origen and Epiphanius (the latter consistent with the position he takes on his canon lists, as discussed elsewhere), and Athanasius, Hilary of Poitiers, and Gregory of Nazianzus (all inconsistent with the positions taken on their canon lists, and yet all to confirm doctrines—in fact, Athanasius cites it in his Defense before Constantius) also cite to Wisdom Chapter 1.[427]

Tertullian cited to Wisdom Chapter 1 in his Prescription against the heretics, Against the Valentinians, and Against Marcion; Cyprian cited to it Against the Jews; Origen cited to it many times Against Celsus; Epiphanius also cited to it many times against heresies in his Panarion; and Augustine cited to it in his Morals of the Catholic Church, his Answer to the Letters of Petilian (five times), his Letter Against the Donatists, his Answer to Maximinus the Arian, and his Reply to Faustus. [428]

So, that would be dozens of times that the first chapter alone is used to fight major heresies and determine fundamental doctrines, including citations by Jerome and Athanasius (two of the three (the other being Rufinus) who would later claim that Wisdom is only being read by the Church and/or not being used to establish doctrine). Below, I show two such uses, from names we have not already brought up endlessly: Archelaus in 278 AD against the Manichaeans and Basil the Great defending himself and his own Faith. Notable is the silence from the alleged heretics or from the rest of the Church regarding these citations that (some claim) are contrary to all precedent, practice, and Scripture of the early Church.

By Chapter 2, the flood of possible New Testament citations has begun in earnest, so I devote little space to annotating "mere" citations after Chapter 1.

---

[427] Athanasius Festal Letter 3, 4 quoted Wisdom 1:5 to confirm that evil works drives out the indwelling Holy Spirit. www.newadvent.org/fathers/2806003.htm; and www.newadvent.org/fathers/2813.htm, 5; Hilary ccel.org/ccel/schaff/npnf209.iii.iv.ii.xxviii.html Gregory Oration 28, 8 quoted Wisdom 1:7 to confirm that God pervades all things and fills all. www.newadvent.org/fathers/310228.htm

[428] Tertullian www.newadvent.org/fathers/0311.htm, 7; www.newadvent.org/fathers/0314.htm, 2; ccel.org/ccel/schaff/anf03.v.iii.vii.html; Cyprian www.newadvent.org/fathers/050712c.htm 3, 53; Origen www.newadvent.org/fathers/04163.htm 3,60; 4,5; 5,29; 7,8; Epiphanius Panarion, Section 3, Heresy 44, 28, 2; Section 3, Heresy 44, 39, 6; Section 3, Heresy 44, 54, 4; Section 4, Heresy 54, 1, 4; Augustine www.newadvent.org/fathers/1401.htm 16, 29; www.newadvent.org/fathers/14092.htm 2, 26; 2, 61; www.newadvent.org/fathers/14093.htm 3, 29; 3, 31; 3, 35; Answer to Maximinus the Arian XXI, 2; www.newadvent.org/fathers/140621.htm 21, 9.

Wisdom: Annotated

1:1 Love righteousness, ye that be judges of the earth: think of the Lord with a good (heart,) and <u>in simplicity of heart seek him</u>.

Chromatius 407 AD Tractate on Matthew 41, 5 [Referred to as prophecy in 41, 1:] This accords with what Solomon says in the persona of wisdom: ..." Not available online.

Jerome 420 AD Against the Pelagians, Bk I, 33: Do you expect me to explain the purposes and plans of God? ... In wisdom and simplicity of heart seek God. You will perhaps deny the authority of this book; listen then to the Apostle blowing the Gospel trumpet..." www.newadvent.org/fathers/30111.htm

1:2 For he will be found of them that tempt him not; and sheweth himself unto such as do not distrust him. 1:3 For froward thoughts separate from God: and his power, when it is tried, reproveth the unwise. 1:4 For into a malicious soul wisdom shall not enter; nor dwell in the body that is subject unto sin. 1:5 For the holy spirit of discipline will flee deceit, and remove from thoughts that are without understanding, and will not abide when unrighteousness cometh in. 1:6 <u>**For wisdom is a loving spirit**</u>; and will not acquit a blasphemer of his words: for <u>**God is witness of his reins, and a true beholder of his heart**</u>, and a hearer of his tongue.

Galatians 5:22: But the fruit of the Spirit is love, joy, peace, longsuffering, gentleness, goodness, faith... (Per the notes included with the original King James Bible).

Hebrews 4:12: For the word of God ... is a discerner of the thoughts and intents of the heart, per E. H. Plumptre.

Tertullian 198 AD On the Soul 15: "We are taught by God concerning both these questions ... For, when one reads of God as being the searcher and witness of the heart..." www.newadvent.org/fathers/0310.htm

1:7 For the Spirit of the Lord filleth the world: and <u>**that which containeth all things**</u> hath knowledge of the voice.

Paul says uses the same language in Colossians 1:17, but the KJV makes it hard to see that. www.biblegateway.com/verse/en/Wisdom%201%3A7 shows many alternate translations, e.g., that which "holds all things together;" compare to www.biblegateway.com/verse/en/Colossians%201%3A17 (e.g., "He is before all things, and by him all things hold together").

Basil the Great 379 AD Letter 8, 10: "Now let us examine, and to the best of our ability explain, the meaning of the words of Holy Scripture, which our opponents seize and wrest to their own sense, and urge against us for the destruction of the glory of the Only-begotten....How then can the two following passages stand? The Spirit of the Lord fills the world..." www.newadvent.org/fathers/3202008.htm

1:8 Therefore he that speaketh unrighteous things cannot be hid: neither shall vengeance, when it punisheth, pass by him. 1:9 For inquisition shall be made into the counsels of the ungodly: and the sound of his words shall come unto the Lord for the manifestation of his wicked deeds. 1:10 For the ear of jealousy heareth all things: and the noise of murmurings is not hid. 1:11 Therefore beware of murmuring, which is unprofitable; and refrain your tongue from backbiting: for there is no word so secret, that shall go for nought: and the mouth that belieth slayeth the soul. 1:12 Seek not death in the error of your life: and pull not upon yourselves destruction with the works of your hands. 1:13 For God made not death: neither hath he pleasure in the destruction of the living.

Archelaus 278 AD Acts of the Disputation with Manes 29: "Archelaus said: You err, not knowing the Scriptures,...you may now advance others of like tenor, and bring forward any passages which may seem to you to be written against the law, to any extent you please...Manes

said: It is written, that death reigned from Adam to Moses. (Romans 5:14) ... in that way it would also follow that God was its maker. Archelaus said: By no means; away with such a supposition! For God made not death; neither has He pleasure in the destruction of the living." www.newadvent. org/fathers/0616.htm

Eusebius of Caesarea 339 AD Preparation of the Gospel, Book 13, 1: "you would find that the Hebrew Scripture does not contain disgraceful tales about the God of the universe.... It is also a doctrine of the Hebrews that God is not the author of evils, inasmuch as God made not death, neither hath He pleasure in the destruction of the living..." www.tertullian.org/fathers/ eusebius_pe_13_book13.htm

1:14 For he created all things, that they might have their being: and the generations of the world were healthful; and there is no poison of destruction in them, nor the kingdom of death upon the earth: 1:15 (For righteousness is immortal:) 1:16 But ungodly men with their works and words called it to them: for when they thought to have it their friend, they consumed to nought, and made a covenant with it, because they are worthy to take part with it.

2:1 <u>For the ungodly said, reasoning with themselves, but not aright, Our life is short and tedious, and in the death of a man there is no remedy: neither was there any man known to have returned from the grave</u>.

1 Corinthians 15:32: "If after the manner of men I have fought with beasts at Ephesus, what advantageth it me, if the dead rise not? let us eat and drink; for to morrow we die." Per the notes included with the original King James Bible.

Matthew 22:23: "The same day came to him the Sadducees, which say that there is no resurrection..." Per the notes included with the original King James Bible.

2:2 For we are born at all adventure: and we shall be hereafter as though we had never been: for the breath in our nostrils is as smoke,

and a little spark in the moving of our heart: 2:3 Which being extinguished, our body shall be turned into ashes, and our spirit shall vanish as the soft air, 2:4 And our name shall be forgotten in time, and no man shall have our works in remembrance, and our life shall pass away as the trace of a cloud, and shall be dispersed as a mist, that is driven away with the beams of the sun, and overcome with the heat thereof. 2:5 For our time is a very shadow that passeth away; and after our end there is no returning: for it is fast sealed, so that no man cometh again. 2:6 <u>Come on therefore, let us enjoy the good things that are present: and let us speedily use the creatures like as in youth. 2:7 Let us fill ourselves with costly wine and ointments: and let no flower of the spring pass by us: 2:8 Let us crown ourselves with rosebuds, before they be withered: 2:9 Let none of us go without his part of our voluptuousness: let us leave tokens of our joyfulness in every place: for this is our portion, and our lot is this.</u>

1 Corinthians 15:32: "If after the manner of men I have fought with beasts at Ephesus, what advantageth it me, if the dead rise not? let us eat and drink; for to morrow we die." Per the notes included with the original King James Bible.

2:10 Let us oppress the poor righteous man, let us not spare the widow, nor reverence the ancient gray hairs of the aged. 2:11 Let our strength be the law of justice: for that which is feeble is found to be nothing worth. 2:12 <u>Therefore let us lie in wait for the righteous; because he is not for our turn, and he is clean contrary to our doings: he upbraideth us with our offending the law, and objecteth to our infamy the transgressings of our education</u>.

There are many New Testament fulfillments of the prophesies in Wisdom 2:12-24, e.g.:

John 7:19: Did not Moses give you the law, and yet none of you keepeth the law? Why go ye about to kill me?

Luke 11:44: ...your inward part is full of ravening and wickedness. Ye fools... But woe unto you, Pharisees! ... Woe unto you, scribes and Pharisees, hypocrites!

Luke 11:52: Woe unto you, lawyers! for ye have taken away the key of knowledge: ye entered not in yourselves, and them that were entering in ye hindered.

Mark 7:9: And he said unto them, Full well ye reject the commandment of God, that ye may keep your own tradition.

Mark 12:26: And as touching the dead, that they rise: have ye not read in the book of Moses, how in the bush God spake unto him, saying, I am the God of Abraham, and the God of Isaac, and the God of Jacob?

Matthew 12:3: But he said unto them, Have ye not read what David did, when he was an hungred, and they that were with him;

Matthew 12:5: Or have ye not read in the law, how that on the Sabbath days the priests in the temple profane the Sabbath, and are blameless?

Matthew: 19:4: And he answered and said unto them, Have ye not read, that he which made them at the beginning made them male and female,

Matthew 23:4: Then spake Jesus to the multitude, and to his disciples, Saying, The scribes and the Pharisees sit in Moses' seat: All therefore whatsoever they bid you observe, that observe and do; but do not ye after their works: for they say, and do not. For they bind heavy burdens and grievous to be borne, and lay them on men's shoulders; but they themselves will not move them with one of their fingers.

Matthew 23:31: Wherefore ye be witnesses unto yourselves, that ye are the children of them which killed the prophets.

Epistle of Barnabas 135 AD Chapter VI: Since, therefore, He was about to be manifested and to suffer in the flesh, His suffering was foreshown. For the prophet speaks against Israel, "Woe to their soul, because they have counselled an evil counsel against themselves (Isa. iii. 9.), saying, Let us bind the just one, because he is displeasing to us." ccel.org/ccel/schaff/anf01.vi.ii.vi.html

2:13 He professeth to have the knowledge of God: and he calleth himself the child of the Lord.

There are many New Testament fulfillments of the prophesies in Wisdom 2:12-24, e.g.:

John 5:20: For the Father loveth the Son, and sheweth him all things that himself doeth: and he will shew him greater works than these, that ye may marvel.

John 10:15: As the Father knoweth me, even so know I the Father: and I lay down my life for the sheep.

John: 12:50: And I know that his commandment is life everlasting: whatsoever I speak therefore, even as the Father said unto me, so I speak.

Luke: 10:22: All things are delivered to me of my Father: and no man knoweth who the Son is, but the Father; and who the Father is, but the Son, and he to whom the Son will reveal him.

Mark: 14:36: And he said, Abba, Father, all things are possible unto thee; take away this cup from me: nevertheless not what I will, but what thou wilt.

Matthew: 11:27: All things are delivered unto me of my Father: and no man knoweth the Son, but the Father; neither knoweth any man the Father, save the Son, and he to whomsoever the Son will reveal him.

2:14 He was made to reprove our thoughts.

Ephesians: 5:14: "But all things that are reproved are made manifest by the light: for whatsoever doth make manifest is light." Per the notes included with the original King James Bible.

John 7:7: "The world cannot hate you; but me it hateth, because I testify of it, that the works thereof are evil." Per the notes included with the original King James Bible.

There are also many New Testament fulfillments of the prophesies in Wisdom 2:12-24, e.g.:

Luke: 5:22: But when Jesus perceived their thoughts, he answering said unto them, What reason ye in your hearts?

Luke:11:17: But he, knowing their thoughts, said unto them, Every kingdom divided against itself is brought to desolation; and a house divided against a house falleth.

Mark: 2:8: And immediately when Jesus perceived in his spirit that they so reasoned within themselves, he said unto them, Why reason ye these things in your hearts?

Matthew: 9:4: And Jesus knowing their thoughts said, Wherefore think ye evil in your hearts?

2:15 He is grievous unto us even to behold: for his life is not like other men's, his ways are of another fashion.

There are many New Testament fulfillments of the prophesies in Wisdom 2:12-24, e.g.:

Luke: 4:32: And they were astonished at his doctrine: for his word was with power.

Mark:1:22: And they were astonished at his doctrine: for he taught them as one that had authority, and not as the scribes.

Matthew: 7:29: And it came to pass, when Jesus had ended these sayings, the people were astonished at his doctrine: For he taught them as one having authority, and not as the scribes.

2:16 We are esteemed of him as counterfeits: he abstaineth from our ways as from filthiness: he pronounceth the end of the just to be blessed, and maketh his boast that God is his father.

There are many New Testament fulfillments of the prophesies in Wisdom 2:12-24, e.g.:

John: 5:17: But Jesus answered them, My Father worketh hitherto, and I work.

Luke: 11:44: ...your inward part is full of ravening and wickedness. Ye fools... But woe unto you, Pharisees! ... Woe unto you, scribes and Pharisees, hypocrites!

Mark: 14: 36: And he said, Abba, Father, all things are possible unto thee; take away this cup from me: nevertheless not what I will, but what thou wilt.

Matthew: 5:10: Blessed are they which are persecuted for righteousness' sake: for theirs is the kingdom of heaven.

Matthew: 11:27: All things are delivered unto me of my Father: and no man knoweth the Son, but the Father; neither knoweth any man the Father, save the Son, and he to whomsoever the Son will reveal him.

Matthew: 23:3 All therefore whatsoever they bid you observe, that observe and do; but do not ye after their works: for they say, and do not.

2:17 Let us see if his words be true: and let us prove what shall happen in the end of him.

Hebrews: 13:7: Remember them which have the rule over you, who have spoken unto you the word of God: whose faith follow, considering the end of their conversation. (Per E. H. Plumptre, as part of showing that Apollos may have written the Book of Wisdom as a Jew and the Epistle of the Hebrews after converting to Christianity).

There are many New Testament fulfillments of the prophesies in Wisdom 2:12-24, e.g.:

Matthew: 27:42: He saved others; himself he cannot save. If he be the King of Israel, let him now come down from the cross, and we will believe him.

Matthew: 27:49: The rest said, Let be, let us see whether Elias will come to save him.

2:18 For if the just man be the son of God, he will help him, and deliver him from the hand of his enemies.

There are many New Testament fulfillments of the prophesies in Wisdom 2:12-24, e.g.:

Matthew 27:43: "He trusted in God; let him deliver him now, if he will have him: for he said, I am the Son of God." Per the notes included with the original King James Bible, and as discussed in depth above.

2:19 Let us examine him with despitefulness and torture, that we may know his meekness, and prove his patience.

There are many New Testament fulfillments of the prophesies in Wisdom 2:12-24, e.g.:

John 18:22: And when he had thus spoken, one of the officers which stood by struck Jesus with the palm of his hand, saying, Answerest thou the high priest so?

Matthew 27:12 And when he was accused of the chief priests and elders, he answered nothing.

2:20 Let us condemn him with a shameful death: for by his own saying he shall be respected.

There are many New Testament fulfillments of the prophesies in Wisdom 2:12-24, e.g.:

Galatians 3:13: Christ hath redeemed us from the curse of the law, being made a curse for us: for it is written, Cursed is every one that hangeth on a tree.

Hebrews 12:2: Looking unto Jesus the author and finisher of our faith; who for the joy that was set before him endured the cross, despising the shame, and is set down at the right hand of the throne of God.

Matthew 4:11: Then the devil leaveth him, and, behold, angels came and ministered unto him.

Matthew 26:53: Thinkest thou that I cannot now pray to my Father, and he shall presently give me more than twelve legions of angels?]

2:21 Such things they did imagine, and were deceived: for their own wickedness hath blinded them.

There are many New Testament fulfillments of the prophesies in Wisdom 2:12-24, e.g.:

Matthew 15:14: Let them alone: they be blind leaders of the blind. And if the blind lead the blind, both shall fall into the ditch.

Matthew 23:24: Ye blind guides, which strain at a gnat, and swallow a camel.

2:22 As for the mysteries of God, they knew them not: neither hoped they for the wages of righteousness, nor discerned a reward for blameless souls.

There are many New Testament fulfillments of the prophesies in Wisdom 2:12-24, e.g.:

1 Corinthians 2:8: Which none of the princes of this world knew: for had they known it, they would not have crucified the Lord of glory.

John 7:49: But this people who knoweth not the law are cursed.

John 8:55: Yet ye have not known him; but I know him: and if I should say, I know him not, I shall be a liar like unto you: but I know him, and keep his saying.

Romans 10:3: For they being ignorant of God's righteousness, and going about to establish their own righteousness, have not submitted themselves unto the righteousness of God.

2:23 For God created man to be immortal, and made him to be an image of his own eternity.

There are many New Testament fulfillments of the prophesies in Wisdom 2:12-24, e.g.:

1 Corinthians15:45: And so it is written, The first man Adam was made a living soul; the last Adam was made a quickening spirit.

Matthew 19:16: And, behold, one came and said unto him, Good Master, what good thing shall I do, that I may have eternal life?

2:24 Nevertheless through envy of the devil came death into the world: and they that do hold of his side do find it.

The first time in Scripture/Apocrypha that the serpent of Genesis 3 is clearly identified with the devil, or Satan, as then later identified throughout the New Testament:

John 8:44: Ye are of your father the devil, and the lusts of your father ye will do. He was a murderer from the beginning, and abode not in the truth, because there is no truth in him. When he speaketh a lie, he speaketh of his own: for he is a liar, and the father of it.

Romans 16:20: And the God of peace shall bruise Satan under your feet shortly. The grace of our Lord Jesus Christ be with you. Amen.

Revelations 12:9: And the great dragon was cast out, that old serpent, called the Devil, and Satan, which deceiveth the whole world: he was cast out into the earth, and his angels were cast out with him.

Paul alludes to this verse many times:

Romans 5:12: Wherefore, as by one man sin entered into the world, and death by sin; and so death passed upon all men, for that all have sinned.

Hebrews 2:14 (For as much then as the children are partakers of flesh and blood, he also himself likewise took part of the same; that through death he might destroy him that had the power of death, that is, the devil), per E. H. Plumptre.

Lastly, the Greek word for "envy" is phthonos, which never appears in the Protestant Old Testament. In the Book of Wisdom, envy is directly opposed to wisdom (Wis 6:23 "Neither will I go with consuming envy; for such a man shall have no fellowship with wisdom") and is depicted as the evil behind the Devil's actions in Genesis (Wis 2:24). Envy was also the motivation behind the Crucifixion:

Matthew 27:18: 17Therefore when they were gathered together, Pilate said unto them, Whom will ye that I release unto you? Barabbas, or Jesus which is called Christ? 18For he knew that for envy they had delivered him.

Mark 15:10: 9But Pilate answered them, saying, Will ye that I release unto you the King of the Jews? 10For he knew that the chief priests had delivered him for envy.

In addition there is a linkage between envy/phthonos, murder, and the Devil (e.g., John 8:44 "Ye are of your father the devil, and the lusts of your father ye will do. He was a murderer from the beginning..."), which may explain so word choices and orderings in the New Testament:

Romans 1:29: Being filled with all unrighteousness, fornication, wickedness, covetousness, maliciousness; full of envy, murder, debate, deceit, malignity; whisperers,

Galatians 5:21: Envyings, murders, drunkenness, revellings, and such like: of the which I tell you before, as I have also told you in time past, that they which do such things shall not inherit the kingdom of God.

It may also explain what James is paraphrasing in James 4:5, a 'quotation' from Scripture that is not found in Scripture:

James 4:5-7 5Do ye think that the scripture saith in vain, "The spirit that dwelleth in us lusteth to envy?" ... 7Submit yourselves therefore to God. Resist the devil, and he will flee from you.

Clement of Rome 96 AD: 1 Clement, 3: every one abandons the fear of God, ... walks after his own wicked lusts, resuming the practice of an unrighteous and ungodly envy, by which death itself entered into the world.

www.newadvent.org/fathers/1010.htm

3:1 But the souls of the righteous are in the hand of God, and there shall no torment touch them. 3:2 In the sight of the unwise they seemed to die: and their departure is taken for misery, 3:3 And their going from us to be utter destruction: but they are in peace. 3:4 For though they be punished in the sight of men, yet is their hope full of immortality.

1 Peter 1:13 (Wherefore gird up the loins of your mind, be sober, and hope to the end for the grace that is to be brought unto you at the revelation of Jesus Christ), per the notes included with the original King James Bible.

2 Corinthians 5:1 (For we know that if our earthly house of this tabernacle were dissolved, we have a building of God, an house not made with hands, eternal in the heavens), per the notes included with the original King James Bible.

Romans 8:24 (For we are saved by hope: but hope that is seen is not hope: for what a man seeth, why doth he yet hope for?), per the notes included with the original King James Bible.

3:5 And having been a little chastised, they shall be greatly rewarded: for God proved them, and found them worthy for himself. 3:6 As gold in the furnace hath he tried them, and received them as a burnt offering. 3:7 And in the time of their visitation they shall shine, and run to and fro like sparks among the stubble.

Matthew 13:43 (Then shall the righteous shine forth as the sun in the kingdom of their Father. Who hath ears to hear, let him hear), per the notes included with the original King James Bible.

3:8 They shall judge the nations, and have dominion over the people, and their Lord shall reign for ever.

1 Corinthians 6:2 (Do ye not know that the saints shall judge the world? and if the world shall be judged by you, are ye unworthy to judge the smallest matters?), per the notes included with the original King James Bible.

Matthew 19:28 (And Jesus said unto them, Verily I say unto you, That ye which have followed me, in the regeneration when the Son of man shall sit in the throne of his glory, ye also shall sit upon twelve thrones, judging the twelve tribes of Israel), per the notes included with the original King James Bible.

3:9 They that put their trust in him shall understand the truth: and such as be faithful in love shall abide with him: for grace and mercy is to his saints, and he hath care for his elect. 3:10 But the ungodly shall be punished according to their own imaginations, which have neglected the righteous, and forsaken the Lord.

Matthew 25:41 (Then shall he say also unto them on the left hand, Depart from me, ye cursed, into everlasting fire, prepared for the devil and his angels), per the notes included with the original King James Bible.

3:11 For whoso despiseth wisdom and nurture, he is miserable, and their hope is vain, their labours unfruitful, and their works unprofitable: 3:12 Their wives are foolish, and their children wicked: 3:13 Their offspring is cursed. Wherefore blessed is the barren that is undefiled, which hath not known the sinful bed: she shall have fruit in the visitation of souls.

Hebrews 7:26 (For such an high priest became us, who is holy, harmless, undefiled, separate from sinners, and made higher than the heavens), per E. H. Plumptre, as part of showing that Apollos may have written the Book of Wisdom and the Epistle of the Hebrews.

3:14 And blessed is the eunuch, which with his hands hath wrought no iniquity, nor imagined wicked things against God: for unto him shall be given the special gift of faith, and an inheritance in the temple of the Lord more acceptable to his mind. 3:15 For glorious is the fruit of good labours: and the root of wisdom shall never fall away. 3:16 As for the children of adulterers, they shall not come to their perfection, and the seed of an unrighteous bed shall be rooted out. 3:17 For though they live long, yet shall they be nothing regarded: and their last age shall be without honour. 3:18 Or, if they die quickly, they have no hope, neither comfort in the day of trial. 3:19 For horrible is the end of the unrighteous generation.

4:1 Better it is to have no children, and to have virtue: for the memorial thereof is immortal: because it is known with God, and with men. 4:2 **When it is present, men take example at it; and when it is gone, they desire it: it weareth a crown, and triumpheth for ever, having gotten the victory, striving for undefiled rewards.**

Hebrews 7:26 (For such an high priest became us, who is holy, harmless, undefiled, separate from sinners, and made higher than the heavens), per E. H. Plumptre, as part of showing that Apollos may have written the Book of Wisdom and the Epistle of the Hebrews.

4:3 But the multiplying brood of the ungodly shall not thrive, nor take deep rooting from bastard slips, nor lay any fast foundation. 4:4 **For though they flourish in branches for a time; yet standing not last, they shall be shaken with the wind, and through the force of winds they shall be rooted out.**

Matthew 7:19 (Every tree that bringeth not forth good fruit is hewn down, and cast into the fire), per the notes included with the original King James Bible.

4:5 The imperfect branches shall be broken off, their fruit unprofitable, not ripe to eat, yea, meet for nothing. 4:6 For children begotten of unlawful beds are witnesses of wickedness against their parents in their trial. 4:7 But though the righteous be prevented with death, yet shall he be in rest. 4:8 For honourable age is not that which standeth in length of time, nor that is measured by number of years. 4:9 But wisdom is the gray hair unto men, and an unspotted life is old age. 4:10 **He pleased God, and was beloved of him: so that living among sinners he was translated**.

Hebrews 11:5 (By faith Enoch was translated that he should not see death; and was not found, because God had translated him: for before his translation he had this testimony, that he pleased God), per the

notes included with the original King James Bible.

Also per E. H. Plumptre, as part of showing that Apollos may have written the Book of Wisdom and the Epistle of the Hebrews.

In addition, Plumptre also identifies as a cross reference Hebrews 12:28: Wherefore we receiving a kingdom which cannot be moved, let us have grace, whereby we may serve God acceptably with reverence and godly fear.

4:11 Yea speedily was he taken away, lest that wickedness should alter his understanding, or deceit beguile his soul. 4:12 For the bewitching of naughtiness doth obscure things that are honest; and the wandering of concupiscence doth undermine the simple mind. 4:13 **He, being made perfect in a short time, fulfilled a long time:**

Hebrews 2:10: For it became him, for whom are all things, and by whom are all things, in bringing many sons unto glory, to make the captain of their salvation perfect through sufferings, per E. H. Plumptre.

4:14 For his soul pleased the Lord: therefore hasted he to take him away from among the wicked. 4:15 This the people saw, and understood it not, neither laid they up this in their minds, That his grace and mercy is with his saints, and that he hath respect unto his chosen. 4:16 Thus the righteous that is dead shall condemn the ungodly which are living; and youth that is soon perfected the many years and old age of the unrighteous. 4:17 For they shall see the end of the wise, and shall not understand what God in his counsel hath decreed of him, and to what end the Lord hath set him in safety. 4:18 They shall see him, and despise him; but God shall laugh them to scorn: and they shall hereafter be a vile carcase, and a reproach among the dead for evermore. 4:19 For he shall rend them, and cast them down headlong, that they shall be speechless; and he shall shake them from the foundation; and they shall be utterly laid waste, and be in sorrow; and their memorial shall perish. 4:20 And when they cast up the accounts of their sins, they shall come with fear: and their own iniquities shall convince them to their face.

5:1 **Then shall the righteous man stand in great boldness before the face of such as have afflicted him, and made no account of his labours.**

Hebrews 10:19 (Having therefore, brethren, boldness to enter into the holiest by the blood of Jesus), per E. H. Plumptre, as part of showing that Apollos may have written the Book of Wisdom and the Epistle of the Hebrews.

5:2 When they see it, they shall be troubled with terrible fear, and shall be amazed at the strangeness of his salvation, so far beyond all that they looked for. 5:3 And they repenting and groaning for anguish of spirit shall say within themselves, This was he, whom we had sometimes in derision, and a proverb of reproach: 5:4 We fools accounted his life madness, and his end to be without honour: 5:5 How is he numbered among the children of God, and his lot is among the saints! 5:6 Therefore have we erred from the way of truth, and the light of righteousness hath not shined unto us, and the sun of righteousness rose not upon us. 5:7 We wearied ourselves in the way of wickedness and destruction: yea, we have gone through deserts, where there lay no way: but as for the way of the Lord, we have not known it. 5:8 What hath pride profited us? or what good hath riches with our vaunting brought us?

There are many New Testament fulfillments of the prophesies in Wisdom 5:1-8, e.g.:

Matthew 27:54 (Now when the centurion, and they that were with him, watching Jesus, saw the earthquake, and those things that were done, they feared greatly, saying, Truly this was the Son of God).

5:9 All those things are passed away like a shadow, and as a post that hasted by; 5:10 And as a ship that passeth over the waves of the water, which when it is gone by, the trace thereof cannot be found, neither the pathway of the keel in the waves; 5:11 Or as when a bird hath flown through the air, there is no token of her way to be found, but the light air being beaten with the stroke of her wings and parted with the violent noise and motion of them, is passed through, and therein afterwards no sign where she went is to be found; 5:12 Or like as when an arrow is shot at a mark, it parteth the air, which immediately cometh together again, so that a man cannot know where it went through: 5:13 Even so we in like manner, as soon as we were born, began to draw to our end, and had no sign of virtue to shew; but were consumed in our own wickedness. 5:14 **For the hope of the ungodly is like dust that is blown away with the wind; like a thin froth that is driven away with the storm; like as the smoke which is dispersed here and there with a tempest, and passeth away as the remembrance of a guest that tarrieth but a day.**

James 1:11: But the rich, in that he is made low: because as the flower of the grass he shall pass away. For the sun is no sooner risen with a burning heat, but it withereth the grass, and the flower thereof falleth, and the grace of the fashion of it perisheth: so also shall the rich man fade away in his ways. Per the notes included with the original King James Bible.

5:15 But the righteous live for evermore; their reward also is with the Lord, and the care of them is with the most High. 5:16 Therefore shall they receive a glorious kingdom, and a beautiful crown from the Lord's hand: for with his right hand shall he cover them, and with his arm shall he protect them. 5:17 **He shall take to him his jealousy for complete armour, and make the creature his weapon for the revenge of his enemies. 5:18 He shall put on righteousness as a breastplate, and true judgment instead of an helmet. 5:19 He shall take holiness for an invincible shield.**

5:20 His severe wrath shall he sharpen for a sword, and the world shall fight with him against the unwise.

Ephesians 6:13-17: 13Wherefore take unto you the whole armour of God, that ye may be able to withstand in the evil day, and having done all, to stand.14Stand therefore, having your loins girt about with truth, and having on the breastplate of righteousness; 15And your feet shod with the preparation of the gospel of peace;16Above all, taking the shield of faith, wherewith ye shall be able to quench all the fiery darts of the wicked. 17And take the helmet of salvation, and the sword of the Spirit, which is the word of God.

(Ephesians uses a Greek word for the armor (of God) that is only found in the Book of Wisdom, not in Isaiah 59).
5:21 Then shall the right aiming thunderbolts go abroad; and from the clouds, as from a well drawn bow, shall they fly to the mark. 5:22 And hailstones full of wrath shall be cast as out of a stone bow, and the water of the sea shall rage against them, and the floods shall cruelly drown them. 5:23 Yea, a mighty wind shall stand up against them, and like a storm shall blow them away: thus iniquity shall lay waste the whole earth, and ill dealing shall overthrow the thrones of the mighty.
6:1 Hear therefore, O ye kings, and understand; learn, ye that be judges of the ends of the earth. 6:2 Give ear, ye that rule the people, and glory in the multitude of nations. 6:3 **For power is given you of the Lord, and sovereignty from the Highest, who shall try your works, and search out your counsels.**

Romans 13:2: Let every soul be subject unto the higher powers. For there is no power but of God: the powers that be are ordained of God. Whosoever therefore resisteth the power, resisteth the ordinance of God: and they that resist shall receive to themselves damnation. Per the notes included with the original King James Bible.

6:4 Because, being ministers of his kingdom, ye have not judged aright, nor kept the law, nor walked after the counsel of God; 6:5 **Horribly and speedily shall he come upon you: for a sharp judgment shall be to them that be in high places. 6:6 For mercy will soon pardon the meanest: but mighty men shall be mightily tormented.**

Luke 1:51-53: 51 ... he hath scattered the proud in the imagination of their hearts. 52He hath put down the mighty from their seats, and exalted them of low degree. 53He hath filled the hungry with good things; and the rich he hath sent empty away.

6:7 **For he which is Lord over all shall fear no man's person, neither shall he stand in awe of any man's greatness: for he hath made the small and great, and careth for all alike.**

1 Peter 1:17 And if ye call on the Father, who without respect of persons judgeth according to every man's work, pass the time of your sojourning here in fear: Per the notes included with the original King James Bible.

Acts 10:34 Then Peter opened his mouth, and said, Of a truth I perceive that God is no respecter of persons. Per the notes included with the original King James Bible.

Colossians 3:25 But he that doeth wrong shall receive for the wrong which he hath done: and there is no respect of persons. Per the notes included with the original King James Bible.

Ephesians 6:9 And, ye masters, do the same things unto them, forbearing threatening: knowing that your Master also is in heaven; neither is there respect of persons with him. Per the notes included with the original King James Bible.

Galatians 2:6 But of these who seemed to be somewhat, (whatsoever they were, it maketh no matter to me: God accepteth no man's person:) for they who seemed to be somewhat in conference added nothing to me. Per the notes included with the original King James Bible.

Romans 2:11 For there is no respect of persons with God. Per the notes included with the original King James Bible.

6:8 But a sore trial shall come upon the mighty. 6:9 Unto you therefore, O kings, do I speak, that ye may learn wisdom, and not fall away. 6:10 For they that keep holiness holily shall be judged holy: and they that have learned such things shall find what to answer. 6:11 Wherefore set your affection upon my words; desire them, and ye shall be instructed. 6:12 Wisdom is glorious, and never fadeth away: yea, she is easily seen of them that love her, and found of such as seek her. 6:13 She preventeth them that desire her, in making herself first known unto them. 6:14 Whoso seeketh her early shall have no great travail: for he shall find her sitting at his doors. 6:15 **To think therefore upon her is perfection of wisdom: and whoso watcheth for her shall quickly be without care.**

Hebrews 6:1 Therefore leaving the principles of the doctrine of Christ, let us go on unto perfection; not laying again the foundation of repentance from dead works, and of faith toward God. Per E. H. Plumptre, as part of showing that Apollos may have written the Book of Wisdom and the Epistle of the Hebrews.

6:16 For she goeth about seeking such as are worthy of her, sheweth herself favourably unto them in the ways, and meeteth them in every thought. 6:17 For the very true beginning of her is the desire of discipline; and the care of discipline is love; 6:18 **And love is the keeping of her laws; and the giving heed unto her laws is the assurance of incorruption;**

Hebrews 6:6 If they shall fall away, to renew them again unto repentance; seeing they crucify to themselves the Son of God afresh, and put him to an open shame. Per E. H. Plumptre, as part of showing that Apollos may have written the Book of Wisdom and the Epistle of the Hebrews.

6:19 And incorruption maketh us near unto God:

Irenaeus of Lyon 180 AD Against Heresies 4, 38, 3: cited along with 1 Corinthians etc. without qualification: "...the beholding of God is productive of immortality, but immortality renders one near unto God."

Eusebius 324 AD Church History 5, 8, 8: [Re: Irenaeus] And he uses almost the precise words of the Wisdom of Solomon, saying: The vision of God produces immortality, but immortality renders us near to God. He mentions also the memoirs of a certain apostolic presbyter, whose name he passes by in silence, and gives his expositions of the sacred Scriptures.

6:20 Therefore the desire of wisdom bringeth to a kingdom. 6:21 If your delight be then in thrones and sceptres, O ye kings of the people, honour wisdom, that ye may reign for evermore. 6:22 As for wisdom, what she is, and how she came up, I will tell you, and will not hide mysteries from you: but will seek her out from the beginning of her nativity, and bring the knowledge of her into light, and will not pass over the truth. 6:23 Neither will I go with consuming envy; for such a man shall have no fellowship with wisdom. 6:24 But the multitude of the wise is the welfare of the world: and a wise king is the upholding of the people. 6:25 Receive therefore instruction through my words, and it shall do you good.

7:1 I myself also am a mortal man, like to all, and the offspring of him that was first made of the earth, 7:2 And in my mother's womb was fashioned to be flesh in the time of ten months, being compacted in blood, of the seed of man, and the pleasure that came with sleep. 7:3 And when I was born, I drew in the common air, and fell upon the earth, which is of like nature, and the first voice which I uttered was crying, as all others do. 7:4 I was nursed in swaddling clothes, and that with cares. 7:5 For there is no king that had any other beginning of birth. 7:6

For all men have one entrance into life, and the like going out.

1 Timothy 6:7 For we brought nothing into this world, and it is certain we can carry nothing out. Per the notes included with the original King James Bible.

Hebrews 10:19 Having therefore, brethren, boldness to enter into the holiest by the blood of Jesus. Per E. H. Plumptre, as part of showing that Apollos may have written the Book of Wisdom and the Epistle of the Hebrews.

7:7 Wherefore I prayed, and understanding was given me: I called upon God, and the spirit of wisdom came to me. 7:8 I preferred her before sceptres and thrones, and esteemed riches nothing in comparison of her. 7:9 Neither compared I unto her any precious stone, because all gold in respect of her is as a little sand, and silver shall be counted as clay before her. 7:10 I loved her above health and beauty, and chose to have her instead of light: for the light that cometh from her never goeth out. 7:11 **All good things together came to me with her, and innumerable riches in her hands.**

Matthew 6:33 But seek ye first the kingdom of God, and his righteousness; and all these things shall be added unto you. Per the notes included with the original King James Bible. Compare the preceding verses plus 7:14 (seek Wisdom first) to Matthew 6:25-33 (seek first the Kingdom of God).

7:12 And I rejoiced in them all, because wisdom goeth before them: and I knew not that she was the mother of them. 7:13 I learned diligently, and do communicate her liberally: I do not hide her riches. 7:14 For she is a treasure unto men that never faileth: which they that use become the friends of God, being commended for the gifts that come from learning. 7:15 **God hath granted me to speak as I would, and to conceive as is meet for the things that are given me: because it is he that leadeth unto wisdom, and directeth the wise.**

Beginning (7:15-7:21) of a declaration that the Book of Wisdom is Divinely inspired.

7:16 For in his hand are both we and our words; all wisdom also, and knowledge of workmanship. 7:17 For he hath given me certain knowledge of the things that are, namely, to know how the world was made, and the operation of the elements: 7:18 The beginning, ending, and midst of the times: the alterations of the turning of the sun, and the change of seasons: 7:19 The circuits of years, and the positions of stars: 7:20 The natures of living creatures, and the furies of wild beasts: the violence of winds, and the reasonings of men: **the diversities of plants and the virtues of roots:**

Matthew 15:22 As discussed above, the title "Son of David" was part of a Solomon typology that identified Jesus as a healer and particularly as an exorcist. ... By addressing Jesus as "son of David," the woman ["Have mercy on me, O Lord, thou Son of David; my daughter is grievously vexed with a devil"] may have been expressing her confidence in Jesus's authority over demons.

7:21 **And all such things as are either secret or manifest, them I know. 7:22 For wisdom, which is the worker of all things, taught me: for in her is an understanding spirit holy, one only, manifold, subtil, lively, clear, undefiled, plain, not subject to hurt, loving the thing that is good quick, which cannot be letted, ready to do good,**

There are many New Testament fulfillments of the prophesies in Wisdom 2:21-30, e.g.:

John 1:3 All things were made by him; and without him was not any thing made that was made.

John 1:14 And the Word was made flesh, and dwelt among us, (and we beheld his glory, the glory as of the only begotten of the Father,) full of grace and truth. Per Gary G. Michuta's "Case for the Deuterocanon"), the word for "only-begotten" (monogenes) appears only in John and the Book of Wisdom, 7:22.

John 1:18 No man hath seen God at any time; the only begotten Son, which is in the bosom of the Father, he hath declared him.

1 John 4:9 In this was manifested the love of God toward us, because that God sent his only begotten Son into the world, that we might live through him.

Colossians 1:16-17 Who is the image of the invisible God, the firstborn of every creature: For by him were all things created, that are in heaven, and that are in earth, visible and invisible, whether they be thrones, or dominions, or principalities, or powers: all things were created by him, and for him: And he is before all things, and by him all things consist.

Hebrews 1:1 God, who at sundry times and in divers manners spake in time past unto the fathers by the prophets. Per E. H. Plumptre, as part of showing that Apollos may have written the Book of Wisdom and the Epistle of the Hebrews. (Divers manners = manifold).

Hebrews 1:2 Hath in these last days spoken unto us by his Son, whom he hath appointed heir of all things, by whom also he made the worlds. (For wisdom, which is the worker of all things...).

Hebrews 4:12 For the word of God is quick, and powerful, and sharper than any twoedged sword, piercing even to the dividing asunder of soul and spirit, and of the joints and marrow, and is a discerner of the thoughts and intents of the heart. (discerner of the thoughts and intents of the heart = ...for in her is an understanding spirit ...subtil...).

Galatians 4:6 And because ye are sons, God hath sent forth the Spirit of his Son into your hearts, crying, Abba, Father. (...for in her is an understanding spirit ...)

Ephesians 3:10 To the intent that now unto the principalities and powers in heavenly places might be known by the church the manifold wisdom of God,

Matthew 15:22 Per the Evangelical Biblical Theology Commentary (i.e., that God taught Solomon the secrets of casting out demons and that Solomon recorded these secrets for the benefit of others; see 7:20).

7:23 Kind to man, steadfast, sure, free from care, having all power, overseeing all things, and going through all understanding, pure, and most subtil, spirits.

There are many New Testament fulfillments of the prophesies in Wisdom 2:21-30, e.g.:

John 1:50 Nathanael saith unto him, Whence knowest thou me? Jesus answered and said unto him, Before that Philip called thee, when thou wast under the fig tree, I saw thee. Nathanael answered and saith unto him, Rabbi, thou art the Son of God; thou art the King of Israel. Jesus answered and said unto him, Because I said unto thee, I saw thee under the fig tree, believest thou? thou shalt see greater things than these. (... overseeing all things...).

John 5:20 Then answered Jesus and said unto them, Verily, verily, I say unto you, The Son can do nothing of himself, but what he seeth the Father do: for what things soever he doeth, these also doeth the Son likewise. For the Father loveth the Son, and sheweth him all things that himself doeth: and he will shew him greater works than these, that ye may marvel. (... having all power...).

John 16:31 Now are we sure that thou knowest all things, and needest not that any man should ask thee: by this we believe that thou camest forth from God. Jesus answered them, Do ye now believe? (... overseeing all things...).

Revelation 1:8 I am Alpha and Omega, the beginning and the ending, saith the Lord, which is, and which was, and which is to come, the Almighty. (... having all power...).

James 3:17 In Jas 3:17, wisdom from above is designated by seven qualities, recalling the famous twenty-one qualities of wisdom in Wis 7:22- 23.

7:24 <u>For wisdom is more moving than any motion: she passeth and goeth through all things by reason of her pureness.</u>

There are many New Testament fulfillments of the prophesies in Wisdom 2:21-30, e.g.:

Hebrews 4:12-13 For the word of God is quick, and powerful, and sharper than any twoedged sword, piercing even to the dividing asunder of soul and spirit, and of the joints and marrow, and is a discerner of the thoughts and intents of the heart. Neither is there any creature that is not manifest in his sight: but all things are naked and opened unto the eyes of him with whom we have to do.

James 3:17-18 17But the wisdom that is from above is first pure, then peaceable, gentle, and easy to be intreated, full of mercy and good fruits, without partiality, and without hypocrisy. 18And the fruit of righteousness is sown in peace of them that make peace.

7:25 <u>For she is the breath of the power of God, and a pure influence flowing from the glory of the Almighty: therefore can no defiled thing fall into her.</u>

There are many New Testament fulfillments of the prophesies in Wisdom 2:21-30, e.g.:

1 Corinthians 1:24: But unto them which are called, both Jews and Greeks, Christ the power of God, and the wisdom of God.

Hebrews 1:1-3 God, who at sundry times and in divers manners spake in time past unto the fathers by the prophets, Hath in these last days spoken unto us by his Son, whom he hath appointed heir of all things, by whom also he made the worlds; Who being the brightness of his glory, and the express image of his person, and upholding all things by the word of his power, when he had by himself purged our sins, sat down on the right hand of the Majesty on high.

Hebrews 4:15 For we have not an high priest which cannot be touched with the feeling of our infirmities; but was in all points tempted like as we are, yet without sin.

James 4:8 Draw nigh to God, and he will draw nigh to you. Cleanse your hands, ye sinners; and purify your hearts, ye double minded.

John 14:9 Jesus saith unto him, Have I been so long time with you, and yet hast thou not known me, Philip? he that hath seen me hath seen the Father; and how sayest thou then, Shew us the Father?

Mark 10:18 And Jesus said unto him, Why callest thou me good? there is none good but one, that is, God.

Revelation 21:22-27 And I saw no temple therein: for the Lord God Almighty and the Lamb are the temple of it. And the city had no need of the sun, neither of the moon, to shine in it: for the glory of God did lighten it, and the Lamb is the light thereof. And the nations of them which are saved shall walk in the light of it: and the kings of the earth do bring their glory and honour into it. And the gates of it shall not be shut at all by day: for there shall be no night there. And they shall bring the glory and honour of the nations into it. And there shall in no wise enter into it any thing that defileth, neither whatsoever worketh abomination, or maketh a lie: but they which are written in the Lamb's book of life.

7:26 <u>For she is the brightness of the everlasting light, the unspotted mirror of the power of God, and the image of his goodness.</u>

There are many New Testament fulfillments of the prophesies in Wisdom 2:21-30, e.g.:

Hebrews 1:3 Who being the brightness of his glory, and the express image of his person, and upholding all things by the word of his power, when he had by himself purged our sins, sat down on the right hand of the Majesty on high; Per the notes included with the original King James Bible. Discussed above; the Greek word for reflecting (as in a mirror: reflecting God) is used only in Hebrews 1:3 and Wisdom 7:26

Also per E. H. Plumptre, as part of showing that Apollos may have written the Book of Wisdom and the Epistle of the Hebrews.

John 1:14 Per R.C.H. Lenski John 1:14: The phrase "from the Father"' is coordinate with "as of the Only-begotten," both equally modifying "glory." What these witnesses beheld was "glory from the Father," a glory so great, so truly divine, resulting from the eternal relation of the Logos to the Father and thus shining forth in the Incarnate Son. This was the kabod Yaweh revealed in the Old Testament in a variety of ways, because of which also the Son is called "the effulgence of his glory, and the very image (impress) of his substance," Heb. 1:3.

Colossians 1:15 Who is the image of the invisible God, the firstborn of every creature.

7:27 And being but one, she can do all things: and remaining in herself, she maketh all things new: and in all ages entering into holy souls, she maketh them friends of God, and prophets.

There are many New Testament fulfillments of the prophesies in Wisdom 2:21-30, e.g.:

Revelation 21:5 And he [Jesus, the Divine Word] that sat upon the throne said, Behold, I make all things new.

2 Corinthians 5:17 Therefore if any man be in Christ, he is a new creature: old things are passed away; behold, all things are become new

Hebrews 6:6 If they shall fall away, to renew them again unto repentance; seeing they crucify to themselves the Son of God afresh, and put him to an open shame. Per E. H. Plumptre, as part of showing that Apollos may have written the Book of Wisdom and the Epistle of the Hebrews.

Hebrews 13:8 Jesus Christ the same yesterday, and today, and forever.

John 5:20 Then answered Jesus and said unto them, Verily, verily, I say unto you, The Son can do nothing of himself, but what he seeth the Father do: for what things soever he doeth, these also doeth the Son likewise. For the Father loveth the Son, and sheweth him all things that himself doeth: and he will shew him greater works than these, that ye may marvel.

Matthew 19:26 But Jesus beheld them, and said unto them, With men this is impossible; but with God all things are possible.

7:28 For God loveth none but him that dwelleth with wisdom. (Some modern translations of Wisdom 7:28: And passing into holy souls from age to age, she produces friends of God and prophets).

There are many New Testament fulfillments of the prophesies in Wisdom 2:21-30, e.g.:

John 8:58 Jesus said unto them, Verily, verily, I say unto you, Before Abraham was, I am.

1 John 1:7 But if we walk in the light, as he is in the light, we have fellowship one with another, and the blood of Jesus Christ his Son cleanseth us from all sin.

1 John 5:12 He that hath the Son hath life; and he that hath not the Son of God hath not life.

Hebrews 13:21 Make you perfect in every good work to do his will, working in you that which is wellpleasing in his sight, through Jesus Christ; to whom be glory for ever and ever. Amen.

James 2:23 And the scripture was fulfilled which saith, Abraham believed God, and it was imputed unto him for righteousness: and he was called the Friend of God.

Romans 8:10 But ye are not in the flesh, but in the Spirit, if so be that the Spirit of

God dwell in you. Now if any man have not the Spirit of Christ, he is none of his. And if Christ be in you, the body is dead because of sin; but the Spirit is life because of righteousness.

7:29 <u>For she is more beautiful than the sun, and above all the order of stars: being compared with the light, she is found before it.</u>

There are many New Testament fulfillments of the prophesies in Wisdom 2:21-30, e.g.:

1 John 1:7 This then is the message which we have heard of him, and declare unto you, that God is light, and in him is no darkness at all. If we say that we have fellowship with him, and walk in darkness, we lie, and do not the truth: But if we walk in the light, as he is in the light, we have fellowship one with another, and the blood of Jesus Christ his Son cleanseth us from all sin.

1 Timothy 6:16 Which in his times he shall shew, who is the blessed and only Potentate, the King of kings, and Lord of lords; Who only hath immortality, dwelling in the light which no man can approach unto; whom no man hath seen, nor can see: to whom be honour and power everlasting. Amen.

John 1:4 In him was life; and the life was the light of men.

John 1:9 That was the true Light, which lighteth every man that cometh into the world.

7:30 <u>For after this cometh night: but vice shall not prevail against wisdom.</u>

There are many New Testament fulfillments of the prophesies in Wisdom 2:21-30, e.g.:

John 1:5 And the light shineth in darkness; and the darkness comprehended it not.

8:1 Wisdom reacheth from one end to another mightily: and sweetly doth she order all things. 8:2 I loved her, and sought her out from my youth, I desired to make her my spouse, and I was a lover of her beauty. 8:3 In that she is conversant with God, she magnifieth her nobility: yea, the Lord of all things himself loved her. 8:4 For she is privy to the mysteries of the knowledge of God, and a lover of his works. 8:5 If riches be a possession to be desired in this life; what is richer than wisdom, that worketh all things? 8:6 And if prudence work; who of all that are is a more cunning workman than she? 8:7 And if a man love righteousness her labours are virtues: for she teacheth temperance and prudence, justice and fortitude: which are such things, as men can have nothing more profitable in their life. 8:8 If a man desire much experience, she knoweth things of old, and conjectureth aright what is to come: she knoweth the subtilties of speeches, and can expound dark sentences: she foreseeth signs and wonders, and the events of seasons and times. 8:9 Therefore I purposed to take her to me to live with me, knowing that she would be a counsellor of good things, and a comfort in cares and grief. 8:10 For her sake I shall have estimation among the multitude, and honour with the elders, though I be young. 8:11 I shall be found of a quick conceit in judgment, and shall be admired in the sight of great men. 8:12 When I hold my tongue, they shall bide my leisure, and when I speak, they shall give good ear unto me: if I talk much, they shall lay their hands upon their mouth. 8:13 Moreover by the means of her I shall obtain immortality, and leave behind me an everlasting memorial to them that come after me. 8:14 I shall set the people in order, and the nations shall be subject unto me. 8:15 Horrible tyrants shall be afraid, when they do but hear of me; I shall be found good among the multitude, and valiant in war. 8:16 After I am come into mine house, I will repose myself with her: for her conversation hath no bitterness; and to live with her hath no sorrow, but mirth and joy. 8:17 Now when I considered these things in myself, and pondered them in my heart, how that to be allied unto wisdom is immortality; 8:18 And great pleasure it is to have her friendship; and in the works of her hands are infinite riches; and in the exercise of conference with her, prudence; and in talking with her, a good report; I went about seeking how to take her to me. 8:19 For I was a witty child, and had a good spirit. 8:20 Yea rather, being good, I came into a body undefiled. 8:21 Nevertheless, when I perceived that I could not otherwise obtain her, except God gave her me; and that was a point of wisdom also to know whose gift she was; I prayed unto the Lord, and besought him, and with my whole heart I said,

1 Corinthians 1:30: But of him are ye in Christ Jesus, who of God is made unto us wisdom, and righteousness, and sanctification, and redemption.

Hebrews 7:25: Wherefore he is able also to save them to the uttermost that come unto God by him, seeing he ever liveth to make intercession for them. Per E. H. Plumptre, as part of showing that Apollos may have written the Book of Wisdom and the Epistle of the Hebrews.

9:1 O God of my fathers, and Lord of mercy, who hast made all things with thy word, 9:2 And ordained man through thy wisdom, that he should have dominion over the creatures which thou hast made,

John 1:1-18 John's Prologue (In the beginning was the Word, and the Word was with God, and the Word was God. ... And the Word was made flesh, and dwelt among us (and we beheld his glory, the glory as of the only begotten of the Father)) identifies Jesus with God's Word (Greek: logos) and with Divine wisdom. Wisdom 9:1-2 related God's "word" to His "wisdom."

1 John 1:1 That which was from the beginning, which we have heard, which we have seen with our eyes, which we have looked upon, and our hands have handled, of the Word of life.

Revelation 19:13 And he was clothed with a vesture dipped in blood: and his name is called The Word of God.

Colossians 1:15-20 also identifies Jesus as the Word of God (implicitly: by him were all things created, etc.), and then makes many allusions to the Book of Wisdom (see 1:7, 7:22-26, 9:9; see also 6:7).

Hebrews 3:4 For every house is builded by some man; but he that built all things is God. Per E. H. Plumptre, as part of showing that Apollos may have written the Book of Wisdom and the Epistle of the Hebrews.

9:3 And order the world according to equity and righteousness, and execute judgment with an upright heart:

Luke 1:75 In holiness and righteousness before him, all the days of our life. (the Greek phrase translated as 'according to equity and righteousness' in Wisdom 9:3 is not found elsewhere in the Old Testament but was used in Luke 1:75 and Ephesians 4:24).

Ephesians 4:24 And that ye put on the new man, which after God is created in righteousness and true holiness. (the Greek phrase translated as 'according to equity and righteousness' in Wisdom 9:3 is not found elsewhere in the Old Testament but was used in Luke 1:75 and Ephesians 4:24).

9:4 Give me wisdom, that sitteth by thy throne; and reject me not from among thy children: 9:5 For I thy servant and son of thine handmaid am a feeble person, and of a short time, and too young for the understanding of judgment and laws. 9:6 For though a man be never so perfect among the children of men, yet if thy wisdom be not with him, he shall be nothing regarded. 9:7 Thou hast chosen me to be a king of thy people, and a judge of thy sons and daughters: 9:8 Thou hast commanded me to build a temple upon thy holy mount, and an altar in the city wherein thou dwellest, a resemblance of the holy tabernacle, which thou hast prepared from the beginning. 9:9 And wisdom was with thee: which knoweth thy works, and was present when thou madest the world, and knew what was acceptable in thy sight, and right in thy commandments.

John 1:1-3: In the beginning was the Word, and the Word was with God, and the Word was God. The same was in the beginning with God. All things were made by him; and without him was not any thing made that was made.

Colossians 1:17: And he is before all things, and by him all things consist.

9:10 O send her out of thy holy heavens, and from the throne of thy glory, that being present she may labour with me, that I may know what is pleasing unto thee. 9:11 For she knoweth and understandeth all things, and she shall lead me soberly in my doings, and preserve me in her power. 9:12 So shall my works be acceptable, and then shall I judge thy people righteously, and be worthy to sit in my father's seat. 9:13 For what man is he that can know the counsel of God? or who can think what the will of the Lord is?

1 Corinthians 2:16: For who hath known the mind of the Lord, that he may instruct him? But we have the mind of Christ. Per the notes included with the original King James Bible.

Romans 11:34: For who hath known the mind of the Lord? or who hath been his counsellor? Per the notes included with the original King James Bible.

9:14 For the thoughts of mortal men are miserable, and our devices are but uncertain. 9:15 For the corruptible body presseth down the soul, and the earthy tabernacle weigheth down the mind that museth upon many things.

Romans 7:24 O wretched man that I am! who shall deliver me from the body of this death?

9:16 And hardly do we guess aright at things that are upon earth, and with labour do we find the things that are before us: but the things that are in heaven who hath searched out?

John 3:12: If I have told you earthly things, and ye believe not, how shall ye believe, if I tell you of heavenly things?

9:17 And thy counsel who hath known, except thou give wisdom, and send thy Holy Spirit from above? 9:18 For so the ways of them which lived on the earth were reformed, and men were taught the things that are pleasing unto thee, and were saved through wisdom.

Romans 8:1-14: The Book of Wisdom 9:17-18 correlates the Holy Spirit with Wisdom, by whom "men were taught the things that are pleasing unto thee, and were saved through wisdom." Compare the point of Romans 8:1-14 (beginning with "There is therefore now no condemnation to them which are in Christ Jesus, who walk not after the flesh, but after the Spirit" and ending with "For as many as are led by the Spirit of God, they are the sons of God").

1 Corinthians 2:6-13 also makes the same point: "... 7But we speak the wisdom of God in a mystery, even the hidden wisdom, which God ordained before the world unto our glory ... 10But God hath revealed them unto us by his Spirit... 11For what man knoweth the things of a man, save the spirit of man which is in him? even so the things of God knoweth no man, but the Spirit of God... 12Now we have received, not the spirit of the world, but the spirit which is of God; that we might know the things that are freely given to us of God. 13Which things also we speak, not in the words which man's wisdom teacheth, but which the Holy Ghost teacheth; comparing spiritual things with spiritual."

10:1 She preserved the first formed father of the world, that was created alone, and brought him out of his fall, 10:2 And gave him power to rule all things. 10:3 But when the unrighteous went away from her in his anger, he perished also in the fury wherewith he murdered his brother. 10:4 For whose cause the earth being drowned with the flood, wisdom again preserved it, and directed the course of the righteous in a piece of wood of small value.

Justin Martyr 155 AD Dialogue with Trypho 137-138: And as they kept silence, I continued: My friends I now refer to the Scriptures as the Seventy have interpreted them; ... I shall add one remark to what I have said, and conclude... Accordingly, when the prophet says, 'I saved you in the times of Noah,' ... he addresses the people who are equally faithful to God, and possess the same signs. ... I mean, that by water, faith, and wood, those who are afore-prepared, and who repent of the sins which they have committed, shall escape from the impending judgment of God. www.newadvent.org/fathers/01289.htm

10:5 Moreover, the nations in their wicked conspiracy being confounded, she found out the righteous, and preserved him blameless unto God, and kept him strong against his tender compassion toward his son. 10:6 When the ungodly perished, she delivered the righteous man, who fled from the fire which fell down upon the five cities. 10:7 Of whose wickedness even to this day the waste land that smoketh is a testimony, and plants bearing fruit that never come to ripeness: and a standing pillar of salt is a monument of an unbelieving soul. 10:8 For regarding not wisdom, they gat not only this hurt, that they knew not the things which were good; but also left behind them to the world a memorial of their foolishness: so that in the things wherein they offended they could not so much as be hid. 10:9 But wisdom delivered from pain those that attended upon her. 10:10 When the righteous fled from his brother's wrath she guided him in right paths, shewed him the kingdom of God, and gave him knowledge of holy things, made him rich in his travels, and multiplied the fruit of his labours. 10:11 In the covetousness of such as oppressed him she stood by him, and made him rich. 10:12 She defended him from his enemies, and kept him safe from those that lay in wait, and in a sore conflict she gave him the victory; that he might know that goodness is stronger than all.

10:13 **When the righteous was sold, she forsook him not, but delivered him from sin: she went down with him into the pit,**

Acts 7:9-10: God was with him, and delivered him out of all his afflictions, and gave him favour and wisdom in the sight of Pharaoh king of Egypt; and he made him governor over Egypt and all his house. Per the notes included with the original King James Bible.

10:14 And left him not in bonds, till she brought him the sceptre of the kingdom, and power against those that oppressed him: as for them that had accused him, she shewed them to be liars, and gave him perpetual glory. 10:15 She delivered the righteous people and blameless seed from the nation that oppressed them. 10:16 She entered into the soul of the servant of the Lord, and withstood dreadful kings in wonders and signs; 10:17 Rendered to the righteous a reward of their labours, guided them in a marvellous way, and was unto them for a cover by day, and a light of stars in the night season; 10:18 Brought them through the Red sea, and led them through much water: 10:19 But she drowned their enemies, and cast them up out of the bottom of the deep. 10:20 Therefore the righteous spoiled the ungodly, and praised thy holy name, O Lord, and magnified with one accord thine hand, that fought for them. 10:21 For wisdom opened the mouth of the dumb, and made the tongues of them that cannot speak eloquent.

11:1 She prospered their works in the hand of the holy prophet. 11:2 They went through the wilderness that was not inhabited, and pitched tents in places where there lay no way. 11:3 They stood against their enemies, and were avenged of their adversaries. 11:4 When they were thirsty, they called upon thee, and water was given them out of the flinty rock, and their thirst was quenched out of the hard stone. 11:5 For by what things their enemies were punished, by the same they in their need were benefited. 11:6 For instead of a perpetual running river troubled with foul blood, 11:7 For a manifest reproof of that commandment, whereby the infants were slain, thou gavest unto them abundance of water by a means which they hoped not for: 11:8 Declaring by that thirst then how thou hadst punished their adversaries. 11:9 For when they were tried albeit but in mercy chastised, they knew how the ungodly were judged in wrath and tormented, thirsting in another manner than the just. 11:10 For these thou didst admonish and try, as a father: but the other, as a severe king, thou didst condemn and punish. 11:11 Whether they were absent or present, they were vexed alike. 11:12 For a double grief came upon them, and a groaning for the remembrance of things past. 11:13 For when they heard by their own punishments the other to be benefited, they had some feeling of the Lord. 11:14 For whom they respected with scorn, when he was long before thrown out at the casting forth of the infants, him in the end, when they saw what came to pass, they admired. 11:15 **But for the foolish devices of their wickedness, wherewith being deceived they worshipped serpents void of reason, and vile beasts, thou didst send a multitude of unreasonable beasts upon them for vengeance;**

Romans 1:23: And changed the glory of the uncorruptible God into an image made like to corruptible man, and to birds, and fourfooted beasts, and creeping things.

(Romans 1:20-1:32 borrows extensively from Wisdom chapters 11-15: see 12:24, 13:2 and 13:7 for KJV cross-references, and 13:1-4, 13:5, 13:8, 14:12, and 14:22-31 for others).

11:16 That they might know, that wherewithal a man sinneth, by the same also shall he be punished. 11:17 For thy Almighty hand, that made the world of matter without form, wanted not means to send among them a multitude of bears or fierce lions, 11:18 Or unknown wild beasts, full of rage, newly created, breathing out either a fiery vapour, or filthy scents of scattered smoke, or shooting horrible sparkles out of their eyes: 11:19 Whereof not only the harm might dispatch them at once, but also the terrible sight utterly destroy them. 11:20 Yea, and without these might they have fallen down with one blast, being persecuted of vengeance, and scattered abroad through the breath of thy power: but thou hast ordered all things in measure and number and weight.

[Cited as early as Justin Martyr (155 AD), this will later become a favorite verse of Augustine, and after him it will then go on to be cited by innumerable pre-modern scientific books.]

11:21 For thou canst shew thy great strength at all times when thou wilt; and who may withstand the power of thine arm? 11:22 For the whole world before thee is as a little grain of the balance, yea, as a drop of the morning dew that falleth down upon the earth. 11:23 But thou hast mercy upon all; for thou canst do all things, and winkest at the sins of men, because they should amend. 11:24 For thou lovest all the things that are, and abhorrest nothing which thou hast made: for never wouldest thou have made any thing, if thou hadst hated it. 11:25 And how could any thing have endured, if it had not been thy will? or been preserved, if not called by thee? 11:26 But thou sparest all: for they are thine, O Lord, thou lover of souls.

12:1 For thine incorruptible Spirit is in all things. 12:2 **Therefore chastenest thou them by little and little that offend, and warnest them by putting them in remembrance wherein they have offended, that leaving their wickedness they may believe on thee, O Lord.**

Hebrews 2:15: And deliver them who through fear of death were all their lifetime subject to bondage. Per E. H. Plumptre, as part of showing that Apollos may have written the Book of Wisdom and the Epistle of the Hebrews.

12:3 For it was thy will to destroy by the hands of our fathers both those old inhabitants of thy holy land, 12:4 Whom thou hatedst for doing most odious works of witchcrafts, and wicked sacrifices; 12:5 And also those merciless murderers of children, and devourers of man's flesh, and the feasts of blood, 12:6 With their priests out of the midst of their idolatrous crew, and the parents, that killed with their own hands souls destitute of help: 12:7 That the land, which thou esteemedst above all other, might receive a worthy colony of God's children. 12:8 Nevertheless even those thou sparedst as men, and didst send wasps, forerunners of thine host, to destroy them by little and little.

Hebrews 6:20 Whither the forerunner is for us entered, even Jesus, made an high priest for ever after the order of Melchisedec. Per E. H. Plumptre, as part of showing that Apollos may have written the Book of Wisdom and the Epistle of the Hebrews.

12:9 Not that thou wast unable to bring the ungodly under the hand of the righteous in battle, or to destroy them at once with cruel beasts, or with one rough word: 12:10 But executing thy judgments upon them by little and little, thou gavest them place of repentance, not being ignorant that they were a naughty generation, and that their malice was bred in them, and that their cogitation would never be changed.

Hebrews 12:17 (The verse in Hebrews and the verse in Wisdom use the same Greek terms found nowhere else in New or Old Testament.) For ye know how that afterward, when he would have inherited the blessing, he was rejected: for he found no place of repentance, though he sought it carefully with tears. Per E. H. Plumptre, as part of showing that Apollos may have written the Book of Wisdom and the Epistle of the Hebrews.

12:11 For it was a cursed seed from the beginning; neither didst thou for fear of any man give them pardon for those things wherein they sinned. 12:12 For who shall say, What hast thou done? or who shall withstand thy judgment? or who shall accuse thee for the nations that perish, whom thou made? or who shall come to stand against thee, to be revenged for the unrighteous men?

Romans 9:20 Nay but, O man, who art thou that repliest against God? Shall the thing formed say to him that formed it, Why hast thou made me thus? Per the notes included with the original King James Bible.

12:13 For neither is there any God but thou that careth for all, to whom thou mightest shew that thy judgment is not unright.

1 Peter 5:7 Casting all your care upon him; for he careth for you. Per the notes included with the original King James Bible.

12:14 Neither shall king or tyrant be able to set his face against thee for any whom thou hast punished. 12:15 Forsomuch then as thou art righteous thyself, thou orderest all things righteously: thinking it not agreeable with thy power to condemn him that hath not deserved to be punished. 12:16 For thy power is the beginning of righteousness, and because thou art the Lord of all, it maketh thee to be gracious unto all. 12:17 For when men will not believe that thou art of a full power, thou shewest thy strength, and among them that know it thou makest their boldness manifest. 12:18 But thou, mastering thy power, judgest with equity, and orderest us with great favour: for thou mayest use power when thou wilt. 12:19 But by such works hast thou taught thy people that the just man should be merciful, and hast made thy children to be of a good hope that thou givest repentance for sins. 12:20 For if thou didst punish the enemies of thy children, and the condemned to death, with such deliberation, giving them time and place, whereby they might be delivered from their malice: 12:21 With how great circumspection didst thou judge thine own sons, unto whose fathers thou hast sworn, and made covenants of good promises? 12:22 Therefore, whereas thou dost chasten us, thou scourgest our enemies a thousand times more, to the intent that, when we judge, we should carefully think of thy goodness, and when we ourselves are judged, we should look for mercy. 12:23 Wherefore, whereas men have lived dissolutely and unrighteously, thou hast tormented them with their own abominations. 12:24 For they went astray very far in the ways of error, and held them for gods, which even among the beasts of their enemies were despised, being deceived, as children of no understanding.

Romans 1:23 And changed the glory of the uncorruptible God into an image made like to corruptible man, and to birds, and fourfooted beasts, and creeping things. Per the notes included with the original King James Bible.

12:25 Therefore unto them, as to children without the use of reason, thou didst send a judgment to mock them. 12:26 But they that would not be reformed by that correction, wherein he dallied with them, shall feel a judgment worthy of God. 12:27 For, look, for what things they grudged, when they were punished, that is, for them whom they thought to be gods; [now] being punished in them, when they saw it, they acknowledged him to be the true God, whom before they denied to know: and therefore came extreme damnation upon them.

13:1 Surely vain are all men by nature, who are ignorant of God, and could not out of the good things that are seen know him that is: neither by considering the works did they acknowledge the workmaster; 13:2 But deemed either fire, or wind, or the swift air, or the circle of the stars, or the violent water, or the lights of heaven, to be the gods which govern the world.

Romans 1:23 And changed the glory of the uncorruptible God into an image made like to corruptible man, and to birds, and fourfooted beasts, and creeping things. Per the notes included with the original King James Bible.

13:3 With whose beauty if they being delighted took them to be gods; let them know how much better the Lord of them is: for the first author of beauty hath created them. 13:4 But if they were astonished at their power and virtue, let them understand by them, how much mightier he is that made them.

Romans 1:25 Who changed the truth of God into a lie, and worshipped and served the creature more than the Creator, who is blessed for ever. Amen. (Wisdom and Paul both define idolatry as worshiping creation rather than the Creator).

13:5 For by the greatness and beauty of the creatures proportionably the maker of them is seen.

Romans 1:20 For the invisible things of him from the creation of the world are clearly seen, being understood by the things that are made, even his eternal power and Godhead; so that they are without excuse. (Wisdom and Paul both contend that God's existence can be perceived from the world that God made).

13:6 But yet for this they are the less to be blamed: for they peradventure err, seeking God, and desirous to find him.

Hebrews 5:12 For when for the time ye ought to be teachers, ye have need that one teach you again which be the first principles of the oracles of God; and are become such as have need of milk, and not of strong meat. Per E. H. Plumptre, as part of showing that Apollos may have written the Book of Wisdom and the Epistle of the Hebrews.

Hebrews 10:36 For ye have need of patience, that, after ye have done the will of God, ye might receive the promise. Also per E. H. Plumptre.

13:7 For being conversant in his works they search him diligently, and believe their sight: because the things are beautiful that are seen.

Romans 1:21 Because that, when they knew God, they glorified him not as God, neither were thankful; but became vain in their imaginations, and their foolish heart was darkened. Per the notes included with the original King James Bible.

13:8 **Howbeit neither are they to be pardoned.**

Romans 1:20 For the invisible things of him from the creation of the world are clearly seen, being understood by the things that are made, even his eternal power and Godhead; so that they are without excuse. (Wisdom and Paul both declare the failure to know the true God an inexcusable error).

13:9 For if they were able to know so much, that they could aim at the world; how did they not sooner find out the Lord thereof? 13:10 But miserable are they, and in dead things is their hope, who call them gods, which are the works of men's hands, gold and silver, to shew art in, and resemblances of beasts, or a stone good for nothing, the work of an ancient hand. 13:11 Now a carpenter that felleth timber, after he hath sawn down a tree meet for the purpose, and taken off all the bark skilfully round about, and hath wrought it handsomely, and made a vessel thereof fit for the service of man's life; 13:12 And after spending the refuse of his work to dress his meat, hath filled himself; 13:13 And taking the very refuse among those which served to no use, being a crooked piece of wood, and full of knots, hath carved it diligently, when he had nothing else to do, and formed it by the skill of his understanding, and fashioned it to the image of a man; 13:14 Or made it like some vile beast, laying it over with vermilion, and with paint colouring it red, and covering every spot therein; 13:15 And when he had made a convenient room for it, set it in a wall, and made it fast with iron: 13:16 For he provided for it that it might not fall, knowing that it was unable to help itself; for it is an image, and hath need of help: 13:17 Then maketh he prayer for his goods, for his wife and children, and is not ashamed to speak to that which hath no life. 13:18 **For health he calleth upon that which is weak: for life prayeth to that which is dead; for aid humbly beseecheth that which hath least means to help: and for a good journey he asketh of that which cannot set a foot forward:**

Hebrews 5:13 For every one that useth milk is unskilful in the word of righteousness: for he is a babe. Per E. H. Plumptre, as part of showing that Apollos may have written the Book of Wisdom and the Epistle of the Hebrews.

13:19 And for gaining and getting, and for good success of his hands, asketh ability to do of him, that is most unable to do any thing. 14:1 Again, one preparing himself to sail, and about to pass through the raging waves, calleth upon a piece of wood more rotten than the vessel that carrieth him. 14:2 For verily desire of gain devised that, and the workman built it by his skill. 14:3 But thy providence, O Father, governeth it: for thou hast made a way in the sea, and a safe path in the waves; 14:4 Shewing that thou canst save from all danger: yea, though a man went to sea without art. 14:5 Nevertheless thou wouldest not that the works of thy wisdom should be idle, and therefore do men commit their lives to a small piece of wood, and passing the rough sea in a weak vessel are saved. 14:6 **For in the old time also, when the proud giants perished, the hope of the world governed by thy hand escaped in a weak vessel, and left to all ages a seed of generation.**

Hebrews 4:6 Seeing therefore it remaineth that some must enter therein, and they to whom it was first preached entered not in because of unbelief. Per E. H. Plumptre, as part of showing that Apollos may have written the Book of Wisdom and the Epistle of the Hebrews.

14:7 For blessed is the wood whereby righteousness cometh. 14:8 But that which is made with hands is cursed, as well it, as he that made it: he, because he made it; and it, because, being corruptible, it was called god. 14:9 For the ungodly and his ungodliness are both alike hateful unto God. 14:10 For that which is made shall be punished together with him that made it. 14:11 Therefore even upon the idols of the Gentiles shall there be a visitation: because in the creature of God they are become an abomination, and stumblingblocks to the souls of men, and a snare to the feet of the unwise. 14:12 **For the devising of idols was the beginning of spiritual fornication, and the invention of them the corruption of life.**

Romans 1:24-32 (Wisdom and Paul both single out idolatry as the root cause of social and sexual immorality – see full quote from Romans at 14:31 below).

14:13 For neither were they from the beginning, neither shall they be for ever. 14:14 For by the vain glory of men they entered into the world, and therefore shall they come shortly to an end. 14:15 For a father afflicted with untimely mourning, when he hath made an image of his child soon taken away, now honoured him as a god, which was then a dead man, and delivered to those that were under him ceremonies and sacrifices. 14:16 Thus in process of time an ungodly custom grown strong was kept as a law, and graven images were worshipped by the commandments of kings. 14:17 Whom men could not honour in presence, because they dwelt far off, they took the counterfeit of his visage from far, and made an express image of a king whom they honoured, to the end that by this their forwardness they might flatter him that was absent, as if he were present. 14:18 Also the singular diligence of the artificer did help to set forward the ignorant to more superstition. 14:19 For he, peradventure willing to please one in authority, forced all his skill to make the resemblance of the best fashion. 14:20 And so the multitude, allured by the grace of the work, took him now for a god, which a little before was but honoured. 14:21 And this was an occasion to deceive the world: for men, serving either calamity or tyranny, did ascribe unto stones and stocks the incommunicable name. 14:22 **Moreover this was not enough for them, that they erred in the knowledge of God; but whereas they lived in the great war of ignorance, those so great plagues called they peace. 14:23 For whilst they slew their children in sacrifices, or used secret ceremonies, or made revellings of strange rites; 14:24 They kept neither lives nor marriages any longer undefiled: but either one slew another traiterously, or grieved him by adultery. 14:25 So that there reigned in all men without exception blood, manslaughter, theft, and dissimulation, corruption, unfaithfulness, tumults, perjury, 14:26 Disquieting of good men, forgetfulness of good turns, defiling of souls, changing of kind, disorder in marriages, adultery, and shameless uncleanness. 14:27 For the worshipping of idols not to be named is the beginning, the cause, and the end, of all evil. 14:28 For either they are mad when they be merry, or prophesy lies, or live unjustly, or else lightly forswear themselves. 14:29 For insomuch as their trust is in idols, which have no life; though they swear falsely, yet they look not to be hurt. 14:30 Howbeit for both causes shall they be justly punished: both because they thought not well of God, giving heed unto idols, and also unjustly swore in deceit, despising holiness. 14:31 For it is not the power of them by whom they swear: but it is the just vengeance of sinners, that punisheth always the offence of the ungodly.**

Romans 1:24-32 24Wherefore God also gave them up to uncleanness through the lusts of their own hearts, to dishonour their own bodies between themselves: 25Who changed the truth of God into a lie, and worshipped and served the creature more than the Creator, who is blessed for ever. Amen. 26For this cause God gave them up unto vile affections: for even their women did change the natural use into that which is against nature: 27And likewise also the men, leaving the natural use of the woman, burned in their lust one toward another; men with men working that which is unseemly, and receiving in themselves that recompence of their error which was meet. 28And even as they did not like to retain God in their knowledge, God gave them over to a reprobate mind, to do those things which are not convenient; 29Being filled

with all unrighteousness, fornication, wickedness, covetousness, maliciousness; full of envy, murder, debate, deceit, malignity; whisperers,30Backbiters, haters of God, despiteful, proud, boasters, inventors of evil things, disobedient to parents, 31Without understanding, covenantbreakers, without natural affection, implacable, unmerciful: 32Who knowing the judgment of God, that they which commit such things are worthy of death, not only do the same, but have pleasure in them that do them. (Wisdom and Paul both single out idolatry as the root cause of social and sexual immorality).

Ephesians 4:17-19 17This I say therefore, and testify in the Lord, that ye henceforth walk not as other Gentiles walk, in the vanity of their mind, 18Having the understanding darkened, being alienated from the life of God through the ignorance that is in them, because of the blindness of their heart: 19Who being past feeling have given themselves over unto lasciviousness, to work all uncleanness with greediness.

15:1 But thou, O God, art gracious and true, longsuffering, and in mercy ordering all things, 15:2 For if we sin, we are thine, knowing thy power: but we will not sin, knowing that we are counted thine. 15:3 For to know thee is perfect righteousness: yea, to know thy power is the root of immortality. 15:4 For neither did the mischievous invention of men deceive us, nor an image spotted with divers colours, the painter's fruitless labour; 15:5 The sight whereof enticeth fools to lust after it, and so they desire the form of a dead image, that hath no breath. 15:6 Both they that make them, they that desire them, and they that worship them, are lovers of evil things, and are worthy to have such things to trust upon. 15:7 **For the potter, tempering soft earth, fashioneth every vessel with much labour for our service: yea, of the same clay he maketh both the vessels that serve for clean uses, and likewise also all such as**

serve to the contrary: but what is the use of either sort, the potter himself is the judge.

Romans 9:22 Nay but, O man, who art thou that repliest against God? Shall the thing formed say to him that formed it, Why hast thou made me thus? Hath not the potter power over the clay, of the same lump to make one vessel unto honour, and another unto dishonour? What if God, willing to shew his wrath, and to make his power known, endured with much longsuffering the vessels of wrath fitted to destruction. Per the notes included with the original King James Bible. (The key here is that both good and bad are made from the same clay. Paul makes the point three times, and that aspect of a potter making something from clay is not found elsewhere outside of the Book of Wisdom).

15:8 **And employing his labours lewdly, he maketh a vain god of the same clay, even he which a little before was made of earth himself, and within a little while after returneth to the same, out when his life which was lent him shall be demanded.**

Luke 12:20 But God said unto him, Thou fool, this night thy soul shall be required of thee: then whose shall those things be, which thou hast provided? Per the notes included with the original King James Bible. (Genesis speaks only of the return of Adam to the earth. Nothing is said of the living breath returning to God, but that is part of the point in the Gospel of Luke ("This very night your life is being demanded of you" Luke 12:20 NRSV). Only in the Book of Wisdom do we have the explicit comparison of death to the return, as if we have a soul only on lease).

15:9 Notwithstanding his care is, not that he shall have much labour, nor that his life is short: but striveth to excel goldsmiths and silversmiths, and endeavoureth to do like the workers in brass, and counteth it his glory to make counterfeit things. 15:10 His heart is ashes, his hope is more vile than earth, and his life of less value than clay: 15:11 Forasmuch as he knew not his Maker, and him that inspired into him an active soul, and breathed in a living spirit. 15:12 But they counted our life a pastime, and our time here a market for gain: for, say they, we must be getting every way, though it be by evil means. 15:13 For this man, that of earthly matter maketh brittle vessels and graven images, knoweth himself to offend above all others. 15:14 And all the enemies of thy people, that hold them in subjection, are most foolish, and are more miserable than very babes. 15:15 For they counted all the idols of the heathen to be gods: which neither have the use of eyes to see, nor noses to draw breath, nor ears to hear, nor fingers of hands to handle; and as for their feet, they are slow to go. 15:16 For man made them, and he that borrowed his own spirit fashioned them: but no man can make a god like unto himself. 15:17 For being mortal, he worketh a dead thing with wicked hands: for he himself is better than the things which he worshippeth: whereas he lived once, but they never. 15:18 Yea, they worshipped those beasts also that are most hateful: for being compared together, some are worse than others. 15:19 Neither are they beautiful, so much as to be desired in respect of beasts: but they went without the praise of God and his blessing.

16:1 Therefore by the like were they punished worthily, and by the multitude of beasts tormented. 16:2 Instead of which punishment, dealing graciously with thine own people, thou preparedst for them meat of a strange taste, even quails to stir up their appetite: 16:3 To the end that they, desiring food, might for the ugly sight of the beasts sent among them lothe even that, which they must needs desire; but these, suffering penury for a short space, might be made partakers of a strange taste. 16:4 For it was requisite, that upon them exercising tyranny should come penury, which they could not avoid: but to these it should only be shewed how their enemies were tormented. 16:5 **For when the horrible fierceness of beasts came upon these, and they perished with the stings of crooked serpents, thy wrath endured not for ever:**

1 Corinthians 10:9 Neither let us tempt Christ, as some of them also tempted, and were destroyed of serpents. Per the notes included with the original King James Bible.

16:6 **But they were troubled for a small season, that they might be admonished, having a sign of salvation, to put them in remembrance of the commandment of thy law.**

Hebrews 3:6 But Christ as a son over his own house; whose house are we, if we hold fast the confidence and the rejoicing of the hope firm unto the end. Per E. H. Plumptre, as part of showing that Apollos may have written the Book of Wisdom and the Epistle of the Hebrews.

16:7 For he that turned himself toward it was not saved by the thing that he saw, but by thee, that art the Saviour of all. 16:8 And in this thou madest thine enemies confess, that it is thou who deliverest from all evil: 16:9 **For them the bitings of grasshoppers and flies killed, neither was there found any remedy for their life: for they were worthy to be punished by such.**

Revelation 9:7 And the shapes of the locusts were like unto horses prepared unto battle; and on their heads were as it were crowns like gold, and their faces were as the faces of men. Per the notes included with the original King James Bible.

16:10 But thy sons not the very teeth of venomous dragons overcame: for thy mercy was ever by them, and healed them. 16:11 For they were pricked, that they should remember thy words; and were quickly saved, that not falling into deep forgetfulness, they might be continually mindful of thy goodness. 16:12 For it was neither herb, nor mollifying plaister, that restored them to health: but thy word, O Lord, which healeth all things. 16:13 **For thou hast power of life and death: thou leadest to the gates of hell, and bringest up again.**

Hebrews 13:20 Now the God of peace, that brought again from the dead our Lord Jesus, that great shepherd of the sheep, through the blood of the everlasting covenant. Per E. H. Plumptre, as part of showing that Apollos may have written the Book of Wisdom and the Epistle of the Hebrews.

Matthew 16:18 And I say also unto thee, That thou art Peter, and upon this rock I will build my church; and the gates of hell shall not prevail against it. Per the Evangelical Biblical Theology Commentary volume on Matthew.

16:14 A man indeed killeth through his malice: and the spirit, when it is gone forth, returneth not; neither the soul received up cometh again. 16:15 But it is not possible to escape thine hand. 16:16 For the ungodly, that denied to know thee, were scourged by the strength of thine arm: with strange rains, hails, and showers, were they persecuted, that they could not avoid, and through fire were they consumed. 16:17 For, which is most to be wondered at, the fire had more force in the water, that quencheth all things: for the world fighteth for the righteous. 16:18 For sometime the flame was mitigated, that it might not burn up the beasts that were sent against the ungodly; but themselves might see and perceive that they were persecuted with the judgment of God. 16:19 And at another time it burneth even in the midst of water above the power of fire, that it might destroy the fruits of an unjust land. 16:20 Instead whereof thou feddest thine own people with angels' food, and didst send them from heaven bread prepared without their labour, able to content every man's delight, and agreeing to every taste. 16:21 <u>For thy sustenance declared thy sweetness unto thy children, and serving to the appetite of the eater, tempered itself to every man's liking.</u>

Hebrews 1:3 Who being the brightness of his glory, and the express image of his person, and upholding all things by the word of his power, when he had by himself purged our sins, sat down on the right hand of the Majesty on high. Per E. H. Plumptre, as part of showing that Apollos may have written the Book of Wisdom and the Epistle of the Hebrews.

Hebrews 3:14 For we are made partakers of Christ, if we hold the beginning of our confidence stedfast unto the end. Also per E. H. Plumptre.

Hebrews 11:1 Now faith is the substance of things hoped for, the evidence of things not seen. Also per E. H. Plumptre.

16:22 But snow and ice endured the fire, and melted not, that they might know that fire burning in the hail, and sparkling in the rain, did destroy the fruits of the enemies. 16:23 But this again did even forget his own strength, that the righteous might be nourished. 16:24 For the creature that serveth thee, who art the Maker increaseth his strength against the unrighteous for their punishment, and abateth his strength for the benefit of such as put their trust in thee. 16:25 Therefore even then was it altered into all fashions, and was obedient to thy grace, that nourisheth all things, according to the desire of them that had need: 16:26 <u>**That thy children, O Lord, whom thou lovest, might know, that it is not the growing of fruits that nourisheth man: but that it is thy word, which preserveth them that put their trust in thee.**</u>

Matthew 4:4 But he answered and said, It is written, Man shall not live by bread alone, but by every word that proceedeth out of the mouth of God. Per the notes included with the original King James Bible.

16:27 For that which was not destroyed of the fire, being warmed with a little sunbeam, soon melted away: 16:28 That it might be known, that we must prevent the sun to give thee thanks, and at the dayspring pray unto thee. 16:29 For the hope of the unthankful shall melt away as the winter's hoar frost, and shall run away as unprofitable water.

17:1 For great are thy judgments, and cannot be expressed: therefore unnurtured souls have erred. 17:2 For when unrighteous men thought to oppress the holy nation; they being shut up in their houses, the prisoners of darkness, and fettered with the bonds of a long night, lay [there] exiled from the eternal providence. 17:3 For while they supposed to lie hid in their secret sins, they were scattered under a dark veil of forgetfulness, being horribly astonished, and troubled with [strange] apparitions. 17:4 For neither might the corner that held them keep them from fear: but noises [as of waters] falling down sounded about them, and sad visions appeared unto them with heavy countenances. 17:5 No power of the fire might give them light: neither could the bright flames of the stars endure to lighten that horrible night. 17:6 Only there appeared unto them a fire kindled of itself, very dreadful: for being much terrified, they thought the things which they saw to be worse than the sight they saw not. 17:7 As for the illusions of art magick, they were put down, and their vaunting in wisdom was reproved with disgrace. 17:8 For they, that promised to drive away terrors and troubles from a sick soul, were sick themselves of fear, worthy to be laughed at. 17:9 For though no terrible thing did fear them; yet being scared with beasts that passed by, and hissing of serpents, 17:10 They died for fear, denying that they saw the air, which could of no side be avoided. 17:11 For wickedness, condemned by her own witness, is very timorous, and being pressed with conscience, always forecasteth grievous things. 17:12 For fear is nothing else but a betraying of the succours which reason offereth. 17:13 And the expectation from within, being less, counteth the ignorance more than the cause which bringeth the torment. 17:14 But they sleeping the same sleep that night, which was indeed intolerable, and which came upon them out of the bottoms of inevitable hell, 17:15 **Were partly vexed with monstrous apparitions, and partly fainted, their heart failing them: for a sudden fear, and not looked for, came upon them.**

Matthew 14:26 And when the disciples saw him walking on the sea, they were troubled, saying, It is a spirit; and they cried out for fear. Per the Evangelical Biblical Theology Commentary: although the CSB translates the Greek term φάντασμα as "ghost," the word refers to any visual manifestation of something or someone that is normally invisible and that inspires fear. A century or two before the time of Christ, the Wisdom of Solomon used the term to describe the monsters that appeared in nightmares (Wis 17:15) ... [combined with other uses of the term it is clear that] the term means "terrifying sight" or "awe-inspiring appearance" and makes the reader more attentive to other features of the narrative that suggest the event should be interpreted as a theophany.

17:16 So then whosoever there fell down was straitly kept, shut up in a prison without iron bars; 17:17 For whether he were husbandman, or shepherd, or a labourer in the field, he was overtaken, and endured that necessity, which could not be avoided: for they were all bound with one chain of darkness. 17:18 Whether it were a whistling wind, or a melodious noise of birds among the spreading branches, or a pleasing fall of water running violently, 17:19 Or a terrible sound of stones cast down, or a running that could not be seen of skipping beasts, or a roaring voice of most savage wild beasts, or a rebounding echo from the hollow mountains; these things made them to swoon for fear. 17:20 For the whole world shined with clear light, and none were hindered in their labour: 17:21 **Over them only was spread an heavy night, an image of that darkness which should afterward receive them: but yet were they unto themselves more grievous than the darkness.**

Hebrews 3:5 (Both the verse in Hebrews and the verse in Wisdom use the same Greek terms found nowhere else in New or Old Testament.) And Moses verily was faithful in all his house, as a servant, for a testimony of those things which were

to be spoken after. Per E. H. Plumptre, as part of showing that Apollos may have written the Book of Wisdom and the Epistle of the Hebrews.

Matthew 8:12 But the children of the kingdom shall be cast out into outer darkness: there shall be weeping and gnashing of teeth. Per the Evangelical Biblical Theology Commentary: "Outer darkness" probably connotes the deepest darkness that is so distant from any source of light that not the slightest ray pierces it. Jewish literature from the intertestamental period taught that the plague of darkness that God used to judge the Egyptians foreshadowed eternal darkness that awaited them (Wis. 17:21)."

18:1 Nevertheless thy saints had a very great light, whose voice they hearing, and not seeing their shape, because they also had not suffered the same things, they counted them happy. 18:2 But for that they did not hurt them now, of whom they had been wronged before, they thanked them, and besought them pardon for that they had been enemies. 18:3 Instead whereof thou gavest them a burning pillar of fire, both to be a guide of the unknown journey, and an harmless sun to entertain them honourably. 18:4 For they were worthy to be deprived of light and imprisoned in darkness, who had kept thy sons shut up, by whom the uncorrupt light of the law was to be given unto the world. 18:5 And when they had determined to slay the babes of the saints, one child being cast forth, and saved, to reprove them, thou tookest away the multitude of their children, and destroyedst them altogether in a mighty water. 18:6 Of that night were our fathers certified afore, that assuredly knowing unto what oaths they had given credence, they might afterwards be of good cheer. 18:7 **So of thy people was accepted both the salvation of the righteous, and destruction of the enemies.**

Hebrews 12:10 For they verily for a few days chastened us after their own pleasure; but he for our profit, that we might be partakers of his holiness. **Per E. H. Plumptre, as part of showing that Apollos may have written the Book of Wisdom and the Epistle of the Hebrews.**

18:8 For wherewith thou didst punish our adversaries, by the same thou didst glorify us, whom thou hadst called. 18:9 For the righteous children of good men did sacrifice secretly, and with one consent made a holy law, that the saints should be like partakers of the same good and evil, the fathers now singing out the songs of praise. 18:10 But on the other side there sounded an ill according cry of the enemies, and a lamentable noise was carried abroad for children that were bewailed. 18:11 The master and the servant were punished after one manner; and like as the king, so suffered the common person. 18:12 So they all together had innumerable dead with one kind of death; neither were the living sufficient to bury them: for in one moment the noblest offspring of them was destroyed. 18:13 For whereas they would not believe any thing by reason of the enchantments; upon the destruction of the firstborn, they acknowledged this people to be the sons of God. 18:14 For while all things were in quiet silence, and that night was in the midst of her swift course, 18:15 **Thine Almighty word leaped down from heaven out of thy royal throne, as a fierce man of war into the midst of a land of destruction, 18:16 And brought thine unfeigned commandment as a sharp sword, and standing up filled all things with death; and it touched the heaven, but it stood upon the earth.**

Hebrews 4:13 For the word of God is quick, and powerful, and sharper than any twoedged sword, piercing even to the dividing asunder of soul and spirit, and of the joints and marrow, and is a discerner of the thoughts and intents of the heart. Neither is there any creature that is not manifest in his sight: but all things are naked and opened unto the eyes of him with whom we have to do.

Revelation 19:13-15 13And he was clothed with a vesture dipped in blood: and his name is called The Word of God. ... 15And out of his mouth goeth a sharp sword, that with it he should smite the nations: and he shall rule them with a rod of iron: and he treadeth the winepress of the fierceness and wrath of Almighty God.

John 1:14 And the Word was made flesh, and dwelt among us, (and we beheld his glory, the glory as of the only begotten of the Father,) full of grace and truth. Wisdom 18:15-16 as fulfilled by Jesus, the Divine Word/Wisdom.

18:17 Then suddenly visions of horrible dreams troubled them sore, and terrors came upon them unlooked for. 18:18 And one thrown here, and another there, half dead, shewed the cause of his death. 18:19 For the dreams that troubled them did foreshew this, lest they should perish, and not know why they were afflicted. 18:20 Yea, the tasting of death touched the righteous also, and there was a destruction of the multitude in the wilderness: but the wrath endured not long. 18:21 For then the blameless man made haste, and stood forth to defend them; and bringing the shield of his proper ministry, even prayer, and the propitiation of incense, set himself against the wrath, and so brought the calamity to an end, declaring that he was thy servant. 18:22 **So he overcame the destroyer, not with strength of body, nor force of arms, but with a word subdued him that punished, alleging the oaths and covenants made with the fathers.**

Hebrews 4:12 For the word of God is quick, and powerful, and sharper than any twoedged sword, piercing even to the dividing asunder of soul and spirit, and of the joints and marrow, and is a discerner of the thoughts and intents of the heart. Per E. H. Plumptre, as part of showing that Apollos may have written the Book of Wisdom and the Epistle of the Hebrews.

18:23 For when the dead were now fallen down by heaps one upon another, standing between, he stayed the wrath, and parted the way to the living. 18:24 **For in the long garment was the whole world, and in the four rows of the stones was the glory of the fathers graven, and thy Majesty upon the diadem of his head.**

Hebrews 9:1 Then verily the first covenant had also ordinances of divine service, and a worldly sanctuary. Per E. H. Plumptre, as part of showing that Apollos may have written the Book of Wisdom and the Epistle of the Hebrews.

18:25 Unto these the destroyer gave place, and was afraid of them: for it was enough that they only tasted of the wrath.

19:1 **As for the ungodly, wrath came upon them without mercy unto the end: for he knew before what they would do;**

Hebrews 3:6 But Christ as a son over his own house; whose house are we, if we hold fast the confidence and the rejoicing of the hope firm unto the end. Per E. H. Plumptre, as part of showing that Apollos may have written the Book of Wisdom and the Epistle of the Hebrews.

19:2 How that having given them leave to depart, and sent them hastily away, they would repent and pursue them. 19:3 For whilst they were yet mourning and making lamentation at the graves of the dead, they added another foolish device, and pursued them as fugitives, whom they had intreated to be gone. 19:4 For the destiny, whereof they were worthy, drew them unto this end, and made them forget the things that had already happened, that they might fulfil the punishment which was wanting to their torments: 19:5 And that thy people might pass a wonderful way: but they might find a strange death. 19:6 For the whole creature in his proper kind was fashioned again anew, serving the peculiar commandments that were given unto them, that thy children might be kept without hurt: 19:7 As namely, a cloud shadowing the camp; and where water stood before, dry land appeared; and out of the Red sea a way without impediment; and out of the violent stream a green field: 19:8 Wherethrough all the people went that were defended with thy hand, seeing thy marvellous strange wonders. 19:9 For they went at large like horses, and leaped like lambs, praising thee, O Lord, who hadst delivered them. 19:10 For they were yet mindful of the things that were done while they sojourned in the strange land, how the ground brought forth flies instead of cattle, and how the river cast up a multitude of frogs instead of fishes. 19:11 But afterwards they saw a new generation of fowls, when, being led with their appetite, they asked delicate meats. 19:12 For quails came up unto them from the sea for their contentment. 19:13 And punishments came upon the sinners not without former signs by the force of thunders: for they suffered justly according to their own wickedness, insomuch as they used a more hard and hateful behaviour toward strangers. 19:14 For the Sodomites did not receive those, whom they knew not when they came: but these brought friends into bondage, that had well deserved of them. 19:15 And not only so, but peradventure some respect shall be had of those, because they used strangers not friendly: 19:16 But these very grievously afflicted them, whom they had received with feastings, and were already made partakers of the same laws with them. 19:17 Therefore even with blindness were these stricken, as those were at the doors of the righteous man: when, being compassed about with horrible great darkness, every one sought the passage of his own doors. 19:18 For the elements were changed in themselves by a kind of harmony, like as in a psaltery notes change the name of the tune, and yet are always sounds; which may well be perceived by the sight of the things that have been done. 19:19 For earthly things were turned into watery, and the things, that before swam in the water, now went upon the ground. 19:20 The fire had power in the water, forgetting his own virtue: and the water forgat his own quenching nature. 19:21 On the other side, the flames wasted not the flesh of the corruptible living things, though they walked therein; neither melted they the icy

kind of heavenly meat that was of nature apt to melt. 19:22 **For in all things, O Lord, thou didst magnify thy people, and glorify them, neither didst thou lightly regard them: but didst assist them in every time and place.**

Matthew 28:20: lo, I am with you always, even unto the end of the world. Amen.

Postscript to Wisdom: Summarizing the Data

The following is a chronological chart of some citations from the Fathers, plus all canon lists and Councils and codices (which are in ALL CAPS, and in **BOLD IF A COUNCIL,** and in *ITALICS IF A CODEX*).

Unfortunately, this is a very incomplete list. It is only those citations which I reviewed, and even of those it is (with only a few exceptions) only the ones which come from works defining Wisdom as Scripture, Prophecy, etc. There are more than a thousand other citations that are not included, and quite possibly thousands more from the 350+ AD period that biblindex.org/citation_biblique/search does not yet index. Even so, there were too many to try to fit online links to them onto the chart. Many works are cited elsewhere herein, and in any event, Google searches will find them if they are available online.

Ch	V	Father	Year	Work
2	24	Clement of Rome	96	1 Clement, 3
12	10	Clement of Rome	96	1 Clement, 7
12	12	Clement of Rome	96	1 Clement 27:5-7
12	12	Clement of Rome	96	1 Clement 27:5-7
2	12	Barnabas	135	Epistle, Chapter VI
10	4	Justin Martyr	165	Trypho 137-138
		MELITO OF SARDIS	170	"WISDOM"
		MURATORIAN CANON	170	CANON
9	13	Irenaeus of Lyon	177	Against Heresies 2, 28, 9
9	17	Irenaeus of Lyon	177	Against Heresies 2, 28, 9
6	19	Irenaeus of Lyon	180	Against Heresies 4, 38, 3
1	6	Tertullian	198	On the Soul 15
2	12	Clement of Alexandria	198	Stromata 5, 14
2	12	Clement of Alexandria	198	Miscellany, v. 14
2	16	Clement of Alexandria	198	Stromata 6, 15
2	25	Clement of Alexandria	198	Stromata 6, 12
3	4	Clement of Alexandria	198	Stromata 4, 16
3	9	Clement of Alexandria	198	Stromata 6, 14
3	14	Clement of Alexandria	198	Stromata 6, 14
4	17	Clement of Alexandria	198	Stromata 6, 14
5	5	Clement of Alexandria	198	Stromata 6, 14
6	7	Clement of Alexandria	198	Stromata 6, 6
6	10	Clement of Alexandria	198	Stromata 6, 11
6	15	Clement of Alexandria	198	Stromata 6, 15
6	18	Clement of Alexandria	198	The Instructor 2, 1
6	20	Clement of Alexandria	198	Stromata 6, 15
7	16	Clement of Alexandria	198	Stromata 6, 11
7	18	Clement of Alexandria	198	Stromata 6, 8
7	24	Clement of Alexandria	198	Stromata 5, 14
7	24	Clement of Alexandria	198	Miscellany, v. 14

11	24	Clement of Alexandria	198	The Instructor 1, 8
14	3	Clement of Alexandria	198	Stromata 6, 11
16	26	Clement of Alexandria	198	The Instructor 2, 1
		CLEMENT OF ALEX.	203	CANON
		ORIGEN (JEWISH LIST)	220	NOT CANON FOR JEWS
1	1	Origen	230	On First Principles 1.2.13
7	16	Origen	230	First Principles 3, 1, 14
7	25	Origen	230	First Principles 1, 2, 5
7	25	Origen	230	First Principles 1, 2, 10
11	20	Origen	230	First Principles 2, 9, 1
18	24	Origen	230	First Principles 2, 3, 6
2	1	Hippolytus of Rome	235	Against the Jews
2	13	Hippolytus of Rome	235	Against the Jews
2	15	Hippolytus of Rome	235	Against the Jews
2	18	Hippolytus of Rome	235	Against the Jews
5	9	Hippolytus	235	Against the Jews 10
		Hippolytus of Rome	235	On Song of Songs
1	1	Tertullian	240	Against the Valentinians, 2
1	1	Tertullian	240	Against Marcion 7
2	12	Tertullian	240	Against Marcion, 3, 22
1	1	Tertullian	240	Prescription v. heretics, 7
1	4	Origen	248	Against Celsus 3, 60
1	4	Origen	248	Against Celsus 5, 29
1	5	Origen	248	Against Celsus 7, 8
1	7	Origen	248	Against Celsus 4, 5
7	26	Origen	248	Against Celsus 3, 72
9	6	Origen	248	Against Celsus 6, 13
10	5	Origen	248	Against Celsus 5, 29
12	1	Origen	248	Against Celsus 4, 37
		ORIGEN (LETTER)	248	N/A
2	1	Commodianus	250	Instructions, 24
		ORIGEN (CITATIONS)	250	CANON
1	2	Origen	253	Homilies on Luke 3 (1:11)
2	20	Origen	253	Homilies on Exodus 6, 1
3	11	Origen	253	Homilies on Jeremiah, 8.1.3
3	16	Origen	253	Homilies on Genesis 1.15
6	6	Origen	253	Comm. on Songs, Book 2, 5
6	17	Origen	253	Comm. on Songs, Book 3, 13
7	17	Origen	253	Comm. on Songs, Book 2, 5
7	20	Origen	253	Homilies on Luke 21 (3:1-4)
7	20	Origen	253	Comm. on Songs, Book 3, 8
7	21	Origen	253	Comm. on Songs, Book 3, 12
7	23	Origen	253	Comm. on John 20.405-6
7	26	Origen	253	Against Celsus, 8, 14
8	2	Origen	253	Comm. on John 20.405-6
8	2	Origen	253	Homilies on Genesis 6.1-2
8	2	Origen	253	Comm. on Songs, Prologue
9	15	Origen	253	Comm. on Romans 3,3,14
9	15	Origen	253	Comm. on Romans 3,3,14
11	17	Origen	253	de Principiis 4.33
11	20	Origen	253	Comm. on Songs, Book 3, 7
11	24	Origen	253	Comm. on Songs, Book 3, 7
11	26	Origen	253	Against Celsus, 4, 28
12	1	Origen	253	Comm. on Songs, Book 3, 7

12	2	Origen	253	Against Celsus, 4, 28
12	2	Origen	253	Against Celsus, 7, 51
16	21	Origen	253	Comm. on Songs 3.8
1	7	Origen	253	Comm. on Romans
1	14	Origen	253	Homilies on Jeremiah, 2.1.1
2	24	Origen	253	Homilies on Jeremiah, 2.1.1
7	26	Origen	253	Homilies on Jeremiah, 9.5
9	6	Origen	253	Commentary on Matthew 69
15	10	Origen	253	Exhortation to Martyrdom 32
1	14	Origen	254	Comm. on John, 20, 235
7	25	Origen	254	Comm. on Hebrews 1:2-4
7	25	Origen	254	Comm. on John, 13, 153
7	26	Origen	254	First Principles 1, 2, 12
7	26	Origen	254	First Principles, 1, 2, 11
7	26	Origen	254	First Principles, 1, 2, 9
7	26	Origen	254	On First Principles 1.2.13
7	26	Origen	254	Comm. on John, 13, 234
10	4	Origen	254	Commentary on John, 20, 26
17	1	Origen	254	Commentary on John, 6, 36
		Origen	254	Against Celsus 6, 7
1	1	Origen	254	Comm. on Romans, 3, 7, 6
1	7	Origen	254	Comm. on Romans, 7, 15, 13
7	25	Origen	254	Comm. on Romans 7, 13, 9
7	26	Origen	254	Comm. on Romans, 1, 5, 2
7	26	Origen	254	Comm. on Romans, 8, 5, 8
7	26	Origen	254	Homilies on Jeremiah, 9, 4, 5
9	6	Origen	254	Comm. on Matthew 10:19
9	6	Origen	254	Comm. on Romans, 5, 3, 8
9	6	Origen	254	Comm. on Romans, 9, 3, 7
10	1	Origen	254	Comm. on Romans, 5, 2, 8
11	20	Origen	254	Comm. on Romans, 2, 3
1	1	Cyprian	258	Treatise 12, 3, 53
2	22	Cyprian	258	Treatise 12, 2, 14
3	4	Cyprian	258	Treatise 11, 12
3	8	Cyprian	258	Treatise 11, 12
3	8	Cyprian	258	Treatise 12, 3, 15
3	11	Cyprian	258	Treatise 2, 1
4	11	Cyprian	258	Treatise 7, 23
4	11	Cyprian	258	Treatise 12, 3, 58
4	11	Cyprian	258	On Mortality 23
4	14	Cyprian	258	Treatise 12, 3, 58
5	8	Cyprian	258	Treatise 2, 10
5	9	Cyprian	258	Treatise 12, 3, 16
6	6	Cyprian	258	Treatise 12, 3, 112
13	4	Cyprian	258	Treatise 12, 3, 59
15	17	Cyprian	258	Treatise 12, 3, 59
1	13	Cyprian	258	LETTER 55.22.18
2	24	Novatian	258	On the Trinity
7	25	Dionysius of Alexandria	265	Letter to Dionysius, 4
7	26	Dionysius of Alexandria	265	Letter to Dionysius, 3
1	13	Archelaus	278	Disputation with Manes 29
7		Pamphilus of Caesarea	310	Apology for Origen, 43-99
3	16	Methodius	311	Banquet of Ten Virgins, 2, 3
4	2	Methodius	311	Banquet of Ten Virgins, 1, 3

4	2	Methodius	311	Banquet of Ten Virgins, 4, 5
4	2	Methodius	311	Banquet of Ten Virgins, 6, 5
4	3	Methodius	311	Banquet of Ten Virgins, 1, 3
4	6	Methodius	311	Banquet of Ten Virgins, 2, 6
7	9	Methodius	311	Banquet Ten Virgins, 11, 1
7	22	Methodius	311	Banquet of Ten Virgins, 7, 1
15	11	Methodius	311	Banquet of Ten Virgins, 2, 7
1	14	Methodius	311	Discourse Resurrection, 1, 8
2	23	Methodius	311	Discourse Resurrection, 1, 11
7	21	Methodius	311	Discourse Resurrection, 1, 15
15	3	Methodius	311	Concerning Anna Simeon, 6
16	24	Methodius	311	Discourse Resurrection, 1, 13
6	19	Eusebius	324	Church History 5, 8, 8
		EUSEBIUS (APPROVAL)	324	CANON
2	22	Lactantius	325	Divine Institutes, 4, 8
		~~THE NICENE COUNCIL~~	~~325~~	~~UNKNOWN~~
2	23	Athanasius	330	On the Incarnation, 5
6	19	Athanasius	330	On the Incarnation, 4
9	2	Athanasius	335	4 Discourses Arians 2, 45
13	5	Athanasius	335	Against the Heathen 2, 44
13	5	Athanasius	335	4 Discourses Arians 2, 32
14	12	Athanasius	335	Against the Heathen 1, 9
14	12	Athanasius	335	Against the Heathen 1, 11
14	21	Athanasius	335	Against the Heathen 1, 17
1	13	Eusebius of Caesarea	339	Prep. Gospel, Book 13, 1
2	24	Eusebius of Caesarea	339	Prep. Gospel, Book 13, 1
6	22	Eusebius of Caesarea	339	Prep. Gospel, Book 7, 12
6	22	Eusebius of Caesarea	339	Prep. Gospel, Book 11, 14
7	12	Eusebius of Caesarea	339	Prep. Gospel, Book 7, 2
7	17	Eusebius of Caesarea	339	Prep. Gospel, Book 11, 7
7	21	Eusebius of Caesarea	339	Prep. Gospel, Book 11, 14
7	22	Eusebius of Caesarea	339	Prep. Gospel, Book 7, 12
7	22	Eusebius of Caesarea	339	Prep. Gospel, Book 11, 14
8	1	Eusebius of Caesarea	339	Prep. Gospel, Book 7, 12
8	1	Eusebius of Caesarea	339	Prep. Gospel, Book 11, 14
8	5	Eusebius of Caesarea	339	Prep. Gospel, Book 12, 52
14	12	Eusebius of Caesarea	339	Prep. Gospel, Book 1, 9
7	22	Council of Sardica	343	Thedoret Ch. History, 2, 6
		CLAROMONTANUS	349	CANON
		CODEX VATICANUS	*350*	*CANON*
		CODEX SINAITICUS	*350*	*CANON*
		CYRIL OF JERUSALEM	350	NOT CANON
		ST CATHERINE'S SYRIAC	350	CANON
3	57	Athanasius	358	Defense of his Flight, 19
7	25	Athanasius	360	Opinion of Dionysius 9
7	25	Athanasius	360	Opinion of Dionysius 9
7	25	Athanasius	360	De Sententia Dionysii, 15
7	25	Athanasius	360	De Sententia Dionysii, 9
7	26	Athanasius	360	De Sententia Dionysii, 15
1	11	Athanasius	360	Defense of Constantius, 5
		CHELTENHAM LIST	360	CANON
2	24	Lucifer of Caligari	361	Concerning Athanasius 1, 32
6		Lucifer of Caligari	361	Concerning Athanasius 1, 33
		~~COUNCIL AT LAODICEA~~	~~363~~	~~NOT CANONICAL~~

1	13	Hilary of Poitiers	367	Orthodox Faith, II, XXVIII
		ATHANASIUS	367	VERSION 3.1
		HILARY OF POITIERS	367	NOT CANON
7	1	Hilary of Poitiers	368	Tractate on Psalm 135, 11
7	27	Hilary of Poitiers	368	Psalm 118, Let. 19, 8
13	5	Hilary of Poitiers	368	On the Trinity 1, 7
17	1	Hilary of Poitiers	368	Tractate on Psalm 118, 8
1	5	Athanasius	373	Festal Letter 3, 4
2	21	Athanasius	373	History of the Arians, 8, 71
7	25	Theognostus	373	Nicene Def., 6, 25
7	26	Athanasius	373	Nicene Definition, 5, 20
7	26	Athanasius	373	De Synodis, 41-42
7	27	Athanasius	373	Festal Letter 1
7	27	Athanasius	373	Festal Letter 10, 4
7	26	Pope Damasus I	374	Letter to the Eastern Bishops
1	4	Basil the Great	379	Letter 8, 12
1	7	Basil the Great	379	Letter 8, 10
7	26	Basil the Great	379	Letter 38, 8
1	7	Basil the Great	379	On the Holy Spirit, 23, 54
3	1	Apostolic Constitutions	380	Bk 6, Ch 6
		GREGORY NAZIANZUS	380	NOT CANON
		AMPHILOCHIUS	380	NOT CANON
		APOSTOLIC CANONS	380	CANON
4	8	Gregory of Nazianzus	381	Oration 43, 73
		~~THE COUNCIL OF ROME~~	~~382~~	~~CANON~~
		Epiphanius	385	Panarion, 6, 76, 22, 5
		EPIPHANIUS PAN. 8.6.1-4	385	DISPUTED FOR JEWS
		EPIPHANIUS PAN. 76.22.5	385	CANON
1	4	Gregory of Nyssa	386	On Virginity 15
7	18	Gregory of Nyssa	386	Against Eunomius 8, 5
7	25	Gregory of Nyssa	386	Against Eunomius 2, 9
7	25	Gregory of Nyssa	386	Against Eunomius 8, 4
		Gregory of Nyssa	386	Against Eunomius 8, 5
13	5	Cyril of Jerusalem	386	Catechetical Lectures 9, 2
14	10	Didymus the Blind	386	Comm. on Zechariah 13:2
4	3	Optatus	387	Against the Donatists 4.8
1	5	Augustine	388	Morals Catholic Ch. 16, 29
6	20	Augustine	388	Morals Catholic Ch. 16, 32
8	3	Augustine	388	Morals Catholic Ch. 16, 28
9	9	Augustine	388	Morals Catholic Ch. 16, 28
9	17	Augustine	388	Morals Catholic Ch. 16, 28
9	17	Augustine	388	Morals Catholic Ch. 16, 29
9	19	Augustine	388	Morals Catholic Ch. 16, 28
5	11	Gregory of Nazianzus	389	On Saint Caesarius 19
7	26	Gregory of Nazianzus	390	Oration 29, 17
1	7	Gregory of Nazianzus	390	Oration 28, 8
3	7	Gregory of Nazianzus	390	Oration 40, 6
1	6	Gregory of Nazianzus	390	Oration 41, 14
3	15	Gregory of Nazianzus	390	Oration 7, 14
5	10	Gregory of Nazianzus	390	On, Caesarius 7, 20
5	11	Gregory of Nazianzus	390	On Caesarius 7, 19
9	15	Gregory of Nazianzus	390	Oration 16, 15
		JEROME (HELMETED)	390	NOT CANON
		EPIPHANIUS DE MENS. 4-5	392	BENEFICIAL FOR JEWS

		THE COUNCIL OF HIPPO - 70 BISHOPS	393	CANON
5	6	Augustine	394	Sermon on Mount 1, 23, 79
7	26	Augustine	394	Sermon on Mount 1, 23, 79
16	14	Gregory of Nyssa	394	Against Macedonians
1	1	Augustine	394	Sermon on Mount 2, 14, 48
13	5	Gregory of Nyssa	394	Answer to Eunomius 2d
13	5	Gregory of Nyssa	394	Answer to Eunomius 2d
1	4	Ambrose	397	3 Books Holy Spirit 3, 128
1	4	Ambrose	397	3 Holy Spirit, 3, 11, 69-70
1	7	Ambrose	397	3 Books Holy Spirit 1, 87
3	13	Ambrose	397	Concerning Virgins 1, 35
4	11	Ambrose	397	2 books Satyrus 1, 30
7	22	Ambrose	397	3 Books Holy Spirit 3, 135
7	22	Ambrose	397	3 Books Holy Spirit 3, 169
7	23	Ambrose	397	Duties of the Clergy 2, 65
7	23	Ambrose	397	3 Books Holy Spirit, 3, 6, 36
7	26	Ambrose	397	Exposition of Faith 1, 49
7	27	Ambrose	397	Exposition of Faith 4, 145
7	30	Ambrose	397	Duties of the Clergy 2, 64
7	30	Ambrose	397	Exposition of Faith 4, 145
8	7	Ambrose	397	Duties of the Clergy 2, 65
8	13	Ambrose	397	Exposition of Faith 3, 18
7	22	Ambrose	397	On Abraham 2.10.76.
8	8	Ambrose	397	On Abraham 2.10.76.
		AUGUSTINE	397	CANON
		COUNCIL CARTHAGE - 44-48 BISHOPS	397	CANON
1	4	Didymus the Blind	398	Comm. on Zechariah 12:9-10
1	10	Didymus the Blind	398	Comm. on Zechariah 11:6-7
11	24	Didymus the Blind	398	Comm. on Zechariah 11:6-7
11	26	Didymus the Blind	398	Comm. on Zechariah 11:6-7
		Didymus the Blind	398	Comm. on Zechariah 8:10
		JEROME (SOLOMON)	398	VERSION 3.2
2	21	Augustine	400	Reply to Faustus 12, 44
6	23	Augustine	400	Reply to Faustus 22, 54
7	26	Augustine	400	Reply to Faustus 22, 2
9	15	Augustine	400	Reply to Faustus 22, 78
14	15	Augustine	400	Reply to Faustus 22, 17
		RUFINUS	400	VERSION 3.3
1	7	Theophilius of Alexandria	402	Festal Letter AD 402 98, 13
1	4	Epiphanius	403	Panarion, 3, 44, 54, 4
1	7	Epiphanius	403	Panarion, 4, 54, 1, 4
1	13	Epiphanius	403	Panarion, 3, 44, 28, 2
1	14	Epiphanius	403	Panarion, 3, 44, 39, 6
2	23	Epiphanius	403	Panarion, 3, 44, 28, 2
2	23	Epiphanius	403	Panarion, 3, 44, 42, 4
2	24	Epiphanius	403	Panarion, 3, 44, 28, 2
2	24	Epiphanius	403	Panarion, 3, 45, 1, 2
3	4	Epiphanius	403	Panarion, 3, 44, 44, 1
3	7	Epiphanius	403	Panarion 3, 44, 48, 4
3	14	Epiphanius	403	Panarion, 2, 6, 15, 7
4	12	Epiphanius	403	Panarion, 3, 45, 1, 2
4	12	Epiphanius	403	Panarion, 4, 47, 4, 7

4	13	Epiphanius	403	Panarion, 4, 47, 4, 8
4	14	Epiphanius	403	Panarion, 4, 47, 4, 8
7	2	Epiphanius	403	Panarion, 3, 31, 29, 6
7	2	Epiphanius	403	Panarion, 3, 44, 18, 1
14	2	Epiphanius	403	Panarion, 1, 3, 3, 9
14	2	Epiphanius	403	Panarion, 1, 8. 2, 1
		JEROME (TOBIT/JUDITH)	404	**CANON**
1	5	Augustine	405	In Answer to Petilian 2, 61
1	5	Augustine	405	In Answer to Petilian 3, 29
1	5	Augustine	405	In Answer to Petilian 3, 31
1	5	Augustine	405	In Answer to Petilian 3, 35
1	11	Augustine	405	In Answer to Petilian 2, 35
12	23	Augustine	405	In Answer to Petilian 2, 19
		Innocent I	405	Letter to Bishop of Toulouse
		POPE INNOCENT I	405	**CANON**
1	1	Chromatius	407	Tractate on Matthew 41, 5
1	5	Chromatius	407	Tractate on Matthew 43.7
1	11	Chromatius	407	Tractate on Matthew 31.15.4
1	11	Chromatius	407	Tractate on Matthew 24, II, 4
2	24	John Chrysostom	407	Homilies on Gen. 46.15-17
4	9	John Chrysostom	407	Homilies on Hebrews 7, 9
5	10	Chromatius	407	Tractate on Matthew 42, 5
6	6	Chromatius	407	Tractate on Matthew 56, 4
6	7	Chromatius	407	Tractate on Matthew 57, 3
6	17	Chromatius	407	Tractate on Matthew 41, 5
10	21	Chromatius	407	Tractate on Matthew 49, 1
16	12	Chromatius	407	Sermon 31, 2
16	12	Chromatius	407	Tractate on Matthew 39, 1
16	12	Chromatius	407	Tractate on Matthew 47, 2
16	13	Chromatius	407	Tractate on Matthew 47, 4
18	15	John Chrysostom	407	Homilies on Matthew, 2
2	24	John Chrysostom	407	Homilies on Genesis, 22, 7
3	1	John Chrysostom	407	Homilies on Matthew, 28, 3
11	23	John Chrysostom	407	Homilies on Philippians, 4
1	4	Chromatius	407	Tractate on Matthew 11, 2
1	5	Chromatius	407	Tractate on Matthew 11, 2
1	5	John Chrysostom	407	Homily 41
3	7	Rufinus	409	Apostles' Creed, 46
7	26	Rufinus	411	Apostles' Creed, 8
8	21	Augustine	414	On Widowhood, 21
8	21	Augustine	416	Perfection Righteousness, 5
9	15	Augustine	416	Perfection Righteousness, 6
1	4	Cyril of Alexandria	418	Comm. John, 1, Intro
1	5	Cyril of Alexandria	418	Commentary on John, 2, 1
13	5	Cyril of Alexandria	418	Commentary on John, 1, 10
1	4	Cyril of Alexandria	418	Commentary on John, 1, 4
		COUNCIL CARTHAGE - 217 BISHOPS	**419**	**CANON**
1	1	Jerome	420	Against Pelagians, Bk I, 33
1	4	Jerome	420	Six Books on Jeremiah 4.8.2
1	11	Augustine	420	On Lying 31 [16]
1	11	Augustine	420	On Lying 5.6
2	24	Augustine	420	Tractates on John 12, 10
4	9	Jerome	420	6 Books on Jeremiah 1.4.1-2

7	26	Augustine	420	Tractates on John 21, 2
8	1	Augustine	420	Tractates on John 21, 2
8	2	Jerome	420	6 Bks on Jeremiah 5.63.8-12
8	21	Augustine	420	On Continence, 28
9	15	Augustine	420	Tractates on John 21, 1
12	11	Augustine	420	On Marriage 2, 20
1	1	Jerome	420	Commentary on Isaiah 15.14
2	24	Augustine	420	On Marriage 2, 45
4	11	Jerome	420	Letter 39, 3
4	14	Jerome	420	Letter 39, 3
6	21	Augustine	420	On Marriage 2, 52
12	11	Augustine	420	On Marriage 2, 32
1	5	Augustine	421	On the Soul 3, 2
4	11	Augustine	421	On the Soul 3, 22
4	11	Augustine	421	On the Soul 3, 14
13	9	Augustine	421	On the Soul 4, 6
1	9	Augustine	426	City of God 20, 26
1	13	Augustine	426	On the Trinity 4, 12
2	1	Augustine	426	On the Trinity 15, 17
2	21	Augustine	426	City of God 17, 20
4	3	Augustine	426	Christian Doctrine 2, 12, 18
6	20	Augustine	426	City of God 14, 7
6	24	Augustine	426	On Christian Doctrine, 4, 5, 8
6	24	Augustine	426	On the Trinity, 14, 1
7	16	Augustine	426	Christian Doctrine, 4, 30, 63
7	22	Augustine	426	City of God 11, 10
7	26	Augustine	426	On the Trinity 4, 27
7	26	Augustine	426	On the Trinity 4, 28
7	27	Augustine	426	City of God 8, 1
8	1	Augustine	426	City of God 12, 25
8	1	Augustine	426	City of God 15, 3
9	10	Augustine	426	On the Trinity 4, 28
9	14	Augustine	426	City of God 22, 29
9	15	Augustine	426	City of God 12, 15
9	15	Augustine	426	City of God 14, 3
9	15	Augustine	426	City of God 19, 4
9	15	Augustine	426	City of God 19, 27
11	20	Augustine	426	City of God 11, 30
11	20	Augustine	426	City of God 12, 18
11	20	Augustine	426	On the Trinity 11, 11
12	18	Augustine	426	On the Trinity, 13, 16
13	5	Augustine	426	On the Trinity 15, 3
13	9	Augustine	426	Christian Doctrine 2, 21, 32
16	25	Augustine	426	On the Trinity 3, 6
		Augustine	426	On the Trinity 14, 11
		Augustine	426	Christian Doctrine 2, 8, 13
6	22	Augustine	428	Reply to Faustus, 19, 29
3	5	Augustine	429	Reply to Faustus, 19, 29
4	11	Augustine	429	Predestination of Saints 26
4	11	Augustine	429	Predestination of Saints 27
4	11	Augustine	429	Predestination of Saints 28
4	11	Augustine	429	Predestination of Saints 29
4	11	Hilary (layman)	429	Augustine Letter 226, 12
1	1	Augustine	430	Exposition on Psalm 4, 9

1	5	Augustine	430	Letter 185, 11, 50
1	5	Augustine	430	Sermon 292, 7
1	5	Augustine	430	In Answer to Petilian 2, 26
1	5	Augustine	430	Against the Donatists, VI, 19
1	5	Augustine	430	Against the Donatists, I, 12
1	7	Augustine	430	Letter 187, 4, 14
1	7	Augustine	430	Answer Maximinus XXI, 2
1	9	Augustine	430	Sermon 12, 3
1	9	Augustine	430	Exp. 24 of Psalm 118, 6
1	9	Augustine	430	Exposition of Psalm 57, 1
1	9	Augustine	430	Sermon 125, 8
1	11	Augustine	430	Sermon 65, 6
1	11	Augustine	430	Sermon 81, 5
1	11	Augustine	430	Sermon 180, 8
1	11	Augustine	430	Sermon 162C, 5
1	16	Augustine	430	Reply to Faustus 21, 9
1	16	Augustine	430	Exposition of Psalm 51, 2
2	1	Augustine	430	Exposition of Psalm 52, 3
2	10	Augustine	430	Exposition of Psalm 52, 3
2	15	Augustine	430	Exposition 3 of Psalm 36, 12
2	20	Augustine	430	Exposition of Psalm 56, 4
2	21	Augustine	430	Reply to Faustus, 12, 44
2	21	Augustine	430	Letter 140, 7, 20
2	21	Augustine	430	Exposition of Psalm 56, 4
2	23	Augustine	430	Enemy of Law Prophets I, 48
2	24	Augustine	430	Reply to Faustus 21, 9
2	24	Augustine	430	Exposition of Psalm 50, 9
2	24	Augustine	430	Sermon 294, 15
2	25	Augustine	430	Letter 157, 3, 21
2	25	Augustine	430	Against Donatists, IV, 8, 12
2	25	Augustine	430	Against Donatists, IV, 8, 14
2	25	Augustine	430	Merits Forgiveness Sins I, 9
3	5	Augustine	430	Sermon 306, 1
3	6	Augustine	430	Exposition of Psalm 69, 5
3	6	Augustine	430	Sermon 62, 12
3	6	Augustine	430	Questions on Judges 49.2-4
3	8	Augustine	430	Sermon 306, 7
4	7	Augustine	430	Sermon 335M, 1
4	11	Augustine	430	Letter 217, 4, 15
4	11	Augustine	430	Letter 217, 6, 22
4	11	Augustine	430	Letter 217, 6, 22
4	11	Augustine	430	Merits Forgiveness Sins I, 30
5	1	Augustine	430	Letter 185, 9, 41
5	1	Augustine	430	Treatise Donatists, 9, 41
5	3	Augustine	430	Exposition of Psalm 57, 20
5	4	Augustine	430	Letter 55, 5, 9
5	4	Augustine	430	Exposition 2 of Psalm 48, 4
5	6	Augustine	430	Letter 55, 5, 8
5	8	Augustine	430	Exposition of Psalm 111, 8
5	8	Augustine	430	Exposition of Psalm 52, 7
5	9	Augustine	430	Exposition 3 of Psalm 36, 10
5	9	Augustine	430	Exposition of Psalm 57, 19
5	9	Augustine	430	Sermon 58, 7
5	17	Augustine	430	Reply to Faustus, 19, 29

6	21	Augustine	430	Exp. 8 of Psalm 118, 20
6	23	Augustine	430	Reply to Faustus 22, 54
6	26	Augustine	430	Letter 193, 1, 2
7	1	Pelagius	430	in Augustine's On Pelagius, 6
7	7	Pelagius	430	in Augustine's On Pelagius, 7
7	16	Augustine	430	Sermon 48, 1
7	22	Augustine	430	Letter 169, 2, 7
7	25	Augustine	430	Against the Manicheans, 29
7	25	Augustine	430	Reply to Faustus 6, 3
7	25	Augustine	430	Letter 187, 3, 7
7	25	Augustine	430	On the Trinity, 4, 13
7	25	Augustine	430	On the Trinity, 4, 20, 27
7	26	Augustine	430	Reply to Faustus, 22, 8
7	26	Augustine	430	Letter 119, 3
7	26	Augustine	430	Enemy Law Prophets I, 15
7	26	Augustine	430	Homilies on John, 21, 2
7	26	Augustine	430	Sermon 117, 11
7	26	Augustine	430	On the Trinity, 4, 20, 27
7	27	Augustine	430	Concern. Nature of Good, 24
7	27	Augustine	430	Sermon 12.10
7	27	Augustine	430	Sermon 12, 10
7	27	Augustine	430	Sermon 187, 2
7	27	Augustine	430	Sermon 212, 1
7	27	Augustine	430	On the Trinity, 2, 8
7	27	Augustine	430	On the Trinity, 4, 20, 27
7	27	Augustine	430	On the Trinity, 4, 20, 27
8	1	Augustine	430	Letter 187, 3, 7
8	1	Augustine	430	Letter 187, 4, 14
8	1	Augustine	430	Letter 205, 3, 17
8	1	Augustine	430	Sermon 8, 1
8	1	Augustine	430	Ans. to Arian Sermon IV, 4
8	1	Augustine	430	Homilies on John, 21, 2
8	1	Augustine	430	Sermon 52, 5
8	1	Augustine	430	Sermon 20, 2
8	1	Augustine	430	On the Trinity, 2, 5
8	1	Augustine	430	On the Trinity, 3, 1, 6
8	1	Augustine	430	Treatise Faith Creed, 3
8	1	Augustine	430	Sermons on NT, Sermon 2
8	20	Augustine	430	Merits Forgiveness Sins I, 38
8	21	Augustine	430	Letter 177, 5
8	21	Augustine	430	Letter 144, 2
8	21	Augustine	430	Letter 157, 2, 9
8	21	Augustine	430	On Spirit and the Letter 56
8	21	Augustine	430	On Spirit and the Letter 22
8	21	Augustine	430	Sermon 283, 2
8	21	Augustine	430	Merits Forgiveness Sin II 5
8	21	Augustine	430	Sermon 283, 8
8	21	Augustine	430	Sermon 348A, 14
8	21	Augustine	430	Sermon 354A, 12
9	10	Augustine	430	On the Trinity, 4, 20
9	10	Augustine	430	On the Trinity, 4, 20, 27
9	15	Augustine	430	Reply to Faustus, 22, 78

9	15	Augustine	430	Exposition on Psalm 4, 9
9	15	Augustine	430	Letter 131
9	15	Augustine	430	Letter 185, 9, 39
9	15	Augustine	430	Exposition of Psalm 35, 1
9	15	Augustine	430	Exposition of Psalm 111, 2
9	15	Augustine	430	Exposition of Psalm 119, 1
9	15	Augustine	430	Exposition of Psalm 57, 10
9	15	Augustine	430	Exposition 2 of Psalm 68, 18
9	15	Augustine	430	Sermon 52, 5
9	15	Augustine	430	Sermon 299, 9
9	15	Augustine	430	On Baptism, VI, 2
9	15	Augustine	430	On Baptism, VII, 1, 1
10	2	Augustine	430	Letter 164, 3, 6
10	2	Augustine	430	Letter 164, 3, 6
10	2	Augustine	430	Sermon 159B, 5
10	4	Augustine	430	Sermon 63, 1
10	19	Augustine	430	Letter 185, 9, 40
10	19	Augustine	430	Letter 185, 9, 37
11	20	Augustine	430	Sermon 8, 1
11	21	Augustine	430	Reply to Faustus 21, 6
11	21	Augustine	430	Tractates on John, 1, 13
12	2	Augustine	430	Concern. Nature of Good 48
12	10	Augustine	430	On Baptism, II, 10
12	12	Augustine	430	Exposition 1 of Psalm 70, 1
12	18	Augustine	430	Exposition of Psalm 57, 20
13	2	Augustine	430	Sermon 68, 4
13	9	Augustine	430	Letter 55, 4, 7
13	9	Augustine	430	Sermon 68, 4
14	11	Augustine	430	Sermon 113A, 9
14	11	Augustine	430	Sermon 299A, 7
14	11	Augustine	430	Sermon 360A, 5-6
14	13	Augustine	430	Sermon 360A, 5-6
14	15	Augustine	430	Reply to Faustus 22, 17
16	25	Augustine	430	On the Trinity, 3, 1, 6
16		Augustine	430	On Spirit and the Letter 62
4	11	Augustine	430	Letter 194, 9, 42
5	9	Nilus of Ancyra	430	Commentary on Songs, 64+
12	19	Augustine	430	Sermon 198, 63
13	1	Augustine	430	Confessions VIII, 1, 2
1	10	Cyril of Alexandria	444	Commentary on John 4.5.96
13	1	Cyril of Alexandria	444	Commentary On Hosea 13
15	10	Cyril of Alexandria	444	Festal Letter 6
1	10	Eucherius	449	Book of Formulas I.97
9	15	Peter Chrysologus	450	Sermon 2
		CODEX ALEXANDRINUS	*450*	*CANON*
		CODEX EPHRAEMI R.	*450*	*CANON*

CANON LISTS

FATHER/LIST/BOOK	Year	WISDOM CANONICAL?	OTHER CITATIONS
MELITO OF SARDIS	170	"WISDOM"	NONE
MURATORIAN CANON)	170	CANON	NOT APPLICABLE
CLEMENT ALEXANDRIA	203	CANON	DIVINE SCRIPTURE
ORIGEN (JEWISH LIST)	220	NOT CANON FOR JEWS	NOT APPLICABLE
ORIGEN (LETTER)	248	N/A	HOLY SCRIPTURE
ORIGEN (CITATIONS)	250	CANON	HOLY SCRIPTURE
EUSEBIUS (APPROVAL)	324	CANON	HEBREW SCRIPTURE
~~THE NICENE COUNCIL~~	~~325~~	~~UNKNOWN~~	~~NOT APPLICABLE~~
CLAROMONTANUS	349	CANON	NOT APPLICABLE
CODEX VATICANUS	*350*	*CANON*	*NOT APPLICABLE*
CODEX SINAITICUS	*350*	*CANON*	*NOT APPLICABLE*
CYRIL OF JERUSALEM	350	NOT CANON	SOLOMON
ST CATHERINE'S SYRIAC	350	CANON	NOT APPLICABLE
CHELTENHAM LIST	360	CANON	NOT APPLICABLE
~~THE COUNCIL AT LAODICEA~~	~~363~~	~~NOT CANONICAL~~	~~NOT APPLICABLE~~
ATHANASIUS	367	VERSION 3.1	DIVINE SCRIPTURE
HILARY OF POITIERS	367	NOT CANON	PROPHECY
GREGORY NAZIANZUS	380	NOT CANON	ORACLES OF GOD
AMPHILOCHIUS	380	NOT CANON	2 CITES
THE APOSTOLIC CANONS	380	CANON	CITED
~~THE COUNCIL OF ROME~~	~~382~~	~~CANON~~	~~NOT APPLICABLE~~
EPIPHANIUS PAN. 8.6.1-4	385	DISPUTED FOR JEWS	SACRED SCRIPTURE
EPIPHANIUS PAN.76.22.5	385	CANON	SACRED SCRIPTURE
JEROME (HELMETED)	390	NOT CANON	SCRIPTURE
EPIPHANIUS DE MENS. 4-5	392	BENEFICIAL FOR JEWS	SACRED SCRIPTURE
THE COUNCIL OF HIPPO - 70 BISHOPS	393	CANON	NOT APPLICABLE
AUGUSTINE	397	CANON	OLD TEST. PROPHECY
COUNCIL CARTHAGE - 44-48 BISHOPS	397	CANON	NOT APPLICABLE
JEROME (SOLOMON)	398	VERSION 3.2	SCRIPTURE
RUFINUS	400	VERSION 3.3	PROPHECY
JEROME (TOBIT/JUDITH)	404	CANON	SCRIPTURE
POPE INNOCENT I	405	CANON	NONE
COUNCIL CARTHAGE - 217 BISHOPS	419	CANON	NOT APPLICABLE
CODEX ALEXANDRINUS	*450*	*CANON*	*NOT APPLICABLE*
CODEX EPHRAEMI R.	*450*	*CANON*	*NOT APPLICABLE*

Version 3.1: Wisdom (and Esther (but not Baruch, which is canon)) not canonical but to be read.
Version 3.2: Wisdom (unlike Esther (which is canon) or Baruch (which is not canon)) read for strengthening but not canonical or for confirming the authority of ecclesiastical dogmas.
Version 3.3: Wisdom (unlike Esther or Baruch (both of which are canon)) not canonical but "Ecclesiastical."

SIRACH (ECCLESIASTICUS)

There is always confusion about the Book of Sirach—Ecclesiasticus is the Latin name for it, which is, of course, easy to confuse with Ecclesiastes. On the other hand, the Book of Sirach is not infrequently called the Book of Wisdom, or even Solomon, which multiplies the confusion.

And yet, relative to other Old Testament works, a surprising amount is known with certainty about Sirach: we know who wrote it (Yeshua ben Eleazar ben Sira (Ben Sira), a Jewish scribe), when (175 BC, or thereabouts), and who translated it into Greek (his grandson, around 117 BC).[429] The original Hebrew text has also been rediscovered—at least, in part.

It is also a very long Book (1372 verses, more verses than our previous five Apocrypha combined) and is an anthology: a collection of poems, advice, and wise sayings. In fact, it looks a lot like Proverbs in places, with the addition of psalms, prayers, and hymns, except that the last nine chapters of the Book are a recapitulation of Jewish history. That last piece is notable for our purposes because, like all historical Books, that portion is much less cited by early Fathers.[430] Accordingly, the citations per verse metric for Sirach is reduced. However, after all this playing around in the data, I see the relatively few citations to that part of Sirach as "deep cuts"—anyone quoting from it shows that they really, really, *really* studied their Sirach.[431]

On the other hand, the rest of the Book is as well referenced in the Bible as the Book of Wisdom (over 64 times in the KJV alone); and it is almost as well-cited by the early Fathers as the Book of Wisdom was (1432 citations to

---

[429] To some, such specific certainty excludes Sirach automatically from the Divinely-inspired Scriptures. But Christianity makes very specific claims of Divine inspiration for known people (particularly the Epistles: if nothing else, the recipients knew who Paul was). To me, if you can believe Paul was inspired, then you can believe Sirach was inspired. In fact, of course, this was once raised as an objection to Jesus as well, e.g., Matthew 13:57: "Jesus said unto them, A prophet is not without honour, save in his own country, and in his own house;" and John 7:27: "Howbeit we know this man whence he is: but when Christ cometh, no man knoweth whence he is;" etc.

[430] 32 citations per chapter for the first 42 chapters, 12 per chapter for the last nine. "The historical books, for example, never seem to have been in the least controversial, yet neither Jews nor Christians ever used them much in their writings ... in much the same position as Acts for early Christian writers: undoubtedly authoritative, scarcely ever used..." *The Spirit and the Letter: Studies in the Biblical Canon*, by John Barton, p. 23-24.

[431] An example of a serious student of Sirach: Origen First Principles 2, 8, 3 "Now the north wind is described in holy Scripture as cold, according to the statement in the book of Wisdom, "That cold north wind" (Sirach 43:20)..." www.newadvent.org/fathers/04122.htm.

1798). Once again, I stopped looking after I had found 500 times that it had been cited by early Fathers in works specifically declaring it to be Sacred Scripture, Prophecy, the word of God, etc. It is, likewise, alluded to very early (e.g., in the Didache, the Shepherd of Hermas, the Epistle of Barnabas, etc.), with full citations earlier than many canonical Books. The first full citations come from Clement of Alexandria. Recall what Kruger told us about Clement:

> Clement of Alexandria, and others - were astute "literary critics" who carefully analyzed the literary merits and historical origins of canonical and noncanonical books... As a result, they took the task of distinguishing between canonical and apocryphal books very seriously, giving us reason for greater confidence in their final conclusions. (P. 201).
>
> The ability of Patristic writers to distinguish between scriptural books and merely useful books is particularly evident in the writings of Clement of Alexandria and Origen. (P. 263).

Clement cited to Sirach as Prophecy and Scripture, and 82 times per Biblindex.org/citation_biblique/search. For comparison, Song of Songs is also a Poetic Book, the same category as Sirach, and we find clear citations to Sirach well before we find clear citations to Songs (which Clement never once cites, per Biblindex).

And yet, through 350 AD, Biblindex shows 1,066 citations to Songs versus 431 for Sirach. But 743 of the citations to Songs (70% of them) come just from Origen, who wrote a commentary/collection of homilies on it (and we still have them, which is not a minor point when making comparisons like this). Origen also cited to Sirach 130 times.[432] So, if we extract Origen from both, we have 323 citations from others to Songs and 301 to Sirach. Ecclesiastes is also a Poetic Book, with 296 citations by 350 AD, of which 144 are from Origen. So, Sirach holds up well enough:

Book	Cites	Origen	Others
Songs	1066	743	323
Sirach	431	130	302
Ecclesiastes	296	144	152

---

[432] E.g., Against Celsus 6, 7: let us show from the holy Scriptures that the word of God also encourages us to the practice of dialectics: ... Jesus the son of Sirach, who has left us the treatise called Wisdom, declaring in another, that the knowledge of the unwise is as words that will not stand investigation. www.newadvent.org/fathers/04166.htm. Plus the quotation in the preceding footnote, as no doubt you forgot, because it is hard to remember the last few chapters of Sirach.

After 350 AD, there is continued support for Sirach: e.g., Ecclesiastes will be cited another 766 times, Sirach/Ecclesiasticus 794. However, we cannot take exact numbers too seriously, as biblindex.org/citation_biblique/search is incomplete after 350 (e.g., it does not even begin to cover Augustine's enormous volume of works (he cites to Sirach hundreds of times)).[433] But other comparisons confirm this, e.g., "There are a total of 65 individual verses cited from Sirach in John [Chrysostom (d. 407 AD)]'s New Testament homilies, only slightly fewer than the 77 verses cited from Proverbs."[434]

Citations to Sirach 34:25 as Scripture were a matter of great importance in the Donatist Controversy, as a scribal error became critical to the dispute:

> It was not Donatus of Carthage[435] who established that Christians had to be rebaptized, as I thought when I responded to his letter.[436] Nor is it true that he drew the words necessary for his purpose directly from an expression of Ecclesiasticus, where it is written, "If a person is baptized after touching a dead person and touches him again, what good was it for him to wash." He claims it reads, "If someone is baptized by a dead person, what good was it for him to wash?" We later ascertained that even before the Donatist party existed, many codices —mostly, to be honest, African— did not have in this context the words "and touches him again." Augustine *Retractions* 1.21.3 [Per Ancient Christian Commentary on Scripture, not available online.]

The scribal error occurred centuries earlier, e.g., in the works of Cyprian, 245-258 AD (who cites to Sirach 42 times, e.g., Treatise 8, 2: "The Holy Spirit speaks in the sacred Scriptures, and says, ... Moreover, He says again, As water extinguishes fire, so almsgiving quenches sin." Sirach 3:30).[437] In any event, we have a case where not only is Sirach long established as Scripture, but also used to establish doctrine; in fact, a mistake in a copy of Sirach led to a heretical doctrine contrary to both the true Sirach and the true doctrine.

---

[433] Numbers for shorter date ranges do not equal the totals (when I search without a date range). This may be because the "search by date" feature excludes works whose date range might be within the parameter or might not (i.e., it crosses over the parameter). But the methodology is the same across the books, and it is all taken from the same data set, so it remains a valid "apples to apples" comparison (but you may get different results with different parameters).

[434] John Chrysostom's Use of the Book of Sirach in his *Homilies on the New Testament* (p. 1-6), de Wet, Chris, U. of Pretoria, 2010 (quoted indirectly from Google, not the actual book/article).

[435] Meaning it was a case of mistaken identity. It was a different Donatus and not Donatus "of Carthage" (there were a bunch of Donatuses in the Donatist hierarchy). The rest of the translation is a bit awkward, but the point is that the error predated the Donatists. Therefore, they did not misinterpret the real Sirach; instead, the problem was that they had a bad copy.

[436] www.newadvent.org/fathers/14086.htm, Chapter 34.

[437] www.newadvent.org/fathers/050708.htm

Sirach, as true doctrine, was also a matter of dispute with the Manicheans. Augustine (a converted Manichean) devoted Sermon 164A (before 396 AD) to disputing the Manichean interpretation of Sirach 12:4-7:

> 4Give to the godly man, and help not a sinner. 5... give not to the ungodly: hold back thy bread, and give it not unto him... 7Give unto the good, and help not the sinner.

They took the words literally, and refused to aid such people; Augustine corrects them: we are to give alms to all, including sinners—but not because they are sinners and not in aid of their sin. We are all sinners, no one is cut off from all charity because of sin (Luke 6:27: Love your enemies, do good to them which hate you); but we are also not to cooperate with their sins.

Sirach will also appear on most of the canon lists, will be accepted by every certain Council, and will be included in every existing early Bible (i.e., the four Great Uncial Codices). Sirach was, of course, also read in the liturgy of the early Churches.[438]

As for the Jewish view of Sirach, recall that we were told by Geisler and the Apologetics Study Bible that "Judaism, which produced these books, has never accepted them into its Bible (the Hebrew Scriptures, corresponding to our Old Testament)." The Jewish Study Bible, on the other hand, says that "different Jewish groups ... may have had different ideas of what comprised scripture..." and that "the Wisdom of Jesus ben Sirach ... was thus, in some sense, canonical for some Rabbis..." (p. 2157). The NIB gives specific details:

> Although Sirach was excluded from the Hebrew Bible, it was frequently cited in rabbinic circles until the tenth century CE, occasionally introduced by the formula "it is written," which indicates Scripture. Akiba, the noted rabbi of the second century (d. C. 132 CE), thought it belonged among the ... extra-canonical books, those that did not, in the language of the day, "defile the hands." A severe penalty accompanied their reading, forfeiture of any participation in the next life. ... Nevertheless, Sirach is quoted eighty-two times in the Talmud and other rabbinical writings.[439]

So, some Jews thought it was Scripture, while others said you would go to Hell/forfeit immortality for reading it. This was an extremely polarized debate. And the dispute goes on for 1000 years after Christ. Recall that Epiphanius, a

---

[438] See, e.g., Rufinus Commentary on the Apostles' Creed 38 newadvent.org/fathers/2711.htm.

[439] Introduction to Sirach, p. 684. Also, at www.sefaria.org/Yevamot.63b.13?lang=bi—you can search for "Sira," and you will see two examples of the Talmud citing Sirach; intertextual.bible/text/sirach-13.15-bava-kamma-92b has another.

Jewish Christian, tells us that the Books of Sirach and Wisdom are "disputed" among the Jews in 385 AD. Now, we have confirmation in the Talmud and other rabbinical writings that Epiphanius (and not Jerome) knew what he was talking about.[440] And it would have been impossible for the early Church to match "the" Jewish canon—they would have to pick "a" Jewish canon from among several. Jerome seems to have consulted one group (the Hebrew purists) and took their side not only in the debate over Christian Scripture but also in the debate over Jewish Scripture and what qualified as Judaism.

Also, notice the confluence of those two things: despite the claim of some Rabbis that one forfeits any participation in the next life by reading it, we still have other Rabbis in the Talmud citing to the Book of Sirach almost 800 years later. Rabbis held onto the Book of Sirach tenaciously for almost a thousand years after Christ. Earlier, the story of the Maccabean martyrs had been successfully suppressed—forgotten and replaced by a falsified version in the Talmud. The fight over Sirach lasted much longer, showing the strength of the pro-Sirach side. Still, it was ultimately rejected, not replaced—showing the strength of the anti-Sirach side that eventually won out.

Lastly, let's go back to claims like "the extent of the Hebrew canon was clear to everyone at the time of Christ." (Don Stewart, Blue Letter Bible).[441] Just on Sirach alone, we have the Jewish Study Bible saying otherwise, plus Akiba's comment less than 100 years after the death of Christ (which comment implies that others disagreed), the Talmud and its citations, other Rabbinical writings until 1000 AD, and several lists, including from Jewish Christians listing the Jewish canon.[442]

Moving from the Jews to the Bible, there are over 150 possible New Testament references to Sirach to consider.[443] The fact that some Jews

---

[440] There is other evidence, as well—e.g., Jerome received Hebrew texts of Sirach, presumably from Jews, and Sirach was still being copied as late as the 12th century C.E. See The Septuagint: the Bible of Hellenistic Judaism, by Albert C. Sundberg, Jr., in The Canon Debate, p. 88.

[441] www.blueletterbible.org/Comm/stewart_don/faq/right-books-in-old-testament/question17-new-testament-quote-old-testament.cfm.

[442] And other evidence, e.g., the inclusion in the Septuagint, the findings at Qumran, etc. Wikipedia also says that "The Book of Sirach may have been used as a basis for two important parts of the Jewish liturgy. In the Mahzor (High Holiday prayer book), a medieval Jewish poet may have used the Book of Sirach as the basis for a poem, [and]... the vocabulary and framework used by the Book of Sirach formed the basis of the most important of all Jewish prayers, the Amidah." wikipedia.org/wiki/Book_of_Sirach.

[443] Per my spreadsheet. However, in moving things to this book, I combined some short citations into longer, aggregate citations; e.g. James 3:1-18 is shown as one long reference to Sirach 24:1-34, rather than many short ones.

accepted Sirach would make references all the more meaningful, especially since never does the Bible warn anyone away from Sirach (a Book that claims to be Scripture[444] and was so "dangerous" that a "severe penalty accompanied their reading, forfeiture of any participation in the next life"). Sixty-four possible references are noted in the KJV: 60% more than even Wisdom.

Unfortunately, Sirach is far too long for me to include it all, let alone annotate it with the more than 500 citations I found from early Church Fathers who identify it as Scripture, Prophecy, etc. Even just annotating with all the possible New Testament references is impractical. Accordingly, I organized things differently: from the New Testament back to Sirach, in order to see which Evangelists and books reference it, how often, for what purpose, etc.

I mentioned above "deep cuts," i.e., anyone referencing the last nine chapters of Sirach really knows the Book well. The Ancient Christian Commentary on Scripture tells us that "the final chapters containing a recapitulation of Israel's history were little read."[445] But as we will see, Jesus Himself, and the Gospel to the Jews, and Paul the Perfectly Taught Jew, and the Epistle to the Hebrews, all seem to reference those last nine chapters.

For example, when we were discussing Biblical references and their relation to the question of the Jewish canon, I quoted this from the Evangelical Biblical Theology Commentary (Example 10, above):

> Although Matthew does not explicitly identify Jesus as the "Wisdom of God" ... Jesus's teaching makes repeated allusions to the words of personified Wisdom from an intertestamental Jewish book called the Wisdom of Ben Sira or Sirach (Sir 51:23, 26, 28). By speaking like personified Wisdom spoke, Jesus identifies himself as Wisdom. ... This background forms a bridge between the descriptions of Wisdom in Proverbs and Jesus's identification of himself as Wisdom. The title affirms Jesus's deity and his roles in both creation (Col 1:16) and the exodus (Jude 5). (pp. 72-73).

---

[444] Chapter 24:32-34: 32I will yet make doctrine to shine as the morning, and will send forth her light afar off. 33I will yet pour out doctrine as prophecy, and leave it to all ages for ever. 34Behold that I have not laboured for myself only, but for all them that seek wisdom.

[445] Intro to the Volume on Apocrypha, page xxvi. Note that the author presumably means in comparison to the rest of Sirach. We have seen many times already that historical Books are cited less, and by that comparison, the end of Sirach holds up. The last nine chapters of Sirach were cited 116 times, which is 13 citations per chapter. Compare that to another historical Book, Esther: 143 citations, 10 chapters, 14 citations per chapter. Per biblindex.org/citation_biblique/search.

Sirach 51:23, 26, 28 is a deep cut, at the very end of Sirach, amidst the chapters almost never cited by the Fathers.[446] But Jesus makes repeated allusions to it, which means that both His audience and the audience of the Gospel to the Jews (including many Priests, Acts 6:7) were so thoroughly familiar with Sirach that they, too, saw these "deep cut" allusions.

In fact, recall that we drilled down to discuss these allusions in Matthew as Example 11. Matthew 11:25-30 are six verses whose similarities to Sirach 51 "are too striking and numerous to be accidental, and indicate a definite literary dependence."[447] The verses start with a Christian hymn that predates the Bible and end with statements perhaps too Jewish for Luke to include, since he was not writing the Gospel to the Jews. Recall that in Judaism, the teacher did not seek out or invite students; the disciple had to find his master. "The sole instance of a teacher's invitation in the so-called apocryphal and pseudepigraphical literature of Second Temple Judaism occurs in Sirach 51..." (Deutsch p. 114). Sirach is, thus, the only possible work that Jesus could be referring to. In fact, if both Jesus' audience and Matthew's audience did not understand via Sirach that this "role-reversal" occurs with (and only with) the personified Wisdom of God, it would have made no sense in their culture for a teacher to make an invitation. But it makes sense for Jesus because, in so doing, He is claiming to be God—by making a deep reference to a "deep cut."

Multiple strands of evidence point to the conclusion that Sirach was being read aloud in the Synagogues of those Jesus and Matthew are speaking to. Long after Jesus, "Akiba, the noted rabbi of the second century (d. C. 132 CE)... protested strongly against the canonicity of certain of the Apocrypha, the Wisdom of Sirach, for instance ... Akiva's utterance reads, "He who reads aloud in the synagogue from books not belonging to the canon..."[448] Akiba's statement implies a need to prohibit, i.e., that Jews were reading Sirach aloud in the Synagogue prior to the prohibition. We also saw that the estimates are that 97% of Roman Palestine was illiterate, so the Book had to be read aloud to the people. And yet they had to understand the least interesting, least read, least cited portion of Sirach—a Book that (a) declares itself to be Scripture, (b)

---

[446] Chapter 51 received only 6 citations from the Fathers. The final 9 chapters were cited 116 times, per Biblindex: 13 citations per chapter, versus an average of 32 for all other chapters.

[447] *Hidden Wisdom and the Easy Yoke*, by Celia Deutsch, p. 13, quoting an article in the *Journal of Religion* by Rist, M. ("Is Matt. 11.25-30 a Primitive Baptismal Hymn?" FR 15 (1935): 63-77).

[448] wikipedia.org/wiki/Rabbi_Akiva.

was "canonical for some Rabbis," (c) was found at Qumran, the Cairo Genizah, Masada, etc., and (d) is quoted in the Talmud as Scripture.

And consider Paul. Per the KJV, the Perfectly Taught Jew made:

> Nine references to Sirach in the Epistle to the Romans,
> Two references to Sirach in the Epistle to the Philippians,
> Two references to Sirach in the 1st Epistle to the Corinthians,
> Two references to Sirach in the 2nd Epistle to the Corinthians,
> One reference to Sirach in the 1st Epistle to Timothy,
> Five references to Sirach in the 2nd Epistle to Timothy,
> Two references to Sirach in the Epistle to the Colossians,
> One reference to Sirach in the Epistle to the Ephesians,
> Three references to Sirach in the Epistle to the Galatians, and
> Three references to Sirach in the Epistle to the Hebrews.

This totals 30 references, made in 10 of the 13 Pauline Epistles. And those are just the ones that the KJV points out.

In addition to the focus shown in the Gospel to the Jews and by the Perfectly Taught Jew (and also John (the Beloved Disciple, "known unto the High Priest")), the greatest focus actually comes from the Epistle of James, the Brother of the Lord. John F. MacArthur Jr. tells us that:

> The epistle's distinctively Jewish character is in keeping with the picture of James given in Acts 15 and 21.[449]

Per the NIB, "James ... shows the influence of the Septuagint (LXX) not only in its explicit citations and allusions but also in its diction." The first verse of the Epistle also identifies James' audience as "the twelve tribes which are scattered abroad," i.e., the Jews of the diaspora, who spoke Greek and used the Septuagint—the Greek Scriptures, of which Sirach was part.[450]

William Barclay's introduction to the Letter of James in his Daily Study Bible gives us more detail:

> James was the leader of the Jerusalem Church ... even after James became a Christian, he remained in complete loyalty to the orthodox Jewish Law. So loyal that the Jews regarded him as one of themselves. ... He was the leader of what might be called Jewish Christianity; he was the head of that part of the Church which remained centered in Jerusalem. There must have been a time when the Church was very close to

---

[449] The MacArthur New Testament Commentary volume on James, p. 3-5
[450] wikipedia.org/wiki/Book_of_Sirach.

Judaism and it was more a reformed Judaism than anything else. ...The letter of James may well represent a kind of Christianity which had remained in its earliest form.

The Epistle of James consists of 108 verses. Below, we will see 29 possible cross-references to the Book of Sirach, or one allusion for every 3.7 verses.[451] Recall that (as part of his claim that Hebrews was written by the same author as Wisdom), E. H. Plumptre found 31 possible allusions to the Book of Wisdom from the Epistle to the Hebrews—31 allusions out of Hebrews' 303 verses, a rate of one allusion for every 9.8 verses. James, the Brother of the Lord, "so loyal that the Jews regarded him as one of themselves ... the leader of what might be called Jewish Christianity" makes allusions to Sirach nearly three times as frequently. He does so in an Epistle to "the twelve tribes which are scattered abroad" and at a time "when the Church was very close to Judaism and it was more a reformed Judaism than anything else."

MacArthur tells us that "The book of James contains four direct quotes of the Old Testament and more than forty Old Testament allusions." That's over 40 allusions to the 39 Books of the Protestant canon, barely one per Book— plus 29 possible allusions to Sirach, a single Book of the Apocrypha.

Moreover, Craig L. Blomberg, in his "The Historical Reliability of the Gospels," identifies the true source of James' writing:

> Of all the New Testament epistles, none contains as many passages that verbally resemble the teaching of Jesus as does James. One need look no further than the first main paragraph of his letter to observe a pattern of allusions that remains constant throughout the work. ... three of the four [allusions] come from the Sermon on the Mount/Plain. Both of these trends continue throughout the rest of the epistle ... there are good reasons for dating James very early, in the mid-to-late 40s, making it the earliest of all the New Testament writings ... That this letter is couched in the form of wisdom literature means that its author functions as a sage, and the role of a sage is to express as his own wisdom in his own formulation the wisdom he has gained from his intensive study of the tradition'. Moreover, Peter Davids argues persuasively that the allusions to Jesus' teaching form the backbone around which James's entire epistle is structured. Thus Jesus' words were not only carefully preserved but commanded great respect, playing a central and authoritative role in the life of the early church. (pp. 292-293, footnotes omitted).

---

[451] Per my spreadsheet. However, in moving things to this book, I combined some short citations into longer aggregate citations, e.g., James 3:1-18 is shown as one long reference to Sirach 24:1-34, rather than many short ones.

No other Epistles resemble the teachings of Jesus more than the Epistle that makes 29 possible references to Sirach, which (a) declares itself to be Scripture, (b) was "canonical for some Rabbis," (c) was found at Qumran, the Cairo Genizah, Masada, etc., and (d) is quoted in the Talmud as Scripture.

Sirach:
New Testament Citations

KJV cross references are in bold.

JAMES

James 1:2-4 2My brethren, count it all joy when ye fall into divers temptations; 3Knowing this, that the trying of your faith worketh patience. 4But let patience have her perfect work, that ye may be perfect and entire, wanting nothing.

James 1:5 If any of you lack wisdom, let him ask of God, that giveth to all men liberally, and upbraideth not; and it shall be given him.

> Sirach 18:18 A fool will upbraid churlishly, and a gift of the envious consumeth the eyes.

James 1:6 But let him ask in faith, nothing wavering. For he that wavereth is like a wave of the sea driven with the wind and tossed.

And James 1:8 A double minded man is unstable in all his ways.

> Sirach 1:28 Distrust not the fear of the Lord when thou art poor: and come not unto him with a double heart.
>
> Sirach 2:12 Woe be to fearful hearts, and faint hands, and the sinner that goeth two ways!

James 1:13-15 13Let no man say when he is tempted, I am tempted of God: for God cannot be tempted with evil, neither tempteth he any man: 14But every man is tempted, when he is drawn away of his own lust, and enticed. 15Then when lust hath conceived, it bringeth forth sin: and sin, when it is finished, bringeth forth death.

> Sirach 2:1 My son, if thou come to serve the Lord, prepare thy soul for temptation.
>
> Sirach 15:11-20 11Say not thou, It is through the Lord that I fell away: for thou oughtest not to do the things that he hateth. 12Say not thou, He hath caused me to err: for he hath no need of the sinful man. ... 16He hath set fire and water before thee: stretch forth thy hand unto whether thou wilt. 17Before man is life

and death; and whether him liketh shall be given him. ... 20He hath commanded no man to do wickedly, neither hath he given any man licence to sin.

James 1:14 But every man is tempted, when he is drawn away of his own lust, and enticed.

> Sirach 18:30 Go not after thy lusts, but refrain thyself from thine appetites.

James 1:19 Wherefore, my beloved brethren, let every man be swift to hear, slow to speak, slow to wrath:

> **Per the notes included with the original King James Bible, see Sirach 5:11: Be swift to hear; and let thy life be sincere; and with patience give answer.**

James 1:21 Wherefore lay apart all filthiness and superfluity of naughtiness, and receive with meekness the engrafted word, which is able to save your souls.

> Sirach 23:13 Use not thy mouth to intemperate swearing, for therein is the word of sin.

James 1:19-25 19Wherefore, my beloved brethren, let every man be swift to hear, slow to speak, slow to wrath: ... 22But be ye doers of the word, and not hearers only, deceiving your own selves. 23For if any be a hearer of the word, and not a doer, he is like unto a man beholding his natural face in a glass: 24For he beholdeth himself, and goeth his way, and straightway forgetteth what manner of man he was. 25But whoso looketh into the perfect law of liberty, and continueth therein, he being not a forgetful hearer, but a doer of the work, this man shall be blessed in his deed.

> Sirach 4:29 Be not hasty in thy tongue, and in thy deeds slack and remiss.

James 2:13 For he shall have judgment without mercy, that hath shewed no mercy; and mercy rejoiceth against judgment.

> Sirach 28:2 Forgive thy neighbour the hurt that he hath done unto thee, so shall thy sins also be forgiven when thou prayest.

James 2:14-26 14What doth it profit, my brethren, though a man say he hath faith, and have not works? can faith save him? 15If a brother or sister be naked, and destitute of daily food, 16And one of you say unto them, Depart in peace, be ye warmed and filled; notwithstanding ye give them not those things which are needful to the body; what doth it profit? 17Even so faith, if it hath not works, is dead, being alone. 18Yea, a man may say, Thou hast faith, and I have works: shew me thy faith without thy works, and I will shew thee my faith by my works. 19Thou believest that there is one God; thou doest well: the devils also believe, and tremble. 20But wilt thou know, O vain man, that faith without works is dead? 21Was not Abraham our father justified by works, when he had offered Isaac his son upon the altar? 22Seest thou how faith wrought with his works, and by works was faith made perfect? 23And the scripture was fulfilled which saith, Abraham believed God, and it was imputed unto him for righteousness: and he was called the Friend of God. 24Ye see then how that by works a man is justified, and not by faith only. 25Likewise also was not Rahab the harlot justified by works, when she had received the messengers, and had sent them out another way? 26For as the body without the spirit is dead, so faith without works is dead also.

Sirach 3:30-4:10 30Water will quench a flaming fire; and alms maketh an atonement for sins. 31And he that requiteth good turns is mindful of that which may come hereafter; and when he falleth, he shall find a stay. 1My son, defraud not the poor of his living, and make not the needy eyes to wait long. 2Make not an hungry soul sorrowful; neither provoke a man in his distress. 3Add not more trouble to an heart that is vexed; and defer not to give to him that is in need. 4Reject not the supplication of the afflicted; neither turn away thy face from a poor man. 5Turn not away thine eye from the needy, and give him none occasion to curse thee: 6For if he curse thee in the bitterness of his soul, his prayer shall be heard of him that made him. 7Get thyself the love of the congregation, and bow thy head to a great man. 8Let it not grieve thee to bow down thine ear to the poor, and give him a friendly answer with meekness. 9Deliver him that suffereth wrong from the hand of the oppressor; and be not fainthearted when thou sittest in judgment. 10Be as a father unto the fatherless, and instead of an husband unto their mother: so shalt thou be as the son of the most High, and he shall love thee more than thy mother doth.

Sirach 15:15 If thou wilt, to keep the commandments, and to perform acceptable faithfulness.

James 3:1-12 1My brethren, be not many masters, knowing that we shall receive the greater condemnation. 2For in many things we offend all. If any man offend not in word, the same is a perfect man, and able also to bridle the whole body. 3Behold, we put bits in the horses' mouths, that they may obey us; and we turn about their whole body. 4Behold also the ships, which though they be so great, and are driven of fierce winds, yet are they turned about with a very small helm, whithersoever the governor listeth. 5Even so the tongue is a little member, and boasteth great things. Behold, how great a matter a little fire kindleth! 6And the tongue is a fire, a world of iniquity: so is the tongue among our members, that it defileth the whole body, and setteth on fire the course of nature; and it is set on fire of hell. 7For every kind of beasts, and of birds, and of serpents, and of things in the sea, is tamed, and hath been tamed of mankind: 8But the tongue can no man tame; it is an unruly evil, full of deadly poison. 9Therewith bless we God, even the Father; and therewith curse we men, which are made after the similitude of God. 10Out of the same mouth proceedeth blessing and cursing. My brethren, these things ought not so to be. 11Doth a fountain send forth at the same place sweet water and bitter? 12Can the fig tree, my brethren, bear olive berries? either a vine, figs? so can no fountain both yield salt water and fresh.

Sirach 1:29: Be not an hypocrite in the sight of men, and take good heed what thou speakest.

Sirach 5:13: Honour and shame is in talk: and the tongue of man is his fall.

Sirach 8:3 Strive not with a man that is full of tongue, and heap not wood upon his fire.

Sirach 14:1: Blessed is the man that hath not slipped with his mouth, and is not pricked with the multitude of sins.

Sirach 23:12-13 12There is a word that is clothed about with death: God grant that it be not found in the heritage of Jacob; for all such things shall be far from the godly, and they shall not wallow in their sins. 13Use not thy mouth to intemperate swearing, for therein is the word of sin.

Sirach 28:10-26 10 As the matter of the fire is, so it burneth: and as a man's strength is, so is his wrath; and according to his riches his anger riseth; and the stronger they are which contend, the more they will be inflamed. 11An hasty contention kindleth a fire: and an hasty fighting sheddeth blood. 12If thou blow the spark, it shall burn: if thou spit upon it, it shall be quenched: and both these come out of thy mouth. 13Curse the whisperer and doubletongued: for such have destroyed many that were at peace. 14A backbiting tongue hath disquieted many, and driven them from nation to nation: strong cities hath it pulled down, and overthrown the houses of great men. 15A backbiting tongue hath cast out virtuous women, and deprived them of their labours. 16Whoso hearkeneth unto it shall never find rest, and never dwell quietly. 17The stroke of the whip maketh marks in the flesh: but the stroke of the tongue breaketh the bones. 18Many have fallen by the edge of the sword: but not so many as have fallen by the tongue. 19Well is he that is defended through the venom thereof; who hath not drawn the yoke thereof, nor hath been bound in her bands. 20For the yoke thereof is a yoke of iron, and the bands thereof are bands of brass. 21The death thereof is an evil death, the grave were better than it. 22It shall not have rule over them that fear God, neither shall they be burned with the flame thereof. 23Such as forsake the Lord shall fall into it; and it shall burn in them, and not be quenched; it shall be sent upon them as a lion, and devour them as a leopard. 24Look that thou hedge thy possession about with thorns, and bind up thy silver and gold, 25And weigh thy words in a balance, and make a door and bar for thy mouth. 26Beware thou slide not by it, lest thou fall before him that lieth in wait.

James 3:2 For in many things we offend all. If any man offend not in word, the same is a perfect man, and able also to bridle the whole body.

Per the notes included with the original King James Bible, see Sirach 14:2: Blessed is the man that hath not slipped with his mouth, and is not pricked with the multitude of sins.

Sirach 25:8 Well is him that dwelleth with a wife of understanding, and that hath not slipped with his tongue, and that hath not served a man more unworthy than himself:

James 3:1-18 (See above for 3:1-12): 13Who is a wise man and endued with knowledge among you? let him shew out of a good conversation his works with meekness of wisdom. 14But if ye have bitter envying and strife in your hearts, glory not, and lie not against the truth. 15This wisdom descendeth not from above, but is earthly, sensual, devilish. 16For where envying and strife is, there is confusion and every evil work. 17But the wisdom that is from above is first pure, then peaceable, gentle, and easy to be intreated, full of mercy and good fruits, without partiality, and without hypocrisy.

18And the fruit of righteousness is sown in peace of them that make peace.

Sirach 24:1-34: 1Wisdom shall praise herself, and shall glory in the midst of her people. 2In the congregation of the most High shall she open her mouth, and triumph before his power. 3I came out of the mouth of the most High, and covered the earth as a cloud. 4I dwelt in high places, and my throne is in a cloudy pillar. 5I alone compassed the circuit of heaven, and walked in the bottom of the deep. 6In the waves of the sea and in all the earth, and in every people and nation, I got a possession. 7With all these I sought rest: and in whose inheritance shall I abide? 8So the Creator of all things gave me a commandment, and he that made me caused my tabernacle to rest, and said, Let thy dwelling be in Jacob, and thine inheritance in Israel. 9He created me from the beginning before the world, and I shall never fail. 10In the holy tabernacle I served before him; and so was I established in Sion. 11Likewise in the beloved city he gave me rest, and in Jerusalem was my power. 12And I took root in an honourable people, even in the portion of the Lord's inheritance. 13I was exalted like a cedar in Libanus, and as a cypress tree upon the mountains of Hermon. 14I was exalted like a palm tree in En-gaddi, and as a rose plant in Jericho, as a fair olive tree in a pleasant field, and grew up as a plane tree by the water. 15I gave a sweet smell like cinnamon and aspalathus, and I yielded a pleasant odour like the best myrrh, as galbanum, and onyx, and sweet storax, and as the fume of frankincense in the tabernacle. 16As the turpentine tree I stretched out my branches, and my branches are the branches of honour and grace. 17As the vine brought I forth pleasant savour, and my flowers are the fruit of honour and riches. 18I am the mother of fair love, and fear, and knowledge, and holy hope: I therefore, being eternal, am given to all my children which are named of him. 19Come unto me, all ye that be desirous of me, and fill yourselves with my fruits. 20For my memorial is sweeter than honey, and mine inheritance than the honeycomb. 21They that eat me shall yet be hungry, and they that drink me shall yet be thirsty. 22He that obeyeth me shall never be confounded, and they that work by me shall not do amiss. 23All these things are the book of the covenant of the most high God, even the law which Moses commanded for an heritage unto the congregations of Jacob. 24Faint not to be strong in the Lord; that he may confirm you, cleave unto him: for the Lord Almighty is God alone, and beside him there is no other Saviour. 25He filleth all things with his wisdom, as Phison and as Tigris in the time of the new fruits. 26He maketh the understanding to abound like Euphrates, and as Jordan in the time of the harvest. 27He maketh the doctrine of knowledge appear as the light, and as Geon in the time of vintage. 28The first man knew her not perfectly: no more shall the last find her out. 29For her thoughts are more than the sea, and her counsels profounder than the great deep. 30I also came out as a brook from a river, and as a conduit into a garden. 31I said, I will water my best garden, and will water abundantly my garden bed: and, lo, my brook became a river, and my river became a sea. 32I will yet make doctrine to shine as the morning, and will send forth her light afar off. 33I will yet pour out doctrine as prophecy, and leave it to all ages for ever. 34Behold that I have not laboured for myself only, but for all them that seek wisdom.

Sirach 19:20-25 20The fear of the Lord is all wisdom; and in all wisdom is the performance of the law, and the knowledge of his omnipotency. 21If a servant say to his master, I will not do as it pleaseth thee; though afterward he do it, he angereth him that nourisheth him. 22The knowledge of wickedness is not wisdom, neither at any time the counsel of sinners prudence. 23There is a wickedness, and the same an abomination; and there is a fool wanting in wisdom. 24He that hath small understanding, and feareth God, is better than one that hath much wisdom, and transgresseth the law of the most High. 25There is an exquisite subtilty, and the same is unjust; and there is one that turneth aside to make judgment appear; and there is a wise man that justifieth in judgment.

James 4:6 But he giveth more grace. Wherefore he saith, God resisteth the proud, but giveth grace unto the humble.

Sirach 7:4-7 4Seek not of the Lord preeminence, neither of the king the seat of honour. 5Justify not thyself before the Lord; and boast not of thy wisdom before the king. 6Seek not to be judge, being not able to take away iniquity; lest at any time thou fear the person of the mighty, an stumbling block in the way of thy uprightness. 7Offend not against the multitude of a city, and then thou shalt not cast thyself down among the people.

James 5:3 Your riches are corrupted, and your garments are motheaten. Your gold and silver is cankered; and the rust of them shall be a witness against you, and shall eat your flesh as it were fire. Ye have heaped treasure together for the last days.

Sirach 29:10-11: 10Lose thy money for thy brother and thy friend, and let it not rust under a stone to be lost. 11Lay up thy treasure according to the commandments of the most High, and it shall bring thee more profit than gold. Per the King James Version, the Gospel to the Jews also references Sirach 29:10-11 (Matthew 6:19-20: 19Lay not up for yourselves treasures upon earth, where moth and rust doth corrupt, and where thieves break through and steal:

20But lay up for yourselves treasures in heaven, where neither moth nor rust doth corrupt, and where thieves do not break through nor steal). [452]

Sirach 12:11 Though he humble himself, and go crouching, yet take good heed and beware of him, and thou shalt be unto him

---

[452] John F. MacArthur Jr., in the MacArthur Study Bible volume on James, makes no mention of James' possible reference to Sirach; he says, instead, that "Even such seemingly indestructible commodities, James noted, can become rusted. ... James may have meant that the gold and silver could literally become rusted; some evidence suggests the coinage of his day was not pure but contained alloys and could rust under conducive circumstances. Or James may have been speaking figuratively, declaring that in the day of God's judgment, gold and silver will be as useless as if they were rusted. The utter inability of riches to deliver individuals from God's judgment is a frequent theme in Scripture (e.g., Prov. 11:4; Isa. 2:20-21; Ezek. 7:19; Zeph. 1:18; Matt. 16:26)." I, too, think it was meant figuratively, but I would get there via a more obvious and applicable citation to Scripture than those MacArthur lists: Sirach is talking about it figuratively, and James is alluding to that. The idea that both writers are referring to gold rusting seems farfetched, given the lack of others ever doing so; the simple answer is the allusion from James to Sirach.

The MacArthur Study Bible volume on Matthew 6:20 explains the reference to rust as "Wealth was also often held in grain, as we see from the parable of the rich farmer who said, "I will tear down my barns and build larger ones, and there I will store all my grain and my goods" (Luke 12:18). Brosis (rust) literally means "an eating," and is translated with that meaning everywhere in the New Testament but here (see Rom. 14:17; 1 Cor. 8:4, "eating"; 2 Cor. 9:10, "food"; and Heb. 12:16, "meal"). It seems best to take the same meaning here, in reference to grain that is eaten by rats, mice, worms, and insects." The KJV, on the other hand, sees it as a reference to Sirach, as noted above.

as if thou hadst wiped a looking glass, and thou shalt know that his rust hath not been altogether wiped away.

PETER

1 Peter 1:17 And if ye call on the Father, who without respect of persons judgeth according to every man's work, pass the time of your sojourning here in fear:

> Per the notes included with the original King James Bible, see <u>Sirach 35:12</u>: Do not think to corrupt with gifts; for such he will not receive: and trust not to unrighteous sacrifices; for the Lord is judge, and with him is no respect of persons.

1 Peter 1:24 For all flesh is as grass, and all the glory of man as the flower of grass. The grass withereth, and the flower thereof falleth away:

> Per the notes included with the original King James Bible, see <u>Sirach 14:17</u>: All flesh waxeth old as a garment: for the covenant from the beginning is, Thou shalt die the death.

1 Peter 4:12 Beloved, think it not strange concerning the fiery trial which is to try you, as though some strange thing happened unto you:

> Per the notes included with the original King James Bible, see <u>Sirach 2:1</u>: My son, if thou come to serve the Lord, prepare thy soul for temptation.

2 Peter 3:8 But, beloved, be not ignorant of this one thing, that one day is with the Lord as a thousand years, and a thousand years as one day.

> Per the notes included with the original King James Bible, see <u>Sirach 18:10</u>: As a drop of water unto the sea, and a gravelstone in comparison of the sand; so are a thousand years to the days of eternity.

2 Peter 3:10 But the day of the Lord will come as a thief in the night; in the which the heavens shall pass away with a great noise, and the elements shall melt with fervent heat, the earth also and the works that are therein shall be burned up.

> Per the notes included with the original King James Bible, see <u>Sirach 16:18</u>: Behold, the heaven, and the heaven of heavens, the deep, and the earth, and all that therein is, shall be moved when he shall visit.

PAUL

1 Corinthians 6:12 All things are lawful unto me, but all things are not expedient: all things are lawful for me, but I will not be brought under the power of any.

> <u>Sirach 37:28</u> For all things are not profitable for all men, neither hath every soul pleasure in every thing.

1 Corinthians 10:23 All things are lawful for me, but all things are not expedient: all things are lawful for me, but all things edify not.

> <u>Sirach 37:28</u> For all things are not profitable for all men, neither hath every soul pleasure in every thing.

1 Corinthians 11:7 For a man indeed ought not to cover his head, forasmuch as he is the image and glory of God: but the woman is the glory of the man.

> Per the notes included with the original King James Bible, see <u>Sirach 17:1</u>: The Lord created man of the earth, and turned him into it again.

1 Corinthians 11:31 But let a man examine himself, and so let him eat of that bread, and drink of that cup. ...For if we would judge ourselves, we should not be judged.

> Per the notes included with the original King James Bible, see <u>Sirach 18:20</u>: Before judgment examine thyself, and in the day of visitation thou shalt find mercy.

1 Timothy 6:6 But godliness with contentment is great gain.

> Per the notes included with the original King James Bible, see <u>Sirach 40:18</u>: To labour, and to be content with that a man hath, is a sweet life: but he that findeth a treasure is above them both.

<u>1 Timothy 6:9</u> But they that will be rich fall into temptation and a snare, and into many foolish and hurtful lusts, which drown men in destruction and perdition.

Per the notes included with the original King James Bible, see <u>Sirach 11:11</u>: There is one that laboureth, and taketh pains, and maketh haste, and is so much the more behind.

<u>1 Timothy 6:9</u> But they that will be rich fall into temptation and a snare, and into many foolish and hurtful lusts, which drown men in destruction and perdition.

Per the notes included with the original King James Bible, see <u>Sirach 27:2</u>: As a nail sticketh fast between the joinings of the stones; so doth sin stick close between buying and selling.

<u>1 Timothy 6:10</u> But they that will be rich fall into temptation and a snare, and into many foolish and hurtful lusts, which drown men in destruction and perdition. For the love of money is the root of all evil: which while some coveted after, they have erred from the faith, and pierced themselves through with many sorrows.

Per the notes included with the original King James Bible, see <u>Sirach 31:1</u>: Watching for riches consumeth the flesh, and the care thereof driveth away sleep. (As discussed above, Don Stewart[453] says that "While Ecclesiastes does not have any direct quotes from it in the New Testament, there are a number of passages that allude to it. For example, Paul wrote to Timothy: "For the love of money is at the root of all kinds of evil. And some people, craving money, have wandered from the faith and pierced themselves with many sorrows. (1 Timothy 6:10 NLT)" This seems to depend upon the

following verse in Ecclesiastes. It reads: The lover of money will not be satisfied with money; nor the lover of wealth, with gain. This also is vanity. (Ecclesiastes 5:10 NRSV)" - But the notes included with the original King James Bible actually say otherwise. There is no cross-reference with Ecclesiastes. Instead it is Sirach 31:1 ("Watching for riches consumeth the flesh, and the care thereof driveth away sleep") that was cross-referenced with 1 Timothy 6:10. Thus the website's claim that "there seems to be direct dependence upon this book in a number of places in the New Testament" should apply to Sirach (Ecclesiasticus), not Ecclesiastes, per the KJV.

<u>1 Timothy 6:19</u> That they do good, that they be rich in good works, ready to distribute, willing to communicate; Laying up in store for themselves a good foundation against the time to come, that they may lay hold on eternal life.

Per the notes included with the original King James Bible, see <u>Sirach 29:11</u>: Lay up thy treasure according to the commandments of the most High, and it shall bring thee more profit than gold.

<u>2 Corinthians 2:6</u> Sufficient to such a man is this punishment, which was inflicted of many.

Per the notes included with the original King James Bible, see <u>Sirach 8:5</u>: Reproach not a man that turneth from sin, but remember that we are all worthy of punishment.

<u>2 Corinthians 9:7</u> Every man according as he purposeth in his heart, so let him give; not grudgingly, or of necessity: for God loveth a cheerful giver.

Per the notes included with the original King James Bible, see <u>Sirach 35:9</u>: In all thy gifts shew a cheerful countenance, and dedicate thy tithes with gladness.

---

[453] blueletterbible.org/Comm/stewart_don/faq/right-books-in-old-testament/question17-new-testament-quote-old-testament.cfm

2 Corinthians 9:7 Every man according as he purposeth in his heart, so let him give; not grudgingly, or of necessity: for God loveth a cheerful giver.

> Sirach 35:9 In all thy gifts shew a cheerful countenance, and dedicate thy tithes with gladness.

2 Timothy 3:12 My son, if thou come to serve the Lord, prepare thy soul for temptation.

> Per the notes included with the original King James Bible, see Sirach 2:1: My son, if thou come to serve the Lord, prepare thy soul for temptation.

Colossians 3:10 And have put on the new man, which is renewed in knowledge after the image of him that created him:

> Per the notes included with the original King James Bible, see Sirach 17:1: The Lord created man of the earth, and turned him into it again.

Colossians 3:25 But he that doeth wrong shall receive for the wrong which he hath done: and there is no respect of persons.

> Per the notes included with the original King James Bible, see Sirach 35:12: Do not think to corrupt with gifts; for such he will not receive: and trust not to unrighteous sacrifices; for the Lord is judge, and with him is no respect of persons.

Ephesians 6:9 And, ye masters, do the same things unto them, forbearing threatening: knowing that your Master also is in heaven; neither is there respect of persons with him.

> Per the notes included with the original King James Bible, see Sirach 35:12: Do not think to corrupt with gifts; for such he will not receive: and trust not to unrighteous sacrifices; for the Lord is judge, and with him is no respect of persons.

Galatians 2:6 But of these who seemed to be somewhat, (whatsoever they were, it maketh no matter to me: God accepteth no man's person:) for they who seemed to be somewhat in conference added nothing to me:

> Per the notes included with the original King James Bible, see Sirach 35:12: Do not think to corrupt with gifts; for such he will not receive: and trust not to unrighteous sacrifices; for the Lord is judge, and with him is no respect of persons.

Galatians 3:8 And the scripture, foreseeing that God would justify the heathen through faith, preached before the gospel unto Abraham, saying, In thee shall all nations be blessed.

> Per the notes included with the original King James Bible, see Sirach 44:21: Therefore he assured him by an oath, that he would bless the nations in his seed, and that he would multiply him as the dust of the earth, and exalt his seed as the stars, and cause them to inherit from sea to sea, and from the river unto the utmost part of the land.

Galatians 6:7 Be not deceived; God is not mocked: for whatsoever a man soweth, that shall he also reap.

> Per the notes included with the original King James Bible, see Sirach 8:5: Reproach not a man that turneth from sin, but remember that we are all worthy of punishment.

Hebrews 3:1 Wherefore, holy brethren, partakers of the heavenly calling, consider the Apostle and High Priest of our profession, Christ Jesus;

And Hebrews 8:2 Now of the things which we have spoken this is the sum: We have such an high priest, who is set on the right hand of the throne of the Majesty in the heavens; A minister of the sanctuary, and of the true tabernacle, which the Lord pitched, and not man.

> Sirach 24:10 In the holy tabernacle I served before him; and so was I established in Sion. (describing the Wisdom of God as our High Priest:)

Hebrews 11:5 By faith Enoch was translated that he should not see death; and was not found, because God had translated him: for before his translation he had this testimony, that he pleased God.

Per the notes included with the original King James Bible, see Sirach 44:16: Enoch pleased the Lord, and was translated, being an example of repentance to all generations.

Hebrews 11:5 By faith Enoch was translated that he should not see death; and was not found, because God had translated him: for before his translation he had this testimony, that he pleased God.

Per the notes included with the original King James Bible, see Sirach 49:13-14: And among the elect was Neemias, whose renown is great, who raised up for us the walls that were fallen, and set up the gates and the bars, and raised up our ruins again. But upon the earth was no man created like Enoch; for he was taken from the earth.

Hebrews 11:7 By faith Noah, being warned of God of things not seen as yet, moved with fear, prepared an ark to the saving of his house; by the which he condemned the world, and became heir of the righteousness which is by faith.

Per the notes included with the original King James Bible, see Sirach 44:17: Noah was found perfect and righteous; in the time of wrath he was taken in exchange for the world; therefore was he left as a remnant unto the earth, when the flood came.

Philippians 2:3 Let nothing be done through strife or vainglory; but in lowliness of mind let each esteem other better than themselves.

Per the notes included with the original King James Bible, see Sirach 3:18: The greater thou art, the more humble thyself, and thou shalt find favour before the Lord.

Philippians 4:12 Not that I speak in respect of want: for I have learned, in whatsoever state I am, therewith to be content. I know both how to be abased, and I know how to abound: every where and in all things I am instructed both to be full and to be hungry, both to abound and to suffer need.

Per the notes included with the original King James Bible, see Sirach 40:18: To labour, and to be content with that a man hath, is a sweet life: but he that findeth a treasure is above them both.

Romans 2:11 For there is no respect of persons with God.

Per the notes included with the original King James Bible, see Sirach 35:12: Do not think to corrupt with gifts; for such he will not receive: and trust not to unrighteous sacrifices; for the Lord is judge, and with him is no respect of persons.

Romans 6:6 Knowing this, that our old man is crucified with him, that the body of sin might be destroyed, that henceforth we should not serve sin.

Per the notes included with the original King James Bible, see Sirach 18:30: Go not after thy lusts, but refrain thyself from thine appetites.

Romans 6:14 Neither yield ye your members as instruments of unrighteousness unto sin: but yield yourselves unto God, as those that are alive from the dead, and your members as instruments of righteousness unto God. For sin shall not have dominion over you: for ye are not under the law, but under grace.

Per the notes included with the original King James Bible, see Sirach 18:30: Go not after thy lusts, but refrain thyself from thine appetites.

Romans 9:21 Nay but, O man, who art thou that repliest against God? Shall the thing formed say to him that formed it, Why hast thou made me thus? Hath not the potter power over the clay, of the same lump to make one vessel unto honour, and another unto dishonour?

Per the notes included with the original King James Bible, see <u>Sirach 33:13</u>: As the clay is in the potter's hand, to fashion it at his pleasure: so man is in the hand of him that made him, to render to them as liketh him best.

<u>Romans 11:34</u> For who hath known the mind of the Lord? or who hath been his counsellor?

Per the notes included with the original King James Bible, see <u>Sirach 1:6</u>: To whom hath the root of wisdom been revealed? or who hath known her wise counsels?

<u>Romans 12:3</u> For I say, through the grace given unto me, to every man that is among you, not to think of himself more highly than he ought to think; but to think soberly, according as God hath dealt to every man the measure of faith.

Per the notes included with the original King James Bible, see <u>Sirach 3:21</u>: Seek not out things that are too hard for thee, neither search the things that are above thy strength.

<u>Romans 12:10</u> Be kindly affectioned one to another with brotherly love; in honour preferring one another;

Per the notes included with the original King James Bible, see <u>Sirach 25:1</u>: In three things I was beautified, and stood up beautiful both before God and men: the unity of brethren, the love of neighbours, a man and a wife that agree together.

<u>Romans 12:19</u> Dearly beloved, avenge not yourselves, but rather give place unto wrath: for it is written, Vengeance is mine; I will repay, saith the Lord.

Per the notes included with the original King James Bible, see <u>Sirach 28:28</u>: Mockery and reproach are from the proud; but vengeance, as a lion, shall lie in wait for them.

<u>Romans 14:5</u> One man esteemeth one day above another: another esteemeth every day alike. Let every man be fully persuaded in his own mind.

Per the notes included with the original King James Bible, see <u>Sirach 32:23</u>: In every good work trust thy own soul; for this is the keeping of the commandments.

JOHN

<u>John 1:1-2</u> 1In the beginning was the Word, and the Word was with God, and the Word was God. 2The same was in the beginning with God.

<u>Sirach 1:1</u> All wisdom cometh from the Lord, and is with him for ever.

<u>Sirach 24:4</u>: I dwelt in high places, and my throne is in a cloudy pillar.

<u>Sirach 24:9</u>: He created me from the beginning before the world, and I shall never fail.

<u>John 1:1-3</u> In the beginning was the Word, and the Word was with God, and the Word was God. The same was in the beginning with God. All things were made by him; and without him was not any thing made that was made.

<u>Sirach 24:3</u> I came out of the mouth of the most High, and covered the earth as a cloud.

<u>John 1:10</u> He was in the world, and the world was made by him, and the world knew him not.

<u>Sirach 24:7-8</u>: 7With all these I sought rest: and in whose inheritance shall I abide? 8So the Creator of all things gave me a commandment, and he that made me caused my tabernacle to rest, and said, Let thy dwelling be in Jacob, and thine inheritance in Israel.

<u>John 1:14</u> And the Word was made flesh, and dwelt among us, (and we beheld his glory, the glory as of the only begotten of the Father,) full of grace and truth.

<u>Sirach 24:8</u> So the Creator of all things gave me a commandment, and he that made me caused my tabernacle to rest,

and said, Let thy dwelling be in Jacob, and thine inheritance in Israel. (The same Greek word for tabernacle is translated as "dwelt among" in the KJV John 1:14).

Sirach 24:16 As the turpentine tree I stretched out my branches, and my branches are the branches of honour and grace. (The same Greek words for honour and grace are translated as glory and grace in the KJV John 1:14).

John 1:18 No man hath seen God at any time; the only begotten Son, which is in the bosom of the Father, he hath declared him.

Per the notes included with the original King James Bible, see Sirach 43:31: Who hath seen him, that he might tell us? and who can magnify him as he is?

Sirach 24:3 I came out of the mouth of the most High, and covered the earth as a cloud. (re" He hath declared Him).

John 4:10-14 10Jesus answered and said unto her, If thou knewest the gift of God, and who it is that saith to thee, Give me to drink; thou wouldest have asked of him, and he would have given thee living water. 11The woman saith unto him, Sir, thou hast nothing to draw with, and the well is deep: from whence then hast thou that living water? 12Art thou greater than our father Jacob, which gave us the well, and drank thereof himself, and his children, and his cattle? 13Jesus answered and said unto her, Whosoever drinketh of this water shall thirst again: 14But whosoever drinketh of the water that I shall give him shall never thirst; but the water that I shall give him shall be in him a well of water springing up into everlasting life."

Sirach 24:19-22: "19Come unto me, all ye that be desirous of me, and fill yourselves with my fruits. 20For my memorial is sweeter than honey, and mine inheritance than the honeycomb. 21They that eat me shall yet be hungry, and they that drink me shall yet be thirsty. 22 He that obeyeth me shall never be confounded, and they that work by me shall not do amiss.

John 6:35 And Jesus said unto them, I am the bread of life: he that cometh to me shall never hunger; and he that believeth on me shall never thirst.

Sirach 24:19-22: "19Come unto me, all ye that be desirous of me, and fill yourselves with my fruits. 20For my memorial is sweeter than honey, and mine inheritance than the honeycomb. 21They that eat me shall yet be hungry, and they that drink me shall yet be thirsty. 22 He that obeyeth me shall never be confounded, and they that work by me shall not do amiss.

John 15:1 I am the true vine, and my Father is the husbandman.

Per the notes included with the original King James Bible, see Sirach 24:17: As the vine brought I forth pleasant savour, and my flowers are the fruit of honour and riches.

LUKE

Luke 1:52 He has put down the mighty from their thrones, and exalted the lowly

Sirach 10:14 The Lord overthrows the thrones of rulers, and enthrones the lowly in their place

Luke 6:24 But woe unto you that are rich! for ye have received your consolation.

Per the notes included with the original King James Bible, see Sirach 31:8: Blessed is the rich that is found without blemish, and hath not gone after gold.

Luke 6:34-35 And if ye lend to them of whom ye hope to receive, what thank have ye? for sinners also lend to sinners, to receive as much again. But love ye your enemies, and do good, and lend, hoping for nothing again; and your reward shall be great, and ye shall be the children of the Highest: for he is kind unto the unthankful and to the evil.

Per the notes included with the original King James Bible, see Sirach 29:2: Lend to thy neighbour in time of his need, and pay thou thy neighbour again in due season.

Luke 11:2 And he said unto them, When ye pray, say, Our Father which art in heaven, Hallowed be thy name. Thy kingdom come. Thy will be done, as in heaven, so in earth.

> Sirach 23:14: O Lord, Father and Ruler of my life, do not abandon me to their counsel, and let me not fall because of them! ... O Lord, Father and God of my life, do not give me haughty eyes, and remove from me evil desire. Sirach is the first time where prayer is addressed to God, calling him Father.

Luke 11:4 And forgive us our sins; for we also forgive every one that is indebted to us. And lead us not into temptation; but deliver us from evil.

> Per Manners and Customs of the Bible, by James M. Freeman (d. 1900): The accompanying phrase, "as we also have forgiven," reflects the Jewish teaching found in Sirach 28:2: "Forgive the wrong of your neighbor, and then your sins will be forgiven when you pray."

Luke 11:41 But rather give alms of such things as ye have; and, behold, all things are clean unto you.

> **Per the notes included with the original King James Bible, see Sirach 29:11: Lay up thy treasure according to the commandments of the most High, and it shall bring thee more profit than gold.**

Luke 12:19 And I will say to my soul, Soul, thou hast much goods laid up for many years; take thine ease, eat, drink, and be merry.

> **Per the notes included with the original King James Bible, see Sirach 5:1: Set not thy heart upon thy goods; and say not, I have enough for my life.**
>
> **Per the notes included with the original King James Bible, see Sirach 11:19: Whereas he saith, I have found rest, and now will eat continually of my goods; and yet he knoweth not what time shall come upon him, and that he**

must leave those things to others, and die.

Luke 12:33 Sell that ye have, and give alms; provide yourselves bags which wax not old, a treasure in the heavens that faileth not, where no thief approacheth, neither moth corrupteth.

> **Per the notes included with the original King James Bible, see Sirach 29:11: Lay up thy treasure according to the commandments of the most High, and it shall bring thee more profit than gold.**

Luke 14:13 But when thou makest a feast, call the poor, the maimed, the lame, the blind:

> **Per the notes included with the original King James Bible, see Sirach 14:13: Do good unto thy friend before thou die, and according to thy ability stretch out thy hand and give to him.**

Luke 15:21 And the son said unto him, Father, I have sinned against heaven, and in thy sight, and am no more worthy to be called thy son.

> **Per the notes included with the original King James Bible, see Sirach 21:1: My son, hast thou sinned? do so no more, but ask pardon for thy former sins.**

Luke 18:11 The Pharisee stood and prayed thus with himself, God, I thank thee, that I am not as other men are, extortioners, unjust, adulterers, or even as this publican.

> **Per the notes included with the original King James Bible, see Sirach 7:5: Justify not thyself before the Lord; and boast not of thy wisdom before the king.**

Acts 3:19 Repent ye therefore, and be converted, that your sins may be blotted out, when the times of refreshing shall come from the presence of the Lord;

> **Per the notes included with the original King James Bible, see Sirach 17:24: But unto them that repent, he granted them return, and comforted those that failed in patience.**

Acts 10:4 And when he looked on him, he was afraid, and said, What is it, Lord? And he said unto him, Thy prayers and thine alms are come up for a memorial before God.

> **Per the notes included with the original King James Bible, see <u>Sirach 29:11</u>: Lay up thy treasure according to the commandments of the most High, and it shall bring thee more profit than gold.**

<u>Acts 10:34</u> Then Peter opened his mouth, and said, Of a truth I perceive that God is no respecter of persons:

> **Per the notes included with the original King James Bible, see <u>Sirach 35:12</u>: Do not think to corrupt with gifts; for such he will not receive: and trust not to unrighteous sacrifices; for the Lord is judge, and with him is no respect of persons.**

<u>Acts 12:21</u> And upon a set day Herod, arrayed in royal apparel, sat upon his throne, and made an oration unto them.

> **Per the notes included with the original King James Bible, see <u>Sirach 11:4</u>: Boast not of thy clothing and raiment, and exalt not thyself in the day of honour: for the works of the Lord are wonderful, and his works among men are hidden.**

Acts 20:35 I have shewed you all things, how that so labouring ye ought to support the weak, and to remember the words of the Lord Jesus, how he said, It is more blessed to give than to receive.

> Sirach 4:31 Let not thine hand be stretched out to receive, and shut when thou shouldest repay.

MARK

Mark 4:5 Other seed fell on shallow soil with underlying rock. The seed sprouted quickly because the soil was shallow,

> Sirach 40:15 The children of the ungodly won't grow many branches, and are as unhealthy roots on a sheer rock.

Mark 9:46 And if thy hand offend thee, cut it off: it is better for thee to enter into life maimed, than having two hands to go into hell, into the fire that never shall be quenched: 44Where their worm dieth not, and the fire is not quenched. 45And if thy foot offend thee, cut it off: it is better for thee to enter halt into life, than having two feet to be cast into hell, into the fire that never shall be quenched: 46Where their worm dieth not, and the fire is not quenched.

> Sirach 7:17 Humble thyself greatly: for the vengeance of the ungodly is fire and worms. (Often cross referenced with Isaiah 66:24, however that is an earthly, temporal punishment: And they shall go forth, and look upon the carcasses of the men that have transgressed against me: for their worm shall not die, neither shall their fire be quenched; and they shall be an abhorring unto all flesh.)

MATTHEW

Matthew 5:7 Blessed are the merciful: for they shall obtain mercy.

> **Per the notes included with the original King James Bible, see <u>Sirach 3:30</u>: Water will quench a flaming fire; and alms maketh an atonement for sins.**

<u>Matthew 5:11</u> Blessed are ye, when men shall revile you, and persecute you, and shall say all manner of evil against you falsely, for my sake.

> **Per the notes included with the original King James Bible, see <u>Sirach 2:1</u>: My son, if thou come to serve the Lord, prepare thy soul for temptation.**

<u>Matthew 5:25</u> Agree with thine adversary quickly, whiles thou art in the way with him; lest at any time the adversary deliver thee to the judge, and the judge deliver thee to the officer, and thou be cast into prison.

> **Per the notes included with the original King James Bible, see <u>Sirach 8:2</u>: Be not at variance with a rich man, lest he overweigh thee: for gold hath destroyed**

many, and perverted the hearts of kings.

Matthew 5:33 Again, ye have heard that it hath been said by them of old time, Thou shalt not forswear thyself, but shalt perform unto the Lord thine oaths:

> **Per the notes included with the original King James Bible, see Sirach 23:9: Accustom not thy mouth to swearing; neither use thyself to the naming of the Holy One.**

Matthew 5:42 Give to him that asketh thee, and from him that would borrow of thee turn not thou away.

> **Per the notes included with the original King James Bible, see Sirach 29:2: Lend to thy neighbour in time of his need, and pay thou thy neighbour again in due season.**

Matthew 6:5 And when thou prayest, thou shalt not be as the hypocrites are: for they love to pray standing in the synagogues and in the corners of the streets, that they may be seen of men. Verily I say unto you, They have their reward.

> **Per the notes included with the original King James Bible, see Sirach 7:14: Use not many words in a multitude of elders, and make not much babbling when thou prayest.**

Matthew 6:7 But when ye pray, use not vain repetitions, as the heathen do: for they think that they shall be heard for their much speaking.

> **Per the notes included with the original King James Bible, see Sirach 7:14: Use not many words in a multitude of elders, and make not much babbling when thou prayest.**

Matthew 6:9 After this manner therefore pray ye: Our Father which art in heaven, Hallowed be thy name.

> Sirach 23:14: O Lord, Father and Ruler of my life, do not abandon me to their counsel, and let me not fall because of them! ... O Lord, Father and God of my life, do not give me haughty eyes, and

remove from me evil desire. Sirach is the first time where prayer is addressed to God, calling him Father.

Matthew 6:12 And forgive us our debts, as we forgive our debtors.

> Per Manners and Customs of the Bible, by James M. Freeman (d. 1900): The accompanying phrase, "as we also have forgiven," reflects the Jewish teaching found in Sirach 28:2: "Forgive the wrong of your neighbor, and then your sins will be forgiven when you pray."

Matthew 6:14-15 14For if ye forgive men their trespasses, your heavenly Father will also forgive you: 15But if ye forgive not men their trespasses, neither will your Father forgive your trespasses.

> Per Manners and Customs of the Bible, by James M. Freeman (d. 1900): The accompanying phrase, "as we also have forgiven," reflects the Jewish teaching found in Sirach 28:2: "Forgive the wrong of your neighbor, and then your sins will be forgiven when you pray."

Matthew 6:20 But lay up for yourselves treasures in heaven, where neither moth nor rust doth corrupt, and where thieves do not break through nor steal:

> **Per the notes included with the original King James Bible, see Sirach 29:11: Lay up thy treasure according to the commandments of the most High, and it shall bring thee more profit than gold.**

Matthew 7:16-17 16Ye shall know them by their fruits. Do men gather grapes of thorns, or figs of thistles? 17Even so every good tree bringeth forth good fruit; but a corrupt tree bringeth forth evil fruit.

> **Per the notes included with the original King James Bible, see Sirach 27:6: The fruit declareth if the tree have been dressed; so is the utterance of a conceit in the heart of man. (See also the discussion at James 5:3, above).**

Matthew 9:22 But Jesus turned him about, and when he saw her, he said, Daughter, be of good comfort; thy faith hath made thee whole. And the woman was made whole from that hour.

Per the notes included with the original King James Bible, see Sirach 11:20: Be stedfast in thy covenant, and be conversant therein, and wax old in thy work.

Matthew 11:29 Take my yoke upon you, and learn of me; for I am meek and lowly in heart: and ye shall find rest unto your souls.

Per the notes included with the original King James Bible, see Sirach 6:24-25: And put thy feet into her fetters, and thy neck into her chain. Bow down thy shoulder, and bear her, and be not grieved with her bonds.

Matthew 11:25-30 25At that time Jesus answered and said, I thank thee, O Father, Lord of heaven and earth, because thou hast hid these things from the wise and prudent, and hast revealed them unto babes. 26Even so, Father: for so it seemed good in thy sight. 27All things are delivered unto me of my Father: and no man knoweth the Son, but the Father; neither knoweth any man the Father, save the Son, and he to whomsoever the Son will reveal him. 28Come unto me, all ye that labour and are heavy laden, and I will give you rest. 29Take my yoke upon you, and learn of me; for I am meek and lowly in heart: and ye shall find rest unto your souls. 30For my yoke is easy, and my burden is light.

Sirach 51:28 23 Draw near unto me, ye unlearned, and dwell in the house of learning. 24Wherefore are ye slow, and what say ye to these things, seeing your souls are very thirsty? 25I opened my mouth, and said, Buy her for yourselves without money. 26Put your neck under the yoke, and let your soul receive instruction: she is hard at hand to find. 27Behold with your eyes, how that I have but little labour, and have gotten unto me much rest. 28Get learning with a great sum of money, and get much gold by her. (Discussed in depth above).

Matthew 13:54-56 54And when he was come into his own country, he taught them in their synagogue, insomuch that they were astonished, and said, Whence hath this man this wisdom, and these mighty works? 55Is not this the carpenter's son? is not his mother called Mary? and his brethren, James, and Joses, and Simon, and Judas? 56And his sisters, are they not all with us? Whence then hath this man all these things?

Per the Evangelical Biblical Theology Commentary volume on Matthew (by Charles L. Quarles): p. 355-56: Interestingly, Sirach had described the wise scribe in detail about two centuries before the ministry of Jesus. ... But, although Jesus fit these descriptions well, he had not attained this wisdom in the way Sirach thought necessary. ... Yet, Jesus astonished those who had attended synagogue all their lives with his wisdom as an interpreter of the Hebrew Scriptures. The attendees asked the obvious question, "Where did this man get this wisdom?" His wisdom did not come from the respected rabbinic schools of Hillel or Shammai. Yet Jesus implied that he had greater wisdom than even Solomon (Matt 13:54). In fact, he not only claimed to have wisdom, but he also claimed to be Wisdom (Matt 11:19 [But wisdom is justified of her children]).

Matthew 25:35 Then shall the King say unto them on his right hand, Come, ye blessed of my Father, inherit the kingdom prepared for you from the foundation of the world: For I was an hungred, and ye gave me meat: I was thirsty, and ye gave me drink: I was a stranger, and ye took me in:

Per the notes included with the original King James Bible, see Sirach 17:23: Afterwards he will rise up and reward them, and render their recompence upon their heads.

Postscript to Sirach: Summarizing the Data

The following is a chronological chart of some citations from the Fathers, plus all canon lists and Councils and codices (which are in ALL CAPS, and in **BOLD IF A COUNCIL,** and in *ITALICS IF A CODEX*). As with Wisdom, this is a very incomplete list. It is only those citations which I reviewed, and even of those it is (with only a few exceptions) only the ones which come from works defining Sirach as Scripture, Prophecy, etc. There are many hundreds of other citations that are not included, and quite possibly thousands more from the 350+ AD period that Biblindex.org/citation_biblique/search does not yet index. Even so, there were too many to try to fit online links to them onto the chart. Many works are cited elsewhere herein, and in any event, Google searches will find them if they are available online.

Ch	V	Father	Year	Work
16	19	Clement of Rome	96	1 Clement, 59
4	31	Barnabas	100	Epistle of Barnabas, 19, 9
4	31	Didache	100	Didache 4.5
4	31	Didache	150	Didache 4, 3-5
		MELITO OF SARDIS	170	NOT CANON (FOR JEWS?)
		MURATORIAN CANON	170	UNKNOWN
1	18	Clement of Alexandria	198	The Instructor 1, 8
1	22	Clement of Alexandria	198	The Instructor 1, 8
5	6	Clement of Alexandria	198	The Instructor 1, 8
7	24	Clement of Alexandria	198	The Instructor 1, 9
16	12	Clement of Alexandria	198	The Instructor 1, 8
16	12	Clement of Alexandria	198	The Instructor 1, 8
16	12	Clement of Alexandria	198	The Instructor 1, 9
18	14	Clement of Alexandria	198	The Instructor 1, 9
21	7	Clement of Alexandria	198	The Instructor 1, 8
22	8	Clement of Alexandria	198	The Instructor 1, 8
30	8	Clement of Alexandria	198	The Instructor 1, 9
30	12	Clement of Alexandria	198	The Instructor 1, 9
32	21	Clement of Alexandria	198	The Instructor 1, 9
33	6	Clement of Alexandria	198	The Instructor 1, 13
34	15	Clement of Alexandria	198	The Instructor 1, 8
9	9	Clement of Alexandria	198	The Instructor 2, 7
9	15	Clement of Alexandria	198	The Instructor 2, 7
9	18	Clement of Alexandria	198	The Instructor 2, 7
11	4	Clement of Alexandria	198	The Instructor 2, 11
14	1	Clement of Alexandria	198	The Instructor 2, 7
18	30	Clement of Alexandria	198	The Instructor 2, 10
18	32	Clement of Alexandria	198	The Instructor 2, 1
20	5	Clement of Alexandria	198	The Instructor 2, 6
20	8	Clement of Alexandria	198	The Instructor 2, 6
21	20	Clement of Alexandria	198	The Instructor 2, 5
23	18	Clement of Alexandria	198	The Instructor 2, 10
23	19	Clement of Alexandria	198	The Instructor 2, 10

26	8	Clement of Alexandria	198	The Instructor 2, 2
31	18	Clement of Alexandria	198	The Instructor 2, 7
31	20	Clement of Alexandria	198	The Instructor 2, 2
31	25	Clement of Alexandria	198	The Instructor 2, 2
31	26	Clement of Alexandria	198	The Instructor 2, 2
31	27	Clement of Alexandria	198	The Instructor 2, 2
31	29	Clement of Alexandria	198	The Instructor 2, 2
31	31	Clement of Alexandria	198	The Instructor 2, 7
32	11	Clement of Alexandria	198	The Instructor 2, 7
39	14	Clement of Alexandria	198	The Instructor 2, 8
39	27	Clement of Alexandria	198	The Instructor 2, 8
9	7	Clement of Alexandria	198	The Instructor 3, 4
9	8	Clement of Alexandria	198	The Instructor 3, 11
9	8	Clement of Alexandria	198	The Instructor 3, 11
9	16	Clement of Alexandria	198	The Instructor 3, 4
11	29	Clement of Alexandria	198	The Instructor 3, 4
19	30	Clement of Alexandria	198	The Instructor 3, 3
21	21	Clement of Alexandria	198	The Instructor 3, 11
25	6	Clement of Alexandria	198	The Instructor 3, 3
26	8	Clement of Alexandria	198	The Instructor 3, 11
1	1	Clement of Alexandria	198	Stromata 1, 4
19	22	Clement of Alexandria	198	Stromata 1, 10
1	27	Clement of Alexandria	198	Stromata 2, 15
6	33	Clement of Alexandria	198	Stromata 2, 5
15	10	Clement of Alexandria	198	Stromata 2, 5
27	12	Clement of Alexandria	198	Stromata 5, 3
		CLEMENT ALEXANDRIA	203	CANON
		ORIGEN (JEWISH LIST)	220	NOT CANON FOR JEWS
7	21	Origen	230	On First Principles 1.2.13
26	4	Origen	230	On First Principles 1.2.13
6	4	Origen	230	First Principles 2, 8, 3
43	20	Origen	230	First Principles 2, 8, 3
16	21	Origen	230	First Principles 4, 1, 26
18	13	Origen	248	Against Celsus 4, 28
39	21	Origen	248	Against Celsus 4, 75
21	18	Origen	248	Against Celsus 6, 7
21	18	Origen	248	Against Celsus 7, 12
10	4	Origen	248	Against Celsus 8, 68
10	19	Origen	248	Against Celsus, 8, 50
		ORIGEN (LETTER)	248	N/A
		ORIGEN (CITATIONS)	250	CANON
8	5	Origen	253	Homily 16 on Jeremiah, 6.2
39	16	Origen	253	Against Celsus, 4, 75
39	17	Origen	253	Against Celsus, 4, 75
28	25	Origen	253	Commentary on Matthew 11, 12
18	30	Origen	253	Commentary on Matthew 12, 22
27	11	Origen	253	Commentary on Matthew 13, 4
		Origen	253	Commentary on Romans 1, 18, 7
2	12	Origen	253	Homilies on Exodus, 8, 4
10	10	Origen	253	Homily 9 on Ezekiel 2
10	12	Origen	253	Comm. on Romans 9, 19, 17
10	12	Origen	253	Comm. on Romans 9, 19, 17
10	14	Origen	253	Homilies on Judges 3, 2
15	9	Origen	253	Commentary on Romans 3,7,13

15	9	Origen	253	Commentary on Romans 3,7,13
22	19	Origen	253	Homilies on Genesis 12, 5
22	19	Origen	253	Homilies on Exodus 4, 5
25	4	Origen	253	Homilies on Judges 3, 2
		Origen	253	Homily on 1 Samuel 1, 4
3	18	Origen	253	Comm. on Matthew 12
48	1	Origen	253	Comm. on John 6.297-98
50	16	Origen	253	Homilies on Joshua 7.1
15	17	Origen	254	Comm. on Romans, 1, 18, 7
27	5	Origen	254	Comm. on Romans, 7, 17, 5
7	29	Cyprian	258	Epistle 64, 2
7	31	Cyprian	258	Epistle 64, 2
2	1	Cyprian	258	Treatise 7, 9
2	5	Cyprian	258	Treatise 7, 9
7	25	Cyprian	258	Treatise 7, 13
3	30	Cyprian	258	Treatise 8, 2
22	12	Cyprian	258	Treatise 8, 2
2	5	Cyprian	258	Treatise 9, 17
27	5	Cyprian	258	Treatise 11, 11
24	7	Cyprian	258	Treatise 12, 2, 1
1	14	Cyprian	258	Treatise 12, 3, 20
3	30	Cyprian	258	Treatise 12, 3, 1
4	29	Cyprian	258	Treatise 12, 3, 96
5	4	Cyprian	258	Treatise 12, 3, 35
5	7	Cyprian	258	Treatise 12, 3, 97
6	2	Cyprian	258	Treatise 12, 3, 51
6	16	Cyprian	258	Treatise 12, 3, 95
7	35	Cyprian	258	Treatise 12, 3, 109
9	16	Cyprian	258	Treatise 12, 3, 95
10	29	Cyprian	258	Treatise 12, 3, 51
14	11	Cyprian	258	Treatise 12, 3, 1
23	11	Cyprian	258	Treatise 12, 3, 12
27	5	Cyprian	258	Treatise 12, 3, 6
28	15	Cyprian	258	Treatise 12, 3, 110
29	12	Cyprian	258	Treatise 12, 3, 1
34	16	Cyprian	258	Treatise 12, 3, 56
34	24	Cyprian	258	Treatise 12, 3, 111
16	27	Dionysius the Great	265	On Nature 3
6	36	Methodius	311	Banquet of the Ten Virgins, 1, 1
18	30	Methodius	311	Banquet of the Ten Virgins, 1, 3
19	2	Methodius	311	Banquet of the Ten Virgins, 1, 3
1	2	Methodius	311	Working of Things Created, 9
		EUSEBIUS (APPROVAL)	324	Prep. of the Gospel, Book 12, 34
24	5	Lactantius	325	Divine Institutes, 4, 8
		THE NICENE COUNCIL	**325**	~~UNKNOWN~~
3	22	Alexander of Alexandria	326	Theodoret's Church History 1, 3
		Alexander of Alexandria	328	Epistles on Arianism/Arius, 5
30	4	Alexander of Thessalonica	335	Athanasius Defense 2, 66
6	28	Eusebius	339	Prep. of the Gospel, Book 12, 34
		CLAROMONTANUS	349	CANON
		CODEX VATICANUS	*350*	*CANON*
		CODEX SINAITICUS	*350*	*CANON*
		CYRIL OF JERUSALEM	350	NOT CANON
		ST CATHERINE'S SYRIAC	350	CANON

15	9	Athanasius	356	Bishops of Egypt and Libya, 3
		CHELTENHAM LIST	360	CANON
		~~COUNCIL AT LAODICEA~~	**363**	**~~NOT CANON~~**
		ATHANASIUS	367	VERSION 3.1
		HILARY OF POITIERS	367	NOT CANON
1	10	Athanasius	373	4 Discourses Arians 2, 79
27	11	Basil the Great	379	Hexaemon Homilies, 6, 10
43	30	Basil the Great	379	On the Holy Spirit, 28, 70
		GREGORY NAZIANZUS	380	NOT CANON
		AMPHILOCHIUS	380	NOT CANON
		APOSTOLIC CANONS	380	CANON
		~~THE COUNCIL OF ROME~~	**382**	**~~CANON~~**
		Epiphanius	385	Panarion, 6, 76, 22, 5
		EPIPHANIUS PAN. 8.6.1-4	385	DISPUTED FOR JEWS
		EPIPHANIUS PAN. 76.22.5	385	CANON
3	22	Cyril of Jerusalem	386	Catechetical Lectures, 6, 4
3	22	Cyril of Jerusalem	386	Catechetical Lectures, 11, 18
4	31	Cyril of Jerusalem	386	Catechetical Lectures, 13, 8
43	20	Didymus the Blind	386	Commentary on Zechariah 2:6-7
2	5	Augustine	388	Morals Catholic Church 23, 43
19	1	Augustine	388	Morals Catholic Church 24, 45
27	6	Augustine	388	Morals Catholic Church 23, 43
25	9	Gregory of Nazianzus	390	Oration 2, 50
38	16	Gregory of Nazianzus	390	Oration 7, 1
3	11	Gregory of Nazianzus	390	Oration 37, 6
32	3	Gregory of Nazianzus	390	Oration 40, 18
		JEROME (HELMETED)	390	NOT CANON
		EPIPHANIUS DE MENS, 4-5	392	BENEFICIAL FOR JEWS
		THE COUNCIL OF HIPPO - 70 BISHOPS	**393**	**CANON**
5	6	Augustine	394	Sermon on the Mount 2, 14, 48
27	11	Ambrose	397	Hexameron 4, 8, 31
4	9	Ambrose	397	Duties of the Clergy 1, 63
20	7	Ambrose	397	Duties of the Clergy 1, 5
23	18	Ambrose	397	Duties of the Clergy 1, 54
23	31	Ambrose	397	Duties of the Clergy 1, 54
23	31	Ambrose	397	Duties of the Clergy 1, 172
28	25	Ambrose	397	Duties of the Clergy 1, 11
6	16	Ambrose	397	Duties of the Clergy 2, 39
22	31	Ambrose	397	Duties of the Clergy 2, 38
22	31	Ambrose	397	Duties of the Clergy 2, 42
29	10	Ambrose	397	Duties of the Clergy 2, 37
31	9	Ambrose	397	Duties of the Clergy 2, 66
6	16	Ambrose	397	Duties of the Clergy 3, 128
22	25	Ambrose	397	Duties of the Clergy 3, 128
22	26	Ambrose	397	Duties of the Clergy 3, 129
24	3	Ambrose	397	3 Books on Holy Spirit, 2, 5, 42
24	3	Ambrose	397	Exposition Christian Faith 1, 110
28	28	Ambrose	397	Exposition Christian Faith 1, 47
24	5	Ambrose	397	Exposition Christian Faith 4, 88
3	22	Ambrose	397	Exposition Christian Faith 5, 235
17	1	Ambrose	397	Exposition Gospel of Luke
33	10	Ambrose	397	Exposition Gospel of Luke
		AUGUSTINE	397	CANON

		COUNCIL CARTHAGE - 44-48 BISHOPS	397	CANON
34	9	Rufinus	398	12 Patriarchs, 3
18	7	Didymus the Blind	398	Comm. on Ecclesiastes 42.24
		JEROME (SOLOMON)	398	VERSION 3.2
30	11	Apostolic Constitutions	400	Book 4, 2, 11
30	12	Apostolic Constitutions	400	Book 4, 2, 11
1	33	Augustine	400	Reply to Faustus 22, 35
		RUFINUS	400	VERSION 3.3
3	18	Augustine	401	On Holy Virginity 31
3	18	Augustine	401	On Holy Virginity 44
3	23	Epiphanius	403	Panarion 7, 77, 15, 3
10	11	Epiphanius	403	Panarion 3, 44, 18, 1
12	24	Epiphanius	403	Panarion, 3, 39, 7, 1
13	16	Epiphanius	403	Panarion 2, 13, 8, 1
14	5	Epiphanius	403	Panarion, 3, 22, Scholion 70a
17	24	Epiphanius	403	Panarion, 3, 39, 6, 1
20	4	Epiphanius	403	Panarion 3, 38, 4, 14
45	12	Epiphanius	403	Panarion 3, 44, 6, 1
		JEROME (TOBIT/JUDITH)	404	N/A
15	17	Augustine	405	In Answer to Petilian 2, 185
		POPE INNOCENT I	405	CANON
1	28	Augustine	407	Homilies on 1 John, 9, 2
9	8	John Chrysostom	407	Homilies on Matthew 17, 2
28	3	John Chrysostom	407	Homilies on Matthew 79, 5
23	10	John Chrysostom	407	Homilies on Acts 10
1	22	John Chrysostom	407	Homilies on Acts 29
10	14	John Chrysostom	407	Homilies on Acts 29
16	12	John Chrysostom	407	Homily 9 on 1 Corin. 3:12-15, 3
5	6	John Chrysostom	407	Homilies on Ephesians 4, 2
2	4	John Chrysostom	407	Homilies on Ephesians 19
11	3	John Chrysostom	407	Homilies on Ephesians 20
25	1	John Chrysostom	407	Homilies on Ephesians 20
40	23	John Chrysostom	407	Homilies on Ephesians 20
18	13	John Chrysostom	407	Homilies on Philippians, 4
11	1	John Chrysostom	407	Homilies on Philippians 15
12	13	John Chrysostom	407	Homily 9 on 1 Thessalonians
3	12	John Chrysostom	407	Homilies on 2 Timothy, 2
7	31	John Chrysostom	407	Homilies on 2 Timothy, 2
5	7	John Chrysostom	407	Homilies on John, 28, 1
16	12	John Chrysostom	407	Homilies on John, 28, 1
1	22	John Chrysostom	407	Homilies on John 48, 3
10	9	John Chrysostom	407	Homilies on John 48, 3
3	30	John Chrysostom	407	Homilies on John, 73, 3
1	22	John Chrysostom	407	Homilies on Hebrews 2, 1:5
1	22	John Chrysostom	407	Homilies on Hebrews 5, 8
9	15	John Chrysostom	407	Homilies on Hebrews 8, 9
3	30	John Chrysostom	407	Homilies on Hebrews 9, 8
28	3	John Chrysostom	407	Homilies on Hebrews 9, 8
2	18	John Chrysostom	407	Homilies on Hebrews 20, 4
5	6	John Chrysostom	407	Homilies on Hebrews 20, 4
1	28	Chromatius	407	Tractate on Matthew 41, 1
4	21	Chromatius	407	Tractate on Matthew 41, 5
4	34	Chromatius	407	Tractate on Matthew 20.2.4

7	14	Chromatius	407	Tractate on Matthew 28, VI, 2
9	8	Chromatius	407	Tractate on Matthew 23, II, 2
9	8	Chromatius	407	Tractate on Matthew 23, II, 3
9	10	Chromatius	407	Tractate on Matthew 18, IV, 4
12	6	Chromatius	407	Tractate on Matthew 33, 3
14	1	Chromatius	407	Tractate on Matthew 21, II, 2
18	31	Chromatius	407	Tractate on Matthew 23, II, 2
19	1	Chromatius	407	Tractate on Matthew 20.2.1-3.6
19	15	Chromatius	407	Tractate on Matthew 58, 1
20	2	Chromatius	407	Tractate on Matthew 58, 1
21	9	Chromatius	407	Tractate on Matthew 43, 8
21	28	Chromatius	407	Tractate on Matthew 21, II, 4
23	9	Chromatius	407	Tractate on Matthew 31.15.3
23	9	Chromatius	407	Tractate on Matthew 24, II, 2
23	10	Chromatius	407	Tractate on Matthew 20.2.1-3.7
23	11	Chromatius	407	Tractate on Matthew 24, II, 2
23	17	Chromatius	407	Tractate on Matthew 21, II, 3
24	5	Chromatius	407	Tractate on Matthew 31.15.2
24	5	Chromatius	407	Tractate on Matthew 52.2
24	15	Chromatius	407	Tractate on Matthew 5, 1
24	21	Chromatius	407	Tractate on Matthew 17, V, 4
24	45	Chromatius	407	Tractate on Matthew 15, 2
25	1	Chromatius	407	Tractate on Matthew 59.1.14
26	18	Chromatius	407	Tractate on Matthew 56, 3
28	2	Chromatius	407	Tractate on Matthew 28, VII, 9
28	2	Chromatius	407	Tractate on Matthew 59, 7
28	4	Chromatius	407	Tractate on Matthew 28, VI, 3
28	5	Chromatius	407	Tractate on Matthew 21, III, 4
28	6	Chromatius	407	Tractate on Matthew 21, III, 5
28	6	Chromatius	407	Tractate on Matthew 59, 7
28	26	Chromatius	407	Tractate on Matthew 41, 2
28	29	Chromatius	407	Tractate on Matthew 21, II, 3
29	21	Chromatius	407	Tractate on Matthew 28, V, 2
35	17	Chromatius	407	Tractate on Matthew 27.2.3
38	1	Chromatius	407	Tractate on Matthew 45, 2
2	1	John Chrysostom	407	Catena
41	2	John Chrysostom	407	Commentary on Job 3.20-23
2	2	John Chrysostom	407	Against the Jews 8, 6, 6
13	24	Augustine	416	Perfection in Righteousness 15
13	24	Augustine	416	Perfection in Righteousness 15
15	8	Augustine	416	Perfection in Righteousness 12
15	16	Augustine	416	Perfection in Righteousness 19
18	30	Augustine	416	Perfection in Righteousness 11
38	10	Augustine	416	Perfection in Righteousness 15
38	10	Augustine	416	Perfection in Righteousness 15
39	25	Augustine	416	Perfection in Righteousness 14
10	13	Augustine	417	On Nature and Grace 33
10	9	Augustine	417	On Nature and Grace 72
18	30	Augustine	417	On Nature and Grace 57
10	12	Augustine	417	On Nature and Grace 33
15	17	Augustine	418	On the Proceedings of Pelagius 7
19	16	Augustine	418	On the Proceedings of Pelagius 4
23	6	Augustine	418	On the Proceedings of Pelagius 7
1	25	Cyril of Alexandria	418	On Luke, Sermon 152

		COUNCIL CARTHAGE -	**419**	**CANON**
		217 BISHOPS		
18	30	Augustine	420	On Marriage 1, 32
18	30	Augustine	420	On Marriage 1, 25
21	1	Augustine	420	On Marriage 1, 29
40	1	Augustine	420	On Marriage 2, 50
10	9	Augustine	420	Tractates on John 25, 15
3	21	Augustine	420	Tractates on John 53, 7
3	22	Jerome	420	Against the Pelagians, Bk I, 33
2	1	Jerome	420	Commentary on Matthew 4:4
8	10	Jerome	420	Commentary on Isaiah 11, 36
11	27	Jerome	420	Commentary on Isaiah 18, 13
11	29	Jerome	420	Commentary on Isaiah 18, 13
40	1	Augustine	421	Enchiridion 66
3	22	Augustine	421	On the Soul and its Origin 4, 5
3	22	Augustine	422	On the Care of the Dead 21
46	20	Augustine	422	On the Care of the Dead 18
3	27	Augustine	426	City of God 1, 27
20	24	Augustine	426	City of God 10, 6
33	15	Augustine	426	City of God 11, 18
7	13	Augustine	426	City of God 14, 8
10	13	Augustine	426	City of God 14, 13
15	17	Augustine	426	City of God 16, 27
36	5	Augustine	426	City of God 17, 20
2	7	Augustine	426	City of God 20, 10
7	17	Augustine	426	City of God 21, 9
21	1	Augustine	426	City of God 21, 27
27	5	Augustine	426	City of God 21, 26
30	24	Augustine	426	City of God 21, 27
40	1	Augustine	426	City of God 21, 14
30	12	Augustine	426	City of God 22, 22
37	20	Augustine	426	On Christian Doctrine 2, 31, 48
		Augustine	426	On Christian Doctrine 2, 8, 13
7	27	Augustine	426	On Christian Doctrine 3, 17, 25
37	19	Augustine	426	On Christian Doctrine, 4, 27, 59
24	21	Augustine	426	On the Trinity 15, 1-2
15	15	Augustine	426	On Grace and Free Will 31
15	17	Augustine	426	On Grace and Free Will 3
22	27	Augustine	426	On Grace and Free Will 32
23	4	Augustine	426	On Grace and Free Will 32
23	5	Augustine	426	On Grace and Free Will 32
23	6	Augustine	426	On Grace and Free Will 32
24	3	Augustine	427	On the Trinity 4, 28
3	1	Augustine	430	Letter 36, 11, 26
11	7	Augustine	430	Letter 43, 3, 11
27	12	Augustine	430	Letter 55, 5, 8
4	21	Augustine	430	Letter 93, 13, 52
23	6	Augustine	430	Letter 130
36	4	Augustine	430	Letter 130
36	18	Augustine	430	Letter 130
18	6	Augustine	430	Letter 137, 1, 3
5	10	Augustine	430	Letter 220, 5
38	16	Augustine	430	Letter 263, 3
24	5	Augustine	430	On the Trinity, 1, 6

28	5	Augustine	430	Reply to Faustus, 19, 28
11	14	Augustine	430	Reply to Faustus 21, 9
1	33	Augustine	430	Reply to Faustus 22, 53
3	18	Augustine	430	Against the Donatists, III, 3, 5
34	25	Quietus of Burug	430	Against the Donatists, VI, 34
15	17	Petilianus	430	Augustine's Petilian, 2, 85, 185
25	24	Augustine	430	Merits Forgiveness Sins I, 21
18	30	Augustine	430	Merits Forgiveness Sins II, 5
7	21	Augustine	430	On the Spirit and the Letter 65
18	30	Augustine	430	On the Spirit and the Letter 65
10	13	Augustine	430	On Nature and Grace, 33
6	37	Augustine	430	Tractates on John, 7, 9
10	12	Augustine	430	Exposition on Psalm 7, 4
10	13	Augustine	430	Exposition on Psalm 7, 4
2	1	Jerome	430	Letter 118, 4
22	6	Jerome	430	Letter 118, 2
1	1	Augustine	430	Enchiridion 1, 1
1	16	Augustine	430	Exposition 2 of Psalm 101, 2
1	16	Augustine	430	Exposition of Psalm 119, 2
1	26	Augustine	430	Exposition 22 of Psalm 118, 8
2	1	Augustine	430	Exposition of Psalm 59, 5
2	3	Augustine	430	Sermon 38, 5
2	4	Augustine	430	Letter 204, 7
2	5	Augustine	430	Sermon 23B, 11
2	5	Augustine	430	Sermon 38, 6
2	14	Augustine	430	Sermon 23B, 11
2	14	Augustine	430	Sermon 20, 2
2	14	Augustine	430	Sermon 47, 17
2	16	Augustine	430	Exposition of Psalm 99, 12
2	16	Augustine	430	Sermon 157, 1
3	18	Augustine	430	Sermon 292, 8
3	19	Augustine	430	Confessions XIII, 21, 23
3	19	Augustine	430	Exposition of Psalm 114, 6
3	22	Augustine	430	Exposition 22 of Psalm 118, 8
3	22	Augustine	430	Answer to Maximinus II, XI
3	22	Augustine	430	To Orosius 11, 14
4	28	Augustine	430	Sermon 306E, 6
4	28	Augustine	430	Sermon 284, 5
4	28	Augustine	430	Sermon 286, 1
5	7	Augustine	430	Sermon 94A, 7
5	7	Augustine	430	Sermon 339, 8
5	7	Augustine	430	Sermon 87, 11
5	7	Augustine	430	Sermon 20, 4
5	7	Augustine	430	Sermon 39, 1
5	8	Augustine	430	Letter 127, 1
5	8	Augustine	430	Letter 2*, 7
5	8	Augustine	430	Exposition of Psalm 102, 16
5	8	Augustine	430	Sermon 339, 7
5	8	Augustine	430	Sermon 40, 5
5	9	Augustine	430	Letter 2*, 6
5	9	Augustine	430	Homilies on John, Homily 33, 8
5	11	Augustine	430	Sermon 8, 6
6	18	Augustine	430	Exposition 5 of Psalm 118, 2
6	32	Augustine	430	Exposition 2 of Psalm 101, 2

9	13	Augustine	430	Sermon 142, 1
10	9	Augustine	430	Homilies John, Homily 25, 15
10	10	Augustine	430	Letter 140, 24, 61
10	11	Augustine	430	Sermon 123, 1
10	12	Augustine	430	Exposition of Psalm 37, 8
10	13	Augustine	430	Sermon 360B, 17
10	13	Augustine	430	Sermon 159B, 11
10	13	Augustine	430	Homilies John 25, 15
10	14	Augustine	430	Letter 140, 28, 68
10	14	Augustine	430	Exposition of Psalm 112, 1
10	15	Augustine	430	Letter 140, 24, 61
10	15	Augustine	430	Letter 140, 28, 68
11	30	Augustine	430	Exposition of Psalm 67, 20
12	6	Augustine	430	Exposition of Psalm 102, 13
12	7	Augustine	430	Sermon 164A, 1
14	5	Augustine	430	Letter 204, 5
15	9	Augustine	430	Sermon 15A, 1
15	9	Augustine	430	Exposition of Psalm 47, 2
15	9	Augustine	430	Exposition of Psalm 49, 29
15	9	Augustine	430	Exposition of Psalm 64, 3
17	26	Augustine	430	Exposition 2 of Psalm 113, 12
17	26	Augustine	430	Exposition of Psalm 67, 8
17	26	Augustine	430	Exposition 1 of Psalm 68, 19
17	28	Augustine	430	Sermon 67, 2
17	31	Augustine	430	Confessions VII, 8, 12
18	30	Augustine	430	Confessions X, 31, 45
18	30	Augustine	430	Sermon 151, 3
18	30	Augustine	430	Sermon 154, 8
19	4	Augustine	430	Confessions VI, 5, 8
22	23	Augustine	430	Sermon 41, 1
23	6	Augustine	430	Confessions X, 31, 45
24	21	Augustine	430	Sermon 170, 9
24		Augustine	430	Sermon 223A, 1
25	24	Augustine	430	Sermon 318, 2
27	6	Augustine	430	Letter 140, 15, 37
27	6	Augustine	430	Enchiridion 18, 68
27	6	Augustine	430	Exposition of Psalm 120, 14
27	29	Augustine	430	Letter 88, 5
28	8	Augustine	430	Sermon 16A, 2
28	14	Augustine	430	Homilies on John 25, 7
29	12	Augustine	430	Sermon 209, 2
29	27	Augustine	430	Sermon 105, 2
30	23	Augustine	430	Sermon 113A, 11
30	24	Augustine	430	Letter 247, 2
30	24	Augustine	430	Sermon 161, 6
31	10	Augustine	430	Sermon 311, 9
31	10	Augustine	430	Sermon 311, 10
31	10	Augustine	430	Sermon 178, 7
34	30	Augustine	430	Letter 108, 2, 6
35	26	Augustine	430	Exposition on Psalm 41, 16
35	26	Augustine	430	Exposition 2 of Psalm 68, 1
36	6	Augustine	430	Sermon 126, 4
39	16	Augustine	430	Sermon 29B, 2
39	16	Augustine	430	Sermon 68, 2

39	21	Augustine	430	Exposition of Psalm 117, 1
39	21	Augustine	430	Exposition 4 of Psalm 118, 4
40	1	Augustine	430	Letter 2*, 10
42	18	Augustine	430	Confessions X, 2, 2
2	10	Augustine	430	Sermon 76, 8
3	17	Augustine	430	Letter 140, 22, 55
2	10	Augustine	430	Sermon 77 A. I.
2	5	John Cassian	435	Conference 7, 25
2	1	John Cassian	435	12 Books on the Institutes 4, 38
33	29	John Cassian	435	12 Books on the Institutes 10, 21
11	30	John Cassian	435	Conferences 6, 16
29	15	John Cassian	435	Conferences 1, 9, 34
34	11	John Cassian	435	Conferences 1, 9, 23
3	30	John Cassian	435	Conferences 20, 8
2	1	Cyril of Alexandria	444	Homily 7
2	14	Cyril of Alexandria	444	Festal Letter 14, 2
3	22	Cyril of Alexandria	444	Letter 15, 2
11	20	Cyril of Alexandria	444	Commentary on Hosea 14
13	23	Cyril of Alexandria	444	Commentary on Amos 3
13	23	Cyril of Alexandria	444	Commentary on Nahum 2
41	14	Cyril of Alexandria	444	Fragment 216
8	14	Vincent of Lerins	445	Commonitories 21
11	28	Hilary of Arles	449	Life of Honoratus, Preface 3
23	9	Anonymous	450	Opus Imperfect Matthaeum 12
23	11	Anonymous	450	Opus Imperfect Matthaeum 12
		CODEX ALEXANDRINUS	*450*	*CANON*
		CODEX EPHRAEMI R.	*450*	*CANON*

CANON LISTS

FATHER/LIST/BOOK	Year	SIRACH CANONICAL?	OTHER CITATIONS
MELITO OF SARDIS	170	NOT FOR JEWS?	NONE
MURATORIAN CANON	170	UNKNOWN	NOT APPLICABLE
CLEMENT ALEXANDRIA	203	CANON	SCRIPTURE
ORIGEN (JEWISH LIST)	220	NOT FOR JEWS	NOT APPLICABLE
ORIGEN (LETTER)	248	N/A	SACRED SCRIPTURE
ORIGEN (CITATIONS)	250	CANON	SACRED SCRIPTURE
EUSEBIUS (APPROVAL)	324	CANON	SOLOMON
~~THE NICENE COUNCIL~~	325	~~UNKNOWN~~	~~NOT APPLICABLE~~
CLAROMONTANUS	349	CANON	NOT APPLICABLE
CODEX VATICANUS	*350*	*CANON*	*NOT APPLICABLE*
CODEX SINAITICUS	*350*	*CANON*	*NOT APPLICABLE*
CYRIL OF JERUSALEM	350	NOT CANON	CITED W/O QUALIFICATION
ST CATHERINE'S SYRIAC	350	CANON	NOT APPLICABLE
CHELTENHAM LIST	360	CANON	NOT APPLICABLE
~~COUNCIL AT LAODICEA~~	363	~~NOT CANON~~	~~NOT APPLICABLE~~
ATHANASIUS	367	VERSION 3.1	SPOKEN BY THE SPIRIT
HILARY OF POITIERS	367	NOT CANON	13 CITES
GREGORY NAZIANZUS	380	NOT CANON	OUR PHILOSOPHY
AMPHILOCHIUS	380	NOT CANON	1 CITE
APOSTOLIC CANONS	380	CANON*	HOLY SCRIPTURE
~~THE COUNCIL OF ROME~~	382	~~CANON~~	~~NOT APPLICABLE~~

EPIPHANIUS PAN. 8.6.1-4	385	DISPUTED FOR JEWS	SCRIPTURE
EPIPHANIUS PAN. 76.22.5	385	CANON	SCRIPTURE
JEROME (HELMETED)	390	NOT CANON	HOLY SCRIPTURE
EPIPHANIUS DE MENS. 4-5	392	BENEFICIAL FOR JEWS	SCRIPTURE
THE COUNCIL OF HIPPO - 70 BISHOPS	**393**	**CANON**	**NOT APPLICABLE**
AUGUSTINE	397	CANON	SCRIPTURE
COUNCIL CARTHAGE - 44-48 BISHOPS	**397**	**CANON**	**NOT APPLICABLE**
JEROME (SOLOMON)	398	VERSION 3.2	HOLY SCRIPTURE
RUFINUS	400	VERSION 3.3	SCRIPTURE
JEROME (TOBIT/JUDITH)	404	N/A	HOLY SCRIPTURE
POPE INNOCENT I	405	CANON	NONE
COUNCIL CARTHAGE - 217 BISHOPS	**419**	**CANON**	**NOT APPLICABLE**
CODEX ALEXANDRINUS	*450*	*CANON*	*NOT APPLICABLE*
CODEX EPHRAEMI R.	*450*	*CANON*	*NOT APPLICABLE*

Version 3.1: Sirach (and Esther (but not Baruch, which is canon)) not canonical but to be read
Version 3.2: Sirach (unlike Esther (which is canon) or Baruch (which is not canon)) read for strengthening but not canonical or for confirming the authority of ecclesiastical dogmas.
Version 3.3: Sirach (unlike Esther or Baruch (both of which are canon)) not canonical but "Ecclesiastical."

*   Arguably, the Apostolic Canons put Sirach in a third category by itself ("And besides these, take care that your young persons learn the Wisdom of the very learned Sirach"). But the book that the list is part of (the Apostolic Constitutions) quotes from Sirach as Holy Scripture elsewhere, and there is a reference on the canon list to the Five Books of Solomon (which usually would include Sirach). It can be debated as to what everything means, all of which depends on whether the same person wrote both the book and the canons, etc. The textual history for that book is a mess of contradictions, and different ancient translations of it contradict each other. See Gallagher and Meade, p. 134-41.

1 MACCABEES

1 Maccabees is a historical book telling the story of the Maccabean revolt.

> 1 Maccabees is only very rarely quoted or referenced by the Church Fathers in the era of early Christianity. ... As 1 Maccabees has very little to say about the martyrs, it correspondingly was not cited or read.[454]

"Not read"—what scientific method was used to prove that, exactly?

But I do know how to check how well it was cited: compare it to something similar. As mentioned many times already, John Barton, in his book *The Spirit and the Letter: Studies in the Biblical Canon* (p. 23-24), notes that "historical books, for example, never seem to have been in the least controversial, yet neither Jews nor Christians ever used them much in their writings ... in much the same position as Acts for early Christian writers: undoubtedly authoritative, scarcely ever used..." And if we compare 1 Maccabees to other historical Books (via biblindex.org/citation_biblique /search), we see that it does, indeed, rank near the bottom—but not at the very bottom by any fair metric:

Book	Verses	Cites	Rate
Ruth	85	201	2.36
Ezra	280	592	2.11
1 Chronicles	943	787	0.83
1 Maccabees	**922**	**596**	**0.65**
Nehemiah	405	256	0.63
Esther	272	143	0.53

In addition, the citations were of comparably early dating: Tertullian ca. 200 and Hippolytus, Origen, Julius Africanus, and Cyprian by 250 AD. Clement of Alexandria (198 AD) mentioned the Book of the Maccabees and appears to cite 1 Maccabees 2:59-60—but for some reason, that is not noted at Biblindex (which would seem to be a mistake).[455] Once he is included, that list

---

[454] wikipedia.org/wiki/1_Maccabees

[455] Clement says, "During the captivity lived Esther and Mordecai, whose book is still extant, as also that of the Maccabees. During this captivity Mishael, Ananias, and Azarias, refusing to worship the image, and being thrown into a furnace of fire, were saved by the appearance of an angel. At that time, on account of the serpent, Daniel was thrown into the den of lions; but being preserved through the providence of God by Ambacub, he is restored on the seventh day..." [The

of Fathers is basically all the usual suspects; in fact, Nehemiah is cited by the exact same list of Fathers. Nehemiah was cited 43 times, 1 Maccabees 66 times. Among their citations to 1 Maccabees, I found Origen,[456] Hippolytus,[457] and Cyprian[458] all referring to it as Scripture.

Even the claim that "As 1 Maccabees has very little to say about the martyrs, it correspondingly was not cited" does not hold up well. Many Fathers (including Tertullian, Chrysostom, and Ambrose) cite the heroes of 1 Maccabees; it is just that they do so as exemplars who remain faithful to God in their own way (as "living martyrs," so to speak, totally devoted to God).

I will go into more detail on the citation evidence below. But other evidence for the acceptance of 1 Maccabees includes the fact that it was read as part of the liturgy in the early Churches.[459]

As for the Bible, the original KJV gives us just one cross-reference, already discussed above, and no quotations. But recall that Don Stewart says:

> All Old Testament books are quoted as authoritative works by the New Testament writers with four exceptions: Ezra/Nehemiah, Esther, Ecclesiastes, and the Song of Solomon. However, the absence of any quotations of these books does not speak against their canonicity.[460]

Ezra, Nehemiah, and Esther are three of the six little-cited historical books in the chart above—and they have zero references using Stewart's standards.

For KJV cross-references, Esther has zero; 1 Maccabees has one; Nehemiah has two; and Ruth has four—however, those last six are references

---

quote is also noted below.] Cf. 1 Maccabees 2:59-60: "Ananias, Azarias, and Misael, by believing were saved out of the flame. Daniel for his innocency was delivered from the mouth of lions."

[456] Against Celsus 8, 46: What need is there to quote all the princes and private persons in Scripture history who fared well or ill according as they obeyed or despised the words of the prophets? ... And the books of the Maccabees relate what punishments were inflicted upon those who dared to profane the Jewish service in the temple at Jerusalem. www.newadvent.org/fathers/04168.htm

[457] 2nd fragment: of the visions: Since, then, the angel Gabriel also recounted these things to the prophet, as they have been understood by us, as they have also taken place, and as they have been all clearly described in the books of the Maccabees, let us see further what he says... www.newadvent.org/fathers/0502.htm

[458] Letter 54, 3: Holy Scripture meets and warns us, saying, ... And again: And fear not the words of a sinful man, for his glory shall be dung and worms. Today he is lifted up, and tomorrow he shall not be found, because he is turned into his earth, and his thought shall perish. 1 Maccabees 2:62-63. www.newadvent.org/fathers/050654.htm

[459] See, e.g., Rufinus Apostles' Creed 38 at www.newadvent.org/fathers/2711.htm.

[460] www.blueletterbible.org/Comm/stewart_don/faq/right-books-in-old-testament/question17-new-testament-quote-old-testament.cfm

to things that are mentioned in the Books, not the Books. E.g., Ruth's all relate to the mention of the woman Ruth in the genealogy of Jesus given at the beginning of the Book of Matthew. (Which is probably why the Stewart's analysis of mentions of Old Testament Books does not even note Matthew's mention of Ruth; instead, he focuses entirely on the possibility that Ruth was attached to Judges.)[461] Nehemiah's cross-references are to the pool at Shiloh (Nehemiah discusses the reconstruction of it at 3:15, and in John 9:7, Jesus tells the formerly blind man to go wash in it), and Nehemiah 9:19 mentions God's manifestation as the pillar of cloud in Exodus 13:22, which 1 Corinthians 10:1 also mentions.

Meanwhile, as discussed above, the exact same reasoning that supports the inclusion of Esther (a possible mention of Purim in John 5:1) supports including 1 Maccabees to a far greater degree. The Gospel of John clearly references Hanukkah by one of its names, and according to the KJV notes, that is a reference to 1 Maccabees 4:59,[462] whereas Purim is never named, and there is no cross reference between John 5:1 to Esther 9:28.

The possibility that John 5:1 is a reference to Purim is minor compared to the importance of Hanukkah in John 9-10. The Apologetics Study Bible includes an essay ("Does the New Testament Misquote the Old Testament?") by Paul Copan, past president of the Evangelical Philosophical Society, that discusses how the Evangelists understood the fulfillment of Prophecy:

> ... "fulfill" (pleroo) in the NT is used to portray Jesus as bringing to full fruition OT events or experiences (the exodus, covenant), personages (Jonah, Solomon, David), and institutions (temple, priesthood, sacrifices, holy days). ... a theological point is being made ... fulfillment of the OT generally refers to the broader idea of perfectly embodying, typifying, epitomizing, or reaching a climax. ... NT writers (and Jesus) interpreted the OT in a Christocentric a manner: Jesus is the embodiment or completer of foreshadowed OT historical events, images, and personages. While fulfillment includes literal predictions of Christ and the new covenant, it goes far beyond to a richer theological embodiment of what the OT foreshadowed. [Emphasis added.]

---

[461] If, on the other hand, you disagree and feel that a reference to Ruth is sufficient, then 1 Clement cited the Book of Judith as Scripture before much of the New Testament was even written, and long before Josephus. See the above discussion about Judith, and how that reference ties back to the four Biblical allusions relating to Corinth.

[462] Both Hanukkah and Purim are ordained/proclaimed by the verses that are being cited to, so the references to the Books are stronger than mentions of a thing (i.e., as with Ruth or Nehemiah).

First, John 9:5 (As long as I am in the world, I am the light of the world) is Jesus saying that He is the true light of the world. He has fulfilled the holy days of Hanukkah, the Festival of Lights: He is the true Menorah.

Second, Antiochus was called "Epiphanes" (epiphany) because he claimed that he was "God Manifest" on Earth. Jesus, thus, declares Himself to be the true Epiphany at the Festival celebrating the victory over Antiochus.

Third, multiple verses in 1 Maccabees were expressly awaiting fulfillment, and were then fulfilled by Jesus—for example, the rededication of the altar in 4:46 and the expectation of the arrival of a faithful prophet in 14:41. These are express declarations that the actions of the Maccabees are just "temporary fixes," and that the true prophet is coming: Jesus.

But let's also look at it in reverse. John's Gospel is 21 chapters long, with almost 10% of it dedicated to this allusion—not a small amount of effort was involved in making his point.

David Limbaugh's *The Emmaus Code* provides an Appendix listing all the Messianic Prophecies of the Old Testament and their New Testament Fulfillment. Of the 120 Prophecies he lists, only one is fulfilled by John Chapter 9: Proverbs 30:4 ("…what is his [the Creator's] name, and what is his son's name, if thou canst tell?"), which he labels "Declared to be the Son of God" and says is fulfilled by "Matt. 3:17; Mark 14:61- 62; Luke 1:35; John 3:13; 9:35-38; 11:21; Rom. 1:2-4; 10:6-9; 2 Pet. 1:17."

I 100% agree that Proverbs 30:4 is fulfilled by John 9:35-38: "35Jesus heard that they had cast him out; and when he had found him, he said unto him, Dost thou believe on the Son of God? 36He answered and said, Who is he, Lord, that I might believe on him? 37And Jesus said unto him, Thou hast both seen him, and it is he that talketh with thee. 38And he said, Lord, I believe. And he worshipped him."

But I believe that is almost coincidental. John's purpose when writing the long story spanning two chapters was not to show "only" the fulfillment of a Prophecy fulfilled in eight other passages of Scripture, including two others elsewhere in his own Gospel. John went to great lengths to show that Jesus is the true Light of the World, the true God Manifest, and the one the Jews were expecting when they rededicated the Temple.

Furthermore, many in the early Church considered Antiochus as one of the "types" for the Antichrist (E.g., Jerome: "Antiochus… is to be regarded as a type of the Antichrist, and those things which happened to him in a preliminary way are to be completely fulfilled in the case of the Antichrist").[463] That conception would seem to add even more depth to what is going on in this scene, as Jesus counters the type of the Antichrist—which, then, of course, leads to seeing Judas Maccabee as a type of Christ, since he countered the type of the Antichrist.

As also discussed above, another possible reference is not noted by the KJV: Hebrews 11:38 ("they wandered in deserts, and in mountains, and in dens and caves of the earth") is often seen as a reference to those who fled Antiochus (including Mattathias and his sons). They are described in 1 Maccabees 1:53 ("And drove the Israelites into secret places, even wheresoever they could flee for succor"), 2:28-31 ("28So he and his sons fled into the mountains, and left all that ever they had in the city. 29Then many that sought after justice and judgment went down into the wilderness, to dwell there: 30Both they, and their children, and their wives; and their cattle; because afflictions increased sore upon them. 31Now when it was told the king's servants, and the host that was at Jerusalem, in the city of David, that certain men, who had broken the king's commandment, were gone down into the secret places in the wilderness"), and 2 Maccabees 5:27, 6:11, and 10:6.

In fact, the entire chapter of Hebrews 11 seems to be modeled after the list of Israel's heroes in 1 Maccabees 2:51-61.

In addition to this Biblical evidence that the Jews accepted 1 Maccabees, Jerome obtained Hebrew texts of 1 Maccabees, presumably from Jews, and translated them into Latin.[464]

1 Maccabees was cited by the Fathers 596 times per biblindex.org/ citation_biblique/search. But the references come in floods, followed by droughts. When a historian (e.g., Eusebius) is summarizing that particular era of history, he can write 30 sentences, each a citation to a verse or collection of verses in 1 Maccabees. But those who never explained that bit of history in their works may make only a single reference to 1 Maccabees in their entire

---

[463] From his long discussion in his commentary on Daniel, at www.tertullian.org/fathers/jerome_ daniel_02_text.htm, esp. Chapter 11. Jerome placed the Books of the Maccabees in his third category of books that "one may read ... for the strengthening of the people, (but) not for confirming the authority of ecclesiastical dogmas"—apparently that allowed typology, or possibly, his third category idea was used inconsistently, or it was not fully thought out (my vote).

[464] Sundberg in the Canon Debate, p. 88.

corpus of writings—or even zero. Bear in mind, that would be any allusion at all; it need not be a quotation, or even a mention, of the Maccabees.

Accordingly, 1 Maccabees is mentioned a lot by the historians but not by anyone else. And that is to be expected: compare to 1 Chronicles, with 787 total references, of which 290 references are by Theodoret, and 174 are by Eusebius (who account for a large majority of references to both Books). Whereas, Athanasius never once in his whole life cited to 1 Chronicles, even though it was certainly canon to him.[465]

By my count, the Books are mentioned by essentially the same number of Fathers (19) who are in the database,[466] with nearly two-thirds of each such list consisting of 12 Fathers who appear on both lists. Nearly all the other seven on each list only mentioned one of the books in only one work (which means there is a lot of randomness involved in why they make the mentions—and also in how we come to still have a copy of that work).

Looking at it by era, the references to 1 Chronicles from the very early Church came from Clement of Alexandria but not Tertullian; for 1 Maccabees, it is Clement and Tertullian.

Neither book gets much action until the Church historians start writing:

References by 300 AD: 1 Chronicles 90, 1 Maccabees 73.[467]

References by 350 AD: 1 Chronicles 267, 1 Maccabees 471.

References by 400 AD: 1 Chronicles 424. 1 Maccabees 503.

After that, the database results include only one single Father who is writing entirely after 400, which is Theodoret, whose totals are 1 Chronicles 290 and 1 Maccabees 41. In the database as a whole, the citations are 1 Chronicles 787 and 1 Maccabees 596; but without Theodoret (which seems like a more coherent data set given the gap between his late date and all the other data[468]), it would be 1 Maccabees = 555 to 1 Chronicles = 497.[469]

---

[465] Numbers should always be taken with a grain of salt, especially zeros: per the database, Cyril of Jerusalem never cited to either 1 Macc or 1 Chron; however, I found one of his for 1 Macc.

[466] Plus, I found five outside of the database for 1 Maccabees.

[467] The numbers seem to exclude works with date ranges that are not certainly within the range. The methodology and data set are the same, so it is an apples-to-apples comparison. In any event, the subtotals do not equal the final total because such things are not counted in the subtotals.

[468] Jumping over Augustine is bound to massively distort the numbers for all Books (Protestant canon and Apocrypha). There are also other Fathers not included (Rufinus, notably).

[469] Eight of the references to 1 Chronicles are from Philo and should be excluded as well (he was a Jew, not a Christian). I also ignore (but keep in the data) the 1 citation to 1 Maccabees by Procopius, 490 AD+, which puts it outside of our date range. These make no real difference, and I feared that changing things would lead me to commit more errors than simply keeping them in.

The claim that no one read or cited to 1 Maccabees is a classic case of judging by the standard of perfection—and not a true comparable. 1 Maccabees was cited barely 1% as many times as was Psalms, but so was 1 Chronicles, and that is the relevant point.

The other aspect to consider is that many citations to a historical Book are as history, not Scripture. But the nature of references to 1 Maccabees and 1 Chronicles is such that we can review them all relatively easily because so many of them come in floods.

On the following pages, I have included what I found by looking into every citation to both of them, in one chart, sometimes using Latin names from the database. Finds of mine that are not in the database are in italics.

The way I see it, the citation evidence is basically the same—roughly the same numbers of Fathers, works, citations, mentions as Scripture, manner of use, context in which it is used, etc. The vast majority are just allusions to events detailed in the Books. But be your own judge.

Father	Year	Notes on 1 Maccabees	Notes on 1 Chronicles
Justin Martyr	155	No citations to 1 Maccabees, per the database.	Justin said, "And you are aware that David said, 'The gods of the nations are demons." This might (?) be a reference to 1 Chronicles 16:26: For all the gods of the people are idols: but the LORD made the heavens.

Father	Year	Notes on 1 Maccabees	Notes on 1 Chronicles
Clement of Alexandria	198	*Cited 1 Maccabees, but it is mistakenly not included in Biblindex. Stromata 1, 21: Jeremiah and Ambacum [Habakkuk] were still prophesying in the time of Zedekiah. In the fifth year of his reign Ezekiel prophesied at Babylon; after him Nahum, then Daniel. After him, again, Haggai and Zechariah prophesied in the time of Darius the First for two years; and then the angel among the twelve. After Haggai and Zechariah, Nehemiah, the chief cup-bearer of Artaxerxes, the son of Acheli the Israelite, built the city of Jerusalem and restored the temple. During the captivity lived Esther and Mordecai [Malachi], whose book is still extant, as also that of the Maccabees. [The rest of the quote is noted above] www.newadvent.org/fathers/02091.htm*	Two citations, and both appear to be just a mention of the reigns of a king whose name appears in 1 Chronicles (Amasias) www.newadvent.org/fathers/02101.htm
Tertullian	198	Two citations, both in Against the Jews, 4: Cited 1 Maccabees 1:38 to prove that the doctrine of the Sabbath had been superseded: Nor is it doubtful that they wrought servile work, when, in obedience to God's precept, they drove the preys of war. For in the times of the Maccabees, too, they did bravely in fighting on the Sabbaths…" www.newadvent.org/fathers/0308.htm	No citations to 1 Chronicles, per the database.

Father	Year	Notes on 1 Maccabees	Notes on 1 Chronicles
Hippolytus	220	Forty-six citations to 1 Maccabees in two works, one on Daniel and one on the Antichrist. Cited with Daniel and other Scripture without qualification and used as part of the typological analysis portraying Antiochus as the type of the Antichrist, etc.	Thirteen citations to 1 Chronicles, in three works. Two are unavailable online, but one is in the same work as the references to 1 Maccabees. It seems to relate to counting the ten kings ("By the toes of the feet he meant, mystically, the ten kings that rise out of that kingdom") and is an allusion to 1 Chronicles 3:15 (And the sons of Josiah were, the firstborn Johanan, the second Jehoiakim, the third Zedekiah, the fourth Shallum.)
Julius Africanus	221	Eight citations in his Chronography, of which we only have fragments. I could not find the fragments that cite to 1 Maccabees online.	Four citations in the Chronography, none of which I could find in what is available online.
Origen	245	Eight citations in three works, including Against Celsus 8, 46: What need is there to quote all the princes and private persons in Scripture history who fared well or ill according as they obeyed or despised the words of the prophets? ... And the books of the Maccabees relate what punishments were inflicted upon those who dared to profane the Jewish service in the temple at Jerusalem. www.newadvent.org/fathers/ 04168.htm; In addition, his list claims the Jews give the Books Maccabees some sort of status.	Forty-eight cites in several works, including Commentary on John, Book 6, where he also calls 1 Chronicles "Scripture." www.newadvent.org/ fathers/101506.htm

Father	Year	Notes on 1 Maccabees	Notes on 1 Chronicles
Cyprian	248	10 citations. Treatise 12 (Ad Quirinum), Book 3, quotes several sections of 1 Maccabees as "Holy Scripture" (see sections 4, 15, 53, but not 17, which is a cite to 2 Macc: www.newadvent.org/fathers/05 0712c.htm); as does Letter 54, 3: Holy Scripture meets and warns us, saying, ... 1 Maccabees 2:62-63. www.newadvent.org/fathers/ 050654.htm. Several other letters make allusions to events in 1 Maccabees.	No cites to 1 Chronicles, per the database.
Pamphilius Caesariensis	280	No citations to 1 Maccabees.	Two citations to 1 Chronicles in one work, both apparently allusions to 1 Chron 21:7 (And God was displeased with this thing; therefore he smote Israel.) and 21:30 (But David could not go before it to enquire of God: for he was afraid because of the sword of the angel of the LORD.) I found the book online but not the allusions, which may be obscure.
Victorinus	304	Three citations from the Creation of the World, 7th day: cited 1 Maccabees 2:31 to confirm the doctrine that the Sabbath obligations have been superseded. ccel.org/ccel/ schaff/anf07.vi.i.html	No citations to 1 Chronicles, per the database.
Lactantius	304	No citations to 1 Maccabees, per the database.	One citation to 1 Chronicles, an allusion to the fact that Solomon followed David (1 Chronicles 29:28: And he died in a good old age, full of days, riches, and honour: and Solomon his son reigned in his stead.) newadvent.org /fathers/07014.htm Ch. 13.

Father	Year	Notes on 1 Maccabees	Notes on 1 Chronicles
Athanasius	329	Letter 3, Section 5 makes three allusions to actions (prayers when facing attacks, etc.) described in 1 Maccabees, but no one is named. www.newadvent.org/fathers/2806003.htm	Never once cited 1 Chronicles, even though he lists it as canon.
Eusebius	339	There are 394 citations, in many works—many of them double-counted (as is the case for his citations to 1 Chronicles, as well, so at least it is apples-to-apples, even if not numerically correct). In his Chronicle, a history of the world, Eusebius states that "I thought it would be appropriate to write down everything in brief, especially the beneficial and important things, and further to put adjacent to [these accounts] the history of the Hebrew patriarchs as revealed in the Bible." He seems to place the Books of the Maccabees in the Bible category. In his Preparation of the Gospel, he cites the Book of Maccabees as proof of prophetic interpretation, saying that "Psalm lxxviii., was fulfilled in the time of Antiochus... It is therefore to that time, and to Antiochus' successors who emulated his deeds, that Asaph's prophecies in Psalm lxxviii. refer. And the Book of those called Maccabees confirms what I say, which has this passage: "And to Jakeimon and Bacchides there came a (c) deputation of scribes asking for justice." And it proceeds to say: "And he sware to them saying, We will not bring evil on yourselves and your friends. And they believed him. And he took of them sixty men and slew them in one day, according to the word of Asaph, which he wrote, They	There are 174 citations, in many works, many of them double-counted; in his Preparation of the Gospel, he calls 1 Chronicles one of the Hebrew Oracles (as he also calls the Book of Wisdom (and asserts that it is Divine Prophecy fulfilled by Christ)).

Father	Year	Notes on 1 Maccabees	Notes on 1 Chronicles
		gave the dead bodies of thy servants to be meat for the birds of the air, and the flesh of thy saints to the beasts of the land, their (d) blood have they poured out like water on every side of Jerusalem, and there was no man to bury them." www.ccel.org/ccel/pearse/more fathers/files/eusebius_de_12_b ook10.htm Chapter 1. In addition he cites Origen's list as "When expounding the first Psalm he gives a catalog of the Sacred Scriptures of the Old Testament as follows...And outside of these there are the Maccabees, which are entitled Sarbeth Sabanaiel," which implies some sort of status for 1 Maccabees.	
Didymus Alexandrinus	350	*Cited 1 Maccabees, but it is mistakenly not included in the Biblindex database. On the Holy Spirit 27-28: ... we find the Holy Spirit performing the office of intercessor with the Father, as when ... And the Savior... pours consolation into those hearts that need it, as in Maccabees, he strengthened those of the people who were brought low." (Per Ancient Christian Commentary on Scripture, not available online.)*	Thirteen citations to 1 Chronicles, in the date range of 350-398 AD, which I could not find online.
Cyril of Jerusalem	350	Lecture XIV, 25: Elias went as into heaven [used 1 Maccabees 2:58 to confirm the doctrine that the ascension was possible.] ccel.org/ccel/schaff/ npnf207.ii.xviii.html	No citations to 1 Chronicles, per the database.
Hilary	353	no citations to 1 Maccabees, which he did not list as canon.	Eleven citations to 1 Chronicles in two works, Commentary on Matthew (353 AD) and Tractates on Psalms (360-367 AD), none available online.

Father	Year	Notes on 1 Maccabees	Notes on 1 Chronicles
Lucifer of Caligari	361	*On not Sparing those who Commit Offences Against God, 15: Introduces 1 Maccabees 2:49-68 as "the Holy Scripture says" per Gary G. Michuta in* The Case of the Deuterocanon. *Not available online.*	*Not in the database.*
Ambros-iaster	363	"Would be Ambrose"—a work that was once mistakenly thought to be a work of Ambrose, but it was actually written by some unknown person (as early as 363 AD, which is actually before the writings of Ambrose). He makes three citations to 1 Maccabees, one inexplicable (that the Jews were named for Judas Maccabeus, p. 290) and the others as proof to confirm the doctrine that the Sabbath could be broken for necessity (p. 185). archive.org/details/ambrosiaster-questions-and-answers-on-the-old-and-new-testaments/page/310/mode/2up	Cited 1 Chronicles 20 times, 16 of them in the same work as 1 Maccabees. As with 1 Maccabees, the book is clearly providing Scriptural proofs but never actually says that 1 Chronicles is Scripture. It just uses it as such.
Basil	363	Made one citation in a work I could not find. Homiliae in Psalmos, 363 AD, p.225.	cited six times in one homily (unavailable) and one letter; section 3 makes an allusion to the events of 1 Chronicles 11:1 and 11:3 without mentioning the Book. www.newadvent.org/fathers/3202236.htm
Epiphanius	377	His Panarion (30, 25, 9) makes one citation to 1 Maccabees but only as history to use linguistics to prove the ethnicity of Alexander the Great. Not available online.	Thirteen citations to 1 Chronicles; one in the Panarion mentions 1 Chronicles as canonical Scripture.

Father	Year	Notes on 1 Maccabees	Notes on 1 Chronicles
Gregory of Nyssa	379	One possible allusion in his *Answer to Eunomius' Second Book,* "Noah was a righteous man, says the Scripture, Abraham was faithful," (www.newadvent.org/fathers/ 2902.htm); see 1 Maccabees 2:52: "Was not Abraham found faithful in temptation, and it was imputed unto him for righteousness?"	Seven citations in four works; none available online.
Gregory of Nazianzus	380	Two citations to 1 Maccabees in one Oration, not available online.	Five citations to 1 Chronicles in three Orations. None available online.
Apostolic Constitutions	380	*At least three citations, used to confirm the doctrine that God accepts gifts and sacrifices from the righteous: Book 7, Section 2, Chapter 37: Thou who hast fulfilled Thy promises made by the prophets, and ... didst accept of the gifts of the righteous in their generations. In the first place Thou did respect the sacrifice of ... of Mattathias and his sons in their zeal... www.newadvent.org/fathers/07 157.htm. Its canon list accepts 1 Maccabees.*	*Not in the database.*

Father	Year	Notes on 1 Maccabees	Notes on 1 Chronicles
Ambrose	397	Twenty-four citations. Letter XL, 33 it is the voice of a Saint which says: "Wherefore was I made to see the misery of my people?" (1 Maccabees 2:7) ccel.org/ccel/schaff/ npnf210.v.ix.html. In "On the Duties of the Clergy," he also makes 20 citations to 1 Maccabees in a two-chapter exposition on martyrs and their virtues.	Forty-three citations in many works, although 21 come in one commentary on Psalm 12. Only a handful were available online, and they are only allusions without mention of the Book 1 Chronicles. E.g., On The Holy Spirit, Book 3, Chapter 17, Section 120 makes a full citation to John Chapter 9: "In this passage too He was walking, as we read, in Solomon's porch on the day of the dedication, that is, Christ was walking in the breast of the wise and prudent, to dedicate his good affection to Himself." That is noted in the database as an allusion to 1 Chronicles 22:9: (Behold, a son shall be born to thee, who shall be a man of rest; and I will give him rest from all his enemies round about: for his name shall be Solomon, and I will give peace and quietness unto Israel in his days), but is also an allusion (not recorded in the database) to the fulfillment of 1 Maccabees.

Father	Year	Notes on 1 Maccabees	Notes on 1 Chronicles
John Chrysostom	407	Seven citations, including Homily on Romans 19, cited to confirm the doctrine that God did not abandon the Jews: "He brought you [the Jews] back again to your former freedom… and there were prophets again, and the gift of the Spirit. Or rather, even in the season of your captivity you were not deserted, but even there were Daniel, and Ezekiel, and in Egypt Jeremiah, and in the desert Moses. After this you reverted to your former vice again, and wast a reveller [2 Maccabees 14:33], therein, and changed your manner of life to the Grecian in the time of Antiochus the impious [1 Maccabees 4:54]. But even then for a three years and a little over only were ye given up to Antiochus, and then by the Maccabees ye raised those bright trophies again. www.newadvent.org/fathers/210219.htm	Three citations to 1 Chronicles in two works, neither available online.
Jerome	417	Cited to 1 Maccabees 41 times—one allusion in a letter, then 40 times in his commentary on Daniel, where (as noted above) he cites Antiochus as a type of the Antichrist.	Nine citations to 1 Chronicles, some as part of a list of "quotations from the Old Testament (newadvent .org/fathers/30111.htm)
Sulpitius Severus	420	*Sacred History 2, 20-26 (Ch 1, 1:) I address myself to give a condensed account of those things which are set forth in the sacred Scriptures from the beginning of the world ... At that time, Matthathias, the son of John, was high-priest. (1 Maccabees 2:1) www.newadvent.org/fathers/35052.htm*	*Not in the database.*

Father	Year	Notes on 1 Maccabees	Notes on 1 Chronicles
Theodoret	423	Forty citations in four works, including Commentaries on Daniel, Ezekiel, and Paul's Epistles. Not available online.	Two hundred and ninety citations, in many works, with many of them double-counted, as with Eusebius. None are available online, but one is a book I own (Commentary on Jeremiah). Six allusions, all to 1:29 and 1:32, which are just the names in the genealogy down from Adam.
Augustine	430	*Contra Gaudentium, 1, 31, 38 [The Books of the Maccabees] will not have been received by the Church in vain if they are read or listened to calmly, and especially those parts that deal with the Maccabees themselves who, for the sake of God's Law, were true martyrs and suffered terrible and humiliating things. Not available online. In addition, his canon list accepts 1 Maccabees.*	*Not in the database.*
Procopius	490	Not in our timeframe.	
Philo			Jewish, not Christian.
Anonymous			Three citations in two books by unknown authors; one is a book on Ezra from the third century, and the other is a fourth-century work that appears to be heretical ("Christian borderline," per database). Not available online.

For your reference, here is a summary chart, looking just at 1 Maccabees and the 24 Fathers we have citations from:

Father	Year	Citation Evidence
Clement Alexandria	198	Cited with Scripture without Qualification
Tertullian	198	Cited to confirm doctrine
Hippolytus	220	Cited with Scripture w/o Qualification, typology
Julius Africanus	221	8 citations
Origen	245	Scripture
Cyprian	248	Holy Scripture
Victorinus	304	Cited to confirm doctrine
Athanasius	329	3 allusions
Eusebius	339	"Bible" category, proof of prophetic interpretation
Didymus	350	Cited to confirm doctrine
Cyril of Jerusalem	350	Cited to confirm doctrine
Lucifer of Caligari	361	Holy Scripture
Ambrosiaster	363	Cited to confirm doctrine
Basil	363	1 cite
Epiphanius	377	1 cite
Gregory of Nyssa	379	1 allusion
Gregory Nazianzus	380	2 cites
Apostolic Const.	380	Cited to confirm doctrine
Ambrose	397	Voice of a saint
John Chrysostom	407	Cited to confirm doctrine
Jerome	417	Used for typology
Sulpitius Severus	420	Sacred Scripture
Theodoret	423	40 cites
Augustine	430	Received by the Church

AGGREGATE CHART

The following is a chronological chart of the summary citation evidence from the Fathers, plus all canon lists and Councils and codices (which are in ALL CAPS, in **BOLD IF A COUNCIL,** and in *ITALICS IF A CODEX*). The symbol "*" denotes a Father who created a list as well as cited 1 Maccabees in his works.

FATHER/LIST/BOOK	Year	1 MACC CANONICAL?
MELITO OF SARDIS	170	NOT CANON (FOR JEWS?)
MURATORIAN CANON	170	UNKNOWN
Clement of Alexandria*	198	Cited with Scripture w/o Qualification
Tertullian	198	Cited to confirm doctrine
CLEMENT ALEXANDRIA	203	UNKNOWN
ORIGEN (JEWISH LIST)	220	"OUTSIDE OF THESE" (?)
Hippolytus	220	Cited w/o Qualification, typology
Julius Africanus	221	8 citations
Origen*	245	Scripture
ORIGEN (LETTER)	248	N/A
Cyprian	248	Holy Scripture

ORIGEN (CITATIONS)	250	CANON
Victorinus	304	Cited to confirm doctrine
EUSEBIUS (APPROVAL)	324	"OUTSIDE OF THESE"
~~THE NICENE COUNCIL~~	325	~~UNKNOWN~~
Athanasius*	329	3 allusions
Eusebius*	339	"Bible" category, prophetic interpretation
CLAROMONTANUS	349	CANON
CODEX VATICANUS	350	*NOT CANON?*
CODEX SINAITICUS	350	*CANON*
CYRIL OF JERUSALEM	350	NOT CANON
ST CATHERINE'S SYRIAC	350	CANON
Didymus	350	Cited to confirm doctrine
Cyril of Jerusalem*	350	Cited to confirm doctrine
CHELTENHAM LIST	360	CANON
Lucifer of Caligari	361	Holy Scripture
~~COUNCIL AT LAODICEA~~	363	~~NOT CANONICAL~~
Ambrosiaster	363	Cited to confirm doctrine
Basil	363	1 cite
ATHANASIUS	367	VERSION 3.1
HILARY OF POITIERS	367	NOT CANON
Epiphanius*	377	1 cite
Gregory of Nyssa	379	1 allusion
GREGORY NAZIANZUS	380	NOT CANON
AMPHILOCHIUS ICONIUM	380	NOT CANON
APOSTOLIC CANONS	380	CANON
Gregory of Nazianzus*	380	2 cites
Apostolic Constitutions*	380	Cited to confirm doctrine
~~THE COUNCIL OF ROME~~	382	~~CANON~~
EPIPHANIUS PAN. 8.6.1-4	385	NOT CANON FOR JEWS
EPIPHANIUS PAN. 76.22.5 (	385	NOT CANON
JEROME (HELMETED)	390	NOT CANON
EPIPHANIUS DE MENS. 4-5	392	NOT CANON FOR JEWS
THE COUNCIL OF HIPPO - 70 BISHOPS	393	**CANON**
AUGUSTINE	397	CANON
COUNCIL CARTHAGE - 44-48 BISHOPS	397	**CANON**
Ambrose	397	Voice of a saint
JEROME (SOLOMON)	398	VERSION 3.2
RUFINUS	400	VERSION 3.3
JEROME (TOBIT/JUDITH)	404	N/A
POPE INNOCENT I	405	CANON
John Chrysostom	407	Cited to confirm doctrine
Jerome*	417	Used for typology
COUNCIL CARTHAGE - 217 BISHOPS	419	**CANON**
Sulpitius Severus	420	Sacred Scripture
Theodoret	423	40 cites
Augustine*	430	Received by the Church
CODEX ALEXANDRINUS	450	*CANON*
CODEX EPHRAEMI R.	450	*UNKNOWN*

CANON LISTS

The following is a chronological chart of just the canon lists and Councils and codices (which are in **BOLD IF A COUNCIL** and in *ITALICS IF A CODEX*).

FATHER/LIST/BOOK	Year	1 MACC CANONICAL?	OTHER CITATIONS
MELITO OF SARDIS	170	NOT FOR JEWS?	NONE
MURATORIAN CANON	170	UNKNOWN	NOT APPLICABLE
CLEMENT ALEXANDRIA	203	UNKNOWN	W/O QUALIFICATION
ORIGEN (JEWISH LIST)	220	OUTSIDE OF THESE	NOT APPLICABLE
ORIGEN (LETTER)	248	N/A	SCRIPTURE
ORIGEN (CITATIONS)	250	CANON	SCRIPTURE
EUSEBIUS (APPROVAL)	324	OUTSIDE OF THESE	BIBLE, PROPHECY
~~THE NICENE COUNCIL~~	~~325~~	~~UNKNOWN~~	~~NOT APPLICABLE~~
CLAROMONTANUS	349	CANON	NOT APPLICABLE
CODEX VATICANUS	*350*	*NOT CANON?*	*NOT APPLICABLE*
CODEX SINAITICUS	*350*	*CANON*	*NOT APPLICABLE*
CYRIL OF JERUSALEM	350	NOT CANON	CONFIRMED DOCTRINE
ST CATHERINE'S SYRIAC	350	CANON	NOT APPLICABLE
CHELTENHAM LIST	360	CANON	NOT APPLICABLE
~~COUNCIL AT LAODICEA~~	~~363~~	~~NOT CANON~~	~~NOT APPLICABLE~~
ATHANASIUS	367	VERSION 3.1	3 ALLUSIONS
HILARY OF POITIERS	367	NOT CANON	NONE
GREGORY NAZIANZUS	380	NOT CANON	2 CITES
AMPHILOCHIUS	380	NOT CANON	NONE
THE APOSTOLIC CANONS	380	CANON	PROPHECY
~~THE COUNCIL OF ROME~~	~~382~~	~~CANON~~	~~NOT APPLICABLE~~
EPIPHANIUS PAN. 8.6.1-4	385	NOT FOR JEWS	1 CITE
EPIPHANIUS PAN. 76.22.5	385	NOT CANON	1 CITE
JEROME (HELMETED)	390	NOT CANON	TYPOLOGY
EPIPHANIUS DE MEN. 4-5	392	NOT FOR JEWS	1 CITE
THE COUNCIL OF HIPPO - 70 BISHOPS	**393**	**CANON**	**NOT APPLICABLE**
AUGUSTINE	397	CANON	SCRIPTURE
COUNCIL CARTHAGE - 44-48 BISHOPS	**397**	**CANON**	**NOT APPLICABLE**
JEROME (SOLOMON)	398	VERSION 3.2	TYPOLOGY
RUFINUS	400	VERSION 3.3	NONE?
JEROME (TOBIT/JUDITH)	404	N/A	TYPOLOGY
POPE INNOCENT I	405	CANON	NONE
COUNCIL CARTHAGE - 217 BISHOPS	**419**	**CANON**	**NOT APPLICABLE**
CODEX ALEXANDRINUS	*450*	*CANON*	*NOT APPLICABLE*
CODEX EPHRAEMI R.	*450*	*UNKNOWN*	*NOT APPLICABLE*

Version 3.1: 1 Maccabees is not canon and not to be read, unlike Baruch (which is canon) or Esther (which is not canonical but to be read).

Version 3.2: 1 Maccabees (unlike Esther (which is canon) or Baruch (which is not canon)) read for strengthening but not canonical or for confirming the authority of ecclesiastical dogmas.

Version 3.3: 1 Maccabees (unlike Esther or Baruch (both of which are canon)) not canonical but "Ecclesiastical."

2 MACCABEES

The good news for those of us who are lazy (i.e., all of us) is that all the work we just did on 1 Maccabees is about to pay immediate bonus dividends: we have already compared the evidence for 1 Maccabees against 1 Chronicles, and 2 Maccabees is inarguably better evidenced as Scripture than either of them (in terms of citation evidence).[470] 2 Maccabees has more verses of theological importance, and hence, more citations as Scripture, more use as Scriptural proof, and more reasons for more Fathers to cite to it. Eusebius and Theodoret cite to 2 Maccabees a lot, but they combine for barely a third of the citations in the database—a far cry from the substantial majority they were for both 1 Maccabees and 1 Chronicles. The database lists 32 Fathers who cited to it, which is a lot more than the 19 for both of the others. Combined with those I found outside of the database, the total became 41. I found over 70 instances where a Father cited to 2 Maccabees as Sacred Scripture, etc.

So, rather than cover the data at the end in a postscript, let's get right to it. To save space, I have left out those whose citations I could not find to read.

Father	Year	Notes
Hermas	90	One citation. The Shepherd of Hermas alludes to 2 Macc 7:28: ...there is one God who created and finished all things, and made all things out of nothing. www.newadvent.org/fathers/02012.htm
Clement of Alexandria	198	Two citations. Stromata 1, 21: in a Chronological list of Scripture, Clement writes: During the captivity lived Esther and Mordecai [Malachi], whose book is still extant, as also that of the Maccabees. www.newadvent.org/fathers/02091.htm
Origen	230	Forty citations, at least seven as Scripture, incl. First Principles 2, 1, 5 But that we may believe in the authority of holy Scripture that such is the case, hear how in the book of Maccabees... www.newadvent.org/fathers/04122.htm
Hippolytus	235	Six citations, using 2 Maccabees to prove the fulfillment of Daniel's Prophecies, and as typology (Antiochus as the type of the Antichrist). www.newadvent.org/fathers/0516.htm and www.newadvent.org/fathers/0502.htm
Pseudo-Tertullian	*240*	*Allusions to the Maccabean Martyrs are made in a martyrdom account that was once attributed to Tertullian. Who wrote it is unknown. www.newadvent.org/fathers/0324.htm*
Tertullian	*240*	*Used to confirm the doctrine that work can be done on the Sabbath, when arguing against the Jews: For in the times of the Maccabees, too, they did bravely in fighting on the Sabbaths. www.newadvent*

---

[470] 2 Maccabees is not a sequel to 1 Maccabees; it actually begins a few years before 1 Maccabees starts and may even have been written earlier. The "2" is just an identifier, nothing more.

		.org/fathers/0308.htm
Cyprian	258	Twenty citations, at least 13 as Holy Scripture or Sacred Scripture, incl. in his Three Books of Testimonies Against the Jews. "You asked me to gather out for your instruction from the Holy Scriptures... Of this same thing in the Maccabees... www.newadvent.org/fathers/050712c.htm
Eusebius	339	One hundred and thirty-two citations, including uses to confirm doctrine: from his Preparation of the Gospel, Book 12, 3: In the Book of the Maccabees, it is said that Jeremiah the Prophet, after his departure from life, was seen praying for the people, as one who took thought for men upon Earth.
Aphrahat	*345*	*At least six citations to prove the fulfillment of Daniel's prophecies, including Demonstration 5, 19: For Daniel said:... For this was accomplished at that time, when the venerable and aged Eleazar was slain, and the sons of the blessed Samuna, seven in number, and when Judas (Maccabeus) and his brethren were struggling on behalf of their people, when they were dwelling in hiding-places. 2 Macc 5:27 ... www.newadvent.org/fathers/370105.htm*
Lucifer of Caligari	*361*	*Introduces quotes from 2 Maccabees as "the Scripture says..." per Gary G. Michuta in* The Case of the Deuterocanon. *Not online.*
Hilary of Poitiers	368	Does not include 2 Maccabees on his list yet cites to it 17 times and seems to allude to it as Scripture and Prophecy. On the Trinity 4, 16: "Such suggestions are inconsistent with the clear sense of Scripture. For all things, as the Prophet says 2 Maccabees 7:28, were made out of nothing; it was no transformation of existing things, but the creation into a perfect form of the non-existent. www.newadvent.org/fathers/330204.htm
Ephrem the Syrian	*373*	*Commentary on Hebrews. In order not to repeat all the details in his review of the works of faith, Paul stopped relating the stories of these ancient fathers... who were given to death despised their own life, like the seven brothers together with their mother... [Per Ancient Christian Commentary on Scripture]. Not online.*
Gregory of Nazianzus	381	Twenty-four citations. Not on his list but seems to include it in his Old Testament anyway. Orations 43, 74 recounts the "men of old days" who were "illustrious for piety, as lawgivers, generals, prophets, teachers, and men brave to the shedding of blood, Let us compare our prelate [Basil] with them and, thus, recognize his merit." He references Adam, Enos, Enoch, Noah, Abraham, Isaac, Rebecca, Jacob, Twelve Patriarchs, Joseph, Job, Moses, Aaron, Joshua, Judges, Samuel, David, Solomon, Elijah, Jonah, and the Maccabean martyrs. Then: "I turn to the New Testament..." www.newadvent.org/fathers/310243.htm
Ambrose	397	Ninety citations, including as teaching of Sacred writings [1, 1, 3]. From Duties of the Clergy, 3, 18, 107: Moses said, as is written in the book of the Maccabees: Because the sacrifice for sin was not to be eaten, it was consumed. 2 Macc 2:11
Theophilius of Alexandria	*404*	*Says that the victories of the Maccabees (2 Maccabees 7) are praised throughout the whole world in the Churches of Christ, per Gary Michuta in* The Case of the Deuterocanon. *Festal Letter of AD 404, in Jerome, Letter 100, 9. Not online.*
Chromatius	*407*	*Tractate on Matthew 57, 2 Now we can know ... not only on the basis of the present passage, but also from other testimonies, ... In the Books of Maccabees, too, repeatedly we read that angels came to the defense of the people to fight against the enemy [see 2Macc*

3:25; 11:6; 15:23]. [Per Chromatius of Aquileia, Sermons and Tractates on Matthew] Not available online.

John Chrysostom	407	Eighteen citations, including as Prophecy: And Jeremiah prevailed not for the Jews, but some one else he did haply cover from evil by his prophecy. ... 2 Maccabees xv. 13–16. Homilies on the Gospel of St. Matthew 1. 22, 23. Not available online.
Jerome	420	Eighteen citations. 2 Maccabees is not on his list; however in one case, he seems to cite it as Scripture, but is perhaps confused: Read the Scriptures and you will never find holy women bearing children in pain, with the exception of Rachel, who, when she was on a journey and in the hippodrome, that is, in the course for horses which had been sold to Egypt,' suffered while delivering her son, whom his father later called "son of the right hand." [the events fit 2 Maccabees; how he connects them to Rachel is unclear] [Per Ancient Christian Commentary on Scripture]. Not available online.
Sulpitius Severus	*420*	*Sacred History 2, 17-23 cites 2 Macc as sacred Scripture many times, e.g. (Ch 2, 20:) At this time, there occurred that well-known and remarkable suffering of the seven brothers and their mother. www.newadvent.org/fathers/35052.htm*
Augustine	426	Cited as Scripture at least 20 times. His canon list includes 2 Maccabees, though he acknowledges that the "faithless people" do not agree. City of God 18, 36: ...the reckoning of their dates is found, not in the Holy Scriptures which are called canonical, but in others, among which are also the books of the Maccabees. These are held as canonical, not by the Jews, but by the Church, on account of the extreme and wonderful sufferings of certain martyrs, who, before Christ had come in the flesh, contended for the law of God even unto death, and endured most grievous and horrible evils." www.newadvent.org/fathers/120118.htm
Vincentius Victor	*430*	*Cites 2 Macc 12:43 as Scriptural proof that sacrifice can be offered for the departed who were not baptized: "in this example of the Maccabees who fell in battle that I ground the necessity of doing this... sacrifices were offered up to liberate their souls, which had been bound by the guilt of their forbidden conduct. [Augustine accepts this as Scripture in 13 and 19] in Augustine's On the Soul 2, 13, 15 and 18. www.newadvent.org/fathers/15082.htm*
Theodoret	435	Forty-eight citations, including Commentary on Daniel, 11, which cites 2 Maccabees as proof that the prophecies of Daniel were fulfilled: The second book of the Maccabees teaches us this when it says, "And about this time Antiochus sent a second expedition to Egypt." ... [Per Ancient Christian Commentary on Scripture]. Not online.

Here is a handy summary chart:

Father	Year	Notes
Shepherd of Hermas	90	1 Allusion
Clement of Alexandria	198	Scripture
Origen	230	Holy Scripture
Hippolytus	235	Used In Typology
Pseudo-Tertullian	240	Allusions
Tertullian	240	Used To Confirm Doctrine
Cyprian	258	Holy Scripture

Eusebius	339	Used To Confirm Doctrine
Aphrahat	345	Fulfills Prophecy
Lucifer of Caligari	361	Scripture
Hilary of Poitiers	368	Not on list; Prophecy
Ephrem the Syrian	373	Sees Hebrews as cite
Gregory of Nazianzus	381	Not on list; Old Testament
Ambrose	397	Teaching of Sacred Writings
Theophilius of Alex.	404	Praised throughout the Churches
Chromatius	407	Scripture
John Chrysostom	407	Prophecy
Jerome	420	Not on list; Scripture
Sulpitius Severus	420	Sacred Scripture
Augustine	426	Holy Scripture
Vincentius Victor	430	Scripture
Theodoret	435	Fulfills Prophecy

AGGREGATE CHART

The following is a chronological chart of the summary citation evidence from the Fathers, plus all canon lists and Councils and codices (which are in ALL CAPS, in **BOLD IF A COUNCIL,** and in *ITALICS IF A CODEX*). The symbol "*" denotes a Father who created a list, as well as cited 1 Maccabees in his works.

FATHER/LIST/BOOK	YEAR	2 MACC CANONICAL?
Shepherd of Hermas	90	1 Allusion
MELITO OF SARDIS	170	NOT CANON (FOR JEWS?)
MURATORIAN CANON	170	UNKNOWN
Clement of Alexandria*	198	Scripture
CLEMENT ALEXANDRIA	203	UNKNOWN
ORIGEN (JEWISH LIST)	220	OUTSIDE OF THESE (?)
Origen*	230	Holy Scripture
Hippolytus	235	Used In Typology
Pseudo-Tertullian	240	Allusions
Tertullian	240	Used To Confirm Doctrine
ORIGEN (LETTER)	248	N/A
ORIGEN (CITATIONS)	250	CANON
Cyprian	258	Holy Scripture
EUSEBIUS (APPROVAL)	324	CANON
~~THE NICENE COUNCIL~~	~~325~~	~~UNKNOWN~~
Eusebius*	339	Used To Confirm Doctrine
Aphrahat	345	Fulfills Prophecy
CLAROMONTANUS	349	CANON
CODEX VATICANUS	*350*	*NOT CANON?*
CODEX SINAITICUS	*350*	*CANON?*
CYRIL OF JERUSALEM	350	NOT CANON
ST CATHERINE'S SYRIAC	350	CANON
CHELTENHAM LIST	360	CANON
Lucifer of Caligari	361	Scripture
~~COUNCIL AT LAODICEA~~	**~~363~~**	**~~NOT CANONICAL~~**
ATHANASIUS	367	VERSION 3.1
HILARY OF POITIERS	367	NOT CANON

Hilary of Poitiers*	368	Not on list; Prophecy	
Ephrem the Syrian	373	Sees Hebrews as cite	
GREGORY NAZIANZUS	380	NOT CANON	
AMPHILOCHIUS	380	NOT CANON	
APOSTOLIC CANONS	380	CANON	
Gregory of Nazianzus*	381	Not on list; Old Testament	
~~THE COUNCIL OF ROME~~	~~382~~	~~CANON~~	
EPIPHANIUS PAN. 8.6.1-4	385	NOT CANON FOR JEWS	
EPIPHANIUS PAN. 76.22.5	385	NOT CANON	
JEROME (HELMETED)	390	NOT CANON	
EPIPHANIUS DE MENS. 4-5	392	NOT CANON FOR JEWS	
THE COUNCIL OF HIPPO - 70 BISHOPS	**393**	**CANON**	
AUGUSTINE	397	CANON	
COUNCIL CARTHAGE - 44-48 BISHOPS	**397**	**CANON**	
Ambrose	397	Teaching of Sacred Writings	
JEROME (SOLOMON)	398	VERSION 3.2	
RUFINUS	400	VERSION 3.3	
JEROME (TOBIT/JUDITH)	404	N/A	
Theophilius of Alexandria	404	Praised throughout the Churches	
POPE INNOCENT I	405	CANON	
Chromatius	407	Scripture	
John Chrysostom	407	Prophecy	
COUNCIL CARTHAGE - 217 BISHOPS	**419**	**CANON**	
Jerome*	420	Not on list; Scripture	
Sulpitius Severus	420	Sacred Scripture	
Augustine*	426	Holy Scripture	
Vincentius Victor	430	Scripture	
Theodoret	435	Fulfills Prophecy	
CODEX ALEXANDRINUS	*450*	*CANON*	
CODEX EPHRAEMI R.	*450*	*UNKNOWN*	

CANON LISTS

The following is a chronological chart of just the canon lists and Councils and codices (which are in **BOLD IF A COUNCIL** and in *ITALICS IF A CODEX*).

		2 MACC	
FATHER/LIST/BOOK	**YEAR**	**CANONICAL?**	**OTHER CITATIONS**
MELITO OF SARDIS	170	NOT FOR JEWS?	NONE
MURATORIAN	170	UNKNOWN	NOT APPLICABLE
CLEMENT ALEXANDRIA	203	UNKNOWN	1 CITE
ORIGEN (JEWISH LIST)	220	OUTSIDE OF THESE	NOT APPLICABLE
ORIGEN (LETTER)	248	N/A	HOLY SCRIPTURE
ORIGEN (CITATIONS)	250	CANON	HOLY SCRIPTURE
EUSEBIUS (APPROVAL)	324	CANON	132 CITES; DOCTRINE
~~THE NICENE COUNCIL~~	~~325~~	~~UNKNOWN~~	~~NOT APPLICABLE~~
CLAROMONTANUS	349	CANON	NOT APPLICABLE
CODEX VATICANUS	*350*	*NOT CANON?*	*NOT APPLICABLE*
CODEX SINAITICUS	*350*	*CANON?*	*NOT APPLICABLE*

CYRIL OF JERUSALEM	350	NOT CANON	2 ALLUSIONS TO 7:28
ST CATHERINE SYRIAC	350	CANON	NOT APPLICABLE
CHELTENHAM LIST	360	CANON	NOT APPLICABLE
~~COUNCIL LAODICEA~~	**363**	~~NOT CANON~~	~~NOT APPLICABLE~~
ATHANASIUS	367	VERSION 3.1	7 ALLUSIONS, 5 TO 7:28
HILARY OF POITIERS	367	NOT CANON	SCRIPTURE (7:28)
GREGORY NAZIANZUS	380	NOT CANON	OLD TESTAMENT
AMPHILOCHIUS	380	NOT CANON	1 CITE?
APOSTOLIC CANONS	380	CANON	VENERABLE, HOLY
~~COUNCIL OF ROME~~	**382**	~~CANON~~	~~NOT APPLICABLE~~
EPIPHANIUS PAN. 8.6.1-4	385	NOT FOR JEWS	3 ALLUSIONS, 2 TO 7:28
EPIPHANIUS PAN. 76.22.5	385	NOT CANON	3 ALLUSIONS, 2 TO 7:28
JEROME (HELMETED)	390	NOT CANON	SCRIPTURE
EPIPHAN.DE MENS. 4-5	392	NOT FOR JEWS	3 ALLUSIONS, 2 TO 7:28
THE COUNCIL OF HIPPO - 70 BISHOPS	**393**	**CANON**	**NOT APPLICABLE**
AUGUSTINE	397	CANON	HOLY SCRIPTURE
COUNCIL CARTHAGE - 44-48 BISHOPS	**397**	**CANON**	**NOT APPLICABLE**
JEROME (SOLOMON)	398	VERSION 3.2	SCRIPTURE
RUFINUS	400	VERSION 3.3	NONE?
JEROME (TOBIT/JUDITH)	404	N/A	SCRIPTURE
POPE INNOCENT I	405	CANON	NONE
COUNCIL CARTHAGE - 217 BISHOPS	**419**	**CANON**	**NOT APPLICABLE**
CODEX ALEXANDRINUS	*450*	*CANON*	*NOT APPLICABLE*
CODEX EPHRAEMI R.	*450*	*UNKNOWN*	*NOT APPLICABLE*

Version 3.1: 2 Maccabees is not canon and not to be read, unlike Baruch (which is canon) or Esther (which is not canonical but to be read).

Version 3.2: 2 Maccabees (unlike Esther (which is canon) or Baruch (which is not canon)) read for strengthening but not canonical or for confirming the authority of ecclesiastical dogmas.

Version 3.3: 2 Maccabees (unlike Esther or Baruch (both of which are canon)) not canonical but "Ecclesiastical."

2 Maccabees supports various theological doctrines, notably:

the afterlife (6:26: yet should I not escape the hand of the Almighty, neither alive, nor dead);

the resurrection of the body (7:10-11: holding forth his hands manfully [he] said courageously, These I had from heaven; and for his laws I despise them; and from him I hope to receive them again);

prayers for the dead (12:40-45, including: Now under the coats of every one that was slain they found things consecrated to the idols of the Jamnites, which is forbidden the Jews by the law. Then every man ... Betook themselves unto prayer, and besought him that the sin committed might wholly be put out of remembrance); and

the intercession of the saints (15:14: "Then Onias answered, saying, This is a lover of the brethren, who prayeth much for the people, and for the holy city, to wit, Jeremias the prophet of God).

that the suffering undergone by martyrs benefits others because it can lead God to intervene on their behalf (2 Maccabees 7:38: And that in me and my brethren the wrath of the Almighty, which is justly brought upon our nation, may cease). This belief, of course, leads up to Jesus Christ (Matthew 26:28: For this is my blood of the new testament, which is shed for many for the remission of sins).

Of course, some try to use the substance of these verses from 2 Maccabees as a reason to exclude it from the Bible. That theology is really outside my focus, which is on whether the Jews accepted it, what evidence the Bible gives about its canonicity, and whether the early Church accepted it. However, there are a few points I will make about that decision-making process.

As noted above, 2 Maccabees is still evidence of prayer and sacrifice for the dead among Jews before the time of Christ. In addition, the New Testament contains a possible instance of prayer for the dead. After praying for the household of a man named Onesiphorus, Paul goes on to pray, "The Lord grant unto him that he may find mercy of the Lord in that day" (2 Timothy 1:18). Paul twice mentions "the household of Onesiphorus" but does not greet him with the rest of his household and speaks of him only in the past tense. So, perhaps Onesiphorus had passed away and, thus, Paul was praying for the departed. If so, then this would be a New Testament allusion to the practice of prayers for the dead in 2 Maccabees.

Not everyone interprets 2 Timothy 1:18 that way, and how you interpret it is up to you—but the point I wish to make is that 2 Maccabees is evidence of the default, the background, the baseline for analyzing 2 Timothy 1:18. One cannot say that the Bible itself is evidence of anything, unless you consider that 2 Maccabees is evidence that the Jews before Christ prayed for the dead.

Given that, it sets the baseline for 2 Timothy 1:18—and so the presumption should be that Saul prayed for the dead. The real question is not whether Paul believed in prayers for the dead after he was Christian; it should be whether he stopped believing in prayers for the dead once he became a Christian.

Debate the evidence, believe against the evidence, whatever you want; but recognize that 2 Maccabees is evidence.[471]

The Christian Basilica to the Holy Maccabees in Antioch (the city of Antiochus, the King who killed them and made them the Maccabean Martyrs) is gone, but relics from the martyrs' bodies were taken to Istanbul, Cyprus, Rome, and Cologne, Germany.

The Christians also devoted a feast day to them—as Christian martyrs, not Jewish. They repeatedly cited to 2 Maccabees as Scripture, read 2 Maccabees at Mass,[472] and preached sermons on it. Augustine's sermon was quoted above. Theophilus of Alexandria, in his Festal Letter of AD 404, says that the victories of the Martyrs are praised in the churches of Christ throughout the entire world.[473] In addition, we have additional sermons from Augustine, three homilies St. John Chrysostom when he was serving in Antioch (386 AD),[474] Oration 15 from Gregory of Nazianzus,[475] and others.

There are also many references to the Maccabean Martyrs in all the Martyrologies. E.g., Polycarp's last words (d. 155 AD) before being sentenced include "What are you waiting for?" (2 Maccabees 7:30);[476] and regarding the martyrs of Lyon (177 AD), Eusebius records that "the blessed Blandina … encouraged her children and sent them before her victorious to the King,

---

[471] And Simon Greenleaf (Christian apologist, Law Professor and author of the book on Evidence) would agree. See, e.g., Examination of the Testimony of the Four Evangelists, Sec. 9.
[472] www.bible-researcher.com/rufinus.html, 38
[473] In Jerome, Letter 100, 9. Not available online.
[474] One at www.johnsanidopoulos.com/2018/08/homily-on-holy-maccabees-and-their.html, two available in a book (*Homilies on the Maccabees*) from Amazon a.co/d/5jYcg8o
[475] iconandlight.wordpress.com/2021/01/24/in-praise-of-the-maccabees-saint-gregory-the-theologian-nazianzus/
[476] Martyrdom of Polycarp 11, 2 www.newadvent.org/fathers/0102.htm

endured herself all their conflicts and hastened after them, glad and rejoicing in her departure ..."[477] etc.

In addition, the Gospel to the Jews and the Epistle to the Hebrews may both refer to 2 Maccabees Chapter 7, per the Evangelical Biblical Theology Commentary and the KJV, as mentioned above. And not to be forgotten in the following discussion: among the Jews and Hebrews were "a great company of the priests" (Acts 6:7).

But to the modern Jews, the story of 2 Maccabees 7 is not canon. Instead, the "Talmud tells a similar story, but with refusal to worship an idol replacing refusal to eat pork. ... In this version of the story, each son goes to his death while citing a different verse from the Torah prohibiting idolatry. ... The Josippon version of the story ... was notable as the first major exposure of medieval Jewish audiences to the story."[478]

There is further corroborating evidence of this progression, as well. A first-century Jewish author took Chapters 6-7 out of 2 Maccabees and "recast them" as a standalone story, 4 Maccabees.[479] So, we have evidence of it being extracted from 2 Maccabees prior to its 'plagiarization.'

Here, then, is a line-by-line comparison of the original and the copy as it is included in the Talmud (from halakhah.com/gittin/gittin_57.html).

	2 Maccabees Chapter 7	**Babylonian Talmud, Gittin 57b**
King	1It came to pass also, that seven brethren with their mother were taken, and compelled by the king [Antiochus Epiphanes of the Seleucid Empire, capital at Antioch] ...	Rab Judah, however, said that this refers to the woman and her seven sons. They brought the first before the [Roman] Emperor [Caesar] ...
Law	against the law to taste swine's flesh, and were tormented with scourges and whips.	and said to him, Serve the idol.
First Son	2But one of them that spake first said thus, What wouldest thou ask or learn of us? we are ready to die, rather than to transgress the laws of our fathers. 3Then the king, being in a rage, commanded pans and caldrons to be made hot: 4Which forthwith being heated, he commanded to cut out the tongue of him that spake first, and to cut off the utmost parts of his body, the rest of his brethren and his mother looking on.	He said to them: It is written in the Law, I am the Lord thy God. So they led him away and killed him.

---

[477] Church History 5, 1, 55: www.newadvent.org/fathers/250105.htm.
[478] wikipedia.org/wiki/Woman_with_seven_sons.
[479] See wikipedia.org/wiki/4_Maccabees.

5Now when he was thus maimed in all his members, he commanded him being yet alive to be brought to the fire, and to be fried in the pan: and as the vapour of the pan was for a good space dispersed, they exhorted one another with the mother to die manfully, saying thus,

6The Lord God looketh upon us, and in truth hath comfort in us, as Moses in his song, which witnessed to their faces, declared, saying, And he shall be comforted in his servants.

Second Son

7So when the first was dead after this number, they brought the second to make him a mocking stock: and when they had pulled off the skin of his head with the hair, they asked him, Wilt thou eat, before thou be punished throughout every member of thy body?

8But he answered in his own language, and said, No. Wherefore he also received the next torment in order, as the former did.

9And when he was at the last gasp, he said, Thou like a fury takest us out of this present life, but the King of the world shall raise us up, who have died for his laws, unto everlasting life.

They then brought the second before the Emperor and said to him, Serve the idol. He replied: It is written in the Torah, Thou shalt have no other gods before me. So they led him away and killed him.

Third Son

10After him was the third made a mocking stock: and when he was required, he put out his tongue, and that right soon, holding forth his hands manfully.

11And said courageously, These I had from heaven; and for his laws I despise them; and from him I hope to receive them again.

12Insomuch that the king, and they that were with him, marvelled at the young man's courage, for that he nothing regarded the pains.

They then brought the next and said to him, Serve the idol. He replied: It is written in the Torah, He that sacrifices unto the gods, save unto the Lord only, shall be utterly destroyed. So they led him away and killed him.

Fourth Son

13Now when this man was dead also, they tormented and mangled the fourth in like manner.

14So when he was ready to die he said thus, It is good, being put to death by men, to look for hope from God to be raised up again by him: as for thee, thou shalt have no resurrection to life.

They then brought the next before the Emperor saying, Serve the idol. He replied: It is written in the Torah, Thou shalt not bow down to any other god. So they led him away and killed him.

Fifth Son

15Afterward they brought the fifth also, and mangled him.

16Then looked he unto the king, and said, Thou hast power over men, thou art corruptible, thou doest what thou wilt; yet think not that our nation is forsaken of God;

17But abide a while, and behold his great power, how he will torment thee and thy seed.

They then brought another and said to him, Serve the idol. He replied: It is written in the Torah, Hear, O Israel, the Lord our God, the Lord is one. So they led him away and killed him.

Sixth Son

18After him also they brought the sixth, who being ready to die said, Be not deceived without cause: for we suffer these things for ourselves, having sinned against our God: therefore marvellous things are done unto us.

19But think not thou, that takest in hand to strive

They then brought the next and said to him, Serve the idol. He replied; It is written in the Torah, Know therefore this day and lay it to thine heart that the Lord He is God

against God, that thou shalt escape unpunished.

Seventh Son

20But the mother was marvellous above all, and worthy of honourable memory: for when she saw her seven sons slain within the space of one day, she bare it with a good courage, because of the hope that she had in the Lord.

21Yea, she exhorted every one of them in her own language, filled with courageous spirits; and stirring up her womanish thoughts with a manly stomach, she said unto them,

22I cannot tell how ye came into my womb: for I neither gave you breath nor life, neither was it I that formed the members of every one of you;

23But doubtless the Creator of the world, who formed the generation of man, and found out the beginning of all things, will also of his own mercy give you breath and life again, as ye now regard not your own selves for his laws' sake.

24Now Antiochus, thinking himself despised, and suspecting it to be a reproachful speech, whilst the youngest was yet alive, did not only exhort him by words, but also assured him with oaths, that he would make him both a rich and a happy man, if he would turn from the laws of his fathers; and that also he would take him for his friend, and trust him with affairs.

25But when the young man would in no case hearken unto him, the king called his mother, and exhorted her that she would counsel the young man to save his life.

26And when he had exhorted her with many words, she promised him that she would counsel her son.

27But she bowing herself toward him, laughing the cruel tyrant to scorn, spake in her country language on this manner; O my son, have pity upon me that bare thee nine months in my womb, and gave thee such three years, and nourished thee, and brought thee up unto this age, and endured the troubles of education.

28I beseech thee, my son, look upon the heaven and the earth, and all that is therein, and consider that God made them of things that were not; and so was mankind made likewise.

29Fear not this tormentor, but, being worthy of thy brethren, take thy death that I may receive thee again in mercy with thy brethren.

30Whiles she was yet speaking these words, the young man said, Whom wait ye for? I will not obey the king's commandment: but I will obey the commandment of the law that was given unto our

in heaven above and on the earth beneath; there is none else. So they led him away and killed him.

They brought the next and said to him, Serve the idol. He replied: It is written in the Torah, Thou hast avouched the Lord this day ... and the Lord hath avouched thee this day; we have long ago sworn to the Holy One, blessed be He, that we will not exchange Him for any other god, and He also has sworn to us that He will not change us for any other people. The Emperor said: I will throw down my seal before you and you can stoop down and pick it up, so that they will say of you that you have conformed to the desire of the king. He replied; Fie on thee, Caesar, fie on thee, Caesar; if thine own honour is so important, how much more the honour of the Holy One, blessed be He! They were leading him away to kill him when his mother said: Give him to me that I may kiss him a little. She said to him: My son, go and say to your father Abraham, Thou didst bind one [son to the] altar, but I have bound seven altars.

fathers by Moses.

31And thou, that hast been the author of all mischief against the Hebrews, shalt not escape the hands of God.

32For we suffer because of our sins.

33And though the living Lord be angry with us a little while for our chastening and correction, yet shall he be at one again with his servants.

34But thou, O godless man, and of all other most wicked, be not lifted up without a cause, nor puffed up with uncertain hopes, lifting up thy hand against the servants of God:

35For thou hast not yet escaped the judgment of Almighty God, who seeth all things.

36For our brethren, who now have suffered a short pain, are dead under God's covenant of everlasting life: but thou, through the judgment of God, shalt receive just punishment for thy pride.

37But I, as my brethren, offer up my body and life for the laws of our fathers, beseeching God that he would speedily be merciful unto our nation; and that thou by torments and plagues mayest confess, that he alone is God;

38And that in me and my brethren the wrath of the Almighty, which is justly brought upon our nation, may cease.

39Than the king' being in a rage, handed him worse than all the rest, and took it grievously that he was mocked.

40So this man died undefiled, and put his whole trust in the Lord.

Mother — 41Last of all after the sons the mother died.

42Let this be enough now to have spoken concerning the idolatrous feasts, and the extreme tortures.

Then she also went up on to a roof and threw herself down and was killed. A voice thereupon came forth from heaven saying, A joyful mother of children.[480]

At the time of Christ, the Jews believed the story in 2 Maccabees to be true: "… Although such an interpretation may sound strange to the modern reader, it would not to Matthew's original Jewish-Christian readers. Antiochus Epiphanes had maimed the heroes of the Maccabean era…"[481] The only

---

[480] It is interesting to note that the modern Jewish version ends in suicide, because the suicide of Razis in 2 Maccabees 14:37-46 was a major topic of theological discussion within the Church (e.g., Augustine Letter 204, 8: "though this man [Razis] was praised in the Books of the Maccabees, his action was reported, not praised…" Per The Works of Saint Augustine, A Translation for the 21st Century, not available online). It makes me wonder if it was merged into the story of the Martyrs in order for the Talmud to retain that aspect of 2 Maccabees, as well.

[481] Per The Evangelical Biblical Theology Commentary, Matthew, p. 458.

candidate meeting all three parts of the Epistle to the Hebrews 11:35 is 2 Maccabees 7:7 et seq. But by the time of the Talmud, the Rabbis taught a fake story instead. The exact same Talmud gives the first ever list of the modern Jewish/Protestant canon, which does not include 2 Maccabees. The original story, then, disappeared from Jewish memory, while the fake story has continued within Judaism. Eventually, the Jews were reintroduced to the Maccabean Martyrs in the Middle Ages.

Using the 'well-proven scientific technique for selecting a statistically valid random sample' (i.e., the first three things on my Google search), I found three Jewish websites detailing the Talmud's story:

1) www.sefaria.org/Gittin.57b.15?lang=bi. Hebrew to English translation of the Talmud, with no comments.

2) halakhah.com/gittin/gittin_57.html#PARTb. English translation, with dozens of footnotes. Footnote 22 claims that, "The same story is related of Antiochus Epiphanes in the second book of the Maccabees"—which is misleading. The Talmud story is not the same story; it only has the same plot. There is a huge difference between four Gospels telling the story of the Resurrection, and four Books, each describing four different "resurrections" of four different alleged Messiahs. Nevertheless, this footnote exists, as do probably a thousand similarly confusing claims in books, other websites, articles, etc. (I linked to another one up above).

3) koltorah.org/halachah/the-mother-and-her-seven-sons-by-rabbi-chaim-jachter.   A modern Rabbi's detailed inspirational comments on the Talmud's story, which makes no mention at all that it is a copy taken from 2 Maccabees.

Several points would seem to be clear. First, the story is very important to Judaism. The Rabbi on website three tells us that:

> "The iconic story of the mother and her seven sons recounted in Gittin 57b is well-known and often repeated. It is most certainly etched in the minds of Jews of faith as a standard bearer for dedication and devotion to Hashem and His Torah. It is even incorporated in poetic form in the Tisha BeAv Kinnot recited by Sephardic Jews."

Iconic, well known, often repeated, etched in the minds, a standard bearer, recited as poetry. And yet "borrowed" from 2 Maccabees.

> …The brothers are not mere "copy cats".

Ouch. Of course, the Rabbi just means that the brothers are not all saying the same thing… but in our context, the words read very differently. Much like the inadvertent message included in the jeers from the Jews at the Crucifixion (Matthew 27:43: He trusted in God; let him deliver him now, if he will have him: for he said, I am the Son of God).

... The mother is ... a powerful role model. She indeed surpasses Avraham Avinu in his dedication sevenfold. Her sacrifice and complete dedication are a foundational component of Jewish identity at least as much as Avraham Avinu and the Akeida.

The new and improved Jewish story of the Mother and her Seven Sons "[is] a foundational component of Jewish identity at least as much as" Abraham and the story of the binding and near sacrifice of Isaac. That is how important the story is and was to the Jews.

Second, website two (similar to the website discussed above as Example 12 in the New Testament references section) explains the truth, but it does so dismissively—in a footnote, using unclear language.[482]

And, thus, the bubble. A reader can read a hundred books, but need never take the footnotes seriously, follow up on them, and see where they lead. If they just read the "scholarly discussion," they may never realize what the truth is. Scholars use abstractions, generalizations, and dismissive references all the time, as we have seen, which are not the same thing as the truth.

But thirdly, Wikipedia explains it, so it is not hard to find. One must be careful trusting Wikipedia, of course, but then, anyone could follow its links or the website's footnote to the story in 2 Maccabees to see that, in this case, it is correct. It takes five minutes of research to end the delusion forever.

And yet, the bubble survives. How many people actually know this "trivia" and understand its implications? Jews, Christians, skeptics, others? No one else I know. Nor do I recall ever seeing it in a single book discussing the canon, nor any book I have on 2 Maccabees, let alone books on the case for Christianity.

Burying it in misleading footnotes has successfully hidden it in plain sight from millions of readers and billions of believers and non-believers.

Meanwhile, Origen told us that "the canonical books, as the Hebrews have handed them down, are twenty-two ... And outside of these there are the Maccabees, which are entitled Sarbeth Sabanaiel."[483] What exactly he meant

---

[482] The least likely explanation of "why" it was done this way is that the Rabbi is a dishonest fraud. Far more likely is that the Rabbi has trivialized the detail in his own mind, and is not trying to carefully communicate the precise facts to those reading him. Never jump to bad motives as the answer. Mark 3:22: And the scribes ... said..."he is driving out demons by the prince of demons."

[483] Gallagher and Meade (p. 95) say Origen "surely has in mind the book we know as 1 Maccabees," since it "probably" originated in Hebrew. I take that as inclusive of 1 Maccabees and not exclusive of the other Books, since their own translation of Origen's words is "there are the

by that (in terms of canonicity among the Hebrews) is unknowable, but Origen shows us that they had some sort of status in his time. It is only later that the Jews had no knowledge of the Books and had to be reintroduced to "the heroes of the Maccabean era."

Thus, the eventual fate of 2 Maccabees is corroborating evidence of several things: one is that Origen was a knowledgeable source when he said there was this "second tier" view among the Jews—the process of erasing them had begun. In fact, that some writers in later centuries make no mention of the Maccabees when discussing the Jewish books is exactly what we would expect: in Origen's day the Books were being erased from Jewish memory, in later centuries they were gone.

But also, Origen's list is, indeed, a list of Jewish books, not the Christian canon. Origen's list includes a mention of the Maccabees as set off in a second tier—because something was going on, and he indicated as much.

Origen certainly considered 2 Maccabees to be full Christian Scripture: in his On the First Principles (the first ever systematic exposition of Christian theology) 2, 1, 5 (230 AD), he wrote "But that we may believe in the authority of holy Scripture that such [that all matter was created by God] is the case, hear how in the book of Maccabees, where the mother of seven martyrs exhorts her son to endure torture, this truth is confirmed; for she says, I ask of you, my son, to look at the heaven and the earth, and at all things which are in them, and beholding these, to know that God made all these things when they did not exist. (2 Maccabees 7:28)."[484]

This quote from 2 Maccabees 7:28 had enormous importance in the history of Christianity: the quote was repeatedly used to prove the doctrine that God created everything from nothing.[485] It is one of the sections of the Book that is truly quoted and cited, and that single verse is cited by the Fathers 74 times (per biblindex.org/citation_biblique/search), including by Origen, Eusebius, Hilary, Epiphanius, Cyril of Jerusalem, and Athanasius—six of Kruger's 10 Fathers—and always to prove the same fundamental Christian doctrine.[486]

Maccabees, which are entitled..." not "there is" or "which is." Of course, which of the other Books is also included is unprovable, but all probability would focus on 2 Maccabees.
[484] www.newadvent.org/fathers/04122.htm
[485] See wikipedia.org/wiki/Creatio_ex_nihilo. The concept is not actually clear just from Genesis. Of course Protestants (and others) can perhaps justify the concept in other ways, but the point is that the ancients used 2 Maccabees, as do modern Catholics and Orthodox.
[486] Origen is the first to cite to it, but there are allusions to this verse from the very beginning of Christianity, e.g., in the Shepherd of Hermas (90 AD?): "First of all, believe that there is one God

In addition, in 235 AD, Origen wrote his "Exhortation to Martyrdom" to preach to the persecuted, using the story of the seven brothers and their mother as his Scriptural basis. Innumerable Christians followed Origen's preaching, e.g., the mother of Marian was "exalting with a joy like that of the mother in the days of the Maccabees" when her son was martyred in 258 AD.[487]

Nor was Origen a hypocrite. In 246 AD, Origen made what might be his last reference to the Book: "But what will they do about the fact that we find many martyrs even under the law? They ought to read the books of Maccabees, where a blessed mother endured martyrdom with complete constancy together with her seven sons."[488] Shortly thereafter, per Wikipedia:

> In c. 249, the Plague of Cyprian broke out. In 250, Emperor Decius, believing that the plague was caused by Christians' failure to recognise him as divine, issued a decree for Christians to be persecuted. This time Origen did not escape. Eusebius recounts how Origen suffered "bodily tortures and torments under the iron collar and in the dungeon; and how for many days with his feet stretched four spaces in the stocks". The governor of Caesarea gave very specific orders that Origen was not to be killed until he had publicly renounced his faith in Christ. Origen endured two years of imprisonment and torture, but obstinately refused to renounce his faith. In June 251, Decius was killed fighting the Goths in the Battle of Abritus, and Origen was released from prison. Nonetheless, Origen's health was broken by the physical tortures enacted on him, and he died less than a year later at the age of sixty-nine.

Meanwhile, in Carthage, Cyprian cites to 2 Maccabees as Scripture eight times in his Testimonies Against the Jews—most notably in 3, 17, where he uses five quotes from 2 Maccabees 6-7 to explain Paul's statement in Romans 8:18 that "The sufferings of this present time are not worthy of comparison with the glory that is to come after, which shall be revealed in us."

> Of this same thing in the Maccabees: "O Lord, who hast the holy knowledge, it is manifest that while I might be delivered from death, I am suffering most cruel pains of body, being beaten with whips; yet in spirit I suffer these things willingly, because of the fear of your own self." Also in the same place: "You indeed, being powerless, destroy us out of this present life; but the King of the world shall raise us up who have died for His laws into the eternal resurrection of life." Also in the same place: "It is better that, given up to death by men, we should expect hope from God to be raised

who created and finished all things, and made all things out of nothing." First Commandment, 1 www.newadvent.org/fathers/02012.htm.
[487] Martyrdom of Marian and James 13, 1: archive.org/details/owen-1927-authentic-acts-of-the-early-martyrs/page/116/mode/2up
[488] Commentary on Romans, 4.10.2. The whole text is not available online, but it is cited at vivacatholic.wordpress.com/2007/08/14/origen-and-canon-of-old-testament/.

again by Him. For there shall be no resurrection to life for you." Also in the same place: "Having power among men, although you are corruptible, you do what you will. But think not that our race is forsaken of God. Sustain, and see how His great power will torment, you and your seed." Also in the same place: "Do not err without cause; for we suffer these things on our own accounts, as sinners against our God. But think not that you shall be unpunished, having undertaken to fight against God."[489]

Cyprian wrote that in 248 AD. This was shortly before the persecution that would lead to Origen's death, and a decade later, Cyprian and eight of his disciples would also be martyred. According to the disciples' own last letter, and the testimony of an eyewitness, "Flavian['s]… mother stuck close by his side with the constancy of the mother of the holy Maccabees."[490]

On the chart above, you can also see that Hippolytus had used 2 Maccabees as part of his typological belief that Antiochus (the King who tortured and killed the Maccabean Martyrs) was a type of the Antichrist. You may also recall that Hippolytus wrote a full Scriptural commentary on Susanna, as part of Daniel; and it is also one of the writings where he used 2 Maccabees as proof of Daniel's typology and shows that Antiochus was a type for the Antichrist. From the commentary on Susanna:

> Verse 8 "These things the rulers of the Jews wish now to expunge from the book, and assert that these things did not happen …"
> Verse 12 "…For up to the present time both the Gentiles and the Jews of the circumcision watch and busy themselves with the dealings of the Church, desiring to suborn false witnesses against us"
> Verse 22 "And Susannah sighed… Now it is in our power also to apprehend the real meaning of all that befell Susannah. For you may find this also fulfilled in the present condition of the Church. For when the two peoples conspire to destroy any of the saints, they watch for a fit time, and enter the house of God while all there are praying and praising God, and seize some of them, and carry them off, and keep hold of them, saying, Come, consent with us, and worship our Gods; and if not, we will bear witness against you. And when they refuse, they drag them before the court and accuse them of acting contrary to the decrees of Caesar, and condemn them to death."[491]

In 235, during the persecution of Emperor Maximinus Thrax, Hippolytus and his rival, Pope Pontian, were exiled together to Sardinia, where they were worked to death in the mines (reconciling prior to their deaths).

---

[489] www.newadvent.org/fathers/050712c.htm
[490] wikipedia.org/wiki/Martyrs_of_Carthage_under_Valerian
[491] www.newadvent.org/fathers/0502.htm.

SIDEBAR 8: 1 ENOCH

1 Enoch is not Apocrypha as defined for this book (because it is not accepted as Scripture by modern Catholics, and I do not have space to do it full justice), but it still relates to our inquiry, since it speaks to whether or not the Apostles actually limited their Scriptures to the 22-Book Protestant/Jewish canon. First, recall this observation from Don Stewart at the Blue Letter Bible website (the logical error of which is discussed in Sidebar 4 above):

> No other book outside of the Hebrew canon is ever cited with the formula, "Thus says the Lord," "It is written," or "Scripture says." While some non-canonical writings may have been alluded to by the New Testament writers, these works are never quoted as Scripture or as having some sort of divine authority. This is further testimony that the extent of the Hebrew canon was clear to everyone at the time of Christ.[492]

And yet the Epistle of Jude says:

> 14 Enoch ... prophesied of these, saying, Behold, the Lord cometh with ten thousands of his saints, 15To execute judgment upon all, and to convince all that are ungodly among them of all their ungodly deeds which they have ungodly committed, and of all their hard speeches which ungodly sinners have spoken against him.

So, the Epistle of Jude quotes a book (called 1 Enoch) and says the words of the quote had been "prophesied" by Enoch, the purported author of the Book.[493] Stewart of course rejects 1 Enoch, and goes through several attempts to argue that Jude rejected it too:

> [1 Enoch and others] ...are not called "Scripture." Neither are they introduced with such phrases as "God said," "the Holy Spirit said," or "it is written." Therefore, we learn two important truths: First, the writers of the New Testament were aware of other written works apart from the Old Testament Scripture. However, though they knew of them, alluded to them, and perhaps quoted from them, they never cited them as divinely authoritative Scripture. This again demonstrates the distinction between the Scriptures and all other writings.[494]

---

[492] www.blueletterbible.org/Comm/stewart_don/faq/right-books-in-old-testament/question17-new-testament-quote-old-testament.cfm

[493] 1 Enoch says: "And behold! He cometh with ten thousands of His holy ones to execute judgement upon all, and to destroy all the ungodly: and to convict all flesh of all the works of their ungodliness which they have ungodly committed, and of all the hard things which ungodly sinners have spoken against Him." www.ccel.org/c/charles/otpseudepig/enoch/ENOCH_1.HTM

[494] www.blueletterbible.org/Comm/stewart_don/faq/right-books-in-old-testament/question18-new-testament-old-testament.cfm

But notice how Stewart speaks of 1 Enoch as one of the "other written works apart from the Old Testament Scripture" when the question is whether 1 Enoch was one of those Scriptures, at least to Jude. This is circular reasoning of course, and begs the question of whether quoting 1 Enoch as "Prophecy" was a fourth way that a Divinely inspired Evangelist identified Scripture.

After all, Stewart told us that the Book of Jeremiah is Scripture because:

> Matthew cites a passage from Jeremiah the prophet (Jeremiah 31:15). This is in the context of the slaughter of the innocents in Bethlehem. He wrote:
>> Then was fulfilled what was spoken by Jeremiah the prophet, saying: "…" (Matthew 2:17-18 NKJV)
> Jeremiah's authority is assumed in the New Testament.

Jude also cites a passage from Enoch the Prophet—so Enoch's authority is likewise "assumed" in the New Testament, by any fair standard.[495]

Next among Stewart's attempted explanations for 1 Enoch:

> … it is possible that Jude is not citing from the Book of Enoch, but rather from a common source that he, as well as the writer of the Book of Enoch, had access. Indeed, some have argued that the quotation is similar but not the same as found in the Book of Enoch. There are some minor differences between the two statements.[496]

Most New Testament citations do not perfectly match the exact words of the Old Testament. In fact, the proof he offered above where Stewart says that Matthew "cites" Jeremiah does not actually involve Matthew quoting Jeremiah. The Apologetics Study Bible says "Matthew loosely translated the Hebrew of Jeremiah 31:15;" he did not quote it.

> …Even if Jude is citing from the Book of Enoch, he is not treating the entire writing as divinely inspired, or for that matter, even true. All he is doing is citing one statement from this work. Thus, what we have is Jude citing a truthful statement in a written work which contains truth mixed with error. There is nothing in his citation that indicates Jude believed the Book of Enoch to be divinely inspired.

---

[495] Especially since Stewart also told us that "Malachi is believed to be God's prophet," showing the entire Book of Malachi to be Scripture, even though Matthew does not even quote from it (he just alludes to it). And the Book of Zechariah is Scripture, Stewart says, because Matthew 21:4-5 quotes a single verse of it as Prophecy (without naming the Prophet): "This important prophecy was cited on Palm Sunday. Zechariah was, indeed, God's prophet." Etc.

[496] www.blueletterbible.org/Comm/stewart_don/faq/books-missing-from-old-testament/question11-new-testament-quote-writings.cfm?a=1167014

Of course, Stewart himself wrote an entire essay claiming that New Testament citations of a single verse assure us that every single word of each Old Testament book is inerrant Divinely-inspired truth. I noted a few situations earlier, so just to pick one more example, "These Four Books May Be Alluded To: In fact, there is some evidence that these four books were considered divinely inspired."—i.e., mere allusions to one statement in a work could prove that the entire work is Divinely inspired, he says, let alone actual quotations as Prophecy.

> Jude says Enoch prophesied about the coming of the Lord. This verb, to prophesy, is used some twenty-eight times in the New Testament. However, on only two occasions, Mark 7:6 and First Peter 1:10, does it refer to predictions found in the Old Testament canon. All of the other references are to prophetic utterances which did not find their way into the canon of Scripture. To the New Testament writers, prophesying was not limited to canonical Scripture. There were valid prophetic utterances made which were not recorded in the Scripture. Therefore, it is consistent with the rest of the Bible that Enoch could make a valid prophetic utterance, which was not part of canonical Scripture, but could still be true.

Stewart appears to be distinguishing between the verb "to prophesy" and the noun "prophecy," given that, in the above analysis, he himself seems to accept translations of the noun "prophecy" to mean Scripture. Otherwise, I do not want to be accused of showing off my fluency in Koine Greek, so I will just assume his linguistic details are correct.

However, how many of his 28 examples were quotes taken from pre-existing books?[497] Of course, the answer is exactly three: this quote from 1 Enoch plus the two examples he mentions where the New Testament quotes to Divinely-inspired Scripture. Lumping those three similar examples in with the other 25 dissimilar examples is not false, but it does not lead one to truth either. You can trust me on this, as much as you should trust my Greek translations—after all, I did my Ivy League Doctoral Thesis in Statistics.[498]

The other utterances "did not find their way into the canon of Scripture" because they were not written down prior to the New Testament, and thus there is no writing that could have found its way into the canon. But every

---

[497] It had been claimed that 1 Enoch must have copied from Jude, but that was disproven. They have found copies of 1 Enoch from before Christ, so that fanciful explanation did not survive.

[498] My doctorate is a law degree; our theses are a joke compared to a PhD's; and my focus was on uncovering lies told with statistics, not actually conducting PhD-level statistical analyses. So I am indeed an expert on the topic of misleadingly lumping disparate things together.

single Prophecy quoted in the New Testament that had been previously written down came from canonical Scripture, except with this quote to 1 Enoch.

Consider also how apologists explain Matthew 2:23 (that it might be fulfilled which was spoken by the prophets, He shall be called a Nazarene). From Geisler and Howe, *When Critics Ask*:

> "[Problem:] Didn't Matthew make a mistake by claiming a prophecy that is not found in the OT?...[Solution:] Matthew did not say that any particular OT "prophet" (singular) stated this. He simply affirmed that the OT "prophets" (plural) predicted that Jesus would be called a Nazarene. So we should not expect to find any given verse, but simply a general truth found in many prophets to correspond to His Nazarene-like character. There are several suggestions..."

Notice how Matthew's reference to the Prophets is understood by even apologists to be a clear reference to the Old Testament Scriptures. Notice further that even though it says the Prophesy was "spoken" by such Prophets then it is understood by all that it will therefore be found in writing in the Old Testament Scriptures. Notice the conspicuous absence of the idea that Prophecy and the Old Testament Scriptures are completely unrelated. Etc.

As it is, Jude quoted the words of a Book purporting to be written by a Patriarch, and Jude declares it Prophecy—which is also what 1 Enoch declares itself to be: "The words of the blessing of Enoch ... whose eyes were opened by God, saw the vision of the Holy One in the heavens, which the angels showed me, and from them I heard everything, and from them I understood as I saw, but not for this generation, but for a remote one which is for to come. Concerning the elect I said, and took up my parable concerning them: ..." Jude skipped over eight verses and selected verse 9 of Chapter 1, after which the Book goes on for 108 chapters, all of which are "Enoch" Prophesying.

> ... Jude quoted Enoch, not the Book of Enoch. How well the Book of Enoch reproduced Enoch's actual words is not relevant. Both the Book of Enoch, as well as Jude, basically say the same thing.

Jude and Enoch say the same thing because Jude quoted 1 Enoch. Stewart had no problem concluding that "The writer to the Hebrews quotes the Book of Joshua (Joshua 1:5) as Scripture. He cited it in the following manner: "... for he has said, "I will never leave you ...""" If we took Stewart's 1 Enoch standard seriously, then the author of Hebrews quoted nothing, he merely notes that someone (not even Joshua) said it, and the fact that it can be found in the Book of Joshua is a random coincidence that proves nothing.

Moving on, consider what *When Critics Ask* by Geisler and Howe has to say about Jude:

> ... the external evidence for Jude is extensive from the time of Irenaeus (ca. A.D. 170) onward. It is in the Bodmer papyri (P72) of A.D. 250, and traces of it are found even earlier in the Didache (2:7) which probably dates from the second century. So there is evidence for the authenticity of the Book of Jude ...

Neither Kruger, nor F.F. Bruce (quoted in the above discussion re: Irenaeus), nor I, nor even Wikipedia consider the possible reference by Irenaeus to Jude as worth mentioning. For the record, however, it is:

> And it was He who rained fire and brimstone from heaven, in the days of Lot, upon Sodom and Gomorrah, "an example of the righteous judgment of God," that all may know, "that every tree that bringeth not forth good fruit shall be cut down..."

The part that tracks Jude is just Sodom and Gomorrah as "an example of the righteous judgment of God;" the other, longer quotation is from Matthew 3:10. So that is matching eight words, and it is in the same context, so that may, indeed, qualify as an allusion; however, Jude is not the only place to find Sodom and Gomorrah mentioned, and the wording that matches is the sort of thing that might be an accidental match. So, it is not a clear allusion.

For comparison, Jude's citation to 1 Enoch is a quote of 47 words. Geisler and Howe tell us that "First, it is not certain that Jude is actually citing the Book of Enoch..."—and that is with a 47-word quote specifically mentioning Enoch. And yet they determine that Irenaeus is certainly citing Jude from just eight words with no mention of this "Jude" person, let alone a Book, or even an indication that the author is actually quoting something.

As for the Didache, it could only be making an allusion. 2:7 says "You shall not hate any man; but some you shall reprove, and concerning some you shall pray, and some you shall love more than your own life," which might be alluding to Jude 1:23: "And others save with fear, pulling them out of the fire; hating even the garment spotted by the flesh." There are far stronger allusions to Apocrypha in the Bible, let alone in the Didache.[499]

The key takeaway, as usual, is that Geisler and Howe think that allusions are solid evidentiary support for the acceptance of the entire Epistle of Jude as

---

[499] E.g., Didache 4.5 "Be not a stretcher forth of the hands to receive and a drawer of them back to give." www.newadvent.org/fathers/0714.htm. Sirach 4:31 "Let not thine hand be stretched out to receive, and shut when thou shouldest repay."

Scripture, without even a reference to the name Jude or a declaration that it is Prophecy; etc. Yet like Stewart and others, they simultaneously try to claim that the extensive and explicit quote from 1 Enoch as "Prophecy" made in that Divinely inspired Epistle of Jude is not clear evidence of anything.

Whether 1 Enoch actually is or should be Scripture is not my present concern.[500] But this reference is one more piece of Biblical evidence, and it should be considered when judging the claim that "the extent of the Hebrew canon was clear to everyone at the time of Christ."

Finds at Qumran evidence that some Jews considered 1 Enoch Scripture. Which Jews, and whether they were in power, or in the majority, are interesting but irrelevant questions. The relevant question is whether the evidence including the Epistle indicates that Jude the Divinely inspired Evangelist was such a Jew, and whether his audience and peers were as well. The words of Scripture written by Jude himself certainly seem to indicate that they were, and even if you could prove that other Jews held to a limited canon, what evidence overrules Jude's own words with respect to himself?

A generation after Jude's death (martyred in Beirut by axe in 65 AD, per traditional accounts), Josephus will claim that the Jewish canon is limited to a number of Books (22). This is the main piece of evidence used to claim that the 22 Book canon is not just what the Jews accepted, but what the Evangelists accepted—even Jude. The Divinely-inspired words of Jude are not considered evidence that Josephus did not speak for Jude; instead the much later words of Josephus (who himself claimed to be Divinely-inspired) are the text used to overrule the plain meaning of the inerrant Scripture of Jude the Evangelist.

The Scriptural evidence is not ambiguous or hard to interpret; it is perfectly straightforward. This situation has parallels, and all were interpreted the exact same way, over and over: it is a reference to Scripture and authenticates the work as Scripture. Paul quoting a poem does not mean Paul saw the poem as Scripture—but Paul did not say the words quoted were "Prophecy," and the words are not from a Book purportedly written by a legendary Patriarch from Sacred history, one who Paul says "by faith was translated that he should not see death; because he pleased God." (Hebrews 11:5).

In addition, Jude referenced 1 Enoch as prophecy in an Epistle that "condemns in fierce terms certain people the author sees as a threat to the early

---

[500] The canon lists do not support 1 Enoch; but the later Church's views are not our present concern, which is just whether the Epistle shows that Jude accepted 1 Enoch.

Christian community ... these opponents are within the Christian community, but are not true Christians: they are scoffers, false teachers..."[501] So, in the midst of writing a letter condemning false teaching among Christians, Jude pulled out 1 Enoch and quoted it as Prophecy. That seems inexplicable if "the extent of the Hebrew canon was clear to everyone at the time of Christ."

Also, why would Jude even own these works if he did not consider them Scripture? We know how expensive these things were, and here he quotes an expensive Book that clearly speaks "as if" it were Scripture—a Book found at Qumran (evidencing that some Jews considered it Scripture), a Book accepted and used as Scripture by both Jews and Christians long after Christ.[502]

1 Enoch played an important role in Jewish mysticism both before and after Christ, still being cited by Rabbis in the eighth century. Josephus and Philo both used 1 Enoch to explain Genesis 6:1-5 (...There were giants in the earth in those days; and also after that, when the sons of God came in unto the daughters of men, and they bare children to them, the same became mighty men which were of old, men of renown...). Some of the earliest Christian works explicitly call it Scripture, including the Epistle of Barnabas (latest date 135 AD, but the dating range goes back to 40 AD).[503] Justin Martyr, Irenaeus, Athenagoras, Clement of Alexandria, Tertullian, and Origen all use it as Scripture, sometimes designating it Prophecy, Divinely inspired, etc.

Moreover, Jude's audience apparently could be expected to recognize the quotation and agree that he was quoting authentic Prophecy. And Jude also makes an extensive allusion to another work called the Assumption of Moses: corroborating evidence showing Jude's and his audience's way of thinking. Again, the illiterate could be expected to recognize all this, meaning 1 Enoch was being read aloud to them. And it is not the kind of work that would be read except as Scripture, as anyone can see for themselves by trying to read it.

The idea that Jude actually held to a strict 22-Book canon and somehow quoted from 1 Enoch without accepting 1 Enoch, is simply not the plain meaning of the words of Jude, as proven in numerous other instances where no one forces fanciful readings onto similar passages.

---

[501] wikipedia.org/wiki/Epistle_of_Jude

[502] wikipedia.org/wiki/Reception_of_the_Book_of_Enoch_in_premodernity

[503] Barnabas 4:3: The last offence is at hand, concerning which the scripture speaketh, as Enoch saith... www.earlychristianwritings.com/text/barnabas-lightfoot.html. What Enoch saith can be found at 1 Enoch 80:2: www.ccel.org/c/charles/otpseudepig/enoch/ENOCH_3.HTM.

And not to be forgotten, many believe that Jude was another Brother of the Lord, since he begins his Epistle by calling himself the brother of James (and Jude the Brother of the Lord is mentioned with James the Brother of the Lord in Matthew 13:55 and Mark 6:3).[504] There are two Epistles possibly from Brothers of the Lord, and only two such Epistles. One is from James and seems to reference Sirach an astonishing number of times, and one is from Jude and quotes 1 Enoch as Prophecy. If the writer of James was his brother, regardless of whether they were brothers of Jesus, then that too would support the conclusion that Jude saw 1 Enoch as Scripture.

Earlier, we discussed the standard of proof:

> "Many proofs of Christianity can be shown, and proofs have been given over and over again. Evidences can be given, but is that the real issue? Do those who reject the Bible refuse to believe because the evidence is not convincing? … lack of information is not the problem. Nor is lack of evidence the problem. The reason for unbelief is simple. Unbelievers start from the presupposition that the claims of the Bible are not true."[505]

The eye witness testimony of the Gospels is clear and convincing evidence. As long as that is the standard of proof, Christianity wins the case. But the Epistle of Jude is also clear and convincing evidence that the canon of the Evangelists was not limited to the 22-Book canon. The Apologetics Study Bible admits why they do not accept the evidence as proof:

> … the book of 1 Enoch was in circulation in Jude's day and was well known in Jewish circles. Jude almost certainly derived the citation from the book of 1 Enoch, and the latter is clearly pseudepigraphical. We would be faced with having to say that Jude knew that this specific quotation from 1 Enoch derived from the historical Enoch. It is better to conclude that Jude quoted the pseudepigraphical 1 Enoch and that he also believed that the portion he quoted represents God's truth. Jude's wording does not demand that he thought he had an authentic oracle from the historical Enoch.

"Does not demand" is not a standard of proof based on the evidence. It is a demand that one's opponent disprove one's presupposition.

---

[504] Kruger sees the case for Jude being the brother of James and Jesus as compelling, p. 270. Among other things, the very fact that the Epistle of Jude was preserved would seem to be based more on the importance of the author than the contents.
[505] everlastingtruths.com/2016/02/26/do-people-not-believe-the-bible-because-of-a-lack-of-evidence/

350 AD

TO

450 AD

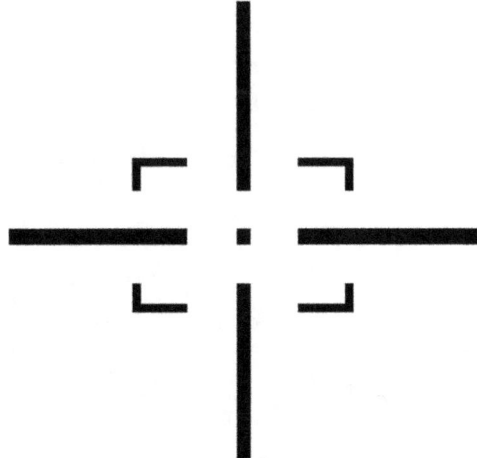

350 AD-450 AD

Let's consider the evidence for the Canon at the start of 350 AD. We, of course, have no formal declaration, so our standard is consensus.

Susanna and Baruch are clearly still canon and have been unanimously so for more than three centuries—far longer than the United States has existed.

Wisdom is very nearly the same: the word is on Melito's list, and the Book is listed on the Muratorian canon and in the Codex Claromontanus, the only certainly-Christian canons to date. There is a massive amount of citation evidence and Biblical evidence, plus it is part of both fourth century Great Uncial Codices.

The other five Apocrypha (Sirach, Tobit, Judith, and 1 and 2 Maccabees) are not far off from that. They are not on Melito's list, which is a point against them if, indeed, Melito's list is a Christian list. And the Muratorian canon does not mention them, which is meaningless (as a New Testament list, it is merely helpful for Wisdom that it is on it). But the other five Apocrypha are also on the Codex Claromontanus list, and that is the only certain Christian list to include the Old Testament. They also have citation evidence and Biblical evidence that ranges from "acceptable in comparison" to "very strong." Sirach, Tobit, and Judith are all included in both of the surviving Codex Bibles, while 1 and 2 Maccabees are included in one and missing in one.[506]

There are some mentions of Apocrypha being disputed, for example the (now long ago) exchange of letters among Origen and Africanus on Susanna. Eusebius (324 AD) says, "[Clement of Alexandria, in his Stromata] makes use also in these works of testimonies from the disputed Scriptures, the so-called Wisdom of Solomon, and ... Sirach..."[507] Clement and Eusebius, however, both accept Wisdom, so what is meant by "disputed Scriptures" is not clear.

Another example is from Origen (253 AD):

> ... we have spoken to the best of our ability in the preceding pages, for the sake of those who are accustomed to seek the grounds of their belief in our religion, and also for those who stir against us heretical questions, and who are accustomed to bandy about the word matter, which they have not yet been able to understand; ... it is to be noted that we have nowhere found in the canonical Scriptures, up to the present time, the word matter used for that substance which is said to underlie bodies. ... And if this word matter should happen to occur in any other passage, it will never be found, in my opinion, to have the

---

[506] Again, 2 Maccabees is missing in both, but it seems like scholars believe it was in Sinaiticus.
[507] Church History 6, 13, 6: www.newadvent.org/fathers/250106.htm

signification of which we are now in quest, unless perhaps in the book which is called the Wisdom of Solomon, a work which is certainly not esteemed authoritative by all. In that book, however, we find written as follows....[508]

Origen is clearly speaking to heretics and others who do not accept Wisdom as Scripture. For himself, in the same work, he quotes from it ten times that I found, citing to it specifically as Scripture in Bk 2,Ch 3, Sec 6; Bk 2,Ch 9, Sec 1; and Bk 3, Ch 1, Sec 14; in addition, Bk 1, Ch 2, Sec 5-13 is an extensive discourse on the Book of Wisdom after he had clearly indicated its Scriptural status in Bk 1, Sec 2, Ch 9.

In sum, before the coming of the canon lists after 350 AD, there is actually very little to debate. It seems that a consensus exists that all the Apocrypha are Scripture, with some rumblings in some cases and no rumblings at all in others. In fact, the idea that a consensus did not exist is not consistent with the standards we see applied to the New Testament canon, or the canonicity of Esther, or the rest of the Old Testament canon.

The Apocrypha compare well to the Jews and their canon. At 350 AD, the Jewish canon has the number of Books (22) from Josephus; a list from the Talmud (if correctly dated to before 350) that may not be consistent with what Josephus may have been thinking; plus inconsistent lists from Christians listing the Jewish canon (Melito, possibly, and Origen), that among them exclude Esther, possibly mention the Book of Wisdom, mention the Epistle of Jeremiah (Baruch Ch. 6), and attribute some sort of status to the Books of the Maccabees. Jewish citation evidence is presumably growing,[509] and certainly Christian citations evidence Jewish acceptance of all the Books of the Jewish canon by this date. But when we make fair comparisons, we see that Christian citations also evidence the Apocrypha in very comparable ways.

And let's compare with the New Testament again. Kruger (p. 269-273):

> ... James clearly did not enjoy the same popularity in the early church as the core New Testament books (like Paul's epistles), as is evidenced by the paucity of explicit Patristic citations of the book. However, its impact can be seen more indirectly as it appears to have influenced a number of other early Christian writings, such as 1 Clement and the Shepherd of Hermas. In addition, James is cited by Irenaeus, Clement of Alexandria wrote a commentary on it which is now lost, and it was recognized as canonical Scripture by Origen, who cites it frequently and refers to it as from "James, the brother of the Lord." Eusebius acknowledges that some had doubts about it, but

---

[508] de Principiis 4.33. www.newadvent.org/fathers/04124.htm
[509] I have done no research on Jewish citations, so that is solely a guess.

counts it among the canonical books "known to most," and the letter is fully received by Jerome, Augustine, and the councils of Hippo and Carthage. Moreover, as noted above, we possess several early manuscripts of James: P20, P23, P100 are all third century and suggest that the book was known and used by early Christians. While James's canonical path was not as smooth as that of other books, these factors give no reason to doubt its place in the canon.

The Book of James has 279 citations (biblindex.org/citation_biblique /search) through 350 AD. Wisdom has 758, Sirach 431, 1 Maccabees 471, 2 Maccabees 213, Baruch 103, Susanna 235, Tobit 75, and Judith 28.

Since our last check-in at 200 AD, Kruger notes some later Fathers: "Origen, who cites it frequently" cites to James 83 times. Compare that with 270 to Wisdom, 130 to Sirach, 40 to 2 Maccabees, 40 to Tobit, and 108 to Susanna. "Eusebius acknowledges that some had doubts about it, but counts it among the canonical books "known to most""—acknowledging doubts is also the worst that Eusebius has to say about any Apocrypha (e.g., "[Clement of Alexandria, in his Stromata] makes use also in these works of testimonies from the disputed Scriptures, the so-called Wisdom of Solomon, and ... Sirach..."). And while Eusebius never provides his own Old Testament canon, he cites to Apocrypha as Scripture himself and cites canon lists that include Apocrypha with approval, as discussed above. Total citations from Eusebius tally to: 1 Maccabees 394, 2 Maccabees 132, Wisdom 206, Sirach 86, Baruch 44, and the Epistle of James 48.[510]

Looking ahead in time beyond 350 AD, Kruger mentions Augustine and the councils of Hippo and Carthage: all accepted all of the Apocrypha. Jerome accepted only Susanna, but we could replace his name with many others who accepted any or all of the other Apocrypha, such as Rufinus and Athanasius who accept Baruch, or Epiphanius who accepts Sirach and Wisdom, Pope Innocent I who accepts all of them, etc.

> Jude. ... we have good reason to think that this letter stems from apostolic circles and would therefore contain apostolic teaching. Like the book of James, Jude was also largely overlooked by many Patristic authors. Of course, as with many of these "disputed" books, the small size of the writing becomes a significant factor in why these books have received less attention. Jude is particularly small-containing only 602 words-which makes the lack of extant evidence for the book less surprising. Also, according to Jerome, Jude's use of Enoch may explain why some had doubts about it.

---

[510] As discussed above, for Susanna, Judith and Tobit, he also cites Origen's response to Africanus with approval, which included support for Susanna, Judith, and Tobit within it.

Nevertheless, Jude's reception is remarkably positive: it was included in our earliest canonical list (the Muratorian canon), Tertullian acknowledged it as apostolic Scripture, "Clement of Alexandria clearly cited it and wrote a commentary on it," Origen received it as fully canonical, and Eusebius placed it firmly in the canonical Catholic Epistles as a book "used publicly with the rest in most churches."

Alas, all attempts to search for citations on the Book of Jude lead to errors in the database search form that I am stuck using, so I have no data for you. I agree with Kruger that citations should be judged per verse, but at the same time, bear in mind that the New Testament works are also cited many times more often than Old Testament works (Kruger tells us that, overall, Christians cited to the New Testament up to fifty times as often as the Old (p. 224)).

But since I have no numbers for Jude, I will mention that James had 279 citations out of 108 verses—so 2.58 citations per verse at 350 AD. Susanna, at 3.67, is even better; Wisdom is close at 1.74. The historical works (which are not comparable at all) come in at 0.08-0.51; Sirach totals 0.31 and Baruch 0.48—all respectable given that this is a comparison of Old Testament to New Testament..

Also, as noted before, that first sentence ("we have good reason to think that this letter stems from apostolic circles and would therefore contain apostolic teaching") is particularly illuminating in comparison to Baruch. The first citations to Jude come decades after Irenaeus quoted 200 words of Baruch and certified it as authentic Apostolic preaching. And the citations to Jude come from Fathers who are early, certainly—but without the "one single step removed from John" that Irenaeus had. By any fair standard, Baruch has much better evidence for being Apostolic teaching than Jude.

Perhaps no book has had a more difficult journey into the canon than 2 Peter. ... Hippolytus also seems to show knowledge of it.... Origen cited it six times and clearly received it as canonical Scripture, and Eusebius considered it to be part of the "disputed" books in the canon that were nevertheless known to most of the church. Despite some initial hesitancy toward 2 Peter from some quarters of the church, in the end it was widely received by such figures as Jerome, Athanasius, Gregory of Nazianzus, and Augustine." Thus, even with its slow start, it is important to remember that 2 Peter still has significantly more support for its inclusion in the canon than the best of those books that have been rejected.

That last point is interesting: there is a large gap between this evidence and the rejected New Testament Books, and yet the Apocrypha seem similar and, in some cases, better evidenced than 2 Peter. Compare the six citations from Origen (biblindex.org/citation_biblique/search says 42, including allusions) to

Origen's cites to Apocrypha: 1 Maccabees 8, Judith 15, Baruch 15, 2 Maccabees 40, Tobit 40, Susanna 108, Sirach 130, Wisdom 270. Augustine accepted all the Apocrypha; the other named Fathers accepted only a few each (and Jerome only Susanna). But note the use of new names and how Kruger is changing the Fathers he mentions as he goes. That is not to dismiss his evidence for 2 Peter, which I certainly agree is sufficient (albeit less than for Baruch, as shown above). My point is that the list of Fathers for individual Apocrypha need not always include the same names either.

> 2 and 3 John. ... Irenaeus (Haer. 3.16.18) and Clement of Alexandria (Strom. 2.15.66) attribute at least 1 John to John the son of Zebedee, there is solid external support for the traditional view that the apostle is the author of all three letters. ... Polycarp appears to know both 1 and 2 John, and there are also reasons to think that Ignatius knew 2 John. By the end of the second century, our first canonical list, the Muratorian fragment, mentions at least two of the epistles of John (and possibly all three). Irenaeus received at least the first and second epistle, and Clement of Alexandria cited from 2 John and wrote commentaries on 2 and 3 John that are now lost. Hippolytus accepted at least 1 and 2 John (but is silent about 3 John), Cyprian was familiar with 2 John, and Dionysius of Alexandria mentions 2 and 3 John quite confidently as canonical Scripture. Although Origen recognized that some had doubts about 2 and 3 John, it appears most in his day regarded the two letters as genuine-including Origen himself. By the time we reach Eusebius in the fourth century, as noted above, 2 and 3 John have found a firm home as part of the seven "Catholic Epistles." Hill has made the case that the reception of two tiny epistles like 2 and 3 John by the third century, though they were not used as much as other books, suggests that they were likely bound together with 1 John (and maybe other Johannine works) at a much earlier point. In other words, we are hard-pressed to think that these two letters would have made it into the Catholic Epistles if they had been circulating independently and were latecomers to the canonical scene. Their historical and textual association with the other Johannine works-even though they were not cited as frequently—is the best explanation for their preservation and eventual reception.

Hippolytus accepted Baruch, Wisdom, 1 and 2 Maccabees, and Tobit, and also wrote a full Scriptural commentary on Susanna. Cyprian accepted Sirach, Wisdom, 1 and 2 Maccabees, Susanna (those quotes I reviewed), and maybe Tobit and Baruch (he made citations to them per the database, but I could not access what he said). Dionysius accepted Sirach, Wisdom, Tobit (all of which I reviewed), and maybe Susanna.

But also notice the critical importance of being bound together with John's works. 1 John is accepted; therefore, these other two letters that are claimed to be from John have a chance. And that acceptance is based on the testimony of Irenaeus and Clement, which "is solid external support." The mere fact that

Polycarp "appears to know" both 1 and 2 John is notable, as well. (All extremely relevant to the case for Baruch.)

By any reasonable analysis, the Apocrypha have very comparable evidence to the case for these New Testament Books.

But now, during the period 350-400 AD, we are going to find divisions among the canon lists.

First, why the 50-year explosion of lists after 350? As always, it is debated. But one inarguable influence was that the persecutions had ended, and things were settling down. People had time and energy to devote to such things and could now be Christian without fear. Accordingly, there was a natural impulse to come together and seek unity and orthodoxy in a way that was not feasible before (e.g., the First Ecumenical Council was held at Nicea in 325 AD). As part of that, people wanted one official list, and various "proposals" were put forth (I put the word proposals in quotes because they are clearly a combination of "this is the history as I understand it," "this is how my Church here does it," and "this is how I think everyone should do it").

I cannot imagine that anyone disagrees with me so far. But then, why the divergence among these lists? Personally, I submit that it is because some of the feelings toward Jews (and vice versa) lessened as the persecutions stopped. Recall that Hippolytus wrote that "when the two peoples [Jews and Pagans] conspire to destroy any of the saints, they watch for a fit time, and enter the house of God while all there are praying and praising God, and seize some of them, and carry them off, and keep hold of them, saying, Come, consent with us, and worship our Gods; and if not, we will bear witness against you. And when they refuse, they drag them before the court and accuse them of acting contrary to the decrees of Caesar, and condemn them to death."

Hippolytus was one of many of the earlier Fathers killed by persecution. From the usual suspects through 300 AD (the names we have heard often): Clement of Rome, Polycarp, Justin Martyr, Irenaeus (possibly), Origen (died later from injuries), Hippolytus, Cyprian—all martyred. Clement of Alexandria, Africanus, Tertullian—not martyred.

The metric is 70% martyred. Seven out of ten died agonizing deaths.

In such circumstances, facing the shockingly likely and extremely real threat of a horrifyingly painful death, with Jews seen as lying frauds and hateful murderers conspiring against them, few Christians would have conceived of or explored the concept of a canon matching what the Jews themselves accepted, if in fact the Jews had themselves agreed on a single unified canon.[511] After the Edict of Milan, the concept starts to find support. I personally believe that is causation, not just correlation.

That is my belief, and of course, I could be wrong. But I find it notable that it is Cyril in Jerusalem who is the first creator of this new batch of lists—and the first that seems to almost match the modern Jewish canon;[512] Athanasius in Alexandria (a city with a gigantic Jewish population) comes soon after with a list that is also close, and puts other books in a separate category. A generation later (380+ AD), many more lists come from elsewhere, some of them with something like the same idea—although always differing in details.

Of course, there is a reaction to all this, leading others to produce lists that are not as tied to the restrictive Jewish-oriented lists. In point of fact, part of the reason for so many lists (relative to the period before 350 or after 400) is precisely that people are disagreeing: they are having an argument. The question of "why so many lists?" is part and parcel of the question of why the lists disagree.

In the midst of all this comes Jerome, who is not so much different in his limited canon lists as he is forceful in explaining and defending the "why" of his lists. Thus, his real innovation is the express concept: Hebraica Veritas.

The North African Councils are then held, where large numbers of Bishops reject Jerome's view and the restrictive approach, and vote for a broader canon, including all the Apocrypha. After this, things settle down again.

With respect to the Apocrypha, the canon debate in the early Church is a 50-year period, and the canon list period is 70 years. For the first 350 years, there is no real debate, and after 400, there is no real debate. Gallagher and Meade cut off their book in 405 AD, thereby avoiding listing the 419 Council of Carthage, with 217 Bishops attending, which accepted all the Apocrypha. Perhaps they see the Pope's list in 405 as the true end rather than Carthage: after all, both lists include all the Apocrypha and are just approving the lists accepted at the two earlier African Councils (Hippo 393 AD, Carthage 397). But the Pope's and the Council's confirmations seem to be the only lists between 400 and 550 AD.[513]

Once we focus on dates, we see just how limited these lists are; they represent only one brief period in the early Church. Otherwise, lists are few

---

[511] The persecution of Jews also abated and that might explain why any of their own canonical differences started to disappear as well.

[512] He specifically includes Baruch and implicitly includes Susanna.

[513] See e.g., bible-researcher.com/canon8.html.

and far between. Melito's list was just a personal letter, seemingly unknown to anyone, until Eusebius republished it for the world to see; the Muratorian fragment is a scrap of paper written in barbaric Latin that is thought to be translating an early Greek list of unknown provenance. After that, Origen gives a list of Jewish Books, cut and pasted by Eusebius, so that we still have it.[514] That is it. That is the entirety of list evidence before the edict of Milan. After 400, there is the Pope and a Council agreeing with earlier councils. Then, there is silence until 550.

In addition, the debate over Apocrypha occurs only via lists. There are no extensive debates that I could find. We have the letters and apologies regarding Susanna. Otherwise, it is just a few acknowledgments and mentions of disputes (out of thousands of mentions of Apocrypha) plus the varying lists.

Meanwhile, the lists disagree: that "all the Apocrypha" are not accepted on many lists is true, but that is not the same as saying the lists reject the Apocrypha. They all accept some: the only question is which.

In fact, the debate clearly does not extend to all of the Apocrypha. Everyone accepts Susanna, and everyone except Jerome accepts Baruch. That is not debate—that is absolute unanimity for one and unanimity but one (maybe) for the other. Any change for those Books comes later, after 450 AD.

Most lists accept Wisdom, and in particular, the early lists may be unanimous in that. And even just "counting lists, not Fathers" does not really result in a negative vote for even the Maccabees (we would have to debate what is included in the count, but it is not hard to get to a 50-50 count for all the Apocrypha across all the lists).

Moreover, once we account for the weight of Councils (early Councils with dozens of Bishops each, the last Council with over 200) the "list case, but counting the actual numbers of Fathers" actually shows overwhelming acceptance of all the Apocrypha.

I submit that the evidence shows clear consensus before 350 AD, 50 years of low-level debate, and clear consensus after 400 AD. I also submit that the evidence shows (a) a broad canon that (b) some try to limit with restrictive canon lists after 350, leading to (c) reactionary canon lists defending the broad canon, and ending with (d) overwhelming numbers in support of a broad

---

[514] Eusebius wrote shortly before the explosion in lists. Perhaps it is Eusebius publishing Melito's, Origen's and Clement's lists that touches everything off. The lists differ, after all, so maybe people wanted to settle the differences.

canon. When exactly Jerome's influence grows and (perhaps) begins to upset that consensus is a matter for those who research the Middle Ages.

Those are my views and conclusions. Right or wrong, between 350 and 400 AD, the canon lists flourish.

GREAT UNCIAL CODICES

To begin our review, recall that two Great Uncial Codices date after 400 and so were made during this period. Codex Alexandrinus included 1 and 2 Maccabees, Wisdom, Sirach, Baruch, Judith, Tobit, and Susanna. Codex Ephraemi Rescriptus included Wisdom and Sirach, but most of the Old Testament is missing, so we do not know what else might have been included.

COUNCILS

Also, there were six Church councils that may have produced canon lists:

> The Nicene Council (325 AD)[515] occurred, with 318 Bishops attending. But with respect to the canon, we only know of a determination from Jerome, writing much later, and he only indicates that they voted to include Judith—and most agree he was mistaken.

> The Council at Laodicea (363 AD) occurred, with 22-32 Bishops attending, but whether they actually voted on a canon is disputed. If they did, it was the same as Cyril of Jerusalem (who had written his list earlier in 350 AD): the Septuagint versions of the Hebrew Books (and thus, Susanna), plus Baruch and the Epistle of Jeremiah.[516]

> The Council of Rome (382 AD) occurred, with 70 Bishops attending, but any vote on a canon is also disputed; if it did occur, they accepted

---

[515] It occurs before this time period, but I list it here because I believe Jerome was mistaken—i.e., his mention of it is evidence relating to Jerome; it is not evidence relating to Nicea.

[516] wikipedia.org/wiki/Council_of_Laodicea. Nearly everyone (ancient and modern) is mistaken in what they call the Septuagint Daniel (and Susanna): they think of it as the Septuagint because it is in Greek, but what they are talking about is the Theodotion version. There is no real debate about what anyone meant after 150 AD (when the Theodotion replaces the Septuagint version), it is a lack of precision. E.g., the Orthodox Study Bible (Intro, p. vi, 2008 ed.) claims to have the original Bible—but they are wrong, they too have the Theodotion Daniel, and not the Septuagint.

all the Apocrypha: 1 and 2 Maccabees, Wisdom, Sirach, Baruch, Judith, Tobit, and Susanna.[517]

I personally assign zero weight to those three, although I added them to the chronologies for your own consideration. For me, they are simply too disputed to bother with, particularly since all the evidence for them consists of single scraps of paper written long afterwards. If it matters, from what I can tell, the authenticity of the Council of Rome gets more support than the Council of Laodicea (which gets support from Gallagher and Meade), but both get very little. The Nicene Council gets almost no support (I saw it argued "for" just one time, and I am not sure how knowledgeable the arguer actually was). However, the writings claiming the votes show at least what the writer was thinking at that later time—but for Rome and Laodicea, those writings come from outside of my time frame, so I ignore them.

However, Jerome was writing in 405 AD and might have induced some readers before 450 AD to believe that the Nicene Council had so voted. Perhaps that would have a supplemental, reinforcing influence, given that the votes of the African Councils also accepted Judith (before Jerome was writing). However, I am also not sure how many would have even read what Jerome wrote about Nicea/Judith before 450 AD. It is in his "prologue," which is basically a cover letter; I am sure his translation of Judith went out to the world, but I have never seen anything indicating whether the prologue was also being copied and distributed (if you read it, it would seem to be a waste of time, effort, and ink to bother with—but who knows).[518] In any event, I never found any Father discussing it.

What Jerome's mistake was is debated—I personally think he just meant one of the more recent African Councils and mistakenly said, "Nicene." Two of the African Councils (see below) had occurred recently and voted on the canon, and they both accepted Judith. Note that (somewhat contemporaneously) Bishops also ask Jerome to translate Tobit, and he gives into the demand without citing the Nicene Council (but still with his typical whining about it, which is how we know that it happened).[519]

---

[517] wikipedia.org/wiki/Council_of_Rome.
[518] tertullian.org/fathers/jerome_preface_judith_e.htm.
[519] Gallagher wrote a paper speculating on Jerome's motivations for making the translations of Judith and Tobit www.academia.edu/14345165/_Why_Did_Jerome_Translate_Tobit_and_Judith_Harvard_Theological_Review_108_2015_356_75). There is one thing that touches on our present

The Council of Hippo in 393 voted to accept all the Apocrypha.[520] Seventy Bishops are thought to have attended.

The Council of Carthage in 397 voted to accept all the Apocrypha. Between 44 and 48 Bishops attended.

The Council of Carthage in 419 reaffirmed the canons of both Hippo and Carthage, i.e., to accept all the Apocrypha. This Council was attended by 217 Bishops, which is a stunning number of voters to consider when we are determining the dominant position—numerically, they are far more than all the early Church Fathers whose writings we still have, and well over ten times as numerous as individual named Fathers who wrote lists (which might be as few as ten, depending on who wrote Christian lists, etc.).[521]

For our purposes, the point of these last three councils is not that they are binding on anyone (that discussion is a red herring) but that they are massive

---

inquiry, which is the importance of making fair comparisons: Gallagher says that, "Jerome cites Wisdom of Solomon and Sirach much more often than the other four deuterocanonical books, so that if one were to guess two noncanonical books to be candidates for translation by Jerome, it would certainly be these two." But once again, that is an apples-to-oranges comparison. Tobit and Judith are historical works, and we would expect few citations compared to wisdom/poetic Books. Biblindex.org uses different data than Gallagher's paper (which cites to a German language book that I will not be reading anytime soon) but lists ten times as many citations across all authors for Sirach and Wisdom combined than for Tobit and Judith combined, and 76 to 10 for Jerome (vs. 154 to 12 using Gallagher's data); Jerome makes 2267 citations to Psalms, 163 to Job, 245 to Proverbs, 146 to Songs, 75 to Ecclesiastes (all Poetic/Wisdom Books, like Sirach and Wisdom), and just nine citations to 1 Chronicles (a historical Book like Tobit and Judith, but far longer than both of them combined); Jerome also cites other historical Books (Ruth 8, Nehemiah 8, Esther 12) as rarely as he cites 1 Chronicles, Tobit, and Judith. So, I would not blindly accept the claim of a "lack of citation;" to the contrary, it seems to be in line with all Fathers and par for the course with historical works. I am not sure this point matters much to Gallagher's overall theory, but my point in mentioning it here is that, once again, we see the need to look for fair comparisons. We have seen many times that authors do not always look for them, so it is we, the readers, who must do so.
[520] With counsel lists, some argue about Baruch, since there had been some separation between it and the label "Jeremiah" via Origen, etc. I view that as a perfectly proper pedantic point, but there is no evidence for a sentiment for excluding it among relevant Fathers/Bishops in Africa (in fact, other than Jerome, I found no evidence for that view at all). So, if there was debate about Baruch, it would seem to relate to the definition of the label "Jeremiah" and not to excluding it, and apparently the label "Jeremiah" won. E.g., I would note that Theodoret's commentary on Baruch is a generation later (448 AD) and Baruch is still part of Jeremiah to him.
[521] wikipedia.org/wiki/Synod_of_Hippo and wikipedia.org/wiki/Councils_of_Carthage

data and evidence to consider regarding what the Church was actually doing at that time. A vast swath of the Church was accepting all of the Apocrypha—and doing so despite the writings of Jerome, Rufinus, Athanasius, etc.

Still, a vast swath of Christendom outside of North Africa was not in attendance at those councils, so it is not the end of the inquiry either. With no other canon list after 400 AD except that of Pope Innocent[522] (who affirmed the decisions of the Council of Hippo and the first Council of Carthage), the answer to whether the rest of the Church accepted any of the Apocrypha comes from the citation evidence.

Another aspect to note is that no early Council (disputed or not) ever once voted for any form of "third category" of Ecclesiastical Books to be read but not used to confirm doctrine, etc.

CANON LISTS

350 AD: Cyril of Jerusalem[523] gives us a canon list, which expressly accepts Baruch and implicitly accepts Susanna. The other Apocrypha are not mentioned, and exactly what Cyril intends with them is debated. He says, "[b]ut let all the rest be put aside in a secondary rank. And whatever books are not read in Churches, these read not even by thyself, as thou hast heard me say." However, that comment might only relate to a second tier of New Testament Books (it comes after the New Testament list, not the Old). Cyril himself cites to Sirach and Wisdom only a dozen times, but one time, he does refer to Wisdom as coming "from Solomon." His use of them even once runs counter to the interpretation that he means that the Books are never to be read by anyone, of course—but he would hardly be the first to tell people not to do what he had done.

To me, the lack of clarity is, in fact, the answer: no one really followed Cyril's idea, or we would know what people were doing and, hence, what he meant. So, the list is just what it says: he accepted two Apocrypha; he does not support the rest; and otherwise, it is just his ambiguous list.

However, although I generally avoid discussion of the Septuagint, note that what Cyril's canon list actually says is, "Read the Divine Scriptures, the twenty-two books of the Old Testament, these that have been translated by the

---

[522] www.bible-researcher.com/innocent.html
[523] www.bible-researcher.com/cyril.html

Seventy-two Interpreters. ... For the process was no word-craft, nor contrivance of human devices: but the translation of the Divine Scriptures, spoken by the Holy Ghost, was of the Holy Ghost accomplished." In other words, Cyril does not evidence Jerome's Hebraica Veritas. He would not view the Protestant Books as the same as those named on his canon list; his express statement is that the Greek versions are the Divinely-inspired versions, not the Hebrew (and he was not alone, that view was common in the early Church).[524]

Cyril's views have several implications—the first and most obvious of which relates to Susanna being inarguably Scripture. His full actual quote (i.e., his list of Books plus his ode to the Septuagint) is literally saying that the word Daniel on his list absolutely, positively means the Greek Daniel (with Susanna) and definitely not the Hebrew Daniel (without Susanna).[525] So, even if we lacked citation evidence to confirm it, Susanna is on the list.

Second is that he expressly lists Baruch as part of Jeremiah, which itself evidences that the Septuagint did indeed include Baruch (either as part of "Jeremiah" or separately).

But third, his entire concept is (for us) a strange hybrid: he accepts only the Septuagint versions, but also only the 22 Books, although his 22 include two Apocrypha. In point of fact, Cyril supports no modern Church's Bible.

The entire canon discussion is often a matter of labels over contents: the names on a canon list may match the names of Protestant Books, but many a Father plainly states somewhere that the Protestant Books (the Masoretic Hebrew texts) are not his Books.[526] That two Books share a name does not make them the same Book, or make both of them "the" Book identified by that name. E.g., the Christian Bible and the Jewish Study Bible both say "Bible."

Of course, the ground rules of the canon debate essentially exclude this point as 'out of bounds'—everyone is supposed to understand that the canon is

---

[524] E.g., Rufinus: "The seventy translators, each in their separate cells, produced a version couched in consonant and identical words, under the inspiration, as we cannot doubt, of the Holy Spirit..." newadvent.org/fathers/27052.htm, II 33.

[525] And yet despite his Ode to the Septuagint he actually means the Theodotion Daniel: his quotes of Susanna/Daniel come from the Theodotion. This is an often-confused discrepancy, both among ancients (as we saw with Rufinus) and moderns: basically, everyone assumes their Greek version of Daniel is the Septuagint, but actually, starting after 150 AD, the Greek version people are using is the Theodotion. It might seem trivial, but, for example, the Orthodox Study Bible (Intro, p. vi, 2008 ed.) claims to have the original Bible because (they claim) they have the Septuagint as their Old Testament—but they are wrong, they too have the Theodotion Daniel, and not the Septuagint.

[526] I mention this with Cyril because his list actually includes it, but other Fathers with lists sing the same Odes (as I call them) elsewhere in their writings.

an esoteric discussion of names only. However, in the case for Christianity, the ground rules do not apply, and this ignored aspect of the canon debate would cause many other complications. The Septuagint problem, as I think of it, is a bit outside of my own arcanely-defined scope because I do not have space to cover all the aspects. So I will just pick one, and pick on Kruger again.[527]

Recall that his model is that the sheep heard the Shepherd's voice as spoken through the canonical Books, which caused the early Church to accept the correct Books. The Shepherd's voice came through a book, not a name on a canon list. Kruger's model actually has nothing at all to do with the canon and the 'correct list of names of Books.' Instead, the model relates to the actual set of Books, through which the Shepherd spoke.

So which versions of Daniel, Jeremiah, etc. are the correct ones? The longer Septuagint[528] versions (with Susanna, Baruch, etc.): those are the versions the early Church accepted and thereby authenticated, so those are the versions the Shepherd spoke through. The names on the canon lists merely help us identify Books; what the Church accepted were Books, not names.

After all: which version of Luke is the true one, the shorter version of the heretic Marcion or the longer version authenticated by Irenaeus? Kruger's model points us to the long form, because that is the document the Shepherd spoke through, as authenticated by the corporate reception of the early Church. They share a name, but what the model points to is the Book, not its name.

One last thing is that Cyril is not known as "of Jerusalem" for nothing. But he is not alone: Melito went "to the East" for his list; Epiphanius was from just outside of Jerusalem; Rufinus lived in Jerusalem for a while; and Jerome set up operation in Bethlehem. Eusebius was nearby, too. A disproportionate number of lists seem to derive from the Holy Land, and yet they give us different canon lists—even the ones expressly giving us Jewish lists (or expressly matching the Jewish list). Melito says Wisdom and skips Esther, using Greek names that imply Susanna and Baruch; Cyril includes Baruch and Susanna; Epiphanius includes Wisdom, Sirach, Susanna, and Baruch; Rufinus accepts Baruch and Susanna; and Jerome accepted Susanna. None matched the modern Jewish/Protestant list. Jerome is almost there, almost 400 years after

---

[527] Which I feel terrible about. He only gets singled out because he built a case rather than just discussed the canon. I honestly think of myself as Kruger's biggest fan (who else considered his ideas this carefully?)—but in a Kathy Bates/James Caan sort of way.

[528] Or what they thought of as the Septuagint, since that is what they mistakenly called the Theodotion Daniel, as just noted above.

Christ, but someone else will have to take that final step. As it is, all five lists accepted Susanna; four of five accepted Baruch; perhaps two accepted Wisdom; one accepted Sirach; one was missing Esther.[529]

350 AD: St. Catherine's Syriac List MS 10.[530] A stichometric list, but one with known errors that make the stichometry hard to rely on. The list specifically includes 1 and 2 Maccabees, Judith, Wisdom, and Sirach. Susanna seems to be included in Daniel; Baruch might be part of Jeremiah, but that is not clearly proven by the numbers. Tobit is not on the list.

360 AD: Cheltenham List.[531] Another stichometric list. Between names and verse counts, it is clear enough to me that all the Apocrypha are included. However, the canonical Books of Ezra-Nehemiah are notably missing.

367 AD: Athanasius of Alexandria.[532] "Because Athanasius' canon is the closest canon of any of the Church Fathers to the one used by Protestant Churches today, many Protestants point to Athanasius as the Father of the Canon."[533] Note that it says "the closest"—and even he does not match it (what his list matches is the New Testament, not the Old). Notably, his "full canon" includes Baruch and excludes Esther; he also implicitly includes Susanna (given citations to it in his other works).

In addition, he is, of course, the first to give us a third category: "There are other books besides these, indeed not received as canonical but having been appointed by our fathers to be read to those just approaching and wishing to be instructed in the word of godliness: Wisdom of Solomon, Wisdom of Sirach, Esther, Judith, Tobit, and that which is called the Teaching of the Apostles, and the Shepherd. But the former, my brethren, are included in the Canon, the latter being merely read…"

There is no corroborating evidence for this limitation having been in place before 367 AD, even though Athanasius says it has been handed down from the Fathers—which is what everyone always claims. It goes against innumerable claims made by others before 367 AD. In particular, Athanasius is Bishop of Alexandria, and we have heard from other Fathers from

---

[529] So too in Alexandria with its large population of Jews: Origen's and Athanasius' lists differ.
[530] 4marksofthechurch.com/biblical-canon-of-st-catherines-monastery/
[531] www.bible-researcher.com/cheltenham.html
[532] www.bible-researcher.com/athanasius.html. There is another list (the Synopsis of Sacred Scripture) once attributed to Athanasius, but it is now thought to be spurious and to have come much later. See www.bible-researcher.com/sss.html
[533] wikipedia.org/wiki/Athanasius_of_Alexandria

Alexandria—including Clement and Origen, who are two of the most prodigious writers of the early Church.

One thing to note on this point is that there are old translations of Athanasius that do not stress this. E.g., if you check out bible-researcher.com/athanasius.html, they give us an 1892 translation that begins the list with "In proceeding to make mention of these things, I shall adopt, to commend my <u>undertaking</u>..." But a modern translation (from Gallagher and Meade) says, "... in order to commend my <u>audacity</u>..."

In the end, scholars (including Gallagher and Meade) usually note somewhere that there is no reason to think Athanasius is telling us what was actually done to that point.[534] He is telling us what he wants done (and he is a powerful Bishop, so within his sphere, we can assume it was done—while questioning what that sphere was and how long it lasted, etc.). Athanasius also gives no basis for his list: no precedents, no names from the past, no fellow supporters, not even any arguments or reasoning—just the claim that it was handed down from the Fathers, while naming no Fathers.

Athanasius himself was an old man when he said it and had been writing for decades without ever once mentioning the third category or actually showing that he treated the Books on his list all that differently. He had already cited to the Apocrypha as Scripture many times, in many works, over many years, in a consistent fashion. Consider the Book of Wisdom:

> ... as the wisdom of God testifies beforehand when it says... Wisdom 14:12
> He [Jesus] teaches us and says ... Wisdom 13:5
> Scripture taught us beforehand long ago, when it said ... Wisdom 14:12
> ... what Scripture calls... Wisdom 14:21
> ... divine Scripture recognizes... Wisdom 9:2.
> ...such illustrations and such images has Scripture proposed... Wisdom 13:5
> hearing the Scriptures we believe... Wisdom 13:5
> ...to which I suppose the divine Scripture refers, when it says: Wisdom 6:19

He says the Book of Wisdom is the work of God, the Divine word of God, Scripture, the Divine Scripture, the wisdom of God, etc.[535] Athanasius cites to Wisdom 48 times.[536] The date ranges for 45 of those citations end before 367, the year of the letter that includes the canon list. The three remaining citations

---

[534] And my statistical analyses confirm that Apocrypha are not treated differently.
[535] The citations are shown above in my chart for the Book of Wisdom.
[536] Not every citation expressly states that it is Scripture, but many do. Others use it to confirm doctrine, while others are made along with canonical Scripture without qualification, etc.

occur in two works: two were in *Epistula ad uirgines* (*Letter to the Virgins*, not available online) with a date range of 350-373 (and thus, much more likely to have been written before 367 than after), and one was in *Epistula ad Afros*, which is given a very specific date of 371-372. That would, of course, be after the canon list. However, Biblindex took that date from an 1857 translation, and a more modern translation of the same work gives it a date of 366-367,[537] which (presumably) is more accurate.

Athanasius also does not apologize for having misled readers by not having done what he claims the earlier fathers told him to do. Athanasius spent his whole life attacking others and defending himself (he was exiled five times and was known as Athanasius Contra Mundum—one of history's great nicknames: Latin for "Athanasius Against the World") yet not once was he called out for his "heretical" claims that Apocrypha were Scripture, canon, etc. In fact, he and others use Apocrypha as canonical Scriptural proofs when Athanasius was arguing over heresy:

> when arguing Against the Heathen Athanasius quotes ten entire verses (an exceptionally long quote for the Fathers) from the Book of Wisdom 14:12-21 as "Scripture taught us beforehand long ago, when it said ...;"
>
> when Discoursing Against the Aryans, he says "... the word of truth confutes them as follows:...God is not as man, as Scripture has said" (Judith 8:16);
>
> in his Defense against Arius, he quotes a letter from his supporter, Alexander of Thessalonica, that says, "as the Holy Scripture somewhere says, 'though his father die, yet he is as though he were not dead'" (Sirach 30:4);
>
> when Lucifer of Caligari defends him in Concerning Saint Athanasius, he quotes the Book of Wisdom as Prophecy from the Holy Spirit;
>
> when the opponents of the Nicene Council quote Baruch 3:14 and Wisdom 7:26 to describe the Son, Athanasius counters with the orthodox view;
>
> and a council of Bishops ruling in Athanasius' favor cite Tobit as providing a command that his accusers violated (See 12:7); etc.[538]

Note that Athanasius himself never says that the Apocrypha are "not to be used to confirm doctrine" (that comes later from Rufinus and Jerome), and all of these uses would seem to be contrary to such a concept in the exact context where orthodox proof is most critical: arguing over heresy.

---

[537] see www.degruyter.com/document/doi/10.1515/9783110866261/html?lang=en

[538] Respectively: www.newadvent.org/fathers/2801.htm; www.newadvent.org/fathers/28162.htm; www.newadvent.org/fathers/28082.htm; the next two are per Gary G. Michuta in the Case for the Deuterocanon, not available online; and the last is at www.newadvent.org/fathers/28081.htm.

Still, Gallagher and Meade feel that there is a distinction between Athanasius' canon category and his "to be read" category in frequency of use over Athanasius' lifetime: "Although Athanasius described these books positively, he used them comparatively fewer times than the books he designated canonical."[539] They cite to "Ernest, James D. 2004. The Bible in Athanasius of Alexandria. The Bible in Ancient Christianity 2. Leiden: Brill, Appendix B, 380-418, in which all of the deuterocanonical and noncanonical references are listed on one page, while the references to the canonical books comprise thirty-seven pages."

That seems like a dubious methodology, if only because it does not seem to distinguish the Old Testament from the New (cited as much as fifty times as often, per Kruger). Here are the numbers from biblindex.org/citation_biblique /search for Poetic/Wisdom Books by citations from Athanasius per 100 verses (i.e., by size), the method that seems to have the most scholarly support:

Cites	Book	Verses	Rate
32	Song of Songs	117	27.4
648	Psalms	2526	25.7
220	Proverbs	915	24.0
48	Wisdom	436	11.0
24	Ecclesiastes	222	10.8
62	Job	1068	5.8
19	Sirach	1372	1.4

Wisdom does not seem to be "discriminated against," although Sirach might well be (but bear in mind that there are occasional weird results in citations by individual Fathers that do not seem to mean anything).

For historical Books:

Cites	Book	Verses	Rate
74	1 Kings	817	9.1
58	1 Samuel	810	7.2
47	2 Kings	719	6.5
21	Joshua	658	3.2
17	Judges	618	2.8
17	2 Samuel	695	2.4
6	Ezra	280	2.1
3	Esther	272	1.1
6	2 Maccabees	556	1.1
3	Judith	340	0.9
2	Tobit	245	0.8
2	Nehemiah	405	0.5

---

[539] P. 129 and footnote 274.

4	1 Maccabees	922	0.4
3	2 Chronicles	821	0.4
0	Ruth	85	-
0	1 Chronicles	943	-

So, all the historical Books in Athanasius' "to be read" category rate pretty well, including Esther. (Note the complete lack of even a single citation to either Ruth or 1 Chronicles—an apparently random circumstance, as just mentioned regarding Sirach).

Athanasius did not treat the "to be read" Books differently until after he came up with his list idea, except, perhaps, Sirach—and something he did not like about Sirach might well be part of his inspiration for the "only to be read" idea in the first place.

Thus, there is no evidence for a "third category" canon being in existence before 367 AD, not even in Athanasius' own head. And that is more than 300 years after Christ.[540] So to me, his claim that "[t]here are other books besides these, indeed not received as canonical but having been appointed by our fathers to be read" means that (a) the Fathers did appoint them, but (b) it is Athanasius who is now saying they are "only to be read" and not received as Canon. He is the one drawing that distinction.

In any event, the list remains, and I definitely see it as defining Athanasius' views from 367 on. I did not find any other evidence to show people following his lead—at least regarding his specific canon. I take it for granted that, even without evidence, there was some use of his canon in Alexandria for at least a little while. But it is the idea and not the specifics that starts to gain followers (as we will see, the idea gets used differently by each Father that adopts it).

One last thing to stress here, is that Athanasius meant for us to learn these Books in Sunday School before we graduated to the Bible: "not received as canonical but having been appointed by our fathers to be read to those just approaching and wishing to be instructed in the word of godliness." They are important and not being minimized—to the contrary, they are used to teach. Athanasius is clear that these were not dangerous heretical Books to avoid.

---

[540] Three hundred and thirty-four years to be exact, assuming Christ died in 33 AD. As I write this, 334 years ago was the year before the Salem witch trials, and the great grandchildren of anyone born in that year would probably be the ones to join up with George Washington (born only 293 years ago) and fight in the American Revolution—my point being that even in reading the Fathers from Athanasius' era, we are no longer anywhere close to the Apostles.

367 AD: Hilary of Poitiers.[541] An interesting list because it seems copied from Origen's list for the Jews (as given to us by Eusebius), but with a few changes. Hilary implicitly accepts Baruch and Susanna (as discussed above), and explicitly says that "some add" Tobit and Judith. Origen did not mention those two, he had included the Maccabees instead. Hilary makes no mention of the Maccabees, nor of Wisdom or Sirach. However, in his writings, he does cite to them—e.g., he cites to Wisdom as Prophecy several times.

The fact that he copied Origen's list and yet made his own personal changes to it is both (a) passed over without the slightest analysis in every book on the canon I have read and (b) by far the most notable aspect to consider about Hilary's list, in my opinion. That would seem to be pretty good evidence that Hilary saw these lists as proposals and/or a reports on what the Church was then doing—and not as the universal and eternal "Gospel truth" being passed down from generation to generation. Perhaps he saw Origen's list as a Jewish list (that he was free to mark up) or Origen's conception (so not universal or eternal, thus also free to mark up). But it was definitely not "The Canon" to him.

Lastly, Hilary produced his list in the same year as Athanasius, which would make it contemporaneous evidence that the claims made by Athanasius should not be taken too seriously, at least for the entire Church.

380 AD: The Apostolic Canons.[542] The writer of the Apostolic Constitutions—whoever he was or they were—does Athanasius one better: rather than pass on what came from the Fathers, he just pretends to be the Apostles themselves, as "they" give us another unique canon that no one else had ever given us before. If you take the claims of the Apostolic Constitutions too seriously, you end up with New Testament Scripture (the Constitutions, as they claim themselves to be) clearly identifying Judith, Tobit, Wisdom, Sirach, Baruch, Susanna, and 1 and 2 Maccabees as Old Testament Scripture. Of course, no one takes the claim that the Book was written by the Apostles seriously today. But it is a list and it shows what someone thought at the time—and shows how claims of Apostolicity are not to be accepted without corroborating evidence to prove them.

Arguably, the Apostolic Canons put Sirach in a third category by itself (it says "And besides these, take care that your young persons learn the Wisdom

---

[541] www.bible-researcher.com/hilary.html
[542] www.bible-researcher.com/apostolic.html

of the very learned Sirach"). But the Book that the list is part of (the Apostolic Constitutions) quotes from Sirach as Holy Scripture. It can be debated as to whether that should be seen as evidence of the intent with the canon list, or contradictory, which depends on whether the same person wrote both.[543]

380 AD: Gregory of Nazianzus;[544] and
380 AD: Amphilochius of Iconium[545]

Gregory and Amphilochius were cousins, and both left poems on the canon (it was once thought that Gregory had written them both). They are similar in that they include Baruch and Susanna (implicitly), and either exclude Esther (Gregory) or say that only "some include" it (Amphilochius).

As for the other Apocrypha, they are not mentioned. Gregory cites the Books a lot (Wisdom 50 times, Sirach 25, etc.), and there is enough ambiguity in his wording (the poem is distinguishing between genuine and spurious works, and the Apocrypha are not really "spurious") that one could read him as having them in a third category, but it is not certain either way. Personally, I think he meant that they are Books, period. Plato is neither spurious nor third category—he simply is not canon or Scripture. On that basis, I just treat them as excluded by Gregory for purposes of my own listings.

Amphilochius definitely has intermediate categories, but we do not know what exactly they are and what is included in them. Gallagher and Meade go through the Greek/Syriac linguistics of his citations to Sirach, Tobit, and Wisdom and think they may be in the third category based on his use of them; but still, we do not have express inclusion of them as a third category Book (or which type of category: Amphilochius' wording is itself ambiguous; he may have six or seven categories, actually). I view everything as uncertain enough to, again, just treat them as excluded for purposes of my own listings.

385 AD:[546] Epiphanius. Epiphanius is the Romaniote Jewish Christian mentioned earlier. He gives us multiple Jewish canons and one Christian list.

---

[543] In addition, textual variations for this work are severe and, sometimes, conflicting. Sirach, in particular, is set out as educational for children, almost like Athanasius' categories, but there is also a reference to the Five Books of Solomon as canon. Such a reference usually means Sirach is included as one of those Books (along with Ecclesiastes, Proverbs, Songs, Wisdom)—so maybe it is to be seen as both, or maybe two different people wrote those sections, etc.; moreover, the Ethiopic version specifically lists Sirach as one of the Solomon Books. So, for my purposes, it is included as full Scripture, but it can be debated if you wish. Tobit has a similar debate about it, but is specifically listed as canon in the Ethiopic and Syriac versions of the text.

[544] www.bible-researcher.com/gregory.html

[545] www.bible-researcher.com/amphilocius.html

For my purposes, Baruch and Susanna are accepted (by both Christians and Jews, per Epiphanius[547]); Wisdom and Sirach, I will discuss momentarily; and the other four Apocrypha are excluded.

Wisdom and Sirach are mentioned in every list. De Mensuris et Ponderibus 4-5 says, "And the twenty-two books were filled according to the number of the twenty-two letters of the Hebrews. For the two books in verse, both the one of Solomon, being called the Excellent, and the one of Jesus son of Sirach, and the grandson Jesus (for his grandfather was called Jesus), who wrote the wisdom in Hebrew, which his grandson, Jesus, wrote by translating it into Greek. And these are useful and beneficial, but they are not offered up to the number of the specified books. Therefore neither were they placed in the ark, that is, in the ark of the covenant."[548] Here he is speaking of the Jews, since the Ark is in the time of the Jews, not the time of Christians (plus there is other context to make it clear if you read more of his book).

Panarion 8.6.1-4: "These are the twenty-seven books given by God to the Jews; now these are numbered twenty-two just as their letters in Hebrew characters because ten books are double, being reckoned as five. Now we have spoken clearly concerning this in another place. Now they also have two other books in dispute, the Wisdom of Sirach and the one of Solomon, separate from some other apocryphal books." Again, "they," speaking of the Jews.

Panarion 76.22.5: "For if you were begotten from the Holy Spirit and instructed in the prophets and apostles, you must have gone through (the record) from the beginning of the genesis of the world until the times of Esther in twenty-seven books of the Old Covenant, which are numbered as twenty-

---

[546] Gallagher and Meade use a 376 date and probably have a better basis for that, but I did not notice that they did so until I was already almost finished. So, I stick with 385, taken from www.bible-researcher.com/epiphanius.html. In any event, De Mensuris et Ponderibus is dated 392 AD.

[547] Other Fathers also imply that Baruch and Susanna are accepted by the Jews when they write their odes to the Divinely-inspired Septuagint, saying that the Jews view it as inspired as well, etc. Epiphanius clearly separates Jews from Christians with his lists, identifies the Septuagint as the versions of the Books on his Jewish lists, and has a background whereby he should know what some Jews are actually and truly accepting. So, it is noteworthy that Epiphanius believed that the Greek translation was actually 'more Divinely inspired' than the Hebrew text: "the seventy-two handed down a more accurate reading that could not be expressed as concisely in Hebrew; their additions gave clarity to the text" (Sundberg, in the Canon Debate, p. 72). And Epiphanius was not alone in that view; we see it above with Cyril of Jerusalem, and with many others.

[548] The actual Ark is said to have disappeared before many Old Testament works were written (or in some cases, finalized); but this is at least a figure of speech, with the point being what is/is not Jewish Scripture. Note that 2 Maccabees 2:4-10 says that Jeremiah hid the Ark in a cave prior to the Babylonian invasion. So, if you hold to a literal understanding of Epiphanius' concept, then 2 Maccabees, by its own terms, cannot be in the Ark.

two, and in the four holy gospels, and in fourteen epistles of the holy apostle Paul, and in the general epistles of James, Peter, John, and Jude before these [and] with the Acts of the Apostles in their times, and in the Revelation of John, and in the Wisdom books, I mean of Solomon and of the son of Sirach, and in short having gone through all the Divine Scriptures, I say, you should have condemned yourself ..." Now, he is speaking of the Christian Bible.

That is what Epiphanius said, which (to me) is easy to understand: the Jews do not fully accept them, and Christians do. What makes things hard is not what Epiphanius said; it is what others claim he said. Gallagher and Meade:

> The Wisdom books of Solomon and Sirach are not included in the twenty-seven books of the Old Testament and appear at the end of the summary lists of the Old and New Testaments. This placement of Sirach and Wisdom at the end of the NT list coheres with a wider patristic practice of listing the useful non-canonical books after the canons of the Old Testament and the New Testament (see Horbury 1994). (p. 168, FN 162).

As an example, it is, indeed, in Athanasius' seventh and last paragraph that he says, "There are other books besides these, indeed not received as canonical but having been appointed by our fathers to be read ... Wisdom of Solomon, Wisdom of Sirach, Esther, Judith, Tobit ..."[549] It is not Athanasius' "coherence to a Patristic pattern" that identifies those Books as "not canonical but to be read," but his actual use of the words "not received as canonical but having been appointed by our fathers to be read." The order of the Books does not override the words Epiphanius wrote.

> That he refers to them collectively as the Wisdom books, fit for instruction of Christians, accords with his previous description of these books as useful and beneficial. They are in dispute, and not established. (Ibid.)

Nowhere does Epiphanius say this. He said "they"—not we. They the Jews, not we the Christians "also have two other books in dispute" and "these are useful and beneficial..." In his Christian list, he identifies that same 27 Book list of the Jews, plus all the other books the Christians accept as Divine Scripture, including the New Testament and Wisdom and Sirach. Nowhere does he say the Books are in dispute among Christians or only useful and beneficial among Christians; instead, he identifies them as Divine Scripture.

---

[549] www.bible-researcher.com/athanasius.html

> However, they are separate from the apocryphal books, which may indicate a middle category of useful Scripture, which is between canonical Scripture and apocryphal books. They are useful Scripture for the training and instruction of Christians, but they are not canonical Scripture according to Epiphanius, for they are only mentioned as useful and not as among the number of specified and established books. (Ibid.)

Epiphanius does not say any of that when referring to the Christian Scriptures. The blurring of Jewish and Christian Scripture is entirely in the mind of those who insist on reading their own presupposition into what Epiphanius wrote.

391 AD, 398 AD, 404 AD: Jerome. Jerome's personal views are pretty clear: he thought the Jewish canon and the Hebrew versions of those books should be the Christian Old Testament as well. Exactly who agreed with him, if anyone, is unclear. He had some high-level support, but (as we saw from Chromatius) that meant support in his translations and his right to hold his views, but not always actual agreement with those views. He had peers who agreed with him sometimes and in some ways, while not at other times or in other ways (Rufinus, notably). And he had various lower-level supporters (lay people, etc.), which I did not find much about (in terms of their views on the canon). The broader field of "the Church" or "Churches" clearly disagreed with him, as Council votes are promptly held, and they roundly reject his views every time. One can use lack of evidence outside of North Africa to debate how broad that consensus was in terms of geography, but numerically, the evidence we do have is that the Fathers were overwhelmingly opposed to Jerome's view in the timeframe we are discussing.

Later, the Reformers loved Jerome's Hebraica Veritas viewpoint—when the topic was the canon. But when the topic changed, then they, too, thought he had "gone native" and gullibly believed the Jews:

> "Jerome, in his manner, imposes Jewish blindness on us... Shall we then suffer this most beautiful and invincible text against Freewill to be polluted with Jewish filth, such as Jerome and Diatribe have daubed on it? God forbid! ... Unless a special grace has interposed, Jerome has earned hell rather than heaven for this..." Martin Luther, *Bondage of the Will* (1521).[550]

But let's forget all discussions of the Apocrypha, the Jewish canon, Hebraica Veritas, or anything else. Just focus on Judith for a moment:

---

[550] www.monergism.com/bondage-will-ebook: Part 4, Section 39 and Part 5, Section 10.

In 391 AD, Jerome wrote: "what is outside of them must be placed aside among the Apocryphal writings. ...Judith ... are not in the canon."[551]

In 398 AD, Jerome wrote: "Therefore, just as the Church also reads the books of Judith, ... but does not receive them among the canonical Scriptures, so also one may read these two scrolls for the strengthening of the people, (but) not for confirming the authority of ecclesiastical dogmas."[552]

In 404 AD or so, Jerome wrote: "... the Book of Judith ... is found by the Nicene Council to have been counted among the number of the Sacred Scriptures ..."[553]

That is Jerome giving us all three of the major views on Judith today and claiming each as the historical practice of the Church: truly Apocryphal and not part of the Bible (391AD) (the usual Baptist/Evangelical/etc. view); not canon but could/should be read (398 AD) (kind of a Lutheran/Anglican view); and Sacred Scripture since 325 AD (Nicene Council) and, thus, full canon (404 AD) (the Catholic/Orthodox view).[554]

Ignore Jerome's personal views: which one of those writings accurately states what the Church was and had been doing? Did Christians at that time reject Judith? Put it in a third category? Or accept it?

Jerome's inconsistency makes his statements somewhat worthless for telling us what was really going on. But on the other hand, once you ignore his statements from an "actual factual description" perspective, and, instead, focus on why he says them and what else he is complaining about, he actually paints a very clear picture. Jerome's Church did not agree with his own strongly-held views of what ought to be done. Start with his famous "Helmeted Preface:"

This preface to the Scriptures may serve as a helmeted [i.e. defensive] introduction [*Why would he need to be defensive if what he says has always been?*]... what is outside of them must be [*Must be? Not "has been"?*] placed aside among the Apocryphal writings. ... as can be proved [*Why is proof now needed if the Church has always seen it this way? Would he not, at least, quote someone or something as a second piece of proof?*] from the very style. ... I beseech you, my reader, not to think that my labours are intended to disparage the ancients [*Sounds like he and the ancients disagree*]...I beg you to confront with the shields of your prayers the dogs who bark and rage against me with rabid mouths, and who go about the city, and think

---

[551] www.bible-researcher.com/jerome.html.

[552] www.tertullian.org/fathers/jerome_preface_solomon.htm.

[553] www.tertullian.org/fathers/jerome_preface_judith_e.htm

[554] Few believe the Nicene Council actually did this, as discussed earlier, but the point is that it is what Jerome says.

themselves learned if they disparage others. [*Jerome has lots of enemies, presumably because he is advancing new ideas against entrenched old ideas*].[555]

Nor is there corroborating evidence to support the idea that the Church was actually doing things the way Jerome claims. Let's move ahead a few years and focus on the middle view—that the Church "does not receive them among the canonical Scriptures," however, they may be "read for the strengthening of the people, (but) not for confirming the authority of ecclesiastical dogmas." What other evidence have we seen to confirm that this statement is true?

We have a statement from Athanasius in 367 AD, and statements from Jerome and Rufinus around 400 AD. But none of the statements match— Athanasius accepts Baruch but puts Esther in the third category; Jerome fully accepts Esther but rejects Baruch (i.e., it is not even in his third category); Rufinus fully accepts both Baruch and Esther.

We do not have a single other canon list before 450 AD matching any one of these—nor did I find anyone else simply mentioning these as the way things were, in fact, being done. No one, when citing to any Books, distinguishes them as being in a third category. There is no mention of these things except via these competing lists.[556]

Even the three Fathers do not actually do things the way they claim everyone does. E.g., Jerome, during his spat with Rufinus, while they are calling each other heretics, defends himself by quoting Origen, who was citing to Judith as Scriptural proof[557]—without anyone (Origen, Jerome, or Rufinus) mentioning that Judith is not really Scripture and can only be read "for the strengthening of the people, (but) not for confirming the authority of ecclesiastical dogmas," etc.

---

[555] www.bible-researcher.com/jerome.html

[556] I mention some vague claims of evidence of a third category with some earlier canon lists; I think the evidence is worthless, but that is just my opinion—you be the judge. In any event, that still only gives you vague and conflicting evidence going all the way back to 350 AD, 17 years before Athanasius gives the first clear mention. That is 317 years after Christ. As I write this, Thomas Jefferson's father was born 317 years ago.

[557] "Now take the words of Origen: '… a man on whom necessity imposes the responsibility of lying is bound to use very great care, and to use falsehood as he would a stimulant or a medicine, and strictly to preserve its measure, and not go beyond the bounds observed by Judith in her dealings with Holofernes, whom she overcame by the wisdom with which she dissembled her words.'" www.newadvent.org/fathers/27101.htm—Section 18, from 402 AD. Note that this is after the African councils, so perhaps Jerome is ok with it for that reason; he writes it two years before the preface to Judith where he mentions the Nicene Council. On the other hand, Rufinus says it is "Ecclesiastical" and not canon but does not seem to call Jerome out for using it.

So, what are these Fathers doing when they say these things? Well, consider that the lists give us three different canons, each of which was "handed down from the beginning"—and yet, each is also a perfect match for the ideas, beliefs, and desires of the particular Father claiming that it had been handed down from the beginning. Rufinus gives it to us in very flowery prose:

> These are the books which the fathers have included in the canon; on which they would have us establish the declarations of our faith. But it should also be known that there are other books which are called not "canonical" but "ecclesiastical" by the ancients... They were willing to have all these read in the churches but not brought forward for the confirmation of doctrine. The other writings they named "apocrypha," which they would not have read in the churches. These are what the fathers have handed down to us, which, as I said, I have thought it opportune to set forth in this place, for the instruction of those who are being taught the first elements of the Church and of the Faith, that they may know from what fountains of the Word of God they should draw for drinking.[558]

Which ancients? When? Where? No one has found a single mention of the "Ecclesiastical" label before Rufinus. Personally, I have to give credit where credit is due: I find it very noble—in fact, rather uncharacteristically noble—of Rufinus to put aside his own thoughts and desires and selflessly give us the exact list that the ancients gave him, without letting any of his own bias or "spin" influence him in any way, shape, or form...[559]

We see this stuff over and over, among the ancients and the moderns. It is the usual trick. Someone claims (perhaps as part of an honest belief, perhaps not) that their personal view is direct from the Fathers, or the original Church, or the long lost first Gospel, or the true Jesus, or the real Christianity, or the forgotten facts, or the hidden history, or the secret truth, or the Q Source, or the M Logion, or whatever else.

It works like a charm, unless we double check and look for corroborating evidence. Sure, they say it goes back to the beginning and was what everyone was doing, but is that actually true?

That Jerome *said* that the Church reads them "for example of life and instruction of manners" is absolutely true.

---

[558] www.bible-researcher.com/rufinus.html

[559] See e.g., Gallagher and Meade, p. 91: "Unfortunately, the passage [something else, not what I have quoted] is available only in the Latin translation made by Rufinus, whose notoriously loose translation technique was criticized in Antiquity as in the Modern Period. Some scholars have doubted that the passage [meaning the entire passage of relevance, not just a few words] derives from Origen, attributing its creation instead to the translator [Rufinus]..."

That the Church (at the time of Jerome) actually did read them only "for example of life and instruction of manners"? Sorry, but you are going to have to show corroborating evidence to prove it, and quoting one of Jerome's contradictory statements is not proof of anything.[560]

Rufinus and Athanasius do not support Jerome, either, because they each have a different list of books. The only thing they have in common is a manipulative style of "persuasive" writing.[561] They each claimed that their view is what the Church was doing and had always done. They each spoke definitively, and with great confidence. Which is why it is called a con game. And as with all cons, it all breaks down because the stories conflict.[562]

But no matter what, Jerome was always valued for his translations. And from that work, his writings and ideas would become more beloved by monks and scholars as time went on.[563] In the meantime there will be an immediate backlash on the topic of the canon, via the Councils.

For our purposes, let us not forget Jerome himself: he certainly believed in the Protestant canon (except for Susanna[564] and a few inconsistencies along the way). But which Protestant canon? Did he want the books "placed aside among the Apocryphal writings and not in the canon;" or "not received among the canonical Scriptures, and only read for the strengthening of the people, (but) not for confirming the authority of ecclesiastical dogmas;" or did he

---

[560] If Athanasius, Rufinus, and/or Jerome were accurately describing what was really being done, there should be a lot of evidence to back them up by this time period—but there is no such thing. In addition, what Jerome says about the Apostles has already become "research into ancient times," not actual testimony based on knowledge (and "research" is me being mighty generous). Christ was 350 years before Jerome's earliest writings—the same distance as 1675 is from us. William Penn was alive but had not yet founded Pennsylvania.

[561] The ancients studied rhetoric and were not gentle about using it. (Read Rufinus (www.newadvent.org/fathers/2709.htm) and Jerome (www.newadvent.org/fathers/2710.htm) attack each other, for example). The real lesson is not to take the persuasive techniques of the Fathers too seriously: a mix of hyperbole, disingenuousness, and pugnacity is just how things were done back in the day. This sort of practice has many ancient parallels and is often understood and accepted by modern Christians (e.g., the "pseudepigraphical" explanations for who actually wrote Biblical Books). Ehrman, of course, sees much of it as forgery and fraud.

[562] Which happens to be the plot of Susanna, by the way.

[563] E.g., Gallagher maintains sanctushieronymus.blogspot.com/ —meaning Saint Jerome.

[564] An always forgotten detail. E.g., Gallagher and Meade claim Jerome's Epistle 53 and Epistle 107 "match precisely the modern Protestant Old Testament," but Jerome's Daniel included Susanna. They do note that Jerome prefixes an "obelus" to Susanna, but Jerome himself says he did not call for its deletion from Daniel. What he said to Rufinus is as applicable to anyone else who claims Jerome matched the Protestant canon: "But when I repeat what the Jews say against the Story of Susanna ... the man who makes this a charge against me proves himself to be a fool and a slanderer; for I explained not what I thought but what they commonly say against us."

think those two were the same view? Scholars support all three guesses. My guess is that deep down he wanted them removed completely never to be seen again. But when that was not well received, he moderated his view to the "third category" in hopes that at least that might happen – but then later when his financial backers demanded that he translate Judith and Tobit, he gives in and does so (making his mistake about Nicea amidst his complaining).

In any event, it is your decision as to what to make of Jerome. To help you, I list all the variations as separate line items in my chronologies.

400 AD: Rufinus:[565] His list implicitly includes Baruch and Susanna as canon. As for the other Apocrypha, "there are other books which were called by our predecessors not 'canonical' but ecclesiastical.' Thus, there is Wisdom...Sirach ... Tobit ... Judith and the books of the Maccabees. They desired that all these should be read in the churches, but that appeal should not be made to them on points of faith." Gallagher and Meade note that, "Despite Rufinus's assertion that his predecessors labelled this category ecclesiastical, we have no evidence for this designation prior to Rufinus's own canon list."

Otherwise, this is my last opportunity in this book to point out the enormous importance of focusing on Susanna and Baruch. Gallagher and Meade tell us that Jerome's and Rufinus' "disagreement revolved around which textual form of the canonical books ... but they agreed completely on which books were canonical." First, they did agree that Susanna was canon— which is not at all what Gallagher and Meade actually think they are saying.

And second, the statement that "they agreed completely on which books were canonical" is also false, because of Baruch. Was Baruch part of their canon, yes or no? For Rufinus: yes; for Jerome: no. Given those answers, the statement "they agreed completely on which books were canonical" is simply false and misleading.[566] They agreed completely that Jeremiah was canonical. They disagreed completely over whether Baruch was canonical.

"Textual form" is only relevant when discussing Jeremiah. They agree on Jeremiah despite differences in the "textual form." They disagree on Baruch despite the attempt to distract us with talk of the "textual form of Jeremiah."

With that, I have to resign the field: it is now up to you to fight that battle whenever you read these things. Just be relentless; do not let people confuse

---

[565] www.bible-researcher.com/rufinus.html

[566] Of course, to Gallagher and Meade, the mutual inclusion of Jeremiah is an important point. My point is that the way they discuss these things is part of what confuses the issue on Baruch.

you. There are very good reasons why courts allow lawyers to tell a scholar (i.e., an expert witness) to "shut up and answer the question, yes or no?" Use that power yourself (politely, of course), as it can clarify things in a hurry.

Lastly, Rufinus says that "They desired that all these should be read in the churches, but that appeal should not be made to them on points of faith," but note that his sponsor, Bishop Chromatius of Aquileia, was both reading them in the Churches and making repeated appeals to Apocrypha on points of faith.

397 AD: Augustine accepted all the Apocrypha.[567] But see this quote:

> In the second case he [Augustine] expressly lowers the authority of the books of the Maccabees by remarking that "the Jews have them not like the Law, the Psalms, and the Prophets to which the Lord gives His witness" (Aug. l. c.).[568]

The author is not quoting any words of Augustine to the effect of "lowering authority." All he quotes is Augustine saying that the Jews do not have the Maccabees in their books. (And that is the best quote he could find.)

Augustine himself cites 2 Maccabees as plain, simple Scripture without any qualification or differentiation in at least 17 different works.[569] There is no evidence that Augustine wanted to "lower the authority" of 2 Maccabees because the "faithless people" (as Augustine himself referred to them in his Sermon 300, quoted above when discussing 2 Maccabees) no longer accept it four hundred years after Christ. The concept of "lowering of authority" comes from the author imposing his own worldview on what Augustine wrote. Always look out for such things. You may or may not agree with them, but you do not even get to decide unless you first notice it.[570]

405 AD: Pope Innocent I[571] accepts all the Apocrypha as full Scripture. As with the African Councils, one could be pedantic about the lack of explicit mention of Baruch, but there is no reason to think it was meant to be excluded and every reason to believe he considered it part of Jeremiah.

---

[567] www.bible-researcher.com/augustine.html.

[568] B.F. Westcott, "Canon of Scripture," in vol. 1 of Dr. William Smith's Dictionary of the Bible: Comprising Its Antiquities, Biography, Geography, and Natural History; revised and edited by Professor H.B. Hackett, D.D., etc. (Cambridge, 1881), p. 362-3. Cribbed from www.bible-researcher.com/augustine.html.

[569] Just my own count from what I have found, which is not exhaustive on Augustine. His innumerable works do not appear in the version of Biblindex that I can access.

[570] And Westcott said "*expressly* lowers the authority" when Augustine does not expressly do so.

[571] www.bible-researcher.com/innocent.html

LIST OF CANON LISTS

Lists broken out by Book were included above, so this is one complete summary list:

FATHER/LIST/BOOK	YEAR	ACCEPTED APOCRYPHA	"THIRD CATEGORY"?
MELITO OF SARDIS	170	SOME APOCRYPHA (JEWS?)	NO
MURATORIAN CANON	170	SOME APOCRYPHA	NO
CLEMENT ALEXANDRIA	203	SOME APOCRYPHA	NO
ORIGEN (JEWISH LIST)	220	SOME APOCRYPHA: JEWS	YES FOR JEWS
ORIGEN (LETTER)	248	SOME APOCRYPHA	NO
ORIGEN (CITATIONS)	250	ALL APOCRYPHA	NO
EUSEBIUS (APPROVAL)	324	SOME APOCRYPHA	N/A
~~THE NICENE COUNCIL~~	~~325~~	~~SOME APPOCRYPHA~~	~~NO~~
CLAROMONTANUS	349	ALL APOCRYPHA	NO
CODEX VATICANUS	*350*	*SOME APOCRYPHA*	*NO*
CODEX SINAITICUS	*350*	*ALL APOCRYPHA?*	*NO*
CYRIL OF JERUSALEM	350	SOME APOCRYPHA	MAYBE?
ST CATHERINE'S SYRIAC	350	SOME APOCRYPHA	NO
CHELTENHAM LIST	360	ALL APOCRYPHA	NO
~~COUNCIL AT LAODICEA~~	~~363~~	~~SOME APPOCRYPHA~~	~~NO~~
ATHANASIUS	367	SOME APOCRYPHA	VERSION 3.1
HILARY OF POITIERS	367	SOME APOCRYPHA	NO
GREGORY NAZIANZUS	380	SOME APOCRYPHA	MAYBE?
AMPHILOCHIUS	380	SOME APOCRYPHA	MAYBE?
THE APOSTOLIC CANONS	380	ALL APOCRYPHA	MAYBE
~~THE COUNCIL OF ROME~~	~~382~~	~~ALL APOCRYPHA~~	~~NO~~
EPIPHANIUS PAN. 8.6.1-4	385	SOME APOCRYPHA: JEWS	NO
EPIPHANIUS PAN. 76.22.5	385	SOME APOCRYPHA	NO
JEROME (HELMETED)	390	SOME APOCRYPHA	NO
EPIPHANIUS DE MENS. 4-5	392	SOME APOCRYPHA: JEWS	YES FOR JEWS
THE COUNCIL OF HIPPO - 70 BISHOPS	**393**	**ALL APOCRYPHA**	**NO**
AUGUSTINE	397	ALL APOCRYPHA	NO
COUNCIL CARTHAGE - 44-48 BISHOPS	**397**	**ALL APOCRYPHA**	**NO**
JEROME (SOLOMON)	398	SOME APOCRYPHA	VERSION 3.2
RUFINUS	400	SOME APOCRYPHA	VERSION 3.3
JEROME (TOBIT/JUDITH)	404	SOME APOCRYPHA	NO
POPE INNOCENT I	405	ALL APOCRYPHA	NO
COUNCIL CARTHAGE - 217 BISHOPS	**419**	**ALL APOCRYPHA**	**NO**
CODEX ALEXANDRINUS	*450*	*ALL APOCRYPHA*	*NO*
CODEX EPHRAEMI R.	*450*	*SOME APOCRYPHA (ALL?)*	*NO*

THE END

I am Alpha and Omega,
the beginning and the ending,
saith the Lord.

THE END

And that's it. There was a flurry of competing lists from 350-400 AD. Toward the end of that period, two African Councils voted to accept all the Apocrypha, then everything stopped. The only lists anyone writes from 400 until 550 AD[572] are from (a) Pope Innocent I in 405 AD and (b) the second Council of Carthage in 419 AD (the one with 217 Bishops attending), both of which endorse the list approved at each of the two earlier African Councils: i.e., all the Apocrypha.

After that Council in 419 AD come 131 years of silence—a good five generations, as long ago now as 1895 is to me as I write this: the year of the first automobile race, the first American battleship, a ruling from the U.S. Supreme Court declaring that Congress and the U.S. federal government have no power at all under the Constitution to regulate manufacturing in any way, shape, or form.

Seems like a long time has passed.

During that 131-year period, the fifth century Great Uncial Codices are made—one with all the Apocrypha, and the other known to contain at least Wisdom and Sirach (with the rest of the Old Testament mostly missing).

Meanwhile, the number of sermons and treatises on the Apocrypha continued to grow after 400, as did citations to them as full Scripture.

I remind you that Kruger, when speaking on the New Testament, set forth the standard:

> "... it took a while for the church to reach a consensus about all of these books. ... there was no formal, official declaration of the church that closed the canon. ..." (p. 286-287).

And that seems like a good place to end it.

---

[572] See, e.g., www.bible-researcher.com/canon8.html and biblecanon.org/lists/. Gallagher and Meade basically end with Pope Innocent I in 405 AD but with some much later additional material on ancillary topics (Codices, medieval manuscripts, Syriac canons, etc.).

THE FINAL RULING:
IS CHRIST RISEN AND WERE APOCRYPHA SCRIPTURE?

There are at least a thousand and one ways to explain the evidence. Of course there are. In fact, many of the old arguments still exist, and nothing "demands" that one give them up.

There is never only one way to explain the evidence, but an infinite number of ways. Amateur sleuth Father Brown makes this point in comic fashion in G.K. Chesterton's classic story *The Honor of Israel Gow*.[573]

So focus on what is actually true, not what you want to prove is true. If it is true, then it will survive attack from your smartest and most diabolical opponent: thine very own self. Wake up tomorrow and take the other side of the argument. We often know that we are wrong, we just do not realize it, because we keep arguing for our side and never against it. So play Devil's advocate, using everything you know to prove it wrong. If it is actually true, then it will still be true the next day; if not, it was never true in the first place.

Then shift gears and try to predict the outcome: stop thinking about your own choice and consider what a reasonable, unbiased and thoroughly competent judge would decide. It is a thought experiment that may allow you to see your own cognitive biases, and should help you to think in terms of what the evidence shows, rather than what you assume the facts are.

As for me, years ago I nearly died. As I was recovering, I looked back on my life without a single real regret: it was a good life, no complaints, and we all have to leave sooner or later. (If that sounds shallow, that is because so I was.) But there was one stupid little thing: I was always going to read those books I was named after, but I had never done so. I ordered a box of various "textual variations" from Amazon; one thing led to another; and I eventually found myself immersed in the case for Christianity.

In the end, after arguing with myself for a long time, I came to believe that a judge would rule that the best and most reasonable explanation of all the evidence is that Christianity's historical claims are indeed true. In other words (and after several philosophical steps which I just pass over), she would decide that she has to convert—which is exactly why I did so.

---

[573] gutenberg.org/files/204/204-h/204-h.htm#chap06. The money quote for present purposes is "Ten false philosophies will fit the universe; ten false theories will fit Glengyle Castle. But we want the real explanation of the castle and the universe."

But I had bought a box of Bibles—plural. The Who, What, When, Where, Why and How of the Bible are absolutely fundamental questions, and the answers are not trivia. Because not every Christian Bible is "The" Bible—and not every Bible can win the case for Christianity.

Simon Greenleaf was not wrong about the evidence, and Lionel Luckhoo has still not been out argued. They are but two of the many great legal minds who analyzed the case for Christianity and concluded that that the evidence and the arguments are on the side of Christianity. But they did not focus on the "Achilles' heel of Protestant Christianity" (D. F. Strauss), the "hidden, dragging illness of the Church" (Herman Ridderbos), and what could be "the single thread that unravels the entire garment of the Christian faith" (Kruger).

I believe that a fair judge would accept as proved both (a) the case for Christianity and (b) the Apocrypha as authentic Apostolic teaching. But Luke 16:31 ("neither will they be persuaded, though one rose from the dead...") works in reverse as well. And if the Christians in the case insist upon maintaining their pre-supposition, and "admit" that the evidence is not enough to prove that the Apocrypha were authentic Apostolic teaching, then the evidence will not be enough to authenticate the Resurrection either.

In such a case, I believe a fair, neutral judge would rule that Christ is not raised, our faith is in vain, they which are fallen asleep in Christ are perished, and we are of all men most miserable. (1 Corinthians 15:16-19).

But that is just my view. Good luck to you in your own research and decisions. God bless.

If you learned anything from this book, please leave an honest review on Amazon and/or social media. This is my first book, so (a) I will be reading all reviews, and (b) reviews are crucial to spreading the word about this "outsider scholarship." That you hate all my opinions is only to be expected, but I am hoping to at least make people aware of my research. I sincerely hope that you learned something you did not know already, and I would appreciate you saying so. Thank you very much!

ADVICE FOR THOSE WHO RESEARCH THE CANON

Having the experience of doing all this research, I offer the following lessons learned for anyone else who tries to do their own research:

1. Focus on individual books; try not to think of the Apocrypha as a set.
2. Review evidence chronologically and focus on eras. The year 200 AD is worlds apart from 400 AD.
3. Try to drill down to original sources as much as possible, and in particular, do so on key issues; do not just assume that someone is correctly describing the past.
4. Look at pieces of evidence individually, in detail, but judge it all together at the end—not piecemeal.
5. Search for corroborating evidence until you can search no more.
6. Seek out comparables to judge by; never compare to perfection.
7. Apply the same standard across the possible Scriptures, not a different standard for Apocrypha.
8. Consider all arguments in light of arguments for the New Testament, the Protestant canon, etc. Have you ever seen this argument argued against in another context?
9. Always read both sides before deciding anything.
10. Double-check everything. Triple-check whatever you agree with.
11. Never let a lawyer talk you into looking at only their preferred pieces of evidence. The other side is entitled to introduce evidence too.
12. Proceed with caution when:
    a. Someone does not cite to something—very suspicious;
    b. "Most scholars agree"—that is not the same as proof;
    c. Relatively neutral parties do not concur with someone's argument—if they do not, why would you agree with it?;
    d. Someone shows even the slightest emotion, even "righteous anger." We are all blind as bats when we are emotional; or
    e. Someone reads minds to show what was thought or meant— especially when that is a perfect match for their own views, or disparaging the mind being read.

QUESTIONS NO OTHER BOOKS SEEM TO ADDRESS

Who read these Apocrypha to illiterate Jews so that they would know all the things it is claimed they knew—and where was that done, and why, if they were not being read as Scripture during religious services?

Why would the Gospel to the Jews be far more focused on Apocrypha than the other Gospels?[574]

Why is the Epistle with the greatest focus on Apocrypha either the Epistle to the Hebrews (Wisdom), or the Epistle of James the Brother of the Lord (Sirach), or the Epistle of Jude the (possible) Brother of Lord (1 Enoch)?

Collectively, those are the two books most devoted to Jewish thoughts and concerns, plus the two books written by possible family members of Jesus. Of the 27 Book New Testament, why would those four books be the ones most focused on Apocrypha (that claim to be Scripture, but allegedly are not)?

What reason is there for the Book of Wisdom (which says it is Scripture) to be referenced more than any comparable canonical Book (per the KJV)—by Evangelists who allegedly did not see it as Divinely inspired?

Is there any other explanation for Jude quoting 1 Enoch that holds up to honest scrutiny?

Why would the Divinely inspired Evangelists incorporate wording from Apocrypha (many of which claim to be Scripture) into hymns and creeds, when canonical Scripture could have been incorporated instead?

Why would Jesus repeatedly allude to Apocrypha (many of which claim to be Divinely inspired Scripture) to prove His divinity if they were not accepted as authentic Scripture by His audience?

From the Jews, to Jesus, to John, to Polycarp, to Irenaeus: who introduced Baruch into Christianity? Why? Why was there no protest?

Why should we continue to trust the early Church, let alone Irenaeus, to identify authentic Apostolic teaching?

What specifically is the error that leads the Jews to wrongly reject the claim that their canon was settled at 22 books at the time of Christ?

Who first excludes Susanna, and who first put Baruch in a third category?

---

[574] I drop the "seems to refer" wording for this list because I had these question when reading Protestant Bible commentaries: they did not address this when their own work shows it.

POSSIBLE ERRATA

Assessing my own work-product, the main problem is that Biblindex starts to become incomplete in the fourth century, and I was forced (by my own technological incompetence, no doubt) to use the old search form.[575] My work used other sources and databases (finding many later citations beyond the Biblindex data) and is an upgrade to the existing scholarship (e.g., a 2017 book counted pages of an index from a 2004 book), but still, better analyses can always be performed with better data. I think my own finds are reasonably complete and my conclusions should hold up through 450 AD—but if you want to confirm or dispute that, you just have to do all the work yourself.

In addition, all such data is flawed, dependent as it is upon proper indexing. There are duplicates, mistaken omissions, etc., let alone actual gaps from missing Fathers and works. I note problems where I found them. But exact numbers are just fake certainty; there is already a large margin of error simply in terms of what documents we still possess to try to index.[576]

There is one category of evidence discussed herein that I believe is indeed complete to the best of my knowledge after all due investigation: no Protestant books or websites I reviewed showed me additional "negative evidence" from the early Church against any of the Apocrypha as Scripture. What I discuss is all anyone I read mentioned. I am by no means claiming that there is not more out there somewhere, but I am claiming that I looked and did not find it.

Otherwise, there are basically three types of evidence discussed herein. First, there are impeccably Protestant books that provide all the main background details and analysis. For the most part, they are also the sources which identify the several hundred possible Biblical references to the Apocrypha noted herein. Unless noted, I found no one who disagreed with any such points they made (which is not to say that all spoke to the point), and I checked an awful lot of books (e.g., over 100 commentaries just on Matthew).

Second, I cite to the Jewish Study Bible and other basic, secondary Jewish sources. The Jews are in no way pro-Apocrypha and have every reason to agree with all the Protestant claims if they thought there was any basis for

---

[575] biblindex.org/citation_biblique/search; vs. biblindex.org/en/quotations/search.
[576] That Augustine is missing from the database I can search is notable. If nothing else, it kept him (the main man often accused of promoting the Apocrypha) from biasing the data toward the Apocrypha; I do not know that it is actually true that he would have cited to them more, but it might be; and yet without his cites in the database, the Apocrypha still hold up under analysis.

them. I viewed simply noting their views on their own canon as sufficient, since a discussion of primary sources would not fit in this book anyway.

And third, I used original source data (well, translations with many footnotes) from the Fathers. I cite to online sources (e.g., the New Advent site) so that you do not have to buy a book just to see a quote in context. Still, I consulted other sources to confirm translations (more for major works of major Fathers, and less for the more obscure sources). Quibbles can be made over individual instances, but in bulk, such quibbling is not being honest.

Beyond those categories, the quality of my evidence varies, and of course starts to involve unscholarly sources like Google and Wikipedia. Everything I cited seems to be the common view, but by all means double check all such things to your heart's content. Questioning the credibility of such sources is not the problem, the problem is not questioning scholarly sources.

The scope of this work is also incomplete: First, I do not really discuss Esther, the Epistle of Jeremiah, or the other additions to Daniel. But they should never be forgotten when discussing the Apocrypha. E.g., Josephus uses the parts of Esther that Protestants claim were never part of his canon.

Second, there were other Books that had at least a little support in the early Church (including some Books accepted by the Orthodox and some rejected even by them; and definitely including 1 Enoch). But showing and analyzing the support (and limits to the support) for those books would make this a two-volume work. Sufficient unto the day is the evil thereof. (Matthew 6:34). It is crucial to note, however, that those books lack any serious canon list support, which made the Catholic books the obvious cut off point.

Third, I do not cover the Septuagint evidence/debate, or the physical scraps of paper that have been found, etc. To me, the core of a Bible-based Christian analysis is the New Testament and the writings of the early Church, the rest of the evidence is more ancillary (and, as noted many times, the Jews do not feel it all adds up to a certain 22 Book canon at the time of Christ).[577]

Fourth, I use a 450 AD cut-off date, which fully covers Jerome, Rufinus, and the various Councils, plus a few decades to track the aftermath of all that. 450 AD is also within the range of dates that one could pick for the beginning of the Middle Ages (Rome was sacked on 24 August 410 AD; the Huns

---

[577] Note, however, that the "Apocryphal pieces" of Daniel, Jeremiah and Esther have an additional Biblical claim attached to them, regarding whether a Biblical reference to the "canonical pieces" of the Septuagint versions of the Books implies that the Septuagint versions with their "Apocryphal pieces" are the real Scriptures.

invaded Italy in 452 AD; the last Emperor of Rome in the West was deposed in 476 AD). And 450 AD also avoids the Oriental Orthodox schism that occurs in 451 AD (they accept all the Apocrypha, incidentally).[578] Lastly, nothing happens with the canon lists after 419 AD until 550 AD. Thus, 450 AD seems like the best place to end my "early" Church analysis. Beyond that, none of the claims I was researching were based on the idea that it was the Church of the Middle Ages that correctly determined the canon (in fact, Kruger's entire model is based on vilifying the Church of the Middle Ages).[579]

Otherwise, there is all my bias. If I saw it as bias, I would not have said it. So, I am afraid that all of it is up to you to notice and sort out. However, personally, I do not see endless repetition of inconvenient facts as bias. It is simply a technique to drill those facts into the brain (Matthew is the Gospel to the Jews, as perhaps you have heard?), and like most lawyers, I just see it as presenting all the evidence in context: that you do not like hearing the fact being mentioned is exactly why it needs to be said over and over.

Finally, I presume that minor mistakes, inconsistencies, and illogic are plentiful herein. All I can say is that (a) I have been finding incredibly stupid errors in my own work product every day while writing this, (b) if I knew where the remaining errors were, then they would not be there, and (c) if I thought such things had any chance at all to change the final outcome, then I never would have started to write this book, let alone finished it.

But then my journey began with a Book that explained the "why" of a truth that I had been proving my entire life: it is a simple trick to deceive a man. Most especially when "thou art the man."

---

[578] The schism occurred over the nature of Christ. They hold to Miaphysitism, while we heretics (as they see us) hold to Dyophysitism. A Bible-based Christian should actually start by proving to herself that Dyophysitism is correct, then move on to minor disputes among Dyophysites, like Protestantism versus Catholicism.

[579] William Webster has assembled dozens of quotes from the sixth to fifteenth centuries where Fathers agreed with Jerome (christiantruth.com/articles/canon/); Gary G. Michuta's *Why Catholic Bibles are Bigger* contains quotes from dozens more who disagreed with Jerome. Gallagher's upcoming *The Apocrypha through History: The Canonical Reception of the Deuterocanonical Literature* might also be a helpful resource for such an analysis. Otherwise, the Middle Ages are beyond my scope, but many of the claims about them actually relate back to the era I am covering. For example, you can see that Webster claims that "Those books were permissable to be read in the Church for the purposes of edification but were never considered authoritative for the establishing of doctrine," then quotes medieval writers saying the same thing. Yet, as their own proof, they were all just citing to Jerome, Rufinus, Athanasius, etc. Such claims are not good evidence of the actual facts on the ground in the Church before those Fathers, as we have seen. Still, the quotes would have value for counting medieval monks to figure out what the evidence shows about the Middle Ages.

CORE BIBLIOGRAPHY

BIBLES
The Apologetics Study Bible, Holman Bible Publishers 2017.
The Holy Bible, King James Version. Cambridge Edition. 1769.
The Holy Bible, King James Version. 1611.
    King James Bible Online, 2025. www.kingjamesbibleonline.org.
The Jewish Study Bible, Second Edition, Oxford University Press 2014.

CANON—PROTESTANT
The Biblical Canon Lists from Early Christianity,
    Edmon L. Gallagher and John D. Meade, Oxford University Press 2019.
The Canon Debate, Lee Martin McDonald and James A. Sanders, Editors.
    Baker Academic 2002.
Canon Revisited, Michael J. Kruger, Crossway 2012.
The New Testament Canon, Harry Y. Gamble,
    Wipf and Stock Publishers, March 2002.
The Spirit and the Letter: Studies in the Biblical Canon,
    John Barton, SPCK 1997.

CANON—SKEPTIC
Forged, Bart D. Ehrman, HarperCollins 2011.

CANON—CATHOLIC
15 Myths, Mistakes and Misrepresentations about the Deuterocanon,
    Gary Michuta, Nikaria Press 2017.
The Case for the Deuterocanon, Gary Michuta, Nikaria Press 2017.
Why Catholic Bibles Are Bigger, Gary Michuta, Catholic Answers Inc. 2017.

THE CASE FOR CHRISTIANITY
The Case for Christ, Lee Strobel, Zondervan 2016.
The Case for the Resurrection of Jesus,
    Gary R. Habermas and Michael R. Licona, Kregel Publications 2004.
Did Jesus Really Rise From The Dead? Carl E. Olson, Ignatius Press 2016.
Evidence for Christianity, Josh McDowell, Thomas Nelson, Inc. 2006.
The Historical Reliability of the Gospels, Second Edition,
    Craig L. Blomberg, InterVarsity Press 2007.
Jesus and the Eyewitnesses, The Gospels as Eyewitness Testimony,
    Second Edition, Richard Bauckham, Eerdmans 2017.

APOLOGETICS
Encyclopedia of Bible Difficulties, Gleason L. Archer, Zondervan 1982.
When Critics Ask, Norman Geisler and Thomas Howe, SP Publications, Inc. 1992.

INDEX

CANON CROSSFIRE

So, What Do You Think?
**Does The Protestant Bible
Blow Up The Case for Christianity?**
Or Not?

Please leave an honest review on
Amazon and/or social media!